OZ CLARKE'S
new essential
WINE BOOK

An Indispensable Guide to the Wines of the World

Third Edition

Fully Revised and Updated

A Fireside Book

Published by Simon & Schuster

NEW YORK   LONDON   TORONTO   SYDNEY

CONTENTS

FIRESIDE
Rockefeller Center
1230 Avenue of the Americas
New York, NY 10020

Copyright © 1996–2005 by Websters International Publishers and Octopus Publishing Group

Text copyright © 1985–2005 by Oz Clarke

Published simultaneously in Great Britain by Mitchell Beazley Publishers, Ltd.

For information regarding special discounts for bulk purchases, please contact Simon & Schuster Special Sales at 1-800-456-6798 or business@simonandschuster.com.

10 9 8 7 6 5 4 3 2

Library of Congress Cataloging-in-Publication Data is available.

ISBN-13: 978-0-7432-8668-8
ISBN-10:   0-7432-8668-5

Colour separations by PT Repro, Multi Warna, Indonesia
Printed and bound in China
Phoenix Offset/The Hanway Press Ltd

Editorial Director   Fiona Holman
Art Director   Nigel O'Gorman
Editor   Margaret Rand
Maps   Andrew Thompson
Photography   Mick Rock/Cephas Picture Library
Desktop Publishing   Keith Bambury
Indexer   Naomi Good
Production   Sara Granger

Photographs:
Page 2 *New plantings on the shore of Lake Wanaka, in New Zealand's Central Otago region, are the world's most southerly vineyards.*
Page 3 *Chardonnay is undoubtedly the world's most popular white grape variety.*

INTRODUCTION

Looking back to the first edition of this book, I marvel at how much has changed in 15 years, how many wine regions then thought of as unimportant now play vital roles in our wine-making, how many grape varieties then unheard of now proudly offer us an ever-growing choice of flavours, and how many winemakers and wineries that barely existed then, if indeed they did at all, are now exciting players in the thrilling, challenging modern world of wine.

But one thing hasn't changed, and that is my attitude to wine and wine-drinking. I love to exult in it! I love to find the fun in it before I check the facts of it. I love to immerse myself in the endless varieties of flavours and scents, I love to feel my heart beat with the sheer joy of it before I settle into the whys and wherefores of the world of wine. My approach has always been one of unashamed enthusiasm, hedonism if you like. I see wine as fun, as friendship, as laughter and jokes, frivolity and passion all hurled into the cauldron of pleasure – and what will the end result be? I don't always know, but I do know I will have had fun.

Of course, part of the pleasure I gain from wine is increasing my knowledge, not only of the old classic regions and their wines, where you reach back into the experience of generations past as you attempt to understand that quality, but also of the new. For me, a new wine region may be one where a dozen years ago there was nothing but virgin soil, uncleared forest and scrub and yet a lone visionary gazed upon the vacant slopes and dreamed of greatness. Or it may be vineyards neglected and forlorn, rejected by fashion, abused rather than used by whoever still deigned to harvest their grapes and make their wine. Until someone determines to resurrect past glories, maybe in an ancient style, maybe in a style that is radical and new and completely unrelated to what went before.

Ancient and modern, radical or reactionary, I try to cover it all in this book. And I try to cover everything from the viewpoint of the consumer. Many wine books are written from the viewpoint of the producers and sellers of wine. I write about wine as a consumer, because I love wine and all it stands for. When I first wrote about wine I was a singer on London's West End stage seeking out bargains for myself and my cronies to drink at our backstage parties. Actors and singers are a demanding lot, and I quickly learnt there was no point in bringing them back anything that was overpriced and underflavoured. I've never lost that attitude. I still care more about the flavour than the label, more about the wine's personality than the pedigree of the owner's family.

Even so, you'll find it all in here – the good, the bad and the ugly. The areas that are exciting, the areas that are underperforming - you'll find them in here. The vintages that are generally delicious, and the ones that bombed – you can find out here. The wines that need to age, the wines that wouldn't dream of it – you'll get my views on every page.

And hopefully they will all lead you to making up your own mind about what you like and don't like – and developing both the courage to stand up for your preferences and the openmindedness to accept that just because you don't like a wine, it doesn't mean that someone else won't find it delightful. And so long as we do all stand up for our rights as wine drinkers, the world of wine can only get better and better. Less than a generation ago, wine producers rarely considered the consumers' likes and dislikes. A mere decade ago the new age of wine consumer was born – opinionated, knowledgeable, enthusiastic yet demanding; prepared to pay for what they liked and pay well, prepared to refuse the stale, the musty, the lazily concocted and the dishonest – however famous the region, however pretentious the label. This consumer army now leads the world of wine, and the producers react by bringing out better flavours at fairer prices than ever before.

That's the modern world of wine, and this book is your essential guide to that modern world of wine.

THE WORLD OF WINE

The world of wine. What a modern phrase that is. That wine – good wine, wine that I want to drink – should come from every continent in the world – I still find that astonishing. The main reason it's so surprising is that a generation, two generations ago, wine didn't come from the whole world at all. It came from a handful of places: France, Portugal, Spain, Germany. That was about it.

But a look at the map below shows that while the world of wine has expanded dramatically, wine is still made in the same sorts of places as ever it was – even if those places are now more numerous. Basically, the vine is a Mediterranean plant that relishes warm summers and mildish winters. Nothing too baking hot, nothing too wet, nothing too freezing. Look at the way the vineyard areas of the

world steer clear of the Equator and are concentrated, instead, between about 30 and 50°N and 30 and 40°S. Look also at the way they tend to hug coastal areas.

The reason that vines like to be near the coast is very simple: the climate is more moderate there. California's Napa Valley, just north of San Francisco, would be as roasting as the interior of that state if it wasn't for the Pacific fogs that roll in from the sea, day after day, and cool things down in the coastal areas. South Africa, too, would be too hot; and Bordeaux, conversely, too cool.

The finest wine is made where it is only just warm enough to ripen the grapes properly. Overripe grapes, with a few exceptions, do not give fine wine. What the vine needs is a long, slow ripening season, extending well

Right: Australia and California are the most influential places in the world of wine today – simply because they're busy showing the rest of us how modern technology can make wines that are reliable, delicious, and yet taste of where they come from. The irony is, of course, that they took their inspiration, in the main, from Europe's classic wine areas.

Below: The selected list shows that despite the rise of several newcomers most of the world's wine still comes from Italy, France and Spain, as it has done for centuries.

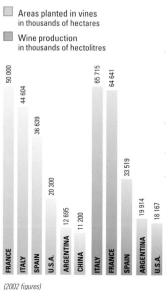

□ Areas planted in vines in thousands of hectares

□ Wine production in thousands of hectolitres

FRANCE	ITALY	SPAIN	U.S.A.	ARGENTINA	CHINA	ITALY	FRANCE	SPAIN	ARGENTINA	U.S.A.	HUNGARY
50 000	44 604	36 639	20 300	12 695	11 200	65 715	64 641	33 519	19 914	18 167	10 974

(2002 figures)

SAN FRANCISCO

NEW YORK

NORTH ATLANTIC OCEAN

PACIFIC OCEAN

SANTIAGO

■ Main vineyard areas of the world

into the autumn, so that the grapes can gradually concentrate their flavours. Ripen a grape fast and furiously and you'll get one-dimensional flavours of little interest. Ripen it slowly, risking autumn rains and hail, and you'll get complex, fascinating flavours that will repay the risk a hundredfold.

Making fine wine is risky. It means seeking out the most marginal conditions – in a warm climate, perhaps a high hilltop, where the days and nights will be cooler but where, equally, there will be less shelter from the wind and where the soil will be thinner and poorer. That's what Australian growers do: increasingly they are planting at higher altitudes to escape the limitations of latitude. In regions like France's Chablis it is already cool; the problem there is not overripening but frost and cold summers. So the growers react by seeking out the sunniest, south-facing slopes. In Germany, where it's even colder,

the finest vine is the Riesling, which is unusually resistant to cold winters. Even so, it's often only possible to grow it in the warmest spots along the steep banks of Germany's great rivers, the Mosel and Rhine, and their tributaries. An expanse of water like this can also help to temper extremes of climate, acting as a heat store to ward off frosts at night.

The point I want to make is that within the comparitively narrow bands of latitude that form the world's possible grape-growing regions there are an infinite number of different climates. Add to that differences of soil – and any gardener knows how much soil can vary within quite a small area – as well as the several dozen grape varieties used to make good wine today, and you have some idea of the number of variables with which the grower and winemaker has to deal. No wonder wine is so endlessly different. No wonder it's so fascinating.

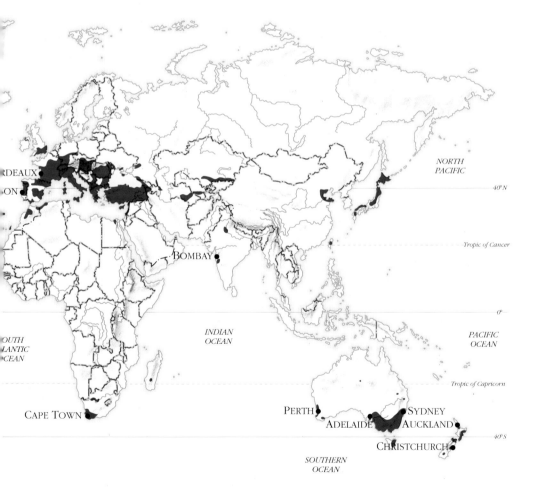

CHOOSING WINE

The world of wine used to be a pretty simple place. Wine-making was a parochial affair, and a winemaker would be unlikely to know much about the wine styles from over the next range of hills, let alone from over the barrier of country and continent.

The few original styles of wine – the Rheingau and Mosel Riesling in Germany, Bordeaux, Burgundy, Champagne and Hermitage in France, Rioja and sherry in Spain, Barolo and Chianti in Italy, Port and Madeira in Portugal – all created recognizable styles without rivalry from anywhere else.

How things have changed. The classic wines are still there, but every year – every month, almost – brings new alternatives. Some of these start as straightforward me-too exercises – not to be despised now that the classics are so expensive – but sometimes they're the result of good wine-making being applied to a region for the very first time.

It all makes for a very exciting picture, but a confusing one for the uninitiated as great wines are bursting out all over the place. So I'm going to pick out some of the main wine styles, and then check out the alternatives.

REDS
Red Bordeaux/Cabernet Sauvignon blends
This is probably the most classic red wine style of today. The reasons for this are twofold: red Bordeaux has been immensely popular on both sides of the Atlantic for generations; and the Cabernet Sauvignon variety, on which much red Bordeaux is based, is an extremely obliging traveller. It will grow in a great range of conditions all over the world, and always give wine with a recognizable varietal character. This means that if your ideal wine would be the one illustrated here – the classically elegant Château Léoville-Barton from St-Julien in Bordeaux – but you can't run to the price, you have a colossal choice of alternatives. In every wine-making continent Cabernet Sauvignon has become a byword for full-flavoured, reliable red wine.

Most obvious are the Cabernet Sauvignon and Bordeaux-style blends from Australia and the USA. Both tend to be softer, riper and more approachable at a young age than top red Bordeaux, and they won't age as long. Californian Bordeaux-style blends are sometimes labelled 'Meritage'. Leaner versions come from the Pacific North-West, or from New York State. Australian Cabernet is often blended with Shiraz. Hotter climates like much of South Australia and Victoria will produce rich wines; if you want lighter, leaner ones, look to cooler climates like Western Australia, Tasmania or New Zealand. In Italy, Tuscany boasts some top-class (and expensive) Cabernets, perhaps blended with Sangiovese; in Spain's Penedés the blending partner, if there is one, might be Tempranillo. South African Cabernet can be straight or blended; Chilean is usually bottled straight. Israel makes some good stuff on the Golan Heights, and there is even some (usually blended) from Greece. And don't forget the array of Cabernet wines from Eastern Europe, particularly Bulgaria. They're still turning them out here, and Bulgarian Cabernet is still good value, though Moldova is also producing some delightful versions.

Some of the best alternatives come from within France itself. Bergerac, the neighbouring region to Bordeaux, produces lighter lookalike wines that are good value; the South makes richer, juicier versions that can be stunning. Appellation wines from Provence may only be part-Cabernet, so look as well to varietal Vins de Pays from Languedoc labelled by grape variety. The lightest, freshest styles of all come from Chinon or Bourgueil in the Loire Valley, where the dominant grape is the Cabernet Franc.

Juicy, fruity reds
I've picked a Chilean Merlot as the modern archetype of this style; I'd have chosen Beaujolais in the past, but these days there are other regions doing this style of wine so much better. There's no particular grape name to look for, although Cabernet seldom makes this style of wine. Gamay, the grape of Beaujolais, can be a good bet: it should be juicily plummy, with marvellous bubblegum fruit. As well as Beaujolais, look to the Loire Valley for Gamay de Touraine. Lots of producers in the south of France and in the Côtes du Rhône region are using the same Beaujolais technique of carbonic maceration; Vins de Pays can give good examples of this style of wine, as can Côtes du Ventoux on the eastern side of the Rhône Valley.

Zinfandel, California's very versatile red grape is also sometimes made in a fresh, fruity, gluggable style for drinking young. Young Pinotage from South Africa can be like a smoky version of Beaujolais. Navarra, Valdepeñas and La Mancha in Spain, light reds from southern Portugal, young Chianti and Trentino's Teroldego in Italy, and grassy young Loire reds from France are also worth trying.

Pinot Noir/red Burgundy

The key to red Burgundy is fragrance and a gentle, strawberry or cherry fruit and this style is hard to imitate – but not impossible. Pinot Noir is a difficult grape to grow even in its home, the Côte d'Or. California has the most and usually the best examples: choose Carneros for wines with bright, fragrant fruit and Santa Barbara for ones with more substance. Pinot Noir is an Oregon speciality, and the top ones are good; New Zealand and Australia are also improving fast, with ripe, supple wines. Germany is making more and more good Spätburgunders, especially from Baden, and Romania makes jammy, good-value versions. Austria and Spain each have a few attractive Pinot Noirs; those from Italy's Alto Adige or France's Alsace are the lightest styles of all.

Syrah/Shiraz: spicy, warm-hearted reds

This is a style of wine where you don't have to stick to the specified grape variety, though I've picked Tim Adams' Shiraz from Australia as the archetype. France's Rhône Valley produces the wildest, smokiest, most herbal Syrah flavours, particularly in the north; in the southern Rhône Syrah is subdued by blending with earthier grape varieties. There are lots of good, bargain Syrah Vins de Pays in the Languedoc-Roussillon, too. These are often more Australian in style, with rich, leathery, berried fruit. In California 'Rhône Ranger' grapes are high fashion, and blends of Shiraz (or Syrah) with Mourvèdre, Grenache and others can be found, though they're seldom cheap. Good Zinfandel, particularly that made from old vines, also offers spicy, berried fruit. Rich, earthy reds at lower prices can be found in Portugal, particularly from the Douro Valley and the South, though top Bairradas can also deliver. In Spain, Toro and Ribera del Duero, both in Castilla y León, are places to look, and in the Lebanon, Chateau Musar, a blend of Cabernet Sauvignon, Cinsaut and Syrah, is marvellously spicy and long-lived. Mexico's Petite Sirah (not the same grape) is also a contender for this style.

But I haven't yet talked about Australian Shiraz. This is the place to look for utterly approachable wines at all price levels: you can pay a lot for distinguished wines from the Hunter or Barossa valleys, often from very old vines, or you can pay less for equally well-made versions that will still keep well.

WHITES
White Burgundy

Yes, I know white Burgundy is made from Chardonnay, and Chardonnay is made just about everywhere that wine is made. But because it's so ubiquitous I've split it into three different styles that reflect the versatility of the grape.

White Burgundy is the original, classic style of Chardonnay. It's nutty, oatmealy and subtle, and that very subtlety makes it the most difficult style to copy. The Côte d'Or still does it best – indeed, does it better than it used to, now that wine-making standards there have improved. Village wines like Meursault or Puligny-Montrachet are the benchmark; Grand Cru wines are superb if you can afford them, and simple, basic white Burgundy from a good grower offers a taste of the style at a lower price (though nothing in Burgundy is cheap). Isolated growers in California, Washington State, Oregon, New York State and Australia make successful lookalikes. Hungary makes some attractive mid-weight Chardonnays, though they don't really have any Burgundian oatmealiness. Wines that taste different, but that have similar balance and subtlety, come from Pessac-Léognan and the Graves in Bordeaux. And unoaked Semillon from the Hunter and Barossa valleys in Australia can with bottle age acquire somewhat Burgundian toastiness.

Steely, dry Chardonnay

This is not the most typical sort of Chardonnay, though it's certainly a benchmark. It's just that few other regions have shown that they can produce the sort of crisp, minerally fruit that Chardonnay develops in the Chablis region of Burgundy. Some Chablis is now aged in new oak, which rather inconveniently takes it out of this bracket – it becomes nearer to a Côte d'Or Chardonnay – and if you want this style from outside the Chablis region you'll be hard put to find anything with the same steely edge. Most have more softness. The best bets are Chardonnay from Italy's Alto Adige, or from Tasmania or New Zealand, or even England. There's not much in England, but Denbies and Valley Vineyards can do it.

Ripe, spicy Chardonnay

Ah, now this is easier. We're talking about ripe, ripe fruit that tastes of peaches, apricots, butterscotch, pineapple and all sort of tropical fruits. And oak: lots of oak, probably of the more pungent, spicy American sort. This style is an Australian invention, and if anybody mentions Australian

Chardonnay, it's ten to one that this is the taste they mean. It's found all over all Australia, except in the coolest places like Tasmania – it's very much a warm-climate style. So it's found, too, in California and in a lighter form in Washington State. Chile's Chardonnays are mostly in this mould, and range from the fairly simple to the quite complex, and South Africa has an increasing number of good ones. Spain has some big buttery Chardonnays, particularly from Penedés, and even Portugal has some good rich Chardonnay. In Italy, Tuscany is the main place to look for international-style versions, but if you want to stick to France, look in the South, where Australian-style wine-making is producing some good, quite inexpensive versions. Moving outside Chardonnay, Australian Semillon is often given a hefty dose of vanilla-flavoured oak, as is old-style white Rioja.

Green, tangy Sauvignon Blanc

I've specified green and tangy here because some New World producers favour aging Sauvignon Blanc in new oak, which gives an entirely different style. But this is the classic – and while it had its origins in the Loire Valley, particularly Sancerre, New Zealand is now doing it even better. Grassy-, nettle- and asparagus-flavoured wines come from many parts of the country, particularly the Marlborough, Hawkes Bay and Martinborough regions; Australia, though, is mostly just too warm to pull off this style successfully. So is much of California, though there are isolated examples there. The Pacific North-West is a better source. Chile is starting to find its feet with this style and there are some smashers from South Africa. In France, Sauvignon from the Loire, especially

Touraine, can be okay but look also to lesser regions like Haut-Poitou. Straight Sauvignon from Bordeaux can be slightly coarse but is usually quite attractive. Bordeaux Sauvignon is often blended with Sémillon. The regions of south-west France, like Bergerac and Côtes de Duras, can be good value, as are Vins de Pays from the Aude in Languedoc.

Non-Sauvignon wines that provide the same feel include bone-dry, aromatic traditional Vinho Verde from the coastal region of northern Portugal and even the lightest Trocken Rieslings from Germany.

Dry or off-dry Riesling

The great white grape of Germany has suffered hugely from copycat competitors – though most of the competition is from Germany itself rather than from outside. The classic Riesling Kabinett style – lowish in alcohol, with a taut streak of acidity running through it, and fruit that starts off flowery and becomes progressively more peachy and petrolly with age – has been imitated by cheap Liebfraumilch, which shares its medium-dry style but not its complexity, nor its ability to improve with age. Liebfraumilch and its cohorts, like Niersteiner Gutes Domtal, usually contain no Riesling at all. Much good Riesling in Germany is now made Halb-trocken (off-dry) or Trocken (dry); alternatives to these are either other German dry wines, like Scheurebe, or Silvaner from Franken or Grauburgunder from Baden, or the Rieslings of Alsace, which are made in a more savoury French style. Austrian Rieslings from the Wachau are dry and peachy and age well; Rieslings from Italy's Alto Adige or Trentino are lighter. English wines can have an attractive grapefruity acidity that is not unlike a young

German Riesling. Elsewhere in the world, Riesling tends to come in a riper and rounder style. The Pacific North-West and New York State produce the most classic US examples, and New Zealand has some good ones, but the Rieslings from the cool-climate regions of Clare and Eden in South Australia have established a style all their own: toasty, limy and long-lived.

Perfumy, off-dry whites

The benchmark wines in this style come from Alsace, from several grape varieties but above all from Gewürztraminer, the wines from which are immensely rich and spice-laden. The name of Gewürztraminer means 'spicy Traminer' and that spice is a smell of roses and lychees, sometimes mangoes. Other Alsace wines like Pinot Gris and Muscat give variations on the style: Pinot Gris is earthier, the Muscat grapier and more flowery. In southern Germany wines made from Gewürztraminer or Ruländer (Pinot Gris) tend to be more flowery, too. Austrian versions are well-structured and dry but seldom luscious with it. Müller-Thurgau provides inexpensive versions of the style in many places, particularly in New Zealand and Germany. Good dry Muscats are hard to find though there are some decent versions in Australia and the south of France; Viognier from the Rhône Valley and the south of France can also deliver lots of perfumed apricot fruit; and Irsay Oliver from Slovakia is quite Muscatty. Otherwise, decent Gewürztraminers come from the Alto Adige in Italy, where it is called Traminer or Aromatico, the Pacific North-West, especially Washington Stae, in the USA, New Zealand, especially Gisborne and Central Otago, and Chile.

Bone dry, neutral whites

These are wines the New World has tended not to copy: people look to the New World for upfront fruit, not reticent, high-acidity whites that won't fight with an oyster. So Muscadet from the Loire and wines made from the Ugni Blanc (alias Trebbiano in Italy) are the leaders in the field. Vin de Pays Charentais or Vin de Pays des Côtes de Gascogne are the Ugni Blancs from south-west France; although sometimes they're aged in oak, which gives them some vanilla richness. Trebbiano is grown all over northern and central Italy in a variety of guises and is sometimes blended. Think of Soave, Frascati, Orvieto, Lugana, Galestro... Apart from these models, proper Vinho Verde as drunk in Portugal (in other words, unsweetened) can be quite neutral or surprisingly aromatic; and dry whites from Austria's Styria can be quite neutral and acidic. Swiss whites from Chasselas are alternatives, as are unoaked Spanish whites.

Luscious sweet whites

Standards of these have improved all over the world in recent years. Sauternes and Barsac produce the most famous, with lesser versions coming from other parts of Bordeaux and Monbazillac in nearby Bergerac. Alsace has its Vendange Tardive and Sélection des Grains Nobles wines, Germany its Auslesen, Beerenauslesen and Eiswein, and Austria has its botrytis-affected wines from around Lake Neusiedl in Burgenland. Even Switzerland makes a few. The Tokaji region in Hungary is benefiting from outside investment and making superb wines, and Australia and the USA both make late-harvest wines from Semillon, Riesling and others. Romanian versions come from the Cotnari and Murfatlar regions and Canada makes excellent Icewine from Vidal or Riesling. Some of the longest-lived of all come from the Loire Valley in France. Non-botrytized sweet wines come from Italy, in the form of Recioto di Soave or Vin Santo, or from Austria in the form of Willi Opitz's Schilfwein, made from dried grapes. And then there are the sweet Muscat wines – France's Vins Doux Naturels from Beaumes-de-Venise and Languedoc-Roussillon; in Italy rose-scented Rosenmuskateller from the Alto Adige, and also some *passito* Moscato; Moscatel de Valencia from Spain and versions from South Africa and Greece. Not forgetting, of course, the superb, dark brown liqueur Muscats and Tokays from Victoria in Australia.

Sparkling wine

Champagne is still the benchmark for sparkling wines – but only just. Inside France, good fizzes are made in Burgundy, the Loire and the Rhône Valley (Crémant de Die), though only Crémant de Bourgogne really captures the style of Champagne. Italian fizzes made from Chardonnay and Pinot Noir can be quite good; Prosecco, the all-purpose fizz of Venice, is light and leafy-tasting, and Piedmont's Asti, lightly sweet and grapy. Spanish Cava still tends to be a bit rooty in flavour. The best rivals to Champagne come from Australia and California, where many a Champagne house has set up its own wine-making operation and now makes super-tasting Champagne-method fizz, often at bargain prices. New Zealand is also a good bet. The best German Sekts, occasionally all Riesling, are excellent, but the lesser ones are usually horrid.

FORTIFIEDS
Port

Port can be white, tawny or deep, deep red, and while a few of the white Ports are dry, most others are medium-sweet to very sweet. Nobody else seems to get the same finesse and complexity, the same spice-rich fruit into their wines as the Port producers do, so I think that this is one style where the original is still many lengths ahead of the rest of the field. Try the Australian and South African port-style wines if they come your way, because they can be quite interesting in their own right.

Sherry

It used to be that sherry could come from places other than Spain, notably Cyprus and Britain, but nowadays Spain has established its right to the sole use of the name – and quite right too, because nobody else does it as well.

The wines from Britain that used to be called British sherry aren't even made from fresh grapes: the producers use imported grape concentrate. South African sherry-style wines can be better, as can Australian ones, but they're still not as good as proper sherry.

Good sherry, whether sweet, medium or dry, has a sharp bite to it and a slightly woody tang. The nearest lookalikes from Spain itself are from the nearby Montilla-Moriles region which makes a similar range of styles and in the same way. Montilla's old sweet wines can be very good indeed. But the region is not thriving. Nobody makes a really convincing alternative to *fino* sherry, though if you want to taste a flor-affected wine with a totally different style, try a bottle of Vin Jaune from France's Jura.

TASTING WINE

Yes, you can enjoy wine reasonably well without ever understanding what you're tasting. But don't you enjoy music more if you know what you're listening to? Come to that, don't you enjoy food more if you understand what you're eating?

Even at the most high-spirited gathering, thinking about what you're drinking only takes a few moments. And it helps if you have some sort of framework in your mind to work from. A vocabulary of tasting terms is a great aid (see below). These descriptions can be as straightforward or as fanciful as you like, providing that each one means something to *you*. And before you say that wine tasters' language is all tosh, let me just point out that the same flavour compounds that give (for exam-

ple) green peppers and fresh-roasted coffee their flavour, also appear (in minute quantities) in Cabernet Sauvignon. So to describe Cabernet in terms of green peppers is fine.

Remember that the tongue can only taste the basic flavours of sourness or acidity, sweetness, bitterness and saltiness. Everything else we perceive as flavour is in fact smell. If you don't believe me, hold your nose and try to tell red wine from white – or coffee from tea. There is no doubt that wine can create passionate comment, because the complexity and changing variety of flavours which wine offers is equalled nowhere in the world of food or drink. And inside broad swathes of taste there is a myriad of differences, tiny, increasingly subtle, yet measurable.

TASTING TERMS

Aromatic Descriptive term for wines of a markedly flowery, spicy or grapy character.

Beefy Term for red wines meaning solid, chunky, four-square.

Buttery Often applied to white Chardonnay and sometimes red Merlot, Pinot Noir or Shiraz. Usually refers to the soft, rich, vanilla flavour imparted by new oak barrels.

Chewy Wine with a lot of tannin and strong flavour.

Clean Wine with no bacterial or chemical faults and a simple, direct flavour.

Deep Term for full-flavoured reds and whites, often applied to wines still not at their peak.

Dusty Usually applied to hot country reds, in particular wines from the southern Rhône.

Earthy A slight root vegetable, muddy flavour, not usually complimentary, except for wines made from Cabernet Franc.

Fat A heavy, sometimes slightly clumsy wine, though if made from fully ripe grapes it can imply a rather unctuous richness in the wine, sweet or dry.

Freshness The youthful aromas in a wine, usually associating good acidity with floral or fruit flavours.

Fruit Term, literally, for the fruit element in a wine. It may not taste of grapes, but it will resemble a fruit of some kind (e.g. apple, blackcurrant, strawberry) and is crucial to the flavour of most wines.

Fullness The feel, or weight, of a wine in the mouth.

Grapy Quite rare flavour of the grape itself in wine. Most common in Muscat, Riesling or Gewürztraminer.

Green Unripe, or tart, not neccessarily an unattractive taste in light, young wine.

Hard Usually applied to reds which have an excess of tannin. In young reds, this is often neccessary to facilitate the aging process.

Honeyed Applied to ripe wines which, sweet or dry, have a taste of honey.

Jammy Rather big, cooked, seemingly sweetish wines, usually red.

Length The way a good wine's flavours continue to evolve in the mouth even after swallowing.

Nutty Usually for dry whites (e.g. a soft Brazil or hazelnut flavour in Chardonnay, a woodier taste in Chenin or Sauvignon Blanc, and a dry richness in medium sherry or Madeira).

Oaky The slightly sweet vanilla flavour imparted by maturation in oak casks. The newer the oak used the more forceful its impact on the wine.

Petrolly An attractive smell applied to mature Riesling wines, and sometimes mature Sémillon.

Plummy Often applied to big, round, ripe reds from Pomerol, St-Émilion, Côte de Nuits and Napa.

Prickly A wine with slight residual gas left in it. Usually attractive in light young whites, but in reds it can be a sign of refermentation in bottle.

Smoky Many wines do have a smoky, aromatic taste, especially when slightly charred oak barrels have been used in maturation.

Spicy Exotic fruit and spice flavours in whites, particularly Gewürztraminer, but also a peppery or cinnamon/clove perfume in some reds and whites aged in oak.

Steely Applied to good quality Rieslings for their very dry, almost metallic flavour.

Stony Usually implying a rather dull, empty dryness in a red or white.

Sweet Tasting term, applied not only to sweet wines, but also to the elements of ripeness or richness which good quality, dry wines can often suggest.

Sweet-sour The slightly sour raisiny taste often found in Italian reds.

Tart Green, unripe wine with excess acidity. Can be desirable in light, dry wines.

Checking the label
They say that one look at the label is worth 30 years blind tasting. That's because the label will tell you the vintage, the alcohol level, the region the wine comes from, its classification (for example, AC or Vin de Pays) and the name and address of the producer. National and international laws set out basic levels of information that labels must convey, but in addition lots of wines have back labels which tell you when to drink the wine, how sweet it is and what sort of food it will go with.

Removing the cork
Wine bottles have corks to exclude the air. Screw caps will do the job as efficiently, but they don't look as nice, and the fact is, we all like playing around with corkscrews. But good-quality corks are expensive, and producers are increasingly using synthetic corks for inexpensive wines. They're sometimes brightly coloured, so we know nobody's trying to fool us. My corkscrew still works on them, so I'm happy. The one I'm using here

is a Screwpull, which is smoothly efficient and seems foolproof; the Waiter's Friend and other level models are also easy. But any corkscrew with an open helix will do the job efficiently. A solid helix is more likely to rip through corks, especially old and fragile ones.

Looking at the wine
The colour and depth will tell you a good deal about whether it comes from a cool country or a hot one (hot country wines have a deeper colour, on the whole), a frail grape or a gusty one (again, frailer grapes tend to have paler colours), and the age of the wine. Tilt the glass against a white background, preferably in daylight and definitely not under neon light. That way you can see the range of colours of the wine, plus any lighter rim that comes with age. Sometimes the colour is so beautiful it's worth gazing at for a while to heighten your expectations.

Swirling the wine
Why do we do this? Because it releases the volatile aromas in the wine so that you can get a

good sniff at them. Remember I said that most of what we perceive as taste is in fact smell? Well, this is how you persuade the wine to start telling you about itself. Don't swirl too vigorously at first – particularly if you're unpractised, the wine is red and the carpet may stain. But you'll soon get into a rhythm – indeed, it's rather soothing. Then stick your nose into the glass fast, before the smell dissipates.

Smelling the wine
This is very important, whether you're tasting critically or for pleasure. Swirl the glass gently, and take a good steady sniff, as if you'd leant over to smell a rose in the garden. Those initial split seconds of inhalation may reveal all kinds of familiar or unfamiliar smells. Always interpret them in words which mean something to *you*. Use similes from everyday life: if the smells remind you of honey, or chocolate, or curry and carrots, fresh apples or rubber tyres – if those or any others are the smells you get – they are sure to be right for you because it is your nose doing the smelling. Another person may interpret the smells differently. That's fine. It is only by honestly reacting to the stimuli of taste and smell in wine that you can build up a memory bank of flavours against which to judge future wines and which will help you recognize wines already tried before. It's also worth jotting down your thoughts at the time, before you forget them – a glance at your notes will bring the flavours careering back weeks later.

Taking a mouthful
Take a reasonable draught of wine – so that your mouth is maybe one-third full and then (if you're by yourself or with friends) feel free to pull a few faces and make some slurping noises. The whole objective is to get the fumes from the wine which is in your mouth to rise up to your nasal cavity, which is where the real tasting goes on. Draw in a little air through your mouth and suck it through the wine – this will help to speed the volatile aroma compounds on their way to your nasal cavity as you then breathe out through your nose.

Assessing the wine
The first thing to do is to pick out any toughness or acidity, which you will feel in your mouth, and then experience all the personality and flavour, which you will 'taste' in your nasal cavity – breathing out carries the aromas to your nasal cavity. Now, quite literally, chew the wine – as if you had a piece of meat between your molars. And concentrate. You want to clock, first your spontaneous impressions, then

the actual taste that will develop after the wine has been in your mouth a few seconds, and finally – after you've swallowed or spat out the wine, which in turn depends on whether you're doing this for fun or work – the persistent, lingering taste which wine-tasters call the 'length' of the wine. The flavours may blast you unchangingly from the first whiff, or they may shift as tantalizingly as sand under the rising tide. In either case, do make notes as you go. It's incredibly difficult to remember a flavour, five or six wines later.

What can you tell from your mouthful?
Basically, what you're trying to do is assess the wine's quality, and its probable development. There are four basic points to look for. First, acidity. Any wine, be it sweet, medium or dry, must have acidity to be refreshing, and to be able to age. But one acid you don't ever want is acetic. That's vinegar. Next, tannin. This comes from the skins and pips of grapes, and is found in red wine: it's the rasping, tooth-furring component that dries your mouth out. It's necessary in greater or lesser amounts if a wine is to age, but it must be in balance with the fruit. The fruit is the next thing to look for – wine is made of fruit and without it wine is no fun. Then there's colour. Lots of colour is not always necessary. Some reds, like those from Pinot Noir, rarely have a deep colour, but may still be full of flavour. Some good whites, especially Rieslings and Sauvignons, have almost no colour at all.

Spitting
Why spit? Well, there are plenty of occasions when spitting would be highly inappropriate: most social situations, for example. But if you've set up a serious tasting with like-minded friends, or you're tasting in a grower's cellar on holiday, then spitting is the order of the day. It's the only way to taste a lot of wines and stay sober. It helps to keep your palate clearer for longer, too. You don't need a special spittoon: a bucket will do. Sawdust in the bottom will make it look less unpleasant. And put newspaper underneath it for those with poor aim.

Summing up
If the flavour lingers in your mouth after you've swallowed or spat out the wine, then that's a sign of quality. And the longer it lingers the better. If the flavour falls away rather quickly – well, don't reckon on laying that wine down for too long. But it isn't just tough, dense wines that can age well. Sometimes a pleasant, approachable, fruity wine just goes on and on – that's quality without tears.

Understanding faults

High wine-making standards in most countries means that faults in wine are rarer than they were. The commonest fault is oxidation, which usually shows as a staleness, a flatness, on the nose and palate. It means the wine has been exposed to too much oxygen. A little is necessary for wine to mature; too much leads to oxidation. Corked wine is recognizable by its mouldy, stale smell – it's caused by a chlorine infection in the cork – and the smell is unmistakable once you've suffered it. Dirty tastes in wine can also be caused by dirty barrels. Too much sulphur (some sulphur is needed to prevent oxidation) smells like spent matches. If the wine fizzes when it shouldn't, and has a yeasty smell, then it may be refermenting. If it's hazy, it may have a chemical problem – but if it's a mature, fine wine you may just have shaken up the sediment. See what it tastes like.

Opening Champagne and other sparkling wines

I love that soft pop of the cork, followed by the wisp of smoky gas curling upwards – and then the great whoosh of bubbles.

But ideally you should control that whoosh of bubbles as much as you can. Otherwise you just waste wine. So hold the bottle firmly, and take off the foil. Then loosen the wire cage and ease it off, keeping one hand firmly over the cork as you do so: some corks can pop out unexpectedly. And never shake the bottle first, unless you want to be mistaken for a Grand Prix champion.

Now hold the bottle at an angle of 45° – but not pointing at anyone because the cork can shooot out at quite a rate. Ease the cork out gently, twisting the cork and the bottle and controlling it as you feel the pressure on your hand. Have a glass ready for the cascade of foaming wine.

THE TASTE OF THE GRAPE

The taste of the grape is intimately bound up with the grape variety. The fundamental balance of sugars, acid and tannin is particular to each variety. Here are some of the classic grape flavours, as well as some of the more bizarre nuances we may think we detect in wine in more fanciful moments.

RED GRAPES

Cabernet Franc Medium, blackcurrant, grassy, sometimes earth and raspberry.

Cabernet Sauvignon Dark, tannic, blackcurrant, cedar, mint.

Gamay Light to medium, strawberry, peach, pepper, going to farmyard earthiness, and Pinot-like strawberry jam.

Merlot Full, soft, blackcurrant, honey, raisins, mint, plum.

Nebbiolo Medium colour, very tannic and difficult to appreciate, prunes, raisins, tobacco, tar, hung game, chocolate – and roses!

Pinot Noir Middleweight, fragrant, often delicate, strawberry, cherry, plum.

Sangiovese Medium to full, tobacco, cherry stone, herbs, sometimes vegetal, raisins.

Syrah Dark, tannic, savage, sometimes, loganberry, redcurrant, blackcurrant, plum, herbs, pepper, smoke, licorice, toffee.

Tempranillo Light to medium, strawberry, vanilla, sometimes blackcurrant, pepper.

WHITE GRAPES

Chardonnay Dry white, from light, appley and acid to full yeast, butter, cream, toast, grilled nuts, sometimes slightly grapy.

Chenin Blanc Very dry to sweet, green apples, lemon, nuts, chalk, to apricots, peach, angelica, honey.

Gewürztraminer Fairly dry to sweet, above all spice, then tropical fruit, cosmetic perfume, freshly ground pepper – and Nivea Creme!

Muscat Dry to very sweet, crunchy, green grapes, peppery yeast, eating apples when dry to deep orange peel, treacle, raisins, toffee and tea leaf when sweet.

Palomino Sherry grape, very dry to sweet, from sharp, almost sour, herbs, to raisin, treacle, toffee, moist brown sugar.

Pinot Blanc Dry, apples, yeasty, cream, spice.

Riesling Very dry to very sweet, steely, slate, apple to lime, petrol, raisins, even honey and tropical fruits.

Sauvignon Blanc Very dry to very sweet, green flavours, grass, nettles, gooseberry, asparagus, elderflower, going to raisin and honey though still with an acid edge.

Sémillon Dry to very sweet, green apple, lemon, lanolin, herbs, to cream, honey, nuts, peaches and sometimes custard and leather.

Viognier Full dry, apricot, pear-skin, may-blossom, musky peaches.

STORING & BUYING WINE

Laying down wine in a cellar. That phrase has a marvellous ring to it. I have visions of the butler gliding into the drawing room of some country house, purring into my ear, 'Would Sir care to view the cellar?'. I'm up in a flash, not even waiting to finish my Pimms or the piece in *Vogue* on this year's croquet fashions, and pad after the keeper of the cellar. Down we go. The stairs get darker, danker, as we descend; cobwebs, the slight glistening of damp fungus on the stone – and then – the iron gate – the paradise. The great rusty key turning grudgingly in the lock, the squeak of the door in the gloom. The butler lights an enormous candle to reveal – as far as the eye can peer – bins and alcoves packed with ancient Bordeaux, dust-covered Burgundy, golden Sauternes. Well, I dream on.

PLANNING YOUR CELLAR

But seriously, the concepts of laying down wine and building up a bit of a cellar both bear some examination. You don't need acres of cellars and a country house (though I'd never refuse either); all you have to do is buy some wine in advance for the convenience of not having constantly to rush out to the local shop, and have somewhere to keep it.

Time can do remarkable things to the colour of a wine. White wines generally darken, becoming deeper yellow as they absorb more oxygen.

Even the deepest red wines fade with age, eventually acquiring a tawny colour which becomes most visible around the rim.

That second point, somewhere to keep it, is the problem for most of us. If you own valuable bottles, there is a strong argument for storing much of your stock with a reputable wine merchant. You will have to pay a storage charge, but the right conditions for really fine wine are hard to find in the average house or flat. For more everyday wines – including those you plan to keep for a year or so, even a couple of years – there are four conditions to try and achieve: correct cool temperature, adequate humidity, relative darkness and relative stillness. This blend of conditions will age the wine slowly, which always results in a slightly more exciting end result. Warm or unstable conditions age wine faster, which almost always results in a less perfect balance of flavour at maturity.

Temperature This should be as stable as possible; changes should be of the gradual seasonal sort rather than huge leaps every time the central heating switches itself on or off. The ideal range is between 10 and 13°C (50 and 55°F), which is slightly cooler than is comfortable for most of us. So keep wine in the coolest part of the house, and certainly away from a radiator.

Humidity Dampness isn't usually a problem for wine, although you might get a bit of mould on the labels. If it's too dry, though, the corks can shrink. It may sound silly but if you have a very dry house, get a humidifier. Your furniture will benefit, too.

Darkness Bright light can damage wines, particularly whites, and particularly Champagne. So if you have to store wines in a light spot, drape a blanket over them. Not pretty, but effective. Keeping bottles in their original cartons or wooden boxes is another solution or wrap tissue paper round individual bottles.

Stillness Vibration can tire a wine, but since some of the best cellars in old cities are underneath railway arches which vibrate frighteningly every time a train goes over, I wouldn't lose sleep over it .

In most homes the ideal storage spot doesn't exist, and it's a question of compromise. The understairs cupboard is a good bet, as are wardrobes, or the garage (but careful the wine doesn't freeze in winter). The kitchen is too warm for more than a few weeks.

BUYING WINE

That only leaves the question of what to buy, and from whom. The style of wine to buy depends on you. What sort of food do you

Me in my favourite room of the house – though you don't have to have such ideal conditions as this to store wine successfully.

like? There's no point in laying down bottles of Cabernet Sauvignon in your cellar if all you eat is fish.

It's also worth remembering that most wines – almost everything in your local store – will be best within a year of buying it. Don't make the mistake of keeping wines too long, or of buying more than you need.

If you fancy some serious aging you may want to sample wines from specialist wine merchants. Tell them what you want, how much you want to spend and ask their advice on what to buy. If you're buying a reasonable amount they'll be happy to let you taste first.

If you buy by mail order it's more difficult to taste in advance, but unless you're going to travel half way across the country it can be the only way of buying wines from particular growers. Most specialist merchants operate a mail order service, and also provide free delivery within their local area.

Some fine wines, notably red Bordeaux, can be bought *en primeur* – that is, in the spring after the vintage. You then take delivery of the wine about 18 months later. It's a way of obtaining scarce wines, but don't assume you'll pay less. And only go to a reliable merchant.

WHEN TO DRINK WINES

WINES TO DRINK YOUNG

Reds Most Beaujolais; basic red Burgundy, e.g. Bourgogne Rouge; Mâcon Rouge; Merlot from the Veneto; simple Rioja; inexpensive reds from the south of Portugal; country wines from Bulgaria; inexpensive Australian reds.

Whites All inexpensive whites, plus Bourgogne Blanc, Mâcon Blanc, Asti; Italian Trebbiano; Vinho Verde.

WINES THAT CAN AGE

Reds Red Bordeaux of Cru Bourgeois quality and upwards; red Burgundy of single-village level upwards; Rhône; Barolo; Brunello di Montalcino; Super-Tuscan Vini da Tavola; Recioto di Valpolicella; Ribera del Duero; top California Cabernet Sauvignon and Zinfandel; top Australian Cabernet Sauvignon and Shiraz.

Whites Top Pessac-Léognan; Sauternes; Burgundy of single-village level upwards; Alsace Vendange Tardive; Savennières; sweet Loire wines; German Riesling; Recioto di Soave; top California Chardonnay; top Australian Chardonnay, Riesling and Semillon.

SERVING WINE

Now, I'm the last person in the world to be pernickety about how wine is served. I'd rather be served an everyday wine in a tin mug with good friends than drink classed growth red Bordeaux out of crystal glasses with people I don't care about. But, on the other hand, if I've gone to the trouble of selecting wine I'm really going to enjoy, and then made the effort to store it properly, it seems silly not to serve it in a way that will make the most of its flavour. So, bearing in mind that not all wines need or want the red-carpet treatment, and there are plenty of picnic and sundowner wines that demand nothing more than a corkscrew and a clean tumbler, let's lay down a few guidelines.

Atmosphere By this I don't mean soft music and the person opposite, I mean the air. The commonest wine-killer is tobacco smoke. You can't smell tobacco and wine at the same time. Some cooking smells, in particular highly spiced oriental food and greasy fried food, do taint the air in a way which makes it impossible to smell good wine. So if you can't avoid having those sorts of smell in the house, open all the windows or don't open any special bottles.

Matching food and wine As for oriental food itself – as well as all the other types of food that used to be considered exotic and

Good bread, unpasteurized cheese and wine made by a producer who cares is the simplest meal of all – and still one of the best.

are now pretty everyday – wine matching is now easier than it's ever been. Partly it's the ever-greater abundance of good flavours from all over the world, and partly, I think, it's because we've all spent so much time thinking seriously about what to drink with chocolate or eggs or Thai food or other supposedly difficult partners for wine. Chocolate still won't flatter any wine, but Australian liqueur Muscat will match it well, as will decent quality (though not the best) young Sauternes. Alsace wine, particularly Gewürztraminer, Tokay-Pinot Gris or Riesling, or good German Riesling goes well with many Chinese dishes; Sauvignon Blanc is good with Thai. Young, fruity reds can be good with Indian food, providing it's spicy but not too hot. Simple unoaked Chardonnay can be nice with eggs.

With more traditional dishes, the old rule of white with white meat and fish, and red with red meat is a reasonable starting point, but remember to take into account the flavour of the whole dish, including the sauce, not just the main ingredient. And match the weight of the flavour, the level of acidity, and of course the occasion.

Serving young wines before old is kind to them both; likewise, serving dry wines before sweet brings out the best in each and is easier on the palate. In the chart (right) I've indicated approximate serving temperatures, but remember that it's always better to serve wine too cold than too hot. You can always warm a glass in your hands, but wine served too warm tastes soupy and over-alcoholic.

Decanting People sometimes worry about this one. Not just should we or shouldn't we, but how long before? An hour before? Two hours before? Well, my advice is, don't worry. Old wines – particularly mature red Bordeaux, red Burgundy, northern Rhônes and vintage or some crusted Ports – may need decanting if they've thrown a sediment, but don't give old wines too much air. Red Bordeaux may develop its bouquet if you give it an hour or two in a decanter, but if in doubt it's better to wait for the the wine to develop in the glass than decant it too early and find the flavour has dissipated by the time you come to drink it. In general, most wines don't need decanting, but if you've got a nice decanter you might as well use it. It'll look lovely and the wine may even soften up a bit.

Keeping wine If you have some left over in the bottle, you can usually recork it, put it in the fridge and drink it the next day. But if you want to keep it longer it may be worth investing in a Winesaver, which is a canister of inert gas which, when squirted into the bottle, sits on top of the wine and prevents oxidation. Kept like this, most wines (not the oldest and most fragile) will keep for several weeks. But, frankly, most young white wines, re-corked, will be alright for a day or two in the kitchen and a week or two in the fridge. Young red wines will last a day or two if kept cool.

Sparkling wine is also pretty easy to keep, though only for a day or so. You can buy Champagne stoppers, and the carbon dioxide in the wine will help to prevent oxidation. But remember that as the carbon dioxide escapes the wine goes flat – and the wine oxidizes.

If you have several open bottles of everyday white wine after a party top them up, recork them and keep them in the fridge. They'll be fine for several weeks. But never, ever, keep wine for longer than a few hours in that elegant, cut-glass decanter that sits so invitingly on your sideboard. Oxygen is the enemy of opened wine. Keep it away from oxygen, and your wine will last much longer.

When decanting this is the moment to stop pouring – the sediment is moving up the bottle and in another moment will have joined the wine in the claret jug.

SERVING TEMPERATURES

in degrees centigrade (°C)

Northern Rhône reds, California Cabernet Sauvignon, Australian Shiraz	
approx. 4 hrs at room temperature	**18°C**
Bordeaux, Châteauneuf-du-Pape, Catalonian and Australian Cabernet, Ribera del Duero, Chilean Cabernet, South African Cabernet and Pinotage	**17°C**
Red Côte d'Or Burgundy, southern French reds, southern Italian reds, Rioja, Toro, Australian and California Pinot Noir	**16°C**
Côte Chalonnaise, Douro red table wines, young Zinfandel, Oregon Pinot Noir, New Zealand Cabernet and Pinot Noir	**15°C**
Chinon, Bourgueil, northern Italian and Washington State Cabernet Sauvignon, Valpolicella, young Chianti	**14°C**
Young Beaujolais, red Sancerre, Bardolino, Lago di Caldaro, young Spanish and Portuguese reds	**12–13°C**
Sauternes, top white Côte d'Or Burgundy, sweet German wines, Tokay, Canadian Icewine, Australian liqueur Muscat	**10°C**
Rhine and Mosel Kabinett and Spätlese, Italian oaked Chardonnay, oaked white Rioja, California and Australian Chardonnay	**10°C**
Good white Pessac-Léognan and Graves, north-eastern Italian whites, Washington State Chardonnay, Chilean Chardonnay, Australian Semillon, New Zealand Chardonnay	**9°C**
Alsace, Chablis, Côte Chalonnaise and Mâconnais whites, dry German wines, Franken wines, Austrian Riesling, English wines, Australian Riesling, Cabernet and Grenache rosé	**8°C**
Good Champagne and sparkling wine, Sancerre, New York State, Chilean and New Zealand Sauvignon Blanc	**7°C**
White Bordeaux, Muscadet, Anjou, other Sauvignons, Asti, unoaked white Rioja, 'flying winemaker' unoaked Chardonnay	**6°C**
Qba German wines, Soave, young Spanish and Portuguese whites, Vinho Verde, Swiss Chasselas, Austrian Grüner Veltliner, cheap rosé	**5°C**
Cheap sparkling wines	
approx. 4 hrs in refrigerator	**2–4°C**

FROM VINE TO WINE

If you leave grapes alone, they'll make wine by themselves. It's easy: the juice is full of sugar, and all it needs is for the skin to break and the yeasts that accumulate on the skins will get to work.

Actually, the yeasts on the skins – they form the bloom on a ripe grape – are too weak to be of much use to the winemaker. When winemakers use wild yeasts, as they do in many regions, it's the ones that are naturally present in the cellars that are called on to get things moving. And here, as in so many areas, the winemaker can intervene.

MODERN WINE-MAKING

The winemaker has a number of choices, from whether the wine is to be red, white, pink or sparkling, to whether or not it is to be aged in new oak barrels, to the precise time it should be bottled. Sometimes the best option for the winemaker is to stand back and let the wine find its own way; sometimes better wine will result if, for example, he or she reduces the temperature, or chooses one cultivated yeast rather than another.

Some of the most remarkable examples of winemaker intervention are embodied in the so-called flying winemakers – internationally minded winemakers, often Australian trained, who jet in to impose higher standards on a winery in some generally underrated part of the wine world, and then jet off to do the same elsewhere. If you want an example of non-intervention, I'd suggest organic wine-making – though, of course, the two methods are not entirely incompatible. To do either well means learning the skill of knowing when to step in, and when not to. Most good winemakers will tell you that the very best they can do is bring out the full potential of their grapes. That's all. You can't make a great wine from poor-quality grapes. With modern technology you can make a clean, fruity one from almost anything, yes, but not a great one.

If you want to make a great wine there's only one place you can start, and if you leave it until the grapes arrive at the winery you've left it too late. You have to start much further back: in fact, with planting your vineyard.

MODERN VITICULTURE

In many parts of the world you can plant a vineyard anywhere. You can dig up your roses, if you like, and plant Chardonnay. (In the EU there is currently a planting ban, and you might find a bureaucrat on your doorstep, but that's another matter.) You can make wine with your Chardonnay, and it might even be drinkable. But if it is to be good, then your Chardonnay will have to have the right sort of climate: one that will ripen the grapes over a long, warm (but not too hot) summer, and one where the summer nights are cool enough to enable the grapes to retain acidity. You'll need to plant them where they get the right exposure to the sun: too little and they won't ripen properly, too much and they'll overripen. You can adjust the amount of foliage on each vine, and manipulate the way the vines are trained to help with this, as well. You'll need soil that is well drained, but bear in mind that in EU countries you can't normally irrigate, so your vines may have to cope with drought on their own. And in countries where you can irrigate, you'll have to be careful not to over-irrigate, or you'll end up with dilute-tasting wines.

Which brings me to the question of yields. I talk a lot about yields in this book. And they matter because if you want intense, concentrated wines you have to restrict the yields – usually by pruning hard, perhaps by removing surplus bunches, certainly by not over irrigating or over-fertilizing. Yields almost everywhere have increased in the last few decades, though vineyard management has improved to keep pace. But there are limits.

Most young vines in the southern hemisphere need irrigation to help them get established. These ones in Chile's Casablanca Valley are using drip irrigation.

In recent years many new trellising methods, seen here at Kenwood Vineyards in Sonoma, have been developed to increase the quality of the fruit.

Encourage your vines to produce too many grapes and you are diluting the flavour. It's as simple as that. But of course if we want great wines we have to pay what they cost. That's simple, as well.

All wine-making consists of four main processes: preparation, fermentation, maturation and bottling. How each is carried out depends on what sort of wine is wanted and what sort of grapes are involved. And the one fundamental thing to remember is that virtually all wine grapes have colourless juice. That applies whether their skins are deepest purple or palest greeny-gold. The colour of red wines comes from the skins, not the juice. The tannin of red wines also comes from the skins, plus the pips and sometimes the stems. It follows that you can, if you separate red grape skins from the juice, make white wine from red grapes. (The impossibility of separating them without some colour seeping into the juice means that most whites of this sort have a pink tinge.)

MAKING RED WINES

On arrival at the winery, the grapes are crushed. Sometimes they are destemmed at the same time: it depends on whether the winemaker wants the extra tannin from the stalks. The only time the grapes are not crushed is when carbonic maceration is to be used. This is the technique responsible for the juicy, bubblegum flavour of good Beaujolais, and it is used with great success with some of the traditionally tough, tannic grapes of the south of France and elsewhere. In carbonic maceration the grapes are put whole into a vat. Obviously, the ones at the bottom get a little crushed, and the juice begins to ferment in the usual way. But the vat is sealed, and carbon dioxide is pumped in. The unbroken grapes undergo an intracellular fermentation which produces some alcohol and a great deal of aroma as well as deep colour, but not much tannin. As the grapes burst, their juice mingles with that of the crushed grapes and completes fermentation in the normal way.

But let's go back to the standard way of making red wine. The crushed grapes – a sticky, slurpy mess – are pumped into vats which can be fibre glass, concrete, stainless steel or wood. The winemaker may rely on the yeasts present in the cellar to start the fermentation, or he may kill them with a dose of sulphur dioxide in the juice (which is now called must) and add some cultivated yeast. Either way, the fermentation gets going.

Red wine is generally allowed to ferment at a higher temperature than white, and it may be left to macerate on the skins for some days after the fermentation has died down. It all depends on whether the winemaker wants a

Chardonnay grapes being tipped straight into the crusher on arrival at Tepusquet Vineyards in Santa Maria Valley, California.

These are the sort of stainless steel fermentation tanks (here at Vergelegen Estate in South Africa) on which many a modern winemaker relies.

It's high-tech to have a computerized control panel like this one at Château Lynch-Bages, Pauillac. The fermentation in every vat can be controlled from here.

deep-coloured, tannic wine or a lighter one; he can run the wine off the skins at any stage if he thinks the colour and tannin are enough. The wine can then finish fermenting without the skins.

What is important is to keep the skins in contact with the wine while they are still there. The pressure of the fermentation tends to push them to the top of the vat, where they form what is called the cap. This must be constantly broken up and pushed back into the wine (or the wine must be pumped up over it). If neither is done, then bacteria can grow on the cap, and in any case, the winemaker is not getting the benefit of the available colour and tannin.

The soggy grape skins are then pressed, and the so-called press wine is usually matured separately from the free-run wine. Some will probably be added when the winemaker puts together his final blend: it is darker, more tannic and coarser but can be useful in small quantities.

The new wine will be run off into vats, or into new oak barrels if the winemaker wants their rich vanilla flavour. The length of time for which a wine is aged, and whether in vat or barrel, depend partly on what sort of wine is wanted (for drinking young or for laying down in bottle) and partly on the characteristics of the individual wine: some wines are gutsy enough to be aged in new oak barrels, some aren't. Either way, the young wine will undergo the malolactic fermentation either soon after the alcoholic fermentation or when the cellar warms up in the spring. This second fermentation is caused by bacteria which change the sharp-tasting malic acid in the wine to the softer-tasting lactic acid, and the wine tastes rounder as a result.

Bottling takes place when the winemaker decides the wine has matured enough. Beaujolais Nouveau is bottled days rather than months after the harvest. With a light red for drinking young, bottling might be within a few months; reds aged in new oak barriques (the small barrels used in Bordeaux and elsewhere) may not be bottled for 18 months or so, and will then need further aging in bottle before they are ready to drink.

MAKING ROSÉ WINES

In the EU you have to do this by starting off as if you were making red wine, and then running the juice off the skins when it has just the right pink colour. You then proceed as for white wines. Only in Champagne can you mix red and white wine together. Outside the EU that rule doesn't apply.

MAKING WHITE WINES

The grapes are usually pressed as soon as they arrive at the winery and the skins discarded. Sometimes, however, they are crushed and left to soak together for a day or two, to extract more flavour and aroma. But white must is not fermented with the skins or stalks. The fermentation temperature of white wine is much lower – between 16° and 18°C (60° and 64°F) compared to 25°–28°C (77°–82°F) for most reds. This is because there is no need for colour or tannin, but every need for freshness and aroma, and these are best preserved at low temperature. The single most important development in modern wine-making has been the introduction of efficient methods of controlling fermentation temperatures – and its effect has been even more dramatic in white wines than in reds.

An increasing number of fine whites are being fermented in barriques. The effect is to give the wines the same toasty vanilla flavour that they gain from being aged in barrique, but if they are fermented in barrique the flavours seem more integrated, more tightly married with the fruit and more subtle.

The finest sweet wines are made from grapes so sweet that sugar is left in the wine after the fermentation stops. Other methods are to add sweet, unfermented must to finished wine (as in Germany for some wines) or to stop the fermentation before all the sugar has been turned to alcohol.

Some whites are allowed to undergo the malolactic fermentation, but often the desire for fruit acidity means that the winemaker filters the bacteria out or stuns them with sulphur dioxide to prevent it.

MAKING SPARKLING WINES

The Champagne method is the one used for all the best fizz (see page 98). But all sparkling wine, unless it is made by pumping carbon dioxide into wine under pressure, involves adding yeast and sugar to base wine, and allowing it to ferment in a closed container. That way the carbon dioxide stays in solution in the wine, ready to foam in the glass when the bottle is opened.

MAKING FORTIFIED WINE

These are made as for reds or whites, with the difference that grape spirit is added – either during the fermentation in order to stop it and leave residual sweetness in the wine (as with Port, Bual or Malmsey in Madeira, and France's Vins Doux Naturels) or afterwards, when the wine has already fermented out to dryness (as with sherry or Sercial in Madeira).

Wines are racked at intervals during their maturation – which means running them into a clean barrel or vat and leaving the sediment behind in an old one.

Assessing the young wines (these, at Robert Mondavi Winery in California, are still cloudy from fermentation) is a difficult, skilled task.

Not all great wines are aged in new oak. These barrels, which have already seen several years' use, are at Vega Sicilia in Spain's Ribera del Duero.

GLOSSARY

ACETIC Vinegary. A sign that a wine is infected by acetobacters and only fit for the vinegar still.

ACID Naturally present in grapes and essential to wine, providing the refreshing tang in white wines and the appetizing 'grip' in reds. Principal wine acids are acetic, carbonic, citric, malic, tannic and tartaric.

AGING Alternative term for maturation. Sometimes term of criticism, as in aging prematurely.

ALCOHOLIC CONTENT The alcoholic strength of wine, usually expressed as a percentage of the total wine.

ALCOHOLIC FERMENTATION The process whereby yeasts, natural or added, convert the grape sugars into alcohol and carbon dioxide. Normally stops either when all the sugar has been converted or when the alcohol level reaches about 15 per cent.

ALMACENISTA Spanish for stockholder. Term used in Jerez for people maturing small individual barrels of sherry. Almacenista sherry is usually dry, dark-coloured and of high quality.

AMERICAN VITICULTURAL AREA (AVA) Appellation system first introduced in the USA in the early 1980s.

AMONTILLADO Generally used to describe a medium sherry.

ANNATA Italian for 'vintage date'.

APPELLATION D'ORIGINE CONTRÔLÉE (AC, AOC) 'Controlled Appellation of Origin.' The French quality control designation.

AUSLESE German term for 'Selected', referring to a QmP wine made from selected bunches of fully-ripe grapes. Normally sweet.

BARREL AGING Time spent maturing in wood, normally oak. The wine takes on flavours from the wood.

BARRIQUE Bordeaux barrel holding 225 litres. Often used loosely now for all oak barrels.

BEERENAUSLESE German term for 'selected single berries', referring to very sweet QmP wine made from overripe, nobly rotted grapes, individually picked.

BEREICH German regional term for a district within a wine region. Usually applied only to QbA wines.

BLANC DE BLANCS Still or sparkling wine made from white grapes.

BLANC DE NOIRS Still or sparkling white wine made from black grapes.

BODEGA Spanish word for 'cellar'. Used to describe wine companies in Spain.

BOTRYTIS CINEREA Fungus, prevalent in cold, wet weather, which attacks grapes. But on healthy, white grapes, in warm, humid conditions, it can become 'noble rot'. Noble rot shrivels the fruit, concentrating the sugars to produced quality sweet wines like Sauternes.

BRUT French for 'unsweetened'. Used to describe the driest type of sparkling wines.

CARBONIC MACERATION Traditional Beaujolais fermentation method whereby whole, uncrushed grapes are fermented in a closed container under a blanket of carbonic gas to produce light fruity red wine. Now widely used in warm areas to keep fruity flavours.

CHAMPAGNE METHOD Traditional method of making wine sparkle by inducing second fermentation in the bottle.

CHAPTALIZATION The legal addition of sugar during fermentation to increase alcoholic strength. More necessary in cool climates where the grapes have insufficient natural sugar.

CHÂTEAU French for castle. Also used for a French wine estate, particularly in Bordeaux.

CLARET English term for red Bordeaux wine.

CLARIFICATION The removal of solid matter from a wine after fermentation.

CLASSICO Italian term for the original central part of a wine area. Usually superior quality.

CLONE Strain of grape species. Grapes like Pinot Noir have hundreds of clones.

COLD FERMENTATION Long, slow fermentation at low temperature to extract maximum freshness from the grapes. Crucial for whites in hot climates.

COMMUNE French term for village. Often used, e.g. in Burgundy, where each major commune has its own appellation.

COOL CLIMATE The areas at the coolest limits of grape-ripening e.g. Germany, England and Washington State in the USA's Pacific North-West.

CO-OPERATIVE Grouping of growers which handles wine-making and, increasingly, marketing on a communal basis.

CÔTE French for 'hillside', incorporated into the name of many wine areas.

CRÉMANT French sparkling wine made outside Champagne but using the Champagne method. Crémants from Alsace, Die and Bourgogne are the best known.

CRU Literally 'growth'. Term used to describe a single vineyard, usually qualified with a quality reference such as 'Grand Cru','Premier Cru', etc.

CULTIVAR South African term for single grape variety.

CUVE CLOSE French for 'closed vat' referring to the method of making sparkling wine in which the second fermentation takes place in closed tanks.

CUVÉE Contents of a *cuvée* or vat. Also refers to a blended wine, often as in 'Tête de Cuvée', 'Cuvée Exceptionelle' and 'Cuvée de Luxe', implying a special quality.

DEMI-SEC Semi-dry, but more accurately translated as 'demi-sweet' in most cases.

DÉGORGEMENT Process in the Champagne method of removing sediment from bottle.

DENOMINACIÓN DE ORIGEN (DO) Spanish equivalent of the French AC system.

DENOMINACIÓN DE ORIGEN CALIFICADA (DOCa) New super-category of Spanish wines above DO which came into force in 1991.

DENOMINAZIONE D'ORIGINE CONTROLLATA (DOC) Italian equivalent of the French AC system.

DENOMINAZIONE DI ORIGINE CONTROLLATA E GARANTITA (DOCG) The top category for Italian wines, above DOC.

DOMAINE French for single vineyard.

DOSAGE A sugar and wine mixture added to sparkling wine after disgorgement which affects how sweet or dry it will be.

DULCE Spanish for 'sweet'.

EISWEIN Very intense sweet wine made in winter from grapes harvested while they are still frozen. Germany and Austria are the chief exponents. See also Icewine.

ESTATE A single property, though this may, as in Germany and Burgundy, encompass several different vineyards.

FILTERING Removal of yeasts, solids and any impurities from a wine before bottling.

FINING Method of clarifying wine by adding albumen-type substances, such as Isinglass, to the surface. As the substance drops it collects impurities.

FINO The dryest type of sherry.

FLOR A film of yeast which forms on the top of *fino* sherries, and a few other wines, inhibiting oxidation and imparting a unique dry flavour.

FORTIFIED WINE Wine which has high-strength spirit added usually before the initial alcoholic fermentation is completed, thereby preserving sweetness.

FRIZZANTE Italian term for semi-sparkling.

FLYING WINEMAKER An international winemaker who travels around the world consulting at different wineries and bringing New World techniques to old-style wines.

GARRAFEIRA Portuguese term for quality wine given extra aging and half a per cent more alcohol.

GRAN RESERVA Quality Spanish wine aged for a specific number of years in wood. Only produced, in theory, in top vintages.

GRAND CRU CLASSÉ 'Classed Great Growth'. Bordeaux has several classifications of quality, and this term is also occasionally used elsewhere, often without justification.

GROSSLAGE A grouping of German vineyards from the same area under a single name.

HYBRID Grape variety bred from an American vine species and a European *Vitis vinifera*; contrary to a crossing, which is bred from two vinifera varieties.

ICEWINE A speciality of Canada; the equivalent of German and Austrian Eiswein.

JUG WINE US term for basic table wine.

KABINETT The lightest category of German QmP wines. Relatively dry and low in alcohol. Kabinett wine cannot have sugar added in Germany (though it can in Austria).

LATE HARVEST The harvesting of grapes after the ordinary harvest date to increase alcoholic strength or sweetness.

LAYING DOWN The storing of wine which will improve with age.

LIEU-DIT Burgundian term for single vineyard below First Growth standard.

MALOLACTIC FERMENTATION Secondary fermentation which converts malic acid to the softer lactic acid. Normal in reds, though hot country whites may arrest it to keep the wine fresher and more acid.

MANZANILLA Very dry sherry.

MATURATION Positive term for the beneficial aging of wine.

MOELLEUX French for 'mellow' or 'sweet', though not quite so sweet as Doux or Liquoreux.

NÉGOCIANT/NÉGOCIANT ÉLEVEUR French for merchant or shipper who buys wine from various sources, matures it, maybe blends it, and then sells it.

'NOBLE ROT' A fungus which in warm, humid autumn weather, can attack white grapes, shrivel them and concentrate the sugar.

NON-VINTAGE A wine without a stated vintage year, usually a blend of more than one harvest.

OIDIUM Powdery mildew, a very dangerous vine disease which rots the stalks, shrivels the leaves and splits the grapes.

OLOROSO Full, rich, aged sherry.

OXIDATION Over-exposure of wine to air, causing loss of fruit and bacterial decay.

PÉTILLANT French term for slightly sparkling.

PETIT CHÂTEAU A minor Bordeaux wine estate, below Cru Bourgeois level.

PHYLLOXERA A louse which attacks vine roots. All European vines are susceptible to it, so they must be grafted on to resistant American rootstocks.

PRESS WINE The wine pressed from the skins after most of the wine has been drawn off after fermentation. Usually hard and dark, and used sparingly to beef up a wine.

QUALITÄTSWEIN BESTIMMTER ANBAUGEBIETE (QBA) German quality designation for wine made in a specified region and from authorized grapes. Between Tafelwein and QmP.

QUALITÄTSWEIN MIT PRÄDIKAT (QMP) Top German quality designation for wine made in defined areas and, more importantly, from grapes not requiring any additional sugar to achieve correct alcohol level. Comprises five categories ranging from the light Kabinett level up to intensely rich Trockenbeerauslese.

RACKING The clarification of quality wine by the transferral of wine off its lees to another barrel.

RESERVA Spanish term indicating wine has been aged for specific number of years according to the DO regulations.

RISERVA Italian term indicating wine aged for specific number of years according to DOC laws.

SEC 'Dry'. When applied to Champagne it actually means medium-dry.

'SECOND' WINES Wines not thought to be up to the level of a property's main production.

SEKT German for sparkling wine.

SÉLECTION DES GRAINS NOBLES Alsace late-picked wine similar to German Beerenauslese.

SOLERA Spanish and Portuguese system for the topping up of older barrels with younger wine of the same style, to ensure continuity.

SPÄTLESE German term for 'late-picked' wine, usually slightly sweet.

SUGAR Naturally present in grapes. Transformed during fermentation into alcohol and carbon dioxide.

SUR LIE French for 'on the lees', meaning wine bottled direct from the cask or fermentation vat to gain extra flavour from the lees. Common with quality Muscadet.

TAFELWEIN German for table wine. Most basic quality designation.

TANNIN The bitter, mouth-drying component in red wines, derived from skins, stalks and sometimes wooden barrels, which is harsh when young but crucial to a wine's ability to age.

TROCKEN German for 'dry'. Applied to new-style German wines made completely dry in an effort to make them better matches for food.

TROCKENBEERENAUSLESE Sweetest category of German QmP wines. Made from late-harvested, nobly rotted single berries.

VARIETAL Wine made from, and name after, a single grape variety.

VENDANGE TARDIVE Alsace term for late harvest similar to German Spätlese/Auslese.

VIN DE PAYS French 'Country Wine' a less stringent French quality designation than Appellation Contrôlée.

VIN DE TABLE 'French Table Wine'. Basic quality designation.

VIN DÉLIMITÉ DE QUALITÉ SUPÉRIEURE (VDQS) This is the second rank of French quality control, between Appellation Côntrôlée and Vin de Pays.

VINIFICATION The process of turning grapes into wine.

VINO DA TAVOLA Italian 'Table Wine'. Basic quality designation, but including some exciting non-conformist wines.

VINTAGE The year's grape harvest, also used to describe the wine of a single year.

VITIS LABRUSCA American vine species making over-powerful wine on its own but crucial in supplying phylloxera-resistant rootstocks for Vitis Vinifera.

VITIS VINIFERA The vine species, native to Europe and Central Asia, which makes all the world's finest wines.

WOOD AGING Aging of wine in barrels, casks or vats. Effects can vary from the highly beneficial to the disastrous.

VINTAGE GUIDE

Vintage guides are only relevant to wines which have personality and individuality – to the top five or ten per cent of any one country's wine. Any mark given to a vintage is a broad generalization to steer you towards the best bottles – there are brilliant wines made in difficult years and disappointing wines in brilliant years. The highest marks are for vintages where the ripeness of the grapes is best balanced by the acidity of the juice – and, for red wines, the proper amount of tannin, giving wines which have the potential to age.

The numerals (1–10) represent an overall rating for each year

♀ Not ready   ♈ Just ready   ♉ At peak   ♊ Past best   ○ Generally not declared

BORDEAUX
The following marks apply only to the leading châteaux in each area.

	04	03	02	01	00	99	98	97	96	95
Pauillac, St-Julien, St-Estèphe	8	9	8	8	10	7	7	6	9	8
Margaux	7	8	7	7	9	7	7	6	8	8
Graves/Péssac-Leognan (R)	7	8	7	8	9	7	8	6	8	8
Graves/Péssac-Leognan (W)	8	6	8	8	8	7	9	5	8	8
St-Émilion, Pomerol	8	8	7	8	9	7	9	6	7	9
Sauternes	6	9	8	10	6	8	7	9	9	7

BURGUNDY
Red Burgundy is desperately unreliable so the vintage has been rated according to what can be expected from a decent single domaine. White Burgundy is generally more reliable.

	04	03	02	01	00	99	98	97	96	95
Côte de Nuits (R)	7	8	9	7	7	9	7	8	9	8
Côte de Beaune (R)	6	7	8	6	5	9	6	7	9	8
Côte de Beaune (W)	9	5	8	7	8	8	5	8	6	9
Chablis	8	7	9	4	9	7	7	7	9	8

CHAMPAGNE
Vintages are usually only 'declared' in the best years, several years after the harvest, but a few Champagne houses will make vintage wine virtually every year.

	04	03	02	01	00	99	98	97	96	95
Champagne	7	5	8	2○	6	7	8	6	9	8

RHÔNE
The reds of the northern Rhône, based on Syrah, take to aging extremely well, and white Hermitage can even outlive the red. Southern reds can age, but do mature sooner.

	04	03	02	01	00	99	98	97	96	95
Hermitage (W)	8	7	4	9	8	8	9	7	9	8
Hermitage (R)	8	7	5	8	8	8	9	8	8	9
Côte-Rôtie	7	7	4	9	7	9	9	6	7	9
Châteauneuf-du-Pape (R)	8	8	2	9	8	8	9	6	7	8

LOIRE
In general Loire wines should be drunk young within a year or two of the vintage but some wines can age, particularly the Cabernet Franc reds and the sweet Chenin whites.

	04	03	02	01	00	99	98	97	96	95
Sancerre/Pouilly-Fumé (W)	8	8	8	7	9	7	7	9	8	8
Bourgueil, Chinon	8	9	8	7	6	6	6	8	10	8
Loire sweet wines	9	9	7	8	5	7	6	9	9	9

ALSACE
Alsace wines should usually be drunk young but can age surprisingly well. The occasional late-harvested sweet wine merits keeping for at least ten years.

	04	03	02	01	00	99	98	97	96	95
Alsace Riesling Grand Cru	8	7	7	7	7	7	9	8	8	8

	04	03	02	01	00	99	98	97	96	95

GERMANY

This chart only applies to the 'Pradikat' or QmP level of special quality wines.

	04	03	02	01	00	99	98	97	96	95
Mosel-Saar-Ruwer Riesling	8	7	8	10	6	8	7	8	6	9
Rheingau Riesling	8	8	8	8	6	7	8	7	8	7
Pfalz Riesling	8	8	7	7	5	7	9	7	8	5

ITALY

Though vintages are of considerable importance for the best Italian wines, wine-making methods differ so widely within the same DOCs that these ratings are only approximates.

	04	03	02	01	00	99	98	97	96	95
Barolo, Barbaresco	9	8	5	9	8	9	8	9	10	8
Amarone, Recioto, Ripasso	9	8	5	7	9	7	7	10	6	10
Chianti, Brunello, Vino Nobile	9	8	5	9	7	9	7	10	6	8

SPAIN

Vintage charts are relevant to few Spanish wines as the quality is not uniform enough.

	04	03	02	01	00	99	98	97	96	95
Rioja (R)	8	7	7	6	8	7	6	7	8	8
Priorat	6	5	5	7	7	7	7	7	7	8
Penedès	6	7	4	7	7	7	8	7	8	7
Ribera del Duero	8	8	4	8	7	8	7	6	9	8

PORTUGAL

Port is one of the great vintage wines though a vintage is only declared (*) in exceptional years.

	04	03	02	01	00	99	98	97	96	95
Vintage Port	8	9	6	7	9	7	6	8	7	8

USA

So many vineyard areas are still in the exciting experimental stage throughout the USA so I have concentrated on the best known regions. There are major weather variations in California.

	04	03	02	01	00	99	98	97	96	95
Napa Cabernet Sauvignon	8	8	7	8	8	9	7	8	7	9
Napa/Sonoma Chardonnay	8	9	8	8	7	8	7	8	6	8
Carneros/Russian River Pinot Noir	8	7	8	9	9	8	9	8	8	8
Santa Barbara Pinot Noir	8	7	7	8	7	9	6	8	7	8
Oregon Pinot Noir	8	8	8	7	9	9	8	5	7	5
Washington State Merlot/Cabernet	9	8	7	8	9	9	8	8	9	8

AUSTRALIA

The world of wine changes so fast in Australia that in most instances the skill of the wine-maker is more important than the vintage. As new cool-climate vineyards come into maturity, vintage variations will become more marked. I list four important areas which can be susceptable to vintage variations.

	04	03	02	01	00	99	98	97	96	95
Coonawarra Cabernet Sauvignon	8	8	9	9	6	8	10	7	9	5
Hunter Valley Semillon	8	9	7	7	9	8	10	8	9	7
Margaret River Cabernet Sauvignon	8	8	9	10	8	10	7	8	10	9
Yarra Pinot Noir	8	8	9	8	9	8	9	10	7	7

NEW ZEALAND

New Zealand is well suited to whites, but often marginal for reds. Rain is often a problem.

	04	03	02	01	00	99	98	97	96	95
Marlborough Sauvignon	7	8	6	9	9	8	5	8	9	3
Hawkes Bay Cabernet	7	5	9	7	8	7	10	7	7	8

SOUTH AFRICA

South Africa's track record for tough, traditional reds goes back a long way, but it is really only during the 1990s that modern wine-making has gained much of a foothold.

	04	03	02	01	00	99	98	97	96	95
Cape Cabernet	8	9	5	9	8	7	8	9	6	9

FRANCE

*N*obody can do it like the French. Many try, none quite manage it. But the fact that all over the world, winemakers have taken the French model and are moving hell and high water to copy it must mean something.

By a mixture of historical chance, geological peculiarity and climatic conditions, France is still the world's greatest wine-making nation. By historical chance it had a series of natural trading partners to the north. France has some of the coldest and some of the hottest vineyards in the world, and consequently, between the two extremes, an array of wine regions where particular grapes can find virtually perfect conditions to ripen. But not to overripen; and this is the secret of France's success.

In France wine is a way of life. Vines and church rub shoulders at Hunawihr along the scenic Alsace wine route (left), with the Rosacker Grand Cru vineyard beyond; and at Mailly on the Montagne de Reims in Champagne (above) a local grower picks his Pinot Noir grapes to produce one of the most expensive wines in the world.

WINE REGIONS

France started off by influencing the New World – even now, if you ask many an Australian or Californian winemaker about the models for his wine, he will name a village or two in Bordeaux or Burgundy. But then the New World began to have an influence on France. New wine-making techniques filtered in. The use of new oak barriques, introduced to the New World by Bordeaux and Burgundy, became so fashionable that other French regions have decided that they, too, want that rich, buttery taste in their wines. and most recently the south of France has started producing wines, often under simple Vin de Pays labels, that are every bit as upfront and fruity as their equivalents from South Australia or the Napa Valley. The wine world has got smaller. But still, no matter to which style you turn, France is there. And without ever admitting that she cares what other countries do, she still manages to absorb the best of what she sees.

So let's take a quick look around France's wine regions. In the far north Champagne uses classic grape varieties – Pinot Noir, Pinot Meunier and Chardonnay – to make lean, barely ripe still wine which is the perfect base for the greatest of sparkling wines. Just to the east, a rainshadow under the Vosges mountains allows Alsace to make intensely perfumed, yet dry wines from such Germanic grapes as Riesling and Gewürztraminer.

Away from the German border, south of Paris, begins one of the most contentious, passionately involving wine regions of the world – Burgundy. The whites, from the Chardonnay grape, range from the frosty, steely chill of Chablis to the power, ripeness and beauty of the Côte d'Or, where there are wines that combine honeyed richness with savoury fragrance in a way that has had two generations of winemakers across the globe wearing their fingers to the bone trying to reproduce them. Also on the Côte d'Or the Pinot Noir does its best to disprove its reputation as one of the two greatest red wine grapes in the world, but in the hands of the top growers makes wines of such haunting, perfumed brilliance that one is almost prepared to forgive the many mediocre bottles.

A short leap south to the Rhône and it is the Syrah's turn. This dark, strong, pungent grape makes the great red wines of Hermitage and Côte-Rôtie, as well as contributing to a host of others. Along France's warm Mediterranean coast, in Provence and Languedoc-Roussillon, the vine grows almost too easily and vast quantities of ordinary red and white wine are made. But the region is undergoing a revolution and there are many exciting, modern wines being made from international varieties led by Cabernet Sauvignon, Merlot, Syrah and Chardonnay.

On the south-west coast is the Mecca for red wine: Bordeaux. Any red winemaker who wishes to be admitted to the international top rank must sooner or later try his hand at Cabernet Sauvignon. The sweet wines of Sauternes, too, are some of the world's greatest dessert wines. Bordeaux's maritime climate also influences the great rivers of the Dordogne, Lot, Garonne and Tarn and here in the South-West, a colourful ragbag of grape varieties is used to make almost every wine style imaginable. Finally, turning back north again, the Loire Valley offers a wide range of wines from different grapes. Its Sauvignons used to set the standard for tangy, fresh whites; now, since New Zealand has shown what she can do, the Loire must share the honours.

The other way in which France has set the pace for the world is in its Appellation d'Origine Contrôlée laws. Except in Germany and Austria, these have formed the basis for most demarcation systems in Europe and in North America and the southern hemisphere.

CLASSIFICATIONS

French wine is divided into four categories.
Vin de table or table wine is the most basic level and regulations are minimal.

Vin de Pays Literally, 'Country Wine'. This category was created to improve the general level of basic table wine by giving the best of it a regional identity, and in this it has succeeded superbly. There are now almost 100 Vins de Pays. Quality is variable, from the dreadful to the superb, so buy from a reliable retailer. There are limits on yields but regulations are far more relaxed than for VDQS or AC wines. There are three levels: **Vins de Pays Régionaux** are five areas which between them carve up most of France's vineyards: Vin de Pays du Jardin de la France covers the Loire Valley; the Comté Tolosan includes the South-West (but not Bordeaux); the Comtés Rhodaniens applies to the northern Rhône and Savoie; stretching south from here to include Provence is the Portes de Mediterranée; and the Oc (a name appearing on a lot of good-value wines these days) is for

ENGLISH
CHANNEL

CHAMPAGNE LORRAINE

•PARIS STRASBOURG•

ALSACE

RENNES •

TOURS• DIJON•

NANTES LOIRE VALLEY BURGUNDY

JURA

ATLANTIC
OCEAN

SAVOIE
•LYON

**WINE REGIONS
OF FRANCE**

Champagne

Lorraine

Alsace

Burgundy

Jura

Savoie

Rhône Valley

Provence

Corsica

Languedoc-Roussillon

South-West

Bordeaux

Loire Valley

• BORDEAUX
BORDEAUX

RHÔNE
VALLEY

SOUTH-WEST

•TOULOUSE PROVENCE
•MARSEILLE

LANGUEDOC-
ROUSSILLON

MEDITERRANEAN
SEA

▲
N

0 km   100   200   300

0 miles   100

CORSICA

Provence and the Midi. **Vins de Pays Départementaux** cover a single departement: Vin de Pays de l'Aude, for example. **Vins de Pays de Zone** are the most tightly controlled and can apply to areas as small as a single commune. Vin de Pays de l'Uzège, for example, is for wines from the locality of Uzès in the Gard department.

Vin Délimité de Qualité Supérieure (VDQS) This is a kind of junior Appellation Contrôlée. There are rules governing yields, grape varieties and the like, but they are less strict than they would be for AC wines. Usually the general standard of the wines is not yet good enough for promotion to full AC status. Over time many VDQS wines have been promoted to AC; for example Sauvignon de St-Bris was a VDQS wine in Burgundy because it was made from Sauvignon Blanc and in Burgundy the only white wines accorded AC status were Chardonnay and

Aligoté. Sauvignon de St-Bris was promoted to AC in 2003 and changed its name to St-Bris.

Appellation d'Origine Contrôlée (AC) This is the top designation for French wines. The area of each AC is determined by *terroir*, a French term that covers soil, aspect and climate. Appellation rules then govern the grape varieties allowed, the permitted yields (notoriously elastic, this), the alcohol level of the wines, the methods of pruning and picking, the density of planting and the wine-making. Sometimes bottling in the region of production is mandatory. All AC wines have to be submitted to a tasting panel to make sure they are typical of the appellation – but an AC designation is not in any way a guarantee of quality. It merely guarantees that the wine has been produced in accordance with the rules, which is not the same thing at all. The consumer's best guarantee of quality is the name of the producer on the bottle.

BORDEAUX

What a change in recent years. When the first edition of this book appeared in 1985 I wrote, 'Bordeaux is the greatest red wine area in the world.' I could still write that. But if I did I'd be ignoring California and Australia, not to mention the huge improvements in Burgundy. I'd be ignoring, in fact, years of dedicated work by red wine makers all over the world. Bordeaux is still the biggest red wine area in the world. It's still the most famous. At its best, yes, it still produces red wines that can outshine almost anything from anywhere for sheer style and excitement. But the world has changed. All those regions that, in 1985, were just beginning to raise their heads, look at Bordeaux and say to themselves, Hey, we could do that, are now doing it. There is good red wine pouring out of regions we hadn't heard of just a few years ago. It's not so much that Bordeaux has gone

down; it's more that the rest of the world is clamouring for its share of attention.

And is Bordeaux responding to the challenge? Is it saying to the newcomers, Forget it, kids. You want flavour? We'll show you flavour. You want reliability? No problem. Is it saying that? Well, yes and no. The top wines are, to some extent. But by top wines I don't necessarily mean those with the highest position in Bordeaux's official pecking orders, like the Médoc classification of 1855. I mean the wines made by people who care, who are passionate about what they do. Sometimes these are the most famous names in Bordeaux, sometimes they're not. It sounds harsh, maybe, but I'd say there are only around 200 properties in Bordeaux (out of several thousand) that meet those criteria, and even fewer – about 50 – producing wine that is genuinely exciting enough to be called

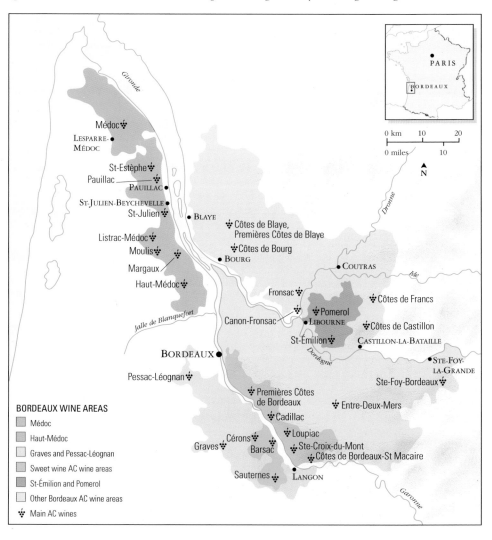

BORDEAUX WINE AREAS
- Médoc
- Haut-Médoc
- Graves and Pessac-Léognan
- Sweet wine AC wine areas
- St-Émilion and Pomerol
- Other Bordeaux AC wine areas
- ❦ Main AC wines

world class. And as for the basic reds – well, I think we have to ask ourselves if basic red Bordeaux really has a role in the world of wine any more. So much of it is thin, stalky stuff, from vines that have been encouraged to overproduce, that it has a failure rate still as high as twenty years ago.

With the white wines, though, the story is different. They've improved at every level. At the top level, the Graves region produces fine dry whites, but basic Bordeaux Blanc is streets ahead of what it was ten years ago. And the sweet whites of Sauternes and Barsac have gone from being ultra-*un*fashionable to ultra-fashionable. The producers have made tremendous improvements in quality (though some properties could still make more) and with the change in their fortunes they have come up against the same problem faced by the producers of red Bordeaux. Other countries – New Zealand, Australia, Hungary – can also make superb botrytis-affected sweet wines. Bordeaux is facing competition on all fronts. But it can count its lucky stars that it's so versatile and part of the reason for this lies in its location in the south-west of France.

Ch. Latour is one of the small number of Bordeaux estates able to combine the power of a New World Cabernet with a perfume that is uniquely Bordelais.

CLIMATE AND SOIL

The Bordeaux region straddles the Garonne and Dordogne rivers, which join up to form the Gironde just north of the city itself, and benefits from several different geological and climatic advantages. First, its proximity to the Atlantic Ocean means that although Bordeaux is on a similar latitude to the Rhône Valley with its harsh, dry climate, it has relatively mild winters and summers. The Landes, a large wedge of forest between the vineyards and the sea, soaks off some of the seaside rain as well as stopping salt winds from blasting the vineyards. South of the city of Bordeaux the rainfall increases, and in the small area of Sauternes the ice-cold spring waters of the river Ciron join the warmer waters of the Garonne. In late summer this conjunction of warm and cold waters causes mists to rise off the water and drift back up the Ciron Valley past the village of Sauternes where they are broken up into hazy warmth by the sun. Here, as in few other wine regions, the warm, humid atmosphere creates the 'noble rot' fungus (see page 63) which in turn creates many of the world's greatest sweet wines.

So Bordeaux's growing season is usually long and warm. But that wouldn't be enough without the soil being right. And, luckily, it is. The most important factor is the gravel banks that are a feature of the Graves and Médoc vineyards. In the best villages, like Margaux and St-Julien, this gravel topsoil can be about 1m (3 feet) deep. Gravel not only drains well, but is poor in nutrients and retains warmth from the sun. The warmth helps to ripen the grapes while the lack of nutrients and the relative dryness force the vine roots deep into the subsoil for food. It is said that vines don't like having wet feet but do like to be made to struggle; this gravel topsoil on a sandy-clay subsoil rich in minerals but well below the surface is ideal, and the Cabernet Sauvignon vine, which thrives on a good battle with its soil, is in its element here.

In Pomerol and St-Émilion, on the right bank of the Dordogne, clay is the dominant feature, sometimes mixed with gravel or limestone, sometimes packed with iron deposits, and the quicker-ripening Merlot grape likes this cooler, damper soil. And in the southern Graves and Sauternes, the soil is mainly limestone and chalk, the two most suitable bases for anyone wanting to make great white wine.

GRAPE VARIETIES AND WINE STYLES

Almost all Bordeaux is made by blending two or more varieties of grape, with the strengths of one balancing the weakness of another.

THE REDS

Cabernet Sauvignon This is possibly the world's most famous grape variety, and it is planted in every single country that has

These rose bushes, planted on Château Le Gay's clay soil in Pomerol, are decorating some of the most valuable vineyard land in France.

enough sun to ripen it. It has small, dark, thick-skinned berries and ripens late, so is ideal in the warm gravel soils of the Médoc and Graves. Cabernet gives dark, tannic wine with a strong initial acid attack, but when aged in new oak barrels it has stark, pure blackcurrant fruit and a cedary, tobaccoey, library-dry perfume which is stunning (new oak barrels give tannin, but at the same time the wine draws out delicious soft, spicy vanilla and butter softness from the wood). It is the main grape in the Haut-Médoc, but is always blended to soften its often austere character.

Cabernet Franc This second Cabernet variety produces lighter-coloured, softer wines than Cabernet Sauvignon, sometimes slightly earthy but also with good blackcurrant fruit. It is used for blending in St-Émilion, Pomerol, the Graves and the Médoc, only being grown for its own virtues in the cool Loire Valley.

Merlot Dominant in St-Émilion and Pomerol, and used to soften Cabernet Sauvignon in the Médoc and the Graves, Merlot ripens early as well as being a big cropper. It gives a gorgeous, succulent, minty, honeyed black-currant or plum-flavoured wine, which explains why Pomerols and St-Émilions take less effort to enjoy than Médocs.

Petit Verdot A tough, acid grape with a licorice and plum taste, and a heavenly perfume, but it ripens late and doesn't crop predictably, so isn't much planted.

Malbec A rather bloated, juicy grape, not much seen, though very important upriver in Cahors where it is known as Auxerrois.

THE WHITES

Sémillon This is Bordeaux's great white grape, and the mainstay of all Sauternes and Barsac. It gives lusciously sweet, honeyed, lanolin-rich wines when affected by noble rot. As a dry wine it can have an excellent full freshness like apple skins and cream that becomes waxy with age, and is often oak-matured.

Sauvignon Blanc Usually blended with Sémillon for its acid bite, though sometimes nowadays it is made very dry and unblended for its sharp, green nettly freshness. Oak aging adds spice and richness.

Muscadelle A musky, exotic grape traditionally used to create a sensation of false noble rot in poor vintages, and used in small quantities to add richness to the sweet wines.

Bordeaux produces enormous amounts of fine wine, but the majority of its production is of basic quality. In whites only a very small fraction of each year's crop reaches the minimum requirements for the appellations of Sauternes, Barsac or Pessac-Léognan/Graves,

while in reds, the vineyards of the Médoc, plus St-Émilion, Pomerol and Pessac-Léognan/Graves – the best areas, in other words – come to under one-third of the total. The overall appellations of Bordeaux and Bordeaux Supérieur (Supérieur simply means the wine has half a degree more of alcohol) account for between a third and a half of the annual yield. The appellations gradually become more and more specific as quality increases. For instance, in the locality of Margaux village, the least suitable land would be classified as AC Bordeaux, the fringes would be AC Haut-Médoc, and the best vineyards would be AC Margaux, even though they might all have the same postal address.

Except in St-Émilion (see page 53) the appellation system in Bordeaux defines the best wine communes and leaves it at that. So, legally, Château Lafite-Rothschild, one of the world's most expensive wines, has the same appellation – Pauillac – as the wine of a peasant proprietor with a few barrowloads of grapes he wheels listlessly to the co-operative. Obviously that makes no sense. There has to be a formal league table of some sort, something that acknowledges that some wines are superb and others merely everyday, even though they may be grown next door to each other on geologically similar soil.

And indeed there is such a league table. In fact there are several of them in Bordeaux: the Médoc has one, the Graves has one, and so on, with the Médoc's being the most famous. Yet, unlike Burgundy, where tiny plots of land have been designated Premier Cru (First Growth) or Grand Cru (Great Growth) and also usually divided between several owners, in Bordeaux it is not the patch of soil that is classified, but the property, or château.

THE CHÂTEAU SYSTEM

Château literally means 'castle' in French, but in Bordeaux the term is applied to any wine-producing estate, no matter how grand or humble its house might be.

Checking the bunches of grapes for rot to ensure that only healthy ones reach the winery is an essential part of quality control in many top Bordeaux properties.

Think of a château name as a brand name. Most Bordeaux wine estates, all called Château This or Château That, have long histories. Some have shrunk over the last few hundred years, some have disappeared altogether and some have expanded. Wealthy, successful châteaux have cast covetous eyes on the best patches of land belonging to their immediate neighbours. Offers have been made, terms negotiated and agreements reached. Land has changed hands, so that patches of vines that 100 years ago might have belonged to Château X now bear the name of Château Y.

Why am I telling you all this? Because in most of Bordeaux it is the château, not the land itself, that is classified – as First Growth, Second Growth and so on (for what these mean in the Médoc, see page 39). So when Château X (which we'll call a Second Growth) agrees terms to buy a nicely sloping patch of gravelly land from Château Y (which we'll call

a Third Growth) that patch of land is instantly and automatically promoted to Second Growth. If Château X sells a corner of vineyard to Château Y, that land is instantly demoted. Unfair? Not necessarily. The Médoc was classified according to the prices for which the different wines sold – which implied some kind of quality differences, which in turn implied better wine-making. It took into account more than just the potential of the vineyard. In that respect, it was rather modern. The trouble is what was bang up to date 140 years ago isn't quite so state-of-the-art now. But I'll come to that later.

It's also totally different from the situation that obtains in Burgundy. There it is the patch of land that is classified; owners may come and go, but they take the land as they find it. It's almost feudal, this idea that in the Médoc a patch of vineyard can be first-rate or not according to who owns it, and indeed the large estates of Bordeaux – and in particular the Médoc – were primarily developed by monied interests and the nobility. Burgundy's fragmentation, on the other hand, can be traced back to the expropriation and redistribution of Church lands after the French Revolution to almost anyone who could hoe a row of vines. Thus the identity of a wine in Bordeaux immediately became associated with the owner and his château, rather than with different patches of field on a particular slope, as in Burgundy.

The concept of the château, with the production of a single wine in single hands, is one of the chief reasons for Bordeaux's position at the epicentre of fine wine. It provides for reliability and consistency, and the development of a particular quality and style, since nowadays, on all leading properties, everything from the care of the vineyards to the making of the wine and the maturing, bottling and sale is in the same hands.

Bordeaux, luckily, has fairly simple natural boundaries which mean that each sub-region is quite self-contained. The Médoc is the whole region stretching north of the city of Bordeaux on the Gironde's left bank. Its chief section is the southern half, the Haut-Médoc, or Upper Médoc, which, as well as being an overall appellation, also contains the greatest wine villages of the region. The appellation Médoc covers the less-regarded but nevertheless important northern section, traditionally known as the Bas-Médoc, or Lower Médoc. St-Émilion and Pomerol make up the most important areas to the east of Bordeaux, while Sauternes and Barsac lie within the Graves region south of the city.

1855 CLASSIFICATION

This is the original 1855 classification of Bordeaux red wines but brought up to date to take account of name changes and divisions of property as well as the promotion of Château Mouton-Rothschild in 1973. In the list below the château name is followed by the commune.

Premiers Crus (First Growths) Lafite-Rothschild, Pauillac; Margaux, Margaux; Latour, Pauillac; Haut-Brion, Pessac/Graves; Mouton-Rothschild, Pauillac (since 1973).

Deuxièmes Crus (Second Growths) Rauzan-Ségla, Margaux; Rauzan-Gassies, Margaux; Léoville-Las-Cases, St-Julien; Léoville-Poyferré, St-Julien; Léoville-Barton, St-Julien; Durfort-Vivens, Margaux; Gruaud-Larose, St-Julien; Lascombes, Margaux; Brane-Cantenac, Cantenac; Pichon-Longueville (Baron), Pauillac; Pichon-Longueville-Comtesse-de-Lalande, Pauillac; Ducru-Beaucaillou, St-Julien; Cos d'Estournel, St-Estèphe; Montrose, St-Estèphe.

Troisièmes Crus (Third Growths) Kirwan, Cantenac; d'Issan, Cantenac; Lagrange, St-Julien; Langoa-Barton, St-Julien; Giscours, Labarde; Malescot-St-Exupéry, Margaux; Boyd-Cantenac, Cantenac; Cantenac-Brown, Cantenac; Palmer, Cantenac; La Lagune, Ludon; Desmirail, Margaux; Calon-Ségur, St-Estèphe; Ferrière, Margaux; Marquis d'Alesme-Becker, Margaux.

Quatrièmes Crus (Fourth Growths) St-Pierre, St-Julien; Talbot, St-Julien; Branaire-Ducru, St-Julien; Duhart-Milon-Rothschild, Pauillac; Pouget, Cantenac; La Tour-Carnet, St-Laurent; Lafon-Rochet, St-Estèphe; Beychevelle, St-Julien; Prieuré-Lichine, Cantenac; Marquis-de-Terme, Margaux.

Cinquièmes Crus (Fifth Growths) Pontet-Canet, Pauillac; Batailley, Pauillac; Haut-Batailley, Pauillac; Grand-Puy-Lacoste, Pauillac; Grand-Puy-Ducasse, Pauillac; Lynch-Bages, Pauillac; Lynch-Moussas, Pauillac; Dauzac, Labarde; Mouton-Baronne-Philippe, Pauillac; du Tertre, Arsac; Haut-Bages-Libéral, Pauillac; Pédesclaux, Pauillac; Belgrave, St-Laurent; de Camensac, St-Laurent; Cos-Labory, St-Estèphe; Clerc-Milon, Pauillac; Croizet-Bages, Pauillac; Cantemerle, Macau.

THE MÉDOC REGION

You can argue against describing the Médoc as the heart of red wine on emotional grounds, and increasingly these days there are hard facts to back that up. You may prefer the silky sweet perfumes of great red Burgundy, you may prefer the tough, black richness of Hermitage, the dry, chocolaty grandeur of Barolo or the concentrated fruit of great Napa wine, but those are all decisions of the palate and the heart.

What cannot be denied is that for hectarage planted, volume produced and (at the top level) exciting quality, the Médoc still stands supreme in the world of red wine.

The Médoc region stretches like a jutting lip to the north-west of the city of Bordeaux. It is flanked to the right by the Gironde estuary (formed by the confluence of the Garonne and Dordogne rivers), and to the left by the Bay of Biscay, which is frequently turbulent, and the prime mover in the heavy black banks of cloud which can roll sullenly in from the sea and wreck a vintage with their downpour. But the Bay of Biscay is far more important for the gentle moderating effect that the presence of water has on a climate, tempering high summer sun and staving off the harshness of mid-winter. And this is significant, because although Bordeaux is in south-west France, it is not tremendously hot and can be subject to cold springs that can damage the prospect for the next vintage.

The Médoc is divided into two main areas. Haut-Médoc is the southern part, closest to the city of Bordeaux. This has all the greatest wine châteaux. Six villages have their own appellations: Margaux, St-Julien, Pauillac, St-Estèphe, Listrac and Moulis (the first four are world-famous in their own right); the last two, Listrac and Moulis, with the smallest production and the least individual wines, are generally thought of as belonging to the Haut-Médoc appellation.

The catch-all Haut-Médoc appellation applies to wines from the less-favoured pieces of land and one or two brilliant vineyards without a village to attach themselves to.

North of St-Estèphe, the Haut-Médoc ends as the predominantly gravelly soil gives way to heavier clay. This northern part of the Médoc is called the Bas-Médoc, or Lower Médoc, but because the growers said that 'lower' sounded like a slight on the quality of their wine, they are allowed to call themselves plain Médoc. This is where quality is currently most marginal.

CLASSIFICATION

It just shows you should never refuse an invitation to a party simply because you can't be bothered. In 1855, Château Lanessan was regarded as one of the top wines of the Haut-Médoc, and was asked to submit samples for the World Exhibition in Paris, where a classification of Bordeaux wines was to be made. Lanessan would certainly have done very well, but the owner felt he had better things to do with his time. On such decisions are fortunes made and lost. That Paris Exhibition produced the 1855 Classification of the Médoc, the most famous and enduring attempt ever made to give a hierarchy of quality to the wines of an area. Lanessan, overnight, had put itself out of the major league, and it has cost the château dear in reduced income and prestige in every single vintage since then.

There was no intention to create a permanent order of merit in 1855. The Bordeaux Chamber of Commerce simply wanted to put on a good show at the Paris Exhibition, and concentrated on the wines most highly

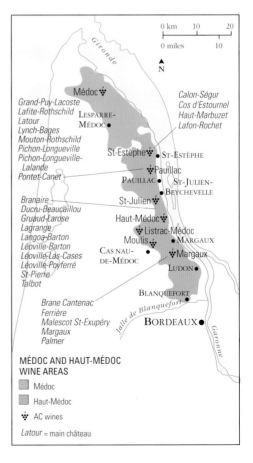

MÉDOC AND HAUT-MÉDOC WINE AREAS

regarded at that time – the reds of the Haut-Médoc, plus Haut-Brion in the Graves, and the whites of Sauternes. They collected up their samples, checked out the prices that the wines had sold for over the preceding vintages and put down five categories of wines, from First to Fifth Growth, based simply on price (see page 38). They argued that the best wine would naturally achieve the highest price. In the modern world of high-pressure marketing this would be a highly questionable premise, because even in wine, the person with the loudest voice is often presumed to make the best wine. Yet they can't have been that far wrong. At the beginning of the eighteenth century, the *London Gazette* carried advertisements for individual Bordeaux estates for the first time. Four wines were offered – Haut-Brion, Lafite, Latour and Margaux – the four First Growths (Premiers Crus) ratified in 1855, and today still regarded as worthy of their position at the top of the tree. However, there is no doubt that some fine vineyards were either excluded altogether or given lower status than they deserved.

The most famous example is Mouton-Rothschild, classified as a Second Growth (Deuxième Cru) only in 1855, but recognized throughout the twentieth century as a First Growth in quality. It finally made it officially to First Growth status in 1973. This is the only change there has ever been in the classification. But there are many other properties which are now asserting their right to a more exalted position by the only expedient which counted in 1855 – they have made the effort to create a finer wine than their neighbours, and charge a higher price accordingly. *Plus ça change...* In today's investment-conscious world, the Fifth Growth Grand-Puy-Lacoste or Lynch-Bages sell at the same price as a Second Growth, and the Second Growths Ducru-Beaucaillou, Léoville-Las-Cases and Pichon-Longueville-Lalande outprice all the other Second Growths with ease. Wines like these are establishing their own unofficial ranking on quality and price alone: the same criteria as were applied in 1855.

Almost since its creation, there has been talk of the injustices of the classification, particularly since 1959 when the late Alexis Lichine, then one of Bordeaux's most influential winemakers and wine writers, published his own revised version. It all makes for excellent conversation and it's a great excuse to keep opening the bottles – just to compare, purely for academic interest, of course – but since fear of

One of the factors in making fine wine is up-to-the-minute equipment and a sparklingly clean cellar, as here at Château Pichon-Longueville-Baron in Pauillac.

demotion is probably a greater spur than desire for promotion, little will change in black and white, though there are always examples of châteaux, taken over by new and enthusiastic owners, emerging from the shadows and producing wine of the highest class again. Châteaux Haut-Bages-Libéral and Sociando-Mallet are recent examples. If we really do need a classification – and any wine buff's life would be simplified but impoverished without it – this one still does pretty well.

The only group of châteaux one does feel a little sorry for are those which were in a state of temporary decline in 1855. Several had been unofficially classified before 1855 – the three most famous examples being Bel-Air-Marquis d'Aligre, d'Angludet and Lanessan – but were being badly run at the crucial moment. Most of these are now making Classed Growth quality wine, and most of them charge Classed Growth prices, too.

Even so modern critics are attempting to 'rewrite' the classification. In 2005 the influential magazines *Wine International* and *La Revue du Vin de France* both published updates to celebrate the 150th anniversary of the 1855 classification. *Wine International*'s was done according to the price criteria of 1855 and included wines from elsewhere in Bordeaux. Because of their scarcity, small production and fashionability at the beginning of the 21st century, various Pomerol and St-Emilion stars appear at the top end and the larger, yet traditionally more famous Haut-Médoc producers are pushed down, or even out of the classification: six of the First Growths are from St-Emilion and Pomerol (in 1855 these weren't even considered), and wines of accepted Second Growth quality like Léoville-Barton and Pichon-Longueville (-Baron) are relegated to Fifth Growth on price alone. Several of the St-Emilion properties – nicknamed 'garagistes' because of their tiny production – are so obscure that even keen wine lovers may not have heard of them. Certainly the reclassification is an accurate snapshot of what was hot in 2005, but far too many serious but large Haut-Médoc estates charging a high but fair price get pushed down or out of the classification

The *Revue du Vin de la France* re-classification concentrates on the Médoc and Haut-Médoc (along with Haut-Brion, from Pessac-Léognan, as in 1855), and is an excellent if opinionated re-education of which properties are performing and which are not. Quality is assessed over a number of vintages, price is taken into account, but so is value for money, several fashionable properties being

The gravel soil of St-Estèphe provides good drainage for these Cabernet Sauvignon vines. The pebbles help retain the heat and keep the vine warm.

flagged as 'too dear' while high quality but less fashionable properties can be marked as very good or excellent in the value for money stakes. If I disagree with a few of the demotions, it's nevertheless the best re-appraisal of the Médoc properties I've yet seen.

However, there is a large band of properties below 'classification' level – the Crus Bourgeois. Some of these were elevated to 'Classed Growth' level in the *Revue du Vin de France* lists, but this isn't an official re-evaluation. However, there was an official re-evaluation in 2003, although, predictably, it was challenged in court by those who were well-heeled but unsuccessful in the quest for Bourgeois classification. From an original list of 444 properties given Bourgeois status in 1932, 247 were still ranked in 2003; 77 lost their Bourgeois status but a French court in 2005 gave them the right to be re-considered. What a surprise in the close-knit world of Bordeaux! Inside the Bourgeois classification there are three levels – Exceptionnel (9 properties), Supérieurs (87 properties) and straight Bourgeois (151 properties before the court ruling). The number of Exceptionnels has been halved from the original 18, but it is a group deserving of its status. After some heavy duty tasting of the Superieurs and Bourgeois categories and inquiries afterwards

I found that the old equation of the best sites being carefully managed still held true in a fairly erratic bunch of wines.

SECOND WINES

Second wines have been around for years, but it was in the 1980s, the decade when Bordeaux quality soared, that they proliferated. There were more produced every year – and as if having a second wine wasn't enough, some châteaux started making a third wine. But in the sober 1990s they came down to earth again. They're still there, but in many cases the quality has slipped. They're beginning to look increasingly like what they should never be: the second-raters, the cast-offs. Instead of being lighter, less age-worthy yet still high quality reds with recognisable characteristics of the property concerned, too many of them are showing signs of young wine greenness and even wine faults. Not good enough at prices which are still high.

But what are second wines? Well, you have a top château, and you want your wine to justify the high prices you're asking for it. So every year you exclude a lot of wine from your 'Grand Vin' – maybe it's not quite good enough, maybe some patches of vines are on the young side, or maybe the style doesn't quite fit. But these wines you're excluding are still decent glassfuls. And there's a whole

world of people out there who'd love to have your wine on their dinner tables but can't afford it. So you make a separate blend of the wines you've judged not quite good enough for your main wine. It'll be lighter than your main wine and more forward, but it'll have some of the château style, and it'll have your name at the bottom of the label.

In the good and plentiful vintages of the 1980s there was an awful lot of good wine slopping around in Bordeaux. The quality of the second wines was high. But the 1990s and early 2000s weren't so kind – and what happens when you bottle the rejects of a poor year? A pretty light, lean wine, that's what. When we get another run of good vintages they'll be worth buying again, but until then...

The following are the best and most reliable second wines from the Médoc:

Pavillon Rouge (Margaux); Les Forts de Latour (Latour); Réserve de la Comtesse (Pichon-Longueville-Lalande); Les Tourelles de Longueville (Pichon-Longueville); Clos du Marquis (Léoville-Las-Cases); Le Sarget de Gruaud-Larose (Gruaud-Larose); Haut-Bages-Avérous (Lynch-Bages); and Dame de Montrose (Montrose).

ORGANIZATION

The dominant unit of production in the Haut-Médoc is the château. These range from those with only a few hectares of vineyards to giants like Larose-Trintaudon with 160 hectares (400 acres). Ideally, a château is a compact piece of land, like La Lagune with 56 hectares (140 acres) in a solid chunk, but more frequently a château gradually acquires land over generations in all corners of the village or commune.

Sometimes, as with Pichon-Longueville-Lalande, for instance, the château's vineyards are in two different appellations (Pauillac and St-Julien). The château had to do some hard bargaining to swap land with its neighbour Léoville-Las-Cases in St-Julien, but still has some in each commune. In true democratic style all its wine is allowed the Pauillac appellation, yet it always has a touch more St-Julien softness and fragrance than its neighbours. Châteaux may be owned by a single individual, by a shipper or by a business consortium more or less concerned with wine. Most wine these days is château-bottled – from the vine's first pruning to the final despatch of the labelled bottle, the wine has never been off the owner's premises.

The finest new French oak and red Bordeaux wine is a marriage made in heaven: Château Margaux is one of the few properties still to retain its own cooper.

THE GOOD YEARS

The vintages of the early 1990s have reminded us, in case we'd forgotten, that Bordeaux is a marginal wine-making area. That means that the climate is only just warm enough to ripen the grapes; the autumns are only just long enough, the springs only just mild enough. Frost is a danger, as is rain at the wrong times, especially in September and October.

Marginal climates produce the finest, most complex wines when the weather obliges, but the other side of the coin is the years when it doesn't: when the summers are just too grey and wet, as happened in Bordeaux in 1992, or when warm summers and ripe grapes suffer the deluge of last-minute rain during the vintage, as in 1993 and 1994.

Even in good years the trend these days in Bordeaux is towards earlier-maturing wines. Partly it's because yields are so much higher nowadays that the concentration needed if a wine is to develop for 20 years or more just isn't there. Partly, conversely, it's a question of better wine-making: the wines are much more attractive when they are young than they ever used to be. They don't need that long, sullen adolescence in order to emerge as fully-fledged beauties.

Most red Bordeaux peaks at five to ten years these days, with only the very top

Ripe Merlot grapes being picked at Château Lamarque in the Haut-Médoc. Merlot blended with Cabernet Sauvignon is the basis of the red Bordeaux blend.

Classed Growths needing longer. (And to those who mourn the passing of the old style, I'd say: 20 years ago, when yields were lower and the wines slower to develop, most of Bordeaux was near-bankrupt. Now they're flush with cash. Can you blame them?)

But some of the old rules still hold. One is that a good château that really cares about quality is still likely to make good wine in a poor year. A lazy winemaker, however, is probably going to make poor wine even in a good year.

2004 Driest year ever recorded in Bordeaux. Good to very good classic wines. Pauillac did particularly well.

2003 Marked by a very hot summer and intermittent drought. Wines have bags of fruit and colour and hefty alcohol levels. Little consistency even within the communes so choose with care. Northern Médoc is most reliable.

2002 Predominantly a Cabernet Sauvignon year, so St-Julien northwards did better than the southern Médoc. Impressive wines.

2001 A late harvest and the Médoc benefited from a dry October.

2000 An exceptionally consistent vintage, especially for the Cabernet Sauvignon wines from the Médoc. Nearly all the wines show irressistible ripeness though there are relatively few standout star wines. For the first time since 1990 it hardly rained during the harvest.

1999 Another rainy vintage giving wines of an acceptable, well-made but basically rather dull style.

1998 Some good to excellent wines despite heavy September rains in the Médoc.

1997 Uneven ripeness due to variable fruit set and rain at harvest time led to varied quality and few standouts. All except the best are starting to fade.

1996 Good sunny conditions through September and into the beginning of October. Some great wines in the Médoc, now just beginning to reach their best.

1995 Rain spoilt what might have been an absolute humdinger of a vintage. Those growers with the courage to wait out the autumn storms made their best wine since 1990.

1994 Oh dear. It would have been superb if rain hadn't come along during September and spoilt the grapes. As it is there are some good but tough, concentrated wines, particularly in St-Estèphe and St-Julien. Choose carefully.

1993 This was an even wetter vintage than 1994. Drink up.

1992 The wettest summer for 50 years and an absolutely massive crop is a recipe for extremely ordinary, insipid wines. Drink up or avoid.

1991 A disastrously hard frost in the spring cut the size of the harvest, and then autumn rain washed it out. Stick to the best names and drink up.

1990 The last in the string of fabulous years that started back in the early 1980s. A roasting hot year of soft, ripe wines, remarkably even in quality and despite their wonderful, heady richness, these wines are well enough balanced to run and run. Many lesser wines are now beginning to lose their lush fruit, so drink up. The top wines are only just ready.

1989 This was another miraculously hot year of rich, ripe red Bordeaux. There are masses of superb wines with good tannin levels, and if any have a problem it is low acidity. Classed Growth Medocs set for the long haul, say 2010–2025.

1988 The most 'classic' of the three great red Bordeaux years of l988, 1989 and 1990. The wines are tougher and more tannic than the '89s and '90s, and the top wines are only just ready. This is the year for the lover of subtle, cedary, tobaccoey red Bordeaux.

1987 These are light but soft wines that need drinking up.

1986 Fine, sturdy, dense reds from the Médoc, tannic but deep and scented. Still evolving fine wines. Solid and tannic, they lack the refinement of 1988. Drink up.

1985 This was a wonderful, luscious, easy-drinking vintage that was a delight from the moment it was bottled. Many top wines are still superb, but the crop was large and lesser wines are fading.

Older vintages

1984 This was the 1980s vintage that didn't make it; unripeness and rain wrecked the Merlot and only a few rather austere Médocs were worth drinking.

1983 Some of these came round quite early, though the very top wines may still last a few more years. It's quite a tannic year, but the wines have a lovely dry, cedary fruit. It was particularly impressive in Margaux.

1982 The first of the great 1980s vintages, and the one that started the boom of that decade. They're rich, supple wines, full of fat, pruny fruit. The top wines have been full of lush fruit from the start, but with good tannin levels they've aged extremely well and still have years of pleasure left. Lesser wines are beginning to dry out.

1981 The top wines are good, classic red Bordeauxs; the others should have been drunk now.

1980 Nice, quite light, grassy, blackcurrant-leaves red Bordeaux that made attractive drinking. Past their best.

1979 Record crop of wines that were initially dismissed as dull, but which have aged remarkably well, and are still a pleasure. Best wines came from St-Julien and Pauillac.

1978 A 'miracle' vintage, saved by a glorious Indian summer after a lousy summer. Initially given very high ratings, but you can't get the better of nature, and the poor summer has left a green rawness in all but the best wines that is now showing through. Drink up.

1975 A vintage that proved that wine can still wrong-foot the greatest experts. They said it would be superb, another year like 1961, but it never did manage to shed its massive tannin.

1970 The top wines are still going strong, and providing lovely mature, ripe drinking.

1966 Some top examples are still fine and cedary but most are now past their best.

1962 Good to very good quality, but rather overshadowed by 1961, and mostly now faded.

1961 This was an extraordinary vintage of intense, perfumed, spicy wines. Top wines are still superb – if you can find them.

1959 Big, rich, superripe vintage that was fabulous young and top bottles can be exciting in their advanced maturity.

MARGAUX

This is the first of the great appellations on the road out from Bordeaux, where the gravel soil which marks out all the finest Médoc vineyards first spreads right across the landscape. It is the gravel which allows the vineyard to drain, and brings out the remarkable depth of flavour and perfume allied to relatively light body which marks out the greatest red Bordeaux. Margaux is a village, dominated by its First Growth wine, Château **Margaux**, but the actual appellation covers 1413 hectares (3490 acres) in all, spread over five villages. Nearly 70 per cent of the vines and most of the top châteaux are in Margaux itself and Cantenac, with smaller plantings in Arsac and Soussans and just 85 hectares (210 acres) in Labarde. Margaux is thus the second-biggest appellation – only just behind St-Estèphe – but it has the largest number of Classed Growths.

There are two styles to the wine. The vineyards round Margaux itself are the finest, and can produce the most 'beautiful' of all red Bordeaux. The perfume of good wines like Ch. **Margaux**, **Palmer**, or **Ferrière** can be ravishingly good. Certainly the flavour is based on blackcurrant fruit, but it's much, much more. It smells as though Christian Dior had sprayed the barrels with his most precious perfume essence, and then the winemakers had emptied bottles of Crème de Cassis into them. That sounds a bit over the top, but really, the perfume is astonishing. The Cantenac end of the appellation is usually a little fuller and less perfumed, but often has a marvellously plummy sweetness to mingle with the blackcurrant fruit. Margaux wines are often quite dry and hard to start with, but the wait for maturity is worth it.

Unfortunately, as well as being home to great wines, Margaux is the most uneven of the top appellations, and has a lot of châteaux that underperform. Properties like **Lascombes**, **Boyd-Cantenac**, **Pouget** and **Rauzan-Gassies** still don't make wine up to the standard their vineyards deserve. Having said that, perennial underperformers such as **Brane-Cantenac** and **Cantenac-Brown** are now producing fine wine, and **Kirwan**, **Giscours** and **Malescot-St-Exupéry** are back on track after some difficult years, as are **du Tertre** and **Marquis de Terme**.

READING THE LABEL
Check to see whether the label says 'Propriétaire à Margaux', or one of the other four

villages, since the actual Margaux wines are far more delicate and fragrant. There are also many good non-Classed Growths in Margaux. Margaux vineyards ripen a week to ten days ahead of the rest of the Médoc, with unpredictable results – 1994 and 1990 were patchy, and 1989 and 1988, too, were more generally successful in other communes; 1983 was tremendous in Margaux.

WHAT DO THEY TASTE LIKE?
From Margaux, the wines of Palmer, Kirwan, **d'Issan**, recent **Rauzan-Ségla**, post-1988 Malescot and **La Gurgue** can give astonishing, sensuous fragrance. **Desmirail** and Ferrière are also wonderfully scented while Cantenac-Brown, du Tertre, Giscours, Rauzan-Ségla and Brane-Cantenac give marvellous plum-rich, gutsy wines. From the hinterland an array of the best Bourgeois wines – **Bel Air Marquis d'Aligre**, **Monbrison**, **Siran**, **Labégorce-Zédé**, **La Tour-de-Mons**, (and others) – combine silky perfume with body and fruit.

ENJOYING THE WINES
The more fragrant Margaux doesn't want too much competition from food. The fuller Cantenac wines are made of sterner stuff and could happily take on more gamy or spicy dishes. But again, nothing too drastic. Some lesser Cantenac and outskirts wines can be drunk young and cool to some effect.

CONSUMER INFORMATION

WHAT DO I GET FOR MY MONEY?

A lot, if you pick a good château – but you'll need a lot of money, too. The Classed Growths are expensive, and nowadays the good Bourgeois wines tend to charge according to their quality, rather than their rank. La Gurgue and d'Angludet are still fairly priced, though, and Marquis d'Alesme doesn't seem to have raised its prices too dramatically yet even though its quality has improved. Siran is another good buy. These wines are certainly a much wiser purchase than any of the underperforming Classed Growths. For the really good Classed Growths – like Margaux itself, Palmer or Rauzan-Ségla – you'll need some pretty serious money.

AVAILABILITY

You'll need to go to a good supplier for the Classed Growths or Bourgeois wines, but some supermarkets stock second wines, or generic Margaux which may well be the second wine of a good château, or perhaps a merchant's blend. It pays here to look closely for the name of the bottler and the vintage, remembering that a good producer might still have made a good wine in a less good year.

CONSUMER CHECKLIST

Château Margaux 1996	Quality 10 ★
	Price 10 ★
	Value 8 ★
Château d'Angludet 2000	Quality 7 ★
	Price 6 ★
	Value 8 ★

Good Years 2004, 2003, 2002, 2001, 2000, 1999, 1998, 1996, 1995, 1990, 1989, 1988, 1986, 1985, 1983, 1982.

Taste Notes Margaux wines are frequently the lightest of the major Médoc appellations, yet are often quite tough and dry when young. Given time to mature, they develop a wonderful exotic perfume and fragrant fruit.

ST-JULIEN

After the roaming expanses of the large Margaux vineyards, one turns the corner outside Soussans – and, suddenly, there are no vines. It's quite a shock, but also easy to explain. The gravel plateau was washed away thousands of years ago, and though it continues to troop through the woods a few kilometres to the west, it doesn't reappear on the banks of the Gironde until St-Julien, 12km (8 miles) further on. When it does resurface with a slab of Classed Growth land, Château Beychevelle, just past a brook called the Chenel du Milieu, it rises and falls in an endless succession of fine vineyards until well past St-Estèphe to the north.

The old saying in the Médoc is that to make great wine you must be able to see the Gironde from the vineyard, and this certainly applies to St-Julien. Every one of the commune's best vineyards is on the pebbly ridge of land which sweeps down to the Gironde's sluggish waters. Vineyards further inland away from the Gironde have slightly heavier soils. St-Julien is the smallest of the great appellations, with 907 hectares (2241 acres), and there's really no centre to it at all, the villages of Beychevelle and St-Julien being entirely unmemorable architecturally.

But the wines are unforgettable, and often seem to be the most perfect of all red Bordeaux, mixing some of the perfume of Margaux with some of the firm body of Pauillac and adding to that a cedary, pine needles scent which is as dry as summer wind, yet as rich as a spice-ship's hold. When they are young some of them have a creamy, honeyed softness, but this is all seductive puppy-fat encasing the taut, pure brilliance of St-Julien when it is mature. However, these wines do suffer from the general Bordeaux problem of

'Remontage' or pumping the fermenting must over the 'cap' at Château Léoville-Barton in St-Julien. Wines from here are absolutely classic red Bordeaux in style.

over-production. Yields are simply far higher than they used to be, and if you produce more you lose concentration. St-Julien suffers less than some communes because there are so many Classed Growths here, eleven to be precise, all of which have the sort of sites which enable them to ripen the grapes, even if yields are high. It's still one of the best-performing communes in the Médoc. If there's such a thing as classic Bordeaux, it's probably a St-Julien.

READING THE LABEL
This appellation is packed sardine-tight with great vineyard names. Even the second wines here are some of the best in the Médoc – look at the small print at the bottom of the label, where it gives the name of the bottler. If it's the name of one of St-Julien's leading châteaux you're probably in safe hands. Nearly all the land in the appellation is classified, but the few non-classified properties are mostly worth a try. Beychevelle, by the way, is the name of a village in the south of the commune, as well as a château.

WHAT DO THEY TASTE LIKE?
The most classic, cedar-fragrant wines are those of **Léoville-Barton** and **Langoa-Barton**, although **Leoville-Poyferré**, after ten years' aging, may equal them, and **Ducru-Beaucaillou** surely will despite being softer and more approachable when young. Leoville-Las-Cases is the most expensive and most intense St-Julien, though not always the most scented. **Gruaud-Larose** is rich and chunky to begin with yet also develops cedar fragrance as does **Beychevelle** in top years. **Talbot** is full, broad and satisfyingly soft, while **Branaire**, after a long period in decline, is back on form. **Lagrange** is a large property set back from the Gironde but consistently produces fine wine. **St-Pierre** is little known, but top quality. **Gloria** and **du Glana** are the best Bourgeois. Talbot produces some good white Caillou Blanc.

ENJOYING THE WINES
Drunk young, the relative fatness of most of these wines means that they go very well with rich duck or wild boar roasts or casseroles, but as St-Julien ages, the food should get simpler and more refined – beef and lamb, carefully roasted, or even free-range poultry, roasted and served simply in its own juices.

CONSUMER INFORMATION

WHAT DO I GET FOR MY MONEY?
St-Julien wines are expensive, though Anthony Barton of Léoville-Barton and Langoa-Barton has stood out against inflated price rises. Both wines are always very fairly priced and are usually the best value in the commune. Léoville-Las-Cases and Ducru-Beaucaillou can be brilliant yet more expensive than almost any other Second Growth wine. Outperformers would include the excellent non-classified Hortevie and Terrey-Gros-Caillou, and second wines from both Barton châteaux, Léoville-Las-Cases and Gruaud-Larose.

AVAILABILITY
The second wines are probably the easiest to find, though any Bordeaux specialist, good independent or upmarket chain should have some Classed Growths.

CONSUMER CHECKLIST
Château Léoville-Las-Cases 2000	Quality 10 ★
	Price 10 ★
	Value 8 ★
Château Léoville-Barton 1996	Quality 10 ★
	Price 8 ★
	Value 10 ★

Good Years St-Juliens benefit from aging. They are reliable in lesser years, and outstanding in great ones. Best years: 2004, 2003, 2002, 2001, 2000, 1999, 1998, 1996, 1995, 1990, 1989, 1988, 1986, 1985, 1983, 1982.
Taste Notes There are two styles – one soft, honeyed and almost slightly sweet, the other dry, taut, and perfumed.

PAUILLAC

Pauillac is separated from St-Julien by the width of a country lane, the width of an old stone wall or a stream, depending where you're standing. But that insignificant boundary line separates two very distinct wines, for Pauillac is the focal point, the quintessence of red Bordeaux, and its principal grape, the Cabernet Sauvignon, summons all its strength in Pauillac to produce wine of great power and remarkable beauty, an unlikely combination which is achieved surprisingly frequently.

Certainly the style is stark, it is often unbending, it is aggressive and uncompromising, it doesn't count on your favours, but in its arrogant way it knows that sooner or later you will come to recognize it for what it is – one of the great flavours of the world. The fruit seems to be all blackcurrant, sometimes thickened with blackberry or raspberry or plum, but at the same time made haunting and memorable by the entwining fumes of lead pencil shavings and late evening cigars which combine with the fruit. Of all red Bordeauxs the Pauillac wines last the longest, and from a hard, rough-necked youth they can untangle tastes almost sweet and perfumed and quite beyond words as they age.

Pauillac is a big commune – with over 5000 inhabitants it is the Médoc's nearest thing to a town centre. Its 1200 hectares (2965 acres) not only harbour good minor châteaux, but also 18 Classed Growths (only the commune of Margaux has more, with 21) and three of the five First Growths: **Latour, Lafite-Rothschild** and **Mouton-Rothschild.**

Predictably, not everything is performing equally well. Among the First Growths, Latour is a star performer with wines of brooding depth but great cedary scent and its reputation for making fine wines in lesser years is well deserved. Lafite is lighter but on top form nowadays and wonderfully scented. Mouton-Rothschild is more erratic but wonderfully rich and exotic when on song, as it seems to have been in recent vintages.

Pauillac only has two Second Growths but both are superb. **Pichon-Longueville** has what is probably the most photographed château in the Médoc with its fairytale turrets and courtyard lake. Since being bought by the AXA insurance company in 1987 there has been a remarkable renaissance of quality and it is now classic, dark, blackcurranty Pauillac. **Pichon-Longueville-Lalande** has been on brilliant form since the 1970s with a succession of lush, hedonistic reds to swoon over

that are gorgeous young and outstanding with age. Pichon-Lalande was the leader of a group called the 'Super-Seconds' – top Second Growths like Ducru-Beaucaillou, Léoville-Las-Cases, Cos d'Estournel and the Third Growth Palmer which tried to push their prices to First Growth levels during the 1980s. Their leaps in quality and price led the way for numerous other properties to follow.

Pauillac also has two Fifth Growths that produce wine of Second Growth quality. **Lynch-Bages** makes lush, seductive, blackcurranty reds that nonethless age superbly well. **Grand-Puy-Lacoste** makes a more reserved style which becomes a perfect Pauillac marriage of cedar and blackcurrant with 10 or more years of age.

Other Classed Growths worth trying are **Pontet-Canet**, now one of the best value of the Classed Growths, the well-priced and satisfyingly blackcurranty **Batailley** and the dark, blackcurranty **Haut-Bages-Libéral**.

Of the non-classed châteaux, **Pibran** is excellent and **Fonbadet** and **Haut-Bages-Averous** are also good.

READING THE LABEL

A large number of Pauillac wines are Classed Growth (in fact, one-third of the 1855 Classification) but only the First Growths state their full rank on the label.

WHAT DO THEY TASTE LIKE?

Latour is renowned for its massive structure, and cigar, cedar and lead pencil scent backed up by deep, dark blackcurrant fruit. Mouton-Rothschild is the other way round, with exotic blackcurrant fruit backed up by spicy, cedar-wood scent, while Lafite treads a fabulously elegant path between the two. Others of the 'blackcurrant and pencil shavings' style are Pichon-Longueville and Pichon-Longueville-Lalande, Lynch-Bages, Pontet-Canet and Grand-Puy-Lacoste, and the second wines Les Forts de Latour and Carruades de Lafite.

There is also a plummier, broader, less perfumed style of Pauillac which is still very good, and which is epitomized by the wines of Batailley, Haut-Bages-Libéral, **Grand-Puy-Ducasse**, Pibran and Haut-Bages-Avérous.

ENJOYING THE WINES

The classic match for mature Pauillac is the local lamb. Rare rib of beef is good too. The Bordelais might well eat steak grilled over vine-cuttings, and a young, sturdy Pauillac would be delicious with this as well as with full-flavoured pheasant and hare.

ST-ESTÈPHE

The famous Haut-Médoc appellations end, as they began at Margaux, in a huddle of hamlets and fields loosely drawn together round a single name – that of St-Estèphe. The finest vineyards look out over a tiny stream to the glories of Château Lafite-Rothschild in Pauillac, but two sharp twists in the road and you feel you have cut all ties with the glitzy showbiz world of Pauillac and returned to the humdrum, labouring life.

There is much truth in this. St-Estèphe is the least glamorous of the main appellations, and makes the least glamorous wine. It has no First Growths and only five Classed Growths, covering 264 hectares (652 acres) out of the total of 1244 hectares (3073 acres). Indeed, the area was planted later than the rest of the Haut-Médoc, and many of the top vineyards

were still young and relatively unknown in 1855 when the Classification was drawn up.

But the lack of Classed Growths has another cause. The soil is different. Those great banks of gravel are becoming exhausted and diluted with clay by now. Clay is colder, drains far less well, and ripens grapes less easily; the wine is heavier, more acid, more likely to have a clumpy solidity than a swishing beauty, to satisfy with fistfuls of flavour rather than tingle with genius. That said, not only is there fine wine in St-Estèphe, but there is trustworthy wine too. And in hot, dry years like 2000 and 2003 that clay can be an advantage, holding water when the deep gravel beds to the south have long since drained dry.

There has been a tendency, too, to take greater advantage of the clay by planting

The *cuverie* at Château Cos d'Estournel has the most exotic architecture in Bordeaux – the pagoda-like roof even has little bells hanging from it.

more Merlot than previously, at the expense of the gravel-loving Cabernet Sauvignon. This has helped to soften the sometimes austere style of St-Estèphe.

WHAT DO THEY TASTE LIKE?

The bragging rights are between St-Estèphe's two Second Growths, **Cos d'Estournel** and **Montrose**. Cos is dark, oaky and slow to reveal its rich, plum and blackcurrant core. Montrose which used to be tough yet cedary, is now lush and exotic almost from the word go but with enough structure to age. The greatly improved but still austere **Calon-Ségur** is also important. **Lafon-Rochet** and **Cos Labory** are less well known but high quality mixing earthiness with good blackcurrant fruit.

To go with these, the top St-Estèphe Bourgeois Growths of **de Pez**, **Haut-Marbuzet**, **Meyney**, **Les Ormes-de-Pez** and **Phélan-Ségur** are often of Classed Growth quality –

the wine is a little sturdy, even earthy sometimes, but dragging enough blackcurrant and tobaccoey cedar perfume from the soil to make fine red Bordeaux only a little bit short on magic and dreams.

READING THE LABEL

St-Estèphe is the home of good Bourgeois Growths, though the actual words may not appear on the label. Some may call themselves 'Cru Exceptionnel' or even just 'Grand Vin' (a term which also appears on some of the most undistinguished wines of Bordeaux). Apart from the leading wines already mentioned they are unlikely to be brilliant, but certainly worth trying.

ENJOYING THE WINES

St-Estèphes are very adaptable. Even the finest wines like Cos d'Estournel can partner fairly highly seasoned dishes, and a St-Estèphe might well be first choice for a traditional Sunday lunch. Red Bordeaux is usually blunted by cheese, but mild Dutch cheese is very popular in the Bordeaux region and St-Estèphe is the best type of local wine to accompany it.

CONSUMER INFORMATION

WHAT DO I GET FOR MY MONEY?

St-Estèphe still represents good value, even though the top performing Cos d'Estournel and Montrose are now verging on the overpriced. Marbuzet, previously Cos's second wine, has been a château in its own right since 1994. So far it is still a good buy, as are Lafon-Rochet, Cos Labory, Les Ormes-de-Pez, Meyney and Haut-Marbuzet.

AVAILABILITY

For the top wines go to specialists, but other good outlets should have some pretty decent Bourgeois Growths.

CONSUMER CHECKLIST

Château Cos d'Estournel 1995

Quality 9 ★
Price 10 ★
Value 8 ★

Good Years In ripe years these wines mature slowly, and need as long as Pauillac to soften. In lighter years, the wines are often drinkable quite young. Best years: 2004, 2003, 2002, 2001, 2000, 1998, 1996, 1995, 1994, 1990, 1989, 1988, 1986, 1985, 1983, 1982.

Taste Notes St-Estèphe wines rarely achieve the heights of the best Pauillacs, but even so they reach a lightly plummy, even cedary style which is very satisfying.

HAUT-MÉDOC

This means 'Upper Médoc', and it covers the vast southern chunk of the Médoc – it's upper in the sense that it's upstream. It's a bit of a catch-all appellation: the best villages have been filleted out and given their own appellations, and the best properties in these villages only use Haut-Médoc as an alternative appellation for their less successful vats which they want to declassify.

Yet this rather haphazard gathering of the less glamorous villages does boast five Classed Growths, and two of these villages do have their own appellations – Moulis and Listrac-Médoc. Of the two, **Moulis** makes the softer and more approachable wine, and has a good ridge of gravel running through it. **Listrac-Médoc** also has some gravel, but it's further away from the river and a fraction higher in altitude, though nothing in the Médoc is frankly all that high. But the combination is just enough to make the wines a little bit harder, a little bit tougher, a little bit more solid.

The Haut-Médoc as a geographical definition runs from south of Margaux near Bordeaux to north of St-Estèphe and accounts, with Moulis and Listrac-Médoc, for about 5940 hectares (14,677 acres). Mostly it applies to vineyards a few kilometres back into the pine forests away from the Gironde estuary, but between Margaux and St-Julien and again for the final gravelly fling north of St-Estèphe, the vineyards do reach down to the estuary. However, **La Lagune**, at Ludon, and **Cantemerle** at Macau are great wines in search of a commune appellation. They used to be described as Margaux, yet now their names and quality are so renowned they have no need to borrow another village's name. Inland from St-Julien, the village of St-Laurent has three little known Classed Growths **La Tour-Carnet**, **Belgrave** and **Camensac**. Both La Tour-Carnet and Belgrave are making increasingly good wine.

Between Margaux and St-Julien, the villages of Arcins, Lamarque and Cussac make relatively light wine, but of a good, fruity style, and north of St-Estèphe, the last gravel outcrop at St-Seurin-de-Cadourne, led by the superb **Sociando-Mallet**, shows that the Haut-Médoc doesn't go down without a struggle, as a crop of quality-conscious châteaux put up their own personal rebuttal of the village's exclusion from consideration in the 1855 classification.

Apart from these good châteaux, the picture is more erratic. The Haut-Médoc boasts a lot of Bourgeois Growths, and these can be good. Unfortunately not only have prices risen but yields, too, have crept up and up. In the best appellations the sites are usually good enough to counteract this, but in the more marginal spots – say, in the north of the Haut-Médoc, some way from the river – the grapes just don't ripen properly. Add to this the dodgy vintages of the early 1990s, and the Haut-Médoc becomes a region where enjoyable quality can in no way be guaranteed and looking at the name of the producer is now very, very important. Best producers: (Listrac-Médoc) **Cap Léon Veyrin**, **Clarke**, **Ducluzeau**, **Fonréaud**, **Fourcas-Dupré**, **Fourcas-Hosten**, **Fourcas-Loubaney**, **Grand Listrac** co-operative. **Mayne-Lalande** and **Saransot-Dupré**; (Moulis) **Anthonic**, **Biston-Brillette**, **Brillette**, **Chasse-Spleen**, **Duplessis**, **Dutruch-Grand-Poujeau**, **Gressier-Grand-Poujeaux**, **Maucaillou**, **Moulin-à-Vent** and **Poujeaux**; (Haut-Médoc) **Beaumont**, **Belgrave**, **Bernadotte**, **Cambon la**

Pelouse, Camensac, Cantemerle, Charmail, Cissac, Citran, Coufran, La Lagune, Lanessan, Malescasse, Maucamps, Peyrabon, Sénéjac, Sociando-Mallet, la Tour-Carnet, la Tour-du-Haut-Moulin and Villegeorge.

READING THE LABEL

The great majority of Haut-Médoc wines are not Classed Growths. Since the appellation covers so much land, the address of the château should give some idea of style. The village of Ludon has several good soft wines; those from Arcins, Cussac and Lamarque are mostly light and slightly earthy but with a rapidly developing blackcurrant perfume, and St-Seurin-de-Cadourne wines combine full, strong fruit with a definite tannic bite. Where new oak is used to age the wine, it should have a softer, more buttery flavour.

WHAT DO THEY TASTE LIKE?

In such a large area the flavours are bound to vary. **La Lagune** is one of the most sumptuous of all Médocs and although it seems overwhelmed by new oak when young, the innate quality always comes through in the end. **Cantemerle** is relatively lighter in texture, but well-balanced and the lovely sweet fruit develops quickly but lasts well.

In general, though, there is an earthiness to the Haut-Médoc taste, sometimes improved by fruit and perfume as in the villages of St-Laurent, Moulis and Listrac-Médoc, or in the land between Margaux and St-Julien. Haut-Médoc is not as reliable an appellation as the smaller village ones – of which Moulis has the highest number of good-quality, good-value wines – simply because it is a catch-all.

ENJOYING THE WINES

Haut-Médoc is pretty all-purpose wine, reasonably tannic and somewhat earthy. It is best served with fairly full-flavoured foods.

CONSUMER INFORMATION

WHAT DO I GET FOR MY MONEY?

The Classed Growths are all fairly priced, and Chasse-Spleen, which tastes like a Classed Growth but isn't, is priced at much the same level.

AVAILABILITY

Most outlets have some.

CONSUMER CHECKLIST

Château Poujeaux 2000	*Quality 8* ★
	Price 7 ★
	Value 9 ★

Good Years Vintage variation is considerable. In general, the hotter years produce measurably finer wines, though Chasse-Spleen has managed to be good even in the off-vintages of the early 1990s. All but the best will mature fairly quickly.
Taste Notes The Classed Growths, along with Chasse-Spleen, Sociando-Mallet and Poujeaux, are often exciting, with a full, oaky softness balancing excellent fruit.

MÉDOC

This is the northern end of the Médoc, jutting upwards into the sea, and traditionally called the Bas, or 'Lower' Médoc. The growers didn't like the sense of inferiority which 'Bas' gave, and so now it's known simply as Médoc, but the simple fact is that this is an inferior region. The gravel outcrops are decidedly few and far between, and the soil is increasingly a rather sickly pale clay.

In the days when yields were lower than they are now the growers could manage to make juicy, fruity, earthy red Bordeaux which had bags of appeal at a low price. But now too many châteaux here are simply allowing their vines to produce too many grapes, and when these high yields are combined with the sort of unforgiving vintages that we have frequently seen since the early 1990s then their chickens start coming home to roost. At the moment too many of the wines are muddy, stalky and frankly not very attractive.

Yes, of course we'll see good vintages again, and the wines will improve. But they won't improve by as much as they need to until the growers start to realize the competition they're up against. Just about every region in the world can now produce low-priced, fruity Bordeaux-style red wines – and they tailor them to what we, the consumers, want to drink. This part of the Médoc doesn't do that. By and large it's a deeply traditional peasant culture, and only a few producers are seriously interested in making the best wine they can for an international market. Best producers: **Bournac, Escurac, Les Grands Chênes, Lafon, Les Ormes-Sorbet, Potensac, Ramafort, Rollan-de-By, La Tour-de-By, La Tour Haut-Caussan** and **la Tour-St-Bonnet**.

ST-ÉMILION

St-Émilion is riddled with wine. Literally. This gorgeous twisting, tumbling cluster of houses on the hillside is the only genuinely picturesque town in all of Bordeaux, and has been a wine centre since Roman times. Squashed into a fold in the steep slope of limestone which marks the southern edge of the St-Émilion/Pomerol plateau, the town is a hive of cellars and tunnels burrowing through the soft rock, many as full of wine now as when the Romans struck camp; and happily the wine area to which it has given its name is one of the greatest in France – St-Émilion.

The name immediately conjures up the acceptable face of red Bordeaux. The softer, juicier fruit, the quick-maturing, rather jammy tastes which are delicious years before the Médoc wines have shifted an ounce of their tannin, these are the flavours which have made St-Émilion world famous. And while neighbouring Pomerol offers similar pleasures, Pomerol is small and sorely tested to meet demand. St-Émilion has no such problems. With nearly 5500 hectares (13,590 acres), this single area fanning out on all sides from the town is appreciably bigger than the entire Côte d'Or in Burgundy, which has just under 4040 hectares (10,000 acres). It also produces more wine than all the major Haut-Médoc appellations put together.

Inevitably, it's a pretty heterogenous area. The vast majority of the vineyards simply produces pleasant enough soft red wine which is easy to drink and sell. The true greatness of St-Émilion, upon the reputation of which the whole enormous area feeds, is a small stretch of land around the town, with the finest vineyards clambering up and down the steep south-facing slopes, and a further stretch of gravel outcrops running like billowing waves in a sea swell up to Château L'Évangile across the Pomerol border. It is also the home of the 'garagiste' movement – tiny, micro-properties on sites both favoured and unheralded producing small amounts of extremely concentrated, absurdly expensive reds for the favoured few.

GRAPE VARIETIES AND WINE STYLES

Except for a sparkling wine made primarily for tourists (of whom between 200,000 and 300,000 visit the town each year) in the cellars under the ancient Couvent de Cordeliers, St-Émilion is primarily red wine country, and the dominant grape, as in Pomerol, is the Merlot, assisted by the Cabernet Franc and Malbec

Le Bon Pasteur
Certan-de-May
Clinet
La Conseillante
L'Église-Clinet
L'Évangile
La Fleur-Pétrus
Gazin
Lafleur
Latour-à-Pomerol
Petit-Village
Pétrus
Le Pin
Trotanoy
Vieux Ch. Certan

Angélus
L'Arrosée
Ausone
Beau-Séjour Bécot
Belair
Canon
Canon-La-Gaffelière
Cheval Blanc
La Dominique
Figeac
Clos Fourtet
Grand Mayne
Magdelaine
Monbousquet
La Mondotte
Pavie
Pave-Macquin
Rol Valentin
Le Tertre-Roteboeuf
Troplong-Mondot
Valandraud

ST-ÉMILION AND POMEROL WINE AREAS

- St-Émilion AC wine area
- Pomerol AC wine area
- Lalande-de-Pomerol AC wine area
- St-Émilion satellite AC wine areas
- AC wines

Canon = main château

and, though only to a small extent, by the Cabernet Sauvignon. This is because much of the area is sand and clay, which Cabernet Sauvignon doesn't like, and on the sun-baked *côtes* (or slopes) near the town, the limestone soil produces dull Cabernet Sauvignon but excellent Merlot. One property has recently replanted the long-forgotten Carmenère, now rediscovered flourishing in Chile.

There are three main areas of vineyards. The most important, producing nearly all the great wines, is the **Côtes St-Émilion**. This area, made up primarily of limestone and clay, has its prize properties on the steep plateau edge near the town itself, but is generally reckoned to run a good way back from this front line. As red wines go, they can be succulently rich, with properties like **Canon**,

Angelus and L'Arrosée able to conjure an amazing honeyed sweetness out of their grapes. They also usually have a tannic toughness which makes them a lot finer than simply gooey, butter-soft reds for gulping. The wines of Ausone, Belair, Magdelaine and Beauséjour-Bécot combine honeyed ripeness with a sometimes minty, eucalyptus fragrance and tannic grip.

The second vineyard area is the Graves St-Émilion. The name implies gravel soil, but most of the area is sandy, with the only decent gravel nourishing the small stretch of vines at Cheval Blanc and Figeac. These are two great wines. The gravel allows Cheval Blanc to have 66 per cent Cabernet Franc, and Figeac 35 per cent each Cabernet Franc and Cabernet Sauvignon. The result is powerful, blackcurranty wine, with the Merlot adding a minty perfume to the blockbusting mouthful of ripe fruit. Of the other Graves properties, only La Dominique really excels.

Third, the Sables St-Émilion is the flatter, sandier area, usually down near the Dordogne river. It is these wines, pale red, quickly turning to orange but with a brief, delicious burst of soft fruit, butter and honey, which have given St-Émilion its reputation for light, easy wine. However, Monbousquet, once a mild, soft red, has been transformed by owner Gerard Perse into a blockbuster that

Harvesting at Château Canon in St-Émilion. This is one of the prettiest parts of Bordeaux, centred on the Roman town of St-Émilion itself.

suggests that the accepted wisdom about St-Emilion soils and the types of wine they can produce may have to be rethought.

Apart from these areas, there is a large hinterland to the north-east and south-east of the town. Much of this area has the appellation St-Émilion, but there are four so-called satellites which can hyphenate their names to that of St-Émilion. These are Lussac, Montagne, Puisseguin and St-Georges. There are over 2800 hectares (7000 acres) of these vineyards. In general the wines are fairly strong and plummy, without being terribly exciting, and as elsewhere in St-Émilion – indeed, as elsewhere in Bordeaux – the question of yields raises its ugly head.

But while some growers in St-Emilion – eespecially in the outlying areas – can be accused of the pervasive Bordeaux vice of overproduction, the group of producers called 'garagistes' and several top Classed Growth producers might be taken to task for yields that are almost too low. Led by properties like Pavie and Valandraud these producers cut yields right down, then super-ripen – over-ripen you might say – their grapes, then vinify them with loads of new oak and the objective of maximum extraction and high alcohol. These styles are very popular in the US but meet with less unanimous approval in Europe.

CLASSIFICATION

Since 1984 St-Émilion has had two appellations, plain St-Émilion and St-Émilion Grand Cru, with the latter comprising some 90 top properties. Grand Cru in turn has two superior ranks, Premier Grand Cru and Grand Cru Classé, of which the former is the higher. Both these ranks are re-examined regularly, and properties applying for them must be subject to various requirements including a lower yield than basic St-Émilion, compulsory château bottling, a commitment not to change the shape of the property in the ensuing ten years (a condition with which many famous Médoc Classed Growths would be unable to comply), and an undertaking that at least 50 per cent of the wine comes from vines of 12 years old or more.

There is also an Association de Propriétaires de Grands Crus Classés de St-Émilion which comprises 31 of the châteaux just below the very top rank. These properties are committed to improving their image and quality through voluntary restriction of yields in the vineyards, compulsory aging in oak barrels and similar assurances of a quality-first approach. A similar approach by the Grands Crus would be no bad thing: there are far too many of them, and some wouldn't even scrape a Bourgeois pass in the Médoc.

ORGANIZATION

The estates in St-Émilion are seldom very large. Over 50 per cent are less than 5 hectares (12 acres). About 800 growers share the 5500 hectares (13,590 acres) of vineyards, and even the major Classed Growths are small by Médoc standards. The lesser properties frequently sell their produce to the local Libourne merchants in bulk, or to one of the five co-operatives. The central one, the Union des Producteurs, is the second biggest in Bordeaux, and vinifies various single properties as well as supplying much of the Libourne and Bordeaux trade in bulk.

READING THE LABEL

Judging the standard of a St-Émilion is complicated by the wide-ranging Grand Cru system (see above). Grand Cru should in theory mean a particular level of quality, but if it does then it starts from a fairly low base.

The narrow spaces between the rows of old vines at Château Magdelaine in St-Émilion mean that horses still have to be used instead of tractors.

WHAT DO THEY TASTE LIKE?

Soft, round, rather generous, sometimes earthy wines are the norm in St-Émilion. They don't always have the minerally backbone of the Pomerol wines, and the sweetness is usually less plummy, and rather more reminiscent of butter, toffee or sometimes raisins. The St-Émilion Grands Crus add a minty, blackcurranty depth.

THE GOOD YEARS

The following notes are applicable both to St-Émilion and its immediate neighbour, Pomerol (see page 57). Vintages here do not always correspond to those of the Médoc in style or quality, owing to different soils, different blends of grapes and generally earlier picking. The wines, particularly St-Émilions, are generally a touch more alcoholic than those of the Médoc, and despite their lower tannin and acidity they still mature very well. The mellow Merlot influence, however, makes them drinkable much younger. Lesser wines are often ready at three to four years old, and even the great wines are usually delicious in six to seven years.

2004 A more typical year after the extraordinary heatwave of 2003. Ideal conditions at vintage time. Good classic wines.

2003 Hottest summer on record and some real blockbusters but not all properties were able to cope with the extreme conditions.

Look out for wines with a high dose of Cabernet Franc.

2002 A difficult year and almost all the Merlot vines on the Right Bank were badly affected by a cold spring. The wines vary from modest to very good.

2001 An exceptional vintage and many producers reckon their wines equal or even exceed the fine 2000s.

2000 A very fine vintage with ripe, concentrated wines.

1999 Some good, ripe wines, but only from those who picked before the September rains.

1998 A very good vintage for Merlot with some fine, rich wines from grapes picked fully ripe. Pomerol did best.

1997 Wines vary in quality due to uneven ripeness and rain at vintage time. Drink up.

1996 Quality more varied than the Médoc. Some enjoyable soft wines. Drink up.

1995 A good, consistent vintage, sometimes even very good but for the third year in a row rain affected the harvest. Even so, there are some lovely luscious reds. Very popular year with investors and prices are high.

1994 Most châteaux in Pomerol increased the percentage of Merlot in the blend, and so made the most successful wines in Bordeaux. They aren't keepers, though.

1993 Another rainy autumn but St-Émilion and Pomerol made better wines than the Médoc and Graves. Drink up.

1992 Terrible vintage. Drink up or give away.

1991 Fearsome spring frosts and little wine made. Drink up.

1990 A very hot, dry year with the early-ripening Merlot becoming so ripe that the wines are very alcoholic too. Top wines are at peak, lesser wines fading.

1989 Wonderful wines of great concentration and richness from a heatwave summer. Excellent now, many will still improve.

Older vintages

Only top wines from the best years (1988, 1986, 1985, 1982, 1979 and 1970) are still worth keeping.

ENJOYING THE WINES

The richness and softness of many of the wines gives them a similar role to Pomerols. Good with pâtés, cheeses and spicy foods, as well as with Burgundian-style meat dishes.

CONSUMER INFORMATION

WHAT DO I GET FOR MY MONEY?

There are few bargains in St-Émilion because demand for the wine is so strong. The best wines are superb, but cost an arm and a leg. The St-Émilion satellite regions – Montagne, St-Georges, Puisseguin and Lussac – trade too heavily on the St-Émilion name to be good value but the co-operatives do produce some reasonably priced, lush though earthy reds.

AVAILABILITY

Not as good as for the wines of the Médoc and Graves, because the estates are smaller and the quantities of wine much less. Most of the St-Émilions readily available to the consumer are the *petit château* wines.

CONSUMER CHECKLIST

Château Angélus 1995   *Quality 9* ★
                                         Price 10 ★
                                         Value 8 ★

Good Years St-Émilions mature more quickly than Médocs because of the far higher proportion of Merlot in the blend, but they can last as well as all but the greatest Pauillacs. Off-vintages can sometimes be a little raw and dilute. Best years: 2004, 2003, 2001, 2000, 1998, 1996, 1995, 1990, 1989, 1988, 1986, 1985, 1983, 1982, 1981, 1978.

Taste Notes Frequently there is an almost sweet flavour to St-Émilions, a gentle, butter, even honeyed softness because of the predominance of Merlot.

POMEROL

It's no use looking on any ordinary map for the village of Pomerol, because there isn't one. Pomerol is just a block of fields on the north side of the river Dordogne 40km (25 miles) east of Bordeaux which, not that long ago, no-one had ever heard of.

On the surface the area still seems to be a featureless, flattish plateau of rather heavy, dull vineyard land, situated just past the small wine town of Libourne, with none of the slopes and escarpments which are supposed to presage great wine.

Pomerol does have natural boundaries, but they lie underneath the surface of the soil, and in certain places these natural features combine with human skill and commitment to produce what are, at their best, some of the greatest red wines in the world. The subterranean boundaries are dictated by the limits of a most unusual subsoil, of dark packed clay, shot through with a remarkably high iron content.

For a couple of hundred hectares in the centre of the appellation the land rises slightly, as though the dark, iron-packed clay subsoil were pushing its way to the surface. It very nearly does. In the finest vineyards this subsoil is only just over 50cm (20in) below the surface. The Merlot grape feeds on this heavy soil like a pirate on rum, and brave braggart wines are the result.

And, of course, the world has taken notice. Pomerol is immensely popular – too popular, really, for its own good. But, in spite of this, the standard of wine-making is very high. It's even getting higher: there are far more good wines made here than there were, say, 15 years ago. I would take issue with only one or two of the top wines as being not quite as good as they used to be.

And Château **Le Pin** is certainly not among them because it didn't exist a generation or so ago and now has overtaken world-famous **Pétrus** – temporarily at least – as the world's most expensive red wine. I do hear it's wonderful but since it only makes about 1000 cases per year, I can't give you a personal tasting note. This is also the home territory of Michel Rolland, the world's most powerful and influential wine consultant, whose enthusiasm for rich, ripe Pomerol styles has influenced properties as far away as India, Argentina and Chile.

GRAPE VARIETIES AND WINE STYLES

Pomerol is small but absolutely solid with vines. North and east of Libourne, the appellation measures only 12km (8 miles) square but has 782 hectares (1932 acres) of vines, so there isn't a lot of room left for back gardens and cabbage patches. The dominant grape here is Merlot, even more than in St-Émilion. Pétrus is 95 per cent Merlot planted on virtually pure clay and iron.

After Merlot, the next most important grape is Cabernet Franc, and occasionally the usually dismissed Malbec, but many vineyards have nothing at all of Bordeaux's most famous grape, Cabernet Sauvignon. Clay soil is cool and damp and Cabernet Sauvignon, which ripens much later than the Merlot, often doesn't ripen at all in clay. (If all of Bordeaux had soil like Pomerol, would growers in Australia and California even have bothered with Cabernet Sauvignon?) There are no white grapes in Pomerol.

The area divides into three approximate styles, according to the soil. To the west of the appellation the soil is sandier, and the wines are lighter, but still have a brilliant sweetness, almost sinfully delicious even when very young. Wines like **Clos René**, **de Sales** and **L'Enclos** epitomize this style.

Tightly packed vineyards and the occasional church spire are the main distinguishing features of Pomerol's flat, open landscape.

Running across the southern part of the region is a much more gravelly soil which links almost imperceptibly with St-Émilion. The resulting wines are drier, tougher when young, which is not a normal Pomerol attribute, and rarely get quite the juicy, plummy richness of the typical Pomerol. However, they have some of the cedary austerity of the Médoc which is otherwise lacking in Pomerol. The gravel also means a lower proportion of Merlot is grown. Good properties from this part of the appellation are **Petit-Village**, **La Conseillante** and **Beauregard**.

Between these two areas is the heart of Pomerol, where a succession of small properties make sensational wine on their iron-clay soil. There is no question that there is a mineral taste to Pomerol from this iron, and it adds an extra dimension to the rich, ripe, plump fruit, the wonderful buttery sweetness of new oak barrel aging, and the silky, perfumy 'well-fed prelate' feel of great Pomerol. The best wines are so sumptuous you can't decide whether to concentrate on the experience or laugh out loud with pleasure.

Château **Pétrus** is the greatest property, though presently hounded by **Le Pin** and followed at a respectful distance by others including **Bonalgue**, **Bon-Pasteur**, **Certan-de-May**, **Clinet**, **Clos L'Eglise**, **Clos René**, **La Conseillante**, **L'Église-Clinet**, **L'Évangile**, **La Fleur-Pétrus**, **Gazin**, **Hosanna**, **Lafleur**, **Latour à Pomerol**, **Petit-Village**, **de Sales**, **Trotanoy** and **Vieux-Château-Certan**.

There is also a 'subsidiary' area, **Lalande-de-Pomerol**, to the north of Pomerol across the river Barbanne. With 1151 hectares (2844 acres) of vineyards, it's far bigger than Pomerol itself. The wines aren't cheap but are generally good, plummy but slightly leaner. Best producers: **Annereaux**, **Bertineau-St-Vincent**, **Borderie-Mondésir**, **la Croix-St-André**, **la Fleur de Boüard**, **Garraud**, **Grand Ormeau** and **la Sergue**.

CLASSIFICATION

There is no classification in Pomerol. This may seem remarkable for an area with so many great wines, but Pomerol's fame is astonishingly recent – post-World War Two – which must give heart to neighbouring areas like Fronsac which are tantalizingly close to breaking into the big time.

A certain Professor Roger did classify 63 châteaux in 1960, but the only universally accepted decision is that Pétrus and Le Pin are out on their own. There follow a good dozen very fine châteaux, led by Trotanoy, La Fleur-Pétrus, Gazin, Lafleur, l'Eglise-Clinet and Vieux-Château-Certan, and perhaps 40 others which usually make wine up to Médoc Classed Growth standard. Pomerol wines may be declassified to the Bordeaux or Bordeaux Supérieur appellations.

ORGANIZATION
There are 180 growers in Pomerol, with one-third of them owning less than 1.5 hectares (3.75 acres) of vines. There are only a couple of properties over 40 hectares (100 acres), and few châteaux are big enough to have second labels. Despite this fragmentation, there is no co-operative. The smaller growers sell their grapes or wine to merchant houses in Libourne, two of whom are called Moueix. A Moueix owns several properties, but it is J-P Moueix, led by the deeply quality-committed Christian Moueix, that matters most. It is the largest proprietor in Pomerol, owning and managing many of its greatest vineyards, including Pétrus, and is chiefly responsible for Pomerol's huge strides towards greatness.

READING THE LABEL
The labels of Pomerol often have a slightly old-fashioned look, as though they're not yet affected by the world of high finance and marketing men (though you have to be in high finance – very high – to afford them). Several châteaux use titles like Grand Cru, and list medals of bygone days. A more reliable pointer is to follow any château with the producer J-P or C Moueix on the label.

WHAT DO THEY TASTE LIKE?
Pomerol is often described as a cross between the Médoc and St-Émilion in flavour, but the description is not really exact. Few of them have the lean, clear definition of top Médocs, yet most have a deeper, rounder flavour than St-Émilion, the plummy fruit going as dark as prunes in great years, but with the mineral backbone of toughness preserving it for a very long time.

THE GOOD YEARS
Pomerol vintages are treated in detail under St-Émilion (see page 53) as climatic conditions are similar. The wines are easy to drink when they are only four to five years old, because of the plummy richness of their fruit. However, they have excellent keeping qualities, and at the top level can last better than most Médoc wines, because of their concentration of finely balanced fruit.

ENJOYING THE WINES
These wines have such rounded, rich fruit to them that of all red Bordeaux they are among the easiest to enjoy without food. At the very top level of Pétrus, Trotanoy and others there are few foods which would not be overwhelmed by their sheer bravura intensity. However, the plummy roundness can also be turned to good account.

The spicier game dishes, such as herby terrines and pâtés, or pheasant, pigeon and duck, blend beautifully with these wines, and the raw Bayonne ham from south of Bordeaux is much better with Pomerol than with most wines. Big casseroles using a lot of red wine in their preparation will also benefit from the sweet-fruit edge of Pomerol.

CONSUMER INFORMATION

WHAT DO I GET FOR MY MONEY?
There is no such thing as a cheap Pomerol: the area's wines are in far too great demand. Yet, thankfully, the standard of wine-making here is tremendously high, so there is little chance of making a bad buy. The famous châteaux sell at inflated prices and even the unknown ones are extravagant but both, in the end, deliver the goods.

AVAILABILITY
Not good. There isn't a lot of wine and there are huge number of thirsty enthusiasts all over the world. Specialist wine outlets will be able to secure the top wines – but at a price. The lesser wines are not often seen, the chief reason being a very high level of direct sales to private individuals, particularly in France and the Low Countries.

CONSUMER CHECKLIST

Château Le Pin	Quality 9 ★
1996	Price 10+ ★
	Value 6 ★

Good Years These are usually the same as St-Émilion. Pomerols are also easy to drink young, but can age well. Lesser vintages are often successful, because the earlier-ripening Merlot is more likely to succeed in a cool year. Best years: 2004, 2003, 2001, 2000, 1998, 1996, 1995, 1994, 1990, 1989, 1988, 1986, 1985, 1983, 1982.

Taste Notes Although there are considerable resemblances between St-Émilion and Pomerol, the latter have a big plummy richness backed up by a positively mineral backbone which is tremendously satisfying.

GRAVES & PESSAC-LÉOGNAN

To those of us brought up on the idea that most Graves is white, flabby, sulphurous and likely to put us off our food, it is a little difficult to grasp, firstly, that most Graves wine is now red, and secondly that for the 300 years between 1152 and 1453 during which Bordeaux owed allegiance to the English Crown, it was red Graves wine, and red Graves wine alone, which the English came to love as claret.

The Graves area is the original fine wine area of Bordeaux. The Médoc, which now bristles with superstars, was merely swamp. Indeed, the claret picked out by name by the diarist Samuel Pepys in 1663, and highly praised, was none other than **Haut-Brion**. The reason for this early fame is that the area surrounds the town of Bordeaux, and in days when travel was tricky, the nearer to the city that you could grow the wine, the better. But Bordeaux expanded rapidly, and most of Graves's original vineyards are now lost under the urban jungle of tarmac and brick. But Haut-Brion still survives, hemmed in on all sides by housing estates, and La Mission Haut-Brion is still there, its vineyards sliced in two by the main Paris to Madrid railway line. These have only been able to fend off the property developers because of the very high prices their wines fetch, and the owner of La Mission Haut-Brion is rather fond of his urban surroundings. He reckons that the houses raise the average temperature of his vineyard by nearly 2°C and allow him to call up hordes of grape-pickers at the last possible moment.

Nowadays the Graves region is in two parts. The most northerly five communes are the best and have been given their own appellation of Pessac-Léognan, totalling 1580 hectares (3904 acres) of vines; had the city of Bordeaux not expanded so far south there would be first-class vineyards where there are now suburban gardens. This is where the gravelly soil is: excellent for Cabernet Sauvignon, not necessarily so good for geraniums.

All the classified Graves châteaux are in the Pessac-Leognan appellation, making both reds and dry whites. The rest of the old Graves area comprises 3816 hectares (9430 acres) to the south, of which some 425 hectares (1050 acres) are given over to the dwindling AC of Graves Supérieures, which is for semi-sweet whites only. And filleting out the best part of the Graves has had huge effects on the rest of the area. For a start, it devalued the name. Suddenly everybody knew that if they wanted the best the region had to offer, they had to look for the words Pessac-Léognan on the label. But then it made the growers of the southern part realize that they had to sink or swim: and they opted to swim. The wines, particularly the whites, have improved by leaps and bounds. Now Graves is a source of reliable, well-made dry white, with properties like **Clos Floridène**, **La Grave** and **Chantegrive** making a name for themselves now that they are no longer in the shadow of the famous classified estates.

GRAPE VARIETIES AND WINE STYLES
The red grape varieties are the same as for the Médoc – Cabernet Sauvignon, Cabernet Franc, Merlot, Malbec and Petit Verdot – and account for about 75 per cent of the vineyards. There is a little less emphasis on Cabernet Sauvignon, and a slightly bigger Merlot presence than in the Médoc to the north which makes for slightly softer styles of wine. Indeed, the Graves reds really do run the gamut of red Bordeaux flavours, and are less easy to generalize about than any of the other main regions. This is partly because while the properties near Bordeaux mostly have good gravelly (Graves means 'gravel') soil, there is also a good deal of clay about and, further south, a fair amount of sand, too.

However, the more important influence is the attitude of the proprietor in his choice of grape varieties and vinification. The description 'earthy' which is often applied is a fair one for many of the wines, because there is an indistinct, dry backbone to the fruit which stops them being razor-sharp in their flavour definitions as the great Médocs often are. Yet they do often have the blackcurrant and cedar flavours of the Médoc, as well as having a little of the full, plummy roundness of Pomerol.

The dry whites are made from Sémillon and Sauvignon Blanc. The two varieties are usually blended together: with a couple of exceptions like the wines from Châteaux **Malartic-Lagravière** and **Couhins-Lurton**, Sauvignon doesn't perform at its best by itself here, often giving rather muddy, tough wine. Sémillon, on the other hand, is well suited to the area, and gives a big, round wine, slightly creamy but with a lovely aroma of fresh apples which is very exciting.

Most white Graves is now fermented at a low temperature, and new oak barrels are increasingly used, for the fermentation as well as for the crucial 6–12 month aging period which gives wonderful, soft nutty wines, often with a nectarine flavour when young and which become honeyed, custardy and smoky as they age over a period of perhaps seven to 15 years. They are among France's greatest white wines.

Some semi-sweet whites are made as Graves Supérieures, but except for **Clos St-Georges**, they are not very thrilling.

CLASSIFICATION

The top Pessac-Léognan château, Haut-Brion, was the only non-Médoc wine classified in the famous 1855 Classification of Bordeaux's red wines. The rest of the Graves is classified according to a 1959 ministerial decree and between them these Classed Growths produce more than one-third of all Pessac-Léognan.

The châteaux listed below are marked R or W according to whether they were classified for red, white or both – the Graves is the only place in Bordeaux where red and white wines are equally highly regarded – and the château name is followed by its commune.

Bouscaut (Cadaujac) R & W; Haut-Bailly (Léognan) R; Domaine de Chevalier (Léognan) R & W; Carbonnieux (Léognan) R & W; Couhins (Villenave d'Ornon) W; de Fieuzal (Léognan) R; Haut-Brion (Pessac) R & W; Malartic-Lagravière (Léognan) R & W; La Mission-Haut-Brion (Talence) R; Olivier (Léognan) R & W; Latour-Martillac (Martillac) R & W; Laville-Haut-Brion (Talence) W;

Just look at the pebbly soil here at Château de France and it becomes clear how the region of Graves got its name of 'gravel'.

Smith-Haut-Lafitte (Martillac) R; La Tour Haut-Brion (Talence) R; Pape-Clément (Pessac) R.

ORGANIZATION

The lack of famous properties in the southern Graves used to mean that a lot of wine was bottled by merchants. However, as standards improve, châteaux bottling is more common.

READING THE LABEL

Check for château or merchant bottling. Among the generic wines, the best are from Coste and Mau, both large merchants. Graves Supérieures wines are semi-sweet and will be sold in a clear bottle, rather than the dark green used for other Graves wines.

WHAT DO THEY TASTE LIKE?

From a region whose name means 'gravel' it is easy to pretend to detect something earthy or stony in the flavours, yet the reds do often have a rather attractive earthiness, and the whites, if not aged in new oak barrels, often have a very stony dryness. The top reds divide fairly evenly between those with a sweet juicy fruit and lots of buttery oak, and the more reserved, aquiline styles of cedary fragrance and dry fruit. The lesser reds don't often have a great deal of colour but they usually do have a fairly chunky full flavour which is enjoyable rather than memorable.

The top whites, with the vanilla of the new oak barrels adding perfume and depth, do combine quite brilliantly the apple and nectarine freshness of the fruit and the sweetness of the oak, becoming honeyed and almost waxy as they age. Lesser whites are best when marked by the strong, sharp, green tastes of modern cool fermentation methods.

THE GOOD YEARS

In general, the Médoc and Graves produce very similar vintage patterns (they are both on the same bank of the Gironde), and therefore the Médoc vintages (see page 43) can also be applied to the Graves. The Graves has a higher incidence of spring frosts because of the amount of woodland, but this is balanced by a slightly earlier ripening date. Most so-called poor years can produce some fairly good wines, while the hottest years may actually be too hot and give baked wines. The reds mature earlier than Médocs, but will last as long. Some châteaux are experimenting with quick-maturing reds, with some success. Except for the fabled few white Pessac-Léognans, which will age as well as their red counterparts, most white Graves is at its best at several years old.

ENJOYING THE WINES

The reds are adaptable, able to partner the classic Médoc matches of ham, beef and game, as well as the richer dishes associated with Pomerol and St-Émilion. The whites are good with fish and seafood.

GRAVES, PESSAC-LÉOGNAN and SWEET WHITE WINE AREAS

- Graves and Graves Supérieures AC wine areas
- Pessac-Léognan AC wine area
- Sweet white AC wine areas
- AC wines

de Fieuzal = main château

CONSUMER INFORMATION

WHAT DO I GET FOR MY MONEY?

The top reds and whites are very expensive, but the quality is uniformly high. Even below that, modern vinification methods are producing exciting wines.

For the reds, top performers are: Haut-Brion (brilliant, fragrant, almost creamy red); Domaine de Chevalier (the most elegant and cedary); Pape-Clément (dry and light in the Médoc style); Haut-Bailly (sweeter, juicier); La Mission-Haut-Brion (massive, aggressive, imposing). Outperformers are: Malartic-Lagravière (very dry, austere even, but beautifully balanced); Fieuzal (rich, exotic fruit); Latour-Martillac (taut, restrained, eventually delicious). For the whites, top performers are: Haut-Brion, Domaine de Chevalier and Laville-Haut-Brion (three of the greatest dry white wines of France, honeyed, slightly resiny, nutty and busting with old-fashioned class); Couhins-Lurton (tangy and delicious), Smith-Haut-Lafitte; and Fieuzal,

Carbonnieux, Montalivet and La Louvière (fresh, bright, fruity wines).

AVAILABILITY

Not brilliant. The top wines are much sought-after. The lesser wines are easier to find.

CONSUMER CHECKLIST

Domaine de Chevalier red 2000	*Quality 8* ★
	Price 10 ★
	Value 7 ★
Château Smith-Haut-Lafitte white 2002	*Quality 9* ★
	Price 8 ★
	Value 9 ★

Good Years Similar to the Médoc, although very hot years may be too hot in the Graves. Best years: (reds) 2003, 2002, 2001, 2000, 1999, 1998, 1996, 1995, 1990; (whites) 2004, 2002, 2001, 2000, 1999, 1998, 1996, 1995.

Taste Notes Earthy, cedary reds, sometimes sweetly juicy; honeyed, fresh whites.

SAUTERNES

Lucky old Sauternes. In the 1980s it had the best run of vintages for decades. Its prices shot up as a result, and suddenly Sauternes was fashionable, and profitable, again.

Well, not that lucky, actually. Those good vintages came not a moment too soon. Fashion had turned away from sweet wines, and a combination of poor vintages and poor wine-making had led the region lower and lower. Nobody wanted these flat, dreary, sulphury wines. Good wine-making in Sauternes is expensive, and if the vintages aren't there, and the buyers aren't there, where is the money to come from? We all knew the theory – that the morning mists coming off the little river Ciron in autumn provided the humidity (and the sun provided the warmth) that the *Botrytis cinerea*, or noble rot, fungus needed to flourish on the ripe grapes. We all knew that these are conditions that are found in very few parts of the world, and that Sauternes was even rarer in being dedicated to the production of great sweet wines to the virtual exclusion of all else. We all knew that the noble rot would feed on the grapes, sucking out the water until the berries were shrivelled and ugly but full of intensely sweet juice. We knew all that. But when we tasted the wines, we all too often thought: so what?

Then came 1983. This was one of those rare years when noble rot swept through the vineyards and when the weather stayed dry and warm, so that the combination of blue skies and gently browning, shrivelling grapes announced a great vintage. The producers saw their chance, and they grabbed it. Sauternes hit the headlines. More good years followed. Demand rose, prices rose, and suddenly there was money for investment – for the new oak barrels that great Sauternes needs, for the repeated, selective pickings that cost so much more than the single sweep through the vineyards that is the norm for most wines, even for expensive techniques like cryoextraction, introduced in 1985 as a method of artificially freezing the harvested grapes in wet vintages, and thus disposing of the unwanted rainwater. (The grapes are pressed while still frozen, much like the grapes for Germany's Eiswein, so that only the ultra-sweet juice remains unfrozen and runs from the press, leaving any water behind in the form of ice.)

These grapes are in the early stages of noble rot or Botrytis cinerea. *By the time they are ready to pick they will be squidgy and brown.*

Cryoextraction has been controversial, and the danger is that it could be used as a short cut in a perfectly good vintage, a way of dodging the slow, chancy work that produces great Sauternes. But the best châteaux are committed to quality, and if sometimes there still seems to be too much mediocre wine-making about, if some producers are still adding the sulphur dioxide with too heavy a hand, it just shows that no region can ever afford to be complacent. The more they charge, the more we expect for our money.

In any case, great Sauternes can never be made every year. In many vintages, the crucial combination of heat and humidity just doesn't occur. Sometimes the sun doesn't shine, sometimes it even shines too much, and frequently autumn rains arrive just too soon for the pickers to gather all the grapes. Also, the grapes may not rot at a uniform rate. Teams of pickers must comb the vineyard time and time again, only picking off the single berries which are properly shrivelled, or when the owner cannot afford this expense, at least the bunches which are most affected. The top properties may do this between five and ten times, depending on the vintage. These grapes are incredibly high in sugar, often reaching 20° of potential alcohol. However, the yeasts which cause fermentation can only operate up to about 13–14° of alcohol, at

A sight to lift the heart of any Sauternes lover. The 1980s produced a remarkable turnaround in the fortunes of this region.

The most important grape is the Sémillon, which imparts a rich, lanolin feel to the wine, while the Sauvignon Blanc (both are susceptible to noble rot) adds acidity and freshness. There is a little Muscadelle which is quite useful for its heady perfume.

What these nobly rotten grapes combine to produce is a brilliantly rich and glyceriny wine. It coats the mouth with a sticky lanolin fatness, combining honey and cream and nuts when young with something oily and penetrating as it ages, when the sweetness begins to have an intensity of volatile flavours rather like a peach, bruised and browned in the sun. The colour of the wine turns gold with age to a heavenly burnished hue, as the wine sheds sugar yet keeps a toffee-intense beauty for decade after decade.

There are several other areas nearby, less favoured but still affected by noble rot in the best years. Quality is on the up here, and certain properties – **La Borderie** and **Tirecul-la-Gravière** in Monbazillac, **Eyssards** in Saussignac, Ch. **Cérons** and **Grand Enclos du Château de Cérons** in Cérons, **Domaine du Noble** and **Loupiac-Gaudiet** in Loupiac, and **Loubens**, **du Pavillon** and **la Rame** in Ste-Croix-du-Mont offer excellent value in vintages where noble rot infection is widespread.

which stage the alcohol kills them off. So any sugar left unconsumed by the yeasts is straight sweetness, balanced by natural acidity. From grapes picked at 20° of potential alcohol, there will be left between 80 and 100 grams of residual sugar per litre. Yet this tortuous, slow process has taken its toll. The yield is about one-sixth of the normal amount a vineyard could produce, and it has probably taken six times as much care and expense to gather the grapes and make the wine. If we want that sort of quality, we have to be prepared to pay the cost.

GRAPE VARIETIES AND WINE STYLES
Sauternes is the overall appellation for a group of five villages in the south of the Graves region which comprise around 2000 hectares (4940 acres) of vineyards. The villages are Sauternes, Bommes, Fargues, Preignac and Barsac. **Barsac** wines also have their own appellation which they may use if they wish. The soil at Preignac and Barsac is quite chalky and the vineyards are flat, while the other villages, a little further south, are hillier, and the soil is a mix of sand, gravel, clay and limestone. In general this difference produces lighter wines in Barsac and richer, more succulent ones in Sauternes, Bommes and Fargues.

CLASSIFICATION
Sauternes was classified, along with the Médoc, in 1855. Château d'Yquem is accorded First Great Growth status, after which there are 11 First Growths and 14 Second Growths. There were originally nine of each category, but since then some properties have been subdivided.

The finest First Growths are **Rieussec**, **Guiraud**, **Suduiraut**, **Climens**, **Rabaud-Promis** and **Lafaurie-Peyraguey**. The best Second Growths are **Doisy-Védrines**, **Nairac**, **de Malle**, **Doisy-Daëne** and **Broustet**. **Lamothe-Guignard** has greatly improved. There are a number of excellent Bourgeois Growths. Look for **Bastor-Lamontagne**, **Cantegril**, **Chartreuse**, **Cru Barréjats**, **de Fargues**, **Gilette**, **Guiteronde**, **Haut-Bergeron**, **les Justices**, **Liot**, **Ménota**, **Piada**, **Raymond-Lafon** and **St-Amand**.

ORGANIZATION
The great wines are from individual properties, bottled at the château, but many châteaux make dry white wine as well, which is sold under the Bordeaux AC, as an insurance policy against poor Sauternes years. Predictably, there is no co-operative.

READING THE LABEL

You should be able to tell if the wine is of the lighter (Preignac, Barsac) or heavier style (Bommes, Fargues, Sauternes) by checking the address on the label.

WHAT DO THEY TASTE LIKE?

The wine should be luscious. Whether it is intensly, overpoweringly so, or delicately, fragrantly so will depend on the vintage and the style of wine-making. When young, a thrilling, syrupy quality reminiscent of pineapple, nectarines and apricots dominate, often nowadays fattened out even further with spicy new oak. Old Sauternes loses much sweetness but still retains a gorgeous deep flavour of barley sugar, apricots, orange peel and dates.

THE GOOD YEARS

Vintages are of crucial importance. In years with little or no noble rot the wines will have the sweetness of late-harvest wines, but without the characteristic taste of noble rot. Sauternes can be drunk young, but good ones will improve over ten to 20 years.

2004   A classic year but not memorable.

2003   Bumper crop with good potential.

2002   A small but successful vintage and plenty of botrytis.

2001   Excellent, very powerful and concentrated wines, needing at least 15 years to peak.

2000   Heavy October rain spoiled the crop.

1999   Low volumes again but top quality.

1998   Small quantities of very good quality.

1997   The best year since 1990 and the wines now at peak.

1996   Some good wines but overall quality is inconsistent.

1995   Small amounts of good wine but not much botrytis. Drink up.

1994–1991   Rain at vintage time meant these are pleasant, sweet wines, not real Sauternes.

1990   The last and best of a magnificent Sauternes trio. The best wines are only just ready. Nothing as good since then.

1989   An uneven year, with the good ones very good indeed. Stick to the top names.

1988   The noble rot developed slowly but well, and the wines are generally excellent, One of the great years of a great decade.

1986   Another great 1980s year, with noble rot affecting everything in sight. These are lovely wines which are just about ready.

1985   A vintage that might have been outstanding, if the noble rot had arrived earlier. Most properties picked too soon. Drink now.

1983   The year that started the boom. Lovely, rich, long-lived wines that are ready now but will last another 20 years.

CONSUMER INFORMATION

WHAT DO I GET FOR MY MONEY?

A lot more than you used to – but you'll need more money, too. Prices have risen steeply, but so has quality, and Sauternes is not overpriced. D'Yquem is expensive by any standards, and other leading wines are also pricy, but in good years there are lesser wines from Sauternes and the outlying areas that offer excellent value.

AVAILABILITY

Quantities are always small, and the leading wines are hard to find. So good suppliers have been hard at work to find promising *petits châteaux*.

CONSUMER CHECKLIST

Château Suduiraut 1997   Quality 10 ★
                                Price 10 ★
                                Value 9 ★

Good Years   Good years are less frequent than for almost any other French wine: one of the reasons the 1980s were so remarkable was that there were so many good years. Lesser years, though, will often give pleasant wine. Best years: 2003, 2002, 2001, 1999, 1998, 1997, 1996, 1995, 1990, 1989, 1988, 1986, 1983, 1976, 1975.

Taste Notes   The flavours are honeyed, viscous, lanoliny and sometimes nutty, but balanced by good acidity.

OTHER BORDEAUX WINES

The finest wines of Bordeaux are among the finest in the world. The wines whose names we know, whose prices we quail before, are the great Classed Growths of the Médoc, Graves, Sauternes and Barsac and St-Émilion, and the rightly vaunted top wines of Pomerol. Yet these star wines only account for around two per cent of Bordeaux's output, even though they capture 99 per cent of the headlines. Even the entire production of these famous regions is only some third of the Bordeaux total. Outside these appellations there is an enormous amount of wine looking for a direction to run in. There's even some Crémant de Bordeaux and pink Bordeaux Clairet but they're rarely seen.

Most of the wine is red. This is because the bulk price for basic Bordeaux Rouge has just about held up while that for Bordeaux Blanc cannot offer a return on the huge investment needed to make the wine to modern standards. Bordeaux Rouge can be blended to the taste of a major supermarket buyer and labelled 'claret' and it will sell; Bordeaux Blanc was for many years so utterly awful, stale, flat and sulphury that even now that most of it is clean, fresh and well made, we're just not buying it.

Every year I'm more convinced that the lesser vineyard areas of Bordeaux are more suited to growing white wine than red. You can pick earlier if you make white wine. With modern technology there is nothing to stop you making crisp, fruity wine year after year. Good Bordeaux Blanc is unlike any other dry white made in France – or in New Zealand or anywhere else, for that matter – and it's a great deal better than most affordable basic white Burgundy.

And yet the producers can't sell it. So they make red from vines that have yielded too generously, and in good warm years maybe they can get away with it. But in marginal years they can't, and the wines turn out lean, stalky and dilute. All these outlying regions have some good sites and good producers –

and, in many cases, good owners from other parts of Bordeaux have invested in the estates with the greatest potential. They're increasingly showing what can be done.

FRONSAC AND CANON-FRONSAC
The lead here is being taken by the excellent Libournais company of J-P Moueix, which runs Château Pétrus among other Pomerol properties. Fronsac is just west of Libourne, in some of the prettiest countryside in Bordeaux. There are 828 hectares (2046 acres) of **Fronsac** and 311 hectares (768 acres) entitled to the supposedly better **Canon-Fronsac** appellation, on limestone and sandstone planted with the usual red Bordeaux vines.

Moueix has helped to raise quality generally. The wines are concentrated, with some of the rich, plummy fruit of Pomerol together with a typical rough, minerally edge, and they age well – and yet to my mind they're still not as exciting as they should be. But they've got potential. Best producers: **Canon, Canon de Brem, Cassagne Haut-Canon, Dalem, la Dauphine, Fontenil, Grand-Renouil, la Grave, Haut-Carles, Moulin-Haut-Laroque, Moulin Pey-Labrie, la Rivière, la Rousselle, les Trois Croix, la Vieille Cure** and **Villars.**

CÔTES DE BOURG
Bourg is a small, mainly red wine region situated bang opposite the Haut-Médoc on the north bank of the Gironde. The wines were known and sought after long before the great Médoc vineyard was more than a twinkle in its mother's eye. It is this great past which is a mere twinkle in the eye of the Bourg growers now, yet their wines could still be good. They have a fairly full, rather raisiny flavour, backed up by good tannin and acidity. All they need is will and investment and they could be very good. The best wines are from the banks of the Gironde opposite Margaux. Best producers: **Brulesécaille, Bujan, Falfas, Fougas, Haut-Macô, Mercier, Nodoz, Roc de Cambes** and **Tayac.**

CÔTES DE BLAYE

Blaye is a large but rather diffuse area north-west of Bourg. There seems no clear pattern to the wine-making, except in the hinterland where the co-operatives which control two-thirds of the region make a lot of white from a blend of Sauvignon and Colombard. The reds, as Premières Côtes de Blaye, are improving. Best producers: **Bel-Air la Royère**, **Bertinerie/Haut-Bertinerie**, **Gigault**, **Les Jonqueyres**, **Mondésir-Gazin**, **Rolande-la-Garde** and **Segonzac**.

BORDEAUX-CÔTES DE FRANCS

There are stars here, properties bought by the owners of Vieux-Château-Certan in Pomerol, and by the owners of L'Angélus and Cheval Blanc, and yet the region as a whole doesn't shine. Most of the wine is red, based on Merlot, and it definitely has the potential to outdo a lot of St-Émilion. Best producers: **Les Charmes-Godard**, **Laclaverie**, **de Francs**, **Marsau**, **Pelan**, **La Prade** and **Puygueraud**.

PREMIÈRES CÔTES DE BORDEAUX

The Premières Côtes consist of a 50-km (30-mile) long thin sliver of land stretching down the right bank of the river Garonne to the south-east of Bordeaux. It gazes jealously, longingly at the respected and well-established vineyards of Pessac-Léognan, Graves, Barsac and Sauternes within spitting distance over the water.

After spending a long time rather pallidly aping the rich, sweet wines of Sauternes, the area is now doing rather better by turning its hand to dry reds and whites in the Graves style. Much replanting of white with red wine varieties has gone on, and it's not inconceivable that the sweet white wine areas of Cadillac, Loupiac and Ste-Croix-du-Mont might follow. The dry whites already being made are attractive, but it seems to me that reds here have more potential. Their earthiness is balanced by big, raisiny fruit and, now and then, some real Cabernet blackcurrant. Best producers: **Carignan**, **Carsin**, **Grand-Mouëys**, **du Juge**, **Lezongars**, **Plaisance**, **Puy-Bardens**, **Reynon** and **Suau**.

ENTRE-DEUX-MERS

This is a whites-only appellation, but increasingly the properties here are making red as well, which only qualifies for the Bordeaux or Bordeaux Supérieur appellation. Entre-Deux-Mers used to be terribly dull stuff, seemingly designed to repel all boarders. But with modern wine-making, white coats and stainless steel brushing aside the faded blue overalls and old wooden vats, these wines are increasingly good, dry, slightly neutral, but fresh and fairly full-bodied. The reds, although a bit earthy, can also be sharp, dry and good. Best producers: **Bonnet**, **de Fontenille**, **Marjosse**, **Moulin-de-Launay**, **Nardique-la-Gravière**, **Ste-Marie**, **Tour-de-Mirambeau**, **Toutigeac** and **Turcaud**. **Ste-Foy-Bordeaux** is a small appellation making reds and whites at the eastern end of the Entre-Deux-Mers.

CÔTES DE CASTILLON

Head eastwards out of St-Émilion toward Bergerac and you'll pass through Côtes de Castillon. It's worth a pause for the sake of the wines which have quite earthy fruit, combined with some grassiness from Cabernet Franc and a touch of plumminess from Merlot. Best producers: **Dom. de l'A**, **Aiguilhe**, **Cap-de-Faugères**, **Clos l'Eglise**, **Clos Puy Arnaud**, **Poupille**, **Robin**, **Veyry** and **Vieux-Ch.-Champs-de-Mars**.

BORDEAUX/BORDEAUX SUPÉRIEUR

These are two regional appellations, with Supérieur meaning half a degree more alcohol. This should mean riper grapes, but all too often it just means more chaptalization. This is the area where Bordeaux is really underperforming at the moment. Reds and whites in these appellations rely completely on the skill of the winemaker or merchant, and on the grower restricting yields – and as yet not very many of them do. Best producers: **l'Abbeye de Ste-Ferme**, **Barreyre**, **Bonnet**, **de Bouillerot**, **Carsin**, **d:Vin**, **de Courteillac**, **Doisy-Daëne**, **Fontenille**, **Grand-Village**, **Lynch-Bages**, **de Parenchère**, **Penin**, **le Pin Beausoleil**, **Reignac**, Reynon, **Roquefort**, Thieuley, **Tire-Pé** and **Tour-Mirambeau**.

BURGUNDY

Burgundy has been on a rollercoaster for over twenty years. Prices have risen and fallen, reputations have been made and lost, and the structure of the trade has changed. And while in 1985 I could praise the white wines and approach the reds with a mixture of hope and bitter disappointment, now it's the reds that have shot ahead, with ever more producers making wines with the sort of fragrance and exotic, tangled flavours that have made the red wine names of the Côte d'Or, the 'golden slope', more famous than any in the world. And the whites? Too often they've reacted to worldwide competition – because every major wine-producing country has some first-class Chardonnays to its credit – by arranging their laurels more comfortably under their snoozing heads.

It's a region that has long been a minefield for the buyer. On the one hand there are the growers, often tending tiny, scattered patches of vineyard; on the other there are the *négociants*, or merchants, who make a living by buying wine from those growers who don't want to bottle it themselves, blending it in commercial quantities and selling it on. For

years I said – if you want great Burgundy that tastes of the particular piece of ground it was grown on, if you want the characteristic musky fragrance of Musigny, the towering splendour of Chambertin or the mouth-filling beauty of Corton, then go to a grower. The *négociants* have long had a reputation (deserved in some cases but not in all) for levelling all wines to a house style

The last few years have seen a dramatic improvement. First of all, there has been a polarization (reflected in the price) between good growers and less good ones. A village wine from a top grower will cost at least half as much again as one from a less good name. That's all to the good: it sorts out the caring growers from the lazy ones in the most straightforward fashion.

Next, the *négociants* have changed tack. Some were hit badly by recession; there have been takeovers and rescues. But many of them, too, are handling their wines far better than they used to. And some have bought their own vineyards. Some growers, too, have started small *négociant* businesses, blurring the distinction still further. And this renaissance of purpose and quality is happening at a time when the sullen, arrogant yet hauntingly beautiful Pinot Noir grape is beginning to be tamed by grape growers in other parts of the world. California, Chile, Oregon, Australia and New Zealand are all showing, bit by bit and wine by wine, that the grape that we all thought would never give up its secrets to any but a scattered few is gradually being persuaded to do so. The finest Pinot Noirs and Chardonnays – the very finest – still come, in minute quantities, from the best parts of the Côte d'Or. But at every level below that, the rest of the world is challenging Burgundy.

GRAPE VARIETIES AND WINE STYLES
And yet Burgundy is a tiny region. It is, in essence, a long, thin streak of land, heading south down the Saône Valley from Dijon to Lyon. The only exception is the clutch of northerly vineyards below Paris near Auxerre which make up Chablis. The Saône Valley is wide and fertile. In other wine regions you would expect vineyards to feature quite prominently in this valley economy. But Burgundy is no ordinary valley wine and, while

Many Burgundian villages like Chambolle-Musigny have latched onto the fame of their most famous vineyard by hyphenating its name with their own.

the white Chardonnay grape is both relatively adaptable and easy-going, the red Pinot Noir is demanding and pernickety far beyond the behaviour of any other great grape. Were it not that Pinot Noir can occasionally produce wine of peerless beauty, the local Gamay grape, which gives little trouble but less fine wine, would have taken over long ago.

As it is, Gamay is banned from the good vineyards of the Côte d'Or and only flares to a certain fame in Beaujolais and the Mâconnais to the south. Otherwise red wine comes from Pinot Noir, and a quick drive south from Dijon toward Nuits-St-Georges, Beaune and Chagny will show both the heart of Burgundy and the root of its problems, because the very first thing that strikes you is how small the area is, yet how many famous names are squeezed into its narrow confines. To the east, an enormously wide plain stretches across to the Jura mountains and Switzerland, and is almost completely devoid of vines. And to the west there is a gently rolling valley hillside, racing east to south-east. Sometimes, as when the great vineyards of Chambertin appear just past the village of Gevrey-Chambertin, this blanket of vines stretches for only about a kilometre before the shrub-covered brow of the hill cuts across the land and the vines abruptly stop. Sometimes, as in the fine Nuits-St-Georges vineyards of Clos Arlots or Clos de la Maréchale, the thin band of vines shrinks to a width of less than 200m (656ft).

Further south, between Beaune and Pommard, the vineyards stretch briefly to their widest – 1200m (3900ft). Within these limits are the Grand Cru, or Great Growth (the best) and the Premier Cru, or First Growth (the next best) vineyards upon which Burgundy's reputation rests. They exist in closely regulated form only in the central to upper parts of what is a very shallow, short slope. Even the most cautious driver can cover the 50km (30 miles) from Dijon to Chagny in less than an hour, and that is the entire Côte d'Or, comprising the Côte de Nuits as the northern half and the Côte de Beaune as the southern half.

Below this quality level, as the vineyards flatten toward the main road, the N74, and then peter out on to the valley floor, the wines may either take their village name, or simply what are called generic Burgundy titles for the lowest quality wines (see page 72). Some of these wines may be good, and some, from the best growers, may be very good.

Most of the important Burgundy villages have hyphenated names – like Gevrey-Chambertin, Chambolle-Musigny and Puligny-Montrachet. The first word is the original

BURGUNDY WINE AREAS

- Chablis and the Yonne
- Côte d'Or (Côte de Nuits and Côte de Beaune)
- Côte Chalonnaise
- Mâconnais
- Beaujolais

name of that village. The second word is the name of that village's most famous vineyard, which is snapped on to the village name to catch some reflected glory. Nowadays the most prestigious of these vineyards are enshrined as Grands Crus. They do not have to use their village name on the label, but they cannot stop the village using their name, hyphenated, on run-of-the-mill wines.

These Burgundian Grand Cru wines, including Chambertin, Romanée-Conti and Le Montrachet, are among the most famous wine names in the world. But they produce only tiny amounts of wine, for which there is an insatiable demand. Prices are sky-high but even so a queue quickly forms.

CLIMATE AND SOIL

It would be nice to state in black and white exactly why these favoured vineyard sites consistently produce the most remarkable wines, and an army of geologists and viticulturists have tried to analyse the soil, the angle of the vineyards, and the mesoclimates without conclusive results.

Certainly the mixture of marl and limestone which dominates the central band of the Côte de Nuits seems perfect for red wine, and the starker limestone outcrops of the Côte de Beaune are wonderful for white, but since parcels of land inside the same plot, with seemingly identical soils, can produce widely differing wines, I can only say that in this difficult and relatively northerly vineyard area, the climate is always poised on a knife-edge. Something as slight as a marginal increase in the angle of the slope or a momentary dip in the field, giving greater susceptibility to spring frosts or autumn rot, is the almost unclassifiable truth behind those pieces of land which are born great and those which are not.

WINEMAKERS AND WINE-MAKING

And then there is the winemaker. If ever there was an area where it is more important to know who made the wine than where it comes from, it is Burgundy. Quite simply, supply cannot hope to meet demand. Indeed, when buying Burgundy one has the feeling of being swept up in a gold rush. With the heady stench of the massive profits to be made clouding the air, it is difficult to remember that Burgundy has always been a land of low-yielding vines and irregular vintages.

It used to be estimated that Pinot Noir only ripened properly, and only produced a decent quantity, in one vintage out of four. Nowadays with global warming and better vineyard management one in two or three is more like it. It was those one-in-four vintages upon which the fame of the region's wines was originally built, but you don't make much of a living by producing saleable wine this rarely. So ways of increasing the strike rate had to be found.

In the old days the ideal red wine was reckoned to be big, dark, full of rather heavy, plummy fruit. This is the kind of wine that the thin-skinned, basically pale Pinot Noir produces not one year in four, but about once a decade. However, further south in the Rhône Valley or even in the vineyards of North Africa, big, rich red wine was made every year, and in varying degrees the less rich years of Burgundy were made to resemble the ripest, most alcoholic vintages by the addition

of these heavy reds, which not only came from different parts of the world, but also from different grapes.

With the tightening up of restrictions since 1973, modern red Burgundy became at least closer to the produce of the permitted grape varieties in the properly delineated vineyards. However, the need to stretch the tiny produce of Burgundy has not diminished. So sub-varieties, or clones, of the Pinot Noir grape, which ripened more regularly and produced larger crops, were planted and modern fertilizers helped swell the volume. The resulting wine was generally pale in colour, but pale in flavour too, yet at least a certain spurious body could be obtained by adding large amounts of sugar to the grape must so that the wine was sweetish and alcoholic but completely lacking the delicate, lingering perfumes which even quite humble Pinot Noir wine will have if honestly made.

The Mâcon wine from these vineyards at Berze-le-Châtel near Cluny will not be as imposing as the nearby medieval buildings.

Adding sugar is a perfectly normal device in northern vineyards. It is done at the beginning of fermentation and, carefully carried out, it will help to round out the wine. But if profligately added to thin, light wine from overproductive vines it will reduce what flavour there was and leave you with a dull, vapid wine which feels thick in the mouth when you drink it and which leaves you feeling thick in the head the next morning.

Red Burgundy is, however, subject to fashions. In the 1980s an oenologist called Guy Accad hit the headlines with his theories about the extraction of colour and fruit: Pinot Noir didn't have to make light wine, he believed, and wines made with his techniques were considerably bigger and weightier. He influenced many top growers; but now he has moved on leaving in his wake an important movement among young, highly qualified winemakers, many of whom have some inter-national experience, towards gentle handling, minimal filtration and low-yielding vines. Sometimes these young turks take low yields and extraction of colour, flavour and tannin too far, but in general they're making bigger volumes of better quality wine than any previous generation.

Vineyard management or rather misman-agement, too, is at last being tackled and here the current guru is Claude Bourguignon, a soil expert who advocates at the very least semi-organic viticulture. His theories, too, are acquiring converts, and while Burgundy is a difficult place to use fully organic methods – it's a bit damp and cold for that – semi-organic ones – even just cutting back on the vast amounts of nitrogen that have been pumped into the soil over the years in the effort to get ever-higher yields – must be a good thing. Burgundy has suffered hugely from yields that are far too high – and when I say 'suffered' I don't mean the place, which has prospered hugely as a result of such greed, I mean the wine. If you've got a famous vineyard it's only human nature to try to make it yield as much as possible – which is why I say hats off to those who are increas-ingly standing out against overproduction.

Overproduction of the whites also exists, but because Chardonnay ripens more easily the inevitable dilution is less apparent. It's a reliable grape, able to give good wine even in cool years when Pinot Noir fails to ripen, and able to overcome the hottest years by produc-ing something buttery and luscious yet dry.

Chardonnay is at its greatest in the Côte de Beaune. In the villages of Meursault, Puligny-Montrachet and Chassagne-Montrachet many growers both ferment and age their wines in small oak barrels, which add a unique savoury spiciness to the wines; the result is dry white wine at its most spectacular. Yet the demand and the prices are such that shortcuts are taken by the less scrupulous. Yields are pushed up, chaptalization is routine. Chablis is also taking advantage of the craving for white Burgundy with expanded vineyards into less suitable sites.

The Mâconnais in the south is less exciting. Pouilly-Fuissé and the wines from the sur-rounding villages manage to obtain high prices for wines which range from the very good to a flood of the flattest, dullest wine the long-suffering Chardonnay produces any-where in France.

GENERIC BURGUNDY WINES

Although Burgundy is above all a region which packs as many famous names as possible into its fairly limited space, there are vineyards which do not qualify for the top honours and have to content themselves with a more humdrum title. This occurs for several reasons. Either the wrong grape is growing, which means Gamay in Pinot Noir land or Aligoté in Chardonnay land. Or the land is off the main slopes, either in the hinterland behind the Côte d'Or, or in the heavy flat land below the villages down toward the plain and away from the hillsides. Or it may be that a good grower practises a form of self-denial, not putting wine from his young vines or his less successful vats in with his main production and more famous names. This second category is likely to yield the better – and the more expensive – wines.

These wines fall into two groups – the generic appellations, or region-wide general titles with no district identity, and the rather more specific general appellations with a wide-reaching but nevertheless defined catchment area.

GENERIC APPELLATIONS

These general regional wines are the lowest level of Burgundy wine but don't make the mistake of thinking they're going to be cheap. They are if you look upwards at the prices of the village wines of the Côte d'Or, or at the Grands and Premiers Crus; but if you look sideways at other French wines such as Côtes du Rhône or Côtes du Ventoux suddenly they don't look so cheap after all.

The other point is that it is vital to buy from a good producer – which in turn adds to the price of the wine. Basic Burgundy from a basic producer is not likely to be very attractive. Basic Burgundy from a good producer who makes all his wines with immense care is another matter, and might almost be worth the money.

BOURGOGNE GRAND ORDINAIRE/ BOURGOGNE ORDINAIRE

This appellation, at the bottom rung of the Burgundy ladder, uneasily mixes the optimism of 'Grand' with the dismissiveness of 'Ordinaire' and hardly deserves its appellation at all. The clumsiness of the title usually slops over into the style of the wine. It can be produced throughout the region from virtually any grape found growing in most vineyards. The bulk of the red is based on Gamay, and

César and Tressot, two traditional northern grapes, are also allowed in the Yonne area. The white is usually based on Aligoté. I have yet to find one of more than passable, and easily forgettable, quality.

BOURGOGNE PASSE-TOUT-GRAINS

Often lumped in the same cart with Bourgogne Ordinaire, this wine is a far superior product, and can achieve a delicious cherry-fresh burst of fruit. There is a little rosé made, but basically this is a red wine appellation. Legally, it should be two-thirds Gamay and one-third Pinot Noir, but usually the best examples are at least 50 per cent Pinot or more. In a ripe year like 2002 it can make excellent perfumed red to drink young, which will also age well – often to a gentle softness that puts some classier Burgundies to shame. Look for examples from really good growers like **Francois Lamarche** in Vosne-Romanée or **Thierry Mortet** in Gevrey-Cambertin, which will, however, not be the cheapest.

BOURGOGNE ALIGOTÉ

The Aligoté is Burgundy's secondary white grape, giving rather a lot of fairly acid wine. Even so, there are times when it suits the mood better than the superior Chardonnay wines. Ideally, good Aligoté should have a smell of buttermilk soap, yet be tart and lemony to taste. It mixes particularly well with the local fruit liqueurs to make Kir (with the local blackcurrant liqueur Crème de Cassis) and Mure (with the blackberry liqueur Murelle). With oilier local dishes like snails it is also sharp and good.

The best Aligoté comes from the village of Bouzeron in the Côte Chalonnaise where it now has its own appellation. The wines of de Villaine are particularly good. Other Aligotés worth seeking out are from **M Bouzereau**, **Coche-Dury**, **A Ente**, **J-H Goisot**, **Jayer-Gilles**, **Denis Mortet** and **Tollot-Beaut**.

BOURGOGNE BLANC

This is the ordinary white Burgundy from the Chardonnay grape, sometimes with some Pinot Blanc blended in too. Much of it comes from the Mâconnais, and is broad, soft and not especially exciting. If you want a good Bourgogne Blanc then look for the name of a good Côte d'Or producer – preferably one based in the villages of Meursault, Puligny or Chassagne (check the address on the label) who may well be using vines adjacent to classier appellations. Most of these wines should be drunk within two years. Good merchants like **Drouhin**, **Jadot** and **Rodet** are also a good bet, particularly Jadot's reliable Couvent des Jacobins, as well as the **Buxy** and **Caves des Hautes-Côtes** co-operatives.

BOURGOGNE ROUGE

This is a more complicated appellation than Bourgogne Blanc, since its objective is to soak up the excess grapes, and each area of Burgundy uses different ones. Beaujolais, for instance, can use this appellation for wine from its ten Cru villages, which will be Gamay. In practice, whether or not they do so depends on the relative prices of basic Burgundy and basic Beaujolais.

In the Yonne, in the far north of Burgundy between Auxerre and Tonnerre, the few vineyards which commercialize their red grapes can include the César and Tressot varieties with their Pinot Noir. Some of the Yonne wines from the villages of Épineuil and Coulanges-Les-Vineuses are extremely good light reds, though they generally need the riper, warmer years. In the Côte d'Or and Côte Chalonnaise pure Pinot Noir is the norm for Bourgogne Rouge.

Good *négociants* do try to have good quality Bourgogne Rouge, with recognizable Pinot Noir fruit, and in today's world of high prices good Bourgogne Rouge, and Blanc, may be the only way we can afford the joys of fine Burgundy. Merchants like **Drouhin**, **Jadot**, **Maison Leroy** and **Rodet** usually have good examples, as well as the **Buxy** and **Hautes-Côtes** co-operatives. But some of the best buys (though they won't be that cheap) come from good Côte d'Or growers who vinify grapes from their young vines separately, or who take good care of their lesser vineyards outside the main village appellations – **Dugat-Py** in Gevrey-Chambertin, **Anne Gros** and **Méo-Camuzet** in Vosne-Romanée, **Lafarge** in Volnay, **Coche-Dury** in Meursault and **Rion** in Nuits-St-Georges are just a few examples.

Good Bourgogne Rouge can be the quintessence of perfumed, strawberryish Burgundy and is utterly delicious. Drink it young within two to three years.

In general, though, it isn't worth buying the cheap, blended offerings because when Pinot Noir overproduces, the wines can be very thin and pale indeed. From the less reputable producers, anything which can't be squeezed into a more expensive appellation will pay its dues in a vat of Bourgogne Rouge.

There is a small amount of rosé, also from Pinot Noir, which can be very pleasant.

SPARKLING WINE

Burgundy is the source of some of France's best Champagne-method wines, called Crémant de Bourgogne. In fact, I'd go further; I'd say that if you want a Champagne substitute that has the yeasty, bready, vinous character of Champagne, but without the clearer fruit of less expensive New World examples, these are your wines. Most Burgundian Crémants are made from Chardonnay or blended with Pinot Noir – the same grape varieties as Champagne – and they're just over half the price of a decent quality, less expensive Champagne. In flavour they're a little weightier without quite the finesse.

Only a few wines are exported, mainly by co-operatives: Caves de Lugny, based in the Mâconnais, and Caves de Bailly, from near Chablis, are two of the main ones. The best rosés come from the Chablis and Auxerre regions.

Crémant de Bourgogne is best drunk young. It doesn't improve with age in the way that Champagne does, because the base wine is never so painfully lean and acidic. Burgundy's climate is marginal for grape-growing, but it's not as marginal as that of Champagne.

CHABLIS

This northerly outpost of Burgundy is where the greatest see-sawing in price has been. Prices of Chablis tumbled during the recession of the early 1990s, and then started to climb steeply with the resurgence in demand. Add to that the spring frosts which regularly hit these vineyards, thus reducing the vintage to come and providing another reason why prices should be increased (even if, come the harvest, the frosts turn out not to have done quite so much damage as had been feared...) and you have a region that keeps one eye firmly on its market.

But then Chablis has a big market to watch, and it's only a small region, located in the hills where the river Serein glides through the small town of Chablis. True Chablis is made from Chardonnay, it's white, and no other wine produced anywhere else has the right to call itself Chablis. Not that this has stopped people in the past; only quite recently has Australia, as part of a deal with the EU, agreed to cease to use the name for its own white wines. The word Chablis has in fact been debased in so many countries for so long that there's no point in the real Chablis producers gnashing their teeth. They must simply grin and bear it. One grower spoke of his excitement at receiving a 900-case export order for immediate dispatch, cash on the nail. It was only as the cases were being loaded on to the truck that he noticed the small print – equal amounts of white, rosé and red Chablis.

GRAPE VARIETIES AND WINE STYLES

There is only one grape used for Chablis and that is Chardonnay, locally often called the Beaunois. What influences Chablis' style is first the siting of the vineyards, and second the method of wine-making. Traditionally, true Chablis comes from a relatively small group of vineyards which are based on Kimmeridgian limestone. All the **Grand Cru** and **Premier Cru** vineyards are on Kimmeridgian soil. But vines are now being grown on Portlandian limestone soil as well, and this seems to produce a less distinct wine. This wine used to be classified as **Petit Chablis** or Little Chablis. There is something of a war between the traditionalists who say that the marvellous flinty, glinting green flavours of Chablis only come from Kimmeridgian soil, and the revisionists who, purely by chance, mostly own estates away from the centre and argue that their wine is as good as anyone's.

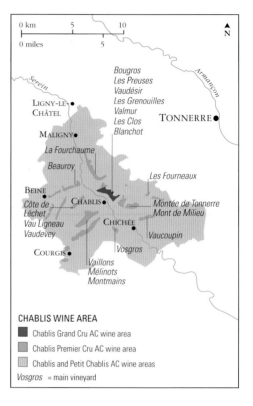

CHABLIS WINE AREA
- Chablis Grand Cru AC wine area
- Chablis Premier Cru AC wine area
- Chablis and Petit Chablis AC wine areas

Vosgros = main vineyard

Perhaps one should go back to the original classifications. All the best vineyards have always been on Kimmeridgian soil. That won't change. Yet no area, be it Burgundy, Bordeaux or the Napa Valley, lives by its Grands Crus alone, so expansion of the basic Chablis appellation should be for the general good. It is when you see woodland being cleared and classified as Premier Cru, and old, derelict vineyards which bear names like Champs des Navets (Turnip Fields) or Verjus (Sour Grapes) being promoted that you wonder about the integrity of the exercise.

There is also a marked but less bitter difference of opinion between producers who swear Chablis should be fresh, bright and lean, and drunk as young as possible, and those who think it is capable of greater things. The first group use stainless steel and concrete to vinify and mature their wines. The second group is less rigid. Some very serious producers, with Grand Cru vineyards, think oak barrels add too much taste to the stark, pure flavours of their wines. Others are convinced that only by the vanilla influence of newish oak, and the less clinical surrounds of a barrel, can Chablis ever get past the merely good to the golden glories of a Grand Cru wine from a great vintage in full flight.

CLASSIFICATION

Chablis is like a microcosm of Burgundy, but its classication system in general works better, with far less variation owed to human factors. There are seven Grands Crus, all on the steep slopes looking out south-west over the little town of Chablis. These often produce wines of power and depth, yet always holding on to a steely acidity, that for once there is no argument about their Grand Cru status. The seven Grands Crus are Blanchots, Les Preuses, Bougros, Grenouilles, Valmur, Vaudésir and Les Clos. (There is one anomaly, a cru called La Moutonne, which straddles the Grands Crus of Les Preuses and Vaudésir.)

There are 39 different vineyards traditionally rated as Premiers Crus, most of which have been rationalized into the following main vineyards: Beauroy, Côte de Léchet, Les Fourneaux, la Fourchaume*, Mélinots, Montée de Tonnerre*, Mont de Milieu*, Montmains*, Vaillons*, Vau Ligneau, Vaucoupin, Vaudevey and Vosgros (*= the most reliable).

The Premiers Crus can be very good, but they depend far more on the attitude of the grower than do the Grands Crus – and with their expansion to previously unproven vineyard sites, it is increasingly necessary to choose the vineyard and the grower with care. Ordinary Chablis is now quite steeply priced but is pretty dependable. But frankly, if you want a crisp, fruity white wine (and most basic Chablis is little more) you might just as well spend half the money in the south of France. The reason Chablis is so wonderful (or can be) is that it ages to nutty complexity; and at the basic level, only the best growers make wines that will age well.

In addition, the classification of basic Chablis has become very diffuse. Originally only wine from Kimmeridgian soil could be included in the appellation, the remainder being classified as Petit Chablis, but the recent expansionist movement which has increased the total vineyard area to 4580 hectares (11,317 acres) – a tenfold increase since the 1950s – has largely taken place on soil which was previously Petit Chablis. Chablis is a marginal northern area and only the best sited vineyards can fully ripen the grapes. The dog-end vineyards with poor drainage, poor exposure to the sun and too little protection from the elements were called Petit Chablis because they could only make Petit wine. That one or two important wine producers in the region, with, shall we say, a surfeit of Petit Chablis on their books, can cavalierly force through an upgrading of such poor land to Chablis and, of course, immediately hike the price of such thin, green wine, makes me despair of the integrity of the *appellation contrôlée* system. The result has been a loss of definition in the taste.

ORGANIZATION

It is not often that a co-operative dominates a fine wine area, but it does in Chablis. The reason is that until recently Chablis growers frequently had a real struggle to make a living, and the co-operative protected them from the worst ravages of poor weather and an indifferent market. The La Chablisienne co-operative is the biggest producer by far in the region. It sells the wines sometimes under its own name and sometimes, confusingly, under the supposed estate name of a member. A lot of Chablis is also sold to merchants or retail groups as own-label Chablis. Best producers: **Barat, J-C Bessin, Billaud-Simon, P Bouchard, Brocard, A & F Boudin, La Chablisienne, Dauvissat, Defaix, Droin, Drouhin, Durup, Fèvre, Domaine Laroche, Long-Depaquit, Louis Michel, Pinson, Raveneau, Servin** and **Vocoret.**

READING THE LABEL

The co-operative's policy of allowing its members whose wines are made in the communal vat to put a domaine-bottled title on the label is an unnecessary confusion – especially since its wines are reliable and the Chablisienne name is nothing to be ashamed of. For Premiers Crus and Grands Crus the best wines are from single growers. Wine labelled simply Chablis Premier Cru will be a blend of several Premier Cru wines.

WHAT DO THEY TASTE LIKE?

Ideally, Chablis at every level should have a steely freshness about it, even though Grand Cru wines from fine years can approach the Côte d'Or wines in their marvellous blend of lusciousness and nuttiness, with an austere savoury bite. Basic Chablis is less stark in taste than it used to be, but is still one of the driest of all Chardonnays. The use of oak barrels for aging makes the wines considerably fuller.

THE GOOD YEARS

Normally, straight Chablis should be drunk within two to three years, though the wine will age, particularly in years with good acidity. Premier Cru and Grand Cru wines must be aged to develop their exciting personalities.

2004 A fine vintage with attractive wines.

2003 The year of the heatwave. Rich, soft, alcoholic wines but not typical Chablis.

2002 Spectacular wines, especially from the top producers.

2001 Cold, wet season. Plenty of lean, green wines, but some successes.

2000 A bumper year of very good quality.

1999 A fine vintage that should still be kept.

1998 Good levels of concentration and acidity despite mixed weather. At peak.

1997 Chablis' long run of good vintages has kept up. At peak.

1996 A good year. The top wines are only just ready.

1995 Excellent wine from ripe grapes. At peak.

1994 A good year but frost reduced the crop and prices rose as a result. Drink up.

1993 A much less exciting year. Drink up.

1992 Excellent, rich and round wines. Drink soon.

Other good years For a taste of how well top Chablis can age try 1990, 1989 and 1988; but hurry up.

ENJOYING THE WINE

Chablis' reputation as a seafood wine, particularly an oysters wine, was founded on its sharpness and relatively unripe flavour. Modern Chablis is rounder and fatter than it used to be, but is still one of the best whites for the job. Premier Cru and Grand Cru Chablis are fine enough to do well with any simple fish dish, and also with roast poultry or white meat. Except for an oaky Grand Cru in a ripe year, they are not usually quite up to the richer concoctions.

RED WINES

There is no red Chablis, but there is red wine in the vicinity: to the west in the Yonne Valley near Auxerre, and to the east in the Armançon Valley near Tonnerre, there are pockets of red wine, made largely from Pinot Noir, sometimes considerably beefed up by an addition of tough, dark wine from the César grape.

Irancy is the finest of these wines, rarely deep in colour, but always perfumed, slightly plummy and attractive. Coulanges Les Vineuses is a little rougher, and Épineuil, near Tonnerre, is light, but fragrant with strawberry fruit. Best producers: **Bienvenu, Colinot, Patrice Fort** (Irancy); **J-H Goissot** (various Yonne wines).

CONSUMER INFORMATION

WHAT DO I GET FOR MY MONEY?

Prices eased in the early 1990s but have since risen again, and the Chablis price see-saw is the most volatile in Burgundy. Any attempt to achieve stability is cast aside as soon as demand hots up.

At the moment it would be difficult to find any bargains. Grand Cru wines are very expensive, Premiers Crus are expensive and basic Chablis costs quite enough, thank you. Good gracious – even Petit Chablis is relatively expensive!

AVAILABLILITY

Ordinary Chablis is easy to find, and is generally reliable. It does, however, pay to select the better, riper years. Premier Cru wines are less common, and Grand Cru wines are rarer and usually obtainable only from specialists.

CONSUMER CHECKLIST

Chablis Premier Cru   *Quality* 7 ★
2002 (La Chablisienne)   *Price* 7 ★
     Value 6 ★

Good Years Because Chablis is very far north for growing grapes, Chardonnay struggles to ripen here and vintages dramatically affect the style of the wine. The hottest vintages produce nutty, honeyed wines to drink young, the cooler vintages steelier, harsher wines which demand a few years' aging. Best years: 2004, 2003, 2002, 2000, 1999, 1998, 1997, 1996, 1995, 1992, 1990.

Taste notes Ideally Chablis should be the driest of all classic Chardonnays. It is often made without using oak barrels, and the result, even in ripe years, is a very dry, nutty but not rich wine. Oak, when it is used, adds a creamy softness.

CÔTE D'OR

Since the mid-1980s there has been a renaissance here – and never was a great wine area so much in need of one. The white wines had survived better, but all too many of the reds were in a sorry state: poorly made and from vines that had been induced to yield every drop they could. Then it was the merchants who were firmly in control, and most of the wines with character and individuality were to be found among the growers.

Nowadays the Côte d'Or is a top-notch Pinot Noir area. Yes, there are still producers who are underperforming. You'll always get that in every area. But there are far more growers who really care, far more growers opting to leave the protection of the co-operatives and merchants and start bottling their own wine – and far more merchants now producing top-class wine. Drouhin and Jadot are merchants both on good form. Bouchard Père et Fils has emerged from the shadows and regularly excels. Boisset, one of the most powerful yet underperforming merchants, is at last converting muscle into quality. And the famous Hospices de Beaune, after years of mediocrity and inconsistency is once again producing expensive but high-quality wine.

One of the crucial ingredients of quality in Burgundy is low yields. It's important for Chardonnay, but it's crucial for Pinot Noir. It's true that the majority of the red wines of the Côte d'Or are light – fragrant, marvellously perfumed with cherry and strawberry fruit, sometimes meatier, sometimes intensely fruity, but light. It's also true that they can be too light. Yields must be kept down if the wines are to have the concentration to develop their wonderfully gamy, vegetal complexity. The current trend is to practise various forms of semi-organic and organic viticulture which should eventually restore the balance of the soil after years of overdosing with chemicals. This idea has taken root with some of the best growers and, so far, the omens are good.

CÔTE DE NUITS

The Côte de Nuits, the northern end of the Côte d'Or, is almost entirely devoted to red wine from Pinot Noir. It contains some of the most famous of all Burgundy's vineyards in the Grands Crus of **Gevrey-Chambertin**, **Vougeot** and **Vosne-Romanée**, all for red wine. The vineyards used to stretch up to Dijon, but now, except for a couple of small sites at Chenôve, they start at Marsannay.

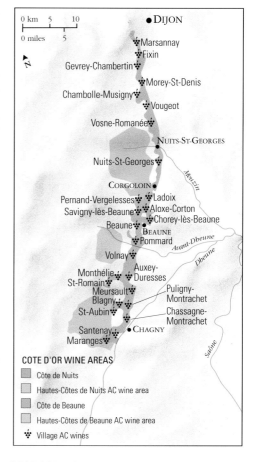

COTE D'OR WINE AREAS
- Côte de Nuits
- Hautes-Côtes de Nuits AC wine area
- Côte de Beaune
- Hautes-Côtes de Beaune AC wine area
- Village AC wines

MARSANNAY

An appellation for reds, whites and rosés from this village which is almost in the suburbs of Dijon. Best known for its pleasant but quite austere rosé but there are an increasing number of light but well-flavoured reds. Best producers: **Bouvier**, **Charlopin**, **B Clair**, **Fougeray de Beauclair**, **Geantet-Pansiot**, **Jadot**, **Méo-Camuzet**, **D Mortet** and **Trapet**.

FIXIN

The neighbouring villages of Fixin and Marsannay are chalk and cheese, because Fixin makes strong, tough red wine. It is still fairly unknown as a wine village, which is a good thing in Burgundy because there is less incentive to stretch the wine. Usually the wines are chunky, fairly tough, lacking a little excitement, yet if you can't afford Gevrey-Chambertin but want to pretend you're drinking it, Fixin is a reasonable substitute. Best producers: **Champy**, **Gelin**, **Alain Guyard**, **Dominique Laurent** and **Naddef**. There is a Premier Cru called Clos Napoléon, but Napoleon's real love was Chambertin wine

from just down the road, and the slightly jilted taste of the Fixin wine reflects this slight.
Best Premiers Crus: Clos du Chapitre, Clos de la Perrière.

GEVREY-CHAMBERTIN

Gevrey has been famous for its wine for over a thousand years, and its eminence is marked by the village's possession of eight Grands Crus. Two of them, Chambertin and Chambertin-Clos de Bèze, can be some of the greatest red wines. They have a rough plumskins and damson strength which is fierce when young, but assumes a brilliant wafting perfume and intense plum richness as it matures.

A Chambertin from a good vintage should need ten to 15 years aging, yet because of the popularity of the name, many are made far too light. The same can be said of all the other wines in Gevrey which, without having the largest vineyard area, has the largest production of the Côte de Nuits. This is very sad, because a strong, sensuous Charmes-Chambertin or an exotically scented Griotte-Chambertin is intensely delicious. Chambertin was Napoleon's favourite wine, and its popularity has been undiminished ever since, so it is essential to buy from a serious grower. The good news is that there are plenty. Best producers: **Bachelet, Boillot, Burguet, B Clair, P Damoy, Drouhin, Dugat, Dugat-Py, Dujac, S Esmonin, Faiveley, Fourrier, Geantet-Pansiot, Jadot, P Leclerc, Mortet, Rossignol, Roty, Rousseau, Sérafin** and **Trapet**.

Grands Crus: Chambertin, Chambertin-Clos de Bèze, Chapelle-Chambertin, Charmes-Chambertin, Griotte-Chambertin, Latricières-Chambertin, Mazis-Chambertin, Ruchottes-Chambertin.
Best Premiers Crus: Combe-aux-Moines, Lavaut, Clos St-Jacques, Clos des Varoilles.

MOREY-ST-DENIS

Morey used to be famous for being the least famous of the Côte de Nuits villages, and consequently was always singled out as being good value. This isn't the case any more. The wines are expensive, and although good growers are now proving the innate quality of the vineyards, too many wines suffer badly from overproduction and oversugaring. The vineyard area is relatively small, but it has four Grands Crus and part of a fifth. These should produce wines with less body and more perfume than Gevrey-Chambertin, and a slight meatiness blending with a rich chocolaty fruit as they age. Too much modern Morey wine is too light for any of those adjectives to apply. Luckily Morey does possess a small number of outstanding growers, whose names are more important on the label than the vineyard designation. Best producers: **Pierre Amiot, B Clair, Dom. du Clos de Tart, Dom. des Lambrays, Dujac, Lignier, Perrot-Minot, Ponsot, Roumier, Rousseau** and **Sérafin**.
Grands Crus: Bonnes Mares (part of), Clos des Lambrays, Clos de la Roche, Clos St-Denis, Clos de Tart.
Best Premiers Crus: La Bussière, Clos des Ormes, aux Monts Luisants, Les Ruchots.

CHAMBOLLE-MUSIGNY

This village has a reputation for producing the lightest, the most fragrant, the most delicate of Burgundies. The scent of a fine Chambolle-Musigny is cherry sweet and as come-hither as roses in bloom – and that's only part of it, because the smoky, dark side of Pinot Noir also adds a fascinating, slightly shadowy depth to this heavenly scented wine. If you want to sample these glories you'd best go to Georges Roumier, who has made every vintage since 1985. There are other stars, too. Best producers: **G Barthod, Drouhin, Dujac, Groffier, Hudelot-Noëllat, Jadot, Dom. Leroy, Marchand-Grillot, D Mortet, J-F Mugnier, Rion, Roumier** and **de Vogüé**.
Grands Crus: Bonnes-Mares (part), Musigny.
Best Premiers Crus: Les Amoureuses, Les Charmes, Les Sentiers.

Harvest time in the Grand Cru vineyard of Grands-Échéchaux, in the village of Flagey-Échézeaux, which produces some excellent red Burgundy.

VOUGEOT

The village of Vougeot is completely dominated by its Grand Cru, Clos de Vougeot, the 50-hectare (125-acre) walled vineyard which seems to many to epitomize Burgundy. Indeed it does, for here, above all, the name of the grower is crucial. Over 80 growers share this enclosure, and while the land at the top of the slope is very fine, the land down by the road is not. Somehow no-one ever admits to owning any of those roadside vines.

The rare bottle of good Clos de Vougeot is a wonderful fat Burgundy, rich, strong, rather unsubtle but exciting for its grandness. The château at Clos de Vougeot is the centre of the Chevaliers du Tastevin, a remarkably successful public relations organization that promotes Burgundy wines. There aren't many vines elsewhere in the village outside the Clos de Vougeot walls, but they're still pretty good, and Clos de la Perrière and Clos Blanc usually give good wines. Best producers: **Bertagna**, **Chopin-Groffier**, **Clerget** and **Vougeraie**. **Grand Cru:** Clos de Vougeot.

VOSNE-ROMANÉE

Vosne-Romanée is the greatest Côte de Nuits village. Its Grands Crus are more renowned, and sell for more money than any red wine on earth, except for top Pomerols from Bordeaux, and remarkably for Burgundy, they are dominated by a single estate, the **Domaine de la Romanée-Conti**. Romanée-Conti itself is a single vineyard of almost 2 hectares (5 acres), capable of a more startling brilliance than any other red wine of France. La Tâche, Richebourg, Romanée-St-Vivant and Grands-Échézeaux all follow close behind Romanée-Conti, producing flavours as disparate yet as intense as the overpowering creamy savouriness of fresh *foie gras* and the deep, sweet, liquorous scent of ripe plums and prunes in brandy. There is also something smoky, something spicy to these wines.

These are Vosne-Romanée's great wines, but in addition there are Premiers Crus which also have a compelling mixture of savoury richness and sweet fruit. The village wines are rather overshadowed by this parade of the immortals and they are not so reliable as once they were but good examples still keep this fascinating savoury/sweet style. Best producers: **Arnoux**, **Cacheux-Sirugue**, **Sylvain Cathiard**, **B Clair**, **B Clavelier**, **R Engel**, **Grivot**, **Anne Gros**, **A-F Gros**, **M Gros**, **Haegelen-Jayer**, **F Lamarche**, **Dom. Leroy**, **Méo-Camuzet**, **Mugneret-Gibourg**, **Rion**, **Dom. de la Romanée-Conti**, **E Rouget** and **Thomas-Moillard**.

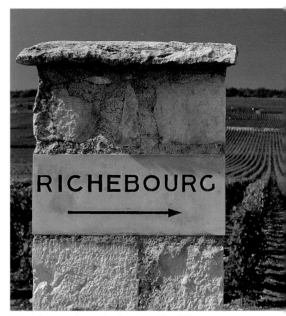

Many famous vineyards along the Côte d'Or are easy to spot by their marker stones. Richebourg is one of six Grands Crus in the village of Vosne-Romanée.

Grands Crus: Échézeaux, La Grande-Rue, Grands-Échézeaux, La Romanée, La Tâche, Richebourg, Romanée-Conti, Romanée-St-Vivant.

Best Premiers Crus: Les Beaux-Monts, aux Brûlées, Clos des Réas, aux Malconsorts, Les Suchots.

Flagey-Échézeaux is a village just over the road from Vosne-Romanée down on the valley floor. Its best wines are Grand Cru (Échézeaux and Grands-Échézeaux and grouped with Vosne-Romanée's Grands Crus), with a small amount of other wine qualifying for the Vosne-Romanée village appellation.

NUITS-ST-GEORGES

The large Nuits-St-Georges appellation is one of the relatively reliable 'village' names in Burgundy. Nowadays it is far better than it used to be, with excellent wines coming from a whole range of producers. It has no Grands Crus, but there are some very good Premiers Crus squeezed in between the road and the hilltop, in this long, narrow commune.

Pinot Noir is a savage, turbulent grape, and at its greatest it often produces a rotting, burnt, decayed kind of flavour which sounds horrible, but is at the heart of great Burgundy. In Nuits-St-Georges this is frequently encountered, but this whiff of cabbage left too long at the bottom of the vegetable tray is balanced by a plummy, pruny sweetness and a brown, smoky depth which can make it one of the most fascinating of all red Burgundies. Prémeaux, to the south, uses Nuits' name.

There is a little white Nuits, the best made in the La Perrière vineyard from a mutation of Pinot Noir that produces white grapes. It is sappy, savoury, and remarkably like a red wine to taste. Best producers: **de l'Arlot, R Arnoux, J Chauvenet, R Chevillon, J-J Confuron, Faiveley, Gouges, Grivot, Jayer-Gilles, Dominique Laurent, Lecheneaut, Méo-Camuzet, A Michelot, Mugneret, N Potel, Rion** and **Thomas-Moillard**.
Best Premiers Crus: Les Argillières, Les Boudots, Les Cailles, aux Chaignots, Clos L'Arlot, Clos de la Maréchale, Les Murgers, Les Pruliers, Les St-Georges, Les Vaucrains.

CÔTE DE NUITS-VILLAGES
This appellation covers the three southern-most villages of Prissey, Comblanchien and Corgoloin, and Brochon and Fixin in the north, although Fixin now usually sports its own name on wine labels. The wines of this appellation aren't usually particularly exciting, though at their best they can conjure up something of the cherryish perfume and delicious decay of good Côte de Nuits red. Best producers: **D Bachelet, Chopin-Groffier, Jayer-Gilles, Rion** and **Rossignol**.

CÔTE DE BEAUNE
The Côte de Beaune is far more evenly divided between red and white wine than the Côte de Nuits, and while it has relatively few of the most famous red wine vineyard sites, it has all of the greatest white wine sites. When people say that white Burgundy is the world's great dry white wine, they are thinking of the top Chardonnay wines from the villages of Aloxe-Corton, Meursault, Puligny-Montrachet and Chassagne-Montrachet.

ALOXE-CORTON
The Côte de Beaune starts in the north with a bang because the village of Aloxe-Corton has the only Grand Cru red in the Côte de Beaune (Le Corton) as well as one of its most famous white Grands Crus (Corton-Charlemagne).

Ideally, red Corton should have something of the savoury strength of Vosne-Romanée to the north, and something of the mouth-watering, caressing sweetness of Beaune to the south. In fact, although it is the cheapest of the Grands Crus, it is difficult to find an outstanding example. There are subdivisions of Le Corton, like Corton-Pougets, Corton-Bressandes and Corton-Clos du Roi as well.

White Corton-Charlemagne which occupies the upper half of the hill where the first of the Côte de Beaune's limestone outcrops becomes apparent, is almost entirely Chardonnay, but a little Pinot Blanc or Pinot Gris (here called Pinot Beurot) is planted which can add an intriguing fatness to the wine. There's rumoured to be a few ancient Aligoté vines as well. Corton-Charlemagne can be a magnificent, blasting wall of flavour, not big on nuance but strong, buttery and ripe enough to blank out any argument and gradually developing a fascinating minerally strength to go with the richness. However, of all the white Grands Crus, this is one you have to age in order to understand its brilliance.

Aloxe-Corton village wines are over-whelmingly red. At their best they have a ripe, soft red fruit and a marvellous savoury flavour, making them some of Burgundy's finest commune wines, but quality is erratic. Best producers: **Ambroise, Bonneau du Martray, Chandon de Briailles, Coche-Dury, Drouhin, Dubreuil-Fontaine, Faiveley, V Girardin, Guyon, Jadot, Dom. Leroy, Méo-Camuzet, Rapet, Rollin, Senard, Tollot-Beaut** and **Voarick**.
Grands Crus: red Corton (part), white Corton-Charlemagne (part).
Best Premiers Crus: Les Chaillots, Les Maréchaudes, Meix, Vergennes.

LADOIX
Under the eastern lee of the hill of Corton, the village of Ladoix sells its best wines under the more prestigious Corton and Aloxe-Corton appellations. The village Ladoix wine, mainly red, is light and pleasant if a little lean in style. Best producers: **Cachat-Ocquidant, Chevalier, E Cornu, Jacob, Prince Florent de Mérode, Nudant** and **Verget**.
Grands Crus: Corton (part), Corton-Charlemagne (part).

PERNAND-VERGELESSES
This is a pleasant little village, snuggling in the lee of the hill of Corton. It has a decent chunk of Grand Cru Corton and Corton-Charlemagne. The reds are sometimes a little lean, but the white Corton-Charlemagne can be outstanding. However, the Pernand's own wines are increasingly good, and this is one of the villages where bargains (if the word is ever appropriate to Burgundy) can be found. It has some of the best Aligoté (see page 72), and its Chardonnays are of the straight, stony type. The reds have a fair amount of body and a rather rich strawberry fruit pastille taste. Best producers: **Chandon de Briailles, C Cornu, Denis, Dubreuil-Fontaine, Laleure-Piot, Pavelot, Rapet** and **Rollin**.

Grands Crus: Corton (part), Corton-Charlemagne (part).
Best Premiers Crus: Île de Vergelesses.

The best vineyards of Auxey-Duresses in the Côte de Beaune catch the last of the evening sun, giving them a crucial extra period of ripening before the harvest.

SAVIGNY-LÈS-BEAUNE

A higgledy-piggledy village up a side valley, Savigny affords the first welcome sight of a vineyard on the thirsty drive south from Paris along the Autoroute du Soleil. The wine is almost entirely red and, while it isn't very full, it should have quite an attractive earthiness to back up the gentle strawberry fruit. Savigny used to be a source of good-quality wine at a fair price, but at the moment many of the wines are lean and stony in style. Best producers: **Bize**, **Bouchard Père et Fils**, **Camus-Bruchon**, **Champy**, **Chandon de Briailles**, **B Clair**, **M Écard**, **J J Girard**, **P Girard**, **Girardin**, **Jacob**, **Leroy**, **Maréchal**, **J-M Pavelot** and **Tollot-Beaut**.
Best Premiers Crus: Dominodes, aux Guettes, Marconnets, aux Vergelesses.

BEAUNE

From having been one of the most flagrantly devalued wine names in Burgundy, the Beaune appellation has pulled itself back to being one of the most reliable in the region, giving a very representative range of wines which show Burgundy at its most enjoyable, and sometimes at its most impressive.

This is excellent news for the drinker, because Beaune, which is the centre of the Côte d'Or trade, and a sizeable town, has the largest amount of vineyards in the Côte d'Or. The vast majority are owned by the merchant houses, and their wines are frequently easy to find. There are no Grands Crus in Beaune, but there are a large number of good and plentiful Premiers Crus. The wines are nearly all red, and have a lovely soft, 'red fruits' sweetness, usually backed by a slightly mineral toughness and, ideally, a certain savoury fragrance which makes them ripe and perfumed yet just sturdy enough to play the Burgundy role in all the big eating the area loves. There's an increasing amount of white – try **Drouhin**'s creamy, nutty Clos des Mouches. Best producers: **Bouchard Père et Fils**, **Champy**, **Chanson**, **Drouhin**, **Jacques Germain**, **Camille Giroud**, **Jadot**, **Jaffelin**, **Labouré-Roi**, **Michel Lafarge**, **Morot** , **Rateau**, **Thomas-Moillard** and **Tollot-Beaut**.
Best Premiers Crus: Les Boucherottes, Les Bressandes, Les Cent Vignes, Le Clos des Mouches, Clos du Roi, Les Épenottes, Les Fèves, Les Grèves, Les Marconnets, Les Teurons, Les Toussaints and Les Vignes Franches.

HOSPICES DE BEAUNE

This charitable institution with its famous Gothic architecture (left) has largely supported itself since 1433 on the proceeds of its vineyards, totalling nearly 60 hectares (150 acres). Each November the famous Hospices de Beaune sale is held, amid a lot of brouhaha. Rises and falls in prices here are not an accurate indication of how the market is moving, but they do show the temper of the times.

The wines themselves are made with tremendous care, and since they come from fabulous sites in the Côte d'Or (mostly in the Côte de Beaune) they can taste pure and delicious from barrel. Sadly, these fine wines cease to be the responsibility of the Hospices after they are auctioned. They are sold into the trade, for aging by *négociants*, some of whom eventually offer for sale wines which bear little resemblance to the original barrels they bought. Given the quality of the original wine, that is little to be proud of. Especially since no wine from here is likely to be cheap.

CÔTE DE BEAUNE/CÔTE DE BEAUNE-VILLAGES

The few outlying vines of Beaune that don't make the Beaune appellation itself can be called **Côte de Beaune**, but there aren't many of them. It's a very rare appellation not to be confused with **Côte de Beaune-Villages** (see page 85). **Dom. de la Vougeraie** is a good producer, of typically lean reds and whites.

CHOREY-LÈS-BEAUNE

The village of Chorey-Lès-Beaune can also produce some very attractive perfumy reds, particularly from **Tollot-Beaut** and **Jacques Germain**, from vineyards that, despite being largely on less than ideal flat valley floor land to the north of the town of Beaune, have better drainage than their neighbours.

POMMARD

While Nuits-St-Georges became the Englishman's idea of the archetypal Burgundy, Pommard filled the same role for the USA. For a small village to satisfy the expectations of an entire nation cannot be healthy, and standards inevitably suffer. In Pommard they certainly did, and among Burgundians the quality of the village's wheeler-dealing is often more praised than the quality of the wine. Even so, Pommard does have good producers, and there can be a strong, meaty sturdiness in the wine, backed by a slightly jammy, but attractive plummy fruit which may not be subtle, but is many people's idea of what red Burgundy should taste like. Best producers: **Comte Armand, Boillot, Carré-Courbin, de Courcel, Dancer, P Garaudet, M Gaunoux, Girardin, Lafarge, Lejeune, de Montille, Parent, Ch. de Pommard** and **Pothier-Rieusset**.

Best Premiers Crus: Les Arvelets, Les Boucherottes, Les Épenots, Les Pézerolles, Les Rugiens (Haut and Bas).

VOLNAY

Volnay's reputation has traditionally been for producing the lightest wine in the Côte d'Or, but with overproduction happening on all sides, this is no longer anything to be proud of. In any case, it isn't that accurate. Up until the eighteenth century, Volnay did produce particularly pale wine, and the higher part of the vineyard slope has a great deal of chalk which reduces the colour, though not the alcoholic strength of the wine. However, it might be truer to say that Volnay is one of the most perfumed red Burgundies, having a memorable cherry and strawberry spice to it, but also, in its Premiers Crus, being able to turn on a big meaty style without losing the perfume. The wine is usually a quick developer, though when from a good producer it can last well.

Best producers: **Ampeau, d'Angerville, H Boillot, J-M Boillot, J-M Bouley, Carré-Courbin, Coche-Dury, V Girardin, Michel Lafarge, Lafon, Matrot, Montille, N Potel, J Prieur, Roblet-Monnot**, and **Voillot**.
Best Premiers Crus: Bousse d'Or, Caillerets, en Champans, Clos des Chênes, Santenots and Taillepieds.

MONTHELIE

It seems to be a rule in Burgundy that if your village is in one of the folds of the hill, rather than on the main slope, your wine will not be well-known, however good it is. The reason is that in the past the wines would have been sold quite happily under the name of your nearest famous neighbour. Monthelie is no exception to this, since it shares boundaries with Volnay and Meursault, but fame with neither. It's a red wine village, and the wine deserves recognition since it is full, dry, rather herby or piney in taste but with plenty of satisfying rough fruit. It's one of the few villages in Burgundy that can actually be a bargain. Best producers: **Bouchard Père et Fils, Boussey, Coche-Dury, Darviot-Perrin, P Garaudet, R Jobard, Lafon, Olivier Leflaive, Monthelie-Douhairet, G Roulot** and **de Suremain**.
Best Premiers Crus: Les Champs Fulliot, Les Duresses, sur la Velle.

AUXEY-DURESSES

Even more tucked away than Monthelie, Auxey-Duresses has always had some reputation for full-blooded reds and soft, nutty whites. They went through a dull patch a few years ago but despite a continuing problem with overcropping leading to dilution, some growers are now making good wine again. Best producers: **Comte Armand, Ampeau, Auvenay, Diconne, J-P Fichet, Gras, Duc de Magenta, M Prunier** and **P Prunier**.
Best Premiers Crus: Climat du Val, Clos du Val, Les Duresses.

MEURSAULT

White wines finally take over from red in Meursault, and they take over in the most spectacular way with by far the largest white production of any Côte d'Or village. The standard, too, has picked up again in recent years, and there are some excellent growers providing leadership for the rest and a pretty high standard from the serious négociants. It is much easier to make good wine from Chardonnay than from Pinot Noir and it's a long time since there was a really disastrous vintage in Meursault.

The limestone runs in a broad band through the middle of the sloping vineyards, and the result is wines of a delicious, gentle lusciousness, big, nutty, sometimes even peachy and honeyed. They perform the great white Burgundy trick of seeming rich and luscious, yet being totally dry. Meursault has no Grands Crus, but some good Premiers Crus, situate to the south of the village. Best producers: **Ampeau, Pierre Boillot, Bouchard Père et Fils, Michel Bouzereau, Boyer-Martenot, Coche-Debord, Coche-Dury, Drouhin, A Ente, J-P Fichet, V Girardin, Jadot, P Javillier, F Jobard, Rémi Jobard, Lafon, Matrot, Pierre Morey** and **G Roulot**.
Best Premiers Crus: Les Bouchères, Les Charmes, Les Genevrières, Les Gouttes d'Or, La Pièce-sous-le-Bois (Blagny), Les Perrières (Dessous and Dessus), Le Poruzot.

The hamlet of **Blagny** is situated up the hill on the boundary with Puligny-Montrachet and usually sells its slightly harsher wine under that name or Meursault's. Meursault red exists, and can be sold as Meursault or Blagny. But the best is called Volnay-Santenots and comes from vineyards on the boundary with Volnay. They're within the Meursault appellation, but they have a historic right to the red wine name of Volnay.

PULIGNY-MONTRACHET

Meursault may have the approachability of style and the high overall standard, but the brilliance, and the genius of everything which Burgundy and Chardonnay stands for comes firmly to roost in Puligny. The great vineyards cling to the upper edge of the hill while the lesser vineyards slip away towards the village down on the plain. Le Montrachet, the village's greatest Grand Cru, is a peerless wine, showing in the most perfect way how humble words like honey, nuts, cream, smoke, perfume and all the rest do no service to a white wine which seems to combine every memory of ripe fruit with a dry savoury tang that leaves your palate restless, your mind amazed and your expectations satisfied.

There are several other Grands Crus, less intense, but whose wines buzz with the mingling opposites of coffee and honey, smoke and cream. And, of course, there is a range of Premiers Crus as well. Unfortunately, apart from the star growers, Puligny offers some of the worst value for money on the Côte. There's too much of it, it's too famous and too easy to sell, so stick to the best growers if possible. Best producers: **J-M Boillot, Carillon, J Chartron, Gérard Chavy, Drouhin, A Ente, B Ente, Jadot, Larue, Latour, Dom.**

Leflaive, **Olivier Leflaive**, **P Pernot**, **Ch. de Puligny-Montrachet**, **Ramonet** and **Sauzet**.
Grands Crus: Bâtard-Montrachet (part), Bienvenues-Bâtard-Montrachet, Chevalier-Montrachet, Le Montrachet (part).
Best Premiers Crus: Le Champ Canet, Clavoillons, Clos de la Mouchère, Les Combettes, Les Folatières, Les Pucelles.

CHASSAGNE-MONTRACHET

Chassagne has a chunk of the great white Montrachet vineyard, but also produces plenty of red (approximately 40 per cent). Although the standard of the Grands Crus is sky-high, neither the red nor the white Premiers Crus dazzle in quite the same way as Puligny's. If anything, the taste of the whites is a little chunkier, inclined to stop short when you had hoped it might reveal one more nuance of flavour. As with Puligny, you should buy single-vineyard wines, and you should get a full-flavoured, slightly nutty dry white of considerable quality. The reds are considerably better than they were a few years ago, but they tend to be a bit heavy, a bit earthy and a bit chewy. Best producers: Allaines, **Amiot**, **Blain-Gagnard**, **Carillon**, **Clerget**, **Colin**, **Colin-Déléger**, **J-N Gagnard**, **V Girardin**, **F & V Jouard**, **Lamy**, **Bernard Morey**, **Morey-Coffinet**, **M Niellon** and **Ramonet**.
Grands Crus: Bâtard-Montrachet (part), Criots-Bâtard-Montrachet, Le Montrachet (part).
Best Premiers Crus: Clos de la Boudriotte, en Cailleret, Les Chenevottes, Clos de la Chapelle, Clos de la Maltroie, Clos St-Jean, Les Grandes Ruchottes, Morgeot.

ST-AUBIN

The Route National 6 slices between the villages of Puligny and Chassagne-Montrachet, and after a dangerously sharp turn at the misleadingly named hamlet of Gamay, St-Aubin appears rather diffidently on the right. It's a backwoods village with only a recent reputation, used to declassifying its strong, tasty, proud Pinot Noirs and full, racy Chardonnays to the basic Bourgogne appellation. Two-thirds of the vineyards are Premiers Crus, and, though the village is at last beginning to earn some respect in its own right, the wines still represent some of Burgundy's best

value. Best producers: **Allaines, D & F Clair**, **Bachelet**, **M Colin**, **Drouhin**, **Jadot**, **Lamy**, **Lamy-Pillot**, **Larue**, **Olivier Leflaive**, **B Morey**, **Ramonet**, **Roux** and **G Thomas**.
Best Premiers Crus: Le Charmois, La Chatenière, les Frionnes, Les Murgers des Dents de Chien, en Rémilly.

ST-ROMAIN

Even more out of the way, St-Romain doesn't produce a lot of wine, although François Frères, one of France's most famous oak barrel-makers is here, sheltering under the steep hills. But the full, rather broad-flavoured, cherry-stone dry red and the flinty dry white are fine wines still sometimes sold more cheaply than they deserve – in comparison to the rest of Burgundy. Best producers: **Bazenet**, **Buisson**, **Chassorney**, **Gras**, **Olivier Leflaive**, **P Taupenot** and **Verget**.

SANTENAY

The southern end comes rather suddenly in the Côte de Beaune. One moment you are flirting with immortality in Chassagne-Montrachet, and a few hundred metres later the hills veer away to the west, the village of Santenay grabs what it can of the disappearing slopes, and that's just about it.

Santenay used to be more famous for its casino, and its wine was largely sold as Côte de Beaune-Villages. However, the wine is better than that. It used to be among the meatiest of Burgundies, having a strong savoury flavour and good ripe strawberry fruit. In general, the savouriness has been replaced by a gentler, fruit pastille softness which is attractive without making you jump with excitement. Even so, the general standard is fairly good, and vineyards like Clos de Tavannes, Les Gravières and La Comme can give you a bit of the beef as well. Best producers: **Belland**, **D & F Clair**, **M Colin**, **J Girardin**, **V Girardin**, **Monnot**, **Bernard Morey**, **L Muzard**, **Prieur-Brunet** and **Roux**.
Best Premiers Crus: Les Gravières, La Comme, Clos de Tavannes, Passetemps.

MARANGES

This appellation covers the string of vineyards that drift away to the west of Santenay. The

wines are developing a sturdy, rustic style. Best producers: **B Bachelet**, **M Charleux**, **Contat-Grangé**, **Drouhin** and **Girardin**.

CÔTE DE BEAUNE-VILLAGES

This is a catch-all but rare red wine appellation for 16 villages on the Côte de Beaune. Only Aloxe-Corton, Beaune, Volnay and Pommard cannot use it. In the past it was used by producers who had small amounts of wine from several villages which could thus be blended into commercial quantities, or by lesser-known villages unable to sell under their own name.

HAUTES-CÔTES DE NUITS/HAUTES-CÔTES DE BEAUNE

This beautiful region is the hilly backwater of the Côte d'Or, making light reds and steely whites. It has potential, but with a few exceptions has yet to realize it. Best producers: **Caves des Hautes-Côtes**, **Michel Gros**, **B Hudelot**, **Jayer-Gilles** and **Verdet**.

CLASSIFICATION

Burgundy is classified into five different levels, with the most basic wine – Bourgogne Rouge or Blanc – coming from inferior, damp valley land in the Côte d'Or – or possibly from young vines in some of the Côte's best vineyards. More specific regional appellations have names like Côte de Beaune-Villages or Hautes-Côtes de Nuits. They cover several villages, and wines from here will often be blended from a number of sources. The next level up is village wines which are appreciably better – or should be. Any wine from a given village that is not entitled to a higher appellation will settle for the village name. Some vineyards which are neither Premier nor Grand Cru may, however, be mentioned on the label: these are known as *lieux-dits*, or stated places.

The Premiers Crus or First Growths are the second-from-top rung of the ladder: in Burgundy, the First Growths are effectively the second growths. These second-best vineyard sites contain some of Burgundy's finest wines. In some villages the majority of the land is classified as Premier Cru, which can devalue the title somewhat. Lesser-known Premier Cru wines may be blended together and sold as Beaune Premier Cru, for example. The Grands Crus are the cream of Burgundy's vineyards and only a few villages possess one. The reds are concentrated in the Côte de Nuits, the whites in the Côte de Beaune, and they can omit the village name on the label.

ORGANIZATION

Vineyard ownership in Burgundy is fragmented, with the average holding per grower only 2 hectares (5 acres), which is often divided between different vineyards in several different villages. The small quantities available from each grower led to the rise of the *négociants-éleveurs*, merchants who buy the wines, mature and blend them. The division between growers and *négociants* is more blurred today, with some growers running *négociant* businesses, and many *négociants* owning vineyards.

READING THE LABEL

Burgundy labels are a mine of information, though you need a good memory to make sense of it all. They also can't tell you about the quality of the wine, which is why the producer's name is of extreme importance here.

WHAT DO THEY TASTE LIKE?

White Côte d'Or Burgundy can vary from good, bone-dry, one-dimensional village wines to the glorious honeyed, rich yet dry top wines. Red Côte d'Or ranges from pale, short, vaguely strawberry-scented wines to those that combine a soft ripeness with a perfumed, exotic fruit, sometimes with a trace of dry, chocolate and, ideally, a smoky, rotting compost richness which is one of the most exciting, unexpected flavours in red wine.

THE GOOD YEARS

Vintages are of enormous importance, but since a good producer will offer something decent even in a poor year, it is better to trust the winemaker than the vintage. In general both the reds and whites can be drunk after two or three years, though the best ones should be kept for ten.

2004 A fine autumn saved the day, especially for the whites.

2003 Reds did better than whites in the extreme heat. Whites are nice, fat but rarely

Sneaking a grape out of the basket now is the nearest most of us will ever get to wine from the prestigious estate of Domaine de la Romanée-Conti.

than in 1997 but quantities lower than normal.

1997 Growing conditions varied so wines will be variable. Not for keeping.

1996 A classic year for reds, ready now but the best will keep. Whites are good, not great.

1995 Excellent year for top whites now at their peak. Reds are firm and lean but tasty.

1994 The reds are light with a fair amount of fruit. Drink up. The whites are past it.

1993 Reds from the best producers are excellent, though others can be chunky and unbalanced. Drink up the whites.

1992 A very good year for whites, less so for the reds. Drink whites now.

1991 Hail and rain-damaged year but good dry reds. Whites less successful. Drink up.

1990 Sumptuously rich reds, the best of the three fine years of 1988, 1989 and 1990. The best will still improve. Some whites were good and are now peaking.

1989 The Côte de Beaune did best among the reds, and the whites are outstanding, with the best still full of life.

1988 Good lean whites now fading. Intense serious reds now at peak.

ENJOYING THE WINE

White Burgundy is the perfect partner for the richer fish dishes of French haute cuisine, and also many poultry and lighter meat dishes. As a wine to turn a snatched lunch into a gastronomic experience, there's nothing like it. Red Burgundy is thought of as a game wine – for venison, pheasant, hare – but only wine from good producers could cope with rich-tasting food. Despite the importance of cheese in the region, the best reds are overpowered by cheese.

distinguished. The best reds are dark and fiery for the long term.

2002 Exciting wines, both red and whites with good colour and acidity.

2001 Generally good for both colours.

2000 Less good for Côte de Beaune reds than whites, which are rich and ripe.

1999 A large, good quality harvest with a number of very fine wines.

1998 Richer and more structured wines

CONSUMER INFORMATION

WHAT DO I GET FOR MY MONEY?

The greatest wines are very expensive, but worth the money for the inimitable sensations they give. However, the lesser villages have not enjoyed or suffered quite the same price explosion. Any quest for quality at reasonable price should include Pernand-Vergelesses, St-Aubin, Monthelie, Ladoix and Chorey-lès-Beaune.

AVAILABILITY

Generic red and white Burgundy is widely available and seldom exciting, unless from a good grower – in which case it's less widely available. The complexities of the region mean that it's worth going to a specialist merchant and paying slightly more for something that's really reliable.

CONSUMER CHECKLIST

Red Gevrey-Chambertin	*Quality 9* ★
Clos St Jacques 1999	*Price 8* ★
(Jadot)	*Value 8* ★
White Meursault Les Charmes	*Quality 10* ★
2002 (Lafon)	*Price 10* ★
	Value 8 ★

Good Years Chardonnay produces fair to excellent wine almost every year. Best years: 2004, 2003, 2002, 2001, 2000, 1999, 1997, 1995. Best years (Pinot Noir): 2004, 2003, 2002, 2001, 1999, 1998, 1997, 1996, 1995, 1993, 1990, 1989, 1988.

Taste Notes From hot vintages the flavours of good white Burgundy are succulent, rich, creamy, honeyed, yet always balanced by acidity. Red Burgundy is plummy, rich, exotic and wonderful when mature.

CÔTE CHALONNAISE

The Côte Chalonnaise has until recently been the forgotten area of Burgundy, with much of its wine going to make up merchants' blends – usually under the generic appellation of Bourgogne. However, since 1973, with the newer and more strictly regulated approach to Burgundy labelling, anywhere with a legal right to a Burgundy appellation, and with vineyards already planted with Pinot Noir and Chardonnay, has become an attractive proposition. A great upsurge in activity in the 1970s and 1980s culminated in 1990, with the new appellation, Bourgogne-Côte Chalonnaise, for the whole area. The villages of Mercurey and Rully have greatly increased their output but so far the results from the whole Chalonnais area have been somewhat inconsistent. The wines should be good. There are some fairly decent sites, yet what we've seen is quality in fits and starts. There are some good producers, like Rodet, the Buxy co-operative and Olivier Leflaive, but there still aren't that many good small growers. Maybe that's why I detect a lack of ambition and focus in the region.

Certainly the Côte Chalonnaise lacks the well-ordered compactness of the Côte d'Or. Its vineyards are splattered rather than spread along the numerous ins and outs of hillside between Chagny, just below the southern end of the Côte de Beaune, and Montagny about 24km (15 miles) south. They're more exposed to the prevailing westerly winds than the Côte d'Or vineyards which keep the temperature down. The grapes are primarily Pinot Noir – which in general here produces rather dry reds that don't seem to have the richness or the juiciness I'm looking for – and Chardonnay, which is better. It can be rather stony and dry when no oak barrel aging is used, but sometimes a soft vanilla succulence creeps over the wine when a grower decides to invest in a few barrels – which, I'm happy to say, more of them are doing. It might well be that in the end the Chalonnais turns out to be a better area for whites than reds, with the exception of Givry and Mercurey whose whites can be a bit flat and dull.

BOUZERON

Aubert de Villaine, whose family owns half of the world-renowned Domaine de la Romanée-Conti, owner of some of Burgundy's most famous red Grands Crus at Vosne-Romanée, has a substantial estate here. Some of this glitter has rubbed off on Bouze-

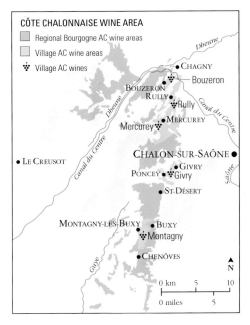

CÔTE CHALONNAISE WINE AREA
- Regional Bourgogne AC wine areas
- Village AC wine areas
- Village AC wines

Dheune
CHAGNY
Bouzeron
BOUZERON
RULLY
Rully
MERCUREY
Mercurey
LE CREUSOT
CHALON-SUR-SAÔNE
GIVRY
PONCEY
Givry
ST-DÉSERT
MONTAGNY-LÈS-BUXY
BUXY
Montagny
CHENÔVES
Canal du Centre
Dheune
Saône
Guye
0 km   5   10
0 miles   5
N

ron where the very good sharp yet buttermilk dry Aligoté (probably the best in Burgundy) is sold under its own appellation, **Bouzeron** (see also page 72). Look for Aligoté wines labelled Vieilles Vignes, as these ones will have the greatest concentration.

The reds and whites from Pinot Noir and Chardonnay are sold under the Bourgogne-Côte Chalonnaise AC and are the quintessence of light Burgundy.

RULLY

Rully is Bouzeron's neighbour, and this is where the Côte Chalonnaise really starts, although there is no great difference in the wine styles between the two villages. The whites are better than the reds, with Chardonnay giving a pale, nutty wine which is delicate and acidic enough to be of great use to Burgundy's sparkling winemakers, but which can be aged in oak for more substance. The reds can be a little too light, but can have some decent strawberry and cherry perfume. There are some Premier Cru vineyards here, but they're not up to Côte d'Or Premier Cru standards so the name on the label doesn't mean very much. All in all, these are good-quality, reasonably priced wines. **Delorme** is the biggest producer: Other best producers: **Allaines, J-C Brelière, Drouhin, Dureil-Janthial, Duvernay, Faiveley, la Folie, V Girardin, Jacqueson, Jadot, Jaffelin, Olivier Leflaive, Ch de Rully/Rodet** and **Aubert de Villaine.**

This is not blackberry sorbet but gorgeous-looking Pinot Noir fermenting in an open cask at Château de Chamirey near Mercurey.

MERCUREY

Mercurey, the next village south, is a positive giant in Chalonnais terms, producing nearly 40 per cent of the region's total wine. This is very much a red wine centre, and the whites are usually rather flaccid afterthoughts from the less good vineyard land.

The red wines have more body than those of Rully, but still manage to retain some strawberry fruit, adding a little smoky spice along the way. There is a considerable difference in style between the lighter wines from the limestone slopes and the chunkier ones from the clay vineyards. At their best they are probably the closest to the Côte d'Or in quality, but their inconsistency is infuriating, especially when I know they could do so much better. The better south-facing sites north of Mercurey have Premier Cru status.

There are some good growers here as well as several large merchants. Best producers: **Ch. de Chamilly, Ch. de Chamirey/Rodet, Brintet, Faiveley, Genot-Boulanger, Jacqueson, E Juillot, M Juillot, de Launay, Olivier Leflaive, Lorenzon, Meix-Foulot, F Raquillet, de Suremain** and **de Villaine**.

GIVRY

Givry has a relatively small vineyard area and one likely to get smaller as the suburbs of Chalon-sur-Saône make increasing demands on the available land and on the growers' scruples. However, the wine is sure to survive, and when well made is the biggest and richest of Chalonnais reds. Decent aging adds a plummy perfume to the strawberry fruit.

There is a little white from Chardonnay, and the best can be attractive, fairly full and nutty. Best producers: **Bourgeon, Chofflet-Valdenaire, B Clair, Clos Salomon, la Ferte, Joblot, F Lumpp, Parize, Ragot** and **Sarrazin.**

MONTAGNY

Further south, Montagny produces some of the driest, chalkiest Chardonnay south of Champagne, and that is all. The appellation applies only to white Chardonnay. It is an excellent bone-dry match for food, but since I am paying Burgundy prices, I'm glad some of the wines are now being aged in new or relatively new oak for several months to deepen the taste. The vineyard sites here are some of the best in the Côte Chalonnaise, with more shelter from the wind than most. Premier Cru on a Montagny label means only that the wine has half a degree more alcohol than straight Montagny. Best producers: **S Aladame, Bouchard Père et Fils, Buxy** co-operative, **Cary Potet, Davenay, Faiveley, Louis Latour, Olivier Leflaive, Rodet, Alain Roy** and **J Vachet**.

CLASSIFICATION

There are five village appellations, Bouzeron, Rully, Mercurey, Givry and Montagny, as well as the regional appellations of Bourgogne-Côte Chalonnaise and straight Bourgogne. The village of Mercurey has five Premier Cru vineyards, while Montagny gaily calls any wine Premier Cru which achieves a half degree more alcohol than the legal minimum, which is pretty silly.

ORGANIZATION

The wines most often seen are those from merchants who control about three-quarters of the region's wine distribution. There are co-operatives too, with the large Buxy co-

Dismal, damp weather at harvest time, here at Rully on the Côte Chalonnaise, is all too common in Burgundy with its marginal climate.

operative near Montagny being one of the most go-ahead and effective in the whole of Burgundy. However, the best, most individual wines will normally be from growers.

READING THE LABEL

Some Côte Chalonnaise wines will bear vineyard names on the label but, except in Mercurey, these do not signify very much, other than being an indication of a more serious producer. Some Mercurey wines may have a Chant-Flûte motif on the label, meaning that the local growers' association has given that particular wine an award for quality.

WHAT DO THEY TASTE LIKE?

Chalonnais wines used to be called the poor man's Burgundy, although these days those of us who can't afford Côte d'Or prices might do better to look elsewhere for our wines. But the flavours of Chalonnais wine are certainly less intense and individual than on the Côte d'Or. The rather lean reds can have some red-fruit fragrance to them, and the whites, though fresh and bright, could still use a little more depth. Oak aging is now improving the best wines.

THE GOOD YEARS

Chalonnais wines are generally ready to drink sooner than those of the Côte d'Or, though given some of the pallid offerings on the Côte d'Or this is not always the case. Chalonnais whites are ready in two to three years, if only because they rarely have the structure to deepen and change during aging. Reds from Givry and Mercurey from a serious grower can age for as much as eight to ten years from good vintages like 2002.

ENJOYING THE WINES

The whites of Rully and Montagny are almost too dry for apéritif drinking, but make excellent all-purpose whites, dry enough for seafood, shellfish and the local trout, and cutting enough for snails, frogs' legs and rich terrines. The Aligoté from Bouzeron at its most concentrated will also cope with these dishes – it can develop a Chardonnay-like intensity with time – but in its lightest, leanest form is often mixed with Crème de cassis to make Kir, the excellent local apéritif.

The reds, if they have some good perfumy fruit, are better with simply cooked meat dishes and some of the milder cheeses.

CONSUMER INFORMATION

WHAT DO I GET FOR MY MONEY?

Value for money in the Côte Chalonnaise used to be excellent, since the prices were well below Côte d'Or levels. However, prices of these wines have risen fast, and except for those from the best growers who don't stoop to oversugaring, they are verging on the expensive. The quality has not risen as much as it should have done and to be honest, there are better wines from other parts of the world – other parts of France even – to be had at the same price or even less.

AVAILABILITY

This is Burgundy's smallest area, so availability is not brilliant. The bigger merchants' wines are fairly well distributed. Any Burgundy specialist should have some growers' wines.

CONSUMER CHECKLIST

Montagny Premier Cru 2004	*Quality 7* ★
(Cave Co-opérative de Buxy)	*Price 6* ★
	Value 7 ★

Good Years The vintages follow a similar pattern to those of the Côte de Beaune to the north (see page 85). Variations in quality between producers are at least as important as those between vintages.
Taste Notes The whites are usually very clean, dry and slightly nutty. The reds should have a delicious fresh strawberry flavour but are too often disappointing.

MÂCONNAIS

With the excessive price of Pouilly-Fuissé (not to mention the way the price can soar and plummet in response to demand) confounding our reason, and the thought of large numbers of Pouilly growers laughing their way to the bank until the tears run down their cheeks (and, hopefully, into the wine, to give it a touch of savoury Chardonnay depth which it will otherwise signally lack), let us step back briefly from the mêlée and work out what the Mâconnais consists of.

It is in southern Burgundy, starting almost at the borders of the Côte Chalonnaise near Buxy, and spreading south until it mingles with the frontiers of Beaujolais just south of its main town of Mâcon. The Mâconnais is easily the biggest producer of white wine in Burgundy (making nearly half the region's annual total), using primarily Chardonnay. Pouilly-Fuissé is certainly the most famous of these wines, but nearly 60 per cent of the production is of simple, unmagical Mâcon Blanc.

Mâcon also produces some red wine, for which it used, once, to be more renowned. In fact it used to be predominantly a red wine area but nowadays, however, only about 15 per cent of the 4800 hectares (11,860 acres) of the Mâconnais vineyards is given over to red vines, and even these don't produce anything very memorable.

In fact, very little Mâconnais wine of whatever colour is memorable. As in the Côte Chalonnaise, there's a lack of ambition in the wine-making (though not, sadly, in the pricing) that means that even though there are some good vineyards here there's not much excitement. Partly it may be the result of the region's extremely efficient co-operative system that seems to level standards. But whatever the reason, the message from the New World doesn't seem to have got through yet – that message being that it's perfectly possible to make tasty Chardonnay, year after year, at the sort of price most people want to pay.

GRAPE VARIETIES AND WINE STYLES
Although there is a little Pinot Noir, **Mâcon Rouge** is almost always made from Gamay. It is usually sold anonymously, although the co-operatives at Igé, Mancey and St-Gengoux have some reputation for the slightly green, earthy wine they produce. Red Mâcon is often used as a Beaujolais substitute but it's drier, rougher and far less attractive. There is also a tiny amount of **Mâcon Rosé** which can be decent. Best producers: **La Combe, La Feuillarde, Duboeuf, Guillot-Broux, Olivier Merlin, de la Sarazinière**.

However, above the basic level, the field is left to the whites. Basic **Mâcon Blanc** is usually a pretty dull wine, okay with food, but somewhat tart and earthy. You need to trade up to **Mâcon Blanc-Villages** before you begin to see the signs of honey and fresh apples and nutty depth normally associated with good Chardonnay – and even then you won't see them as often as you should. Villages wine is limited to 43 communes with the best land. Some of these can add their own village name, like Prissé or Lugny. The whites from these villages can be full, buttery yet fresh and if anything a little fat. This is sometimes because the Chardonnay, which is said to have originated in the Mâconnais village of

All too often the landscape of the Mâconnais (this is the village of Vergisson) is far more appealing than the wines it produces.

As well as lush green vineyards, white Charolais cattle are another feature of the Mâconnais landscape; Charolais beef is famed throughout France.

Chardonnay, has developed a rather exotic, spicy strain in some vineyards, fine in small doses, overbearing by itself. But a greater danger is of paying too much money for a rather broad, simple Chardonnay of no particular distinction. Best producers: **Barraud, Bon Gran, Bonhomme, Bret Bros, Deux Roches, E Gillet, Guffens-Heynen, Guillemot-Michel, Lafon, J-J Litaud, Jean Manciat, O Merlin, R Michel, Rijckaert, Roally, Robert-Denogent, Talmard, Thévenet, Valette, Verget** and **J-J Vincent**.

By now we're closing in on Pouilly-Fuissé, but first we reach **St-Véran**, an appellation created in 1971 to bridge the gap between ordinary Mâcon Blanc-Villages and the stars of Pouilly. It sandwiches the three Pouilly appellations north and south, where it even manages to include some of the vineyards of the St-Amour Beaujolais Cru. St-Véran wines are usually soft, quick-maturing, but quite attractive. Though there are some good wines, like Pouilly it too suffers from the name being used largely by merchant houses and co-operatives more concerned to establish a brand-type name at a certain price point than to show how good these wines could be. Best producers: **Barraud, Corsin, Deux Roches, Drouin, Duboeuf, Guérin, Lassarat, O Merlin, Saumaize-Michelin, Thévenet, Tissier, Verget** and **J-J Vincent**.

And then there's Pouilly. Two villages, Loché and Vinzelles, have gained their own appellations (**Pouilly-Loché** and **Pouilly-Vinzelles**) by hyphenating their names to Pouilly with reasonable effect, but their vineyards are more fertile and flatter than their more famous neighbour, Pouilly-Fuissé. Best producers: **Cave des Grands Crus Blancs, La Soufrandière, Tripoz** and **Valette**.

Pouilly-Fuissé itself comes from four sub-regions and five villages, not all of which are equally good, around the original village of Pouilly in the southern Mâconnais. It's over-hyped but there are some committed growers making buttery, creamy wines that can achieve a delicious deep, honeyed flavour up to the standard of village Meursault but fattened out by the southern sun. Much merchant Pouilly is overpriced and dull. Best producers: **Barraud, Corsin, Drouin, Ferret, Forest, Ch. Fuissé, Guffens-Heynen, Lassarat, Léger-Plumet, Luquet, O Merlin, Robert-Denogent, des Rontets, Saumaize-Michelin** and **Valette**.

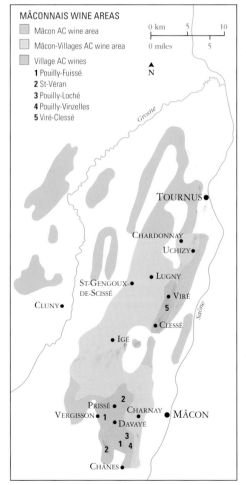

MÂCONNAIS WINE AREAS

- Mâcon AC wine area
- Mâcon-Villages AC wine area
- Village AC wines
  1 Pouilly-Fuissé
  2 St-Véran
  3 Pouilly-Loché
  4 Pouilly-Vinzelles
  5 Viré-Clessé

0 km   5   10
0 miles   5

CLASSIFICATION

The classification of Mâcon wines is an example of a regional wine gradually evolving its own particular hierarchy, and then attempting to consolidate these gains. First there is the catch-all Mâcon appellation, then the more specific Mâcon Blanc-Villages from specific communes, and then particular appellations, such as St-Véran and Pouilly-Fuissé, grouped round one village's reputation. Curiously, it was the village of Vinzelles which tried to delineate its vineyards before Fuissé, but it is Pouilly-Fuissé which has hit the jackpot, particularly on the US market.

ORGANIZATION

The co-operative movement is more effectively organized, and to a higher standard, here in the Mâconnais than almost anywhere else in France. There are 18 different organizations, covering over half the production. This was a very important move at its time of inception, creating disciplined, shared expertise, equipment and marketing, and frankly the chance to earn a living instead of starve.

The trouble is, of course, that this domination by co-operatives who, of necessity, try to level out quality rather than highlight the best growers and the best land, creates a bland safe sameness in the wines, and a complacent approach means the potential for excellence is submerged in the flat reality of mediocrity. All the best Mâconnais wines are from a single grower.

READING THE LABEL

The term Mâcon Supérieur on the label merely shows that an ordinary Mâcon has attained an extra degree of alcohol.

WHAT DO THEY TASTE LIKE?

The red wines are in general a little astringent, and lack the juicy fruit of a good Beaujolais. The whites are the opposite, sometimes too soft and dull-edged, but at their best the single-village wines can have a lovely gentle, honeyed style – Burgundy whites but with a southern touch.

THE GOOD YEARS

In general, these are wines to drink young. Though Chardonnay usually demands time to develop its flavours, Mâconnais Chardonnay is immediately attractive and can quickly tire after two years. Pouilly-Fuissé, properly made, repays keeping and will often develop beautifully for up to ten years. The hottest years are not necessarily the best; 2004, 2003 and 2002 are good vintages.

ENJOYING THE WINES

The reds are best with food – their rather rough-hewn flavours are good with French *andouillettes*, *rillettes* and *boudins*. The good whites have a softness which may slightly blur their personality, but which makes them very good, all-purpose wines, even going well with chicken, veal and pork. The soft but fruity Crémants make ideal apéritifs.

CONSUMER INFORMATION

WHAT DO I GET FOR MY MONEY?

Mâcon wines veer from fairly cheap to very expensive, but at all levels it is not very good value. Cheap Mâcon Blanc is rarely very pleasant and, at the other end of the scale, Pouilly-Fuissé is rarely worth the price. St-Véran is often the best value wine in the region and the emergence of a few growers of quality in the region is encouraging.

AVAILABILITY

All levels of Mâconnais wine are pretty easy to find, though for a top-line Pouilly-Fuisse you will have to go to a specialist merchant.

CONSUMER CHECKLIST

St-Véran 2002   *Quality 8* ★
(Domaine Corsin)   *Price 7* ★
                         Value 8 ★

Good Years Nearly every vintage produces reasonable wine, and they're usually ready to drink within the year. Best years: 2004, 2003, 2002, 2001, 2000, 1998, 1996, 1995.
Taste Notes These are among the softest and broadest of white Burgundies. The basic Mâcons should have a gentle appley flavour, while the single-village wines should have a creamy, round, honeyed taste.

BEAUJOLAIS

Is there any wine that is more French than Beaujolais? Any name which conjures up so potently our visions of bucolic, moustachioed Frenchmen with obligatory beret and blue-and-white striped T-shirt, carousing carelessly with their flagons of foaming red? All the clichéd foreigners' fantasies about the French revolve around this splashing, irreverent red from the southern end of Burgundy.

Of course, it isn't really in Burgundy – the grapes are different, the soils and wine-making methods far removed. And the people of Beaujolais, too, are all richer and rather more sober now that the rest of the world has taken to their local wine in such a big way. They can afford to sit back and enjoy the beauty of those rolling hills which make the region one of the most heart-softening and romantic of the wine areas to visit. Beaujolais was an astonishing marketing success.

I say 'was' because times have changed. It used to be that Beaujolais Nouveau was the first wine of the year, fizzing and grapy and fun. Then other parts of Europe climbed on to the Nouveau bandwagon, and there were *novello* wines from Italy and other *nouveaux* from other parts of France. Then Australia began releasing the first wines of her harvest – and suddenly there we were drinking the first wine of the year in June. And all the while Beaujolais kept getting more expensive.

Suddenly it wasn't so much fun any more to pay a no-longer-low price for a wine that had lost its shine. The rest of Beaujolais began to seem increasingly irrelevant, too. Prices rose, standards seemed to stagnate. And all the while anybody who craved juicy fruit in their wines could find it, at a lower price, from Down Under, or from the Midi, or from Spain. We did begin to look again at the Beaujolais Cru wines, the top level. Some of these wines can be bigger, more serious, more concentrated – but not as serious as the prices they were charging. Things are still scarcely in balance in Beaujolais. Prices are still too high for what is essentially an everyday, unpretentious wine, and despite a pretty good quality level nowadays, a significant chunk of Beaujolais was sent for distillation in 2004 and 2005. The Swiss and the French do still drink the Crus, but many parts of the world seem to have forgotten how much fun Beaujolais used to give them.

GRAPE VARIETIES AND WINE STYLES

There is in fact some **white Beaujolais**, and it is usually quite good, having a stony dryness

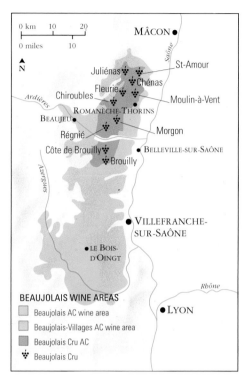

which can be closer in style to the northern wines of Chablis than the fatter, softer, sunny wines of southern Burgundy. And the grape is Burgundy's finest white wine variety – Chardonnay. Best producers: **Charmet**, **Duboeuf** and **Pizay**. You can actually make white Beaujolais out of the black Gamay grape but Gamay has a more important job – it is the only grape allowed to make 'le Beaujolais', which in the eyes of the world is red, red, red.

Gamay produces pretty dull stuff in most other areas of France, and can yield an unattractively hard, tart wine if grown any further north than Beaujolais. But somehow, on these granite slopes chiselled back toward the Massif Central from the Saône Valley, it can give the world's most juicy, gulpable wine.

Since Gamay has no pretensions as a grape, Beaujolais as a wine rarely has any either. It should be drunk young in great draughts of pleasure. Although a few of the top wines improve with age, the vast majority of the wine doesn't. And it doesn't get a chance to, either: a lot of it is drunk as early as Christmas as Beaujolais Nouveau.

CLASSIFICATION

This is very important in Beaujolais, which is divided into three geographical categories.

BEAUJOLAIS/BEAUJOLAIS SUPÉRIEUR

This covers all the basic wines. Supérieur simply means that the wine has a fraction more alcohol; it does not ensure a better wine. Up to two-thirds of this harvest is made into Nouveau, so run-of-the-mill Beaujolais is likely to be pretty thin, reedy stuff. Best producers: **Charmet, Duboeuf, Garlon, de la Madone/ Jadot, Terres Dorées** and **Vissoux**.

BEAUJOLAIS-VILLAGES

This appellation is for 39 villages which make better than average wines (especially Beaujeu, Lancié, Lantignié, Leynes, Quincié, St-Étienne-des-Ouillières and St-Jean-d'Ardières). The wines are certainly a bit better and the cherry-sharp fruit is usually more marked. Best producers: **de Belleverne, Descombes, Duboeuf, Manoir du Pavé** and **P Sapin**.

BEAUJOLAIS CRUS

These Crus or Growths are the top villages, and should all have definable characteristics.

St-Amour This usually has freshness and peachy perfume and good ripe fruit all at once. It is frequently the most reliable and the most enjoyable Cru. Best producers: **L'Ancien Relais, Billards, des Duc** and **des Sablons/Duboeuf**.

Juliénas This can be big wine, but many of the best more closely resemble the mixture of

Harvesting at Chiroubles, one of the ten Cru villages. These gently rolling hills are typical of the Beaujolais region and the Crus have the best vineyard sites.

fresh red fruits and soft, chocolaty warmth which marks good Fleurie. It can age, but is better young. Best producers: **Descombes, Duboeuf, P Granger, Ch. de Juliènas, J P Margerand, R Monnet, Pelletier** and **B Santé**.

Chénas A strong, tough wine. It can easily be as good as Moulin-à-Vent, but if you age it, it will taste more like Burgundy. Best producers: **Benon, Braillon, Champagnon, Lapierre, Manoir des Journets/Duboeuf** and **Santé**.

Moulin-à-Vent Enter the heavy brigade. These wines should be solid and strong, aging for three to five years or more. What one wants here is a big, plummy, slightly Burgundian style. It rarely resembles anyone's view of straight Beaujolais: it takes itself too seriously. Best producers: **Champagnon, Duboeuf, Ch. des Jacques, Ch. du Moulin-à-Vent, Romanesca** and **P Sapin**.

Fleurie Usually gentle and round, its sweet cherry and chocolate fruit just held firm by a little tannin and acidity. Best producers: **Aujoux, Chignard, Clos de la Roilette, Daumas, Depardon, Depres, Duboeuf, Fleurie** co-operative, **Métrat, Morel, Verpoix** and **Vissoux**.

Chiroubles Light, perfumy, cherryish wines ideal for early drinking. Best producers: **Cheysson**, **Méziat**, **A Passot** and **J Passot**.

Morgon These wines can be some of the glories of Beaujolais. They can start out thick and dark, and age to a sumptuous chocolaty, black cherry depth. Too much, though, is light and quick-maturing. Best producers: **Aucoeur**, **Brun**, **Charvet**, **Descombes/ Duboeuf**, **Jonchet** and **Lapierre**.

Régnié In warm years this newest Cru makes attractive wines but the grapes don't ripen in cool years. Best producers: **Duboeuf** and **Dubost**.

Brouilly Usually one of the lightest Crus. It is best drunk at nine months to a year. Best producers: **La Chaize**, **de Nervers/Duboeuf**, **Michaud** and **Thivin**.

Côte de Brouilly This is from the hilly slopes in the centre of the Brouilly area. The wines are fuller and stronger-tasting, since the slopes lap up the sun. Best producers: **Lacondemine**, **Ravier**, **Thivin** and **Viornery**.

BEAUJOLAIS NOUVEAU
Nouveau is the new vintage wine of Beaujolais and goes on sale at midnight on the third Wednesday in November – which makes it around two months old. It will normally improve for several months in bottle.

ORGANIZATION
The co-operatives and merchants play an important part, and some are better than others. The merchant Georges Duboeuf is internationally renowned. A reasonable number of growers bottle their own wines.

READING THE LABEL
If it's a merchant's wine, make sure it has been bottled in the region. Those bottled elsewhere tend to be more anonymous. A label with a single-vineyard name is a good sign.

WHAT DO THEY TASTE LIKE?
Gamay produces a gushing, purple-red, frothy-fresh wine. It reeks of cherries and raspberries and peaches, and it has that rare quality for a red wine – it is thirst-quenching.

THE GOOD YEARS
Most Gamay wine is at its best purple-fresh, full of fruit and so usually the most recent year is best for Beaujolais, though some of the Crus can age for a few years.

ENJOYING THE WINE
You should be able to drink it whenever you want, however you want, with whoever and with whatever you want. You don't even need wine glasses – paper mugs, tea cups or glass slippers will do. You can drink it warm or cold – I'd go so far as putting it in the fridge. However, at the price you've paid nowadays, you may want to drink it more soberly, with charcuterie or a cheese sandwich.

CONSUMER INFORMATION

WHAT DO I GET FOR MY MONEY?
There's a lot of duff Beaujolais on the market, and in the hands of a careless merchant, those ten Crus don't always live up to their reputation either. All the Crus are too expensive, with only the less fashionable Juliénas and Côte de Brouilly lagging slightly behind.

AVAILABILITY
Beaujolais of some sort is to be found in most outlets, although its drop in popularity means that the range to choose from will be less than it used to be.

CONSUMER CHECKLIST
Morgon Jean Descombes 2004 *Quality* 7 ★
(Georges Duboeuf) *Price* 6 ★
Value 7 ★

Good Years There is decent wine every year, though wet years may produce thin basic wine. In general the wines should be drunk within a year, though top Cru wines may age for three to four years. Best years: 2004, 2003, 2000, 1999.
Taste Notes Most Beaujolais is best drunk very young for its delicious burst of purple-fresh, peppery, cherryish fruit. The top Beaujolais Crus can age to a deep, chocolaty, plummy style that resembles Burgundy and yet is still distinctly Beaujolais in flavour.

CHAMPAGNE

There's no conjuring act like it. They take some of the rawest, sourest still wine in all France, and from the magician's hat they draw out the most sumptuous, glittering creation in all the world of wine.

How does Champagne happen? It needs a remarkable combination of climate and geology along with a leavening of human ingenuity and good luck. The natural phenomena could be described as a mixture of chalk and chill. The chalk cliffs which stare at each other over the English Channel between Dover and Cap Gris Nez are part of a long billowing seam roaming across southern England and northern France. There's nothing light white wine seems to thrive on as much as chalk, and round the cathedral city of Reims, northeast of Paris, the chalk manages to find those deep cleft river valleys and tucked-away sites which can ripen wine grapes. Just.

This is the Champagne region – the only one – and it has an average annual temperature just one degree above what is needed to ripen wine grapes. Many years it's a close-run thing and in some years the grapes just never get warm enough to ripen. But this risk element is crucial to the eventual character of the wine since, when they do ripen, the struggle

The great sweep of vines on the Montagne de Reims north of the village of Bouzy contains some of the finest Champagne vineyards.

has given a fresh and a lingering depth to what is still a light wine in much the same way as a cool-climate apple or pear or plum, fighting eternally against wind and rain, will always taste more interesting than the fat-cat table fruit from sunny climes.

Talking of which, this is about 1 degree above what you normally get in southern England, but as global warming begins to radically affect our climate, South England with those identical chalky soils will become more and more like Champagne is nowadays. Champagne itself will become more like Champagne in a really warm vintage – but it'll be occurring almost every year. This would explain why some of the most convincing Champagne look-alikes are now appearing from southern England (see page 234).

That word 'Champagne'. It doesn't just mean a style of wine. It doesn't simply mean something fizzy and fun. It can only legitimately apply to the wine coming from a very distinct, carefully delimited, part of France. The fact that this local wine has been such a whopping international success has meant that 'Champagne' is a term often used to describe any sparkling wine. This is neither accurate nor honest. Champagne can only come from the chalky, chilly hills and valleys centred on the river Marne around Reims. But the Champagne method can be used wherever you want to make a still wine sparkle.

Although nowadays the litigious *champenois* restrict the use of this term on the labels. I almost defiantly still use the term whenever I am talking about a wine made in the same way as Champagne, but on the labels of excellent products from other parts of France (where it is called Crémant), Europe and the world you are likely to see phrases like 'Traditional Method' or 'Classic Method'. That means the wine has been made to sparkle in the same way as Champagne but it comes from somewhere else. But, let's get back to Champagne – the place and the wine.

Champagne – and indeed all sparkling wines – are naturally still. The Champagne region is so far north that the wines ferment very slowly in the late autumn, and, if left to their own devices, would usually fail to finish off the job before the icy winter winds freeze the cellars and put the yeasts to sleep. Traditionally, most wines everywhere used to be made to be drunk within a year of the vintage. This meant that the wines of Champagne were shipped off in barrels during the winter, to Paris first, and later to London. Spring came, the weather warmed up, and the yeasts, which had gone into hibernation, woke up and returned to the task of fermenting out the sugar in the juice. Nobody quite realized why it happened, but it meant that a creamy, foaming mousse appeared in the wine around Easter, and for six to eight weeks into the early summer this laughing, gurgling liquid cascaded and frothed out of the barrels. Louis XIV's court at Versailles loved it. Madame de Pompadour, Louis XV's mistress, declared that it was the only way to get sozzled and stay sexy.

However, it eventually stopped frothing of its own accord when the yeasts had eaten up all the sugar, and it was not until a way was devised of keeping the bubbles in the wine that Champagne could reliably be made sparkling. Ironically, the figure who first properly understood the process, a Benedictine monk called Dom Pérignon who was the cellar master at Hautvillers Abbey near Epernay in the late seventeenth century, in fact spent much of his time trying to stop the sparkle, and the first person who tried scientifically to explain how to keep the bubbles in the wine

rather than get rid of them was an Englishman, Dr Merret, in 1662. All that was needed now were new, stronger glass bottles from England, and cork stoppers from Spain. Even so, a lot of early bottles of Champagne burst, because the pressure inside can build up to five or six atmospheres. The ones that survived produced a wine full of sparkle and also far richer in fruit and perfume than the thin, still wines people had been used to.

Today, the Champagne method means the inducing of a second fermentation of the wine inside the bottle, and the consequent dissolution of carbon dioxide in the wine under pressure. Cheaper fizzes are either pumped full of gas or given their second fermentation in enormous pressurized tanks. The latter needn't be worse than the Champagne method (though in practice they usually are): it's the quality of the base wine that counts.

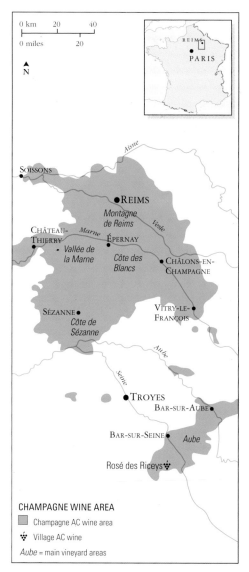

CHAMPAGNE WINE AREA

Champagne AC wine area

Village AC wine

Aube = main vineyard areas

The first pressing of Champagne grapes is very gentle, and afterwards the grapes are heaped up in the centre of the press for the second, harder pressing.

Krug ferments all its wines in oak barrels. Here, wine is being racked from one barrel to another; the tastevin is used to check clarity and taste.

Before the wine is bottled, it must be blended. Henri Krug will blend up to 50 different wines for Krug's non-vintage Grande Cuvée Champagne.

MAKING CHAMPAGNE TODAY

Let's look in more detail at how Champagne is made (much of this will also apply to other Champagne-method wines). The grapes are brought in to the winery and carefully pressed – and I mean carefully, since many of the grapes have black skins and the object is to press them quickly and gently so that the juice – which is normally colourless – is as pale as possible. These basic wines are fermented out to dryness, and then wines from various vineyards are expertly blended into the style required by the producer.

The next stage is to create the bubbles. The still wine is bottled, with a little *liqueur de tirage* of yeast and sugar to start another fermentation. A strong cork or metal stopper is shoved in the bottle, and the newly added yeasts begin eating up the newly added sugar. Creating alcohol. Creating carbon dioxide, which, since it can't escape, dissolves in the wine, biding its time until it reappears as that beautiful twining and twisting tangle of bubbles when the wine is finally poured.

But while this second fermentation has been creating the bubbles, it's also been behaving in a less attractive way. It's been depositing dead yeast cells as a thoroughly unprepossessing light brown gunge on the side of the bottle. Not the right image at society weddings or luxury liner launches, but crucial for imparting flavour.

Let's think about it. There's sludge in the bottle. The bottle only has one opening, so the sludge will have to leave by that exit. There's a cork in this opening. If the bottles were tipped upside down, the sludge would drop on to the cork in a little dollop – which brings us to the second stage, *remuage*, or 'removal'. The bottles are gradually tipped from horizontal to upside down, by being given a slight turn and knock every day for weeks on end. Gradually the sludge moves on to the cork.

Then comes the *dégorgement* or disgorging. With a deft flick of a wrist, you pull out the cork and simultaneously flip the bottle upright, removing the plug of yeast sludge, and probably a few drops of wine too. The wine is topped up with Champagne and a little sugar, according to how sweet it is to be, and given its final cork.

It's much more mechanized nowadays, but here we have the three fundamental principals of the Champagne method. The first, and obviously most crucial, is getting those bubbles into the wine. The second process, shifting the sludge, was invented by an employee of La Veuve Clicquot, the greatest of the many widows who have helped to form the modern

Champagne industry. Ever since, a kind of two-sided rack with holes in it, called a *pupitre*, has been in use for *remuage*. Shove the bottles in the holes, go through the tilt-and-tap routine for three months and you're ready for *dégorgement*. Most Champagne houses now use mechanical *pupitres* called *giropalettes* instead of humans to do the job. These large metal cages click and clunk as they turn the bottles and can do the process in one month, not three.

Dégorgement used to require a large number of men with strong wrists and fast reflexes, popping corks and ejecting sediment, but now the neck of the bottle containing the deposit is frozen, the cap with its frozen plug of sediment is whipped out on a machine production line, and the dosage is added. In fact, technology is becoming more and more evident in this most romantic and evocative of wines. Most wine is now made in shiny, computer-monitored, stainless steel vats by men in white coats – not wooden barrels and the cheeky peasants of yore. There are even experiments with little yeast pellets to create those second fermentation bubbles without any mess. That'll be good-bye to *remuage*. Whatever next?

A word about the dosage. The wine by this stage is still totally dry, and since the basic wine of Champagne is fairly harsh and raw, there are few Champagne houses which don't add some sugar after disgorging to take the edge off the acidity. Even Brut Champagnes, usually the driest on offer, will have usually at least 6g of sugar per litre and can have up to 15g per litre. Only a very few brands, often called Brut Zéro or something similar, have none at all.

Then the special triple-strength Champagne cork is rammed in. This usually consists of three layers of high-quality cork fixed horizontally on to a good chunk of composition cork, made up of little chips of cork and glue. The high-quality end is jammed into the bottle, and the cheaper end is left sticking out. When we remove a Champagne cork it looks like a mushroom, because the cork is actually wider than the neck of the bottle. Compress, shove it two-thirds in, and the bit in the bottle will strain to expand, thus preserving a total seal against the carbon dioxide panting to get out. Gradually the cork in the bottle will weaken and shrink, while the part outside stays the same shape, which produces the mushroom effect.

And that's it. Put a wire over the cork just in case the wine gets over-excited, doll it up with gold foil, age it if you can – but whatever happens from now on, you've just made a Champagne-method wine.

Champagne in pupitres *at Perrier-Jouët. The* remueurs *turn and twist each bottle a little more each day; nowadays this is usually done by machine.*

Champagne ready for remuage *at Louis Roederer. The sediment can be clearly seen in the neck of the bottle, collected in a heap on the cap.*

After disgorging the wine is topped up and given its final cork. Disgorging is the final chance to take a quick sniff and make sure the wine is all it should be.

GRAPE VARIETIES AND WINE STYLES

The grapes of Champagne are primarily black. About two-thirds of the vineyards grow black grapes. However, although the skins are black, the juice is white. The chief grape is Pinot Noir, which makes all the finest red Burgundies. It has difficulty ripening in Burgundy, and further north in Champagne it almost never attains any great depth and strength of colour or alcohol. Which is fair enough, because with the exception of pink Champagne, or the rare, non-sparkling Coteaux Champenois, the general idea is to produce a white sparkling wine. Very careful pressing of the grapes in enormous square vertical presses is the best way to draw off the juice as pale as possible. Even so, the black grape juice does have a fairly big feel to it, and a Champagne relying largely on black grapes is certain to be heavier and take longer to mature.

The other black grape is Pinot Meunier, which makes a softer, fruitier style, important in producing easy, forward wines.

The white grape is Chardonnay of white Burgundy fame. This produces a lighter, fresher juice, and the resulting Champagnes are certainly the most perfumed and honeyed.

In the middle ground (above) is the smalled walled vineyard of Clos de Mesnil, owned by Krug and making fantastically expensive Champagne.

They have been criticized as lacking depth and aging potential. Not true: good Blanc de Blancs has a superb, exciting flavour which is only improved by aging.

Champagne is produced in several styles:

Non-vintage The ordinary, most basic blend. The best Champagne houses and growers pride themselves on providing a continuous house style through the judicious blending of various vintages. In an ideal world a house would not 'declare' a vintage in a good year if they needed the wine to keep up the standard of their non-vintage, but that seldom happens these days. Most non-vintage Champagnes are based on wine from a single year, with added reserve wines from previous vintages. Minimum aging before release is 15 months, but all the good houses are now giving their wines considerably longer, which does wonders for their flavour.

Vintage Wine of a single, usually good quality year. As a rule it is only made in the best years but far too many mediocre years were declared in the 1990s. It's typically fuller, deeper, and a definite leg up the quality scale from non-vintage Champagne, but not necessarily more enjoyable for that. Certainly these are less effective as 'spontaneous celebration' wines, so save your money at parties. To get the best out of a vintage Champagne it's worth taking your time to enjoy it.

Cuvée de Prestige/de Luxe A special, highly prized, and certainly highly priced blend, usually vintage but not always. It encompasses some great wines and some unworthy wannabees. There seems to be a rule that the wines must come in distinctively shaped bottles. This certainly makes them *look* expensive.

Coteaux Champenois Still wines, either red or white from the Champagne region. They sometimes come with a village name, like Bouzy (red) or Cramant (white).

Crémant This used to mean a Champagne with less than the normal amount of fizz, but now that Champagne has won the exclusive use of the term *méthode champenoise* (no other wine made by this method may use the term, and now has to use words like 'traditional method' instead) it has surrendered use of the word *crémant* on labels. Crémant is now used only by Champagne-method sparkling wines from other parts of France, as in Crémant d'Alsace.

Rosé Traditionally the pink colour is gained by a careful and short maceration of the black Pinot Noir and Pinot Meunier skins with the juice. However, this method is unpredictable and more often now a little red wine from the region is added to the white just before bottling. The wines are usually aromatic and fruity, but are usually drunk young.

Blanc de Noirs This less-common style is made from 100 per cent black grapes. The wine is white, usually rather solid, but can be impressive if aged for long enough.

Blanc de Blancs An increasingly common style, from white Chardonnay grapes. The wines are usually fresh and bright when young, getting deeper and richer as they age. Many de luxe Champagnes come in this style.

AGING

Let's get one thing straight – Champagne does age. From time to time people will tell you that it should be drunk as the French like it –

young and tart and as soon as it is put on the market. This is all well and good if you happen to be French, but the British, in particular, have long known what the French have been unwilling to recognize, that certain wines take on a different dimension with long bottle aging, and that they are improved by it. The natural acidity in the grapes gets time to soften, and because two of the world's greatest grapes, white Chardonnay and black Pinot Noir, are involved, you get the benefit of softer, richer, gentler flavours.

Time was when the Champagne houses released their wines on to the market only when they were ready to drink. But that was before high interest rates and an accountant on every board of directors took their toll. The usual time for releasing a vintage wine was at around seven to eight years old, and non-vintages seldom saw the light of day before three or four years. Nowadays non-vintage is is rarely aged that long. In times of shortage far too many Champagnes are still release with less than two years age, but the general quality is good. Even so, another six months' aging after you buy the wine will probably do it the world of good. Sadly, it's still perfectly possible to buy well-known non-vintage brands that are far too green and need longer. Rosé, though, has fresh strawberry flavours and needs less aging.

Vintage Champagnes nowadays are sold at around five to six years old, when they may be drinkable if they're from a soft, ripe vintage, but they certainly won't be at their best. Resist the temptation to drink them so young – it's worth waiting for another five years.

If you want instant sparkling wine there are plenty of good substitutes for Champagne. Crémant de Bourgogne is the nearest French equivalent to Champagne's rich, bready style at a lower price; and there are masses of good Champagne-method sparkling wines from Australia, New Zealand, South Africa, California, Italy and England at various price levels, offering fresh, clean young fruit.

The days of cheap Champagne are over – at least for the time being. It makes sense for the Champenois to make the best fizz they can, to stop us deciding to shop elsewhere.

CLASSIFICATION

The classification system in Champagne is based on vineyards. The land is graded according to its suitability for black and white grapes, ranging from 100 per cent for the 17 finest Grand Cru villages, through 99–90 per cent for the 38 Premier Cru villages, and on to 80 per cent for the least-favoured. Champagne houses boast how high their average percentage of grapes is. One wonders who buys the rest.

ORGANIZATION

The Champagne industry is divided between the houses (large producers like Moët et Chandon) who might own some vineyards of their own but who are rarely self-sufficient in grapes, and the growers, some of whom may make and bottle their own wine but many of whom sell their grapes to the houses or the co-operatives. These growers' Champagnes dominate the French market and are often sold rather green and raw, but growers' Champagnes are now becoming increasingly important abroad as well. The large companies' PR machines used to deny them as inferior since blending of cuvées was seen as vital to Champagne quality. Blending is crucial if you're trying to beef up cuvées from poor sites, farmed by lazy or greedy growers. But all over Champagne there are special sites – just as there are in Burgundy to the south – and where these are owned and worked by dedicated individuals, it makes enormous sense for us to have the chance to appreciate their particular qualities. Surprisingly, however, they are often less good than wines produced by the houses, which can draw on a greater variety of base wines for blending.

The co-operatives, many of which are enormous, are also very important. Many of the own label and cheaper brands of Champagne on the market come from one of the big co-operatives. The standard of own label Champagnes is good at the moment.

The houses used to be organized into a Syndicat de Grandes Marques, which had between 20 and 30 members at any one time, depending on company takeovers and so on. In the mid-1990s unsuccessful attempts to make members agree on some sort of quality charter and whether to admit new members or not led to the Syndicat being dissolved in 1997. Of more relevance, perhaps, was Bollinger's Charter of Ethics and Quality, published in 1999, which has since been welcomed and adapted by various other producers. However, the situation is still in a state of flux and re-organization is on-going.

The Grandes Marques (as in 1997): Ayala, Billecart-Salmon, Bollinger, Canard-Duchêne, Deutz, Gosset, Heidsieck & Co. Monopole, Charles Heidsieck, Henriot, Krug, Lanson, Laurent-Perrier, Mercier, Moët et Chandon, G H Mumm, Perrier-Jouët, Joseph Perrier, Piper-Heidsieck, Pol Roger, Pommery, Louis Roederer, Ruinart, A Salon, Taittinger and Veuve Clicquot.

The chalky soil of the Côte des Blancs produces the best Chardonnay grapes in Champagne: ripe and with plenty of acidity.

Best producers: (houses) Billecart-Salmon, Bollinger, Cattier, Delamotte, Deutz, Drappier, Duval-Leroy, Gosset, Alfred Gratien, Charles Heidsieck, Henriot, Jacquesson, Krug, Lanson, Laurent-Perrier, Bruno Paillard, Joseph Perrier, Perrier-Jouet, Philipponnat, Pol Roger, Pommery, Louis Roederer, Ruinart, Salon, Taittinger and Veuve Clicquot; **(growers)** Michel Arnould, Paul Bara, Barnaut, Beaufort, Beerens, Chartogne-Taillet, Paul Déthune, Diebolt Vallois, Daniel Dumont, Egly-Ouriet, René Geoffroy, Gimonnet, H Goutorbe, André Jacquart, Lamiable, Larmandier, Larmandier-Berniet, Launois, Margaine, Serge Mathieu, J Michel, Moncuit, Alain Robert, Secondé, Selosse, de Sousa, Tarlant and Vilmart; and **(co-operatives)** Beaumont des Crayères, H Blin, Nicolas Feuillatte, Jacquart, Mailly and Union Champagne.

READING THE LABEL

Apart from the various descriptive terms on the label, the letters in small print at the bottom indicate the type of producer. The numbers the individual winemaker. The codes are:

RM (Récoltant-Manipulant) Wine made by a grower, not by a co-operative or merchant.

RC (Récoltant-Coopérateur) A grower sells his grapes to a co-operative and buys some wine out of the communal vats to sell under his own name.

Pruning the vine cuttings is the first vineyard task to be tackled after the harvest and is solitary work, continuing through the long, cold winter.

CM (Co-opérateur-Manipulant) This is wine made and sold by a co-operative.

NM (Négociant-Manipulant) Wine made and sold by a merchant.

MA (Marque d'Acheteur) Wine made by a merchant under a subsidiary label to satisfy a buyer's wish for a special selection, or to sell at a lower price than his chief brand.

SR (Sociéte de Récoltants) Wine made by a family company of growers.

Sometimes the phrase 'Recently Disgorged' will be seen on a Champagne label. These bottles have lain on their yeast deposits for much longer than usual, gaining depth and flavour but keeping maximum freshness. The disgorging takes place only just before the wine is sold. Such wines are frequently of de luxe standard.

WHAT DO THEY TASTE LIKE?

What does it feel like? How does it make you feel? These might be more natural ways of looking at Champagne and its flavours, since it is the effect of Champagne and its bubbles that most people are after.

However, this would be to say that Champagne is just another sparkling wine. It is not,

Wines from the Aube are soft and early-maturing, which makes them popular with many Champagne houses wanting more approachable wines earlier.

although the quality of some of its rivals from the New World, in particular those made in Australia, New Zealand or California by some of the Champagne houses, begin to make that a rather tentative statement. Some of these imitate the bready flavours of Champagne, some go all out for a fruitier style.

All can promote the heady, hectic sensations of good fortune and good company. This is because the carbon dioxide in the wine is absorbed at a particularly frantic rate by the stomach wall, which startles and livens up the circulation, which carries the alcohol to the brain at a faster rate, which makes you feel friskier, feistier... that's the simple explanation of why Champagne really does make a party go with a pop.

The taste. Well, first the still red and white wine from the region, called Coteaux Champenois – it's rarely brilliant, and usually tastes a little thin and unripe; in fact it demonstrates precisely why the Champenois go to such lengths to make their wine sparkle. The fizzy stuff ranges from rather green and raspingly fresh to the deep, honeyed, excitingly soft, ripe wines of high quality that need perhaps ten years' aging.

This ability – indeed, this need – to age sets Champagne apart from other sparkling wines. The high acidity that makes it need to age comes from the chalk soil and the cool climate, and the balance that enables it to age comes from the blending skills of the makers. As many as 30 or 40 different wines from all round the region may be used in a non-vintage blend. Almost none of them on its own is as good as the final blend. And almost none would age so well by itself. Champagne can achieve remarkably rich flavours, and it is worth giving it time to prove itself.

THE GOOD YEARS

2004 A good vintage but a record harvest, with very high yields.

2003 The European heatwave meant this was the earliest harvest since records began in 1822. Small harvest but some houses will probably make a vintage wine.

2002 Good to excellent quality, especially the Pinot Noir. Good potential.

2001 The wettest harvest in over a century. Not a vintage year.

2000 Another unexciting year but because this was the millennium there will probably be some vintage wines.

1999 A large crop marred by rain at harvest and low acidity.

1998 An abundant harvest but variable quality. Some very good wines so choose with care.

1997 Careful producers made good quality wines. Drink before the 1996s.

1996 Thought to be perhaps the best year ever. Perfect harvest conditions and results were great for all three varieties and seriously-made wines will improve for 20 years.

1995 A hot summer produced good-quality, healthy fruit which resulted in some quite rich vintage wine being made.

Older vintages
1990, 1989, 1988, 1985, 1983, 1982, 1976.

ENJOYING CHAMPAGNE

I drink Champagne just about whenever I can get my hands on some. There's no drink more likely to put snap back into the fingers and bounce back into the feet, sparkle back into the eyes, and gurgling, flirting laughter back into the throat. Champagne is a wine which has no rules, except perhaps the general feeling that it should be chilled rather than lukewarm. But even lukewarm, the whoosh of the bubbles and the sharp-edged flavour mean it's easy to make the best of a bad job.

If you want a civilized apéritif or don't feel your bottle is too special you could mess it about a bit. You could add a tiny dash of cassis or mûre or framboise liqueur, but don't, – as so many bars do – use sirop. Adding some fresh orange juice makes Buck's Fizz, although both the fresh-pressed orange juice and the Champagne are so good on their own that I'd keep the Champagne separate and take alternate mouthfuls. And the same goes for Black Velvet, an unbeguiling mixture of Champagne and Guinness.

And with food? Yes, of course, it does go with food. It is rarely the perfect taste combination, but since it is frequently the perfect complement to your mood one could say, yes it goes brilliantly with caviar, foie gras, salmon, roast venison, fish and chips and a bacon double cheeseburger (go easy on the ketchup) – so long as your mood is right. Even a dry Champagne can cope with rich cakes and puddings, though a 'rich' (or sweet) style might go better. Otherwise, Champagne is at its best with lighter dishes rather than with heavy, grand creations. The finely tuned flavours of modern cooking often defy traditional wine partnerships: Champagne fits that bill very well indeed.

CONSUMER INFORMATION

WHAT DO I GET FOR MY MONEY?

Champagne is generally offering fair value for money at the moment. It's expensive, yes, but I don't mind paying if I'm getting the right quality. And if I want to pay less there are reliable own-label Champagnes from the leading supermarket chains. By buying carefully at about the middle of the range (well-chosen growers' wines and the top own labels) there is some excellent value to be had. Of the Grandes Marques, Billecart-Salmon, Joseph Perrier, Pol Roger, Veuve Clicquot, Taittinger, Charles Heidsieck, Bollinger and Roederer should all be stunning. Vintage wines from all these producers will be very good, though they will need extra aging if they are to show themselves worth the money. The de luxe cuvées are hardly good value, though some are very exciting and one or two, like Bollinger RD, Clicquot Grande Dame, Laurent-Perrier Grand Siècle, Taittinger Comtes de Champagne, Krug Grande Cuvée (its standard non-vintage!) or Roederer Cristal are so classy one might be tempted. Might.

AVAILABILITY

Champagne must be the most generally available wine in the world – that is, the non-vintage blends of the major Champagne houses and the own labels – which are normally exactly what we want. The straight vintage styles and the de luxe styles are less widely available and more expensive. Still Coteaux Champenois wines are rarely seen.

CONSUMER CHECKLIST

Cuvée Nicolas-François Billecart *Quality 10* ★
1996
(Billecart-Salmon)   *Price 10* ★
                                            Value 10 ★

Good Years The region is so large that by careful selection it is, in theory, possible to produce some top-quality wine, even if only a little, in most years. In practice most houses wait until they have a sensible quantity of top wine before declaring a vintage. Best years: 2004, 2002, 1999, 1998, 1996, 1995, 1990, 1989, 1988, 1985, 1983, 1982, 1976.

Taste Notes All Champagne should have clear, clean fruit, not aromatic, but very fresh when young and becoming honeyed and mellow as it matures. The higher the quality, the deeper and more thought-provoking the flavour should be. Some people favour Champagnes so old that the fizz is weakening and the wine is taking on a mushroomy note.

RHÔNE

It's not until you've painfully negotiated the wretched highway system in Lyon, plunged south through the sour-smelling parade of grimy factories and refineries that stretches for the next 30km (18 miles) and, gasping for the fresh country air, swung the car over the two bridges spanning the Rhône near Vienne, that you know you're in the south of France. From that moment on, every sign of civilization will seem to be rudely carved by the demands of the beating Mediterranean sun and the harsh summer winds.

The Rhône Valley is both the beginning of the vast drab vinelands of the South, and the pinnacle of their achievement. Beginning with a sliver of narrow, precipitous vineyard rock face tumbling down to the river bed at Côte-Rôtie in the north, and spreading to the immense tarpaulin of stubby, ugly vines to the south around Avignon, this is one of France's most important wine regions, pumping out more wine than Beaujolais and Burgundy, and nearly as much as Bordeaux.

That's a lot of wine. And while the Rhône Valley harbours one of the world's most famous and abused wine names – yes, good old Châteauneuf-du-Pape – just cite me another household wine name from the Rhône. Apart, of course, from equally 'good old' Côtes du Rhône, which can cover just about every eventuality from half-hearted

The steeply terraced vineyards on the hill of Hermitage overlooking the Rhône produce some of France's deepest, darkest brooding red wines.

rosé to thick paintbrush bristle red palate bashers. What else is there? Well, a good deal. It is remarkable how the Rhône's famous names had slipped from view in the past, but now times have changed. Great names like Hermitage, Côte-Rôtie, Condrieu and even Châteauneuf-du-Pape are acknowledged to be some of France's finest wines – and prices have risen accordingly. The very top wines, from a handful of producers, sell for prices I can only describe as Burgundian. Even less fabled names like St-Joseph and Crozes-Hermitage are attracting far more attention – and are showing they're worthy of it, too, with rich, increasingly well-made wines of individuality and character.

Many of these wines are from the thin, northern river slope slice of the region, whose whole tradition is more geared to the production of high-quality, hand-crafted wines from steep, rocky, terraced vineyards, and whose styles are markedly more reserved and 'cool climate' than the sweltering produce of the much flatter, much larger, easier-to-work southern Rhône. So let's divide the Rhône Valley into north and south and try to see what makes each area tick.

NORTHERN RHÔNE

The northern Rhône Valley makes chiefly red wines, dominated by one grape – Syrah. Along with Cabernet Sauvignon, Bordeaux's great grape, Syrah makes France's darkest, most pungent red wine, and it is here that it is traditionally at its most brilliant.

GRAPE VARIETIES AND WINE STYLES

The greatest northern Rhône wines are **Hermitage** and **Côte-Rôtie**, two tiny vineyard areas less than a fifth the size of any of Bordeaux's great wine villages. Hermitage is one of France's burliest wines, while Côte-Rôtie, when helped by the judicious admixture of juice from the white Viognier grape, can be one of France's most perfumed and fragrant reds. The wines of **Cornas**, black and tarry teeth-stainers, and **St-Joseph**, almost smooth and sweet by comparison, are also fine, and the large **Crozes-Hermitage** appellation provides Hermitage-type wine – quite beefy but these days with supple fruit, and occasional scent.

Despite red dominance, there is a white presence. The Viognier grape makes **Condrieu** and **Château-Grillet**, two dreamy-tasting rarities, and the Marsanne and Roussanne grapes not only make white **Hermitage** and **Crozes-Hermitage**, but also white **St-Joseph** and the rarely found **St-Péray**. And if you take a long hike eastwards from Valence to the river Drôme, high in the foothills, the Muscat and the Clairette grapes make **Clairette de Die** – delicious, light, super-fresh fizz.

Côte-Rôtie 'Roasted slope' is an apt name for this appellation, since it is the hot, cliff-like slopes which offer the best wines. It's a tiny area, with only about 216 hectares (534 acres) of vineyards in the best part. Sadly, there has been a massive, cynical extension of appellation rights on to the ambling plateau land behind the river bend. Unless something is done to differentiate wine from the slopes from wine from the flat land, the reputation of this high-priced, highly prized vineyard will fall. At its best, from a few individual growers like **Jasmin**, **Guigal** and **Jamet**, Côte-Rôtie can be an astonishingly scented red, with the fierceness of the Syrah grape tempered by heavenly scent and mellow, autumn-sweet fruit of the white Viognier's sweetness. Rare and delicious. Best producers: **Gilles Barge**, **Bonnefond**, **Bonserine**, **Burgaud**, **Clusel-Roch**, **Cuilleron**, **Delas**, **Duclaux**, **Galet**, **Garon**, **Gérin**, **Guigal**, **Jamet**, **Jasmin**, **S Ogier**, **René Rostaing**, **Tardieu-Laurent**, **F Villard** and **Vins de Vienne**.

Château-Grillet A single property, and one of the smallest appellations in France, at only 4 hectares (10 acres). This white wine should have that magic reek of orchard fruit and harvest bloom about it. If it does, though I've seen little evidence of this recently, the huge asking price is almost worth it.

Condrieu This little appellation has grown from a low point of 10 hectares (25 acres) in the 1960s to 112 hectares (277 acres), with some of the vines planted in the early 1990s not in ideal vineyard sites. Condrieu is situated on the bend of the river just above Château-Grillet, but at least there are quite a few different growers giving it a go, and most of the best French Viognier now comes from Condrieu. It is an amazing taste. That apricot scent leaps out of the glass at you, and the balance between succulent, sweet fruit and gentle nipping acidity in a big, fairly dry white

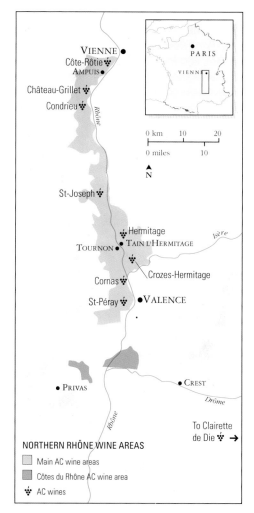

NORTHERN RHÔNE WINE AREAS
- Main AC wine areas
- Côtes du Rhône AC wine area
- AC wines

Wine-making the traditional way is not for the faint-hearted. These men are breaking up the 'cap' of skins on the fermenting must at the firm of Chapoutier.

wine is worth all the effort and expense to root out. However, I have to say that Condrieu is in serious danger of losing its exalted reputation if something is not done to stem overproduction and the granting of appellation rights to unsuitable plateau land above the traditional hillside sites. Best producers: **G Barge, Bonnefond, du Chêne, Colombo, Cuilleron, Delas, Dumazet, Facchin, Gangloff, Guigal, Monteillet, A Paret, Perret, C Pinchon, Rostaing, St-Cosme, Vernay** and **F Villard**.

Hermitage The hill of Hermitage broods over the town of Tain, so steep and angular that it would seem hardly possible to cultivate it. But those 135 hectares (333 acres) of vineyards produce the Rhône's greatest reds, and fine whites too. It was once described as the manliest wine of France. Men should be so lucky, to combine such strength and fiery toughness when young with such a rich, brooding magnificence when mature. There is always a stern, vaguely medicinal or smoky edge to red Hermitage, but Syrah also possesses a depth of raspberry and blackcurrant fruit no other grape can touch. White Hermitage is often a bit heavy and dull, but was once regarded as France's greatest white wine and, curiously, ages tremendously well to a soft, mouthfilling nuttiness. Indeed, after seeming often to be on its last legs before ever reaching maturity, it can often end up outlasting *red* Hermitage. Best producers: **Belle, Chapoutier, J-L Chave, Y Chave, Colombier, Colombo, Delas, B Faurie, Fayolle, Ferraton, Guigal, Jaboulet, J-M Sorrel, M Sorrel, Tain l'Hermitage co-op, Tardieu-Laurent** and **Les Vins de Vienne**.

St-Joseph This is yet another northern Rhône appellation suffering from wanton expansion of vineyard into unsuitable land, although the boundaries have recently been pulled back to exclude the least suitable terrain. Even so, good St-Joseph is a delicious wine, gentler and lighter than Hermitage, and stacked with blackcurrant fruit in a good year. Best producers: **Chapoutier, J-L Chave, L Chèze, Colombo, Courbis, Coursodon, Cuilleron, Delas, Durand, Florentin, Gaillard, Gonon, Graillot, B Gripa, Guigal, Jaboulet, Monteillet, Paret, A Perret, C Pinchon,** the **St-Désirat** co-operative, **Tain l'Hermitage** co-op, **Tardieu-Laurent, Trollat, Vernay** and **Villard**.

Cornas Closer to Hermitage in weight, but lacking a little of the fresh fruit which makes Hermitage so remarkable. The wine is usually rather hefty, jammy even, and needs a bit of patience. Best producers: **Allemand, Balthazar, Clape, Colombo, Courbis, Delas, Durand, Fauterie, Jaboulet, Lemenicier, Lionnet, R Michel, Tain l'Hermitage** co-op, **Tardieu-Laurent, Tunnel** and **Alain Voge**.

Crozes-Hermitage A potentially massive area of wine production, mostly red, which is an increasingly good source of exciting smoky, plummy Syrah wine, sometimes not far off Hermitage in quality. The white is generally rather dullish. Best producers: **Belle, Chapoutier, Y Chave, Colombier, Delas, Fayolle, Desmeure, Graillot, Jaboulet, Pochon, M Sorrel, Tain** co-operative, **Tardieu-Laurent** and **Vins de Vienne**.

St-Péray This was once France's most famous fizz after Champagne. Not any more. Although it's quite good, it always seems rather stolid and short of freshness. The still whites, with a couple of exceptions, also suffer from an honest toiler's dullness. Best producers: **S Chaboud, Clape, Colombo, G Darona, Fauterie, B Gripa, Leminicier, Lionnet, Thiers, Tunnel** and **Voge**.

Clairette de Die This is a delicious, off-dry Muscat fizz of high quality. Crémant de Die, which lacks the aromatic Muscat scent, is not so exciting. Drink young. Best producers: **Achard-Vincent**, the **Die** co-operative and **Raspail**.

Châtillon-en-Diois This is still wine made in the out-of-the-way valleys around Die, where sparkling Clairette de Die is produced. The reds are mostly Gamay, with some Syrah and Pinot Noir, and the whites mostly Aligoté with some Chardonnay. As yet the red wines are a bit harsh, and the whites a bit biting, but this far south these are faults in the right direction, so when Chardonnay and Syrah get more involved, the results could be very interesting. Best producer: the **Die** co-operative.

CLASSIFICATION

Classification in the northern Rhône is largely a matter of simple geographical delineation of vineyard areas around a single name. A couple of producers label their wines 'Grand Cru', but there isn't a cru or 'growth' system as such, and there's not an official classification. Some vineyards are widely recognized as being better than others, but it is quite rare for their names to appear on the labels. In any case, most northern Rhône wines are a blend of several wines from within the appellation.

ORGANIZATION

The northern Rhône is one of the few areas where the honours are fairly evenly shared between merchants' blends and growers' wines, with more growers now bottling their own wines. Most leading merchants own numerous plots of land, and in difficult vintages may even have the upper hand because of the ability to blend wines from different sites. Standards among the growers are high: a few generations of family pride in your small plot of land is a great incentive to strike out for excellence. There are a few co-operatives and the best is probably at St-Désirat.

READING THE LABEL

Rhône labels are fairly easy to interpret. They follow the Burgundian pattern of a general area name or single village name. Some basic wines are offered without a vintage.

Carrying grapes up the steep slopes of Côte-Rôtie, above the town of Ampuis, is backbreaking work as each hod of grapes weighs nearly 40kg (90lb).

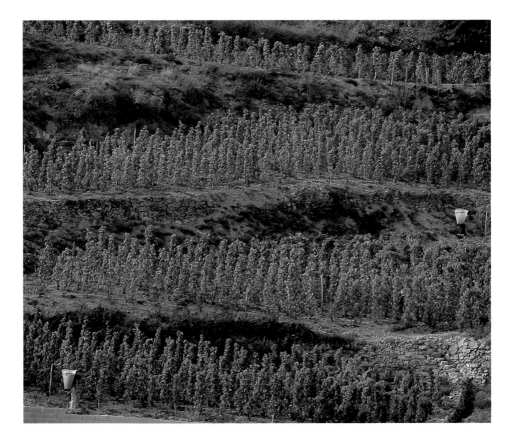

WHAT DO THEY TASTE LIKE?

You'd better be sitting down when you start reading this, because the purple prose is about to flow. The red Syrah and the white Viognier, hidden in their steep-sided, twisting river valley below Lyon, pour out two of the most startling taste sensations the world of wine has to offer. The white Viognier, now planted in the Midi and the Ardèche as well as in Condrieu and Château-Grillet (and now more extensively within Condrieu as well) has such a steamy, exotic flavour of apricot, fresh mayblossom and yet bursts with the muskiness of ripe autumn fruit, that you gasp at the sheer unexpected beauty of the thing.

You gasp at the Syrah, too. In young Hermitage and Cornas, this massive brute of a grape shoves aside the niceties of taste and bellows its presence, rasping with tannin and tar and woodsmoke, and the deep ungainly sweetness of black treacle. Leave it a while. Five years, maybe ten, then try again. The wine will have undergone a sea change. The almost medicinal edge will still be there, but those raw fumes will have become sweet, pungent, full of raspberries, brambles and cassis. Well, I warned you about the purple prose, but good Syrah wine is such exciting stuff, I thought I'd risk going over the top a bit – just to tempt you to try it.

There are no short cuts when you have to carry a load of grapes down the hill of Hermitage. Note the old stone walls that support the steep terraces.

THE GOOD YEARS

The poor years of the early 1990s that afflicted other parts of France took their toll of the northern Rhône, too, bringing to an end a run of good to excellent vintages that had established these wines in the eyes of the world. However, recent years have been kinder and quality improvements continue.

2004 Highly successful reds and whites.

2003 Drought affected the size of the harvest. Weighty, powerful reds with baked flavours.

2002 Heavy rain so choose carefully.

2001 Impressive reds and whites, especially Côte-Rôtie.

2000 A very good year. Côte-Rôtie wines promise to be exceptional.

1999 An outstanding vintage with well-structured, long-lived wines.

1998 Drought and heat produced a reduced crop of good, burly, age-worthy wines.

1997 Good but perhaps not quite up to the standard of 1996.

1996 Very good – similar quality to 1995.

1995 Excellent wines were made despite September rains.

1994 A rainy harvest produced wines for early drinking. But at least they're ripe.

1993 A thin year, generally best avoided.

1992 Not a very successful vintage and only the best names made anything of it. The wines should be drunk up.

1991 Côte-Rôtie was the star here and made excellent wines. The rest of the north was generally fairly good.

1990 A hot, drought-ridden year in which the north made some super wines. Côte-Rôtie was more successful in 1991, though.

1989 A hot year with drought problems. Quality is a bit uneven, but the best wines are rich and powerfully concentrated.

1988 Very tannic wines, at their best in Côte-Rôtie and Hermitage.

Older vintages

1985, 1983, 1979, 1976, 1971, 1970, 1969, 1966, 1964, 1961.

ENJOYING THE WINES

Without exception northern Rhône wines have uncompromising, unsquashable flavours. The reds are quite superb with the most lordly of roasts and game, but are perhaps more used to the highly flavoured casseroles and charcuterie of their own region.

The whites are more difficult to match with food, since they are relatively short on the cutting acid edge which makes white wine so refreshing. But simply prepared chicken, pork, and the local fish go well with most of them. The Muscat Clairette de Die is a marvellously grapy apéritif.

CONSUMER INFORMATION

WHAT DO I GET FOR MY MONEY?

The top wines are now expensive by any standards, although they do deliver some of France's most fascinating flavours. I certainly wouldn't call them overpriced; it's just that we'd all got used to regarding the Rhône as undervalued, and now it's a shock to find that it's not. For good value at a lower price, go for Crozes-Hermitage or St-Joseph.

If you want a Viognier wine and Condrieu and Château-Grillet are too expensive, there's quite a bit of Viognier now from the Midi. It's not quite as exciting, but it's a lot cheaper.

AVAILABILITY

Not great. Crozes-Hermitage is a pretty big appellation, and most good outlets will have a good example. St-Joseph is relatively easy to find. The more expensive, rarer wines tend to be rationed to specialists.

CONSUMER CHECKLIST

Côte-Rôtie Brune et Blonde
1995 (Guigal)

Quality 9 ★
Price 9 ★
Value 8 ★

Good Years Northern Rhône has been very lucky for the past 20 years with only three bad vintages (2002, 1993 and the rain-smitten 1992). A massive price increase in the wines of the northern Rhône has also triggered off a considerable improvement in quality. Best years: 2004, 2003, 2001, 2000, 1999, 1998, 1997, 1996, 1995, 1994, 1991, 1990, 1989, 1988, 1985.

Taste Notes Northern Rhône reds are strong, gutsy wines with flavours of blackcurrant, tar and spice. They repay aging; indeed they can be distinctly unapproachable in youth. Whites from Condrieu can be marvellously exotic; others can be merely heavy. Viognier wines are at their best young; other whites may age.

SOUTHERN RHÔNE

The southern Rhône is awash with permitted grape varieties, barely tolerated grape varieties and distinctly frowned upon grape varieties. Add to this a total change of terrain from the precipitous vineyards of the North to the sprawling ones of the South, with only the best villages pulling a few suitable slopes out of the bag, and a climate which, even as early as March, makes you reach for the sunhat or the tanning lotion – and you have a recipe for wines with full, strong, flavours.

They used to be a bit dull, relying on power for their punch; but lately they've smartened up their act and the southern Rhône is where you're likely to find herby, peppery fruit, full of raspberries and loganberries. It's part of the renaissance that is overtaking the whole of the south of France.

GRAPE VARIETIES AND WINE STYLES

The southern Rhône is still primarily a red wine area. The only white grape of any distinction is the Muscat, centred round Beaumes-de-Venise, though there is now some Viognier in the South. Other white grapes are Clairette, Roussanne and Bour-

boulenc. In reds, the oomph is provided by the dark, but perfumed Syrah or the powerful Grenache plus Mourvèdre and Cinsault.

Châteauneuf-du-Pape This is the great name of the South, and is where the Appellation Contrôlée designation was first tried out in 1923. There are 13 different red and white grape varieties permitted in the vineyards, and the result is a slightly indistinct but, at its best, very satisfying full red, with a characteristic dusty taste on top of the sweet juicy fruit. Roughly a third of the wine sold under the Châteauneuf name matches this description. The rest is too light, or too lean, or too stringy. There is some surprisingly good white. Best producers: **Barrot, Beaucastel, Beaurenard, Bois de Boursan, Bonneau, Bosquet des Papes, du Caillou, les Cailloux, Chante-Perdrix, Chapoutier, la Charbonnière, L Charvin, Clos du Mont-Olivet, Clos des Papes, Font du Loup, Font de Michelle, Fortia, la Gardine, Grand Tinel, la Janasse, Marcoux, Monpertuis, Mont-Redon, La Nerthe, Pégaü, Rayas, Sabon, Tardieu-Laurent, Usseglio, la Vieille Julienne, Vieux Donjon** and **Vieux Télégraphe.**

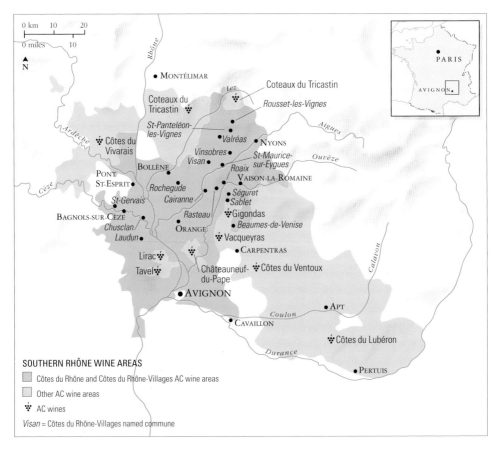

SOUTHERN RHÔNE WINE AREAS

Côtes du Rhône and Côtes du Rhône-Villages AC wine areas

Other AC wine areas

❦ AC wines

Visan = Côtes du Rhône-Villages named commune

Gigondas Often likened to Châteauneuf, but usually bigger, beefier and more likely to have that strong, tough, southern taste of pressed grape skins warring with the considerable fruit. Best producers: **Brusset, Cros de la Mûre, Font-Sane, Les Pallières, Raspail-Ay, St-Gayan, Tardieu-Laurent** and **Trignon**.

Lirac An excellent and often underrated area just across the Rhône from Châteauneuf. The reds and rosés are packed with fruit, often with a not unwelcome mineral edge, and the rosés are remarkably fresh for so far south. The whites can be good. And they're all still quite cheap. Best producers: **Aquéria, Lafond-Roc-Epine, La Mordorée** and **Sabon**.

Tavel Always rosé from mainly Grenache and Cinsaut, the wine is quite expensive, very tasty, and packs rather more of a punch than you'd expect – or want. Best producers: **Aquéria, Forcadière** and **Trinquevedel**.

Côtes du Rhône-Villages Always red, from specific villages making higher-quality wine, these combine the rather earthy, dusty southern heat with a good deal of raspberryish fruit. They are good value, quite chunky reds. Best producers: **Beaurenard, D Charavin, Chaume-Arnaud, Combe, Cros de la Mûre, Gourt de Mautens, Grand Moulas, la Janasse, Pelaquié, Réméjeanne, St-Gayan,** and **Ste-Anne**.

Olives and vines often rub shoulders in the south of France. This is the Côtes du Ventoux with the snow-covered Mont Ventoux in the distance.

Côtes du Rhône The basic appellation. Mostly red, the wines can be tremendously fresh and fruity, not unlike Beaujolais, or they can occasionally be fierce black grape skins and alcoholic monsters. I'd increasingly go for the former style as a source of good cheap reds but, since the labels give no clue, it's trial and error or merchants' recommendations. Best producers: **Brunel, Coudoulet de Beaucastel, Fonsalette, Gramenon, Grand Moulas, Guigal, la Janasse, Lionnet, la Mordoreé, Santa Duc, Ste-Anne** and **Vieux-Chêne**.

Rasteau (Vin Doux Naturel) Rasteau is famous for some strong, sweet fortified red and white but also makes decent dry Côtes du Rhone-Villages. Best producers: **Beaurenard, J Bressy, la Soumade** and **du Trapadis**.

Muscat de Beaumes-de-Venise (Vin Doux Naturel) The village of Beaumes-de-Venise makes good, chewy, berryish reds, promoted to its own AC in 2005, as well as this sweet, aromatic white fortified. It's not as fashionable as it was a few years ago, but it is delicious: grapy, fresh, rich but not cloying. Best producers: **Baumalric, Bernardins, Coyeux, Durban, Jaboulet** and **Pigeade**.

Côtes du Vivarais An area west of the Rhône making pleasant, mostly light, mostly red wines based on Grenache, Cinsaut and Carignan.

Coteaux du Tricastin Parched, scrubby land that produces extremely good and cheap reds from the usual range of grapes. The appellation was virtually invented to cope with the influx of North African grape growers in the 1950s and 1960s; since they had to start from scratch, they've had to try harder. Frequently they succeed, and as simple, full-bodied Rhône reds the wines can be excellent value. Best producers: **Grangeneuve, St-Luc, Tour d'Elyssas** and **Vieux Micocoulier**.

Côtes du Ventoux This appellation is spread out across the wide southern slopes of Mont Ventoux to the east of the Rhône, and these good-value wines are much more like Beaujolais in style than beefy Côtes du Rhône. That is to say, they are light and fruity, and at their best, reeking of fresh strawberry fruit. There is a little white and rosé. Best producers: **Anges**, **La Croix des Pins**, **Jaboulet**, **Pesquié** and **Valcombe**.

Côtes du Lubéron There is decent white wine here, appley-fresh if drunk young enough. Most reds and rosés are also fresh and reasonably fruity at less than a year old. Best producers: **la Citadelle**, **Fontenille**, **l'Isolette** and **la Verrière**.

Vins de Pays Coteaux de l'Ardèche wines are increasingly good varietal wines marked by tremendous fruit. The local co-operatives (especially **Vignerons Ardechois**) are the main producers, and are very good and innovative. Good merchants include **Duboeuf** and **Louis Latour**. Other Vins de Pays in the region make lighter versions of mainstream Rhône wines, mainly red and they are usually light, peppery but fruity too. So long as modern wine-making techniques are used, Vin de Pays de Vaucluse is simple and attractive, while both Coteaux de Baronnies and Principauté d'Orange have a bit more stuffing.

CLASSIFICATION

This is similar to that of the northern Rhône: there is no system of marking out the best wines within an appellation. The majority of wines come under the all-embracing Côtes du Rhône appellation. They may be red, white or rosé. The addition of 'Villages' to the title Côtes du Rhône will usually mean a considerable upward jump in quality and character, and wines from one of the villages that have the right to put their own name on the label should be better still.

ORGANIZATION

The co-operative movement is vitally important here, and has made a dramatic contribution to the quality of the wines: co-operatives like Chusclan, Beaumes-de-Venise, Cairanne and Vacqueyras now make some of the best value wines in the region.

Only weeds and vines can thrive in the stony soil of Châteauneuf-du-Pape. The young vines are protected by plastic from the local rabbit population.

READING THE LABEL

Particularly in Châteauneuf it is important to check that the wine is estate-bottled. Some of the merchants have improved lately.

WHAT DO THEY TASTE LIKE?

The South is giving increasingly juicy, spicy, slightly dusty raspberryish reds. The whole point is the blend, which means that a single grape seldom dominates. They're not wines that need much aging – they're far softer than the tannic reds of the North – though they don't lack concentration.

THE GOOD YEARS

It used to be said that vintages didn't much matter in the southern Rhône, but they can be inconsistent. The chief problem is often the failure of Grenache, the most important grape. It tends to have difficulty flowering successfully, and if there's a difficult spring the crop can be drastically reduced, thus altering the character of the wine. The reds don't on the whole last as long as those from the North. All but the top Châteauneufs should be drunk quite young.

2004 Reds have good balance and should be long lived.

2003 Hot year produced powerful reds.

2002 Heavy rain and floods around Châteauneuf so choose carefully.

2001 Impressive reds and whites, especially Côte-Rôtie.

2000 A relatively small crop of superb quality. Plenty of rich whites and age-worthy reds.

1999 Another good year, especially for Châteauneuf.

1998 Deeply coloured wines with excellent depth and concentration.

1997 Patchy because of rain.

1996 Good for whites but rain affected the red harvest; there will be some good reds.

1995 Quality was very good despite the drought.

Older vintages

1994, 1990, 1989, 1988, 1986, 1985, 1983.

ENJOYING THE WINES

These southern reds are excellent as high-class quaffing wines for casseroles and grills. Good Lirac and Châteauneuf-du-Pape, as well as some of the best Côtes du Rhône-Villages wines, will bear a bit more contemplation, but they'll still be happiest with hearty chunks of lamb rather than dainty morsels eaten off the best Wedgwood.

The whites are often dull, but increasingly attempts at a modern style, while lacking apéritif freshness, can be good first course

Investment in modern, stainless steel equipment has transformed many southern Rhône wines. Although expensive, the results show immediately.

wines. Chilled Muscat de Beaumes-de-Venise (and it must be chilled) is wonderful grapy stuff at any time before or after a meal, or even matched with puddings.

CONSUMER INFORMATION

WHAT DO I GET FOR MY MONEY?

Prices in the South remain generally lower than those in the North. Châteauneuf is the most expensive. The sweet Muscats of Beaumes-de-Venise are some of France's best, though the price is quite high. Basic Côtes du Rhône red can be good value, though the best ones, especially the Villages wines, are worth paying more for.

AVAILABILITY

Straight Côtes du Rhône is one of the world's most widely available wines. Serious merchants will generally have a good example.

CONSUMER CHECKLIST

Châteauneuf-du-Pape 1999	Quality 9 ★
(Grand Tinel)	Price 8 ★
	Value 9 ★

Good Years The ability to blend different grapes means that the good producers usually cope with marginal years. Best years: 2004, 2003, 2001, 2000, 1999, 1998, 1997 1996, 1995, 1994, 1990, 1989, 1986, 1985.

Taste Notes The reds have herby, earthy raspberry fruit, while the aromatic sweet Muscats are the best whites.

LOIRE

The river Loire pours in a great arc across the centre of France, and to a visitor it seems to embrace much of what we all like to think of as the great romantic soul of the country – its history and architecture, its lush agriculture, and the natural French facility for an endless parade of different wines and different foods to match.

Just as the food in the Loire Valley swings from the heights of gastronomic fare to some of the best café eating and simple market produce in the whole of France, so the Loire wines span the great sweet wines of Anjou, the trendy, sharp, tasty wines of the upper reaches around Sancerre and Pouilly, the dry but piercing Cabernet Franc reds of Touraine. And always there's a great wash of everyday wine, red, white and rosé, from Muscadet, Anjou, Touraine and the numerous smaller vineyard areas along the river's length. Vin de Pays du Jardin de la France can come from anywhere in the Loire Valley. Altogether there are about a hundred different wines being made along the Loire's 1000-km (620-mile) course. But not a hundred different styles.

GRAPE VARIETIES

The grapes which predominate in the Loire Valley are not, on the whole, France's most versatile or winsome. Chenin Blanc, though it does (with lots of time) make some wonderful sweet wine, can be unrelentingly harsh in its normal dry state. Sauvignon Blanc is best at uncomplicated tangy dry styles, and the Muscadet grape prides itself on tasting of very lit-

tle indeed. In the reds we have got Cabernet Franc and Pinot Noir, but in the Loire both are almost beyond their northern limits of ripening properly. The same could be said of the heavily planted Gamay (the grape of Beaujolais), and the pale Groslot, both of which make a fair amount of dullish, tart red, and a lot more indeterminate, often sweetish rosé.

In all these, there are probably only six or seven truly different wine styles, so let's try to simplify the Loire Valley by slicing it broadly into four regions with definable styles, plus the great, long-lived (but undeservedly little known internationally) sweet whites.

WINE REGIONS

Three of the four regions do divide roughly into grape types. Certainly the Muscadet region or Pays Nantais at the mouth of the Loire around Nantes is completely dominated by the Muscadet grape.

Anjou-Saumur's white production is heavily slanted towards Chenin Blanc, and its red towards Gamay. Only small outcrops of Sauvignon and Chardonnay help to ameliorate Chenin's generally charmless white. Cabernet Franc is the quality red grape here, but is very much in a minority.

It is in Touraine that Sauvignon Blanc at last shares the spoils with Chenin and Cabernet slowly gets the better of Gamay, but it is not until we attain the upper reaches of the river around Sancerre that Sauvignon finally takes over from Chenin, and Pinot Noir takes up its endless battle to produce decent red.

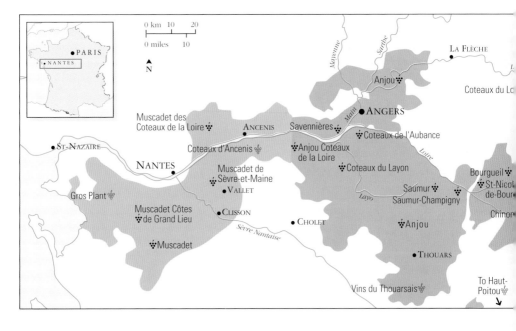

Then there are the sparkling wines. If the Loire is a region that can, in the warmest years and in the warmest spots, produce superbly rich sweet wines, it can also, in less favoured areas, produce large quantities of lean and acidic base wine perfect for fizz. Here this acidity is a positive advantage, and the sparkling wines of Saumur, Vouvray and Crémant de Loire can even age for a few years. All are made by the Champagne method.

The main difference between these wines and Champagne is that whereas barely ripe

Dominated by its fairytale castle overlooking the river, the town of Saumur is also the largest centre of wine production in the Loire Valley.

Chardonnay and Pinot Noir, as in Champagne, have a fairly light flavour, the main Loire grape, Chenin Blanc, has a more assertive character and is notoriously difficult to ripen. It needs careful handling if it is not to have an unripe, earthy character; and it doesn't age as elegantly as Chardonnay. But the best of these wines can be good value.

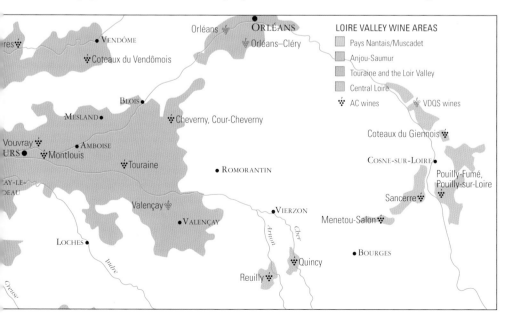

MUSCADET/PAYS NANTAIS

Muscadet isn't the most exciting of wines. It doesn't have flavours which burst and glitter in the glass and have you lunging for your thesaurus in search of a description. Sometimes it seems that all the racy upriver excitement is mirrored in Sancerre, while the heavy sluggish spread of muddy waters into the estuary past Nantes is epitomized by the dullness of most Muscadet.

Well, there is some truth in this, especially for the dumb, deadened commercial blends which, indeed, may well come from the slabby flatlands towards the river mouth. The true virtue of Muscadet is discovered in the Sèvre-et-Maine district further inland, and particular in the twisting, hilly vineyards around St-Fiacre and the more meadowy vineyards of Vallet. In the core of the Sèvre-et-Maine region, the best growers get to work to produce a wine which has managed to make a positive virtue out of its neutrality.

GRAPE VARIETIES AND WINE STYLES
There is only one grape, and its name is the Muscadet, alias Melon de Bourgogne. There used to be others, and at one time the region was even largely given over to black grapes, which can't have been very exciting. But Dutch traders, looking for a light white wine which they could then distil, persuaded growers to plant something simple and innocuous, and the grape they finally settled on was the Melon de Bourgogne, a vine long since kicked out of Burgundy as having no class and lowering the tone of the place.

Muscadet quickly earned itself a reputation as the perfect quaffing wine for all the local seafood, and it might have remained just a pleasant, bright, sharp local white, if the Beaujolais Nouveau drinkers in 1950s Paris hadn't decided they needed a bistro white, as well. The light, rather low-in-acid Muscadet was the perfect wine. Remarkably, it is this *lack* of flavour, this simple neutrality of style which has made Muscadet famous.

There are some serious growers, and domaine-bottled Muscadet can, while remaining fairly neutral, develop a peppery, even peachy fruit in the mouth. The best wines have *Mis(e) en bouteille sur lie* on the label. This means the wines have been bottled directly off their lees, which are the dead yeast cells left after fermentation; it sounds horrid, but they are tremendously important, since they add extra flavour, freshness and depth. The law has recently been tightened up, so any wine that claims to be *sur lie* should have been handled properly, and should be a fresher, fruitier wine. (Significantly, several important producers in the Midi has adopted *sur lie* bottling for some of their whites, to add a bit of freshness and texture.) The standard of non-*sur lie* Muscadet varies, however, from unexciting to poor.

Other wines of the Pays Nantais include the VDQS **Gros Plant**, a tart, harsh white that is, however, an effective thirst-quencher with rock-fresh seafood.

CLASSIFICATION

There are four appellations for Muscadet:
Muscadet The generic appellation. The wine is usually pretty basic and dull. Best producers: **Günther-Chéreau** and **Sauvion**.

Muscadet Coteaux de la Loire A small area. The wine is rarely seen, though quality can be fair. Best producers: **Roland Chevalier** and **Guindon**.

Muscadet Sèvre-et-Maine The biggest and best central area along the Maine and Sèvre rivers south of Nantes. Best producers: **Michel Bahuaud**, **Bossard**, **Chasseloir**, **l'Ecu**, **Günther-Chéreau**, **la Haute Févrie**, **Hautes Noëlles**, **l'Hyvernière**, **Luneau-Papin**, **Louis Métaireau**, **la Ragotière**, **Sauvion** and **la Touche**.

Muscadet Côtes de Grand Lieu A new appellation south-west of Nantes covering nearly half the area that used to make basic Muscadet. Quality is variable, but at least most of it is being bottled *sur lie*. Best producers: **Batard**, **Bel-Air** and **Herbauges**.

ORGANIZATION

Surprisingly, the co-operative movement has never gained sway in the Pays Nantais. This is the land of small, owner-run vineyards, often run in tandem with other crops. The merchants are very important, owning or controlling almost a third of the vineyards. Though their basic blends may be dull, the single-domaine wines are often good.

READING THE LABEL

The 'Sèvre-et-Maine' name is important, as is the *sur lie* tag. Buy estate-bottled wine, and look out for St-Fiacre and Vallet, two of the best villages. Single-domaine wines are almost always the best bet; some merchants, like Sauvion, have mobile bottling lines, to bottle *sur lie* at the grower's cellar.

WHAT DO THEY TASTE LIKE?

Simple, fresh, unquestionably dry, yet with little rasping acidity. A good Muscadet may taste slightly nutty, even honeyed, but never heavy – it is the only appellation in France to impose a maximum alcohol degree (12°).

THE GOOD YEARS

Always buy the most recent year. A few wines can age quite well, but don't count on it.

ENJOYING THE WINE

This wine makes a perfect complement to seafood. Offer me Champagne with my oysters,

Muscadet grapes in the press, soon to be turned into the perfect wine for oysters – providing it is made and bottled properly, and drunk young.

Chablis with my clams, and I'll spurn them all for a good Muscadet. This dry, neutral taste even copes with the seaweedy greenness of Breton oysters. It's dry and light and fits in easily as a cheapish white for most situations.

CONSUMER INFORMATION

WHAT DO I GET FOR MY MONEY?

Muscadet is no longer as cheap as it was, and one or two of the most prestigious wines are inexcusably expensive. The wine couldn't really be called good value, except if you're going to drink it with raw shellfish and actually need its neutrality.

AVAILABILITY

It's pretty well everywhere, especially basic Muscadet.

CONSUMER CHECKLIST

Muscadet de Sèvre-et-Maine	*Quality 6* ★
sur lie 2004	*Price 5* ★
(Dom. de l'Ecu)	*Value 6* ★

Good Years Muscadet is usually best drunk at only a year old.
Taste Notes This is basically a dry, fairly neutral white wine.

ANJOU

Anjou is most famous for its rosé. Most infamous, perhaps I should say, because rosé is a wine style which used to be held up as a gently fruity, vaguely sweet, all-purpose wine for those who were just dipping their toes into the wine-drinking lake. But the advent of an entirely new, modern, stainless-steel-and-white-overalls kind of wine-making in the last couple of decades has flung up numerous easy-drinking wines, and from numerous countries. The beginner doesn't need Anjou rosé any more, and the wine hasn't yet discovered a new identity for itself.

In red and white, too, Anjou is struggling to rid itself of a depressed downmarket image, while in sweet wines (see page 126) it has some of the most exciting and underrated wines in all France. It also makes sparkling wines around the town of Saumur, but here too it has been outpaced by the New World, which is producing rather better flavours.

GRAPE VARIETIES AND WINE STYLES

Though rosé still accounts for over half of Anjou's wine production, there are no fewer than 25 appellations in the region. **Anjou** whites are the most important but they're in a real quandary, due in part to the dominance of the Chenin grape. In a cold, frequently damp part of France, the last thing you want is a grape that needs heat to ripen and which, indeed, ripens so late that all other varieties are judged by the amount of time before the Chenin they ripen. Consequently, the general standing of the dry whites is poor but the grape has shown itself remarkably suitable to skin contact, a method which in the best wines brings out greengagey, full yet dry flavour and global warming means a generally improved climate. Chenin is often seen at its most cussed and mean-minded in Anjou Blanc, one of France's cheapest appellation wines, and often deserves no better in its sulphured, sour state. Yet it can deliver the goods. Best producers: **Mark Angeli**, **Fesles**, **Ogereau**, **Pierre-Bise**, **J Pithon**, **Richou** and **P-Y Tijou**.

Much better is the tiny appellation of **Savennières**, from estates like Nicolas Joly's **Clos de la Coulée-de-Serrant** and **Baumard**, **Clos de Closel**, **Epiré**, **Forges**, **Pierre-Bise** and **P-Y Tijou**. These Savennières producers make some of the steeliest, diamond-dry wines in the world; the eventual honeyed fullness of the wines still only glints coldly through the acidity after a dozen years of aging and more.

Growers in the lesser parts of Anjou are beginning to mix Sauvignon Blanc and, more importantly, Chardonnay with their Chenin Blanc to make better, fresh whites. The simplest Chenins of all come from the **Thouarsais** VDQS area, which also makes fresh Cabernet Franc reds, from **Coteaux du Loir**, which makes mainly red, mostly from Gamay, and from the Vin de Pays du **Maine-et-Loire**.

Rosé wines are mainly from the Gamay or Groslot grapes, although better, drier wines are made from Cabernet Franc and are labelled **Cabernet d'Anjou** or **Rosé de Loire**. Best producers: **Baranger**, **Hardières**, **Richou** and **Valliennes**.

Since rosé is a declining market, many growers now make red wine, much of it raw and Gamay-based, but some light and sharply fruited Cabernet reds from producers like **Brizé**, **Fesles** and **Richou** are very enjoyable under the **Anjou Rouge** label. As with Chenin, modern vinification methods are drawing out exciting, unthought-of fruit flavours from both these grapes and the best villages can use the superior Anjou-Villages appellation. **Saumur-**

These vines at Quarts-de-Chaume in the Layon Valley will, come the late autumn, be heavy with brown, shrivelled grapes to make great sweet wine.

Champigny is the best of these Cabernet appellations, particularly from **Clos Rougeard**, **Filliatreau**, **Hureau**, **Legrand**, **Nerleux**, **la Perruche**, **Roches Neuves** and **Villeneuve**. The **Coteaux du Vendômois** also makes light reds and rosés, and a little dry white.

The sparkling wines are Chenin-based but unless softened by Chardonnay, or the red Cabernet Franc, they can be a little fierce. The most carefully made wines can use the appellation **Crémant de Loire**, which requires more restricted yields from the vineyards, gentler pressing and a longer aging period. Wines from **Baumard**, **Berger**, **Bouvet-Ladubay**, **Brizé**, **Fardeau**, **Gratien et Meyer**, **Grenelle**, **Langlois-Château**, **Michaud**, **la Paleine**, **la Perruche** and the **St-Cyr-en-Bourg** co-operative can be quite stylish.

CLASSIFICATION
The most general appellation is Anjou, with the best villages being entitled to use Anjou-Villages for their red wines. Inside the small Savennières appellation there are two even tinier ones, Savennières-Coulée-de-Serrant and Savennières-La Roche-au-Moines.

ORGANIZATION
The large merchants are the most important influence and it is well worth searching out for growers' own wines. Co-operatives like the one at St-Cyr-en-Bourg are also important.

READING THE LABEL
The term 'Vieilles Vignes' does generally mean higher quality wines with more depth, made from older-than-average vines. Among sparkling wines, 'Brut' means very dry, and 'Sec' means medium-dry.

WHAT DO THEY TASTE LIKE?
These are real cool-climate tastes, with the most obvious flavour being acidity. Reds are light and grassy. Rosés, in general, are sulphurous and stickily sweetish but at their best they are relatively dry, very bright, with a blueish cast to their pale pink colour, and a refreshing tang. The best dry whites can have a delicious, refreshing and highly individual flavour of angelica, greengage plums, apple and orchard leaves, sometimes tempered with a mineral glint and, in maturity, quince.

THE GOOD YEARS
Vintages are crucial in Anjou. Without a fair amount of sun, the red grapes won't ripen, and Chenin needs warmth, too. Reds from a warm vintage can age for a few years. **2004** excellent year for reds; **2003** atypical year produced powerful reds; **2002** was an excellent red wine vintage; **2001** enjoyed a dry vintage and the reds did well; **2000**, a difficult year, turned out some good reds; **1999** was good but not outstanding; **1998** provided decent red wines but less reliable whites; the three vintages of **1997**, **1996** and **1995** all made high-quality wines.

ENJOYING THE WINES
These are very much wines to go with food. The good whites go well with the local river fish, as can the reds, chilled down.

CONSUMER INFORMATION

WHAT DO I GET FOR MY MONEY?
Most Rosé d'Anjou is overpriced at any price. But Saumur-Champigny in a good year is unusual and decent value, and Savennières, being unfashionable, is well worth it if you're prepared to age it a while. Anjou sparkling wine is reasonable value if you like the flavour.

AVAILABILITY
Rosé d'Anjou is widely available, but the interesting wines from Anjou are in short supply. It's worth going to a specialist.

CONSUMER CHECKLIST
Saumur-Champigny Vieilles Vignes 2002 (Filliatreau)

Quality 8 ★
Price 8 ★
Value 9 ★

Good Years Warm years are best: 2004, 2003, 2002, 2001, 2000, 1997, 1996, 1995.

Taste Notes Even if Anjou rosés rarely tempt a wine writer to expand his vocabulary, the steely, stark flavours of the best Anjou whites, with their remarkable ability to soften in maturity, can be tantalizingly good and the top reds from warm vintages in Saumur and the best Anjou-Villages wines mix fresh earthiness with raspberry and blackcurrant – and they can age!

TOURAINE

The high and mighty of France have always seen Touraine as their personal, private vacation spot, and this central swathe of the Loire Valley is dotted with many of France's greatest and most breathtaking castles. But it wasn't just the landscape which has lured them here over the centuries.

The climate is one of the mildest and softest in the country, and the gentle hills and valleys produce some of the best fruit and vegetables, the rivers teem with fish, and the large forests used to be congested with game. So, of course, there is wine here too, but these are not regal wines to match the castles and their history. Rather, Touraine wines are a good example of wine primarily blending with the local food. Although often similar to Anjou's offerings, Touraine wines are just that bit riper, that much more fruity – and there is another crucial difference. We see less of the rather tricky, charmless Chenin Blanc and Gamay grapes, and a good deal more of the finer Sauvignon Blanc and Cabernet Franc.

There are famous wine names here, such as Vouvray and Chinon, but in general the pleasure of Touraine is the abundance of fresh, straight red and wine wine with few pretensions to elegance, and there's even a little rosé, dry and sappy, to keep the balance.

GRAPE VARIETIES AND WINE STYLES

The dominant white grapes are the Sauvignon Blanc and (still) the Chenin Blanc, with – encouragingly – a little Chardonnay as well. Chenin is used in the wines of **Vouvray** and **Montlouis**, ranging in style from bone-dry to full and sweet, to sparkling (one of France's best fizzes). Best producers: (Vouvray) **Aubuisières, Bourillon-Dorléans, Champalou, Clos Naudin, la Fontainerie, Gaudrelle, Gautier, Haute Borne, Huet, Pichon, F Pinon, Taille aux Loups** and **Vigneau Chevreau**; (Montlouis) **Chatenay, Chidaine, Delétang, Levasseur, des Liards** and **Taille aux Loups**. In the tiny appellation of **Jasnières**, the wine is stark and bone-dry, particularly from **Bellivière** and **Gigou**.

Sauvignon Blanc, while lacking a single famous wine name to lean on, produces delicious, grassy-green wine right across Touraine under the **Sauvignon de Touraine** appellation, and frequently behaves like a Sancerre wine, without having the gall to ask a Sancerre price. Some of the best Sancerre substitutes come from **l'Aulée, Beauséjour, la Charmoise, Chenonceau, Corbillières,**

Joël Delaunay, Michaud, Octavie, Oisly-et-Thésée co-operative, **Pibaleau, Pré Baron, Preys, Roche Blanche** and **Vignobles des Bois Vaudon**.

The Sauvignon from the **Haut-Poitou** VDQS can fulfill this function, too, at a still lower price. The local **Haut-Poitou** co-operative is the main producer, and also makes good tangy Chardonnay, a rather ritzy Champagne-method sparkler and some good red Gamay. White **Cheverny** (AC) is also good, especially when made from Chardonnay. Cour-Cheverny is a bone-dry white made from Romorantin (there's some red, rosé and sparkling as well).

The best Touraine reds are based primarily on Cabernet Franc, and found near the Anjou border in **Chinon** and **Bourgueil**. They are usually quite light, but can have a piercing blackcurrant fruitiness, sharp and thirst-quenching, which especially in Chinon can age remarkably well, and end up resembling Bordeaux. Others have a fruit more like raspberry and a cool, earthy quality halfway between chalk and dust. Best producers: (Chinon) **P Alliet, l'Aulée, B Baudry, J & C Baudry, P Breton, Coulaine, Couly-Dutheil, Druet, la Grille, Joguet, la Perrière, Olga Raffault, Raifault, Roncée** and **Sourdais**; (Bourgueil) **l'Abbaye, Y Amirault, T Boucard, P Breton, la Butte, Pierre-Jacques Druet, des Forges, Lamé-Delisle-Boucard, la Lande/Delaunay, Nau Frères, Ouches** and **des Raguenières**; (the tiny enclave of St-Nicolas-de-Bourgueil) **Y Amirault, Clos des Quarterons, Cognard-Taluau, F Mabileau, J-C Mabileau, J Taluau** and **Vallée**.

Elsewhere in Touraine there is still a lot of Gamay, and the best is earthy but as fruity as Beaujolais. Touraine rosés are often dry and good and the sparkling wine companies of Vouvray, Montlouis and straight Touraine lap up the unwanted acid Chenin grapes and transform them into good sharp fizz. There is some attractive Vin de Pays from the **Loir-et-Cher** and **Indre-et-Loire** departments.

CLASSIFICATION

Touraine, like Anjou, is riddled with small appellations, like Touraine Amboise and Touraine-Mesland – both good for reds; and Touraine Azay-le-Rideau – good for whites and rosés. The most general regional appellations, like Sauvignon de Touraine or Touraine Mousseux, are pretty reliable.

ORGANIZATION

The merchants are important in Touraine, particularly in Vouvray. In Chinon and Bourgueil it is easier to find wines from single growers, and these are likely to be the best wines. Co-operatives exist here, and the one at **Oisly-et-Thésée** is one of the best in France.

READING THE LABEL

On Touraine reds, check for the grape variety – Cabernet will usually be better than Gamay. Look out also for the term 'Vieilles Vignes'. It isn't legally defined, but wine made from old vines will have more depth and concentration. It's often the sign of a serious grower, too. For white wines and sparklers check to see whether the label has the words 'Sec' (vaguely dry), 'Demi-Sec' (vaguely semi-sweet) or 'Moelleux' (sweet).

WHAT DO THEY TASTE LIKE?

Most Touraine wines are certainly tart and green, but they also have a lot of fruit. The acidity is an advantage – making the wines thirst-quenching rather than gum-searing. Most of the Vouvray we see is mediocre – sadly, since the appellation can produce some of the finest Chenin Blanc. The sparkling wines often have more fruit than those of Saumur. The reds from Chinon and Bourgueil have lovely, earthy, raspberry fruit.

THE GOOD YEARS

Touraine can produce pleasant Sauvignon almost every year. In general, drink the reds and whites within two years, though top reds age well. But top sweet Vouvray will age for decades, especially from a warm vintage, otherwise the fizz-makers have to take the strain. **2004** an excellent year; **2003** was an atypical year producing powerful reds; **2002** was an excellent red wine vintage; **2001** enjoyed a dry vintage and the reds did well; **2000** was not a good year; **1999** was troubled by September rains but quality was better than average; **1998** produced better red wines than white; **1997** and **1996** were very good; **1995** was the best year since 1990, especially for reds and sweet Vouvray.

ENJOYING THE WINES

The otherwise adaptable Touraine whites actually have too much fruit to be ideal with seafood. Touraine Sauvignon is excellent with fish, though, and goat's cheese, of which the Loire happily produces large quantities. The reds, often best slightly chilled, go well with the local fish, and from a good ripe year also with game. Drink the fizz at any time.

CONSUMER INFORMATION

WHAT DO I GET FOR MY MONEY?

In general the wines are fairly inexpensive, though they are not the Loire's cheapest. Touraine Sauvignon is particularly good value, given the price of Sancerre. Haut-Poitou wines are still a bargain.

AVAILABILITY

Good, but not brilliant. There is much mediocre Vouvray around, and little of the best. Touraine Sauvignon is gradually and deservedly becoming better known.

CONSUMER CHECKLIST

Chinon 2003   *Quality* 7 ★
(J-M Raffault)   *Price* 7 ★
       Value 7 ★

Good Years Good Vouvray can improve for decades and the Chinon and Bourgueil reds age well in warm vintages. Best years: 2004, 2003, 2002, 2001, 1999, 1997, 1996, 1995, 1993, 1990, 1989, 1988, 1985, 1983, 1978, 1976, 1975, 1970.
Taste Notes Touraine Sauvignon is a tangy, green-tasting wine, and refreshing when very young. Vouvray ranges from bone dry to sweet, flecked with angelica and honey. The reds mix raspberry and dry, summer earth in an enticing manner.

CENTRAL & UPPER LOIRE

Some areas seem to have all the luck. In many parts of France, generation after generation of grape growers slave away, painstakingly building a reputation on an endless round of labour and dedication. In others, no reputation is sought, none is won, and the grapes are lovelessly grown and anonymously sold to the handiest bidder. And then there's the little enclave of vineyards south of Orléans in the central and upper reaches of the Loire, centred on one of the wine world's most famous names – Sancerre. Sancerre has the golden touch – in red, white and rosé – and there can be few regions in the whole of France where making a living out of wine has been easier.

GRAPE VARIETIES AND WINE STYLES
Less than 50 years ago, the villages of **Sancerre**, **Menetou-Salon**, **Reuilly**, **Quincy** and **Pouilly** were largely unknown. The vineyards were in decline and patchily planted on the hill of Sancerre and in the ragged fields spreading out east and west from the Loire. A fair amount of dull white wine and a surprising amount of rather thin red and rosé were made. And just a little of one of the sharpest, freshest, most startlingly dry white wines in France, indeed, at the time, in the world.

It was these few top Sauvignon Blanc wines that were taken up by fashionable Parisian circles in the 1960s. The neighbouring villages, in particular Pouilly, were quick to follow suit, hotfooting it up the N7 to the capital. By the late 1970s, the region's run of luck was still on course as its rosés and its reds were seized upon by the exponents of *nouvelle cuisine*; for a time you could hardly find a wine waiter in Paris who wouldn't recommend red Sancerre with the fish. It's a fad which has made a lot of the area's growers wealthy. Yet it's a dangerous fad, hyping red and rosé wines which are at best only quite attractive. And the whites? They became the prototype for a whole generation of winemakers, desperate to achieve lightness and zingy, thirst-quenching fruit in their white wines. They have influenced the renaissance of Bordeaux Blanc Sec and have been the model for good crisp Sauvignons from Chile, South Africa, Spain, Italy and, most important, from New Zealand.

The New Zealand flavour isn't the same as the Sancerre flavour – it's tangier, more gooseberryish – but it is more reliable. Sancerre these days is not only very expensive for what is basically a fairly simple wine, but if you go to the wrong producer you may get infuriatingly flat, flabby flavours. Best producers: **F & J Bailly**, **Balland-Chapuis**, **H Bourgeois**, **H Brochard**, **R Champault**, **F Cotat**, **L Crochet**, **Delaporte**, **Gitton**, **P Jolivet**, **S Lalou**, **A Mellot**, **J Mellot**, **P Millérioux**, **H Natter**, **A & F Neveu**, **V Pinard**, **P & N Reverdy**, **J Reverdy**, **Reverdy-Ducroux**, **J-M Roger**, **Vacheron** and **André Vatan**.

The other whites are generally made from Sauvignon, though **Pouilly-sur-Loire** uses the dull Chasselas grape, which makes good eating but not memorable drinking. The wines are lightest and most fragrant in Menetou-Salon (best producers: **de Chatenoy**, **Chavet**, **J-P Gilbert**, **Pellé**, **J-M Roger**, **Teiller** and **Tour St-Martin**) and in Reuilly (best producer: **Beurdin**); most brilliantly balanced between sharpness and ripe, round body in Sancerre and Pouilly-Fumé (best producers: **Berthiers**, **G Blanchet**, **H Bourgeois**, **A Cailbourdin**, **J-C Chatelain**, **Didier Dagueneau**, **Serge Dagueneau**, **M Deschamps**, **Ladoucette**, **Landrat-Guyollot**, **Masson-Blondelet**, **M Redde**, **Tinel-Blondelet** and **Tracy**), and most assertive in Quincy (best producer: **Rouzé**). The **Coteaux du Giennois** produces cheaper lookalikes.

Further upriver, **St-Pourçain-sur-Sioule** (VDQS) makes sharp, rustic whites from the local Tressallier grape, as well as some rosé and light red, and near Orléans there is some good VDQS **Orléans** (red and rosé from Pinot Meunier and Pinot Noir and tiny amounts of white from Chardonnay) and **Orléans-Cléry** (Cabernet Franc reds). Going further upriver to the Upper Loire, mainly light reds and rosés are produced from Gamay. A new wave of producers in the **Côte Roannaise** and **Côtes du Forez** ACs and the **Côtes d'Auvergne** VDQS are on a quality drive.

A fairytale castle in a region of castles: Château du Nozet, near Pouilly. Like most vineyards here, these ones are planted with Sauvignon Blanc.

CLASSIFICATION

The vineyard sites are not classified but some, such as Sancerre's Clos du Chêne Marchand or Monts Damnés, and Pouilly's Les Loges or Les Berthiers, are definitely superior.

ORGANIZATION

Most of the wine comes straight from the growers but there are some merchants making decent wine. The co-operatives are only of middling quality.

READING THE LABEL

The most important thing to look for as a mark of authenticity is *Mis(e) en bouteille au domaine* or domaine-bottled.

WHAT DO THEY TASTE LIKE?

The best reds can display a bit of strawberry-ish Pinot fruit plus some soft oak. The white wines range in flavours from asparagus, through gooseberries, to nettles and newly cut grass. In the best wines all these flavours mingle, and there can even be a slight whiff of roasted coffee. Pouilly-Fumé is said to smell of gunflint, though only the best does. What you don't want is any smell of sulphur, or anything meaty or flabby and this is, at the moment, all too common. Sancerre and Pouilly wines live by their freshness.

THE GOOD YEARS

The whites are not at their best in the hottest years, although the reds need warmth. None of these wines really improve with keeping. **2004** saw tricky, uneven weather but the top producers made good wines; **2003** was the year of the heatwave so stick to top producers; **2002** was excellent across the board; **2001** was a challenging year for Sancerre and Pouilly Fumé; **2000** saw rigorous producers making some good wines.

ENJOYING THE WINES

The whites have the bite and sharpness to accompany quite rich fish dishes, yet can cope with foods such as seafood and vegetable crudités, both of which make many wines taste sour. They also go well with the local goat's cheese and, with their strong, gooseberry-fresh taste, make good thirst-quenching apéritifs. The rosés are best as apéritifs or as picnic wines, and the reds are very rarely big enough to accompany anything except fairly light meat dishes.

CONSUMER INFORMATION

WHAT DO I GET FOR MY MONEY?

Nearly all the Sauvignons from this part of the Loire Valley are expensive, and it's worth looking at alternatives like Coteaux du Giennois, which have similar flavours though not quite the style. The reds and rosés rarely have much character and are usually overpriced for what they are.

AVAILABILITY

Although the vineyard area is not enormous, the distribution of white Sancerre and Pouilly-Fumé is good. Virtually all outlets will have at least one example. Reuilly, Menetou-Salon and Quincy are rarer but worth seeking out.

CONSUMER CHECKLIST

Sancerre 2004	Quality 8 ★
Croix du Roy	Price 8 ★
(Crochet)	Value 7 ★

Good Years The wines are best drunk young, but occasionally whites are made which develop an intense gooseberry fruit with a few years of aging.

Taste Notes Sancerre and Pouilly should be reasonably full, as well as having a very grassy, even blackcurrant or gooseberry (or even asparagus) green bite which is mouth-tingling and quite delicious.

SWEET LOIRE WINES

Anjou has a secret. It makes some of the greatest sweet wines in the world. Why is it a secret? Quite simply, because nobody seems to want to know. There the growers are, in their little river valleys of the Layon and the Aubance, toiling away at one of the riskiest, most expensive and exhausting challenges the world of wine possesses – the production of naturally sweet, noble rot-affected sweet wines, continuing picking late into November, doing several trips round the foggy, chilly vineyard slopes to pluck the last ounce of overripeness from their grapes, and at every harvest time risking autumn storms, and the destruction of their crop. They're probably so whacked by this commitment that they haven't got the energy left to shout.

Well, in that case I'd better shout. Quarts de Chaume and Bonnezeaux make two of the world's finest sweet wines; they're succulent and rare, yet the price most of them command is still not high. The boom that has swept Sauternes to profitability has yet to affect the Loire to the same extent, although during the 1990s the Loire made some of the best sweet wines for a generation. If it weren't for many vineyard owners having other incomes, and all of them being afflicted by this marvellous mad passion to create great sweet wine, it's difficult to see how most of them could survive. So not only should we buy these classics, but we should willingly pay a proper price for them, or else they will quite simply go out of business and go back to planting pear trees.

GRAPE VARIETIES AND WINE STYLES
Chenin Blanc is the main sweet wine grape, apart from Pinot Gris in **Coteaux d'Ancenis**, a VDQS from Muscadet country near the mouth of the Loire. Here the Pinot Gris, or Malvoisie (unaffected by botrytis) produces gentle, sweet white which performs happily as an apéritif (best producer: **Guindon**).

Chenin Blanc is a rasping, harsh grape, which makes some of France's least charming whites, yet finds its vocation in the pursuit of great sweet wine. In the damp, warm valley vineyards, as the autumn draws in, it is likely to be affected by *pourriture noble*, or noble rot, a fungus which, when it attacks healthy, ripe white grapes, thins the skins, sucks the water out and leaves the sugar. (On unripe grapes it has altogether less satisfactory effects, and merely destroys the crop.) The Layon Valley and the more northerly appellation of **Jasnières** (best producer: **Gigou/la Charrière**) on the Loir river are among the few places in the Loire Valley where noble rot appears naturally.

The styles of wine produced range widely – there are the pleasantly fresh, vaguely sweet, fruity wines of much **Coteaux du Layon** (best producers: **P Aquilas, Baudouin, Baumard, Bergerie, Bidet, Breuil, Cady, Delesvaux, Forges, Guimonière, Ogereau, Passavent, Pierre-Bise, J Pithon, Joseph Renou, Roulerie, Sablonettes, Sauveroy, Soucherie, Yves Soulez** and **Touche Noire**); and **Coteaux de l'Aubance** (best producers: **Daviau/Bablut, Deux Moulins, Haute-Perche, Jean-Yves Lebreton, Montgilet/V Lebreton** and **Richou**). The wines of **Vouvray** are more concentrated, though rarely as luscious (best producers: **Domaine des Aubuisières, Bourillon-Dorléans, Champalou, Clos Naudin, la Fontainerie, Gaudrelle, Gautier, Haute Borne, Huet, Pichot, Pinon, Taille aux Loups** and **Vigneau Chevreau**); with **Montlouis** trailing a little way behind (best producers: **Chatenay, Chidaine, Delétang, Levasseur, des Liards** and **Taille aux Loups**). The gorgeous peachy, quince-rich wines of **Quarts de Chaume** (best producers: **Baumard, Bellerive, Lafourcade, Pierre-Bise, J Pithon, Plaisance, Joseph Renou** and **Suronde**) and **Bonnezeaux** (best producers: **Mark Angeli/Sansonnière, Fesles, Godineau, des Grandes Vignes, Petit Val, Petits Quarts, René Renou, Terrebrune** and **la Varière**), with their perfect mesoclimates for noble-rotten sweet wines, are some of the greatest sweet wines of France. Yet, through all these different wines, Chenin's fierce balancing acidity is never lost.

CLASSIFICATION
There is no Grand Cru system here. However, there are six communes that can sell their wine as Coteaux du Layon-Villages, or add their name to that of Coteaux du Layon.

ORGANIZATION
Making sweet wine demands rare dedication and the majority of the best wine comes from single growers.

READING THE LABEL
With Quarts de Chaume or Bonnezeaux on the label you should get as sweet a wine as the vintage has allowed. Elsewhere the least

sweet wines are sold as 'Demi-sec', the next sweetest as 'Moelleux' and the sweetest of all as 'Liquoreux'.

WHAT DO THEY TASTE LIKE?

Sweet Chenin wines develop their flavours slowly. Because the acidity is so high, even the sweetest great wines don't always taste that sweet when young. (Sauternes has an advantage here, since even young Sauternes is unmistakeably luscious.) Coteaux du Layon and Coteaux de l'Aubance are usually crisp-apple sweet rather than tremendously rich. Great Quarts de Chaumes and Bonnezeaux need ten to 15 years to show their flavours, which then become intensely peachy and apricotty, but never cloying. Their high acidity and slight bitter twist make them some of the most refreshing of all sweet wines. Sweet Vouvray is less luscious but still enjoyable.

THE GOOD YEARS

Vintages are very important. Most years can produce something vaguely sweet, and in less good years ordinary Layon and Aubance wines should simply be drunk fresh and young without too many questions asked.

2004 Perfectly poised sweet whites.

2003 The year of the heatwave produced some excellent sweet whites.

2002 The best vintage since 1997 with good botrytis.

2001 Variable conditions for sweet whites but there are some good wines.

2000 Not a good year for sweet whites.

1999 A small crop but good quality.

1998 A disappointing vintage.

1997 A long, late summer produced some spectacular wines.

1996 Another very good year.

1995 A hot summer and fine autumn meant exciting sweet Anjou and Vouvray.

Older vintages

1990, 1989, 1988, 1985, 1983, 1982, 1976, 1971, 1959, 1949, 1947, 1921.

ENJOYING THE WINES

The lighter wines can be delicious as aperitifs, but will also match certain river fish and chicken dishes, particularly spicy oriental ones. Even the sweetest wines are marvellous with fresh fruit, foie gras or blue cheese, but will be good on their own too. They will also match most puddings, particularly fruit ones and are superb with those made with slightly tart fruit.

CONSUMER INFORMATION

WHAT DO I GET FOR MY MONEY?

Good value. Even these days (and prices have risen) you can still find remarkable bargains. The sweetest wines are the most expensive – but it might still be possible to find some affordable 1997 Coteaux du Layon which will give you an idea of the styles of the other rarer wines.

AVAILABILITY

Very poor. Not only is there not a great deal made, but it's so unfashionable that most outlets simply don't bother stocking any.

CONSUMER CHECKLIST

Bonnezeaux 1997   *Quality 10* ★
(Château de Fesles)   *Price 9* ★
     Value 10 ★

Good Years Sweet Loire wines need a long time to show their best. They are usually at their peak between 15 and 30 years old, though simple Coteaux d'Ancenis is best drunk young. Best years: 2004, 2003, 2001, 1999, 1997, 1996, 1995, 1990, 1989, 1988.

Taste Notes Succulent wines, with a lovely perfume of peaches. The acidity of the Chenin stops them from being cloying.

ALSACE

W hen you go to Alsace, you may think yourself in an eater's and drinker's paradise. The food is wonderful, and everywhere you turn there are vineyards and winemakers offering their wares. The local fare includes such great dishes as *choucroute alsacienne*, the well-bred glutton's favourite meal, as well as *pâté de foie gras, truite au bleu, tarte à l'oignon, coq au Riesling*, various kinds of mountain game, and the redoubtable, terrifying Munster cheese. There's only one problem. These dishes cry out for a good burly red wine, or an intense, lingering, fragrant one – and Alsace, despite all its success with the white wines, can't produce full-bodied reds.

When I've been in Alsace I've actually found myself dreaming of reds above almost anything else – rich, gamy Burgundies and minty, blackcurranty Cabernets – but only dreaming, because this is white wine country. Alsace is too far north to give anything more than a nod towards decent red; its red is pale, though pleasant enough, from Pinot Noir. Thankfully, Alsace whites are some of the most adaptable the world offers.

The Alsace wine region is a long strip of land centred south-west of Strasbourg around the town of Colmar, creeping up into the foothills of the Vosges mountains to the west, and stretching out across the prosperous plain

The vineyard of Schlossberg, beyond the village of Kaysersberg, was the first in Alsace to be classified as Grand Cru. There are now 50 Grands Crus.

to the river Rhine and the border with Germany in the east. Its history has always been confused, and never more so than since 1870, when it was annexed by Germany. World War One surged and ebbed relentlessly across the region, but in 1918 Alsace became French again – for a mere 22 years. World War Two saw Alsace returned to the thick of the fighting, her vineyards churned into muddy wastelands and many of her most beautiful towns and villages razed to the ground.

Looking back now, however, the mixture of German and French influences has created a remarkable people, mixing warmth and good humour with hard work and dedication. They are proud, too, and the towns which were destroyed have been rebuilt in something resembling their ancient manner. The towns that survived the war are so awash with narrow cobbled streets, high, overhanging gabled houses and Romanesque or Gothic churches that they allow a rare glimpse of history still being put to work today, because these little towns and villages are now as dependent for their living upon wine and its mysteries as they have ever been.

GRAPE VARIETIES AND WINE STYLES

The image of Alsace is of fresh, briskly attractive white wines, balanced between the fruity fragrance of the German wine styles, and the commitment to dryness of the French mainstream. In general these are some of the most trustworthy wines to be found in a restaurant or wine shop, though this overall reliability is sometimes at the expense of the brilliant, dangerous tastes which often mark out the truly great wines. Above all, the image is of quality and adaptability.

The white wines range from the light, frothy-fresh and almost neutral wines from **Chasselas** and **Pinot Blanc**, through the remarkable austere steeliness of **Riesling**, to the musky delights of **Pinot Gris** and **Gewürztraminer**. And if you think that all sounds like a curious blend of French and German grape varieties – you're right, it is.

Alsace wines are mostly made from single grape varieties and more details of the individual wines will be found below (see page 131). The exception, apart from **Edelzwicker** and some blends that have their own Cuvée names, are the sparkling wines, called Crémant d'Alsace. These are mostly made from **Pinot Blanc**, usually with additions of the other fairly neutral grapes like **Sylvaner** or **Chasselas**.

CLASSIFICATION

The appellation for the whole region is simply 'Alsace' and is normally used with a grape variety, such as 'Alsace Riesling'. Except for Edelzwicker, a blend, and Crémant d'Alsace, the local Champagne-method fizz, all the wines are from a single grape.

There are now 50 classified vineyard sites which are allowed to call themselves 'Grand Cru' or 'Great Growth'. Most of these are historically excellent, and deserve their promotion; but local politics has inevitably had its way and boundaries were not always drawn quite as severely as they might have been. Some sites that were simply not up to scratch were also given undeserved promotion. The Grands Crus currently represent only 4 per cent of total Alsace wine production and some growers prefer to use the Cuvée names they have always used in the past for particular wines, even if they come from Grand Cru vineyards. Another reason is that not all growers with vines in Grand Cru sites want to reduce their yield to the 55 hl/ha, the current Grand Cru limit.

This Grand Cru yield is itself controversial. Even this latest reduction is still too high if the full potential of the wines is to be realized,

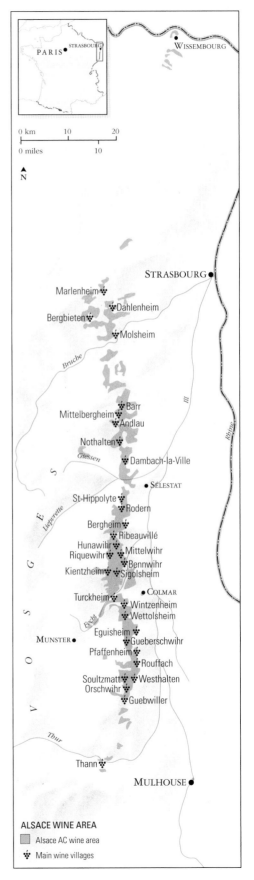

0 km   10   20
0 miles   10

N

WISSEMBOURG

PARIS · STRASBOURG

STRASBOURG ·

Marlenheim ❦
Bergbieten ❦   ❦ Dahlenheim
❦ Molsheim

Bruche

❦ Barr
Mittelbergheim ❦
❦ Andlau
Nothalten ❦
Giessen   ❦ Dambach-la-Ville

Ill

· SÉLESTAT

St-Hippolyte ❦
❦ Rodern
Bergheim ❦
❦ Ribeauvillé
Hunawihr ❦ ❦ Mittelwihr
Riquewihr ❦
❦ Bennwihr
Kientzheim ❦ ❦ Sigolsheim

· COLMAR
Turckheim ❦
❦ Wintzenheim
❦ Wettolsheim
Fecht
Eguisheim ❦
MUNSTER ·   ❦ Gueberschwihr
Pfaffenheim ❦
❦ Rouffach
Soultzmatt ❦ ❦ Westhalten
Orschwihr ❦
❦ Guebwiller

Thur

Thann ❦

MULHOUSE ·

Liepvrette

V O S G E S

Rhine

ALSACE WINE AREA
▢ Alsace AC wine area
❦ Main wine villages

and they are to show the character of the vineyard and the soil – which are the reasons why the Grand Cru sites were considered superior in the first place. But at least it's lower than the basic Alsace yield. This, at a massive 80 hl/ha, is the highest of any appellation in France. The best producers, though, will use lower yields, especially for their better Cuvées.

Only unblended wines from Riesling, Pinot Gris, Gewürztraminer and Muscat, considered Alsace's finest varieties, may have the Grand Cru designation. However, new regulations say that grape names are not needed on Grand Cru wines and this flexibility might lead to blending becoming legal. Some Grand Cru sites have traditionally been excellent for Sylvaner. One of these, the Zotzenberg, is now allowed the Grand Cru designation for Sylvaner and others may follow.

Many producers distinguish their various Cuvées (of which they may make several) with terms like Réserve, Réserve Exceptionelle and Cuvée Exceptionelle. These have no legal definition, so one producer's Réserve is another's Exceptionelle, and perhaps another's basic Alsace. Piling on the superlatives on the label doesn't really help anybody to understand what's going on.

What is easier to grasp is the sweetness definitions. Alsace wine is basically dry (although there seems to have been some sweetening up by quite a few producers), but autumns can be long and warm, and sometimes noble rot swoops on the ripe grapes, concentrating their sweetness in just the same way that it does in Sauternes or the Loire. Wines from late-picked grapes – which will be sweet, but not massively so – are called Vendange Tardive; those from nobly rotten grapes are called Sélection des Grains Nobles. These are the sweetest of all, equivalent to a German Beerenauslese, though seldom with German levels of acidity. From the 2004 vintage to help the consumer all Alsace medium-dry or sweeter wines are labelled *moelleux*.

With a run of good vintages from 1988, especially with 1989, 1990, l994, l995, l996, 1997, 1998, 2000 and 2002 producing ideal late-season conditions to make both Vendange Tardive and Sélection de Grains Nobles, these types of rich to unctuous special Cuvées have achieved something of a cult status. Prices have soared and collectors have scrambled for allocations of the top wines. There is no doubt that some remarkable wines have been made, especially where the grapes were affected by noble rot, but it is difficult to know just how good they are,

Many Alsace villages resemble an operetta stage set: not only are buildings half-timbered, but the timbers are carved and the wrought-iron signs painted.

because one of the characteristics of both Pinot Gris and Gewürztraminer when massively overripened and noble-rotted is that the astonishing perfume and fruit intensity that usually marks out these varieties is stunned by the sweetness. Most of the top wines need ten years' aging to show their hopefully thrilling personalities.

The Champagne-method fizz has its own appellation, Crémant d'Alsace which is reasonable quality if not great value for money. Best producers: **Paul Blanck, Dopff & Irion, Dopff au Moulin, J Gross, Ostertag, P Sparr, A Stoffel** and the **Pfaffenheim** and **Turckheim** co-operatives.

ORGANIZATION
The co-operatives are very important and their wines are of good quality. However, the finest quality will come from the growers or from the best merchants. Wines from the merchants' own vineyards will almost always be of higher quality than their blends.

READING THE LABEL
Most Alsace labels are simple to read, and will usually say Alsace or Vin d'Alsace, followed by the name of the grape, the merchant or grower and the vintage. Some wines will also show a vineyard or a Cuvée name.

WHAT DO THEY TASTE LIKE?

Most of these wines have a slightly spicy smell, rising to very spicy in some varieties. They are nearly always dry, although they have a roundness to them which may disguise the fact. In the very hottest years even the dry wines may have an edge of sweetness to them.

Edelzwicker This is the name given to blends of Alsace's less interesting grape varieties, in particular Chasselas, Sylvaner and Pinot Blanc. Usually it is fresh and nothing more than an everyday slurping wine. Just occasionally it is spicy, and then it is much more interesting.

Sylvaner Light, slightly tart and slightly earthy. It sometimes achieves rather more class than this, but can taste a bit empty and one-dimensional. If you leave it too long, it begins to taste of tomatoes. Best producers: **Hugel, Ostertag, Kientzler, Marc Kreydenweiss, R Muré, Rolly Gassmann, Schaetzel, Schoffit**, the **Turckheim** co-operative, **Weinbach** and **Zind-Humbrecht**.

Pinot Blanc This has taken over from Sylvaner as the basic grape for Alsace's bright and breezy young whites. It's a much better grape, giving clean, rather appley wine – light, quite acid, sometimes with an attractive whiff of honey. Best producers: **J B Adam, P Blanck, Marcel Deiss, Hugel, Charles Koehly, Marc Kreydenweiss, Albert Mann, Ostertag, Rolly Gassmann, Schlumberger, Martin Spielmann, Trimbach**, the **Turckheim** co-operative and **Zind-Humbrecht**.

Riesling This is the grape that produces the great juicy-sweet wines of Germany. In Alsace it is usually startlingly dry – as austere and steely as any wine in France. Indeed it is particularly unfruity here but, for such a dry wine, it is often quite full-bodied to balance the starkly green, lemony acidity. In the best ones there is some honey to give this very dry wine a strangely rich flavour. As it ages it goes petrolly, a taste which is surprisingly delicious. Best producers: **Jean Becker, Beyer, Paul Blanck, Marcel Deiss, Dirler-Cadé, Pierre Frick, Hugel, A Mann, R Muré, Ostertag, Rolly Gassmann, Schueller, Schlumberger, Sick-Dreyer, Jean Sipp, Louis Sipp, Bruno Sorg, Trimbach**, the **Turckheim** co-operative, **Weinbach** and **Zind-Humbrecht**.

Muscat Light, fragrant, wonderfully grapy. Imagine crushing a fistful of green grapes fresh from the market and gulping the juice as it runs through your fingers. That's how fresh and grapy a good Muscat is – yet again, it is completely dry. Best producers: **Jean Becker, Joseph Cattin, Dirler-Cadé, Charles Koehly, Marc Kreydenweiss, A Mann, Ostertag**, the **Pfaffenheim** co-operative, **Rolly Gassmann, Schlumberger, Bruno Sorg**, the **Turckheim** co-operative, **Weinbach** and **Zind-Humbrecht**.

Tokay-Pinot Gris This unwieldy name is the Alsace synonym for Pinot Gris, which was called Tokay d'Alsace until the EU decided that there was a danger of consumers confusing it with the wine of Tokay in Hungary. Some chance! At its best it tastes sumptuously honeyed, and in such an obvious way that the flavour really can resemble a quick lick of the honey spoon. Even the light, young versions have a lusciousness lingering behind the basically dry fruit. The Tokay part of the name is being dropped from 2006. Best producers: **Lucien Albrecht, Léon Beyer, P Blanck, Marcel Deiss, Pierre Frick, Hugel, M Kreydenweiss, A Mann, Ostertag, Schlumberger, Schoffit, Bruno Sorg**, the **Turckheim** co-operative, **Weinbach** and **Zind-Humbrecht**.

Gewürztraminer It is sometimes difficult to believe that these wines are dry because they can be so fat and full of spice. But, with few exceptions, dry they are. Yet they are also big, very ripe and with all kinds of remarkable exotic fruit tastes – lychees, mangoes, peaches – and, if you're lucky, finished off with a slightly rasping twist, just like the tang of black pepper straight from the pepper mill. Best producers: **Beyer, P Blanck, Hugel, A Mann, Ostertag, Schlumberger, Trimbach**, the **Turckheim** co-operative, **Weinbach** and **Zind-Humbrecht**.

Pinot Noir The Burgundy grape here makes light reds and rosés. It often achieves quite an attractive perfume and a light, strawberryish flavour, making a pleasant summer red, to be drunk chilled. Recent attempts to make a darker Pinot have not been a success. Best producers: **J B Adam, Jean Becker, Marcel Deiss, Ginglinger, Hugel, Koehly, A Mann, R Muré**, the **Pfaffenheim** and **Turckheim** co-operatives and **Wolfberger**.

THE GOOD YEARS

The lighter Alsace styles, like Pinot Blanc and Muscat, are ready within a year of the vintage, and most wines are at their best within two. Few basic Alsace wines demand aging, though the better Rieslings and Pinot Gris can be improved by it. Grand Cru wines made from Riesling, Pinot Gris and Gewürztraminer should certainly be able to age, for up to a decade.

The sweeter Alsace wines will also age, but for how long will depend on their acidity. If they have the balance, these wines should keep and improve for a decade or more.

2004   Riesling and Pinot Gris show the most potential among the dry wines. October rains dashed hopes for the sweet wines.

2003   Small harvest and variable wines. Very few sweet wines made.

2002   Good but not spectacular. Late-picked Riesling did best.

2001   Well-balanced wines.

2000   A variable vintage.

1999   Many outstanding Grand Cru wines.

1998   A difficult vintage but with good Riesling, Sylvaner and Pinot Gris.

1997   Soft, plump, forward wines all drinking beautifully now.

1996   A long, dry autumn resulted in very good wines.

1995   A hot year with drought followed by September rain meant that some good, concentrated wines were made.

1994   A good year for late-harvest wines, which are rich and sweet. Those that were picked earlier are generally light.

Older vintages
1990, 1989, 1988, 1985, 1983.

ENJOYING THE WINES

Alsace wines go very well with food. There is almost no classic white wine dish which will not be a good partner for Pinot Blanc or

Riesling. And Pinot Gris and Gewürztraminer have the weight and flavour to go with such tricky dishes as smoked fish or choucroute. As for Muscat, I'd drink it by itself out in the garden on a summer evening. Gewürztraminer and Pinot Gris are excellent with Chinese food – they're probably the best all-rounders you can find for oriental food.

Alsace reds can be good with fish, particularly salmon or red mullet, and are good all-purpose summer wines, particularly the better Cuvées which will have more guts and perhaps some oak-aging.

CONSUMER INFORMATION

WHAT DO I GET FOR MY MONEY?

Alsace wines are good value, although prices are never rock-bottom. Wines from the better co-operatives should show varietal character and typical Alsace spice, but for real individuality you will need to buy one of the better Cuvées from a good grower or merchant – which will be appreciably more expensive. The top dry wines and the rare sweet wines are very expensive. But reliability is good, and these Alsace wines contain wonderful flavours that are duplicated nowhere in the world.

AVAILABILITY

Good at a basic level. Most wine shops will stock some Alsace varietal wines, though the better growers' and merchants' wines are often to be found only in specialists.

CONSUMER CHECKLIST

Vendange Tardive	*Quality 9* ★
Gewürztraminer 2002	*Price 10* ★
(Trimbach)	*Value 8* ★

Good Years   The hottest years with Indian summers suit the late-harvested sweet wines, though some of the dry ones can then lack acidity. Best years: 2002, 2000, 1998, 1997, 1996, 1995, 1994, 1990, 1989 for sweet wines; 2004, 2003, 2002, 2000 for dry wines.

Taste Notes   The most famous Alsace wines are the Gewürztraminers with their intense, spicy fruit. Muscat is very grapy and fragrant, and Pinot Gris is honeyed and soft – yet all these wines, while smelling sweetly spicy, are dry-tasting. Riesling can be very steely and stern, while Pinot Blanc and Sylvaner are softer and lighter.

JURA & SAVOIE

Jura wines are outside the mainstream of French wine, and you only have to attempt a single mouthful of one of their strange, strong reds and whites to see why. Mountain vineyards often harbour curious indigenous grape varieties and wine-making styles out of step with the fast-flowing world of lowland winemakers, and the Jura certainly follows this pattern. Reds, whites, rosés and sparkling wines are made, and a high strength **Vin Jaune** or 'yellow wine'. Many have an uncompromising, often oxidized, flavour and few of the wines reach export markets.

The reds are usually charmlessly heavy, and although Pinot Noir is grown, the local Trousseau variety rules the roost in a hefty, 'no prisoners taken' manner. Similarly, with whites, although Chardonnay is grown, it pales before the fierce raw flavours of the native Savagnin variety. Rosé, sometimes called Vin Gris, from the local Poulsard grape, can be big but good, but the most successful wines are sparkling, with some very good Champagne-method Chardonnay.

And then there's the inimitable Vin Jaune. It's the kind of wine of which more than a small glass makes you quite grateful it is so rare. It grows a flor fungus in barrel, like dry sherry; yet, unlike dry sherry, which is best drunk as soon as it is bottled, this intense, concentrated dry wine demands aging. No-one seems to know for how long, because the wine is virtually indestructible, and as long as the cork is healthy, it should live as long as any of us.

The largest appellations are **Arbois** and **Côtes du Jura**, and **Crémant du Jura** for mainly Chardonnay-based fizz. Jura is also the home of the very rare **Vin de Paille**, made from semi-dried grapes. Vin Jaune, rare and expensive, can be Arbois, Côtes du Jura or, at best, **Château-Chalon**. It comes in 62cl 'clavelin' bottles which managed to defy EU attempts at standardization. The other wines are medium-priced and more widely available but a little too rugged at times.

SAVOIE

This is a mountain district with an array of special grape varieties like Roussette, Jacquère and Mondeuse, and a titillating diversity of character in the wines to show for the multiplicity of grape varieties. Savoie wines are mostly white and very typical of wines from mountain regions – light, sharp, tartly fresh, sometimes very slightly *pétillant*.

Since Savoie embraces much of France's best skiing, much of the wine is knocked off after a hard day on the slopes. This is a pity, because these mountain-meadow flavours do have the ability, even far from their source, to bring back memories of the holiday atmosphere and the stunning scenery.

There used to be a wonderful feather-light, spring snow-fresh sparkling wine from **Seyssel**, made from the Molette and Roussette grapes. This disappeared for a while into a coarse commercial blend, but is now thankfully re-emerging under its own colours. The best wine is **Roussette de Savoie**, the most common is **Vin de Savoie**, perhaps with one of 16 Cru names attached. Mondeuse can make delicious, plummy red.

BUGEY

The **Bugey** VDQS makes nice crisp Chardonnays – some of the local Michelin-starred restaurants have taken to it in a big way. Drink all these on the spot with the local fish.

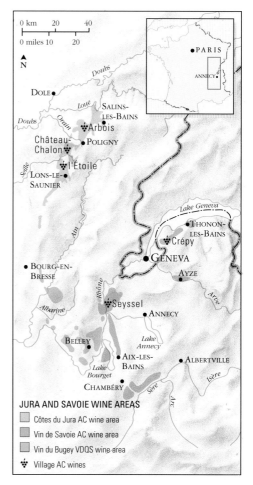

JURA AND SAVOIE WINE AREAS

- Côtes du Jura AC wine area
- Vin de Savoie AC wine area
- Vin du Bugey VDQS wine area
- Village AC wines

PROVENCE & CORSICA

There's never been any doubt that Provence can affect the heart and soul like a magic drug. It stretches from just east of Avignon across to the Italian border, on its way taking in pine-filled gorges, rugged hills, ancient forests, herb-grown *garrigues* and olive groves that look as though they have been there since Roman times. The Romans grew wine here; so did the Greeks before them. Provence has always attracted visitors, and the visitors have always gulped down the local wine – though whether the Greeks and the Romans were as uncritical as today's sun-dazed tourists is another matter. But even Provence is caught up in the revolution sweeping through southern France's vineyards and the wines are at least improving.

GRAPE VARIETIES AND WINE STYLES

This is predominantly a red and rosé wine area. There are some good whites, particularly from the **Cassis** and **Palette** appellations, but the most common white grapes are the undistinguished Ugni Blanc and Clairette, plus superior Bourboulenc and Rolle. The best that can usually be said of these wines is that they're fresh. Chardonnay pops up, though, as do Sémillon, Roussanne and Sauvignon Blanc, but these grapes need the very coolest spots.

Generally speaking, it is the sun-loving red grapes like Syrah, Mourvèdre, Grenache, Cinsaut, Carignan and Cabernet Sauvignon that flourish best. They make herby, rich reds and stone-dry rosés – and while it is the rosés that are mindlessly pounced on by the tourists, there are nevertheless some good ones. The best ones are made by 'bleeding' the red wine vats early on in the fermentation – running off some wine while the colour is still quite pale, which not only gives flavoursome pink, but also concentrates the red.

Côtes de Provence This is a massive appellation which has spent much of its life spewing out uninspiring rosé for a heat-stricken and undemanding clientele, who were, in any case, usually near-horizontal when they drank it, and so were unlikely to

For a long time the scenery was the best thing about the Coteaux d'Aix-en-Provence region and even now only some of the producers are fulfilling their potential.

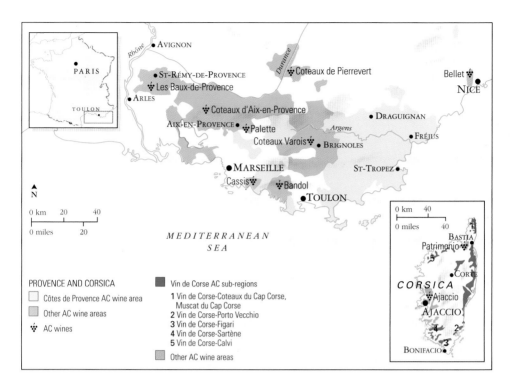

complain, except about the price. Well, things are changing. Tired of being left behind by Provence's more go-ahead appellations, Côtes de Provence can at last boast producers who are making serious wine – usually giving notice of their intentions by planting Syrah and Cabernet Sauvignon. Best producers: **Barbaneau**, **la Bernade**, **Commanderie de Peyrassol**, **la Courtade**, **Coussin Ste-Victoire**, **Dragon**, **Féraud**, **des Garcinières**, **Gavoty**, **Mauvanne**, **Minuty**, **Ott**, **Rabiega**, **Réal Martin**, **Richeaume**, **Rimauresq**, **Roquefort**, **Maîtres Vignerons de St-Tropez**, **Sorin** and **Sumeire**.

Coteaux d'Aix-en-Provence There are still too many under-achievers, although it can boast enough good names to make it interesting. Planting Cabernet Sauvignon and Syrah, again, is one of the keynotes of improved quality. Best producers: **Bas**, **les Bastides**, **des Béates**, **Beaupré**, **Calissanne**, **Fonscolombe**, **Pontet Bagatelle**, **Revelette** and **Vignelaure**.

Les Baux-de-Provence This AC is gaining a reputation for organic farming. The reds can be intense and complex with wild, untamed flavours of herbs and fruit and smoke and even the rosés are good. Best producers: **Hauvette**, **Mas de la Dame**, **Mas de Gourgonnier**, **Mas Ste-Berthe**, **Romanin**, **Terres Blanches** and **de Trévallon** (since 1994 sold as Vin de Pays des Bouches du Rhône).

Coteaux Varois A fairly recent promotion to the Appellation Contrôlée ranks, this large area is a source of good-value reds, whites and rosés. There are lots of new plantings of classic grapes like Cabernet Sauvignon, and lots of producers who seem to know what to do with them, so the future looks bright. Best producers: **Alysses**, **Calisse**, **Deffends**, **Routas**, **St-Esteve**, **St-Jean-le-Vieux** and **St-Jean de Villecroze**.

Bellet This tiny appellation tucked into the hills behind Nice on the Côte d'Azur produces a rather good, unusual, nutty white and some decent reds, but they are ridiculously expensive for what they are. The good people of Nice seem to be undeterred, so I suggest we leave them to it. Best producers: **Bellet**, **Crémat** and **Delmasso**.

Bandol Powerful, herby reds made principally from the heat-loving Mourvèdre grape. They have sweet spicy fruit to match their slightly tannic, herby fragrance and can age well, but are delicious young. There are good spicy rosés too but the whites are pretty dull. Best producers: **Bastide Blanche**, **la Bégude**, **Bunan**, **Frégate**, **le Galantin**, **J-P Gaussen**, **Gros' Noré**, **l'Hermitage**, **Lafran-Veyrolles**, **Mas Redorne**, **la Noblesse**, **Pibarnon**, **Pradeaux**, **Ray-Jane**, **Roche Redonne**, **Romassan**, **Ste-Anne**, **Salettes**, **de Souviou**, **la Suffrène**, **Tempier**, **Terrebrune**, **la Tour de Bon** and **Vannières**.

Cassis Not to be confused with the black-currant drink of the same name, this is chiefly white wine from a small but beautiful vine-yard area tucked into the bluffs by the Mediterranean. Based on Ugni Blanc and Clairette, the whites can have a cool freshness and fruit which is still rare on this coast. But they are overpriced, and only worth paying for if you are about to tuck into a cauldron full of *bouillabaisse*. The red is dull but there are some attractive rosés. Best producers: **de Bagnol**, **Clos Ste-Magdeleine**, **La Ferme Blanche**, **Mas Fontcreuse** and **de Paternel**.

Palette A tiny appellation hidden in the pine forest, with interesting red, white and rosé. Best producer: **Crémade**, **Simone**.

Vins de Pays Bouches-du-Rhône has some fair reds and rosés, and from 1994 the excelent de Trévallon wine (see Les Baux-de-Provence, page 135). Mont Caume is an interesting Vin de Pays, since it often represents the lesser efforts of Bandol growers.

Corsica There are some splendidly idiosyncratic grape varieties, like the red Nielluccio and Sciacarello and the white Vermentino, as well as sweet rich Muscats. The potential for wine-making is there, and standards are improving. The general Corsican appellation is **Vin de Corse**. Other appellations are **Ajaccio** and **Patrimonio** and the Vin de Pays is poetically called L'Île de Beauté.

CLASSIFICATION

There is no single catch-all appellation for Provence and Corsica. Instead there are several large, sprawling ones, like Côtes de Provence, and a handful of smaller ones.

ORGANIZATION

Growers have become increasingly important in recent years. In fact, it is usually easier to find growers' wines than merchants'. Merchants play a bigger part in Corsica.

READING THE LABEL

Quality is so mixed here that the name of a reliable grower is essential.

WHAT DO THEY TASTE LIKE?

The reds are generally herby and rich and the whites neutral and clean, though nowadays they have increasing fruit.

THE GOOD YEARS

For the whites, the rule is drink the most recent year available. Some of the reds, notably Bandol, as well as the wines of individual producers elsewhere, will age well. There is far less vintage variation here than in more marginal wine-making areas.

ENJOYING THE WINES

These wines need strong flavours in food – just the sort of flavours, in fact, that are to be found on their home ground. A table overlooking the Mediterranean helps too.

CONSUMER INFORMATION

WHAT DO I GET FOR MY MONEY?

Sadly, these wines are not bargains. They are too easy to sell on their home ground for that – but you have the consolation, at least with the best wines, of forking out for some of France's most unusual flavours.

AVAILABILITY

Not that great, actually. The Vin de Pays wines are not too difficult to find, but the better ones tend to be available only through specialist wine shops.

CONSUMER CHECKLIST

Côtes de Provence red	*Quality 6* ★
2004 (Richeaume)	*Price 5* ★
	Value 6 ★

Good Years There's not too much vintage variation here, but always go for the youngest whites.

Taste Notes Rich, herby reds; minerally rosés with a herby edge; and whites that tend to be pretty neutral, but they are at least clean and fresh-tasting.

LANGUEDOC-ROUSSILLON

This is where it's all happening. This is where France's wine revolution is sweeping away generations of suspicion, prejudice and inefficiency to be replaced by enthusiasm, initiative and innovation. In the past the Midi was one of France's most scrubby, bedraggled, exhausted-looking regions. It was where France's share of the wine lake had its source; and cheap hooch poured from these vineyards. Nobody wanted it. Increasingly, the producers couldn't sell it as it was only fit for distillation. But the mindless, featureless prairie vineyards, the sullen flat plains and care-worn hillocks continued to be cultivated in the same old way. The wine continued to be made in co-operatives whose winemakers cared no more than the growers if the vats were dirty, the wine-making old-fashioned and the results increasingly undrinkable.

Not now. Now the Midi is known as the California of France – although the Australia of France might be a more accurate title. There are nearly as many Australians here as there are in London's Earl's Court, and rather more trained winemakers. Go into a winery and you're as likely to hear 'G'day mate, how's it going?' as 'Bonjour'.

But let's not give all the credit to the Aussies. They're a recent arrival, but the renaissance of the Midi dates from before they turned up. It's the last twenty years that have really made the difference. The improvement started in the appellations of Fitou, Corbières and Minervois – areas that already had a reputation for the best quality in the Midi. Suddenly the good growers seemed to be in the majority. Suddenly the co-operatives seemed to be waking up to the fact that they had a choice in the modern wine world, and that choice was modernization or bankruptcy.

From there the spirit of change spread to the other appellation areas, and then to the Vin de Pays. It's here in the Vins de Pays where the big changes are now taking place – they're unfettered by appellation rules; they can plant what they like, and make it how they like. That's the sort of thing that appeals to Aussies – and if anybody asks me if these wines are 'typical', my answer is yes. They're typical of good wine-making. They're using local grapes, grown by local growers. How much more typical can you get?

GRAPE VARIETIES AND WINE STYLES

The Languedoc-Roussillon is still mostly a red wine region, though the amount of Chardonnay Vin de Pays d'Oc about might lead one to think otherwise. The appellation areas are tied to traditional grape varieties, though they can manage to extract some tremendously exciting raspberry and blackcurrant flavours, thickened with chocolate and scented with bay leaf and thyme, from varieties like Carignan. Grenache, Syrah, Cinsaut and Mourvèdre also come into play, but Carignan can be excellent on its own – especially if the vines are old and producing

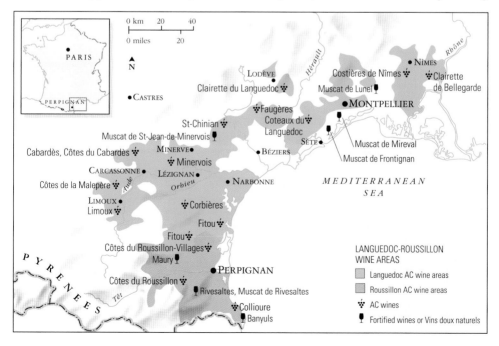

small quantities of concentrated wine. These earthy, peppery flavours, often with good juicy fruit, tend to be typical of the welter of mountains stretching south from Narbonne. Côtes du Roussillon and Côtes du Roussillon-Villages, in particular, are big, beefy wines, but soft with it. The Vin de Pays d'Oc makes the most international-style wines, often from a single, fashionable grape like Cabernet Sauvignon, Merlot, Syrah or Chardonnay, and frequently aged in new wood. Some of these wines have a strong, modern 'New World' ripeness, but the cheap ones are too often inexcusably thin and lean.

There are also more traditional whites and some are excellent. Blanquette de Limoux or Crémant de Limoux, both based on the Mauzac grape, are claimed (by the locals) to have been made sparkling long before Champagne got round to it. And there are fortified wines or Vins Doux Naturels made from Grenache or Muscat – some of which are immediately attractive and some of which are distinctly acquired tastes – emanating from various rocky corners of this dry, wind-swept and sun-scorched land.

Costières de Nîmes Savoury, smoky but juicy reds and good, fresh rosés. Best producers: **L'Amarine**, **Grande Cassagne**, **Mas des Bressades**, **Mourgues du Grès**, **Nages**, **la Tuilerie** and **Vieux-Relais**.

The medieval walled town of Aigues-Mortes, in the Camargue on the Mediterranean coast, is surrounded by large areas of flat vineyards.

Coteaux du Languedoc A huge, sprawling appellation of tremendous potential, producing mainly reds and some whites and rosés that vary in style from fresh, young and fruity to dark and tannic (for the reds) and fresh to not so fresh for the whites. Quality varies hugely – as does the terroir and the climate. **Clairette du Languedoc** applies only to whites made from Clairette; **Picpoul de Pinet** is likewise white, and made from the local Picpoul grape. Various villages are able to add their name after the appellation on labels; the best of these are La Clape, Montpeyroux, Pic St-Loup and St-Saturnin. Best producers: (Coteaux du Languedoc) **l'Aiguelière**, **Aupilhac**, **Calage**, **Capion**, **Clavel**, **La Coste**, **Exindre**, **Grès St-Paul**, **Lacroix-Vanel**, **Mas des Chimères**, **Mas Jullien**, **Peyre-Rose**, **Poujol**, **Prieuré de St-Jean-de-Bébian**, **Puech-Haut**, **St-Martin de la Garrigue** and **Terre Megère**; (La Clape) **Hospitalet**, **Pech-Céleyran** and **Pech Redon**; (Clairette du Languedoc) **de la Condamine Bertrand** and **St-André**.

Faugères An exciting red appellation producing wines bursting with cassis and liquorice. Many will age well. Best producers: **Abbaye Sylva Plana**, **Alquier**, **Barral**, **Chenaie**, **Estanilles**, **du Fraisse**, **Grézan**, **Haut-Fabrègues**, **La Liquière**, **Moulin de Ciffre** and **Ollier-Taillefer**.

St-Chinian   Reds that can be big and beefy, or soft and full according to whether they're grown in the high, arid part of the appellation or the lower-lying, more easy-going part. The grapes are the usual Languedoc mix, and there are some rosés as well. This is good, stylish wine with more personality than the usual Hérault stuff. Best producers: **Borie la Vitarèle**, **Canet Valette**, **Cazal-Viel**, **Clos Bagatelle**, **Jougla**, **Mas Champart**, **Maurel Fonsalade** and **Rimbert**.

Minervois   Rich, often soft and scented reds and quite aromatic whites produced from a blend of grapes: Carignan, Grenache, Mourvèdre and Syrah plus other minor ones for the reds, and Grenache Blanc, Rolle, Bourboulenc, Roussanne, Marsanne and Macabeo for the whites. The reds often show lovely juicy fruit. **La Livinière**, a denomination covering four villages, can be added to the Minervois name. Best producers: **Aires Hautes**, **Bonhomme**, **Borie de Maurel**, **Clos Centeilles**, **Pierre Cros**, **Fabas**, **Maris**, **Piccinini**, **Ste-Eulalie**, **La Tour Boisée** and **Villerambert-Julien**.

Cabardès   These reds (and a few rosés) are caught neatly between the influence of the Mediterranean and that of Bordeaux. Cabardès grows the grapes of both regions: Cabernets Sauvignon and Franc, Merlot and Malbec in its western part, Syrah, Grenache, Cinsaut and Carignan in the east. The resulting wines are aromatic, lively, and entirely original. Best producers: **Auzias**, **Cabrol** and **Pennautier**.

Côtes de la Malepère   Rather like Cabardès, this newly promoted AC is sandwiched halfway between the two different worlds of the Atlantic and the Mediterranean, but Malepère is appreciably more oriented toward Bordeaux wine styles than its northern neighbour. Merlot and Cot (or Malbec) are the main varieties, and there's some Cinsaut and rather less Cabernet Sauvignon, Cabernet Franc, Syrah and Grenache. Most of the wines are red, but there is a little rosé. The flavours

are exciting, concentrated and well worth exploring. Best producers: **Dom. des Cazes**, **Guilhem**, **Plana**, and **Razès** co-operative.

Limoux   Made in a higher, cooler spot than anywhere else in Languedoc-Roussillon, this region makes still, barrel-fermented, Chardonnay-based whites (with some Chenin Blanc) and Merlot-based reds under the Limoux label, Champagne-method sparklers from Mauzac, Chardonnay, Chenin Blanc and Pinot Noir under the Crémant de Limoux name, and under the Blanquette de Limoux name, fizz made from at least 90 per cent Mauzac. There's also some appley, slightly sweet, semi-fizzy, slightly cloudy Blanquette Méthode Ancestrale (when the fermentation is finished off inside the bottle), which sounds wonderfully rustic and is very much a local taste. Best producers: **Aigle**, **Antugnac**, **Collin**, **Fourn**, **Laurens**, **Martinolles**, **Robert** and the **Sieur d'Arques** co-operative.

Fitou   A red wine appellation split into two parts – an inland mountain and a coastal zone – within Corbières. This burly, dark-coloured wine is very good and dominated by Carignan, although Grenache and, increasingly Syrah and Mourvèdre, are being used. One of

Hillside vineyards around the village of Caramany in the Pyrénées-Orientales make Côtes du Roussillon-Villages red wines with ripe, spicy, earthy flavours.

the success stories of the 1980s, the wine dipped in quality but, led by the mountain vineyards, is now back on form. Best producers: **Bertrand-Berge**, **Lerys**, **Nouvelles**, **Roudène** and the **Mont-Tauch** co-operative.

Corbières Carignan rules the vineyards here, making concentrated, spicy reds of great character which from the best producers can age for years, as well as lighter ones made, like Beaujolais, by the carbonic maceration method. The whites can be surprisingly good, too but need drinking young. Best producers: **Baillat**, **Caraguilhes**, **Cascadais**, **Clos de l'Anhel**, **Étang des Colombes**, **Fontsainte**, **Grand Crès**, **Grand Moulin**, **Haut-Gléon**, **Hélène**, **l'Ille**, **Lastours**, **Mansenoble**, the **Mont-Tauch** co-operative, **Les Ollieux**, **Les Palais**, **St-Auriol** and **Voulte-Gasparets**.

Côtes du Roussillon Attractive reds full of dusty, earthy raspberry fruit come from this vast area, spreading inland almost from the coast. The most successful wines are from traditional southern grapes like Carignan; the whites tend to have low acidity. Côtes du Roussillon-Villages can be used in the northern part of the region, and Latour-de-France and Caramany can add their village names to the label. On the whole this is one of the most exciting parts of the Midi, especially since the best wines are from traditional varieties and a surge of new producers are producing thrilling dense, sunbaked reds and windswept whites. Best producers: **Casenove**, **Cazes**, **de Chênes**, **Clos des Fées**, **J-L Colombo**, **Ferrer-Ribère**, **Fontanel**, **Gardiès**, **Gauby**, **de Jau**, **Laporte**, **Mas Amiel**, **Mas Crémat**, **Piquemal**, **O Pithon**, the **Rivesaltes** co-operative, **Sarda-Malet**, **Schistes** and **Vignerons Catalans**.

Collioure Intense, ripe, Grenache and Mourvèdre-based reds, reeking of spice and heady fruit, are made in this beautiful coastal region. The very ripest grapes go into the Banyuls Vin Doux Naturel (see left). Best producers: **Baillaury**, **Cellier des Templiers**, **Clos des Paulilles**, **Mas Blanc**, **la Rectorie**, **La Tour Vieille** and **Vial Magnères**.

Vins de Pays This is where some of the most exciting, best value-for-money flavours are being turned out at the moment – and they're being aided and abetted by winemakers who know how to turn these hot, arid conditions into a positive advantage. They know how to grow Syrah, Cabernet Sauvignon and Chardonnay here and vinify them cool so that they keep all their freshness.

The reds have the edge in quality for the time being but the whites are getting there too now. The regional Vin de Pays d'Oc has some of the best producers, but the Vins de Pays of Val d'Orbieu, Coteaux de Murviel, Côtes de Thongue, Côte de Thau, Côtes Catalanes, L'Hérault, Mont Baudile, Coteaux de Peyriac and Pyrénées-Orientales all have stars. Not

VIN DOUX NATUREL

'Naturally sweet wine' is what this title means. In fact the wines are fortified with the addition of strong grape spirit during fermentation, when about half the natural sweetness of the grape has been converted to alcohol.

White Vins Doux Naturels are made from the Muscat grape; these are the easiest styles for outsiders to appreciate. They have, at their best, all the delicate sweetness and aroma of the Muscat grape, plus enough concentration to make them good either as apéritifs or pudding wines. Muscat de Beaumes-de-Venise from the southern Rhône is the best known, but there are others too: Frontignan, Mireval, Lunel, Rivesaltes and the rare but good St-Jean-de-Minervois, all from the Midi.

Reds are made from Grenache, and the wines are left to mature for between two and ten years to develop deep, intense flavours. There's no question of grapy freshness here; indeed, there's even an oxidized rancio style. Banyuls, Maury and Rivesaltes are the appellations to look for.

Best producers: (whites) Bernardins, la Capelle, Cazes, la Peyrade and the co-operatives at Frontignan, Beaumes-de-Venise and St-Jean-de-Minervois; (reds) Mas Amiel, Mas Blanc, la Rectorie and the Maury co-operative.

The Domaine de la Baume, near Béziers in the Hérault, was one of the leaders of the 'New Wave' modern southern wines.

everything under these names is stunning, of course. Not everything is that good. But it's easy to avoid the bad stuff, because there's so much good. Best producers: **l'Aigle**, **Aupilhac**, **Chais Baumière**, **du Bosc**, **de Condamine-L'Evêque**, **la Croix Belle**, **J-L Denois**, **de la Fadèze**, **des Fontaines**, **Grange de Quatre Sous**, **de Jau**, **de Limbardie**, **J & F Lurton**, **Mas de Daumas Gassac**, **Ormesson**, **Pech-Céleyran**, **Peyrat**, **Skalli-Fortant de France**, **Val d'Orbieu** and **Virginie**.

CLASSIFICATION
The appellations stretch in a long arc around the Mediterranean coast and range from the large regional ones, such as Coteaux du Languedoc to smaller, more specific ones.

ORGANIZATION
This is a land of excellent, small producers and go-ahead co-operatives and merchants. In fact, some of them are among the most innovative in France, and are at the forefront of the great quality revolution here. Good individual estates are becoming more common.

READING THE LABEL
Many new wave Vins de Pays are varietals, and will state the grape name on the label. Appellation and VDQS wines tend to be blends of more traditional grapes.

WHAT DO THEY TASTE LIKE?
The reds have the dusty, herby flavours of the South, mixed with good, spicy raspberry fruit. The softer, juicier ones may be made partly by carbonic maceration. These wines should be drunk young, while some of the more traditional wines, in particular Faugères and Corbières, can age quite well. At their best, the whites are crisp and aromatic, though most (apart from international-style Chardonnays, Viognier and Sauvignons) are fairly neutral.

THE GOOD YEARS
There's not a great deal of vintage variation in this part of France, so with the whites and the lighter reds, choose the most recent year.

ENJOYING THE WINES
The reds will go well with most substantial meat dishes, in particular the strongly flavoured foods of the Mediterranean. The whites are good for most fish dishes and the best of them make good apéritifs, too.

CONSUMER INFORMATION

WHAT DO I GET FOR MY MONEY?
Good value – in fact, some of the best value in France. Even the best of these wines are still underpriced compared to their equivalents in more famous regions, and while the new wave Midi Vins de Pays may look expensive for such wines, they're, in fact, decidedly cheap for the flavours you're getting.

AVAILABILITY
The smaller appellations like Faugères and St-Chinian are not widely distributed – in fact you may have to look quite hard to find them. But wines from Corbières, Fitou and Minervois are pretty widespread. The Vin de Pays wines, too, have become supermarket staples.

CONSUMER CHECKLIST
Coteaux du Languedoc red	*Quality 7* ★
La Clape 2004	*Price 4* ★
(Pech-Céleyran)	*Value 9* ★

Good Years Buy the most recent vintage for whites, in nearly all cases, though reds can improve.
Taste Notes Dusty raspberry fruit with a good lick of spice and herbs is the keynote of the reds; rosés, too, can be quite substantial, particularly from Syrah. Whites are mostly neutral: drink them young.

SOUTH-WEST FRANCE

We talk a lot about discovering new wine areas, and frequently that is exactly what we do – we find new, modern wines, trying to make their mark on the world. The south-west of France is different; it is crying out to be rediscovered. Most of its wines are still hardly known, yet 700 years ago they were better known and more highly thought of than the wines of Bordeaux. Indeed, they were frequently used to beef up and add body to Bordeaux's pale, insipid red wine.

Well, Bordeaux is now famous around the world, as well as being one of the greatest in the world. The other wines of the South-West have long been languishing in an ill-deserved obscurity. Yet they are some of the most individual, memorable wines in France, and though many of their wine traditions have only survived by the skin of their teeth, there is a gradual and welcome resurgence of activity in the region.

GRAPE VARIETIES AND WINE STYLES
The nearer you are to Bordeaux, the more likely you are to find Bordelais grape varieties in the vineyards. This goes for both reds and

whites: Bergerac, Côtes de Duras and Buzet can all be viewed as making mini-Bordeaux – even if quite often the quality of these wines is a definite step up from most basic Bordeaux Rouge or Blanc. That means Cabernet Sauvignon, Cabernet Franc and Merlot predominate for the reds, and Sauvignon Blanc and Sémillon for the whites.

But travel further away from Bordeaux and totally new wine flavours begin to reveal themselves. Cahors takes Bordeaux's Malbec grape, rechristens it Auxerrois and makes strange, deep, ripe reds with it. In Côtes du Frontonnais the Negrette takes over; in Madiran it's Tannat, plus both Cabernets and the local Fer Servadou. Add some new oak barrels and you can have some very arresting flavours indeed.

Most of the reds from the foothills of the Pyrenees – wines like Béarn and Irouléguy – are Tannat-based and more or less rustic, but white Jurançon can be excellent – and quite expensive. The grapes are Petit Manseng, Gros Manseng and Courbu – and they've certainly never heard of those in Bordeaux.

Bergerac There are nine different appellations inside this region, which is, in effect, the eastward extension of the St-Émilion vineyards. Bergerac red at least has a similar reliance on Merlot, with help from Cabernet Sauvignon and Cabernet Franc. However, the best Bergerac reds are a good deal less substantial than St-Émilion's. They have plenty of bite, but without the rough edges of basic Bordeaux, and can have delicious blackcurranty fruit. The best will age well. The rosés can be excellent, with full, dry fruit and good colour. **Côtes de Bergerac** wines have a slightly higher alcohol level. Côtes de Bergerac Moelleux can also be sold as **Saussignac**, but seldom is. Bergerac Sec is white, and is usually good, quite full and grassily dry. Best producers: **l'Ancienne Cure**, **Bélingard**, **Jonc Blanc**, **la Colline**, **Court-les-Mûts**, **Eyssards**, **Tour des Gendres**, **Tour des Verdots** and **Clos d'Yvigne**.

Pécharmant A tiny appellation within Bergerac, making very fine, fully dry reds requiring considerable aging. Good vintages will last easily up to ten years. Best producers: **Costes**, **Haut-Pécharmant**, **Métairie** and **Tiregand**.

Some of the more idiosyncratic reds of south-west France come from Madiran. This is Château de Crouseilles owned by the local co-operative.

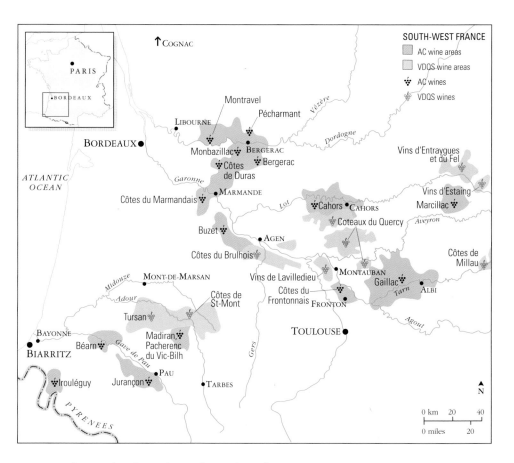

Montravel Mostly dry whites from the western end of the Bergerac region, based on Sémillon, with a little Merlot-based red. They've improved in recent years. Côtes de Montravel is semi-sweet; Haut-Montravel is rarer, and sweeter. Best producers: **Masburel**, **Moulin Caresse** and **Puy-Servain**.

Monbazillac Bergerac's most serious sweet white area. The grape varieties are the same as in Sauternes – Sémillon, Sauvignon Blanc and Muscadelle – and noble rot visits the vineyards, though less than in Sauternes. Lower selling prices also mean that few producers are prepared to take Sauternes-style pains in picking or making their wines – with the result that too many are simply sweet and too few have the rich, spicy character that comes from careful selection of nobly rotten grapes. However, some do have it, especially in the best years. Best producers: **l'Ancienne Cure**, **Bélingard**, **la Borderie**, **Grande Maison**, **Theulet**, **Tirecul-la-Gravière**, **Tour des Verdots** and **Treuil-de-Nailhac**.

Côtes de Duras An appellation in the Lot-et-Garonne bordering Bordeaux's Entre-Deux-Mers region, making light, grassy, usually rather attractive reds and dry whites

from Sauvignon Blanc which are also good. Best producers: **Mouthes le Bihan** and **Duras** and **Landerrouat** co-operatives.

Côtes du Marmandais A Bordeaux satellite making light reds for drinking young, some rosé and a little white. Decent but not outstanding quality. Best producer: the **Beaupuy** and **Cocumont** co-operatives.

Buzet This is the most exciting of the Bordeaux lookalike regions. These reds, from Bordeaux varieties, are surprisingly good, combining a rich blackcurrant sweetness with an arresting grassy greenness. Best producer: the **Buzet-sur-Baïse** co-operative, sold under labels including Château de Gueyze, Château Padère and Baron d'Ardeuil.

Cahors This is a one-wine town, and that wine is red, made from at least 70 per cent Auxerrois (Bordeaux's Malbec). Good Cahors has the remarkable ability to combine a tough, sturdy style with a fruit so gentle, so warm that it is very difficult to persuade yourself to mature it for a while. What Cahors is not is the legendary 'black' wine, the very smell of which would reduce a hardened drinker to tea and sympathy at 50 paces. From

The grape harvest is over at Château La Grave Bechade in the Côtes de Duras but in the vineyards the work of spraying weeds goes on.

a single domaine, and these days from the co-operative as well, Cahors is a fine wine. Some growers make the wine to drink young, when it is marked by a wonderful plummy richness, kept fresh by a distinct appley acidity. More generally, the growers intend the wine to age, and the flavours it develops are often almost honeyed, but kept straight-faced by that plummy fruit going deeper, spicier, darker, often resembling tobacco and prunes – what a combination. But *that* is the modern-day 'blackness', a 'blackness' of deep flavours, unlike almost any other red. Best producers: **la Caminade**, **du Cèdre**, **Clos la Coutale**, **Clos de Gamot**, **Clos Triguedina**, **Gautoul**, **Haute-Serre**, **Lagrezette**, **Lamartine**, **les Laquets**, **les Rigalets**, and the **Côtes d'Olt** co-operative.

Gaillac This is one of the best-known of the south-west wines, and standards are improving, with a fair number of good, go-ahead producers. The whites, which can be sweet or dry, are a little terse and could usually do with softening a bit, though they can have tastes of apple and liquorice fruit. The reds should have an intensely peppery, dry flavour. They're not deep or rich, but the fruit is ripe and this ground pepper taste is surprisingly more-ish. There are various semi-sparkling wines, but the best from the *méthode gaillaçoise* – rather like the *méthode rurale* sometimes used in Limoux (see page 139) – are superb: peppery, honeyed, apricotty, appley, all at the same time. Best producers: **Causses-Marines**, **Dom des Cailloutis**, **de Gineste**, **Labarthe**, **Ch. l'Arlus**, **Mas Pignou**, **Plageoles**, **Rotier**, **des Terrisses**.

Côtes du Frontonnais The nearby city of Toulouse wisely drinks this wine at a great rate. There is some rosé, but the joy is the red, based on the Negrette grape. At its best this is silky smooth, bursting with liquorice and strawberry fruit. Drink it young. Best producers: **Bellevue-la-Forêt**, **Ferran**, **Flotis**, **Montauriol**, **la Palme** and **le Roc**.

Madiran and **Pacherenc du Vic-Bihl** Madiran has been described as the best red of the South-West outside Bordeaux. I would disagree. In general, it has a strangely ill-defined flavour. The fruit is dominated by a slightly green apples sharpness from the mixture of Tannat, Cabernet Franc and Cabernet Sauvignon grapes. But the will to improve is there and there's even some interesting varietal wine from the tannic Tannat grape. The use of new oak barrels is on the increase. The white Pacherenc du Vic-Bihl, made from local grapes like Ruffiac and Courbu, is worth seeking out for its remarkable pear-skin fruit. Best producers: **Aydie**, **Barréjat**, **Bouscassé**, **Capmartin**, **Chapelle L'Enclos**, the **Crouseilles** co-operative, **du Crampilh**, **Laffitte-Teston**, **Montus** and **Viella**.

Béarn, Irouléguy and **Jurançon** All these appellations are found sheltering in the lee of the Pyrenees. Tannat is the grape for the reds and rosés of Béarn and Irouléguy. Petit Manseng, Gros Manseng and Courbu make the sweet, medium or dry whites of Jurançon. Go

for a grower's wine here, for both nutty dry wines and the rare honeyed, raisiny, peachy sweet ones. Best producers: (Béarn) **Bellocq** co-operative and **Lapeyre**; (Irouléguy) **Arretxea**, **Brana**, **Illaria** and **Mignaberry**; (Jurançon) **Bellegarde**, **Bru Baché**, **Castera**, **Cauhapé**, **Clos Lapeyre**, **Clos Thou**, **Clos Uroulat**, **Larrédya** and **Souch**.

Vins de Pays The well-known Vins de Pays of Charentais and Côtes de Gascogne are from the Cognac and Armagnac regions respectively, and use the light, neutral Ugni Blanc and Colombard grapes that would otherwise be used for distillation. Best producers: **Grassa**, **de Plantérieu**, the **Plaimont** co-operative, **les Puts**, **San Guilhem** and **de Tariquet**.

CLASSIFICATION
There are no overall regional appellations here. The South-West is a fascinating area of local appellations often based on interesting ancient grape varieties.

ORGANIZATION
The co-operatives are important here and some, like those at Buzet and Gaillac, are capable of good, interesting wines when they put their mind to it but the most exciting wines generally come from single growers.

READING THE LABEL
With so many different appellations and wine styles look for the name of a good producer.

WHAT DO THEY TASTE LIKE?
The reds and whites from near Bordeaux taste like mini-Bordeaux wines – blackcurranty and tobaccoey for the reds, leafy and crisp for the whites. Further away the wines take on

Not all wineries are fully automated. This Jurançon grower is pressing his grapes right in the vineyard in a small, hand-operated press.

remarkable spicy or nutty flavours that are found nowhere else in France.

THE GOOD YEARS
In general, buy the current year. Some of the reds will age, and in Madiran and Cahors you may find a choice of vintages.

ENJOYING THE WINES
The reds are mostly chunky and rustic, and cry out for duck, goose and casseroles; the white wines make good apéritifs. There are also a few delicious sweet whites, ideal for accompanying foie gras or Roquefort.

CONSUMER INFORMATION

WHAT DO I GET FOR MY MONEY?
Most of these South-West wines are not expensive, and the best ones can offer excellent value for money – that is, if you're prepared for some thoroughly unfamiliar flavours. Bergerac, Côtes de Duras and Buzet are the ones to choose if you want Bordeaux lookalikes. Dry Jurançon is no longer cheap, unfortunately, but it is good.

AVAILABILITY
Variable. The Bergerac wines and the Vins de Pays are not difficult to find. Gaillac, Madiran, Jurançon and the other appellations can be hard to track down.

CONSUMER CHECKLIST
Madiran 2003	*Quality* 7 ★
(Château Montus)	*Price* 8 ★
	Value 6 ★

Good Years The red wines, especially Madiran and Cahors, can need several years to develop. Côtes du Frontonnais and Buzet reds are immediately delicious. Rosés and the white Vins de Pays are best very young.
Taste Notes Many of the old-fashioned wines have flavours as original and memorable as can be found anywhere in France. The newer wines and the Vins de Pays are mostly high quality, to be drunk young.

GERMANY

Some countries have equal reputations for their red wines and their white, their sweet wines and their dry, their still wines and their sparkling. Germany makes all these styles, and yet it is for her still white wines, made dry or, more usually, sweetish, that she is known above all. They are made in a style that no other country can imitate, from one of the world's greatest grapes, in terrain that is some of the most uncompromising in the whole wine world, and often to the very highest standards. And yet outside their native country these wines are hopelessly unfashionable. Should we change our tastes, or should the Germans change the wines they make?

Schloss Vollrads (left) is one of the great aristocratic estates of the Rheingau; most German wine producers are on a less grand scale, like Weingut St Hubertus at Horrweiler, near Bingen in the Rheinhessen (above). Michael Polzer is sampling new wine, still cloudy from fermentation, from a traditional old oak barrel.

WINE REGIONS

The German Wine Law of 1971 has never been popular with quality producers, since it adopted an egalitarian approach to wine production that militated against the best sites and the best producers. Germany is the most northerly of Europe's major wine producers and so maximum exposure to the sun and maximum protection from wine and rain are fundamental to top quality just as dediction on the part of the grower is of paramount importance. After 30 years of stuggle under a law that allows a bog standard sugar water wine concocted from some new-fangled grape variety full of sweetness but devoid of flavour and grown on a patch of mud that would be better use raising a potato crop, the good producers have had enough. They say the same wine law that should be upholding standards is in fact responsible for lowering them to the lowest common denominator. So they've started acting outside the law, making wine the way they want to, and, if necessary, labelling it as base Tafelwein.

The problem is not so much the minute delimitation of the whole of Germany, vineyard by vineyard, and the corresponding morass of single-vineyard names that this produces. Once you know that the first word of a two-word name on a wine label is the village, and the second the vineyard, you've more or less got that system cracked. The problem is that there are larger areas, called Grosslagen, which have names that sound suspiciously like single vineyards – Niersteiner Gutes Domtal, for example. Nierstein is a village that can produce very fine wine indeed – but Gutes Domtal is an area so large, and is sold at a price so low, that the wine is never more than rock-bottom quality. It is most emphatically not to be compared to a single-vineyard wine from Nierstein – but it sounds just the same. Sneaky – or what?

Then there are still larger wine areas called Bereiche. These, again, often borrow the name of their most famous village – like Bereich Bernkastel. The village of Bernkastel produces some of Germany's finest wines – but cheap wine sold under the Bereich Bernkastel name has probably never even been within screaming distance of Bernkastel.

Add to this the enormous yields from inferior grape varieties that are the bane of most German wine regions (of which there are 13 – see the map opposite) and you have a downward spiral of ever-increasing amounts of wine that have to be shipped at ever-lower prices.

What the leading growers are doing is imposing stricter rules on themselves than the law requires. This applies to yields, minimum ripeness levels, how the vines should be pruned and so on. Some are maturing their wines in new oak barrels whose flavours virtually ensure that the official judging panels will refuse them QmP status (see below) – so they take the law into their own hands and sell them as (high-priced) Tafelwein, or table wine. Others have banded together to classify the best vineyards in the best areas – as far as German wine law is concerned, all vineyards are equal, but commonsense tells one that this can't be true.

These growers are also fussy about the vines they grow. In most of Germany the Riesling stands head and shoulders above any other grape: it's one of the world's classic grapes. Only in Franken, where Silvaner can be excellent, and in Baden, where the whole Pinot family flourishes, should the Riesling take a back seat. But one of the German wine industry's biggest projects is research into new vine varieties that will reliably produce large crops in the country's cool climate. Yes, you can do that – but you sacrifice the quality that you get with Riesling. And large yields of inferior wine are the main reason why the reputation of German wine has sunk so low.

CLASSIFICATION

German wine law makes no distinctions of quality between vineyards. Instead the wines are classified according to the ripeness of the grapes and measured by their must weight or sugar level.Sugar levels are measured in degrees Oechsle, a measure of how much heavier a litre of grape juice is than a litre of water. Thus, a reading of 95° Oechsle means that a litre of the grape juice in question is 95 grams heavier than a litre of water. The extra weight is that of the natural grape sugar, so the riper the grapes, the greater the potential alcohol. In 2000 new rules to try to regulate 'dry' wines were brought in with two classifications – Classic for mid-market wines and Selection for top end wines.

Tafelwein is basic table wine, usually a low-quality blend. 'Deutscher Tafelwein' must be German; EU Tafelwein can be a blend of anywhere in the EU and should be avoided.

Landwein The equivalent of France's Vin de Pays. Quality is not exciting.

WINE REGIONS OF GERMANY
Quality wine regions

- Ahr
- Mittelrhein
- Mosel-Saar-Ruwer
- Rheingau
- Nahe
- Rheinhessen
- Pfalz
- Hessische Bergstrasse
- Franken
- Württemberg
- Baden
- Saale-Unstrut
- Sachsen

Qualitätswein bestimmter Anbaugebiete (QbA) Quality Wine from a Designated Region.

Qualitätswein mit Prädikat (QmP) No sugar can be added to these wines. There are six Prädikats, or special attributes – based on ripeness levels in the vineyard – and the wines get steadily rarer, usually sweeter and always more expensive:

Kabinett Wine made from ripe grapes. The driest and lightest of the lot. It will be slightly sweet, yet acidic, unless the label says 'Halbtrocken' (half dry) or 'Trocken' (dry).

Spätlese Wine from late-picked grapes. It is usually sweetish, though not very sweet. Again, it can be Halbtrocken or Trocken.

Auslese Made from selected bunches of extra-ripe grapes. In the warmest years there may well be some noble rot. Auslesen can be pretty sweet; a few are Halbtrocken or Trocken.

Beerenauslese With this level the wines become truly sweet. Made from individually selected berries. They should be nobly rotten, and the wines will be sweet and luscious.

Trockenbeerenauslese Made from individually selected berries that are shrivelled with noble rot. TBAs are intensely sweet and long-lived – and expensive. To make a single bottle requires the grapes of six to eight vines. You'd expect at least 15 to 20 bottles of a cheap wine from that number of vines.

Eiswein Made from grapes that have frozen on the vine, when the temperature drops to -6°C. When they are pressed – still frozen – the water is left behind in the form of ice and only the intensely sweet juice – too full of sugar to freeze – comes off the press. Yields are tiny, and the risk of losing the whole crop is large, since the grapes must stay on the vine until December or even January. The wine is fearfully rare, fearfully expensive.

MOSEL-SAAR-RUWER

The Mosel-Saar-Ruwer region is almost too beautiful to bear. Nature has created such a brilliant combination of gentle, twisting river valley and soaring, broad-shouldered swathes of vines that it would be remarkable if these vineyards, coating the steep valley sides with a wonderful array of greens and golds through half the year, did not produce something altogether exceptional in the way of wine. And they do.

The white wines of the Mosel-Saar-Ruwer are unlike any others in the world – when they are based on the Riesling grape, and when they come from one of the numerous steep, slaty, south-facing vineyard sites nestled into the folds of the river, or strung out for mile upon mile in its golden heart between Bernkastel and Erden and, less breathtakingly, but just as importantly, between Bernkastel and Piesport. These wines can achieve a thrilling, orchard-fresh, spring flowers and autumn apples flavour, often with an alcohol level so low that it leaves your head clear enough, glass after glass, to revel in the flavours of the fruit. This is the joy of Mosel wine at its best, which no one else has succeeded in duplicating.

The great majority of Mosel wine comes from the river valley itself. There are, however, two small tributaries which have been

Even on a bright day the Mosel can look grey. But the Doctor vineyard soars above the town of Bernkastel, soaking up all the available sun.

incorporated into the overall region: the Saar and the Ruwer. These areas are even colder than much of the Mosel Valley and the reason for the difference in climate lies in geography.

Rising in the Vosges mountains of France, the Mosel flows more or less north-east from the German border with Luxembourg to join the Rhine at Koblenz, though in its middle section it winds so obsessively between its steep, slate walls that you'd be hard put to say exactly where it was going. But as the river twists and even sometimes retraces its route those bends provide plenty of steep vineyards that face south, south-east or south-west – these are the ones that receive most of the precious sun, and are sheltered from the wind. Along the Mosel many of the towns and villages lie on the shady, south side facing their vineyards on the opposite bank. As well as being suntraps many of these vineyards rise up almost from the water's edge and so benefit also from the heat reflected from the nearby river. And this warmth is what you need in such a northerly wine region.

The Saar and the Ruwer, by contrast, flow more or less northwards, to join the Mosel either side of the city of Trier, and this south to north direction provides fewer ideal vineyard sites, especially in the Saar, and the cold wind whistles through the vines. There is also the risk of frost in some Saar vineyards.

Along with vital warmth from the sun and shelter from the wind, slate plays a key role. Many of the Mosel vineyards, apart from those in the Upper Mosel or Obermosel, benefit from a stony, grey slate soil which absorbs the heat, reflecting it back on to the vines – and when heat is as precious as it is here, that is a valuable function. Another asset of slate is that it lets all the rain through. It can rain cats and dogs in the Mosel, and if the soil was absorbent it would all wash away down the steep slopes. As it is, the rain pours straight through the soil like water through a sieve. Erosion can be a problem, but even so, in the best slaty parts of the Mosel, the problem is far less than one would expect.

GRAPE VARIETIES AND WINE STYLES

Not all the Mosel is planted with Riesling – Germany's greatest grape accounts for only about half of the Mosel's vineyards, with the balance planted with inferior but higher yielding vines like Müller-Thurgau – but the Saar and the Ruwer valleys are simply too cold for much else to ripen. So here it's Riesling, Riesling, nearly all the way. The wines have higher acidity and a steely edge that is even more pronounced than that of the Mosel – and while **Beerenauslesen**, which need humidity, are a great rarity in the Saar and the Ruwer, **Eisweine**, which need severe cold rather than warmth and humidity, are somewhat more common. Indeed, some producers find that they can make Eiswein almost every year, albeit in small quantities.

The progress of the Riesling in the Mosel-Saar-Ruwer has not been particularly happy over the last few decades. In 1910 it occupied 88 per cent of the vineyards (Elbling has long been grown since Roman times in the Ober Mosel near the Luxembourg border, usually for sparkling wine) and as late as 1964 it still accounted for a proud 80 per cent. But then the rot set in – or rather, the fruit trees that occupied much of the flat alluvial ground by the river and the shady north-facing banks unsuitable for Riesling, were ripped out. Instead in went Müller-Thurgau and other lesser varieties with no regard for suitablility of site, certainly no regard for quality, and,

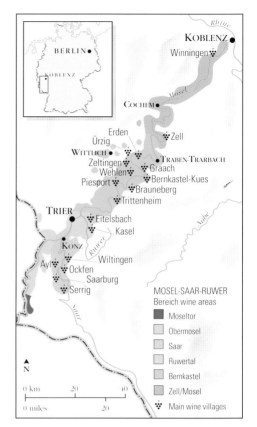

| MOSEL-SAAR-RUWER |
| Bereich wine areas |
| Moseltor |
| Obermosel |
| Saar |
| Ruwertal |
| Bernkastel |
| Zell/Mosel |
| Main wine villages |

This is the slate soil of the Saar, in the Scharzhofberg vineyard. It is composed of little more than shards of rock, from which the vines must find some sustenance.

producing feeble wine that was, disgracefully, allowed to bear the famous names of nearby villages. Riesling now accounts for 57 per cent of the Mosel's vineyards. Today any wine labelled with the regional names of Bereich Bernkastel or Piesporter Michelsberg is likely to come from such mediocre vineyards and these vines. It is very unlikely to originate from the villages of Bernkastel or Piesport themselves. And it will have nothing in common with the delicately steely, uncompromising style of true Mosel Riesling.

The Mosel does make wines right up to the very sweet **Trockenbeerenauslese** level, but they are definitely not as sweet as their equivalents from the Rhine, and the fundamental delicacy of Mosel fruit can be swamped by overripe richness. **Auslesen** are quite often made, but do not always have a noble rot character. The true genius of Mosel wine is usually found in Rieslings of **Kabinett** and **Spätlese** quality. These are sometimes made Halbtrocken (half dry) or Trocken (dry), and even those that make no claim to either style are often made drier (and, accordingly, with more alcohol) than they used to be. This is in response to fashion on the home market, which for some while seemed to crave ever leaner, more acidic wines. The fashionable taste is no longer quite so extreme, but growers all over Germany feel the need to make wines that will go with food – and that means drier than they used to be.

A Mosel **Kabinett** Trocken can, however, be a disaster. Take away the sweetness and you can have a wine that is all bones and no flesh – and only in warm years is there enough alcohol and body to compensate. **Spätlese** Trocken wines can be more successful, since their greater ripeness will fill the gap left by the sweetness. And in the Saar and Ruwer, especially, it is essential to look at the vintage, since in a cold year these wines can be lean in the extreme.

CLASSIFICATION

The same classification system is used for Mosel wines as in the rest of Germany, but with one important difference: all the minimum ripeness levels for the various quality categories are lower. This reflects the fact that it is more difficult to ripen grapes on the steep, slaty valley vineyards of the Mosel, and also that the traditional Mosel style, with its fresh lemony fruit and high natural tartaric acid level, is lighter, fresher and lower in alcohol than an equivalent Rhine wine. Along with the Ahr and Mittelrhein, these are the lowest sugar levels in German wine production.

ORGANIZATION

The merchants and co-operatives control nearly three-quarters of all Mosel wine. Moselland is the name of the huge, central co-operative at Bernkastel and it processes about one quarter of all the region's grapes. All these wine companies offer basic Bereich Bernkastel and Piesporter wine. The standard of all but a few of these mass-market wines is diabolical and the only companies who regularly produce good-quality, basic Mosels are those which own their own vineyards, such as Reh-Kendermann.

For the true taste of Mosel Riesling you need to go to a reliable single grower, most of whom only own a few hectares of vines or less. It's remarkably hard work making great Mosel wine and owning your own piece of land, especially a prized vineyard site, is a great incentive to quality. Best producers: **J J Christoffel, Grans-Fassian, Fritz Haag, Reinhold Haart, Heymann-Löwenstein,**

The steep Sonnenuhr vineyard at Wehlen in the Mittel Mosel is named after its famous sundial, built in 1842 for the vineyard workers.

and Bare Bum beloved of the tourists – and Piesporter Michelsberg. Also avoid wines sold as Bereich Bernkastel. Confusingly, wines from vineyards within the town of Bernkastel itself are some of the best in the region – these ones will be labelled as 'Bernkasteler' followed by the name of a vineyard such as 'Doctor', 'Graben' or 'Lay'.

To help you find an estate wine, look for the words 'Erzeugerabfüllung' or 'Gutsabfüllung', meaning 'estate bottled', in the small print at the bottom of the label. Look at the letters VDP – an association of top quality estates, especially strong in the Mosel.

Look also at the alcohol level. If the wine is a Kabinett with around 7.5 or 8 per cent alcohol, you will be getting a wine with a fair amount of residual sugar. As the alcohol goes up, so the residual sugar goes down.

WHAT DO THEY TASTE LIKE?

Good Mosel is a thrilling taste. There's nothing caressing, gentle, seductive about it, but it simply bursts with the happy, blossoming flavours of spring and early summer. As the first spring buds appear, everyone should whip out a bottle of Mosel Kabinett or Spätlese to remind themselves of the freshness and beauty of a world waking up again after the long dead haul of winter.

What is remarkable about good Mosel wines is that as they age they can still hold on to this freshness in a steely, tautly acidic way. A good Mosel should always have a high acidity level, though the wines of the Mittel Mosel villages of Piesport, Brauneberg, Graach, Zeltingen and Erden are likely to give wines with a softer, honeyed feel to them.

The wines from the side valleys of the Saar and Ruwer are lighter, with a wonderful steely bite which becomes deliciously, dangerously petrolly as they get older.

THE GOOD YEARS

Vintages matter enormously in the Mosel-Saar-Ruwer, since it is by no means possible to ripen the grapes properly every year. And even when ripening is achieved, the high yields which all of Germany pursues can mean the light, delicate flavours are too diluted to have much to say for themselves.

However, the finest estates can still make wonderful steely dry wines in cool years. In warm years (it's hardly ever too hot on the Mosel, though 2003 came close) the wines

Karthäuserhof, **Carl Loewen**, **Dr Loosen**, **Markus Molitor**, **Mönchhof**, **Egon Müller-Scharzhof**, **J J Prüm**, **Max Ferd. Richter**, **St-Urbans-Hof**, **Willi Schaefer**, **Schloss Lieser**, **Schloss Saarstein**, **von Schubert** (Maximin Grünhaus), **Selbach-Oster**, **Dr Thanisch**, **Wegeler**, **Weins-Prüm** and **Zilliken**.

READING THE LABEL

There was a time when you did not expect to see 'Riesling' on a Mosel wine label, since it was automatically assumed that all the wine would be Riesling. Sadly, this isn't so any more. Most cheap Mosel is from Müller-Thurgau, or something with even less claim to quality.

A Riesling wine nowadays will state the fact proudly on the label. As a rule, avoid the general brand names like Moselblümchen – an evocative name likely to be hiding a fairly hideous concoction – and wines sold under Grosslage names such as Zeller Schwarze Katz and Kröver Nacktarsch – the Black Cat will have a fascinating balance between smoky, minerally fruit and acidity.

Good Mosels keep well: a Kabinett will need four or five years to mature, and will last for several years more; a Spätlese will need perhaps seven years to come round and an Auslese probably ten.

2004   A large but classic vintage.

2003   Driest, warmest summer since 1540 and a small vintage. Problems of high alcohol with low acidity levels.

2002   Almost perfect season spoilt by rain at vintage time. Generous yields so quality won't be the equal of the 2001s.

2001   Some great wines from growers who picked late during the Indian summer.

2000   Modest quality, with some dilution due to heavy rain. For early drinking.

1999   The top estates produced aromatic, well-balanced wines but quality is variable.

1998   Classic, racy wines.

1997   Spring frosts reduced quantity. Quality for late-ripening varieties is good.

1996   Quality is unexciting.

1995   Good, balanced wines which should keep well.

Older vintages

1994, 1993, 1992, 1990, 1989, 1988, 1985, 1983, 1976, 1971, 1969, 1959.

ENJOYING THE WINES

There's nothing quite so refreshing as a light, well-made Kabinett from the Mosel, Saar or Ruwer to drink by itself, for the simple pleasure of its flavour. The flowery, apple freshness, the low alcohol, the tangy acidity all make Mosels marvellous anytime refreshment wines. They are generally reckoned to be less good with food, since even up to Auslese level, the flavours of Mosel wine are basically delicate but try a Mosel Kabinett with smoked fish or to sip as the sun goes down.

CONSUMER INFORMATION

WHAT DO I GET FOR MY MONEY?

Mosel wines are often remarkably good value but at the bottom end of the scale, the co-operatives can churn out large quantities of sugar-water and the good estates are increasingly aware of their own value, and charge accordingly. But it is still perfectly possible to find Kabinett (or even, Spätlese) wines from leading growers for roughly the price of a basic Bourgogne Blanc that has far less character and far less interest. The difference is that the Bourgogne Blanc is fashionable, the Kabinett isn't.

AVAILABILITY

The basic wines, like Bereich Bernkastel and Piesporter Michelsberg, are easily available. Ignore them and look in the corners of the fine wine shelves for single-vineyard, single-estate wines.

CONSUMER CHECKLIST

Erdener Treppchen	*Quality 9* ★
Riesling Kabinett 2004	*Price 7* ★
(Dr Loosen)	*Value 10* ★

Good Years   The Mosel has had a remarkable string of vintages in recent years. Best years: 2004, 2003, 2002, 2001, 1999, 1998, 1997, 1995, 1994, 1993, 1992, 1990.

Taste Notes   The impression should be of cool, tingling freshness, sharp as a lime, sweet as an apple, sometimes with a splash of honey. The Kabinett and Spätlese quality levels are usually the best examples of Mosel Riesling.

RHINE VALLEY

Most of Germany's vineyards owe their existence to the river Rhine. It first appears way south where it forms the northern border of Switzerland. At Basle the Rhine flows north through a wide fertile basin past the Baden vineyards (see page 169) to the heart of German wine production. The Pfalz, on the east-facing slopes of the Haardt mountains, is the most southerly of these Rhine wine regions. Next comes the Rheinhessen, with its finest vineyard sites around Nierstein on the so-called Rheinfront or Rheinterrasse, but encompassing a very large, prolific area away from the river to the west in undulating farmland. North of Mainz the Rhine meets the mass of the Taunus mountains and is forced west and here, along a short stretch between Wiesbaden and Assmannshausen, is the

Rheingau. Flowing into the Rhine at Bingen is the Nahe river and along its banks around Bad Kreuznach are some of the most perfect south-facing vineyards in the whole of Germany. North of Bingen, in a beautiful stretch of the Rhine valley, complete with fairytale castles and vineyards snuggling into the rockface overhanging the river, lies the Mittelrhein. Flowing into the Rhine just south of Bonn is the tiny river Ahr, a tourist spot with its own vineyards.

All these regions produce different styles of wine. But in general terms Rhine wine is fuller, broader and richer than Mosel wine. As in the Mosel, the finest grape is the Riesling, but only in the Mittelrhein does it cover the majority of the vineyards. And there's even some red made too.

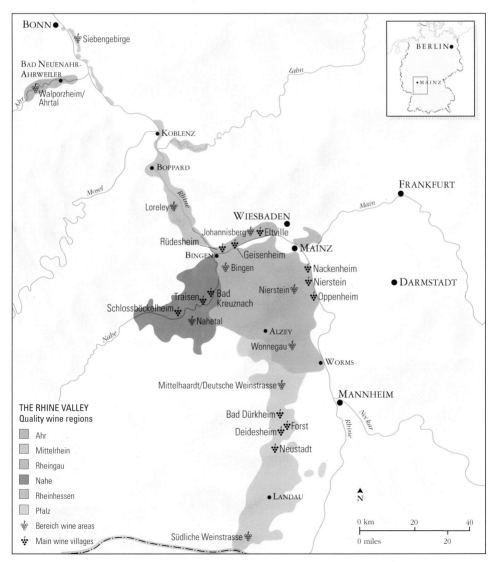

THE RHINE VALLEY
Quality wine regions

- Ahr
- Mittelrhein
- Rheingau
- Nahe
- Rheinhessen
- Pfalz
- Bereich wine areas
- Main wine villages

AHR & MITTELRHEIN

These are among the least known of the German wine regions – outside Germany. Inside Germany – particularly in Bonn and Koblenz, their nearest cities – they are rather better known, as tourist spots. Both the **Ahr** Valley, a tiny northerly tributary of the Rhine, and the **Mittelrhein**, a steep-sided, northern stretch of the Rhine, are extremely beautiful areas. And what could be more enticing for city-dwellers than a breath of mountain air and a bottle of local wine?

Both regions are tiny. The Mittelrhein has 495 hectares (1223 acres) under vine, the Ahr just 529 (1307) and until the early 1990s a steady decline in the Ahr had brought fears that the vineyards might disappear there altogether, in spite of the tourist trade.

GRAPE VARIETIES AND WINE STYLES
The Ahr specializes in red wines, which makes it a rarity in Germany. The Ahr should be too far north to produce anything substantial, and the traditional German taste for light sweetish reds meant it didn't have to. But there is a New Wave of producers whose full deep reds are transforming expectations. Try the reds of **Deutzerhof–Cossmann-Henle**, **Meyer-Näkel** or **Jean Stodden**, made from either Spätburgunder or a rare variant, Frühburgunder.

The Mittelrhein, by contrast, is **Riesling** country. Nearly 70 per cent of its vineyards are planted with Germany's finest grape – which makes it rather a shame that the weather here is too cold to produce the sort of quality found further upriver. The leanest of the wines are snapped up by the Sekt industry for sparkling wine; in the south of the region the wines are riper, sometimes slaty, and may even catch some noble rot.

CLASSIFICATION
In both the Ahr and Mittelrhein there is a fair amount of Qualitätswein, meaning the grape musts have been helped by adding sugar.

ORGANIZATION
Co-operatives are important in the Ahr but in the Mittelrhein it is easier to find wines from single estates.

READING THE LABEL
Look for the words Trocken or Halbtrocken on the labels of red wines, unless you relish something sweet. And look for Spätburgunder, too. It won't be as good as Burgundy's Pinot Noir, but it'll be the best there is.

WHAT DO THEY TASTE LIKE?
The Ahr flavour is pretty light. Mittelrhein wines rarely match up to the scenery, but even so are rather good, slightly sharp wines, with an earthy background.

THE GOOD YEARS
The warm years are the best – years like 2001 – and since then Germany has been generally lucky with the weather.

ENJOYING THE WINES
They are best drunk at a café table overlooking the river (the Ahr or the Rhine, as the case may be) with or without some local food.

CONSUMER INFORMATION

WHAT DO I GET FOR MY MONEY?
Tourist demand ensures high prices.

AVAILABILITY
They are not widely distributed in Germany and almost unavailable outside.

CONSUMER CHECKLIST
Bacharacher Hahn Riesling Spätlese 2004 (Toni Jost)

Quality 7 ★
Price 7 ★
Value 7 ★

Good Years Most are best drunk fairly young. Any recent year should be good.
Taste Notes The reds are light and sweetish; the whites earthy and light.

RHEINGAU

Of all the great vineyard areas of Germany, this is the smallest. There are just 3167 hectares (7825 acres) of vines here, which makes it one-third of the size of the Mosel-Saar-Ruwer, yet a favourable mesoclimate – plus the presence of large estates owned by the Church and the nobility – have meant fame for many of the villages along the northern bank of this stretch of the Rhine. At Wiesbaden the Rhine's rather stately progress north is met by the implacable wall of the Taunus mountains, and the river sullenly veers westwards until Rüdesheim. Rüdesheim to Wiesbaden is not much over 30 km (20 miles), yet between the two towns there is a parade of vineyards of concentrated brilliance on the south-facing riverside slopes.

Potential quality here is some of the highest in all Germany – though there are times when it still disappoints, when the Riesling lacks quite the balance of tension and richness that it should have. Excessive yields are the reason. Yields here are among the lowest in Germany, but frankly that's not saying a lot. A good Rheingau grower will take perhaps 70 or 80 hl/ha from his Riesling vineyards; in much of the flatter, more fertile Rheinhessen yields can easily be twice that, but is that an excuse? The Rheingau should be top quality.

Paradoxically, the presence of aristocratic, governmental, ecclesiastical – and, more recently, big business – ownership of substantial estates may have made it easy for Rheingau wines to acheieve considerable fame and fortune, but has also contributed to a lot of slovenly and uninspired – yet high priced – wines as numerous of the estates fell victim to lazy or exploitative management. In Germany more than perhaps any other country, you need great personal committment to maximize the potential of your vines, and life was too easy in the Rheingau – famous, and near such population centres as Frankfurt, Mainz and Wiesbaden. The recent return to form of the world-famous Schloss Johannisberg and Schloss Vollrads

Typically for a German wine town, the houses of Rüdesheim are squeezed in by the river, leaving south-facing slopes above free for vines.

estates is hopefully a sign that these powerful domaines are now keen to take things seriously again. In the meantime, there *are* good independent growers, and looking for the 'VDP' logo on the label is a good way to find some of the best.

GRAPE VARIETIES AND WINE STYLES

The **Riesling** grape dominates these slopes. It has 78 per cent of the vineyard hectarage, and virtually every great Rheingau is a Riesling wine. There is a little **Müller-Thurgau** – but now down to 2 per cent – and 13 per cent **Spätburgunder** (Pinot Noir), which is far more than there used to be. Spätburgunder – as Pinot Noir, responsible for red Burgundy – is centred on the village of Assmannshausen which, alone of the Rheingau villages, is famous for red wine. But there is some – and it's often better – grown in the main stretch of the Rheingau, too. Here, where it gets all the sun that's going, it may ripen to **Spätlese** or even **Auslese** level. When it's then fermented out dry and perhaps given some aging in new oak barrels, then you can end up with some very good, rich red wine. It's not a Burgundy lookalike – why should it be? – but it's a top glass. It's also another example of the Rheingau's international outlook – making wines to go with food because that's how the rest of Europe expects to drink them.

There are other grape varieties, too. There is a little **Weissburgunder** (Pinot Blanc) and Erbach's Rheinhell vineyard even has some **Chardonnay**. And the wine institute at Geisenheim is the centre of German wine research, which has created many of the new vine hybrids. However, new crossings like **Ehrenfelser**, **Scheurebe** and **Kerner** are more popular in other regions than they are in the Rheingau itself.

Although the region's fame rests of its astonishing sweet wines of **Beerenauslese** standard and higher – which manage to combine an intensity of honeyed sweetness with an acidity which is so strong and clean it is as fresh as a squirt of lime or blood orange into the grape juice – the Rheingau's true worth is measured lower down the scale, with the **Kabinetts** and **Spätlesen**.

These wines give the Riesling the chance to show off not only its floweriness and grapiness, but also the bite it acquires in the Rheingau, the steely, minerally, smoky toughness which is exhilarating and delicious. As the wines get sweeter, the honeyed ripeness takes on a musky beeswax aroma which is unique in the world of wine.

CLASSIFICATION

The Rheingau is the first of Germany's 13 wine regions to have an official vineyard classification. The term ' Erstes Gewächs' or First Growth applies to dry or sweet wines of Auslese quality and upwards from these historically superior classified vineyards.

ORGANIZATION

For fine Rheingau it is always worth buying estate-bottled wine and the VDP and Charta organizations have done much to improve the region's reputation within Germany. Many of the best Rheingau wines now come from the smaller, family-owned estates. Best producers: **J B Becker** (good red), **Breuer**, **Flick**, **von Hessen**, **Johannishof**, **Jung**, **Kesseler**, **Krone**, **Kühn**, **Künstler**, **Lang**, **Josef Leitz**, **Löwenstein**, **Prinz**, **Ress**, **Schloss Johannisberg**, **Schloss Reinhartshausen**, **Schloss Schönborn**, **Schloss Vollrads**, **Spreitzer**, **Staatsweingut Eltville**, **Wegeler**, **Robert Weil** and **Werner**.

READING THE LABEL

Look out for the term 'VDP' as a sign of quality. You may also see wine names that break the usual Germany pattern of village name followed by vineyard followed by grape followed by ripeness level. One variation (it's happening with quality-conscious growers elsewhere in Germany, too) is for producers to use just the village and the grape names for their simplest wines – Rauenthaler Riesling, for example. There may be more information on the back label, but it's a sign of general exasperation with the complexity of the wine laws.

Certain vineyards (e.g. Schloss Vollrads and Schloss Johannisberg) have the right to omit the village name – it generally means they have been so famous for centuries that even the bureaucrats are convinced by their renown. Both are rare German examples of big houses surrounded by their own vineyards.

Price rises in the Rheingau have been as steep as the vineyard slopes. This is the Höllenberg vineyard at Assmannhausen famous for Spätburgunder.

WHAT DO THEY TASTE LIKE?

At their best, Rheingau wines are marked by an astonishing balance between grapiness and slatiness, between perfume and smoke, between luscious honey and austere acidity. They often have the most lingering, endlessly shifting flavours the Riesling is capable of producing, and even the Kabinetts have body and ripeness. The Halbtrocken and Trocken styles can take a bit of getting used to for anyone familiar with the sweeter styles, but they have improved immeasurably over the last few years and do have the body and ripeness to cope with dryness.

THE GOOD YEARS

Most Kabinetts need at least five years, and Spätlesen should be given at least seven. Auslesen will need longer, and if from a good vintage, should still be fine after 20 years. The ultra-sweet wines, the Beerenauslesen and Trockenbeerenauslesen, will need longer.

2004 Large but classic vintage. Indian summer meant that grapes of Beeren- and Trockenbeerenauslese ripeness were picked.

2003 Very hot weather led to some fine sweet wines.

2002 Almost perfect season until rain at vintage time but the wines still excellent.

2001 Wonderful late autumn produced excellent late harvest wines.

2000 Pretty dreadful weather. Modest quality.

1999 The second rainy harvest in a row but many long-lived Auslesen wines were picked.

1998 Torrential rain at vintage time but Kabinett and Spätlesen wines are good.

1997 Good late harvest conditions resulted in excellent Spätlese and Auslese.

1996 Harvesting delayed and, as elsewhere, quality was down.

1995 A Spätlese and Auslese vintage for those who waited to pick after the rain.

Older vintages

1994, 1993, 1992, 1990, 1989, 1985, 1983, 1976, 1971.

ENJOYING THE WINES

Trocken – and even more so, Halbtrocken – wines can be very successful with food, particularly spicy oriental flavours. Go for a Spätlese fermented out dry or half-dry in order to have enough body. Off-dry Kabinett and Spätlese wines are delicious by themselves. The best Spätlese or Auslese reds will cope well with beef or lamb dishes.

CONSUMER INFORMATION

WHAT DO I GET FOR MY MONEY?

Prices have risen steeply in recent years – largely due to the marketing efforts of the same leading estates who have been concerned to raise standards of winemaking. Most Rheingaus are now fairly expensive by German standards, particularly if they are of Auslese level or above. But it is still possible to find Kabinetts – and even Spätlesen, if you're lucky – at affordable prices.

AVAILABILITY

The Rheingau is a small region, and there's not a great deal, even of the basic wines, to go round – and demand within Germany is high. But a reasonable selection of estate wines finds its way abroad.

CONSUMER CHECKLIST

Kiedricher Gräfenberg	*Price 10* ★
Riesling Auslese 2001	*Price 10* ★
(Robert Weil)	*Value 9* ★

Good Years There's hasn't been a really disastrous vintage in the Rheingau for years, even though it is very susceptible to poor weather. Best years: 2004, 2003, 2002, 2001, 1999, 1998, 1997, 1996, 1994, 1993, 1990, 1989, 1985, 1983, 1976, 1971.

Taste Notes Wonderful balance is the keynote, with a slaty, dry edge, and the sweet wines maintain this wonderful refreshing flavour.

NAHE

Where? What did you say it was called? The what? How do you spell that? Okay, that's a bit unfair. The Nahe is far from obscure – in fact it produces some of Germany's finest wines. But it doesn't have one of the biggest reputations – or rather, it doesn't have the long-standing reputation of the Rheingau or the Mosel. Part of the reason for this is that the Nahe only started flying its own flag in a big way relatively recently: until the 1930s much of its wine tended to be sent off to the Rhine or the Mosel for blending.

It's an area of mixed farming, too, so the vine doesn't rule in the way that it does in, say, the Rheingau. Indeed, one of the best vineyards in the Nahe, the Kupfergrube at Schlossböckelheim, was planted from scratch only in the early years of the twentieth century. 'Kupfergrube' means copper mine, and that's exactly what it was: a steep slope of scrub and rock above the entrance to a copper mine. But the beady eye of the then director of the important local State Domaine at Niederhausen-Schlossböckelheim fell on it, and he set convict labour to work on clearing the scrubby ground and building the steep slopes out of the rocky hillside.

Whether the convicts ever got to taste the fruits of their labours I don't know, but somehow I doubt it. These are wonderful Rieslings, full and rich from the influence of the heat-retaining, colourful volcanic porphyry soil on which the vines grow, and very long lived wines they are.

There are three areas of the Nahe that produce top-class wine. The heart of the region lies around the village of Schlossböckelheim and stretches for a short way along the north bank of the Nahe past the villages of Niederhausen, Norheim and Traisen downriver to Bad Münster; here, the south-facing slopes provide some wonderful Riesling sites, including Schlossböckelheimer Kupfergrube and Traiser Bastei which nestles at the foot of the towering Rotenfels cliff.

The second vineyard area is just north of the town of Bad Kreuznach, and the third is across the river from Bingen, where the Nahe flows into the Rhine. There are other good vineyards elsewhere, mainly on the south-facing slopes of the small tributaries that flow into the Nahe, but these three areas are the main ones.

GRAPE VARIETIES AND WINE STYLES

Much of the wine of the Nahe does have an uncanny ability to unsettle the taster by being similar to a Mosel in lightness and freshness, yet even more similar to a Rheingau in the intensity of fruit and the power of the bouquet. One might also detect some Rheinhessen floweriness there. It's a big region, appreciably bigger than the Rheingau, and the majority of the land is in the flatter, lower part of the river valley, where the well-known Rüdesheimer Rosengarten produces a large amount of pleasant, fruity wine hardly distinguishable from Rheinhessen wine.

The **Riesling** is by far the most important grape, both in terms of reputation and plantings, since the great upriver sites are almost exclusively planted with Riesling. Overall in the Nahe 25 per cent of the vineyard area is planted with Riesling and the dreaded **Müller-Thurgau** has fallen to 15 per cent.

Silvaner is also important here, and can make good wines in favourable sites. There are some newer grape varieties, too, of which the most common is **Dornfelder**. But look for Riesling if you want to the best the Nahe has to offer. Rieslings range from basic **Qualitätswein** right up to great **Trockenbeerenauslesen** and **Eisweine**, though the most typical and exciting

The Rotenfels cliff rises sheer above the Traiser Bastei vineyard, with the vines (here being sprayed) packed closely into the scree at its foot.

wines are the **Spätlesen** and **Auslesen**, where an astonishing grapiness blends with a wonderful, minerally, chill vein of flavour to produce full but superbly balanced wines.

CLASSIFICATION

The Nahe occupies a middle position between the Rhine and Mosel as regards the required minimum ripeness for the different categories of QmP wines. For most grape varieties up to Kabinett level the Nahe and Mosel are the same while for Spätlese and Auslese the Nahe creeps ahead, though only by 2° Oechsle. Wines labelled simply Bereich Nahetal or Rüdesheimer Rosengarten should at best be light, fruity wines but in no way resembling the best wines from single vineyards.

ORGANIZATION

Most of the Nahe vineyards are scattered along the valleys and a great deal of the wine is sold at the farm gate. The co-operatives are fairly good but it's best to aim high here – some of Germany's finest Rieslings come from a handful of top producers. Best producers: **Crusius, Schlossgut Diel, Hermann Dönnhoff, Emrich-Schönleber, Göttelmann, Kruger-Rumpf, Gutswervaltung Niederhausen-Schlossböckelheim, Plettenberg, Prinz zu Salm-Dalberg** and **Schäfer-Fröhlich**.

The village of Oberhausen is on the right bank of the Nahe while its top vineyard, the Oberhäuser Brücke, is across the river, on sloping land and facing south.

READING THE LABEL

Top village names to look out for include Bad Kreuznach, Dorsheim, Langenlonsheim, Laubenheim, Monzingen, Münster-Sarmsheim, Niederhausen, Norheim, Oberhausen Roxheim, Schlossböckelheim, Traisen, Wallhausen and Winzenheim. Other villages in the Nahe will probably yield pleasant but unexceptional wines.

WHAT DO THEY TASTE LIKE?

Caught between the acid freshness of the Mosel and the cool, grapy brilliance of the Rheingau, Nahe wines have a freshness which is almost sweet, and yet this steely, mineral edge keeps them startlingly fresh. Of all German wines they accentuate the grapy side of the Riesling's character.

THE GOOD YEARS

The Nahe's relatively southerly position compared with many of Germany's other vineyard areas means that most vintages recently have been pretty good. As with Germany's other leading wine regions, the Rieslings, particularly those from good producers, need time to develop in bottle.

In classic years all the Nahe can produce fine wines, burning with the flavour of the soil and the grape. In lesser years, the flatter, downstream vineyards north of Bad Kreuznach will still produce pleasant wine, but only the best upstream sites will bring out the best from underripe grapes.

The Kabinetts and Spätlesen need five to seven years' aging and Auslesen perhaps eight or more. If you can lay your hands on a Beerenauslese or even a Trockenbeerenauslese, don't touch it for at least a decade. At least. Eiswein, like those from Germany's other regions, can be drunk young, or left for a decade for the acidity to soften.

2004 Good quality Riesling and the Pinot family, despite frost damage, storms and hail.

2003 Older vines coped best with the summer drought and extreme heatwave. Very high ripeness levels and some outstanding wines produced.

2002 Another very good vintage, helped by warm, dry weather at vintage time.

2001 Indian summer right into November produced excellent late-harvest wines. Plenty of good Eiswein, too.

2000 Torrential rain throughout the harvest produced rather dilute wines.

1999 A variable vintage so stick to the top producers.

1998 Good and plentiful Eiswein.

1997 No spring frost in this region. Decent quality.

1996 Good late harvest conditions up to early November. Quality better than elsewhere in Germany.

1995 Probably the best year since 1990.

Older vintages

1993, 1992, 1990, 1989, 1988, 1985, 1983, 1981, 1976, 1971.

ENJOYING THE WINES

I have always eaten pretty massive meals in the Nahe, with which the wines went well enough, but the best combinations were between quite full Kabinett Rieslings and the local, early-season white asparagus. Because of their slight grapy sweetness, allied to just a hint of metallic bite, they make marvellous wines to drink by themselves.

CONSUMER INFORMATION

WHAT DO I GET FOR MY MONEY?

In general the Nahe offers good value for money. The top wines are fairly priced (not cheap, note – just fair) because their names are less well known than those from the more famous Rheingau villages across the Rhine. The most basic cheap and cheerful Nahe wines are almost always pleasant, fruity and nicely balanced. However, they are unlikely to contain many – or even any – Riesling grapes in them.

AVAILABILITY

Not brilliant. A large percentage of the wine is bought direct in the region, and there are relatively few top estates, compared to its neighbours, the Rheingau and the Mosel. Even the most famous basic wine, Rüdesheimer Rosengarten, is not widely seen. You will need to go to a specialist if you want to try something really thrilling like Schlossböckelheimer Kupfergrube.

CONSUMER CHECKLIST

Oberhäuser Brücke	*Quality 10* ★
Riesling Spätlese	*Price 9* ★
2002	*Value 10* ★

Good Years The Nahe can produce pleasant rather than exciting wines in most vintages, but her top wines need a great year like 2001 to do well. In general, the wines from the best growers age very well, but other wines are drinkable almost immediately. Best years: 2004, 2003, 2002, 2001, 1999, 1998, 1997, 1996, 1995, 1993, 1992, 1990, 1989, 1988, 1985, 1983, 1981, 1976, 1971.

Taste Notes There is a lovely fruity freshness about Nahe wines, with more acid balance than those from the Rheinhessen, more fruit than the Mosel, and less weight than the Rheingau. The Mittel Nahe vineyards around Schlossböckelheim produce the wines with the most intense minerally smell and taste which almost overpower the fruit flavours.

RHEINHESSEN

The Rheinhessen is the largest of the Rhine's wine-producing areas, as far as vineyard hectarage and volume go, but if you look on the map (see page 155) you will see that this does not tell the whole story. The Rhine flows north from Worms to Mainz, then angles west to Bingen before forcing its way north again, leaving an enormous hinterland in the southwest. All this is the Rheinhessen, and some 165 villages nestle there in bland anonymity.

But between Mainz and Worms, the names Oppenheim, Nierstein, Nackenheim and Bodenheim appear, and, way round the bend in the far west of the region, Bingen – five villages, on whose fame and limited output rests the reputation of the entire Rheinhessen. These are villages which have their vineyards on the river, the first four sharing a sweep of land called the Rheinterrasse (or Rhine front) and they can make some of Germany's finest wine. Can. Not everything, even from the Rheinterrasse villages, is anything like as good as one would like it to be. Because that's the other problem with wine: even when nature does her bit, you can't rely on people to do theirs.

These five between them comprise the two quality areas of the Rheinhessen and can all produce great whites. Near Bingen the village of Ingelheim produces fairly decent reds from Spätburgunder, though the wines tend to be of the light and strawberryish kind rather than anything more substantial.

Further inland the Rheinhessen can produce decent wines. But the growers never have the same advantages as do those working the slopes of the Rheinterrasse. The gentle inland hills are cooler than the slopes facing the river, making it more difficult for the Riesling to ripen (one reason why there isn't much Riesling here); and of course the lack of any famous villages means that growers here can only ever attach a lower price tag to their wines. And if you can't charge the right price, why bother to take the trouble?

GRAPE VARIETIES AND WINE STYLES

Nearly all the grapes from the 160 lesser wine villages go into the faceless blends of cheap wine, especially **Liebfraumilch**, with which Germany floods the export markets and wines under the regional names of Bereich Bingen and Bereich Nierstein which cover the output of about two-thirds of the whole of the

On the Rheinterrasse, here looking across from the Ölberg vineyard in Nierstein to the Rhine, vineyards take priority over all other crops

Rheinhessen. Bereich Wonnegau mops up the remainder. No wonder the growers of Nierstein in particular feel that their own fame and excellence is being seriously eroded by all the other villages, many of whom offer their own wines labelled as Nierstein yet at half the price and half the quality.

The fault lies partly with the German wine law, which allows the names of good villages like Nierstein to be so shamefully abused. If you see a wine labelled Niersteiner Ölberg, it comes from a single vineyard within the village boundaries of Nierstein. One labelled Niersteiner Gutes Domtal is a blend of wines from no fewer than 15 villages; and only a tiny part of it – fewer than 30 hectares (74 acres) – is in the village of Nierstein.

It gets worse: the Bereich Nierstein, under which name wine can also be sold, covers the whole eastern part of the Rheinhessen. Could a more short-sighted rule have been devised? And who would ensure that such a concept became law? The growers and co-operatives determined to sell large quantities of poor wine by whatever methods they could devise? Or the few growers with a few precious hectares of steep, hard-to-work vineyard land in Nierstein itself? You tell me.

The best wines of the Rheinhessen are made from **Riesling**. A quick glance at the figures is sufficient to indicate how little really good wine is made here: Riesling has just 10 per cent of the vineyard area, while the inferior **Müller-Thurgau**, **Dornfelder** and **Silvaner** are all ahead of it in the pecking order. Silvaner, admittedly, can be good and it is often marketed as a high-quality wine to go with food. Dornfelder, when not over cropped – and it often is in Rheinhessen – makes excellent dark, soft plummy red.

Scheurebe – a Riesling x Silvaner crossing – can be good but it does need a dedicated grower to persuade it to achieve its magic flavour of honey and ripe pink grapefruit. In fact, name me a grape and they're sure to grow it somewhere in the Rheinhessen, because this is the great experimental area of Germany. The idea may have started out as one of adding a little floweriness and excitement to the generally dull tastes of the hinterland Hessen wines, but too often, with grapes like **Ortega**, **Kerner** and **Optima**, the result is a rather coarse, scented pungency with no elegance. Müller-Thurgau can be pleasant, with an undemanding pot-pourri scent, and Silvaner has a more earthy style.

All these go into the bland, sugary concoctions sold as Liebfraumilch. That such a wine can be Qualitätswein – that is, of a level equivalent to the French Appellation Contrôlée – is yet another point to the discredit of the German wine law. Liebfraumilch can come from several German wine regions, but it still accounts for one-fifth of all Rheinhessen wine production. The demands made on Liebfraumilch are few. As long as it is sweetish and of low acidity, is made from at least 70 per cent Müller-Thurgau, Kerner, Silvaner or Riesling and is 'of pleasant character', it's passed the test. In practice, who would put high-quality Riesling grapes into such a cheap wine? The one or two leading brands may have a dribble of Riesling, but don't bank on it. In fact, the market for Liebfraumilch is, happily, in decline.

Liebfraumilch has perfectly respectable origins in Worms, in the south of the region, where there is a Gothic church called the Liebfrauenkirche. The church's own vineyard now distances itself from Liebfraumilch by calling itself the Liebfrauenstift-Kirchenstück – and makes reasonable, though not exciting wine.

CLASSIFICATION

Most Rheinhessen wine is likely to be of fairly basic Qualitätswein standard. However, true Nierstein is a particularly ripe wine and in most years the village will produce a large amount of QmP wines.

ORGANIZATION

Given the predominance of branded Liebfraumilch and Bereich Nierstein, obviously merchants' commercial blends play a dominant role here. The co-operatives are pretty good but they mainly concentrate on producing anonymous blends. However, the serious growers of Nierstein and other Rheinterrasse villages produce some of Germany's finest

On the Rheinterrasse Oppenheim's best vineyards, including the Herrenberg, lie behind the town on a south-east-facing slope slightly away from the Rhine.

wines at all levels up to TbA. Best producers: **Balbach**, **Gunderloch**, **Guntrum**, **Gutzler**, **Heyl zu Herrnsheim**, **Keller**, **Manz**, **Sankt Antony**, **Schales**, **Schneider**, **Villa Sachsen**, **Wagner-Stempel** and **Wittmann**.

READING THE LABEL

This, I'm afraid, is where you have to start looking hard for single-vineyard names – as opposed to those of Grosslagen or Bereiche. Good single-vineyard names include (in Nierstein) Pettenthal, Brudersberg, Hipping, Kransberg, Glöck, Ölberg, Heiligenbaum and Orbel; (in Oppenheim) Herrenberg, Sackträger and Kreuz; (in Nackenheim) Rothenberg; (in Bodenheim) Hoch and Silberberg; and (in Bingen) Scharlachberg.

WHAT DO THEY TASTE LIKE?

Rheinhessen wines at their best have a delicious, scented floweriness to them, nearly always gentle, sometimes slightly grapy, but with the whiff of a rose garden in bloom. The Rheinterrasse wines, particularly of Bodenheim and Nierstein, can be wonderfully scented, rising to some of the richest, sweetest wines in Germany, yet still retaining their acid edge. Bingen wines have a dry, steely, sometimes positively smoky, quality closer to the style of the Rheingau, just across the river.

THE GOOD YEARS.

Only top Rieslings will age.

2004 A late harvest and healthy, ripe grapes for both reds and whites.

2003 Summer of the long heatwave. Healthy grapes and abundant harvest.

2002 Another good vintage.

2001 Pinot varieties did particularly well.

2000 Another vintage badly hit by rain.

1999 Some wines are dilute so trade up.

1998 Classic Kabinett and Spätlesen wines.

1997 Pleasant, but not special, now tiring.

1996 Good quality, age-worthy wines.

Older vintages

1995, 1993, 1990, 1988, 1985, 1983, 1976, 1971.

ENJOYING THE WINES

The best Rheinhessen estate wines are often marvellous by themselves but also have enough flavour to go with the river fish and sausages. The very sweet wines are some of the few in Germany which are really rich and luscious enough to match sweet puddings.

CONSUMER INFORMATION

WHAT DO I GET FOR MY MONEY?

What you pay for, that's what you get. Cheap Liebfraumilch and Bereich Nierstein blends can be reasonable if they're fresh, but basic Kabinetts don't cost much more and are generally better quality. The top wines are fairly expensive, particularly from Bingen and Nierstein, but are high quality if from a good grower.

AVAILABILITY

Liebfraumilch is one of the most easily available wines in the world – outside Germany, that is. The Germans are more likely to demand some kind of provenance for their wines. Top-quality Rheinhessen wines are not easy to find but perservere.

CONSUMER CHECKLIST

Nackenheimer Riesling	*Quality 8* ★
Spätlese 2001 (Gunderloch)	*Price 8* ★
	Value 8 ★

Good Years Most vintages are reasonable to good. The best single vineyard wines of Nierstein, Nackenheim and Bingen age almost as well as Rheingau wines; everyday wines should be drunk young. Best years: 2004, 2003, 2002, 2001, 1998, 1997, 1996, 1995, 1993, 1992, 1990, 1988, 1985, 1983, 1976, 1971.

Taste Notes The best Rheinterrasse wines have a freshness and honeyed sweetness matched by the good structure so lacking in much of the region; Bingen wines resemble the steelier Nahes.

PFALZ

If you want to get to the Pfalz – indeed, if you want to see exactly how French wines differ in style from German – go to Alsace and head north. You'll travel through umpteen Alsace villages all making dry, spicy wine from such grape varieties as Riesling, Tokay-Pinot Gris, Gewürztraminer and Pinot Noir. Then cross the border into Germany. The same range of hills, the Haardt mountains, which the French call the Vosges, continues on your left. The Rhine is to your right, some distance away across the plain. There are umpteen villages, all making wine from, among other vines, Riesling, Pinot Gris, Traminer (alias Gewürztraminer) and Spätburgunder (alias Pinot Noir). The wines are full, rich, and often have a touch of spice. They're even quite often drier than most German wines. But whereas the French versions have a savoury vinosity that is entirely French, these wines from the Pfalz have a floweriness, a muskiness that is entirely German.

As in Alsace, the rain shadow caused by the mountains has an important influence on the climate, making the Pfalz Germany's driest and sunniest region and only a little less warm than Baden just to the south. As well as an advantageous climate, the Pfalz benefits from an extraordinary range of soils, including loam, loess and some weathered sandstone near the mountains.

The northern Pfalz used to be the only place you looked if you wanted top quality: the villages of Wachenheim, Forst, Deidesheim, Ruppertsberg, Bad Dürkheim and Kallstadt would have been the beginning and end of your search. And they're still good.

But these days the south is busy catching up and, indeed, is the centre of a lot of youthful innovation. The southern Pfalz used to be all Liebfraumilch – and it's still the main producer. But it's also the home of individual growers who think to themselves, why shouldn't I age my wine in new oak if the results are good? Why shouldn't I make a good, international-style red from Spätburgunder? Why shouldn't I make, drier, more elegant wines than the rich, somewhat blowsy style for which the Pfalz was known until quite recently?

And having thought it, they do it. The southern Pfalz is one of the least hidebound places in the whole of German wine. And maybe because all the famous estates are in the north, it's a place where ambitious young growers can make their mark.

The Pfalz produces some of Germany's richest, ripest wines. These grapes come from near Neustadt-an-der-Weinstrasse, in the north of the region.

GRAPE VARIETIES AND WINE STYLES

The whole feel of the Pfalz is immensely easy-going, the ancient villages rather chubby and contented, and the vineyards, on gentle, east-facing slopes, joining imperceptibly with the wide, flat, agricultural plain down toward the Rhine. Much of the wine follows the same pattern: broad, soft, rather smugly fruity, memorable for the ripeness of the fruit but not the bite, nor for the racy flash of acidity, except in the best villages of the north. And so the good growers play on this.

Riesling is the most important variety – accounting for 20 per cent of the vineyards – and there are only small quantities of **Pinot Gris** (Grauburgunder or Ruländer) or **Gewürztraminer**. But they can make some terrific wine, ripe and well-structured. There are large plantings of **Müller-Thurgau** and **Kerner** while the reds (**Dornfelder**, **Blauer Portugieser** and **Spätburgunder**) account for nearly 40 per cent of plantings. These used to be merely attractive cherryish reds, especially from Spätburgunder, but there is now an increasing number of deep, ripe, impressive reds, led by Spätburgunder, but amply supported by Dornfelder and, occasionally, Frühburgunder. The lesser grapes, of course, go into the Liebfraumilch vat, or something very like it.

Just as they do in Alsace, white grapes seem to take on fullness and lusciousness here – even Riesling ripens regularly in the Pfalz. A Riesling **Kabinett** from one of the good northern Pfalz villages can be both rich and taut, and will be long-lived. Gewürztraminer can be some of the spiciest in Germany (though it never seems to equal Alsace levels of spice). Pinot Gris attracts noble rot and gets astonishingly sweet – when it is often known as Ruländer. The name Grauburgunder is often (though not always) kept for the drier wines.

CLASSIFICATION

The two Bereich areas of the Pfalz are enormous; while the northern one, Bereich Mittelhaardt or Deutsche Weinstrasse, may house the great names, the southern one, Bereich Südliche Weinstrasse, can boast of some of the most exciting wine-making. All the different levels of wine – Qualitätswein, Kabinett, Spätlese, Auslese, Beerenauslese and Trockenbeerenauslese – are likely to taste bigger and sweeter in the Pfalz than from further north. For this reason, the dry Trocken wines can be reasonably good, having enough ripe body to keep their fruit even when fully dry.

ORGANIZATION

In the Pfalz the co-operatives are enormously important as well as being efficient and motivated, and their general effect on quality is positive. However, the leading Pfalz villages have a large number of growers bottling their own wine, and producing great wine in the process. Best producers: **von Bassermann-Jordan**, **F Becker**, **Bergdolt**, **Bernhart**, **Biffar**, **von Buhl**, **Bürklin-Wolf**, **Christmann**, **Deinhard**, **Kleinmann**, **Knipser**, **Koehler-Ruprecht**, **Mosbacher**, **Müller-Catoir**, **Münzberg**, **Pfeffingen**, **Rebholz**, **Karl Schaefer**, **Siegrist**, **Ullrichshof**, **Weegmüller**, **Wehrheim**, **Wilhelmshof** and **Wolf**.

READING THE LABEL

Dry wines will be labelled 'Trocken', half-dry ones 'Halbtrocken'. Apart from that, and apart from looking for the name of a good grower, look on the label for the following villages: Bad Dürkheim, Wachenheim, Forst, Deidesheim, Kallstadt, Ruppertsberg, Freinsheim, Herxheim, Grosskarlbach and Laumersheim in the north of the region, and Siebeldingen, Leinsweiler and Burrweiler in the south.

Traditional barrels (and traditional lighting) in the cellar at Weingut von Buhl, a large, historic estate in Deidesheim, now leased to the Japanese group, Sanyo.

WHAT DO THEY TASTE LIKE?

Even at the most basic level in the Pfalz, the wine tastes are big, strong and ripe. It's not a joke to say the wines remind you of tropical fruits, because many winetasters use such *aides-mémoires* as a way of identifying Pfalz wines. However, there is usually a decent balance, even when the fruit tends to near-blowsiness. In good Rieslings, the sheer concentration of flavour can be startling, and some of the best producers of the north, such as Bürklin-Wolf and von Buhl, can match their ripe fruit with a delicacy the Rheingau would be proud of.

THE GOOD YEARS

There is hardly such a thing as a bad year in the Pfalz, because even in the coolest, wettest years, a reasonable amount of wine reaches Prädikat level. In any case, many of the producers and co-operatives concentrate on bulk blends and are not attempting to make Prädikat level wines. The information below applies only to serious estate wines. Many of the wines can be drunk young, but should also keep well and develop in bottle.

2004 Producers who controlled yields did best. Deep-coloured reds and whites with fresh acidity and lots of fruit.

2003 Summer of the long heatwave. Ripe grapes with unusually high Oeschle levels.

Flemlingen is like many villages in the southern Pfalz – it has never had any particular reputation of its own and must rely on generally good quality to succeed.

Riesling did particularly well.

2002 A fine vintage, with excellent Riesling and Pinot Noir.

2001 Glorious long Indian summer meant high Oeschle levels and an unprecedented red wine vintage.

2000 Very poor weather hit quality severely.

1999 A bigger vintage than 1998 and quality is better than elsewhere in Germany.

1998 Fine wines right across the board.

1997 Excellent Spätlese and Auslese.

1996 Ideal late harvest conditions.

1995 Rich wines now tiring.

Older vintages

1994, 1993, 1992, 1990, 1989, 1988, 1985, 1983, 1976, 1971.

ENJOYING THE WINES

The Kabinetts and Spätlesen, with their full spicy flavour, are delicious by themselves, but it is also their body and extra fruit which make them excellent summer lunch wines, when the mixture of pâtés, meats, salads and cheeses could scare away a light Mosel. The Trocken wines go very well with fish and fowl, and when from a good vineyard and a ripe year, they even go fairly well with game and strong cheese. The luscious sweet wine often accompany the local fruit and cream concoctions – even figs ripen in the Pfalz.

CONSUMER INFORMATION

WHAT DO I GET FOR MY MONEY?

Pretty good value, on the whole. The famous estates of the north charge fairly high prices for their wines, but the south can offer very good value indeed, since both the villages and the growers are far less well known.

AVAILABILITY

Not fantastic outside Germany. The great estates of the northern Pfalz are probably easier to find. Availability in general suffers from the same problem that afflicts all good German wine abroad: it's unfashionable, nobody buys it, so shops don't stock it. But it's worth perservering.

CONSUMER CHECKLIST

Scheurebe Haardter Mandelring *Quality 10* ★
Spätlese 2001 *Price 8* ★
(Müller-Catoir) *Value 10* ★

Good Years The best villages produce Prädikat wines almost every year, and these will be drinkable early but still age well. The great estates produce powerful wines in good years, which last well. Best years: 2004, 2003, 2002, 2001, 1999, 1998, 1997, 1996, 1994, 1993, 1992, 1990, 1989, 1988, 1985, 1983, 1976, 1971.

Taste Notes The Pfalz's warm, sunny climate means that the wines have an almost exotic, pungent character.

BADEN-WÜRTTEMBERG

Baden-Württemberg is two wine regions, yoked together by German bureaucracy into a single state for non-wine purposes, and in fact making very different sorts of wine. Baden is the one we come across most – the drier style of Baden wines is familiar to anyone who has sampled the wares of the big central co-operative, the Badischer Winzerkeller. Württemberg, conversely, is far better known only to the residents of Stuttgart and it's nearly all drunk close to home.

BADEN

The first thing to say about Baden is that it sprawls all over the place. The main chunk of vineyards, where 80 per cent of the wine comes from, is a long narrow strip across the Rhine from Alsace and sandwiched between the river and the Black Forest. It's quite warm here – in fact, Baden as a whole is warm enough to be in the EU's vineyard Zone B, while the rest of Germany's wine regions are in Zone A. Being in Zone B puts Baden, temperature-wise, on a par with Alsace and the Loire Valley, although in fact this main stretch of vineyard is a touch cooler than Alsace, and a bit damper, too. It stretches from the chi-chi spa town of Baden-Baden right down to the Swiss border, taking in on its way some of Baden's most important areas.

The Bereich **Ortenau** is one such and it is the home of some of Baden's best Rieslings, especially on the granite hills east of Offenburg. Breisgau, Ortenau's neighbour, grows a lot of Müller-Thurgau but also the Pinot family, Grau- and Weissburgunder. Further south, the **Kaiserstuhl** is also well known. The Kaiserstuhl proper (it has given its name to the whole Bereich) is an extinct volcano which still rises, steeply and stumpily, from the surrounding plain, and is covered with vines. It's more or less horseshoe-shaped, and one of the villages tucked into its valleys, Irhingen, is the warmest in Germany. Just to the south-east there's another, smaller, outcrop, the **Tuniberg**, which also gives its name to a Bereich. This one is a crest of limestone and the growers of Baden have pounced on it with as much delight as they did on the Kaiserstuhl.

East of this main strip of Baden vineyards there are other scattered vineyards down near the Swiss border in the **Markgräflerland** district and on the shores of Lake Constance within the Bereich **Bodensee**; in the north, between Heidelberg and Karlsruhe there is the

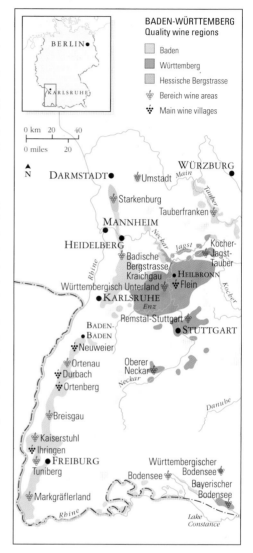

BADEN-WÜRTTEMBERG
Quality wine regions

- Baden
- Württemberg
- Hessische Bergstrasse
- Bereich wine areas
- Main wine villages

Bereich **Badische Bergstrasse** or **Kraichgau**; and north-east of here, there are various vineyards in the Bereich **Tauberfranken** squeezed in between Württemberg and Franken. In wine terms this outpost of vineyards seems to have far more in common with Franken, but for bureaucratic reasons it's treated as Baden.

Winemakers don't often vote en masse to make less wine, but that's what they've done in Baden. The problem was that there was just

The vineyards around Durbach in Baden's Ortenau region are famed for producing good Spätburgunder or Pinot Noir, as the village sign proudly shows.

too much of it. Better methods of viticulture (the vineyard reorganization called Flurbereinigung, by which the old-fashioned, hard-to-work terraces are rebuilt in a more logical fashion and then replanted, has been very popular) have meant that more and more wine was being made. Well, no grower wants prices to fall. So, they said, we'll make 90 hl/ha, no more. It's still a generous limit, but it's an improvement in the right direction, and it has helped the concentration of the wine.

WÜRTTEMBERG

The zigzagging river Neckar and the narrow valleys of its tributaries are where to find vineyards here. Germany's fourth largest wine region, it starts well north of the city of Heilbronn but the main zone is a great swathe of vineyards south of Heilbronn down to Ludwigsberg. There are also vineyards close to Stuttgart and a few on either side of the river Neckar down further south near Tübingen.

The main part of Württemberg does, however, have a distinctive character. It's hotter in the summer and colder in the winter than most of Germany – and those sunny summers mean that red grapes ripen better than they usually do in Germany. (For the same reason, Baden, too, can make some excellent reds.)

GRAPE VARIETIES AND WINE STYLES

This is where the rule that holds true in most of Germany, that **Riesling** is tops, breaks down. Sure, there's good Riesling in Baden – from Durbach, in particular, it is dry, well-structured, and with a minerally edge – but generally in Baden, it is the Pinot family that make the finest wines. That means good, ripe **Spätburgunder** (Pinot Noir), now the most widely planted vine in Baden, traditionally made sweetish but increasingly now being fermented out dry and given some oak aging to produce wines in a more international mould; it also means **Grauburgunder** (Pinot Gris), that here has the same sort of weight that it does across the Rhine in Alsace. **Weissburgunder** (Pinot Blanc) also does well.

Müller-Thurgau has declined to about a fifth of the vineyard. It's pleasant, musky wine but not exactly thrilling.

In Württemberg Riesling gets more of a look in, accounting for 19 per cent of the plantings, but it is outnumbered by red vines, which take up nearly two-thirds of the vineyards. **Trollinger** and **Schwarzriesling** (Pinot Meunier) are the most popular, making light, sweetish traditional German wines. Sometimes red and white grapes are mixed to make Schillerwein, a rosé named after the poet. Mind you, not much of the red rises far above the rosé level, mainly because of high yields.

CLASSIFICATION

Baden's warm climate means that the wines have to reach unusually high Oeschle levels to gain each rung of the Prädikat ladder, in addition to which over half are now dry.

ORGANIZATION

The small size of vineyard holdings means that in both regions the vast majority of the wines are made by the 100 co-operatives or so who make and sell about 85 per cent of Baden's wines, most of it good and sound. Best producers: (Baden) **Bercher, Dr Heger, Huber, Karl-Heinz Johner, Andreas Laible, Salwey, Schloss Neuweier, Schneider**, and the co-operative at **Pfaffenweiler;** (Württemberg) **Aldinger, Graf Adelmann, Dautel, Drautz-Able, Ellwanger, Haidle, Neipperg, Schneitmann, Schwegler** and **Wöhrweg**.

READING THE LABEL

Most of the wines come from a co-operative, or Winzergenossenschaft, though the best reds are from single estates. Look also for Klingelberger, Riesling's name in the village of Durbach.

WHAT DO THEY TASTE LIKE?

In Baden the wines are drier and 'winier' than in most of Germany. They're a cross between the grapiness of most of Germany's wines and the full weightiness of those from nearby Alsace just across the Rhine in France. Dry Spätburgunder can be remarkably good – Germany's top red wine is usually a Spätsburgunder from Baden – though much of it is still made sweetish. Württemberg's light reds are often made in this sweetish mould, as well.

THE GOOD YEARS

Baden wines are reliably good in most years, and most can be drunk young. In Württemberg, drink the latest vintage.

ENJOYING THE WINES

Baden wines, with their ripe but dryish style, are better with food than most German wines. The ripest reds will be good with most meat dishes, while the whites will match fish or poultry, though they don't have enough acidity for raw shellfish. In Württemberg wine has to compete with the excellent Bavarian beer for a place at the table, and it doesn't always win.

CONSUMER INFORMATION

WHAT DO I GET FOR MY MONEY?

Baden wines are reasonably priced for the quality, which is sound. Württemberg wines are expensive, taking into account the air fare to Stuttgart to find them.

AVAILABILITY

Few of Baden's best growers' wines are seen outside Germany. Wines from the large co-operatives are more easily available as the dry white wines appeal increasingly to international tastes. Württemberg wines are rarely seen outside the region.

CONSUMER CHECKLIST

Spätburgunder	*Quality 8* ★
Trocken Alte Reben 2002	*Price 9* ★
(Bernhard Huber)	*Value 7* ★

Good Years Any recent vintage.
Taste Notes Baden white wines are dry and vinous; Württemberg's reds are light and often sweetish.

HESSISCHE BERGSTRASSE

Bergstrasse means 'mountain road'. This part of it, the part in the state of Hessen, is on the route between Heidelberg in the south and Darmstadt in the north; and since the local BMWs prefer the Autobahn these days, the peaceful paths through the hills, where fruit trees alternate with vines, is left to Sunday hikers.

It's a tiny region – just a northerly extension of Baden, plus another, more northerly patch east of Darmstadt – and it's warm enough for the fruit trees, as well as the vines, to flourish. Yields are low here – considerably lower than in the more fertile vineyards of Baden – and the lack of much market for the wines outside the region itself has meant that a lot of growers have succumbed to the temptation to sell their land for housing. The vineyard area is accordingly shrinking, supported only by the local population and the visitors.

GRAPE VARIETIES AND WINE STYLES

It is a pity the vineyard area is diminishing, because the wines are actually rather good. The best are from **Riesling**, which covers just over half the vineyard area, with **Müller-Thurgau**, **Grauburgunder** (Pinot Gris) and others all taking a share. There's a little

Spätburgunder, but red wines aren't really what Hessiche Bergstrasse is about. Instead it is the Rieslings – often dry, rather delicate, with a rustic tinge – that is the most interesting wine, often reaching **Auslese** standard.

CLASSIFICATION

The general German classification applies here. There are no regional extras.

ORGANIZATION

Most of the wines come from Domäne Bensheim, the state domaine; the other main producer is the co-operative in **Heppenheim**.

READING THE LABEL

Look for Rieslings from the vineyards around Heppenheim.

THE GOOD YEARS

Most years are pretty good here, and the wines don't need long aging. Just drink whatever vintage is available.

ENJOYING THE WINES

The gentle fruit of these wines makes them ideal café wines, to be drunk outdoors as the evening sun turns amber in the summer sky.

FRANKEN

Franken always used to be the area which everyone pointed to when the cry went up that 'Germany cannot make dry wines, and no wonder the Germans prefer to drink beer with their meals'. Well, paradoxically, Franken nestles in the top north-west corner of Bavaria, Germany's greatest, most utterly beer-devoted state. This, in part, explains both Franken's isolation from the mainstream of German wine styles. Don't expect the taut floweriness of the Rhine or Mosel here, or the knife-edge balance between sweetness and acidity that makes those wines so endlessly fascinating. Instead look for a dry earthiness, with acidity balanced by extract rather than by sweetness. And look for them in bottles that are a different shape from those used in the rest of Germany. The Franken bottle is the squat, round Bocksbeutel, similar in shape to the Mateus Rosé bottles that launched a thousand lampshades in the swinging 1960s.

Most of the vineyards hug the river Main and its tributaries. They have to: the continental climate here is harsh, with short, warm summer, cold winters, and springs and autumns that can go either way. An early, cold, wet autumn can ruin a year's hopes; equally, a late spring frost can decimate the vintage before it has even got going. This is where the shelter of a river valley can help temper the climate so that the full fury of frost and cold isn't visited on the grapes or the vines.

And away from the city of Würzburg, where most of the vineyards are concentrated, the vines can be so scattered that even the efficient German bureaucrats quailed at the prospect of alloting Grosslage names to them. As a result many of the wines are sold under Bereich names – and two of Franken's three Bereiche take their names from the shape the river Main forms, tacking up and down on its way west to Frankfurt.

First, there's the Bereich Maindreieck where the river forms two sides of a triangle, and where most of the vineyards are. It also contains the vineyard which gave Franken wine its popular name of Stein wine. Really only wine from Würzburger Stein, a steep

You can't get away from bishops in Franken. Behind this statue of one in Würzburg is the Schlossberg vineyard, and the Festung Marienberg castle.

green cliff of vines overlooking the city to the north, should be given the name of Stein wine, but then the name Hock, which is derived from the village of Hochheim in the Rheingau, is used to refer to all Rhine wine. And why should the Rhine enjoy all the perks?

The Stein is the most famous single vineyard in Franken. The village of Randersacker can contribute a few top sites, too, like Teufelskeller, Pfülben or Marsberg, and in the village of Escherndorf is the Lump vineyard – it is a fact of life in Franken that some of the vineyards are individually famous, although the region overall is still so often overlooked.

The other Bereiche are Mainviereck in the west, where the river Main ambles round two sides of a square, and Steigerwald in the east, where one of the star vineyards is the Iphofer Julius-Echter-Berg. Part of this site, as well as parts of Würzburger Stein and Escherndorfer Lump, is owned by the Juliusspital, one of Franken's greatest estates.

GRAPE VARIETIES AND WINE STYLES

Franken is most famous for its **Silvaner** – dry, minerally wine, high in acidity and extract which reaches heights that this grape reaches nowhere else in Germany. But Silvaner is less typical of Franken than it was: the advance of **Müller-Thurgau** in the vineyards means that Silvaner is now grown in only a fifth of the region, and it's also being squeezed out by umpteen new late-budding, early-ripening vine crossings, all developed at the Geisenheim Viticultural Institute in the Rheingau with an eye to helping the grape growers beat Franken's spring frosts and early autumns.

Well, it's true that they do the job. They often ripen early, so avoiding the danger of rain and cold at the very time when both **Riesling** and Silvaner need warm sun for that final push toward ripeness. But frankly the likes of crossings such as **Bacchus**, **Kerner**, **Perle** and **Ortega** can never produce the subtlety of Riesling or good Silvaner. A rather obvious aromatic quality is usually the best they can aspire to – although there's also some **Scheurebe** planted, which is one of the best of the new crosses. Give it a good warm summer and the blessing of a sunny autumn Scheurebe can make very interesting wine.

There is also some Riesling, which can be very good, but there's not much of it and its late ripening can be a problem here, even though it is resistant to Germany's cold winters. And Müller-Thurgau here can also be better and more substantial than elsewhere in Germany. Lastly, this is where the ancient variant of Pinot Noir – Frühburgunder – was discovered.

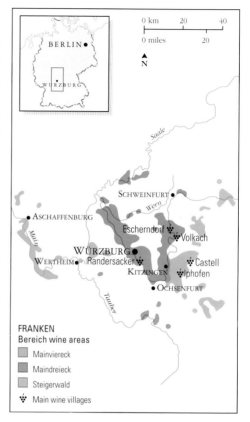

FRANKEN
Bereich wine areas
- Mainviereck
- Maindreieck
- Steigerwald
- ❀ Main wine villages

CLASSIFICATION

Franken follows the same rules as the rest of Germany, yet the wines up to Auslese level are always likely to be drier. The words, Trocken and Halbtrocken are not much used.

ORGANIZATION

Even though the co-operatives are a dominant feature, producing about 40 per cent of the wine, the single growers are the real quality producers. Best producers: **Fürstlich Castell'sches Domänenamt, Fürst, Glaser-Himmelstoff, Löwenstein, Ruck, Sauer, Schmitt's Kinder, Sommerhausen, Stein, Störrlein, Wirsching** and **Zehnthof**. Some of the best wines also come from the ecclesiastical foundations (the **Juliusspital** and the **Bürgerspital zum Heiligen Geist**) and the state (the **Staatlicher Hofkeller**), all based in Würzburg.

READING THE LABEL

The easiest way to recognize Franken wine is by the short green or brown flask or Bocksbeutel – though not all Franken wine is bottled this way. Some producers use the tall narrow bottles seen, with variations, all over the rest of Germany. Checking the grape name is particularly important here – look for Silvaner or Riesling. Don't, however, expect to find much mention of Trocken or Halbtrocken. Franken growers don't usually bother using them: everybody knows their wines are dry, they reason, unless they're of Auslese level, in which case everybody will know they're sweeter. But don't expect even an Auslese to be very sweet in Franken: it will certainly be off-dry, but not luscious.

WHAT DO THEY TASTE LIKE?

Franken wines often taste honeyed and slightly earthy – but that is no bad thing, since many of Germany's wines are markedly aromatic. The earthiness adds a savoury edge to wines which are by nature fuller and drier than a typical Hock from the Rhine.

THE GOOD YEARS

Good years do matter in Franken, because the whole region suffers badly from very harsh winters, a high annual rainfall and early frosts. This cuts down the grape's ripening period, and certainly the Riesling only ripens in hot years. The increasing use of new vine crossings is an attempt to get a ripe crop of grapes every year. Most Franken wines can be drunk young. The best will age – those of Spätlese and Auslese levels will need a few years and the occasional wines at Beerenauslese and Trockenbeerenauslese level will improve glo-

riously for decades – but the simple wines can be drunk immediately.

2004 High quality, particularly the late-ripening Silvaner, Pinot family and Riesling.

2003 Beautiful, healthy grapes that benefited from the long, dry summer.

2002 Excellent ripeness levels.

2001 Good quality and abundant harvest. Plenty of Spätlese and Auslese.

2000 Unlike the rest of Germany, good ripeness and high quality.

1999 Larger quantity than 1998. Many wines were best for early drinking.

1998 A good number of classic wines.

1997 Small quantity, high quality.

1996 Fruity wines with high extract.

1995 Not very exciting, now tired.

ENJOYING THE WINE

Franken wine used to be Germany's most successful dry wine style, though now it's facing stiff competition from the drier Rhine Rieslings. But it does go well with the gutsy local cooking.

When served very young from the barrel, its dryness and almost fizzy freshness make it as effective with the local ham and sausages as any draught of Bavarian beer. Even when bottled, it can certainly be as good with most food as a moderate white Burgundy.

CONSUMER INFORMATION

WHAT DO I GET FOR MY MONEY?

You don't necessarily get value for money, because Franken wines are some of the most expensive in Germany. Until the explosion of Trocken wines we've seen in recent years they were Germany's only French-style dry whites, and commanded high prices, particularly in the north. However, quality is high, and the flavours are interesting, so don't pass them by.

AVAILABILITY

Not very good. In Bavaria and northern Germany they are easily obtainable, but elsewhere only a specialist merchant is likely to stock any. Their price is a deterrent, and there's also the sad fact that expensive German wines from almost anywhere in the country just don't sell well.

CONSUMER CHECKLIST

Würzburger Stein 2004	*Quality 8 ★*
Silvaner Spätlese	*Price 8 ★*
(Juliusspital)	*Value 8 ★*

Good Years Most recent vintages in Franken have produced good wines. The latest real disaster was in 1985, when spring frosts killed 2.5 million vines.

Taste Notes Silvaner, Franken's main quality grape, has a delicious minerally dryness to it, but the more recent vine crossings like Bacchus and Ortega are less interesting and usually have plenty of aroma and little subtlety. Scheurebe, one of the better crossings, can make powerful, sweet wines in good years. Müller-Thurgau covers more than a third of the vineyards but is never as good as Silvaner.

SAALE-UNSTRUT & SACHSEN

These are the wine regions of the former East Germany. Nobody knew much about them before reunification in 1989. Certainly nobody from the West went there. And as far as the winemakers in East Germany were concerned, quantity was a far more important criterion than quality.

Yet even so, the quantity made was not high. Both regions are tiny: Saale-Unstrut, in the state of Sachsen-Anhalt, is the bigger, with 652 hectares (1611 acres) of vineyards; Sachsen, further east in the valley of the Elbe, has just 446 hectares (1102 acres). In both cases the vineyards were revealed to be in a pretty parlous state in 1989 with gaps in the rows where dead vines had not been replaced, and no money to put things right. But then, with reunification, there developed a steady flow of advice eastwards, and though the vineyards and the cellars have got a long way to go, improvements are already visible.

They're still not making much wine, though. Yields, at around 30 to 40 hl/ha may sound impressively low, but they're low for the wrong reasons – not because a dedicated winemaker is purposely pruning hard and discarding surplus grapes, but low because too many of the vines are dead. With investment the yields will increase, though since the vines are still planted on the sort of picturesque, narrow terraces that the rest of Germany has been busy bulldozing they probably won't get all that high.

GRAPE VARIETIES AND WINE STYLES
There is potential for quality in **Saale-Unstrut** – the wines have plenty of extract, naturally high acidity and are fermented dry. **Müller-Thurgau** is the main vine, so it's no good expecting too much, but there's quite a lot of **Weissburgunder** (Pinot Blanc) and **Silvaner**, as well as **Kerner**, **Riesling** and **Gewürztraminer**. The rivers Saale and Unstrut are the focus of the vineyards, and long cold winters and short hot summers mean that late frosts can cut the crop by over half in as many as four years in every ten.

In **Sachsen** they're hoping that the renascent tourist industry will give things a bit of a boost – the tourists are heading for Dresden and Meissen, and presumably need a drink when they get there. The hope is that they might also want to round off a weekend of china shepherdesses with a visit to a vineyard. They'll find most of the vineyards planted with Müller-Thurgau, **Riesling** and Weissburgunder, but there's also some **Grauburgunder** (Pinot Gris), **Gewürztraminer** and others; and while the wines tend to be a little softer than those of Saale-Unstrut, they, too, are dry.

CLASSIFICATION
Both regions have adopted the classification system used elsewhere in Germany.

ORGANIZATIONS
The regional co-operatives at Freyburg and Meissen are important here as there are still few independent wine estates. Best producers: (Saale-Unstrut) **Lützkendorf**, **Pawis**; (Sachsen) **Schloss Proschwitz**, **Schloss Wackerbarth** (the state-owned cellars), and **Klaus Zimmerling**.

READING THE LABEL
There are an increasing number of private producers doing their own bottling, but most of the wines still come from the regional co-operatives and previously state-owned cellars.

WHAT DO THEY TASTE LIKE?
The wines are made dry, and those of Saale-Unstrut have good structure. Sachsen wines tend to be milder. Sweet wines can only be made in exceptionally warm years.

THE GOOD YEARS
The wines are improving year by year, so more recent vintages are a better bet.

ENJOYING THE WINES
So far these are simple, everyday wines, to be gulped rather than pondered over.

SWEET GERMAN WINES

One of the abiding principles of great wine is that it is made at the margin. That means where it is only just warm enough to ripen the grapes. Where that margin occurs varies from grape variety to grape variety, and by such geographical factors as whether a particular vineyard faces north or south, and whether it is a sun trap or a frost pocket.

All this helps to explain why chilly Germany, where the ripeness of the grapes is a matter of such vital importance that it is enshrined in the wine law, and where white wine predominates because few regions are warm enough to ripen red grapes, produces some of the world's most luscious and concentrated sweet wines.

Part of the answer lies in the long, gentle ripening season. This produces subtle, complex flavours where a short, hot summer gives, well, short, hot flavours. Part of the answer is the Riesling grape, which stands up to cold and frost better than most. And part of the answer is *Botrytis cinerea*, or noble rot, which relishes the warm autumns and the humidity provided by Germany's great rivers.

Not all Germany's sweet wines are affected by noble rot. The lightest ones – the **Spätlesen** – may have a touch of it in an exceptionally good year, but Spätlesen are seldom properly sweet. **Auslesen** can be quite sweet, and may well have a little noble rot. Only with **Beerenauslesen** and **Trockenbeerenauslesen** can one really expect the characteristic tang of botrytis on the nose. And Eisweine are not nobly rotten at all: it is the cold that concentrates the sugar, not a fungus, and it is essential to start with healthy grapes.

GRAPE VARIETIES AND WINE STYLES
Riesling is the grape associated with the greatest of Germany's sweet wines, but the fruits of the country's vine research programme have been grapes like **Huxelrebe**, which ripens so fast that it can be picked to make Beerenauslese before the Riesling is ripe enough to make light, dryish Kabinett wines. Does this short ripening period argue wines of complexity and subtlety? No, it doesn't. The long, dangerous ripening period of the Riesling always produces a far more exciting flavour than the fat, musky sweetness of a Huxelrebe or a **Bacchus** or a **Morio Muskat** – all three recent inventions.

The only grapes, apart from Riesling, that are capable of making real quality sweet wines are the **Scheurebe**, which has good acidity and has a fabulous flavour of pink grapefruit soaked in honey, **Silvaner** in Franken and the honeyed **Rülander** (or Pinot Gris) in Baden. **Rieslaner**, a cross between Silvaner and Riesling, can, in the right hands, produce some classy stuff, but it's not widely grown.

The other thing about Riesling is that it needs time to mature. Taste a young Beerenauslese and you'll probably get a mouthful of sweetness and acidity so concentrated that it will make your teeth hurt. Leave it for ten – or preferably 20 – years, and you'll get incredibly rich, oily, honeyed tastes. It's one more reason why Riesling is so unfashionable: we don't expect to have to wait for our wines any more. A Trockenbeerenauslese will take still longer, and will last in bottle for decades. Eiswein can be drunk young, in spite of its piercing, frosty acidity, but bottle age will help to tame it. A decade is about the minimum aging period.

CLASSIFICATION
The minimum Oechsle levels for the different classifications vary according to wine region, with the cold Mosel-Saar-Ruwer having lower thresholds than, say, the Rheingau, and warm Baden having higher ones. Even so, anything above Auslese level is rare in the Mosel.

ORGANIZATION
All the best sweet wines come from single growers as it takes dedication and considerable financial risk to make these wines. The best alternative is likely to come from one of the top co-operatives, such as the Zentralkellerei in the Mosel.

READING THE LABEL
Look for the name of the grape as well as the Prädikat level: Riesling is almost always the best bet. Other grapes may well make cheaper wines, but a lower price doesn't necessarily mean a bargain. The vintage is slightly less important since even if the year as a whole wasn't that great, the grapes may still get wonderfully ripe and nobly rotten in individual sites. Some years, though, have more noble rot than others. Sometimes the quantities made of these very sweet, very rare wines are so small that producers abandon the attempt to bottle single-vineyard wines and will blend several vineyards together in order to have enough to make it worthwhile. These are about the only instances where buying a Grosslage wine is sensible.

WHAT DO THEY TASTE LIKE?

These rarities have higher acidity than any other sweet wine, and this, combined with a deep, honeyed richness and very low alcohol content, makes it impossible to resist a second glass. Don't, though, expect this brilliant complexity of flavours from wines of unfamilar grape varieties. Sweet wines from Huxelrebe, Ortega, Bacchus and Reichensteiner will be sweet but dull. Among Rieslings, the Mosels are the lightest and most elegant. The Rheingau makes fuller wines and the Pfalz often fuller still. Sweet Rheinhessens can lack excitement but top wines from Nierstein, Nackenheim, Bodenheim and Bingen are outstanding. Baden sweet wines can be fat but not quite as thrilling.

THE GOOD YEARS

German sweet wines last a very long time.

2004 Excellent year with top-quality luscious sweet wines, including Eiswein.

2003 Exceptional vintage and plenty of Beeren and Trockbeerenauslese wines.

2002 Especially good in the Pfalz. Fine Eiswein throughout Germany.

2001 Classic year, especially in the Mosel.

2000 A very poor year, but an Indian summer resulted in some good botrytized wines.

1999 A fine vintage for long-lived Auslesen.

1995, 1996 and **1997** Years for Spätlesen and Auslesen.

1994 There are wonderful Beerenauslesen and Trockenbeerenauslesen from the Pfalz.

1993 A good year for Auslesen.

Older vintages

A few top wines from 1959 will still be going

strong. Other classic years for sweet wines are 1990, 1989, 1988, 1983, 1976 and 1971.

ENJOYING THE WINES

Cherish them – these wines are expensive and rare, and their flavours are so satisfying that they don't need any food at all. At most you need some fresh fruit such as a peach or pear.

CONSUMER INFORMATION

WHAT DO I GET FOR MY MONEY?

What we are talking about here is wines made at great expense and in limited quantities mainly by individual growers who charge high prices but even so may not really expect to make a proper profit on their greatest rarities. So in one sense many of these wines are bargains – but the prices will still be high. It is perfectly possible to find very good Auslesen from leading growers at affordable prices, but for anything above that, expect to pay a lot. If it's a Beerenauslese, Trockenbeerenauslese or Eiswein and it seems cheap, check the grape name on the label carefully.

AVAILABILITY

Specialist wine shops are the best bet for hunting down fine sweet German wines above

the level of Auslese. The quantities made are so limited – a grower may sometimes make as few as 200 bottles of a particular wine – that not everything will find its way abroad.

CONSUMER CHECKLIST

Mülheimer Helenenkloster	*Quality 10* ★
Eiswein 1995	*Price 10* ★
(Max Ferd Richter)	*Value 9* ★

Good Years These are rarer in the Mosel and the northern Rhine than further south. Best years: 2003, 2002, 2001, 1999, 1997, 1996, 1995, 1994, 1993, 1990, 1989, 1988.

Taste Notes The taste of these sweet wines is astonishing, deep, honeyed, intense, and yet filled out with a wonderful, shocking, limy acidity which is as thrilling a flavour as the wine world possesses.

PIEDMONT

Piedmont has the dubious distinction of harbouring within her borders the sternest-faced worthies of Italian wines as well as the giggliest of ne'er-do-wells. Barolo and Barbaresco, with the other big, tough, terrifying reds from the Nebbiolo grape, are these giants of propriety, while the charming sparkling wines of Asti are the scallywags everybody can't quite admit to liking, but can't quite resist either. Indeed, the reds of Piedmont can be so massive and unyielding to taste that a slug of Asti is well and truly earned.

The best of Piedmont's wine-making is committed to quality in a self-denying manner that is generally uncommon in Italian viticulture. Many of the hill vineyards are high and bare, the climate is harsh and the grapes, in particular the Nebbiolo, need to hang on late into the foggy autumn to bring their dense tough skins to full ripeness. Asti, often derided as kindergarten stuff, is in fact made with great care under DOCG regulations from the Muscat grape.

GRAPE VARIETIES AND WINE STYLES

There are over 40 DOCs in Piedmont, more than any other region can boast, but it is the Nebbiolo grape that dominates Piedmont's consciousness. The Barbera grape may quench the thirst of the Piedmontese, but Nebbiolo accounts for over half of the reds and is the automatic choice for many of the meals you're likely to enjoy there. But Nebbiolo is a surly, fierce variety, producing wines which are dark, chewy and exhausting for the first few years of their life, yet which can blossom out into a remarkable shower of dark, wild flavours. Behind the almost inevitable cold tea tannin and acidity there is a richness full of chocolate, raisins, prunes and an austere perfume of tobacco, pine and herbs. These flavours all intermingle in **Barolo** and **Barbaresco**, both DOCGs, but while these wines can use plenty of oak aging, the danger is that their fruit and sweetness can be leached out by too much wood.

The answer, for some of the most forward-looking producers, has been to offer less tannic, more easily drinkable wines; Barolos are fermented and aged for a shorter time, but often aged in new oak (rather like red Bordeaux) to bring them to heel faster. That means after about five years in bottle rather than the more traditional 20 – which is good news for those of us who want to drink the wines ourselves, rather than pass them on in our wills.

Nebbiolo grapes are famous for their deep colour and rich tannins. These belong to Roberto Voerzio and come from the top-quality Barolo vineyard of La Serra.

Best producers: (Barolo) **Alario, Alessandria, Altare, Azelia, Boglietti, Bongiovanni, Brovia, Cappellano, Ceretto, Clerico, Colla, Aldo Conterno, Giacomo Conterno, Conterno-Fantino, Corino, Einaudi, Giacosa, Grasso, Marengo, B Mascarello, G Mascarello, Monfalletto- Cordero di Montezemolo, Oberto, Oddero, Parusso, Pio Cesare, Pira, Prunotto, Revello, Rocche dei Manzoni, Sandrone, Scavino, Sebaste, Vajra, Veglio, Vietti, Vigna Ronda, G Voerzio** and **R Voerzio**; (Barbaresco) **Ceretto, Cigliuti, Farina, Fontanabianca, Gaja, Giacosa, Marchesi di Gresy, Moccagatta, Nada, Castello di Neive, Paitin, Pelissero, Pio Cesare, Produttori del Barbaresco, Albino Rocca, Bruno Rocca, Sottimano, La Spinetta** and **Vietti**.

Nebbiolo can be found in a softer, plummier form as **Nebbiolo d'Alba, Langhe Nebbiolo** or **Nebbiolo del Piemonte**, when the fruit often has a remarkable apple or melon freshness to tone down the toughness. Further north, in the Novara and Vercelli hills, **Carema** (DOC), **Gattinara** (DOCG) and **Ghemme** (DOC) give a much softer and more approachable Nebbiolo style. Best producers: (Carema) **Luigi Ferrando**; (Gattinara) **Antoniolo, Nervi** and **Travaglini**; (Ghemme) **Antichi Vigneti di Cantalupo**.

Barbera wines are widespread in Piedmont and are remarkably consistent – **Barbera d'Alba** (best producers: **G Alessandria, Azelia, Boglietti, Cogno, Aldo Conterno, Corino, Correggia, Molino, Oberto, Parusso, Principiano, Prunotto, Albino Rocca, Sandrone, Scavino, La Spinetta, Vajra, Veglio, Vietti, G Voerzio** and **R Voerzio**) and **Barbera d'Asti** (best producers: **La Barbatella, Barbero, Bertelli, Braida, Coppo, Martinetti, Il Mongetto, Prunotto, Scarpa, La Spinetta** and **Vietti**) are the best DOCs. They usually have fairly high acidity, a slightly resiny edge and yet a very sweet and sour raisin taste or even some brown sugar sweetness. Barbera wines have lots of bite, but don't make the gums suffer such a full frontal assault as Nebbiolo.

The **Dolcetto** grape is also good. It makes brash, purple wine, full yet soft, slightly chocolaty, wonderfully refreshing when young – and most *should* be drunk young. The best will age for around four years, but many are best at a year or so old. **Grignolino** is an attractive red, while **Freisa** also pursues the Piedmont sweet 'n' sour trail, and is often fizzy as well. Best producers: (Dolcetto) **Altare, Bongiovanni, Brovia, Aldo Conterno, Einaudi, G Mascarello, Pecchenino, Albino Rocca, Sandrone, Vajra, Vietti** and **G Voerzio;** (Grignolino) **Aldo Conterno** and **Braida;** (Freisa) **Coppo** and **Gilli.**

The still Piedmont whites are only now finding their feet. Fashionable and expensive **Gavi**, and **Cortese di Gavi** are DOCs from the Cortese grape, making fresh, appley wine. Best producers: **Chiarlo, La Giustiniana, San Pietro, La Scolca** and **Castello di Tassarolo;** **Erbaluce di Caluso** (DOC) offers better value – sharp, lemony, nutty wine (best producers: **Ferrando** and **Orsolani**). **Roero Arneis** (DOC) at its best is a fascinating, slightly bitter white, mixing liquorice and peach fruit with a perfume of fresh hops. Best producers: **Correggia, Deltetto, Giacosa, Malvirà, Negro, Prunotto, Vietti** and **G Voerzio.**

The Muscat grape is at its most brilliant in **Moscato d'Asti** and **Asti** (DOCG), both sweet, fizzy and full of the crunchy green freshness of a fistful of ripe table grapes. Both must be drunk young. Best producers: **Bera, Braida, Cascina Fonda, Cascina Pian d'Or, Caudrina, Cinzano, Gancia, Giacosa, Martini & Rossi, Saracco, La Spinetta** and **I Vignaioli di Santo Stefano**.

CLASSIFICATION

Piedmont has a large number of DOCs as well as a third of Italy's DOCGs. The leading candidate for a classification over and above the DOCG designation is Barolo, and with the new law something along these lines could develop. If it does, it will recognize the best individual vineyards in Barolo.

Evening in the hilltop village of Castiglione Falletto in Barolo. Some of these vineyards are candidates for official Cru status, if it happens.

approachable younger, it's getting easier to find its flavours of tar, roses, violets, game and liquorice. Barbaresco is lighter than Barolo but richer than the other Piedmont Nebbiolos, and Barbera comes in all sorts of styles according to the taste of the maker. Expect high acidity, and go for a good grower if you want richness. Dolcetto is Piedmont's answer to the need for a flavoursome but light red, full of chocolaty plumminess.

The whites – both the dry Arneis Roero and Cortese di Gavi, and sweet Moscato – have simple, direct flavours.

THE GOOD YEARS
Vintages are very important for Barolo and Barbaresco, less so for the whites.
2004 Both abundant and of high quality.
2003 Hot summer and a difficult year for Nebbiolo.
2002 Poor summer and serious hail damage in Barolo. Choose with care.
2001 The seventh fine vintage in a row. Potentially outstanding but spoiled by some rain at vintage time.
2000 Good concentration and structure.
1999 Another good year.
1998 The third great vintage in a row.
1997 The greatest since 1990. Outstanding.
1996 A good year but yields were down.
1995 Some fine Barolo and Barbaresco.
Older vintages
1993, 1990, 1989, 1988, 1986, 1985.

ORGANIZATION
The best merchants' wines are reliable but for real quality in Barolo and Barbaresco go to single growers. In Asti the co-operatives and merchants' wines are usually good.

READING THE LABEL
Look for a single-vineyard wine in Barolo (and often on Dolcetto, too). Just as clues, 'Bric' means 'hilltop', 'Sorì' means 'slope' and 'Vigna' means 'vineyard'. The term Riserva indicates the wine has had extra aging.

WHAT DO THEY TASTE LIKE?
The Nebbiolo grape gives memorable tastes, and now that many of the wines are more

ENJOYING THE WINE
Barolo and Barbaresco need big, brawny foods to stand up to them. Dark, spiced beef casseroles, jugged hare, fondues and *bollito misto* are all local dishes. Unlike many reds, Piedmont reds can also handle most cheeses. Sweet Asti is delicious by itself but is also perfect with Christmas pudding and mince pies – especially since by that stage of Christmas lunch its low alcohol is welcome.

CONSUMER INFORMATION

WHAT DO I GET FOR MY MONEY?

There is cheapish Barolo around, but it is usually best avoided. Good Barolo is expensive these days, and great Barolo – a single-vineyard wine from a top producer – is very, very expensive. Straight Nebbiolo can be good value, but choose your vintages carefully because it can be lean and stringy. Barbera is better value – but if you buy wine of a good producer it won't be cheap. Dolcetto can be a very good buy: not dirt cheap by any means, but the best have good depth and complexity and are well worth the money. Of the whites, Gavi and Roero Arneis are generally overpriced. Asti, which used to be a cheap drink, is now much less so, but is pretty good value.

AVAILABILITY

For good Barolo and Barbaresco you must go to a specialist. The other Piedmont reds are also not very widely distributed, and the dry whites are rare outside the region. Asti and other Moscato wines are universally available, and the only important thing is to buy from somewhere that has a quick turnover and avoid dusty bottles.

CONSUMER CHECKLIST

Barolo Granbussia 1999	Quality 10 ★
(Aldo Conterno)	Price 10 ★
	Value 10 ★

Good Years Moscato should be drunk as young as possible; most of the reds need some aging, though most Dolcetto is best young. Best years (reds): 2004, 2001, 2000, 1999, 1998, 1997, 1996, 1995, 1990, 1989, 1988.

Taste Notes Most Piedmont reds are marked by unmistakable, strong flavours, whether they're the tough, dark, plummy reds from Nebbiolo like Barolo and Barbaresco or the softer, bitter-cherry Dolcetto. The whites should also have flavour but not all Cortese or Arneis does. The fizz, especially Moscato d'Asti, are fresh and wonderfully grapy.

VALLE D'AOSTA

Lost in the steep Alpine valleys which twine up toward Mont Blanc or the Great St Bernard or Little St Bernard passes, Valle d'Aosta is Italy's tiniest region, producing the smallest quantity of wine. But thirsty tourists in the local ski resorts and other passing travellers seem willing to pay high prices for any wine that is available.

I always feel it's unfair when mountain people, with their harsh climate and local cooking built on burly, heroic lines can only produce fleeting, delicate wines, but Valle d'Aosta does at least produce tasty stuff.

The wines reflect the region's position, looking across to Switzerland in the north and France in the west, so while there are plenty of Italian grapes growing here – grapes like Dolcetto and Nebbiolo – there are also French vines like Gamay, Syrah, Pinot Noir, Grenache, Pinot Gris (here called Malvoisie), Chardonnay and Pinot Blanc. The Petite Arvine of Switzerland is also found here, as is the Müller-Thurgau of Germany.

This curious mixture of vines – some of which are suited to far higher temperatures than they find here – are grown on hillside terraces on the steep slopes rising from the valley floor. Around Morgex and La Salle are reputedly some of the highest vineyards in Europe, between 900 and 1300m (3000 and 4300 ft). Below them flows the river Dora Baltea, which eventually reaches the Po.

The regional DOC (Valle d'Aosta) covers 17 wine styles, referring either to a specific grape variety or to a sub-region. The wines aren't exported but, consumed on the spot, white **Blanc de Morgex et de la Salle** from the otherwise obscure Blanc de Morgex grape in the upper Aosta Valley, can be delicious, while the red **Donnaz**, made from Nebbiolo from the other end of the region near the border with Piedmont, and **Torrette**, from the Petit Rouge grape in the central Aosta valley, can pack a perceptible punch – in the flyweight division.

The rarities of sweet white **Chambave Moscato** and **Malvoisie de Nus**, **Vin du Conseil**, a dry wine from Petite Arvine and **Enfer d'Arvier**, a dry red, are worth a detour. There's also a red grape called Fumin which is currently occupying a number of growers, who see possibilities for aging it in small oak barrels: it's a grape that makes wine of considerable structure and concentration.

And if you're wondering why so many of these grape names sound French – that's what a lot of the population speaks, up there on the border.

LIGURIA

Liguria is a long, thin sliver of land curving gracefully around the Genoese coastline from France to Tuscany. On a map it looks almost too narrow for many vines to be squeezed in, and indeed it is one of Italy's least productive wine regions. Yet Genoa, its capital, is a great gastronomic centre, working wonders with fish, seafood and some of Italy's most original pasta creations. So what Liguria primarily produces is a fair amount of wine for immediate drinking, from the hills behind the coast. The good stuff goes to the Genoese, and the mediocre stuff goes down the uncomplaining and uncritical throats of the holidaymakers on the Italian Riviera.

In some ways this is a shame, because Liguria does have an astonishing variety of grapes packed into a tiny area. The white **Vermentino** is made into a non-DOC varietal of good delicate flavour, as well as being part of the blend for Liguria's most famous wine, **Cinqueterre**. This comes from precipitous, terraced vineyards perched on the cliffs high above the sea: picturesque yes, high-quality no. It's some years since I've talked to anyone who reckoned they'd drunk an honest bottle.

The white **Pigato**, again often made as a varietal, can be more interesting, though quality is pretty erratic. Of the reds, **Ormeasco** is difficult to find but often good – it's the local name for Dolcetto, and has some of the good

These steeply terraced Ligurian vineyards in the beautiful wine region of Cinqueterre near La Spezia were once accessible only by boat.

bitter-cherry flavour found in Piedmontese versions. The Rossese variety, which is DOC in **Dolceacqua**, is better still, producing flavours ranging from strangely fragrant to jammy-strong.

LOMBARDY

If Liguria is only of passing interest, Lombardy, with the great industrial city of Milan as its capital, is a serious wine area. It is, however, an underrated one, primarily because Piedmont carries all the partisan colours for this part of Italy, and produces twice as much wine. And, remarkably, Milan doesn't seem to realize her good fortune. Fine wines from all over Italy are readily available in Milan – except from her own backyard of Lombardy.

The problem for the rest of us – and perhaps for Lombardy itself – is that there is no single famous wine or great grape on which to hang the reputation of the region. Tuscany has Sangiovese and Chianti; Piedmont has Nebbiolo and Barolo. Lombardy has – what?

Well, quite a lot of everything, actually. Lombardy makes a lot of wine, and roughly a third of it is DOC, so it is by no means to be written off.

Franciacorta is one of the most interesting. Apart from decent fizz, newly promoted to DOCG, there are good Cabernet and Merlot blends, good nutty Chardonnay and even some Pinot Noir. These wines are still DOC and have been renamed **Terre di Franciacorta**. Nebbiolo makes a rare foray outside Piedmont to the **Valtellina** DOC, although it doesn't always excel here and can seem a little stringy. The red Bonarda grape can be more substantial, making plummy, liquoricy wine in **Oltrepò Pavese** (DOC); the Barbera also gives high-acid, chewy reds under the same DOC.

Of the whites, **Lugana** from near Lake Garda is sometimes supposed to have more character than most Trebbiano-based wines, though frankly that's not difficult. Lugana has very good body and though the taste is a little neutral, has decent aroma and good acidity.

NORTH-EAST ITALY

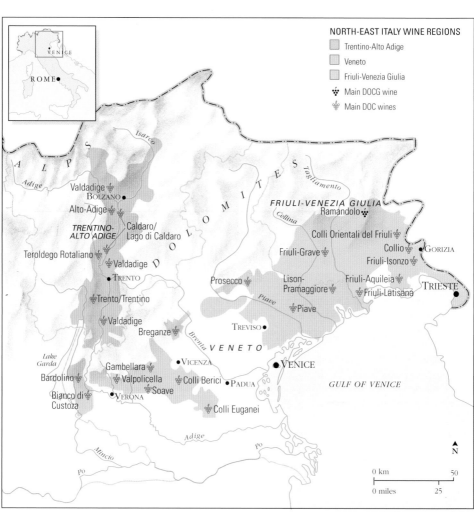

NORTH-EAST ITALY WINE REGIONS

- Trentino-Alto Adige
- Veneto
- Friuli-Venezia Giulia
- ❦ Main DOCG wine
- ❦ Main DOC wines

This is where Italy meets Austria. In fact, Friuli-Venezia Giulia and Alto Adige used to be part of the Austro-Hungarian empire; and in the Alto Adige to this day you'll still find a strong Germanic influence – there is even official bilingualism in the region. Friuli-Venezia Giulia, tucked in between the Austrian and Slovenian borders, continues to make the sorts of wines that might have been popular at the Habsburg court: Sauvignon Blanc, Pinot Bianco, Riesling and Müller-Thurgau. There are reds, too: Merlot, Cabernet Franc and the lean, tarry Refosco.

North-east Italy makes some of the best whites in the country. In the Alto Adige, unless the growers allow the vines to yield too generously, which they often do, there are flavoursome wines from Chardonnay and Gewürztraminer and some lusciously sweet Muscat, grown high up in the mountains. Where the grapes are grown in vineyards down on the flat valley floor the results are never as good. That is land best left to apple orchards.

And then of course there is the Veneto, home of some of Italy's most famous wines: Soave, Valpolicella and Bardolino. They are also the names of some of Italy's most disgracefully abused wines: in the last year I have bought Soave from choice only once. The degradation of Soave and Valpolicella, potentially proud wines of subtlety and individuality, show just what went wrong with the 1963 Italian wine law. Will the new Goria law put things right, and restore the quality of these wines? Partially; only the growers can do that. Luckily there are growers in both areas who care enough about their wines to make them properly, to produce wines that will remind us why they became famous in the first place. But they cost money and we have to decide if we're prepared to pay.

ALTO ADIGE

Although the Alto Adige is officially joined to Trentino to form the region of Trentino-Alto Adige, this conjunction is purely for political convenience, to avoid the embarassment of having one province – Alto Adige – with a German-speaking majority and separatist inclinations. The wine-making traditions and styles of both provinces differ dramatically, and although Trentino was first in the field in trying to upgrade its quality levels, with isolated exceptions, the general standard is not as high as in the Alto Adige.

Alto Adige is one of the most fascinating of Italy's wine regions, as well as being one of the most beautiful. It comprises the northern half of a long, narrow valley, stretching up from Verona – flat as prairie land on its floor, but bounded by magnificent peaks. The valley floor is largely given over to apple-growing, but the dizzily steep mountainsides are planted with vines. It looks impossibly difficult to tend vines at such angles but the majority of these Alto Adige winemakers are Germanic – and have been for 2000 years – and to them steep river valley slopes are accepted as the norm in quality viticulture.

Although geographically within Italy, the Alto Adige is emotionally in Austria. Most of its inhabitants would like to be thought of as Austrian – they even call their region the Südtirol. From 1363 to 1920 this long, steep-sided valley was part of the Austro-Hungarian Empire, until it was forfeited to Italy after World War One. There is a strong Tyrolean feel to the architecture, cuisine and customs, and outside the main town of Bolzano most people speak German as their first language.

GRAPE VARIETIES AND WINE STYLES

The Alto Adige makes every conceivable kind of still wine with considerable success, and some of its wines are unique in style. The vast majority of the vines are red, and the vineyards are chiefly given over to the **Schiava**, or **Vernatsch** as it is locally called. The wine is often derided as feeble and tasteless but this isn't so. It can make wonderfully quaffable light reds when the yields are restrained and is at its best in the wines of **Caldaro** (also called by its German name of Kalterersee) and **Santa Maddalena**. **Lagrein** is another local red grape variety, Lagrein Dunkel (or

'dark Lagrein') being a dark, intense red. **Pinot Noir** and **Cabernet Sauvignon** are increasingly planted but they need warm years to succeed. In Alto Adige Cabernet Sauvignon wine has a fresh, earthy, grassy feel and pure blackcurrant fruit; Pinot Noir can be too light, but at its best can produce a mini-version of the luscious plum and cherry flavour of red Burgundy.

Although they are in the minority, much of the current excitement is centred on the white varieties. There is some **Sauvignon Blanc**, but **Pinot Bianco** and **Chardonnay** are more important. Both make quite light wines, the Pinot Bianco leafy rather than ripe and vinous as it is in Alsace, and the Chardonnay generally made with little or no new oak. Even without oak it is much lighter and yet softer than it is in Chablis. A few growers use oak and produce good, balanced Chardonnay.

Sylvaner and **Müller-Thurgau** both have sharp-fresh flavours here. **Rheinriesling** produces refreshing, steely dry wines. **Gewürztraminer** or **Traminer** is less spicy here than the Alsace version, and can be a little too soft to be satisfying; the different varieties of Muscat make dry wines to rival those of Alsace, and light sweet wines unrivalled in Europe. Look particularly for **Goldmuskateller** or **Rosenmuskateller**.

The pergola system of vine-training (on the left), used in Alto Adige vineyards for centuries, is now giving way to the more standard vertical training on wires.

The majestic Dolomites provide a stunning backdrop to the densely planted Alto Adige vineyards, here at Cortaccia in the Lago di Caldaro DOC zone.

There is also good rosé, produced from the **Lagrein** grape, which makes a marvellously fruity, totally dry wine called Lagrein Kretzer. There is a certain amount of decent fizz, though much of the Pinot Bianco and Chardonnay crop is still shipped southwards to the fizz factories in Trento and Lombardy.

Best producers: **Abbazia di Novacella**, **Haas**, **Hofstätter**, **Lageder**, **Pliger-Kuenhof**, **Muri-Gries**, **Tiefenbrunner**, and the co-operatives at **Colterenzio**, **San Michele Appiano** and **Terlano**.

CLASSIFICATION
The regional Alto Adige DOC covers 25 wine styles, including varietals grown in various sub-zones such as Santa Maddalena.

ORGANIZATION
Most of the best wines are made by single growers but a large proportion comes from the co-operatives, most of them well run.

READING THE LABEL
The labels can be rather confusing. Grape varieties and place names may be in Italian, German, or both, and grape varieties may even occasionally be in French.

WHAT DO THEY TASTE LIKE?
The basic style is light and intensely fresh. Few of the whites need age at all, though some can age quite well if they have to.

THE GOOD YEARS
Most wines should be drunk young. The pale red Vernatsch wines are often at their best within six to nine months of the vintage, and most whites peak at about a year. Some Pinot Bianco, Chardonnay and Traminer wines need at least three years' aging, as does most Cabernet and Pinot Noir. The deep, dark Lagrein needs perhaps five years to blossom. Recent good years include 2004 and 2001.

ENJOYING THE WINES
These wines will fit any bill – Alto Adige can provide almost anything, from apéritifs to big sturdy reds to sweet dessert wines. But the most reliable are the whites, and these are ideal with light dishes – their delicate flavour would be swamped by too many big, creamy sauces. Lagrein Kretzer makes a marvellous picnic rosé, and the reds can be matched to virtually any meat dish.

CONSUMER INFORMATION

WHAT DO I GET FOR MY MONEY?

Since these wines come from hillside vineyards which are more expensive to maintain, they are not as cheap as many better-known Italian wines. They're also not as much of a bargain as they once were: they've become better known and yes, the quality has dropped as well. Yields have gone up and too many of them lack the concentration they once had. Even so, an Alto Adige Chardonnay or Pinot Bianco is still cheaper than an equivalent Chardonnay from Burgundy. This is also one of the best places in the world to obtain unoaked Chardonnay – useful to those consumers who realize there is life beyond oak.

AVAILABILITY

A large proportion of the annual production goes straight to the established export markets of Austria, Germany, Switzerland and the Low Countries. Chardonnay is probably the easiest to find, and Pinot Bianco isn't too difficult. Lagrein is pretty rare abroad, and if you see Goldmuskateller or Rosenmuskateller, snap it up immediately.

CONSUMER CHECKLIST

Alto Adige Pinot Bianco 2004	*Quality 7* ★
(Franz Haas)	*Price 6* ★
	Value 8 ★

Good Years Most should be drunk very young. All the whites are drinkable at six months, but are better at a year old. The best, most concentrated whites (from Pinot Bianco, Chardonnay and sometimes Traminer) need at least three years. Cabernet and Pinot Noir (Blauburgunder) need three years, with the finest wines capable of another dozen years' aging. Only Lagrein Dunkel needs a lot of time, perhaps five years, to mature. Best years: 2004, 2003, 2001.

Taste Notes The whites are very fresh, with sharply defined fruit. The reds are light, yet remarkably intense in flavour, and Lagrein has a tarry roughness jostling with chocolate-smooth ripe fruit.

TRENTINO

South of Alto Adige, the Trentino vineyards are less influenced by the geological structure and climate of the mountain valleys. Most Trentino wines are varietals, and there is a regional DOC (Trentino) covering the whole area, as well as numerous other DOCs.

In Trentino the Germanic influence wanes. Trentino's history is Italian, not Austrian, and Italian is the main language spoken. The Kalterersee DOC that extends across the boundary from Alto Adige into Trentino is more usually known as Caldaro here, and the grape used for this wine is more likely to be called Schiava here than its Germanic name of Vernatsch used in Alto Adige.

Trentino does have one important wine characteristic in common with the Alto Adige, however: high vineyard yields. Yes, the wines are good and can have riper, softer flavours – but they could be so much better if, for example, the growers weren't content to take crops of up to 120 hl/ha for Teroldego Rotaliano, a potentially beefy, chunky red wine that could be excellent if it weren't so diluted.

The red wines are a mixture of international grapes like Cabernet Sauvignon, Merlot and Pinot Noir, along with local varieties like Lagrein, Marzemino and Teroldego. They usually have a fair amount of flavour without any great defininition, but often an attractive smoky dryness.

Among the whites there are some interesting wines from Germanic varieties like Riesling and Müller-Thurgau, but the genuinely exciting wines are from Pinot Bianco and Chardonnay. Especially when made from grapes grown to the north of Trento, they match the austere freshness of the Alto Adige whites with an extra dimension of creamy depth which can make them some of Italy's finest whites.

Such good quality in still dry white wine is a relatively new departure here, because Trentino has up until quite recently preferred to use Pinot Bianco and Chardonnay to make sparkling wine – often made by the Champagne method, when it is called **Trento Classico**, and often good, if expensive. Two of the best fizz producers are **Equipe 5** and **Ferrari** but the **Càvit** co-operative also makes a deliciously dry Chardonnay Spumante – unnervingly like Champagne in style, and very much cheaper.

Best producers: **Cesconi**, **Foradori**, **Maso Cantanghel**, **Pojer e Sandri**, **San Leonardo**, **Simoncelli**, **Spagnolli** and **Vallarom**.

VENETO

The Veneto almost matches Sicily and Puglia in the massive quantities of wine it produces. Around a quarter of its wine is DOC, but don't get too excited: that proportion is reached with the aid of vast quantities of dull Soave, Valpolicella and Bardolino. I wish I could be more enthusiastic about this unholy alliance, but the quality of what are supposed to be light but good, simple, local wines, too often falls below what even their low prices can make acceptable.

GRAPE VARIETIES AND WINE STYLES

The Veneto uses a mixture of indigenous grapes and international varieties, and the most famous wines are basically from the local kind. Until World War Two **Soave** (DOC), based on the Garganega grape, with a little hindrance from Trebbiano, was simply the light local wine of Verona. It was dry, slightly nutty, and perfectly inoffensive. But when the DOC was created in 1968 it included a huge area of alluvial plain, as well as the hillsides that produced the best wine, and then the widespread replanting with the productive but inferior Trebbiano Toscano (as opposed to the much better Trebbiano di Soave) sent production soaring and quality plummetting. In 1988 even the growers decided things had gone far enough: there was a proposal to increase yields still further, which thankfully was defeated. Treat Soave with care, but if you see one from **Bertani**, **Coffele**, **Gini**, **Pieropan**, **Pra**, or **Suavia** –

particularly their single-vineyard wines – buy it, and don't quibble over the price. **Anselmi** makes excellent Soave but uses the local regional IGT denomination. And if you see a sweet **Recioto di Soave** (DOCG) made from dried grapes, buy that, too. Other Veneto whites include the green-apple, fresh **Bianco di Custoza** (DOC), the low-priced **Piave** (DOC) from Verduzzo (soft and nutty) or Tocai (quite full and slightly aromatic), and fresh **Prosecco** (DOC), which can be either still or sparkling.

The reds of **Valpolicella** (DOC) and **Bardolino** (DOC) suffer from overpopularity and overexploitation in the same way as Soave has done. Made from a variety of local grapes, in particular Corvina, Rondinella and Molinara, Bardolino can be the palest of pale reds, with a wispy cherry fruit and a slight bitter snap to finish. Best producers: **Guerrieri-Rizzardi** and **Le Vigne di San Pietro**.

Valpolicella, from the same grape mix, should be just a little bit fuller and deeper and each year we see a few more good examples. Valpolicella Classico from hill vineyards is the best. Valpolicella makes some very good non-DOC table wines – big, strong and full of a strange, intense fruit, the best being **Campo Fiorin** and **Capitel San Rocco**. And, best of all, Valpolicella produces small amounts of **Amarone** and **Recioto della Valpolicella**, two of Italy's most exciting and unusual red wines. *Amaro* means 'bitter' and this remarkable wine, made from half-shrivelled grapes, is bitter, but it also has a brilliant array of flavours – sweet grape skins, chocolate, plums, woodsmoke – all bound up in a wine which is almost sour at the same time. Recioto della Valpolicella is sweet, but with a bitter finish. Best producers: (all Valpolicella styles) **Allegrini**, **Anselmi**, **Bertani**, **Brigaldara**, **Brunelli**, **Cecilia Beretta**, **Bussola**, **Dal Forno**, **Guerrieri-Rizzardi**, **Masi**, **Mazzi**, **Quintarelli**, **Le Ragose**, **Le Salette**, **Speri**, **Tedeschi**, **Viviani** and **Zeni**.

Elsewhere in the Veneto there is good red. North of Venice, in the vast **Piave** DOC, Cabernet Franc and Merlot (often sold as **Merlot del Veneto**) can be good, while Raboso can make tannic, acid wine, bursting with raw fruit. **Breganze** (DOC) is good leafy, blackcurrant stuff, especially from **Maculan**.

The quality of the Valpolicella that will be made from these grapes depends heavily on whether the yields are low or not. After that, it's a question of wine-making.

CLASSIFICATION

Although 'Superiore' appears on labels, in the case of Valpolicella, Bardolino and Soave, it doesn't mean better, merely older. So avoid it. Do, however, look for the word 'Classico': it means the wine comes from the original heartland of the area, and should be much more like the real thing that gave these wines their reputation in the first place.

ORGANIZATION

The merchants and co-operatives dominate production with their commercial blends. Always choose a single grower if possible for wines with more individuality.

READING THE LABEL

The best producers use single-vineyard names for their better wines. These will be a lot more expensive, but worth it.

WHAT DO THEY TASTE LIKE?

Veneto wines should be among the most enjoyable in Italy, since they are nearly all light, refreshing and undemanding. The cherry kernel nip of good Valpolicella or Bardolino is absolutely delicious, yet too many are tart and fruitless. Soave can have a lovely nutty taste with just a flick of liquorice; most doesn't. However, the top growers will rarely let you down, nor will Amarone.

THE GOOD YEARS

Drink most wines young. Rich, intense Recioto will keep for eight to ten years and the Amarones between ten and 20 years or so.

2004 Abundant and high quality.
2003 Hottest, driest vintage for decades. Potentially outstanding wines.
2002 Forget Amarone this year.
2001 Very good year for both Soave and Valpolicella.
2000 Fine, ripe wines.
1999 Another variable vintage.
1998 An uneven year in which the red wines fared best.
1997 An outstanding vintage.
1996 Affected by rain but quite good.
1995 The best year for a long time.

ENJOYING THE WINES

The local cuisine is ideally accompanied by large jugfuls of fresh, light Veneto wine. Strongly flavoured food will swamp most of these wines. Amarone is excellent with strong cheese, and Recioto della Valpolicella can be a good pudding wine for cooked black plums or blackberries. Recioto di Soave is good with bread and butter pudding, among others.

CONSUMER INFORMATION

WHAT DO I GET FOR MY MONEY?

Soave, Valpolicella and Bardolino are too often traded entirely on price, so cheap ones are unlikely to be good value. The growing numbers of single-estate wines are more expensive, and single-vineyard wines are more expensive still, but they are worth it for tastes that can be found nowhere else.

Amarone and Recioto wines are much more expensive again, but they can be so exciting that they really are worth the price for a special occasion. The Vino da Tavola, Venegazzù, is fairly priced for the quality, while the basic Veneto and Piave wines are pretty cheap and often make good buys.

AVAILABILITY

Basic Soave and the other everyday Veneto wines are on sale just about everywhere, and best left there. Go to Italian specialists for a selection of good Veneto growers and top wines. Wines like Raboso, Verduzzo, Prosecco and Tocai are not often seen but are good value and worth seeking out.

CONSUMER CHECKLIST

Soave single-vineyard 2004	*Quality 8* ★	
(Pieropan)	*Price 7* ★	
	Value 8 ★	

Good Years Best years: 2004, 2003, 2000, 1997, 1995, 1993, 1990, 1988, 1985.
Taste Notes The reds have a bitter cherry twist and the whites are clean and nutty. Recioto wines are sweet and concentrated, Amarone della Valpolicella is fascinatingly bitter and rich.

FRIULI-VENEZIA GIULIA

Friuli spreads northwards from the flatlands bordering the Gulf of Venice to the wild jumble of hills which spread along the border with Slovenia. The border has been a tug-of-war here for centuries and it wasn't until 1954 that Trieste, Friuli's capital, was returned to Italy after World War Two. Consequently, there were very few preconceptions about what kind of wine should be made, where, and by whom. The land seemed good, the climate, particularly in the Collio Goriziano hills squeezed up against the border, seemed ideal; what was needed was a sense of direction: the direction they chose was clean, vibrant fruit.

GRAPE VARIETIES AND WINE STYLES
This became possible in the 1960s when Friuli set up what proved to be Italy's least complicated, most logical DOC system. There are now nine different zones – **Collio** and **Colli Orientali del Friuli** in the hillier east and the flatter **Friuli-Grave**, **Friuli-Latisana**, **Friuli-Annia**, **Friuli-Aquileia**, **Friuli-Isonzo** and **Carso**. The wines are simply labelled with their grape variety and the area. Colli Orientali has the biggest range of styles, and the best reds, but the boundary between Colli Orientali and Collio merely reflects the different times at which they joined modern Italy rather than any great difference in style.

The range of wine styles is incredibly wide, but throughout the wines are characterized by something rare in Italian wines – fruit. The international grapes of Cabernet Franc (far more common here than Cabernet Sauvignon), Merlot, Pinot Bianco, Chardonnay and even Sauvignon Blanc and Müller-Thurgau all have a juicy, direct stab of flavour which is absolutely delicious. The Pinot Bianco, which is so often dull in Italy, manages a lemony bite to go with its smoky fruit, and the nutty white Tocai, along with the tough, tarry red Refosco, are also exciting. There is a certain amount of aging in oak barriques, particularly in Collio and Colli Orientali, but results have been a bit mixed thus far.

Most famous of all Friuli wines is **Picolit**. This should be sweet and luscious (it is made

either with dried grapes, or grapes left on the vine and harvested late and overripe) and has been called Italy's d'Yquem, a pointless comparison presumably based on sugar content and rarity value. Nowadays it is certainly sweet, but too often rather insubstantial. Ramandolo (DOCG) is another sweet wine, this time from Verduzzo. Best producers: (Colli Orientali) **Dorigo, Dri, Le Due Terre, Livio Felluga, Miani, Moschioni, Ronchi di Manzano, Ronco di Cialla, Ronco del Gnemiz, Specogna,** and **Zamò del Palazzolo**; (Collio) **Borgo Conventi, Borgo del Tiglio, La Castellada, Livio Felluga, Gravner, Jermann, Keber, Princic, Puiatti, Roncùs, Russiz Superiore, Schiopetto, Tercic, Venica & Venica, Villa Russiz** and **Zuani** (**Gravner** and **Jermann** make wines outside the DOC); (Grave) **Plozner** and **Pradio**; (Isonzo) **Lis Neris-Pecorari, Pierpaolo Pecorari, Ronco del Gelso** and **Vie di Romans**; and (Picolit) **Dorigo** and **Livio Felluga**.

CLASSIFICATION
There is no classification system beyond the normal DOC system.

ORGANIZATION
Single growers and small merchants were responsible for the region's rise to fame in the 1960s and they continue to provide some of the most exciting wines.

READING THE LABEL
'Colli' means 'hills', so expect wines with greater concentration and character from the regions with this word in their name. There are some expensive Vino da Tavolas, particularly in Colli Orientali; the whites have often been aged in new oak barriques. Their price will be the most obvious distinguishing feature on the label.

WHAT DO THEY TASTE LIKE?
Cold fermentation techniques and a clean purity of fruit distinguish these wines – both features were extraordinarily innovative when they were first introduced in the 1960s. Mario

These terraced vineyards are near Prepotto in the better, southern half of the Colli Orientali del Friuli zone and benefit from a warm, dry climate.

Schiopetto is the man credited with establishing the style of wine now made throughout Friuli. The wines have more flavour than central Italian whites, which rely heavily on Trebbiano, but they no longer have the field to themselves: the Alto Adige is now making similar styles, and often from the same grapes.

THE GOOD YEARS

Most of these wines should be drunk young.
2004 Abundant and high quality.
2003 Big, rich wines did well following the summer heatwave.
2002 Not a good year.
2001 Quality mixed. The whites did best.
2000 Another fine vintage.
1999 An exceptionally good year.
1998 A good white wine vintage.
1997 Excellent quality.
1996 Top growers did well.

ENJOYING THE WINES

These are good all-purpose, everyday wines, which go easily with most foods. Avoid any food too hefty, though, as most of the flavours in these wines are fairly light. The reds tend to be fresh and grassy; drink lightly chilled.

CONSUMER INFORMATION

WHAT DO I GET FOR MY MONEY?

Prices are seldom very low for Friulian wines, but they are still pretty good value. Picolit is the exception. Drink it as a curiosity if you want, but try to get somebody else to pay.

AVAILABILITY

The sort of outlets that think that Italian wine begins with Chianti and ends with Soave probably won't have much Friuli to put in between. You might have to go to a specialist, but you'll get a decent range of producers that way, anyway.

CONSUMER CHECKLIST

Friuli-Isonzo Tocai 2004	*Quality 8* ★
(Ronco del Gelso)	*Price 7* ★
	Value 8★

Good Years Most Friulian wines are best drunk young, though the top reds can age for a few years. Best years: 2004, 2002, 2001, 2000, 1999, 1998, 1997, 1996.
Taste Notes The whites have clean, crisp fruit and good varietal definition though use of new oak sometimes blurs this; the reds are mostly fairly light and grassy but that's fine because of their juicy fruit.

CENTRAL ITALY

This great stretch of Italy's calf runs from the south bank of the river Po right down to the south of Lazio and Molise, stopping short of the spur of Puglia. It is a hugely varied place, a peninsula of land washed by the Tyrrhenian Sea on one side and the Adriatic on the other, and ridged down its centre by the Appenines; and these two factors – the proximity of the sea and the altitude of the hills – between them determine where wine can be made, and in what style. Central Italy is hot, and yet by advancing high up into the hills the vines can find some respite from the heat, as well as cool nights to give elegance to the wines; and the sea provides much-needed humidity and a tempering influence on the climate.

For all that, viticulture here is dominated by only a handful of grapes. Sangiovese and Trebbiano, Montepulciano and Lambrusco come and go all over the map. Sangiovese is best known for Chianti, of course, but also for Brunello di Montalcino and Vino Nobile di Montepulciano – all in Tuscany. In Umbria it makes decent reds in Torgiano; and in the Marche it teams up with Montepulciano to make Rosso Conero and Rosso Piceno. In Emilia-Romagna there is Sangiovese (here a high-yielding clone) too, plus endless Lambrusco which is all slightly fizzy and some of it actually rather good. Then there's Albana di Romagna, overpriced, uninspiring, yet the first white to be awarded the DOCG classification. There's good Verdicchio in the Marche and plentiful, usually reliable, Montepulciano in Abruzzo. In Lazio, Trebbiano is used for Frascati, which can be good but usually isn't, and there is improving Orvieto and excellent Sagrantino in Umbria.

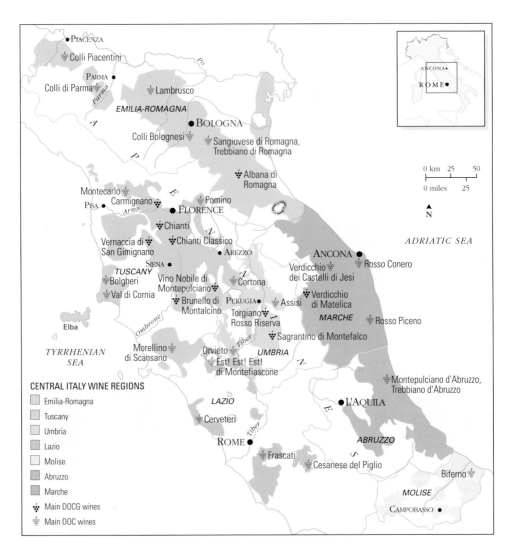

CENTRAL ITALY WINE REGIONS
- Emilia-Romagna
- Tuscany
- Umbria
- Lazio
- Molise
- Abruzzo
- Marche
- Main DOCG wines
- Main DOC wines

TUSCANY

Tuscany should be the most glittering of all Italy's wine regions. After all, Florence and Siena, of all Italy's cities, have a history which shines with achievements in art, philosophy and science, and luckily the astonishing beauty of these two cities is largely unaffected by twentieth-century ugliness. And between them, as the road rises and dips and twists past San Casciano, Greve and Castellina, as every turn in the lane seems to offer a picnic spot even more perfect than the last, flanked by olives, vines, the rough rock of the hills, and the occasional cypress grove hiding another country villa from intrusive eyes, it is easy to sink back and contentedly feel one is slap in the heart of everything Italian wine, Italian life even, should stand for. The dream is nearer than it used to be. In wine terms Tuscany has come a long way in recent years, and some of the most exciting wines in Italy have been emerging from these hills.

Tuscany possesses more vineyard land of potentially brilliant quality than any other province. It possesses in Chianti (DOCG) the most famous of Italian wine names; it's virtually synonymous with all things Italian, from the guttering candlelight in the dingiest trattoria to the majestic flights of Michelangelo. It also possesses, in Brunello di Montalcino (DOCG), a wine which has as its prime objective the title of 'most expensive Italian wine'. Then there is the majestically named Vino Nobile di Montepulciano (DOCG) which now more often rings with the self-confident timbre of its title, and Vernaccia di San Gimignano (DOCG) which at its best can do justice to the remarkable, multi-towered hill town of San Gimignano near Siena which lends its name to the wine.

And there are the iconoclasts – chiefly those who watched in dismay as Chianti set itself on a course of ritual dismemberment, and vowed that they would go their own way to draw out the potential for greatness which quite patently lies in the soil of the Tuscan hills. **Tignanello** (from within the Chianti Classico zone) and **Sassicaia** (from Bolgheri, near the sea) were the groundbreakers: they ignored the rules that dictated grape varieties and aging requirements, and instead made wines the way they wanted, using such forbidden vines as Cabernet Sauvignon or Merlot, or pure Sangiovese, and aging the wines in new small oak barrels. These wines were sold as vini da tavola, and at considerably higher prices than they would have commanded had they been DOC or DOCG. Vino da tavola wines proliferated in the 1980s: they all had snappy names like Sammarco or Solaia or Cepparello, they all came in smart bottles, and nobody could keep track of them all. Then came the Goria Law in 1992. These wines can all now return to the fold, and can sometimes even apply for their own personal DOCs. Sassicaia, from 100 per cent Cabernet Sauvignon, has done so, and from the 1994 vintage is labelled DOC Sassicaia di Bolgheri. The silence of others not rushing to imitate is deafening.

However, Chianti itself made a major bid to improve quality by way of a scheme called 'Chianti 2000'. The idea is that as Chianti vineyards came to be replanted, only the best clones of Sangiovese should be used. Such matters as how many vines should be planted per hectare, and how they should be pruned and trained, also came under close scrutiny.

GRAPE VARIETIES AND WINE STYLES

Tuscany is above all red wine country and the Sangiovese grape is by far the most important influence. The small-berried Sangiovese Piccolo – or Sangioveto – is the mainstay of **Chianti**, while the larger-berried Sangiovese Grosso produces **Brunello di Montalcino** and **Vino Nobile di Montepulciano** (all DOCG). Historically, Sangiovese provided purple-fresh, slightly rasping, herby wines full of thirst-quenching acid fruit, to be drunk young in the bars and trattorias of nearby Florence from the straw-covered *fiaschi* which have now sadly all but disappeared. This is the wine Baron Ricasoli had in mind when he virtually invented modern Chianti over 100 years ago – a wine to be polished off within a year or so of the harvest – but Chianti got grand ideas and started to age its wines in big old wooden barrels. This alone might not have killed all the wines, but crazy laws that allowed up to 30 per cent of the hopeless (white) Trebbiano in the blend led all too often to a thin, orange-tinged wine with little fruit and no pleasure. Thank goodness, the DOCG regulations grasped the nettle and first reduced the permitted amount of white grapes in Chianti to between 2 and 5 per cent, and now allow none, as well as allowing the addition of up to 10 per cent other red grapes.

Antinori's Vino da Tavola wine, Tignanello set the trend and now virtually every top Chianti uses a portion of Cabernet, Merlot or Syrah with Sangiovese or sticks to Sangiovese alone (often with a little Canaiolo). But it's worth remembering that there has been Cabernet in Carmignano (best producers: **Capezzana** and **Villa di Trefiano**), a fine DOCG just west of Florence, from time immemorial. There is no doubt that producers who make such wines, often with the help of small oak barrels, which produce wines that lose less fruit and oxidize more slowly, are taking a path away from traditional Chianti, but at last the conditions exist for world-class wines to be made. Best producers: (Classico) **Castello di Ama**, **Antinori**, **Badia a Coltibuono**, **Capaccia**, **Carpineto**, **Casaloste**, **Castell'in Villa**, **Casa Emma**, **Casa Sola**, **Collelungo**, **Felsina**, **Fonterutoli**, **Fontodi**, **Isole e Olena**, **La Massa**, **Monsanto**, **Castello dei Rampolla**, **Riecine**, **Ruffino** and **Castello di Volpaia**; (Colli Fiorentini) **Castello di Poppiano**; (Rufina) **Basciano**, **Frescobaldi** and **Selvapiana**.

Chianti's Sangiovese grape, which seems to have the ability to change its character according to where it is planted and will only produce rich, deep wine on poor soils and in cool sites, is also the grape which produces **Brunello di Montalcino**, Italy's most effective drain on a wine lover's bank balance. At its best this can indeed be a huge, complex wine, but few examples are worth the asking price, and long, legally-required barrel-aging

for wines that can't always take it means that there's better value to be had from the new **Rosso di Montalcino** DOC where lack of restrictions on the age of release leads to softer, juicier wines. Best producers: **Biondi-Santi**, **Brunelli**, **Casanova di Neri**, **Casanuova delle Cerbaie**, **Case Basse**, **Cerbaiona**, **Col d'Orcia**, **Costanti**, **Fuligni**, **La Gerla**, **Le Gode**, **Il Greppone Mazzi**, **Lambardi**, **Mastrojanni**, **Siro Pacenti**, **Pian delle Vigne**, **Piancornello**, **Pieve Santa Restituta**, **Poggio Antico**, **Il Poggione** and **Talenti**.

Vino Nobile di Montepulciano, which is also no slouch when it comes to emptying wallets of their loose change. Like Brunello, it comes from Sangiovese (here known as Prugnolo) with the help of a little Mammolo. Here again there is a good-value junior version, **Rosso di Montepulciano** DOC, but the best producers are making fine DOCG wines that fall halfway between Brunello and a top Chianti in style. Best producers: **Avignonesi**, **Boscarelli**, **La Braccesca**, **Dei** and **Poliziano**.

Along with Sangiovese in all its guises and the other traditional grapes I've mentioned, there are increasing quantites of Cabernet (Sauvignon and Franc), Merlot and Syrah – even Gamay – grown both for blending into DOCG wines and for the continuing fashion for Vino da Tavolas – every self-respecting estate has at least one – which aspire to be judged on the world stage.

Best red Vino da Tavolas: (Sangiovese and other Tuscan varieties) **Boscarelli**, **Cepparello**, **Coltassala**, **La Corte**, **Flaccianello**, **Fontalloro**, **La Gioia**, **Palazzo**, **Percarlo**, **Le Pergole Torte**, **Sangioveto**, **Il Sodaccio** and **I Sodi di San Niccolò**; (Sangiovese-Cabernet and Sangiovese-Merlot blends) **Il Camartina**, **Casalferro**, **Il Futuro**, **Siepi**, **Solengo**, **Summus** and **Tignanello**; (Cabernet Sauvignon) **Collezione**, **Il Pareto**, **Olmaia**, **Sammarco**, **Solaia** and **Le Stanze**; (Merlot) **L'Apparita**, **Masseto**, **Messorio** and **Redigaffi**; (Cabernet-Merlot blends) **Excelsus**, **Ghiaie della Furba**, **Giusto di Notri**, **Guado al Tasso**, **Ornellaia** and **Le Stanze**.

The most widely planted white variety is Trebbiano Toscano which produces vast quantities of grapes with frightening efficiency. No longer used in Chianti, it is at last being vinified in a modern way to produce clean, refreshing, but still pretty unmemorable wines, including **Galestro**, although the

Trebbiano and Malvasia grapes are left to dry in the winery at Isole e Olena to make Vin Santo, Tuscany's famous apéritif and dessert wine.

addition of Malvasia and Chardonnay can produce decent results. Chardonnay on its own can be superb from top growers. The Vernaccia grape makes Tuscany's potentially most interesting white at **San Gimignano** (DOCG): dry, but nutty and slightly honeyed with a fair amount of fruit. Best producers: **Casale-Falchini**, **Montenidoli**, **Teruzzi & Puthod** and **Vagnoni**. But there is plenty of cynical production here too! And Sauvignon Blanc and even Viognier are making an appearance.

And then there is **Vin Santo** or 'holy wine' – which doesn't have to be Tuscan, but classically is. Made from Trebbiano and Malvasia, the grapes are picked and left under the rafters to shrivel before being crushed and fermented. It can be dry, quite sweet, very sweet or anything in between, and is aged in small sealed barrels for at least three years. Some is DOC, some not. Some is sublime. Some is not. Best producers: **Castello di Ama**, **Avignonesi**, **Basciano**, **Bindella**, **Cacchiano**, **Capezzana**, **Fattoria del Cerro**, **Corzano & Paterno**, **Fontodi**, **Isole e Olena**, **Romeo**, **San Felice**, **San Gervasio**, **San Giusto a Rentananno**, **Selvapiana** and **Villa Sant'Anna**.

CLASSIFICATION

Situated between Florence and Siena, Chianti Classico is the best and most famous of Chianti's seven sub-zones. The other six are Colli

The forward-looking estate of Altesino was one of the first in Montalcino to make a more modern style of Brunello, big wine yet packed with fruit in its youth.

Aretini, Colli Fiorentini, Colli Senesi, Colline Pisane, Montalbano and Rufina, of which Rufina and Colli Senesi are the most important. Much basic wine is simply called Chianti, without any further definition. Riserva means a special selection of wine that has been aged longer before release but these aging requirements have been coming down in recent years. Chianti Classico Riserva must now be aged for at least 27 months (usually in barrel) before release. The 'Riservas' of Brunello di Montalcino and Vino Nobile di Montepulciano require respectively a total of two and a half and three years' aging in barrel and bottle. The headline-grabbing 'Super-Tuscan' Vino da Tavolas should theoretically start to diminish in number as they adopt various DOCs. We'll see! *Siamo in Italia.*

ORGANIZATION

All the finest Tuscan wines, without exception, now come from the estates of committed growers and winemakers. The merchants are finding it increasingly difficult to buy good-quality wine and this is one reason why the standards of basic Tuscan wine have fallen so low, although some producers, like Antinori, manage to combine high standards as growers with quality-orientated merchant businesses. The best co-operatives are trying to improve standards.

READING THE LABEL

'Classico' denotes the central and most tightly controlled Chianti zone. 'Riserva' is supposed to denote a superior wine because of the longer aging requirements. In practice, except with the top producers, it often only guarantees that the wine is drying out and losing its fruit. Stay clear of older wines from unknown producers. The words Vino da Tavola on wines from a single estate are often a sign of extra quality. It means that the grapes and wine-making methods do not conform to DOCG regulations. Confusingly, the cheapest wines are also classified as Vino da Tavola – but the price will put you straight!

WHAT DO THEY TASTE LIKE?

There are arguably now three main red wine styles in Tuscany, assuming we leave aside the still too many examples of the tired and fruitless wines of yesteryear. First, there are the sharp young reds typified by well-made young Chianti which should be fresh, aggressive, bitter-sweet frothing stuff made to be glugged back thoughtlessly with food for a year or so after the harvest. For my taste these are best using the traditional and increasingly rare *governo* method whereby dried grapes are used to start the second fermentation, giving the wine a characteristic and delicious prickle.

Then come regular estate bottlings from Chianti, Montalcino and Montepulciano – together with the Rosso wines of Montalcino and Montepulciano – which take themselves more seriously and should at their best provide fruity, drinkable wines with strong Sangiovese flavours of cherry, blackcurrant and spice underpinned with reasonable tannin and acidity.

And, third, there are the Riserva wines and the Vino da Tavolas – and remember we're talking only about the best estates here – that aspire to be judged on a world stage. The top Chianti Classico Riservas are marked by ele-

gance and structure with rich berry flavours and, one hopes, plenty of traditional Sangiovese bite – although this can be nicely balanced out by the addition of Cabernet Sauvignon or Franc, Merlot or Syrah. Vino Nobile can, at its peak, approach the sheer power of Brunello while retaining the greater finesse associated with the best Chiantis – but sadly this spice and sandalwood style remains the exception rather than the norm. The most successful producers of Brunello can, in a good year, achieve a blockbusting combination of fruit and tannin that can achieve greatness with flavours of raisins, pepper, tannin, liqorice and fierce black chocolate – although few of us can afford the cost or the wait.

The Vino da Tavolas are notable for their pure sweet fragrance of various berries – according to the grape varieties used – and a certain toughness which inspires confidence in the wine's aging potential rather than merely concern about the enamel on one's teeth. Carmignano, too, with its component of Cabernet can achieve a delightful blackcurrant sweetness.

Tuscan whites are less exciting, though good Vernaccia di San Gimignano can have lovely hazelnut and angelica flavours and the occasional Bianco Vergine Valdichiana is a crisp summer quaffer. At their best, the barrel-fermented Chardonnays can successfully blend Old and New World flavours.

THE GOOD YEARS

Vintages matter in this part of Italy: the Tuscan hills are cool and subject to frost, and less-good years can produce lean wines. White wines should generally be drunk young; only the reds are intended to age, and many of these are best young.

2004 High quality, classic wines.

2003 Younger vines suffered from the drought and heatwave. Older vines produced rich, ripe Sangiovese.

2002 Terrible year, including freak tornadoes in Chianti.

2001 Reduced quantities due to hot, dry summer but some excellent Sangiovese.

2000 Very hot August led to high sugar levels and some unbalanced wines.

1999 An early harvest produced some classic wines.

1998 An uneven vintage better for Brunello than Chianti.

1997 Exceptionally healthy and ripe grapes; a great year for Tuscan reds of wonderful balance and ripe tannins.

1996 A fine end to the vintage saved it but yields were down. Drink up.

1995 A good vintage for red wines which are now at peak.

1994 A good year overall, and welcome after several poor ones.

1993 Damp vintage but good concentrated reds; drink up.

1992 A year to forget.

1991 A good year in Tuscany: both reds and whites were ripe, with good structure and concentration.

1990 An excellent vintage. The best reds have plenty of richness and concentration and will keep well (though many are at their peak).

1988 Wonderful reds across the board; the top wines are still drinking well.

ENJOYING THE WINES

Tuscany is very much a wine with food land: the local red wines positively demand food. With everyday Tuscan meat and poultry dishes, *crostini* and other simple fare, especially using the wonderful local olive oil and herbs, I would drink very young Chianti or unclassified Sangiovese, and with more elaborate, stronger-tasting dishes either Rosso di Montalcino or Montepulciano or one of the Cabernet-influenced reds.

The Chianti Riservas and the big, burly Brunellos and Vino Nobiles, providing they have kept their fruit, are best with hearty roast game or local grilled Valdichiana beef. Versions with less fruit can still be good with pasta sauces, casseroles and tangy Pecorino cheese.

Vernaccia di San Gimignano has a fair amount of body and goes well with the local strong, herby salads and bean dishes. Vin Santo is traditionally sipped after a meal with *cantucci* (hard almond biscuits).

CONSUMER INFORMATION

WHAT DO I GET FOR MY MONEY?

Tuscan wines range from some of Italy's cheapest to the most expensive, yet at neither end is the value particularly good. At the top, the flavours of Brunello di Montalcino and Vino Nobile di Montepulciano have to be very good indeed to justify the price. In Chianti there is good, cheap wine available locally, but not all exported Chianti is as good value as it should be. However, quality has gone up in recent years, and if you look for good names you should find something satisfying. Carmignano from Capezzana is good and not too expensive. Sassicaia is prohibitively expensive but world class; this also goes for some of the 'Super-Tuscan' Vino da Tavolas, but even those that aren't excellent are still extremely expensive.

Tuscan whites are neither expensive nor exciting, except for a few 'boutique' wines from Chardonnay and other international varieties, which can be both.

AVAILABILITY

Chianti is possibly Italy's most famous wine, and is available amost everywhere. However, choosing good Chianti requires some care, because there are still too many importers and cheaper Italian restaurants abroad who select the wines solely on price. The other Tuscan reds are not widely available. Brunello di Montalcino, Vino Nobile di Montepulciano, Carmignano and the top Vino da Tavolas are usually found only in specialist shops. The whites are not that easy to find outside Tuscany or Italian restaurants.

CONSUMER CHECKLIST

Chianti Classico 2001	*Quality 9* ★
(Isole e Olena)	*Price 8* ★
	Value 8 ★

Good Years Tuscan white wines are best drunk young. Many more reds are now being released young as well, and only Brunello di Montalcino and the top Vino da tavolas need long aging after they are released for sale. Best years: 2004, 2003, 2001, 1999, 1997, 1995, 1990, 1988, 1985, 1983, 1976.

Taste Notes Chianti veers from the delicious to the basic, but at its herby, rather aggressive best is excellent with Italian food. Brunello, Vino Nobile, Carmignano and the top Vino da Tavolas are richer, denser, more concentrated wines. The white wines are mostly light and more or less nutty.

EMILIA-ROMAGNA

Emilia-Romagna is centred on Bologna, a city often described as the belly of Italy. The food here is rich and appetites are hearty; and the wine that swamps the region is the undemanding thirst-quencher par excellence – **Lambrusco**. Good Lambrusco should be lightly fizzy and low in alcohol; it can range from dry to vaguely sweet, but it should always have a sharp, almost rasping acid bite to it. Most Lambrusco is not DOC and is softened for fear of offending consumers, which is a pity, because this type of baby-juice is often feeble stuff. Real Lambrusco, from one of the four DOC zones, is anything but feeble – purple red and full of acid zing. **Bellei** and **Cavicchioli** are good producers.

However, the region isn't all Lambrusco; Gutturnio reds (an appealing blend of Barbera and Bonarda) from the **Colli Piacentini** DOC are strong and excellent accompaniments to Bologna's big blowouts. Best producers: **La Stoppa** and **La Tosa**. **Sangiovese di Romagna** (DOC) is often good light red for drinking young, and it hasn't been debased like Lambrusco. Best producers: **La Berta**, **Castelluccio**, **L Conti**, **La Palazza**, **Tre Monti** and **Zerbina**.

Among the whites, the rather vapid **Albana di Romagna** (DOCG) achieved brief notoriety when political pressure finally got it accepted as Italy's first white DOCG in 1987. Standards are now improving and **Fattoria**

Albana di Romagna didn't deserve to be Italy's first white DOCG, but they had to have a white wine, and politics is politics…

Paradiso and **Zerbina** make decent versions. **Trebbiano di Romagna** is the region's all-purpose white: neutral, clean and fresh and Pagadebit is a local white variety showing promise as both a dry and sweet wine.

There are also 'foreign' vines in Emilia-Romagna, like Chardonnay, Cabernet Sauvignon and Müller-Thurgau, all usually making quite light wines.

MARCHE

This hilly coastal region has one world-famous wine – **Verdicchio**, made from the Verdicchio grape, with a little Trebbiano and Malvasia. Among Italy's dry whites only Soave produces more wine. Yet the general standard of Verdicchio is far higher than that of Soave – it is reliable, light, dry and fairly neutral, but above all Verdicchio is clean, and justly appreciated for its suitability with fish and shellfish. There are two DOC zones: the bigger **Castelli di Jesi** has a Classico heartland, and **Matelica**, which produces wine with more flavour and depth from lower-yielding, better-sited and higher vineyards. Verdicchio dei Castelli di Jesi often comes in a kitschy, amphora-shaped green bottle which was invented in the 1950s as a sales gambit. Best producers: **Belisario**, **Bisci**, **Brunori**, **Bucci**, **Colonnara**, **Fabrini**, **Fazi-Battaglia**,

Garofoli, **Mancinelli**, **Mecella**, **La Monacesca**, **Moncaro**, **Monte Schiavo**, **Santa Barbara**, **Sartarelli**, **Umani Ronchi** and **Zaccagnini**.

The region's best reds are made from the Montepulciano and Sangiovese grapes, and while the wines can be tasty and interesting they are more often lean, dilute, stringy and overproduced. **Rosso Conero** (DOC) is mostly from Montepulciano with some Sangiovese; **Rosso Piceno** (DOC) is the reverse, mostly Sangiovese with a dollop of Montepulciano (the more the better). Both wines should be sturdy, mixing herbs and fruit with a slight prickle where the *governo* method is practised. Best producers: (Rosso Conero) **Dittajuti**, **Garofoli**, **Mecella**, **Moroder**, **Le Terrazze** and **Umani Ronchi**; (Rosso Piceno) **Boccadigabbia** and **Pilastri**.

UMBRIA

It must be easy to feel overshadowed when you are next door to Tuscany, Italy's most famous wine region. Even Umbria's most famous wine, **Orvieto** (DOC) has seemed to go into decline as Tuscany has pulled itself together. That is, if you mourn its old sweetish, smoky, honeyed incarnation: now it is slick and more anonymous – but too reliant on the feckless Trebbiano grape – and in just the right shape to benefit from Italy's boom in light white wine. Best producers: **Barberani**, **Castello della Sala**, **Decugnano dei Barbi**, **Palazzone** and **Conte Vaselli**.

The prime mover in the resurrection of much of Umbria was Dr **Lungarotti** who, during the 1960s, virutally created the DOC of **Torgiano** single-handed. Torgiano is still best known for Lungarotti's Rubesco, a full, plummy red, but unless you like a disconcerting amount of fizz and a slight sour yeast flavour in your reds, this is no longer the wine it was. Much better are the experiments with Cabernet Sauvignon, showing once again how well-suited central Italy is to this grape, and the excellent Rubesco Riserva from the single Monticchio vineyard. **Torgiano Rosso Riserva** is now DOCG. The Torgiano whites show a welcome freshness and straightforward fruit, and can be excellent, especially from **Lungarotti**. Less well-known Umbrian wines include red **Montefalco Sagrantino** (DOCG), with a tremendous sweet-and-sour richness and Grechetto-based whites, especially from the producer **Caprai**.

ABRUZZO & MOLISE

These two coastal regions rely on the Montepulciano variety for their DOC reds and rosés. Montepulciano is one of Italy's most underrated grapes, because while it has the toughness characteristic of Italian red varieties, it also has masses of fruit. A good **Montepulciano d'Abruzzo** wine manages to be citrus fresh and plummily rich, the fruit sweet yet biting. Prices are not high, and this is one of Italy's more consistent wines. The rosé is called Cerasuolo, and is good, though doesn't make the best of the Montepulciano fruit. Best producers: **Cataldi Madonna**, **Cornacchia**, **Filo-musi Guelfi**, **Illuminati**, **Masciarelli**, **Monti**, **Umani Ronchi**, **Valentini** and **Zaccagnini**. In Molise the reds from **Biferno**, the region's main DOC, have a decent amount of Montepulciano and can be decent, beefy wines.

Trebbiano is the main grape for the whites. **Trebbiano d'Abruzzo** (DOC) is unexciting but adequate wine, and in spite of its name is not necessarily made entirely from Trebbiano. The best producer is **Valentini**, who ages his wine in wood. The Biferno whites are also made from Trebbiano. The best Molise wines come from the producer **Di Majo Norante**.

LAZIO

Most of Lazio's wine comes from the attractive Alban hills south-east of Rome. Nearly all the wine is white, yet it is unlikely that any of us will taste the best ones unless we head into these hills around the towns of Frascati, Marino or Montecompatri, because these bright and breezy whites have always been useless at travelling out of the region.

The best known of these wines, **Frascati** (DOC) is made from Malvasia and Trebbiano, and it should have a lovely fresh feel, nutty, and with an unusual but attractive tang of sour cream about it. But most Frascati found abroad has too much sour cream and not enough nuts. **Colli di Catone** is the main producer. Wines from the neighbouring DOC of **Marino** don't usually have much personality either, but they are usually fresher than Frascati, as are the somewhat peppery, appley-whites from **Montecompatri** (DOC). The soft and slightly *frizzante* white **Colli Lanuvini** (DOC) and the good, fruity white **Cerveteri** (DOC) are also good, but forget **Est! Est!! Est!!! di Montefiascone** (DOC) from northern Lazio around Lake Bolsena. Rarely the real thing, the wine should have a gentle angelica and almond paste fruit.

As for Lazio's reds, **Aprilia** (DOC) has some good Merlot, **Cerveteri** (DOC) produces tough but tasty wines from mainly Montepulciano and Sangiovese and **Velletri** (DOC) reds are dusty, ripe and soft.

SOUTHERN ITALY

Setting out from Rome with the compass taking you south-east, you are heading into the most concentrated and productive vineyard land in the world. But try to think of a single world-famous name, and you will draw an almost total blank. Lacryma Christi we've all heard of, but probably never drunk a bottle which was halfway decent. Marsala we've heard of but never tried a mouthful except in the frothy golden confines of a *zabaglione* dessert. Aglianico del Vulture? If I said it's potentially one of Italy's greatest red wines, would we be any the wiser? Probably not, because great though it could be, it seldom fulfils its potential.

So this sweep through southern Italy is of necessity going to sound a little unfamiliar. But be patient, because wine-making is modernizing all the time here. Already we are

seeing tasty, inexpensive wines from the nooks and crannies of the parched and daunting hillsides and I believe some classic styles are just about to re-emerge.

CAMPANIA

Campania is the most infuriating of places. The Ancient Greeks and Romans were infatuated with the wines of this lovely region based around the Bay of Naples, Sorrento and Mount Vesuvius. Many of their greatest, most fabled wines came from within a day's hike of Naples or Sorrento, and the Falernian draught which Cicero, Horace and the boys grew maudlin and lyrical about in turns, came from the coast north of Naples just a few miles off the road to Rome.

Nowadays only a minuscule proportion of the wine produced in Campania appears

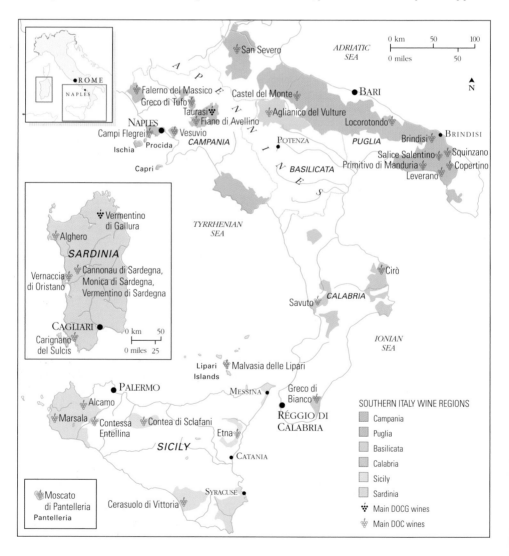

SOUTHERN ITALY WINE REGIONS
- Campania
- Puglia
- Basilicata
- Calabria
- Sicily
- Sardinia
- Main DOCG wines
- Main DOC wines

under a DOC label. Of these DOCs **Capri** is swiftly disappearing as tourism takes over the island and vines prove less profitable than holiday housing and tourist shops. The island of **Ischia** still makes a little DOC wine, though, and Campania's most famous wine, the red or white **Lacryma Christi del Vesuvio**, is DOC, but sells more on its name than on any intrinsic quality of the wine.

However, cooling sea breezes aided by large amounts of volcanic soil and the Apennine foothills that slope gently down to the coast from the inland mountains are all of real benefit to growing quality grapes. Inland behind Mount Vesuvius, centred on the town of Avellino, the chewy, liquoricy white **Greco di Tufo** (DOCG), the more fragrant white **Fiano di Avellino** (DOCG) as well as the remarkable, plummy but strangely austere red **Taurasi** (DOCG) from the Aglianico grape show what potential there is in Campania. The revived Falernian DOC, **Falerno del Massico**, with a white Falanghina and reds from Aglianico and Primitivo, look promising. The venerable **Mastroberardino** is the most famous producer in Campania: his wines are the best in the region but they're not cheap. Several young producers have finally begun to realise the region's potential, especially for Aglianico.

South of Bari around Locorotondo the landscape is dotted with trulli, *curious-looking stone buildings with pointed, conical roofs.*

PUGLIA
Talk to any northern Italian winemaker about the south and it will mean only one thing to him – Puglia. Experienced wine tasters can sometimes be seen spitting out a sample with sour conviction and muttering one of two words – 'concentrato' or 'Puglia', because Puglia is famous as a source of dark, strong, cutting wines, and concentrated grape juice used to add guts to many frail, pale wines in the north. The region's output is massive, but as the consumption of basic, anonymous red and white jug wine declines in Italy, and the demand of the vermouth houses for their neutral but alcoholic whites declines in the face of determined opposition from Sicily, the winds of change are beginning to tease the winemakers into maximizing their resources.

Much of the experimental work has been done on whites and rosés. Certainly, the whites are light and clean, and the advent of international grapes like Sauvignon Blanc, Chardonnay and Pinot Blanc shows the direction in which things are going. The rosés are mostly a little hefty and grape-skinny, though new cool fermentation installations will improve the wine-making. There is Sangiovese and Trebbiano in the northern part of the region, and the red Uva de Troia in the **San Severo** DOC, but none of these grapes is hugely exciting.

For excitement you need to go to the Salento peninsula south of Brindisi. Here the Negroamaro grape (meaning 'bitter black'), often softened with a little Malvasia Nera, makes rich, flavoursome reds in the DOCs of **Salice Salentino**, **Copertino**, **Leverano**, **Squinzano** and **Brindisi**. These are some of the best bargains currently coming out of Italy. Best producers: **Candido**, **Taurino**, **Vallone**.

The Ancient Greeks left behind them on Sicily not only many temples, as here at Segesta in the west of the island, but also the tradition of viticulture.

But Puglia has another trick up its sleeve, as well. The red Primitivo grape ripens incredibly early here, often by mid-August, and as such has always, in the past, been the darling of the northern blenders. But now it's emerging under its own flag as a big, peppery, briar-sweet red. It is the same grape as the Californian Zinfandel and tastes pretty similar here. And as a complete contrast some outstanding Chardonnay is appearing too.

BASILICATA

It comes as a bit of a shock to find that Potenza, the capital of Basilicata, way down in the south of Italy, regularly records lower temperatures than Bolzano, the capital of the Alto Adige within spitting distance of the Dolomites in the far north. This, combined with a barren rock-strewn landscape which, one feels, had all the goodness sucked out of it centuries ago, forms what is probably Italy's poorest region even in the chronically poor far south. And it doesn't even have much of a wine industry to sustain it.

But Basilicata's most important DOC could make it worthwhile: the rare and ominously-named **Aglianico del Vulture**. Planted more than 600m (2000ft) up the side of the gaunt Mount Vulture, an extinct volcano, on wretched, arid land with hardly a scratch of good soil in sight, the Aglianico grapes have the capacity to make great wine. Not only is it cold up there, but the Aglianico is a very late-ripening grape. Benefiting from the long,

slow growing season (the harvest is almost the last in Italy, at the end of October), this big, thick-flavoured red wine can be superb. The colour isn't that deep, but the tremendous flavours of almond paste and chocolate fruit, matched by a tough, dusty feel and quite high acidity, make for a remarkable wine, which is not very expensive. Best producers: **D'Angelo**, **Cantine del Notaio** and **Paternoster**.

CALABRIA

The region of Calabria seems so far removed from the babble and fuss of Italian life. But this wonderfully distant mountainous land occupies the entire toe of Italy in splendid isolation and the mood here is wild and untrained. Because it is almost too mountainous for extensive vineyards, Calabria isn't really a big blending wine producer, and its wines are made for local consumption and seldom seen outside the region. Leading producers are **Librandi** and **Odoardi**.

Cirò (DOC) – the wine offered to champions in the ancient Olympics – is still the most famous wine. It has now been re-invigorated and offers the most exciting Calabrian wines in all three colours.

SICILY

This mountainous, aggressively self-assertive island produces huge quantities of wine. But it also spotted the trend away from the production of vast amounts of undistinguished blending wine earlier than its neighbours on the mainland, and is already producing a good deal of high-quality table wine, as well as its historically famous Marsala and Moscato di Pantelleria.

Marsala (DOC) at its best has a delicious deep brown sugar sweetness allied to a cutting, lip-tingling acidity which makes it surprisingly refreshing for a fortified dessert wine. There are several Moscatos made in Sicily and its off islands but the one from **Pantelleria** (DOC), a tiny island closer to Tunisia than it is to Italy, is the most famous.

The dry Sicilian whites show just what can be done with determination and investment. Most of the best wines are not DOC, but can be tart and apple-fresh, while retaining a decent splash of hot southern body. The **Alcamo** DOC provides some good, dry nutty whites (best producer: **Rapitalà**). The reds can have a lovely, big, old-fashioned flavour of herbs, chocolate and jammy fruit: the wines from **de Bartoli**, the **Duca di Salaparuta**, **Planeta** and **Regaleali** are very interesting. Inycon and Cusumano are good value.

The Regaleali estate has been a pioneer of high-quality modern table wines in Sicily, proving how a harsh climate can be turned to good account.

SARDINIA

If Sicily has rushed into the future with gay abandon, Sardinia has been more circumspect. But then the character of this isolated island, and the strong, brash flavours of her wines, have always been out on a limb, away from the headlong currents of mainland Italy. Even so, the **Sella & Mosca** winery in Alghero, along with some, though not all of the co-operatives, have begun to drag Sardinia into the modern world.

Don't feel you have to see DOC on the label – until the latest wine law reforms many of the best wines didn't sport a DOC – but out of several Sardinian wines with fairly beefy character, the following are worth a try. Red **Cannonau** (DOC and *vino da tavola*) can be sweet or dry, and virtually any strength but can be exciting when sweet and fortified. White **Vernaccia di Oristano** (DOC) has plenty of big, dry sherry taste. The Torbato grape around Alghero is the source of rather good dry whites. They are not wildly cheap, but pack a fair punch; the widely planted, white Nuragus also makes good wine.

CONSUMER INFORMATION

WHAT DO I GET FOR MY MONEY?

Generally speaking, good value. Salice Salentino and Copertino are particularly good, as are Cannonau and Sicily's non-DOC wines.

AVAILABILITY

The supermarkets have taken up some of these wines in quite a big way, so they can be quite easy to find. But for more adventurous selections, try a specialist.

CONSUMER CHECKLIST

Salice Salentino 2003	Quality 6 ★
(Candido)	Price 4 ★
	Value 9 ★

Good Years In general these are not wines to age, and most vintages are fairly similar. Aglianico del Vulture needs six to ten years' aging; Taurasi is fine and deep and needs to age for five to ten years.

Taste Notes The south is producing increasingly good, individual flavours. Many of the reds manage to balance new and old philosophies remarkably well. The whites are, on the whole, less exciting.

SPAIN

*S*pain has more land under vine than any other country in the world. Yet in production terms it's way down the league, plagued as it has been for years by low rainfall and old-fashioned viticulture. But if Spain can't do much about the weather, the wine-making has certainly improved. All over the country the winemakers have been throwing out the musty old vats that produced the tired wines of yore and replacing them with brand new, shiny stainless steel ones. The results are startling. Pick up a bottle of Spanish wine nowadays and you're likely to be confronted with a crisp, white wine with just a touch of tropical pineapple and peach to its fruit, or a red with both juiciness and weight.

High up in the Catalan hills in north-eastern Spain, the Castillo de Milmanda estate (left) produces top-quality Chardonnay for the world-famous firm of Torres; while on the vast monotonous plain of La Mancha in central Spain (above), Airén grapes are grown for everyday table wine. But both rely on the sort of modern wine-making technology that is transforming Spanish wine year by year.

WINE REGIONS

If the truth be told the Spanish taste is still often for wines aged in wooden barrels for what you and I would consider far too long, until the fruit has started to dry out and the freshness has vanished. White wines, in the traditional Spanish view, are best when verging on the...well, darkish. Reds, too, shouldn't be too vibrant and fruity. Such tastes developed from making wine in a hot, dry land that was long relatively isolated from the rest of Europe, and had only to please itself.

But a number of factors in recent years have changed things. A demand from outside Spain for wines that were fresh, fruity and also cheap sent wine buyers scurrying down there to cajole winemakers into humouring their strange foreign tastes. When Spain joined the EU, it started getting subsidies and became more international in attitude. Winemakers started to get seriously interested in the sort of whites that were young and pale and full of fruit, and reds that passed from barrel to bottle far more quickly than they used to.

We don't have to go far to see the results: just down to our nearest wine shop, where there will be any number of inexpensive bottles of cold-fermented white and lightly barrel-aged red, plus a shelf of pricier wines. These latter will be from Rioja, of course, but also from Ribera del Duero, Penedès and possibly from the North-West, if any bottles could be prised away from the fashion-conscious drinkers of Madrid. And the grapes? Tempranillo, Garnacha, Cabernet Sauvignon, Chardonnay, even Pinot Noir. A mixture of old and new, of indigenous Spanish and imported French.

Let's start in the North-West, where Spain juts over the north of Portugal. The wines here are pretty similar to those south of the border, since wine is no respecter of boundaries. Spain's most aromatic whites are made here (this is a country short on aromatic white varieties) from the Albariño grape – think of the best Vinho Verde you've ever drunk, and double the price. Albariño is delicious, but it is expensive. Edging eastwards along the Bay of Biscay we come to País Vasco and Basque country, home of unspellable and unpronouncable words (I'll stick to Spanish spelling here and risk a Basque nationalist kneecapping) and also home to some tasty, entirely individual red and white wines. A short step south brings us to Navarra and Rioja, where some of Spain's most famous reds and best rosés are made. It's still close enough to the Pyrenees here not to be too stiflingly hot. Even Cariñena and Somontano, to the south and the east respectively, aren't really hot in Spanish terms.

On the Mediterranean coast Barcelona and the wine regions to its south-west have just the sort of climate that I like: not too hot, not too cold. And enough variety to plant white vines where they do best, in the coolest spots, and red vines where they get more warmth. Just inland are Calatayud and Campo de Borja with their ripe, crunchy Garnacha reds.

Valencia? Mostly decent everyday stuff, plus some sticky-sweet Moscatel de Valencia, which I'll put in the fridge for later. Go inland just a bit and there are good, beefy reds from Jumilla, on sale at remarkably low prices.

Then it's a long, vineless trek round the corner of Spain into Andalucía. There's fortified wine in Málaga and more in Montilla-Moriles, some of it underrated, some of it not. Then we get to Jerez, and some of the finest wine in the whole country – sherry – and all of it underrated outside south-west Spain.

Further north, along the Duero river, are some more of Spain's best vineyards, producing, in Ribera del Duero, some of her most expensive wines, and in Toro and Rueda, some of her beefiest reds and most interesting whites. These are among Spain's most improved wine regions. They're producing the sort of flavours that the more traditional areas either can't or won't.

Then I'll dive into the centre of the country to La Mancha, a vast central plateau, freezing in the winter, baking hot in the summer and dotted with parched, whitewashed villages, herds of goats and the odd windmill. You passed through it on the way to Madrid, if you chose to drive. But oh, my goodness, you didn't drink the wine then unless you had to. *Now* I'll happily pop into my local supermarket and stock up with fruity young white or red from here – and that, above all, is a measure of how things have changed in Spain.

CLASSIFICATION

Like all EU countries, Spain divides her wines into table wine at the bottom level and quality wine at the top. If I had to criticize the Spanish system, though, I'd say it was too French-based. There's a large emphasis on geographical origin here which is fine if you have umpteen different grape varieties to suit different conditions – but Spain doesn't. The great Spanish skill was always blending; and of course you can't have both.

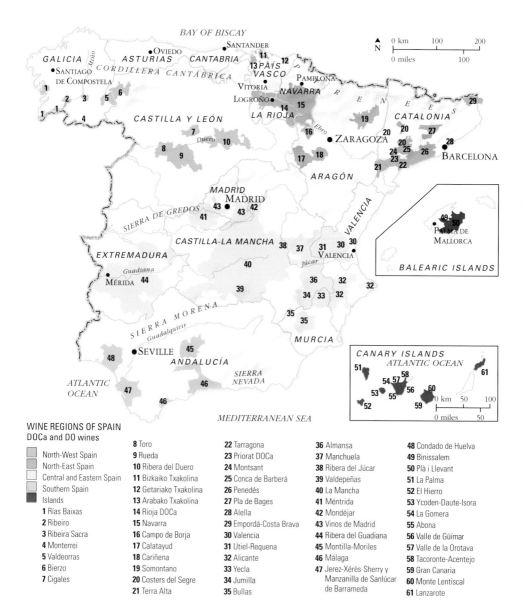

WINE REGIONS OF SPAIN
DOCa and DO wines

- North-West Spain
- North-East Spain
- Central and Eastern Spain
- Southern Spain
- Islands

1 Rías Baixas
2 Ribeiro
3 Ribeira Sacra
4 Monterrei
5 Valdeorras
6 Bierzo
7 Cigales

8 Toro
9 Rueda
10 Ribera del Duero
11 Bizkaiko Txakolina
12 Getariako Txakolina
13 Arabako Txakolina
14 Rioja DOCa
15 Navarra
16 Campo de Borja
17 Calatayud
18 Cariñena
19 Somontano
20 Costers del Segre
21 Terra Alta

22 Tarragona
23 Priorat DOCa
24 Montsant
25 Conca de Barberá
26 Penedés
27 Pla de Bages
28 Alella
29 Empordá-Costa Brava
30 Valencia
31 Utiel-Requena
32 Alicante
33 Yecla
34 Jumilla
35 Bullas

36 Almansa
37 Manchuela
38 Ribera del Júcar
39 Valdepeñas
40 La Mancha
41 Méntrida
42 Mondéjar
43 Vinos de Madrid
44 Ribera del Guadiana
45 Montilla-Moriles
46 Málaga
47 Jerez-Xérès-Sherry y
    Manzanilla de Sanlúcar
    de Barrameda

48 Condado de Huelva
49 Binissalem
50 Plà i Llevant
51 La Palma
52 El Hierro
53 Ycoden-Daute-Isora
54 La Gomera
55 Abona
56 Valle de Güímar
57 Valle de la Orotava
58 Tacoronte-Acentejo
59 Gran Canaria
60 Monte Lentiscal
61 Lanzarote

Vino de Mesa (VdM) These are the basic table wines. They won't have a vintage, or a regional name, and may well be a blend of different regions.

Vino de la Tierra (VdlT) This is approximately equivalent to France's Vin de Pays. The wines are from a defined area, often as large as an autonomous region, and are supposed to have local character. As in Italy, there are also a growing number of winemakers who want to make top quality wine outside the DO regulations.

Vino de Calidad con Indicación Geográfica (VCIG) A new category introduced in 2003 for the best VdlT wines wanting promotion or for struggling DOs. The rules are less stringent than for DO wines.

Denominación de Origen (DO) There are now nearly 60 of these wines, and they include the best-known regions as well as a fair number of less famous ones. DO is the rough equivalent of France's Appellation Contrôlée with fairly strict quality control regulations.

Denominación de Origen Calificada (DOCa) A super-category intended to recognize wines which have a long tradition of high quality. Regulations are more stringent and include rigorous tasting. To date, Rioja and Priorat are the only wines promoted to this level.

Denominación de Origen de Pago Calificada A new category introduced in 2003 for top-quality single estates, whether inside an existing DO or not. Two estates in Castilla-La Mancha have been promoted so far.

NORTH-EAST SPAIN

Think of the north of Spain in wine terms and most people think of Rioja. And yet the grapes that go to make red Rioja – principally Tempranillo and Garnacha Tinta – are found pretty well all over Spain. Forget the French pattern, where each region has its speciality grapes and never, if the AC authorities have their way, the twain shall meet. In Spain the same vines pop up over and over again, sometimes with a local name, sometimes not, but always present in great swathes of stubby vineyards covering the poor, arid soil.

In north-east Spain the wine regions follow one another mainly along the river valleys from the Bay of Biscay across to the Mediterranean. Some hug the foothills of the Pyrenees; some spill on to the edges of the great central plateau. Some of these DO wines have a purely local following, like the Chacolí de Bizkaia and Chacolí de Getaria of the Basque coast. Try them if you're there, just for the fun of trying to pronounce them, but don't expect to find them on sale at home.

Then there are the wines of Rioja and Navarra. For years Navarra has been the humble younger sibling of successful, swanky Rioja. The grapes used are much the same, but Navarra never managed to produce red wines with quite the style and seductiveness of its neighbour. Navarra had to look to its rosés for anything approaching a reputation

of its own. Then it looked as though Navarra might branch out on its own, and set its own agenda with new wines and new styles. Has it done so? Read on.

The wine region I'd currently back as most exciting newcomer is Somontano in Aragón. There are international varieties like Chardonnay, Cabernet and Merlot here, but also the indigenous Moristel and Spain's old favourites, Garnacha Tinta and Tempranillo. Quality is still a bit uneven – the wineries have yet to benefit from as much investment as the vineyards – but things will improve, and already it's looking encouraging.

There's more Garnacha Tinta used in Aragón's other DOs, Campo de Borja, Cariñena and Calatayud, all making beefy, rather solid reds – the first two, in particular, can have staggeringly high alcohol – and as yet not very distinguished whites.

That leaves Catalonia. Believe it or not, this prosperous region which plays such a major part in Spain's modern wine story doesn't just consist of Penedès (and Penedès doesn't just consist of Torres). But a closer look will have to wait until page 215.

I also ought to mention Mallorca in the Balearic Islands, which is home to the DO of Binissalem. The wines, both red and white, are mainly unexciting, but then most of the tourists either don't care or prefer lager anyway.

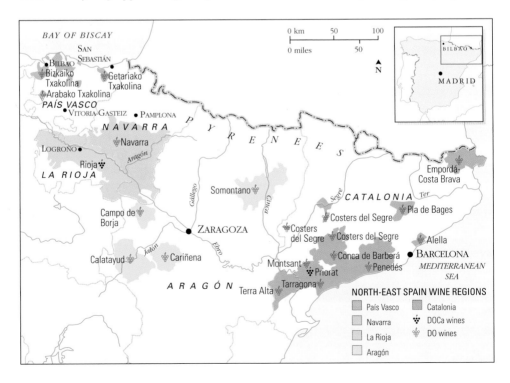

RIOJA

Only 40 years ago, with the exception of a few dedicated specialist outlets, no-one outside the Spanish-speaking world sold Rioja, and very few people even knew what it was. But this isn't some kind of parvenu wine area we're talking about – these are vineyards which may even predate the Romans, and which were certainly thriving before anybody in Bordeaux had ever pruned a vine.

It took Bordeaux to show Rioja the way, though. While the phylloxera vine louse was destroying Bordeaux's vineyards and livelihoods like an avenging flood, Rioja was as yet unaffected. The Bordelais poured south, bringing their know-how, their money and their dreams, building a Bordeaux lookalike south of the Pyrenees.

That boom didn't last long. Phylloxera was defeated and the Frenchmen went home, but leaving behind their methods. And while Bordeaux became one of the centres of modern wine-making, evolving and improving its wines, Rioja slumbered on, simply duplicating the good old original Bordeaux methods.

Throughout Spain and South America, Rioja's unique, smooth, buttery style established itself as the finest wine Spain could produce. Only in the early 1970s did Rioja finally make it to the international limelight – and there eventually followed the inevitable expansion of the vineyard area into flat land better suited to growing wheat, and a reduction of the oak influence that made Rioja so well loved in the first place.

These new, flatter vineyards, if they're going to make wine at all (and frankly I'd prefer them to go back to wheat) should stick to making young, juicy wines without any aging. That should leave the classic areas free to produce the high-quality wines – but at the moment, although there has been a recent rise in quality, yields are too high and quality too patchy. Rioja doesn't seem to know where it's going, and that's a pity.

GRAPE VARIETIES AND WINE STYLES

Rioja is red, white and pink – and there is even a tiny amount of sparkling. However, its fame rests squarely on its red wines, largely because reds in general take more successfully to oak aging than whites.

There are three main sub-regions in Rioja, the most important being the Rioja Alta. Although most merchant bodegas blend their wines from all three regions, the Alta-based reds tend to be firmer and leaner in style. The

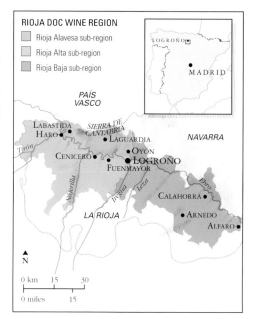

RIOJA DOC WINE REGION
- Rioja Alavesa sub-region
- Rioja Alta sub-region
- Rioja Baja sub-region

Alta-based rosados are Rioja's best. Rioja Alavesa produces the most delicate, perfumed reds. East of Logroño, the Rioja Baja is big, hot and fairly flat, and the wines are similarly stolid. They are used in the blend to give weight to the lighter wines from the other two sub-regions, but they are usually a bit lumpish when used by themselves.

The red grapes are Tempranillo, Garnacha Tinta, Graciano and Mazuelo, of which Tempranillo is the best. It's not intensely coloured, but it gives the strawberry fruit which marks out the best wines. Garnacha is the big, solid, alcoholic Grenache that is found all over southern France. It can be peppery and slightly empty, and blending with Tempranillo does wonders. Garnacha also makes good rosado. Graciano was on the verge of disappearing, but some of the better producers are busy rescuing it for the sake of its quality. Mazuelo is less exciting, and there are also a few patches of Cabernet Sauvignon, a leftover from Rioja's Bordeaux days.

The chief white grape is Viura, traditionally added to the red blend also. Made in the modern, cool and slow way, the white wine develops a remarkable, sharp, grapefruit taste. However, it also takes well to oak and can develop a lovely big, creamy flavour. Malvasía Riojana and Garnacha Blanca are the other white grapes used in Rioja.

Best producers: **Allende, Altos de Lanzaga, Artadi, Campillo, Campo Viejo, Contino, López de Heredia, Marqués de**

Preparations for the harvest start weeks in advance. These oak barrels at Bodegas López de Heredia in Haro must all be repaired and cleaned in plenty of time.

Murrieta, **Marqués de Riscal**, **Marqués de Vargas**, **Martínez Bujanda**, **Abel Mendoza**, **Remelluri**, **Remírez de Ganuza**, **La Rioja Alta**, **Roda**, **Romeo**, **Sierra Cantabria** and **Señorío de San Vicente**.

CLASSIFICATION

Joven wines are sold young, and seldom see any oak aging. These juicy Beaujolais-style wines can be delicious.

Crianza wines must be at least two years old, and have had at least one year in barrel. They can be pleasant, light wines, but sometimes fall uncomfortably between the upfront fruit of Sin Crianza wines and the strawberry oakiness of Reservas.

Reserva wines must be at least three years old, and have had at least one year in barrel. Many will have had more than that, and will be at least five years old on release. These can be the most enjoyable of all Riojas.

Gran Reservas must be at least five years old and have had at least 18 months in barrel. The barrel aging is often longer, and dries out the wine, though Gran Reservas can be great.

ORGANIZATION

In Rioja the merchant bodega rules supreme, mainly because of the expense of making traditional Rioja. The capital sum tied up in those rows and rows of expensive oak barrels, all holding wine that has to be aged for several years before it can be released for sale, must be enormous.

READING THE LABEL

The wine's classification, such as Crianza, is often recorded on the back label in Rioja. Because blending is so important here vineyard names rarely appear on the label.

WHAT DO THEY TASTE LIKE?

The very young reds have a juicy fruit reminiscent of Beaujolais, but apart from these, red Riojas should taste of oak. Vanilla, strawberry and coconut are the flavours I look for, but don't find all that often. Among the whites, the golden, buttery style is on the wane, and the new style is fresh and zippingly full of sharp, breathcatching raw fruit. The rosados are dry and full of soft fruit, and unfairly overlooked.

THE GOOD YEARS

The very old wines may look like bargains, but only the very finest Gran Reservas will improve for more than ten years. 2001, 1998, 1996–1994 were excellent, the best vintages for years; 1991, 1990, 1989 and 1985 were all good for reds. Whites and rosados should be drunk young, except for a few rare, top whites, but even these are usually sold when ready to drink.

ENJOYING THE WINES

The young whites are crisp and fresh and ideal for seafood, and the young reds are good with spicy sausages, cured ham and Spanish-style bean casseroles. Keep the mature reds to go with game, stews and cheese.

CATALONIA

Catalonia, Spain's most north-easterly region, is where the modern Spanish wine revolution began. Miguel Torres of Penedés started it off with a string of increasingly exciting and innovative wines at the 1979 French Gault-Millau Wine Olympics where, amid a potent mixture of disbelief and unfettered enthusiasm, a panel of 27 Frenchmen and just two Spaniards voted the Torres Gran Coronas Black Label 1970 top of the prestigious Cabernet class against the best that Bordeaux had to offer. Torres had arrived with a bang, dragging all of Catalonia and the rest of Spain in his wake.

The change was dramatic, and it lasted for next 15 years or so. The Torres name and style spread to the company's operations in Chile, and suddenly it was showing the Chileans the way, too. And yet at the moment I have my doubts about Catalonia. Somehow the revolution just doesn't seem to be delivering the goods. I don't want to be disappointed by Catalonia – for years I've been singing the praises of the Torres wines and all that have followed in their wake – and yet nowadays they seem to be less exciting than they were.

Maybe it's because Catalonia is still so feudal. It's a region of peasant smallholdings providing dull grapes for cheap sparklers and table wines. If it were going to become the sort of region I'd hoped, with innovation spreading far and wide instead of being limited to the few who started it all in the first place, then we'd be looking at many more individual quality-conscious producers and fewer peseta-counting co-operative members.

GRAPE VARIETIES AND WINE STYLES

I don't want to exaggerate. There has been a vast amount of innovation in Catalonia, which is still continuing. The **Costers del Segre** DO was created to accommodate the vast **Raïmat** operation to the west near Lérida. The Raïmat vineyards are officially classified as experimental, which they have to be in the EU if irrigation is to be permitted – and it's hard to see how these vineyards, dry and roasting in the summer and dry and freezing in the

In contrast with all the oak used in making Rioja, the Torres winery in Penedés is full of spanking new stainless steel.

winter, could survive without it. The grape varieties here mix Spanish die-hards like Tempranillo and the white Parellada and Macabeo with international stars like Cabernet Sauvignon, Merlot, Chardonnay and Pinot Noir.

There is innovation, too, in tiny **Alella**, which is compensating for its increasing urbanization by changing its wine style from white, sweetish and wood-aged to white, young, zippy and fresh; **Marqués de Alella** is the name here and the wines are nutty, apricotty, off-dry and very good. Similar changes have been occuring in **Ampurdán-Costa Brava**, right up against the French border. The wine style here used to be heavy *rancio*-style Garnacha; now, as well as a lot of pretty dull rosado, there's some decent nouveau-style Vi Novell. It's not world-beating but it is a sign of the times, and a sign that the region has finally latched on to having the Costa Brava tourists on its doorstep.

Elsewhere the historical **Priorat** DOCa, high in the hills, remains strange and dark, but is now absurdly trendy. The minimum alcoholic content here is 13.5 per cent, which is high by any standards, and the wines, from low-yielding vines, are extraordinarily concentrated. Best producers: **Cims de Porrera**, **Clos Erasmus**, **Clos Mogodor**, **Mas Doix**, **Mas Martinet**, **Alvaro Palacios**, and **Vall-Llach**. In **Terra Alta** and **Tarragona**, sweet fortifieds are gradually being abandoned for light, dry whites, though Tarragona sells much of its wine in bulk for blending, or for making into sparkling Cava. **Montsant** is a new DO carved out of Tarragona's best zone around Falset. Producers here are aiming to make Priorat-style wines and so far signs are promising. **Conca de Barberá** also produces a lot of base wine for the fizz houses, though the Torres tendrils reach here as well: the company has vineyards of Chardonnay, Pinot Noir and Cabernet here.

Which brings me neatly to **Penedès**. This was one of the first places in Spain, thanks to Torres, to set in motion the stainless steel and cold fermentation mentality that has since taken hold throughout the country. Torres was one of the first companies to plant international varieties and blend them, to great

effect, with native grapes. It still has a greater variety of vines growing than most Spanish regions, with the result that terroir here can, in the right hands, mean more than just about anywhere else. In the warm coastal region there are hot-climate grapes like Monastrell or Garnacha, and the wines tend to be everyday and pretty hefty. Go inland and higher up, to the Medio Penedès, and you'll find vineyard after vineyard of Macabeo, Xarel-lo and Parellada for the huge Cava industry. There is Cabernet here as well, and Tempranillo. Further inland again the land rises to the Penedès Superior, and the temperature drops sufficiently for Parellada, Chardonnay, Riesling and even Gewürztraminer to flourish. Best producers: **Albet i Noya**, **Can Feixes**, **Can Ràfols dels Caus**, **Jean León**, **Masía Bach**, **Puig y Roca**, **Sot Lefriec**, **Torres** and **Jané Ventura**.

And **Cava**? Well, I've always been a bit uncertain about this fizz. All too often it can taste rooty and old before its time but there are many more good ones than there used to be. The increasing use of Chardonnay to give some style to the distinctly unthrilling grapes normally used in the blend is a vast improvement. Of those prescribed grapes, Macabeo gives acidity and not much flavour; Xarel-lo gives some earthiness and alcohol and Parellada, the best, gives some floweriness. Best producers: **Can Rafols dels Caus**, **Codorníu**, **Juvé y Camps** and **Augusti Torelló**. But do drink it young. Although made by the Champagne method, it doesn't age like Champagne. Cava can actually come from some other parts of Spain – there are 159 villages permitted to make it – but in practice most is from Catalonia.

CLASSIFICATION

Catalonia has the most varied wine production in Spain, with a large number of DO wines as well as Cava. Many of the most intersting still wines today are made outside the DO regulations.

ORGANIZATION

The co-operatives are all-important in much of Catalonia. Although the firms of Torres and Raïmat are world-famous, the region really needs more go-ahead small growers if it is to progress in quality terms.

READING THE LABEL

Several of the best Catalan wines are non-DO and may be labelled by their grape variety or wine style. Sparkling Cava will be marked according to sweetness, from Brut Nature or Brut at the dry end, through Seco, Semi-seco and Semi-dulce to the pretty rich Dulce. Tarragona and Priorat still make a little *rancio* wine – sweet and heavily oxidized. Check the label if this adventure into Catalan wine history is not for you.

WHAT DO THEY TASTE LIKE?

The flavours of Catalan wine vary enormously, from tangy, fresh whites and impressive oak-aged reds to the traditional sweet Moscatel flavours of old Sitges and Tarragona, though these are on the wane now. Some of the tastes are familiar – the vanilla of new oak mixed with nutty, tropical fruit Chardonnay or vivid blackcurrant Cabernet Sauvignon, for example – but some of the most original wines are those that mix Spanish grape varieties with more international ones. Torres is a dab hand at this: its Gran Viña Sol Green Label, for example, blends Parellada with Sauvignon Blanc. And Cava, for all my misgivings, is increasing fresh. Don't expect the yeasty, bready character of Champagne:

instead look for fresh, one-dimensional, dry fruit, and if possible avoid the rooty ones that have been hanging around too long. The ones containing Chardonnay are almost always the best.

THE GOOD YEARS

There isn't a great deal of variation in climate to affect the quality of vintages. Vintage differences will mostly affect red wines, in particular those from higher, cooler sites by producers trying to achieve more elegance. The reds age quite well on the whole, though the whites are almost always best young. 2004, 2003 and 2001–1993 all produced very good wines in Catalonia, the best of which will age well.

ENJOYING THE WINE

Catalan whites made by modern winemakers like Torres or Marqués de Alella can be some of Spain's best apéritif wines because of their fresh fruit. The local food is more exciting than in most of Spain, partly because of Catalonia's cosmopolitan outlook. The reds, in particular, are big and tasty enough to go with the local cured hams, *butifarra* sausage, poultry and game casseroles, and meat grilled with herbs. Most whites go well with the abundant local seafood, but light rosados, possibly from Ampurdán-Costa Brava, can be good as well. Cava is probably best served as an apéritif.

CONSUMER INFORMATION

WHAT DO I GET FOR MY MONEY?

Wines from the best producers of north-east Spain are not cheap. Constant price rises in Rioja have meant that it is no longer the good value it once was. Penedès producers also don't see why they should offer any bargains, but tangy whites can be good. All over north-east Spain it is important to look for good producers as quality is not uniformly high anywhere. For good value the best areas to look are probably Calatayud and Campo de Borja. The young, unaged reds of Rioja can also be a good buy.

AVAILABILITY

Very good for the main wines. Rioja, in particular, is a household word in many countries, since it managed brilliantly to fill a quality gap when Bordeaux and Burgundy prices went loony in the 1970s. Gran Reservas are difficult to find, but many shops stock Crianza and Reserva wines.

Cava wines are not difficult to find, and other Penedès still wines are quite widely

available, especially the wines of Torres, although their top-of-the range labels are in more limited distribution. Raïmat wines are not difficult to find. Other Catalan wines are less widely exported, though the selection is improving all the time.

CONSUMER CHECKLIST

Viña Sol 2004	Quality 7 ★
(Torres)	Price 5 ★
	Value 8 ★

Good Years Most wines in north-east Spain are released when they are ready to drink. Vintage variations are greater in Rioja than in most of Catalonia. Best years: 2004, 2003, 2001–1993.

Taste Notes Rioja is usually associated with soft, vanilla-flavoured reds, though there are also fresh young reds and crisp whites. Catalan reds are usually richly fruity, while the whites range from dry and fresh to big, oaky Chardonnays. Cava wines are often unsubtle but getting better.

NORTH-WEST SPAIN

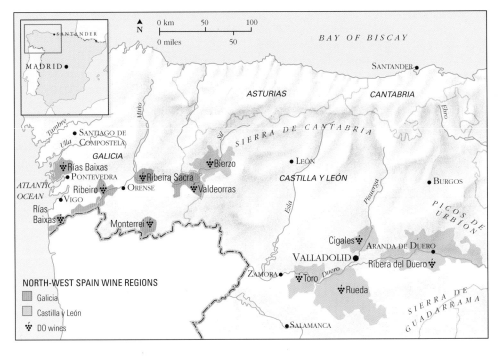

NORTH-WEST SPAIN WINE REGIONS
- Galicia
- Castilla y León
- DO wines

Only because of the accident of geography that placed all these regions in the north-west corner of Spain can they be talked about in the same breath. Rias Baixas? Light, aromatic whites that have more in common with Portuguese Vinho Verde. Toro? Strapping, heavyweight reds, as beefy as the name. Ribera del Duero? Complex, classy reds from the banks of the same river that, just over the border in Portugal, is also the source of some of that country's finest wines – most of them sweet and fortified.

All these wine names have come to international notice only recently. We knew about Vega Sicilia, certainly – rich, fragrant, complex and very slow to mature, this was supposed to be Spain's finest red wine, reserved for royalty (preferably Spanish) and a few favoured others but that was all.

Now it's different. There are red wines from Ribera del Duero, the home of Vega

Sicilia, popping up all over the place, and very good many of them are, too. There are also light whites from nearby Rueda, that are demonstrating some of the most distinctive flavours in Spain today, and some of the most inspired wine-making. The grapes, mainly local crisp, grassy Verdejo and some Sauvignon Blanc, are picked early and fresh and then fermented cool. A few years ago we'd never heard of them at all.

That's another thing that's so astonishing about this part of Spain. In most of the country the improvements in viticulture and winemaking take place quietly, and gradually one or two of the wines might be exported. Only where a major company gathers up the reins of a region and sets about changing things single-handedly, as Raïmat did in Costers del Segre, or Torres did in Penedès, is there a startling explosion. But in the North-West the explosion has also been in quality. Sure, there are some big names here, and they have led the way. But there were fewer ingrained traditions to overcome and there are more wines of individuality than elsewhere.

To me this is one of the most exciting parts of Spain, and I'm going to take you on a trip from the green, rainy north-western corner of Galicia across the Cantabrian mountains and down to the broad river valley of the Duero in the heart of Castilla y León. So excuse me for rushing you, but we've got a long way to go.

GALICIA

Okay, umbrellas up. If it's raining, it must be Galicia. Galicia is quite unlike the rest of Spain in this respect. A wet, humid region draped in lush greenery, it has far more in common with northern Portugal than it does with any other part of Spain. They even speak a different dialect here: Gallego, a mixture of Portuguese and Castilian Spanish.

GRAPE VARIETIES AND WINE STYLES

There are five DOs. The most important and currently the most fashionable both in Spain and outside is **Rías Baixas**. The grape making all the running here is Albariño, found south of the Portuguese border as Alvarinho. It tastes the same in both places: dry, apricotty, aromatic. That makes it a rarity in Spain, a country sadly lacking in aromatic white grapes. No wonder it's popular; and since yields are low it's also expensive. Ten other varieties are permitted in the DO, some of which are red – but such is its popularity these days that Albariño covers around 90 per cent of the vineyards.

Ribeiro has also been making changes to its wines, mostly by uprooting the utterly dull white Palomino, which makes decent wine only in Jerez, and replanting with Treixadura and Torrontés. So the wines are still white, but now they're crisp and have some aroma.

Valdeorras is further inland where Spain starts to warm up. Accordingly, there are more reds, mostly from the unexciting, high-yielding Garnacha Tinta or Alicante grape. The better wines are from the white Godello, which has far more character and heady aroma, and the black Mencía, which is said to be related to the Cabernet Franc – and certainly tastes like it. **Ribeira Sacra**, on the banks of the Miño and Sil rivers, also does well with young reds from Mencía, while tiny **Monterrei** down on the Portuguese border shows some potential with its native white grape, Doña Blanca. Best producers: (Rías Baixas) **Adegas Galegas**, **Agro de Bazán**, **Granja Fillaboa**, **Lagar de Fornelos**, **Lusco do Miño**, **Martin Códax**, **Pazo de Senorans** and **Terras Gauda**; (Ribeiro) **Bodegas Alanis**.

CLASSIFICATION

There is no other classification here other than the Spanish DO system.

By this stage of the autumn the landscape in other parts of Spain will be looking dry and biscuit-brown; here in Galicia, however, the hills are still green.

ORGANIZATION

Many small growers in Galicia tend to sell their grapes to merchants – this is not a land of single-vineyard wines.

READING THE LABEL

In Rías Baixas the unblended varietal Albariño wines are best, and they will state the grape name on the label.

WHAT DO THEY TASTE LIKE?

Albariño can be bitingly sharp and clean, with a raw apricot aroma; with better, more aromatic, local white grapes, new-style Ribeiro should also be very crisp and uncompromising. New-style Valdeorras red is light and fruity, for early drinking; the white, from the Godello grape, is clean and quite aromatic.

THE GOOD YEARS

Drink all these Galician wines young, and choose the most recent vintage. They will only lose freshness if kept.

ENJOYING THE WINES

The high acidity of these white wines makes them good with fish, particularly oily fish like sardines. The reds are good drunk on their own or with light dishes.

CASTILLA Y LEÓN

I love this part of Spain. Not because it is particularly beautiful – on the contrary, it is mostly sparsely populated plateau with only a few flocks of sheep to break the monotony – but because it has some of the best wines in the country. Some of them are sticking firmly to their traditions, but using them well; some have developed entirely new styles.

GRAPE VARIETIES AND WINE STYLES

Rueda is the region I'd pick out for the originality award. The native white Verdejo and Viura grapes are being used to produce wonderfully crisp, aromatic wines, and there's quite a bit of Sauvignon Blanc as well; these styles are supplanting old-style Rueda, which is fortified and heavy. Best producers: **Alvarez y Diez**, **Belondrade y Lurton**, **Marqués de Griñon** and **Vinedos de Nieva**.

Ribera del Duero is the source of the top reds in Castilla y León. Long before it became a DO in 1982, the region was famous for **Vega Sicilia**, but now this intensely concentrated and long-lived wine has been joined by other stars, some of whom are nearly as good: **Aalto**, **Alion**, **Hacienda Monasterio**, **Emilio Moro**, **Pago de los Capellanes**, **Pedrosa**, **Pesquera**, **Pingus**, **Telmo Rodriguez** and **Hermanos Sastre**, to name but a few. Tempranillo is the main grape, known here as Tinto Fino or Tinta del País.

Less expensive reds come from **Toro** (DO), where the arrival of some top Spanish wineries in the late 1990s gave the sleepy area a major boost. The main grape is Tempranillo but called here Tinto del Toro. It gets terrifically ripe and alcoholic. Best producers: **Maurodos**, **J & F Lurton** (El Albar) and **Telmo Rodriguez**. The **Bierzo** DO hasn't undergone the transformation of the leading regions and makes sharply fruity red from the Mencía grape. **Cigales** wines are beginning to be seen outside the region; they are made from Tinta del País (alias Tempranillo) and Garnacha grapes.

CLASSIFICATION

There is no classification here beyond the nationwide DO system.

ORGANIZATION

Many of the large and medium-sized merchants buy in grapes from the small growers.

READING THE LABEL

Fortified Rueda is unlikely to appear on export markets, so the danger of encountering it unexpectedly is small. In Ribera del Duero the grandest bodega of all, Vega Sicilia, makes a lighter, younger, and cheaper, version called Valbuena.

WHAT DO THEY TASTE LIKE?

The Ribera del Duero reds are some of the most complex and long lived in Spain: they mix rich, plummy fruit with an intriguing smokiness. Toro wines are less elegant and chunkier, but Bodegas Fariña wines are aged in small oak barrels and have good vanilla flavours to balance their weight. Rueda whites are beautifully, crisp, grassy and aromatic.

THE GOOD YEARS

Toro has fewer vintage variations than Ribera del Duero, where good years are 2004, 2002, 2001, 2000, 1999, 1996, 1995, 1994, 1991, 1990 and 1989. The best wines can easily live for a decade in bottle. Drink Rueda wines young.

ENJOYING THE WINES

The reds of Ribera del Duero demand fine and flavoursome meat dishes; so does Toro, but on less grand occasions. Rueda will go well with most fish dishes.

CONSUMER INFORMATION

WHAT DO I GET FOR MY MONEY?

Top Ribera del Dueros are expensive, but not all wines are so pricy (nor, indeed, quite so outstanding). It is possible to get a very good red from here at an affordable price. Toro is good value; Rueda is fairly priced, and Albariño is expensive.

AVAILABILITY

Not great. Only the more adventurous outlets will have Toro or Rueda, and for leading Ribera del Duero or Rías Baixas wines, see a specialist.

CONSUMER CHECKLIST

Ribera del Duero 2001	*Quality 8* ★
Gran Reserva	*Price 9* ★
(Ismail Arroyo)	*Value 7* ★

Good Years (Ribera del Duero) 2001, 2000, 1999, 1996, 1995, 1994, 1991, 1990, 1989.
Taste Notes Albariño is assertively acidic, with a delicate apricot aroma; Rueda is clean and often quite grassy. The reds of Ribera del Duero are rich and complex, while Toro is big and chunky.

CENTRAL SPAIN

With the lowest production costs of any major wine-making country in western Europe, the great central swathe of vines which blankets the land from south-west of Madrid right across to Valencia and Alicante in the east has always been able to trade effectively on price. There has, until recently, been little incentive to create any individual image for the wines concerned.

Even now, with the wines improving rapidly and every wine shop full of inexpensive, tasty reds and whites from La Mancha and Valdepeñas, I'd still hestitate over the word 'individual'. But I don't think it matters. That most of these wines come from big co-operatives that are able to afford the equipment necessary to turn La Mancha's oxidized yellowy-orange whites and fruitless reds of yesteryear into wines that are crisp and fresh, and young and fruity respectively, is fine by me. At these prices, I'm not looking for the stamp of the winemaker's personality. But as New World winemakers begin to appear, and

In any New World country a vineyard as hot and dry as this one would depend on irrigation, but here in Valdepeñas the vines must survive on their own.

EU regulations allow irrigation in this bone-dry part of Spain, this could well become the source of some of Europe's best basic wine.

The enormous **La Mancha** DO covers the southern part of Spain's parched central plateau. **Valdepeñas** is a hot, dry enclave in the south of La Mancha where, sheltered by hills, the white Airén and red Cencibel grapes (the same ones that cover La Mancha) have good potential for quality (best producer: Los Llanos). Cencibel is the local name for Tempranillo, and it's generally more exciting than the Garnacha of the **Méntrida** or **Viños de Madrid** DOs in the north (though the **Marqués de Griñon** at Dominio de Valdepusa and **Dehesa del Carrizal** make good wines such as Chardonnay and Syrah near Toledo).

Further east, there are hefty reds in **Alicante**, **Yecla** and **Jumilla** and some rosado in **Bullas**. **Utiel-Requena** and **Almansa** produce more sturdy reds, and **Valencia** makes simple, fruity reds, whites and rosados as well as lusciously sweet, grapy and inexpensive Moscatel de Valencia. Alicante also produces a little known treasure, the Fondillón dry or semi dry fortified wine, from Monastrell (Mourvèdre).

SOUTHERN SPAIN

The south of Spain is overwhelmingly a fortified wine area. **Jerez** is its top wine name, although Montilla and Málaga have been as famous in the past. Table wine is produced, mostly at a fairly basic level (the Canary Islands used to make sweet wine, but now concentrate on dull red from the DO of Tacoronte-Acentejo), and it is often made only because sales of fortified wines from here are falling. Jerez is one of the best examples of a wine area brought to crisis point and reorganizing in order to survive – and survive it will, albeit with less land under vine.

These other regions, without the fame or the quality image of Jerez, are having to find ways of getting by. Crops other than grapes are one solution – in **Condado de Huelva** falling sales of the traditional fortified wine have encouraged the growers to plant wheat, sugar beet or strawberries – or to make light, dry table wine from the Zalema grape, though they grow some of Jerez's grape, Palomino Fino, and Garrido Fino, as well.

The problem is that none of the grapes grown here for fortified wine have any great character. You can make light, dry white from it – given modern technology, you can make light, dry white from practically anything – but it is low in acidity and just not as attractive as other Spanish whitest. La Mancha's new-style Airén wine can outclass anything from here but what it is good at is fortified wine – but we're all drinking less and less of it.

Málaga was hugely popular in the eighteenth and nineteenth centuries. In the middle of the nineteenth century it was Spain's second largest wine region – and then phylloxera struck. This was the first part of Spain to be hit by the louse – and by the time the region started to recover, which wasn't until the 1960s, Málaga was becoming a massive tourist resort. It is now one of Spain's smallest DOs.

Most of the vineyards grow Pedro Ximénez, though there is also some Airén and Moscatel. There are some dry fortified wines, though they're not exactly spectacular; and most range from nutty and medium-dry to big, luscious, smoky, raisiny and very sweet. The label generally states colour and sweetness. The grapes for Málaga have to be brought to bodegas within the city for maturing and to help counter dwindling production a 'sister' DO, **Sierras de Málaga**, was created in 2001 to include wineries outside the city limits.

Montilla-Moriles makes wine similar in style to sherry. Well, similar up to a point. The

SOUTHERN SPAIN WINE REGIONS
- Condado de Huelva DO wine
- Jerez-Xérès-Sherry, Manzanilla de Sanlúcar de Barrameda DO wine
- Montilla-Moriles DO wine
- Málaga DO and Sierras de Málaga DO wines

terminology is different outside Spain (the sherry style called *amontillado* was originally named for its similarity to Montilla – yet these days Montilla may not, outside Spain, be labelled *amontillado*). The main grape is Pedro Ximénez, which can stand up to the region's withering heat. It is often exported (perfectly legally) to Jerez which doesn't grow enough of the stuff any more.

The wines are aged the same way as sherry, in solera. But whereas the film of flor in Jerez transforms the rather dull base wine into *fino* that is miraculously elegant and light, the flor doesn't grow as thickly in Montilla-Moriles, and the equivalent style, Pale Dry, is clumsy by comparison.

Medium Dry, Pale Cream and Cream are the other Montilla styles. On the whole, they lack the finesse of good sherry, though the richer, darker *oloroso* styles (labelled Cream) can be complex and pungent. Aficonados maintain the very best are just as good as anything in Jerez, but you'll need an air ticket to go and check, because the best wines of Montilla-Moriles are not exported. Most of what is exported is aimed at the cheap end of the sherry market – by which I mean fortified wines from Britain, Cyprus and all the other countries which may no longer call their wine 'sherry' in the EU.

SHERRY

Real sherry comes only from Spain. That's what the generic advertising has been telling us for years, and now at last it's true. No other wine can, from 1996 onwards, call itself sherry – at least in the EU. That means that British 'sherry', Cyprus 'sherry' and South African 'sherry' now have to call themselves something else if they're being sold in the EU – and about time too.

Real sherry comes from the town of the same name, or almost: 'sherry' is an anglicization of the name 'Jerez' pronounced 'hereth' by Spaniards but more likely 'sherezh' by the slightly tipsy sailors whose job it was to haul this rough, crass wine back to northern Europe in the centuries when the trade was becoming established. Jerez de la Frontera (the full name reflects its position, for a full hundred years, on the frontier between Christian and Moorish Spain during the Reconquest) is the central town of the sherry-producing region, about 16km (10 miles) from the Bay of Cádiz in the south-west corner of Spain.

As with Port and Madeira in the south of Europe, and Champagne in the north, the basic wine wasn't very nice – in this case dull and flaccid – but at least it was strong in alcohol and therefore found a ready market in the cold north. As with Port and Madeira, much of the business was created by Irish and English traders building up companies in and around Jerez, and as tastes became more sophisticated, they learned how to create a remarkable array of tastes out of this local wine.

The most recent crisis in the sherry trade, and the one which helped to force the region to reduce its production, was a spiral of price-cutting in the 1970s. A company called Rumasa bought up many of the old family-run businesses; in 1983 Rumasa was nationalized and subsequently broken up into its component parts, which were reprivatized. Sales continued to fall even as quality was slowly restored, and many of the vineyards have been uprooted.

But the good news is that quality has continued to rise – and that the old, traditional styles of dry, well-aged sherries are finding a new market. It's now far easier to buy sherry of sensational quality than it was in the days of Rumasa, when cheapness was all.

What gives sherry its remarkable flavours is, first, the presence of a swathe of chalky soil, or *albariza*, which sweeps right across the central growing area. Chalk always produces particularly light, fresh-tasting wines. This means that, with modern techniques, wines of considerable delicacy can be produced, even in such a torrid region as this. Second, there is the remarkable phenomenon of the flor.

After fermentation, the wines are fortified to about 15 per cent and put into 500-litre capacity barrels, called butts. The butts are left four-fifths full. The finest, lightest wines rapidly develop a gungy, creamy film on their surface. This film is called flor, and is in fact a protective layer of yeast which sits on top of the wine and, while imparting a rather pungent herbiness to the wine, also stops it oxidizing. The wines which develop this flor are the ones that will become dry *fino* sherries.

If the flor looks unlikely to grow, the wine is fortified more heavily with brandy to stop any stray growth of flor (the yeast film doesn't like wine with too much alcohol, or too little)

THE SOLERA SYSTEM

All sherry is a blend of different vintages. The object is not to reflect vintage differences (which are not great down here anyway) but to achieve consistency year in year out and produce wine which has a balance of maturity and freshness. Each bottle of sherry, therefore, contains some very old wine and some very young. This is achieved by the solera system.

Imagine a pile of barrels. You take wine out of the bottom barrel, and top it up from the next barrel up. You top up that one, in turn, from the one above it, and so on. The barrel at the top of the pile you top up with new wine. That, basically, is a solera system: mature wine is drawn off at the bottom, new wine added at the top. Strictly speaking, only the final stage is the solera, and all the others are *criadera*, or nurseries – real soleras have hundreds of barrels in each stage, not just one. Some soleras were begun a century or more ago and there are soleras for each different style of sherry.

The best soil in Jerez is albariza *chalk, finely grained and dazzlingly white. These days winemakers know how to match the soil to the style of sherry they want.*

and is put into barrel in order that it can slowly mature and oxidize. It is thus at this moment in a young sherry's life that the path divides for good between the light *fino* wines and the darker, richer *oloroso* ones. Good *fino* is wonderful, but good *oloroso* can eventually achieve even greater heights.

GRAPE VARIETIES AND WINE STYLES
The main grape is Palomino Fino, but whereas a dry *fino* will probably be 100 per cent Palomino, the sweeter styles can be sweetened with Pedro Ximénez which may be concentrated by drying the grapes on grass mats in the sun (the traditional way, and now hardly practised) or in plastic tunnels. Alternative ways of sweetening the wine involve various sorts of grape concentrate or concentrated must. Palomino as well as Pedro Ximénez grapes may be concentrated in this way – in fact Jerez now grows so little Pedro Ximénez that it has to buy some in from neighbouring Montilla-Moriles.

There are two basic styles of sherry, *fino* and *oloroso* and each style has various subdivisions. **Fino** is pale and dry, with a quite unnerving austere bite to it. It should be drunk cool and young. **Manzanilla** is a form of *fino* matured by the sea at Sanlúcar de Barrameda, one of the three sherry towns. It can be almost savoury-dry, and have a definite

whiff of sea salt – if you're lucky to catch *manzanilla* young enough.

The most widely seen sherry is **amontillado**. Usually this simply means a bland, vaguely sweetened drink of no style or interest. However, it is correctly a term applied only to aged *fino* on which the flor has died, enabling the wine to deepen and darken in cask to a tantalizing nutty dryness. One of the most encouraging things in recent years has been the slowly increasing popularity of such genuine wines. Proper *amontillado* should be bone dry – it always is in Spain.

Olorosos in their natural state are deep, dark, packed with violent burnt flavours – yet totally dry. These are some of the most wonderful wines to come out of Jerez, and thanks to the revival of fine sherry we're seeing far more of them than we ever used to. But don't despise the sweetened versions either. Commercially sweetened *oloroso* is a pretty dull, sticky drink, yes, but dessert *olorosos* are a proper style, so make sure you get the real thing. Sherries called Milk, Cream, Amoroso or Brown are likely to be commercial in style. Interestingly, **pale creams** are not *olorosos* but sweetened *finos*.

Palo cortado is a 'half-breed' sherry which got confused and developed both *fino* and *oloroso* characteristics. It is rare and dry and should be superb, with a pungent acid bite. Finally, there is **Pedro Ximénez**. A little is aged separately in solera and bottled as a dessert wine, and it can be extremely good, though it never develops the complex pungency of *oloroso* and has instead a rich, almost overpowering, dark grapiness.

CLASSIFICATION
The vineyards of Jerez are divided into three soil types. *Albariza* is white, chalky soil, with small amounts of clay and sand, and produces the best, most delicate wines. The reduction of the vineyard area has affected mainly the less-good soils: *barros rojos* is heavier clay, producing heavier wine, and *arenas* is sandy soil, better for growing tomatoes and grain.

ORGANIZATION
The shippers who process the wine are very much the dominant feature of Jerez life. Many of them also own large vineyards. There are, even so, large numbers of smallholders who will usually be under contract to a shipper. Best producers: **Barbadillo, Domecq, Don Zoilo, Garvey, Gonzalez Byass, Hidalgo, Lustau** (especially dry *almacenista* sherries from small, private producers), **Osborne, Valdespino** and **Williams & Humbert**.

A guard of honour in traditional Andalucian costume, and carrying a basket of grapes, stands outside Jerez cathedral during the annual harvest festival.

READING THE LABEL

The label will state the wine's basic style. Qualifying terms like Viejo (old), Seco (dry) or Dulce (sweet) may be added also, and are a good sign, if you want a genuine traditional-style of sherry. Manzanilla Pasada is *manzanilla* with extra aging in solera, and is likely to be very good. Look out also for *almacenista* sherries, unblended wine from small stockholders, which can be wonderful.

WHAT DO THEY TASTE LIKE?

Good sherry, dry or sweet, has a bite to it. After all, it is fairly high in alcohol, a lightly fortified *fino* being around 15.5 per cent in strength, while a big *oloroso* may be over 20 per cent. And even the youngest *fino* should be four to five years old, and the wine will have been gaining flavour all that time. Old sherries have a positively painful intensity of flavour, mixing sweet and sour, rich and dry all at once. However, most commercial wines are aiming for mass acceptance and are bland and forgettable. This is a particular problem in the medium-sweet sector, which embraces many famous brand names.

THE GOOD YEARS

Certainly some harvests are better than others, but the solera system is designed to even this out. Occasionally a solera will be named after its starting date, but don't take too much notice of this: the amount of wine still available from those early years is minuscule.

ENJOYING THE WINE

Sherry got itself stuck with a dowdy image, although in its traditional, uncommercial form it is one of the least compromising of wine styles. *Fino* or *manzanilla*, fresh and fridge-cool, is a wonderful anytime drink, strong enough to brighten you up, biting enough to be refreshing. As an appetite-whetter before dinner it is difficult to beat. *Fino* and *manzanilla* must be drunk as soon after bottling as possible, though modern bottling techniques mean that most big brands survive the long trip from Jerez perfectly well, and should stay fresh in bottle for some months. And don't ever decant it – it will only oxidize.

Dry *amontillados* and *olorosos* make wonderful winter apéritifs, or serve them with nuts after dinner. Dessert sherries are best served after dinner, too. Sweet, rich Pedro Ximénez is wonderful poured over vanilla ice cream.

CONSUMER INFORMATION

WHAT DO I GET FOR MY MONEY?

Commercial sherries have to bear the cost of massive advertising campaigns – and all too often the advertisements are far more exciting than the wine itself. But proper dry *finos* and other styles are exceptional value.

In fact, sherry is possibly the only wine in existence where the value gets better as the quality and price gets higher. Certainly the finest, rarest old sherries are quite expensive, but they are of outstanding quality and are some of today's best wine bargains.

AVAILABILITY

The commercial brands are easily available. Nowadays the finer sherries are not too difficult to find.

CONSUMER CHECKLIST

Valdespino Inocente Fino   Quality 9 ★
                               Price 7 ★
                               Value 10 ★

Good Years There are no vintage years as such in sherry. Virtually all sherries are blends of several years.
Taste Notes The available styles of sherry range from cheap, forgettable, medium-sweet blends to fine, handcrafted wines of inimitable, penetrating character.

PORTUGAL

Portugal is the most encouraging and the most infuriating of wine countries. It's encouraging because it has a wealth of vine varieties found nowhere else, and as yet not too many inroads have been made by the international brigade of Cabernet, Chardonnay and the like. These indigenous varieties are Portugal's greatest strength: their innovative use along with blending with international varieties and a touch of modern wine-making, means that Portugal is now a rich source of inexpensive yet characterful wines.

Portugal's vineyards are chaotic. EU subsidies have done wonders for the wineries – and for the wines coming out of them – but until the growers can sort out what vines they know they have in their vineyards, the wines will never realize their full potential.

On the west coast the Atlantic cools and dampens the climate; on the eastern side the land dries out and heats up as it approaches the Spanish border. In the north are the famous wines of Dão and Bairrada, Vinho Verde and Port, but the centre and south of Portugal have famous wines too, in particular those from near Lisbon: Colares, Bucelas, Carcavelos and Setúbal.

But if there is a division between east and west, and between south and north, there has long been a division between those wines the Portuguese drank themselves and those they obligingly allowed others, usually the British, to adapt to their own tastes. Port, Madeira and the sweetish rosados of the twentieth century, like Mateus, fall into the latter category.

CLASSIFICATION

Vinho de Mesa is basic table wine from anywhere, and without a stated region or vintage.
Vinho Regional (VR) These nine regional wines are a new category to parallel France's Vins de Pays and allow producers more flexibility with laws and permitted grape varieties.
Indicação de Proveniência Regulamentada (IPR) Roughly equivalent to the French VDQS level, this is probably quite a snappy name if you're Portuguese. The alternative name is Vinho de Qualidade Produzido em Região Determinada/Demarcada – even less snappy. Many were promoted to DOC level in 1999, leaving just nine.
Denominação de Origem Controlada (DOC) This is the top. Following necessary rationalisation there are now 23 regions, including world famous ones like Port and Madeira and lesser known regions like Tavira.

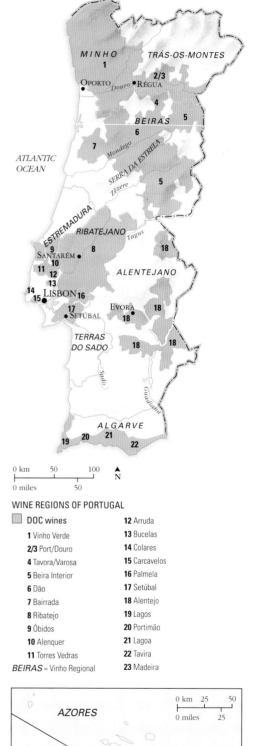

WINE REGIONS OF PORTUGAL

▨ DOC wines

1 Vinho Verde	**12** Arruda
2/3 Port/Douro	**13** Bucelas
4 Tavora/Varosa	**14** Colares
5 Beira Interior	**15** Carcavelos
6 Dão	**16** Palmela
7 Bairrada	**17** Setúbal
8 Ribatejo	**18** Alentejo
9 Óbidos	**19** Lagos
10 Alenquer	**20** Portimão
11 Torres Vedras	**21** Lagoa
BEIRAS = Vinho Regional	**22** Tavira
	23 Madeira

NORTHERN PORTUGAL

Wander through the **Vinho Verde** region and you won't see many vineyards. And yet this is Portugal's largest DOC. You look around, and all you can see is tall, leggy cabbages. What's going on?

The answer is quite simple. Look above the cabbages, and there you'll see the vines. They're grown high on trellises – so high that ladders are needed to pick the grapes. Partly this is to make the best use of space in a land of smallholdings (it's amazing how many cabbages and vines you can fit into a back garden) and partly it's because it rains here. It rains a lot. I won't say all the time, but I've never stayed dry here. If the vines were grown lower the grapes would tend to rot – which is why the rare vineyards, with the vines in rows at a more comfortable height, tend to be owned by large companies who can afford mechanization and the necessary expensive sprays.

'Vinho Verde' means green wine, but this name refers to its youth rather than to its colour – indeed, around half is red. And wow, is it red! It's dark-coloured, with rasping fruit and acidity – perfect for the oily local food, but not so good in the chilly, damp north, which is why very little is exported. Of the white, much of what is exported is sweetened, which is a pity, since it tends to lose its aromatic delicacy and become lumpish. The very best are often varietal wines, from Alvarinho, Loureiro or Trajadura grapes – but like all other Vinhos Verdes, these wines should be drunk within the year. Best producers: **Quinta da Baguinha**, **Quinta da Franqueira**, **Casa de Sezim**, **Quinta da Soalheira**, **Sogrape** and **Quinta de Tamariz**.

Apart from **Port** (see page 228), northern Portugal's other main wines are **Dão** and **Bairrada**. Both have long been established on foreign markets; both needed to improve quality. Dão had suffered because of a misjudged law (no longer in force) that ensured that only co-operatives could buy grapes and make wine. They were less than enterprising, and often less than hygienic; Dão these days is cleaner and fresher than it used to be, but – well, I'm sorry to have to say it, it's just a bit boring. The grapes are okay – nine of them, including Touriga Nacional and Tinta Roriz for the reds, and Encruzado for the whites. But both reds and whites are left in barrel too long. They dry out and become oxidized and fruitless. Only a few companies, principally **Sogrape** but also **Caves São João**, **Caves**

You can sometimes still see vines in the Minho trained up trees in the old-fashioned way. The idea was to avoid as much rot as possible in this damp region.

Aliança, **J M da Fonseca** and **Quinta dos Roques**, are getting it right. **Aliança**, **Caves São João** and **Sogrape** are also the leading names in Bairrada, along with **Luis Pato**, and for the same reason. They're making softer, but still powerful, more approachable red wines from the amazingly tannic Baga grape.

CONSUMER INFORMATION

WHAT DO I GET FOR MY MONEY?
Single-estate wines generally are fairly pricey in Vinho Verde. The best Dão and Bairrada wines are good value.

AVAILABILITY
Sogrape wines are not too hard to find. Good Vinho Verde is very difficult to find.

CONSUMER CHECKLIST
Bairrada 2000   *Quality* 7 ★
(Caves São João)   *Price 5* ★
                              Value 8 ★

Good Years Vinho Verde should be drunk within the year. The best Dão and Bairrada wines age well for some years.
Taste Notes White Vinho Verde is aromatic and bone dry. Red Dão is herby, almost piney; white Dão should be lemony and crisp. Bairrada is sturdy and plummy.

PORT & DOURO TABLE WINES

The Douro Valley is so far removed from the grimy, crazy activity of the city of Oporto at the river's mouth that a child's cry will hang in the still, warm air for a good distance up the hillside terraces above the river banks. The Douro Valley seems even older, more stuck in time than any other area, with a remote beauty to its cruelly angled vineyards that stumble down to the idly lapping river's edge. And from these lovely hills comes Port wine, a wine whose worldwide fame was built in the languid rooms of London's St James' clubs and the raucous chaos of a thousand urban taverns across Britain. But these days there is a new twist to the Douro Valley. Around half the wine made here is unfortified – and these are now some of the best, fruitiest, most exciting reds in Portugal and they are sold under the name of Douro.

Port is very much a British invention. It came about because of increasing friction between England and France in the late seventeenth century. This meant the usual supply of French wines dried up, so England looked to Portugal, her oldest ally, for an alternative source. The red wines were the opposite of the light, easy-going French wines, being harsh and lumpish, but as British merchants pushed up the Douro Valley away from

Oporto, into what was then an untamed wilderness, they began experimenting with the local Douro reds. They found that if you threw in a bucket or two of brandy, the wine seemed to cope with the sea journey back to England fairly well. It didn't taste very good, however, until they began adding brandy before the fermentation of the wine had finished. Since yeasts cease working if the alcohol level is too high, adding brandy when the wine is part-fermented will leave a lot of natural grape sweetness in the wine.

This strong, rich drink proved immensely popular in northern Europe, and to this day the principles of making port wine remain the same. The Douro Valley didn't do much to give Englishmen a red Bordeaux substitute while the bickering with France continued. Instead, it provided the base material for a totally different fortified wine, which has since been copied throughout the world. It took a further two centuries for the table wine to start to realize its full potential; but now, I suspect, there'll be no stopping it.

GRAPE VARIETIES AND WINE STYLES

Grape varieties are tremendously important to the eventual quality of the wine, but their names never appear on the label. There are over 90 different grapes permitted, and about 18 in wide use for Port. Of these the most important in terms of quality and concentration of flavour are Touriga Nacional, Tinta Barroca, Touriga Franca, Tinta Cão and Tinta Roriz for the reds, and Gouveio, Viosinho and Malvasia Fina for the whites. The same varieties are used for the table wines.

White Ports are basically made in two styles, dry and sweet. In general, the flavour is a bit thick and alcoholic, with the sweet ones even tasting slightly of rough grape skins. There are a few good dry ones. All the most exciting wines are red, however, ranging from angry, impenetrable purple to a pale, frail tawny brown, depending on their age and style. Most of the best table wines are red, too, and have wonderful smoky raspberry fruit. The best whites are peachy and crisp.

CLASSIFICATION

Port is one of the most rigidly controlled wines in the world and the production area

The narrow, walled terraces in the Douro Valley, here in the Cima Corgo looking towards the town of Pinhão, hold just two rows of vines each.

was demarcated in 1756. Nowadays every one of the 85,000 vineyards is marked on productivity (the lower the yield, the higher the mark), altitude, soil, geographical position, vine varieties, gradient, shelter, age of vines and distance from root to root. Even the upkeep of the vineyard is tested. The marks are totted up and the vineyard is given a rating from A (the top) to F (the bottom). Only a certain amount of wine is allowed to be made into port in any one year, and 'A' vineyards can make up to 600 litres of Port per 1000 vines; 'F' vineyards are seldom allowed to make any.

In addition, there are various styles of Port, which basically divides into vintage Ports (wines of a single year, aged in barrel for about two years and then aged in bottle) and wood ports (those aged longer in barrel).

Ruby This is the simplest and least expensive Port: it is tangy, tough but warmingly sweet wine to knock back uncritically.

Tawny If it's cheap, tawny is often simply a mixture of ruby and white Ports, and is low in quality. Proper, high-quality tawny usually has an indication of age: 10, 20, 30 or even 40 years old. These are wonderful, nutty wines, increasingly frail with age.

Vintage Port This is the finest of the Ports matured in bottle. It is only made or 'declared' in the very best years: the object is to make a big, impressive, concentrated mouthful rather than the gently fragrant tawny style. Bottled after only two years, it needs at least a dozen years in bottle to mature, and sometimes twice that long.

Single quinta vintage Port This is vintage Port from a single estate and bottled after two years in cask. It is made in the 'second-best' years and matures more quickly than vintage. It is usually released when it is ready to drink.

Crusted or **Crusting Port** Making a comeback, this is a blend of good Ports from several vintages, bottled after about three years in barrel. It throws a sediment, or crust, in bottle and needs decanting. Most are very good and very good value too.

Vintage Character (VC) and **Late Bottled Vintage (LBV) Ports** These styles are bottled after four to six years in barrel. LBV Ports are from one year, which will be on the label along with the year of bottling. VC Ports are a blend of several years. A few (the best) are not filtered and have much more flavour, but most have been browbeaten into early maturity and have lost much of their character.

Colheita Ports These are a speciality of the Portuguese Port houses (as opposed to the British-owned ones). They are wood-aged

The town of Vila Nova di Gaia, facing Oporto across the river Douro, is where the Port houses have their lodges or cellars and do their blending.

wines from a single vintage, and can be marvellously raisiny and nutty in style. They always bear a vintage date.

ORGANIZATION

The Port trade is divided between the farmers, who grow the grapes, and the shippers, who buy either grapes or young wine, though most also own some vineyards themselves. In the spring after the harvest the wine is usually taken from the wineries in the Douro Valley to Vila Nova de Gaia at the mouth of the river, where it is left to mature in the shippers' cellars or lodges. Best producers: (Port) **Cálem, Churchill Graham, Cockburn, Croft, Delaforce, Dow, Ferreira, Fonseca, Graham, Niepoort, Offley, Quinta do Noval, Ramos Pinto, Sandeman, Smith Woodhouse, Taylor** and **Warre**; (Douro table wines) **Chryseia, Quinta do Côtto, Quinta do Crasto, Ferreira, Niepoort, Poeira, Sogrape** and **Quinta do Vale Dona Maria**.

READING THE LABEL

If a branded Port doesn't specify what it is, it can be assumed to be Vintage Character in style, since this is a bit of a catch-all name.

WHAT DO THEY TASTE LIKE?

Except for the rare dry white Ports, the taste will be of varying degrees of sweetness and fieriness. The fieriness is important because although the techniques of aging Port are

designed to reduce its bite, all but the finest old tawnies, which have a gentle, brown sugar softness to them, need some bite to balance the sweetness. The best Ports have a peppery background to a rich fruit which is both plummy and raisiny, getting a slight chocolate sweetness as they become older, and managing to mix perfumes as incompatible as fresh mountain flowers, cough mixture and old leather.

THE GOOD YEARS

Most Port is a blend of various years, and such blends iron out vintage differences. But the quality of the year is crucial in vintage and single-quinta vintage wines: vintage Ports are seldom declared more than about three times in each decade, while single-quinta wines will be released from the years that don't quite make the vintage grade. From a good shipper, a vintage Port should take 15 to 20 years to mellow and mature; single-quinta vintages are ready in eight to ten years.

2004 Yields slightly down but initial tastings promising.

2003 The year of the heatwave. Expect a declaration but not great wine.

2002 Torrential rain at harvest time spoiled a potentially fine vintage. Small quantities of good single-quinta ports made.

2001 Moderately good wines destined for single-quintas.

2000 Widely declared vintage. Yields were low and wines should be long-lived.

1997 A cool year but a miraculous vintage. An almost unanimous declaration.

1996 Some good single quinta port.

1995 Very good but few declarations.

1994 Outstanding; many declarations.

1992 Rich, fruity wines, declared by a few-shippers.

1991 A generally declared year, though quantities are small.

1987 A small but good vintage, declared by four shippers.

1985 Every major shipper declared a vintage. Exceptionally good, juicy wines.

ENJOYING THE WINES

The French drink their Port primarily as an apéritif, the British mainly after meals, the Portuguese before and after meals. White Port is best as a chilled apéritif. Tawny is also best slightly chilled, before or after a meal. The big red Ports are best either as a pick-me-up in cold winters or, ideally, at the end of a meal. Vintage Port is best with nuts and dried fruit, good conversation and the occasional wisp of cigar smoke trailing through the candlelight.

CONSUMER INFORMATION

WHAT DO I GET FOR MY MONEY?

With drastically mounting production costs, Port isn't cheap any longer. Yet good Port is nonetheless excellent value for money. The basic wines are the only ones to avoid. With LBV Ports, do not feel you are getting vintage wine at a cut price, because you're not. Only Fonseca, Niepoort, Ramos Pinto, Smith Woodhouse and Warre offer a good approximation. Crusting is a rare style in which Smith Woodhouse specializes – some wine merchants may offer it as own label.

AVAILABILITY

For basic Ports, very good. Old tawnies are more difficult to find, and vintage Port should be sought at a specialist. Single quinta vintage Port is more widely available.

CONSUMER CHECKLIST

Crusted Port 1999 (Graham's)

Quality 9 ★
Price 8 ★
Value 10 ★

Good Years Best years (vintage Ports): 2000, 1997, 1994, 1992, 1991, 1985, 1983, 1980, 1977, 1970, 1966, 1963, 1960, 1955, 1948, 1947, 1945.

Taste Notes The vast majority of the wines are sweet and red, though a few are white and even dry. Styles range from cheap, rough red ruby to pale, delicate tawny, to massive, rich vintage Ports.

CENTRAL PORTUGAL

If the north of Portugal is home to its most famous wines, the centre and south, with an abundance of IPR regions and lesser-known DOCs, are where some of the most dramatic changes are taking place. Producers here are responding to international demand for fresh, fruity wines in a remarkably flexible way, and the co-operatives that dominate this part of Portugal have installed acres of stainless steel.

I'll start with the four DOC regions, all huddled around Lisbon, that had a glorious past. There's **Carcavelos** – raisiny, nutty, fortified and popular in the eighteenth century but not now; these days it's mostly buried under the bricks and mortar of Lisbon's suburbs. **Quinta dos Pesos** is, glory be, a new producer. Then there's **Colares**: blackstrap red wine grown in the sand dunes on the Atlantic coast from the doughty but scented Ramisco grape but now in slow decline. **Carvalho, Ribeiro & Ferreira** still makes it. **Bucelas** is a decently acidic dry white, popular in Britain in the nineteenth century; best producers: **Quinta da Murta** and **Quinta da Romeira**. **Setúbal**, spirity fortified wine from Moscatel grapes, can still be found from **J M da Fonseca**, but the Setúbal peninsula is more famous now for the activities of Australian consultant winemaker, Peter Bright at - **J P Vinhos** and the table wines of **José Maria da Fonseca Successores**, which use Gewürztraminer and other foreign grape varieties, often blended with native ones.

There are two big regions to the north of here, **Estremadura** and the **Ribatejo**. Estremadura occupies the western, coastal strip and the leading area here is Alenquer, promoted to DOC status along with Arruda, Obidos and Torres Vedras. Much of the wine, including some of the region's best, is simply labelled as Vinho Regional Estremadura. From Estremadura **Arruda** is sturdy, gutsy red from a variety of different grapes, among them João de Santarém and Tinta Miúda; **Alenquer** is softer and more glyceriny – look out here for the wines of **Quinta de Abrigada** and **Quinta de Pancas**, both single estates; the **Óbidos** reds are drier and more cedary and the **Torres Vedras** reds are quite light. Top producers also make fresh, aromatic whites.

The Ribatejo region, straddling the river Tagus (or Tejo in Portuguese), has always been the source of good Garrafeiras, well-aged reds that seldom, in the past, mentioned the name of their region of origin. They are often, in any case, blends of more than one region. Only made in the best years, they can be red or white. **Caves Velhas** and **Carvalho, Ribeiro & Ferreira** are specialists in Garrafeiras, which can be excellent, complex wines. If you want young Ribatejo wines your best bets are the co-operatives at **Almeirim** (their wines use the brand name of Lezíria) and **Benfica do Ribatejo**; other best producers are **Bright Brothers**, **Casa Cadaval**, **D F J Vinhos**, **Fiuza** and **Quinta da Lagoalva**.

The deep south means the **Alentejo** and the **Algarve**. If the latter conjures up images of holiday villas, you're quite right: its DOC regions do not deserve their status. The Alentejo is one of Portugal's fastest improving red wine regions: the sub-regions of **Borba** and **Redondo** are both producing good wines, as are the companies of **Quinta do Carmo**, **Herdade dos Coelheiros**, **Cortes de Cima**, **Vinha d'Ervideira**, **Esporão**, **José Maria da Fonseca**, **J P Vinhos**, **Mouchão**, **Quinta do Mouro**, **J P Ramos** and **Quinta da Terrugem/Caves Alianca** and also the co-operatives at **Borba**, **Redondo** and **Reguengos de Monsaraz**. Expect well-made, soft-centred, full-flavoured wines.

CONSUMER INFORMATION

WHAT DO I GET FOR MY MONEY?
Remarkable value. As so often happens, once we all discovered these wines their quality began to drop a little as prices rose. However, prices are catching up with value slowly and they're still good value.

AVAILABILITY
Very good. The old-fashioned fortified wines are hard to find, but the inexpensive table wines – and the slightly more expensive wines of Fonseca and J P Vinhos – are widely distributed.

CONSUMER CHECKLIST
Grand' Arte 2003	Quality 7 ★
(D F J Vinhos)	Price 6 ★
	Value 8 ★

Good Years Drink these simple wines as young as possible.
Taste Notes Red table wines tend to be fresh and fruity, sometimes sturdy, sometimes light; the whites are fresh when young, but won't keep.

MADEIRA

Even among enthusiastic wine lovers, few people have tasted this remarkable fortified wine from a lonely island that rears steep-sided from the Atlantic waves about 600km (375 miles) from the Moroccan coast. The wine's unique properties were discovered in the seventeenth century, when it was found that long sea voyages actually improved the wine. By the nineteenth century Madeira was highly prized. But the island was fiercely hit by the twin vine scourges of oidium and phylloxera in the nineteenth century, and for most of the twentieth century, great Madeira has been little more than a memory. But since 1979, after a drastic government initiative to improve the quality of the wines, things are once more on the move.

Madeira is the only wine in the world where heat is deliberately applied to age the wine artificially. This heating is done by *estufas*, of which there are two types. Cheaper wines are put into concrete tanks equipped with heating coils, and are heated to between 40 and 50°C for at least three months. This is the fastest, hottest method, and the least gentle. Better wines are put into wooden lodge pipes of 600-litre capacity, and stored in warm rooms, often heated by pipes, for six months to a year. The temperature of the wines rises to between 30 and 40°C. The very best wines are made by the canteiro system, whereby no artificial heating is used at all. The wines are

The Madeira vineyards are squeezed in around the edge of the island, taking advantage of any likely slope, though bananas can be a more profitable crop.

stored under the eaves in 600-litre pipes, warmed only by the sun. They may stay here for years on end.

GRAPE VARIETIES AND WINE STYLES

Each Madeira style takes its name from the grape on which it was originally based, although in recent decades Tinta Negra Mole has supplanted the better varieties in many vineyards. It's a versatile grape but its wines are never as good as the real thing. Portuguese membership of the EU now means that if a grape variety is stated on the label, then 85 per cent of the blend must be that variety. So now if a wine calls itself Sercial it really is from Sercial; those not made from Sercial, Verdelho, Bual or Malmsey grapes now call themselves Seco (dry), Meio seco (medium-dry), Meio doce (medium-sweet) or Doce (sweet).

Sercial is a dramatic dry wine, savoury, spirity, tangy and with a steely, piercing acidity. The grape claims to be related to Riesling.

Verdelho is pungent, smoky, medium-sweet wine, with gentle fruit. It may be the same as the Pedro Ximénez grape of Jerez.

Bual is rich and strong, but less concentrated than Malmsey, sometimes with a faintly rubbery whiff and a slightly higher acidity.

Madeira is one of the longest-lived wines. Vintage wines are rare but can seem virtually indestructible, as this bottle of 1863 Bual shows.

Malmsey is startlingly sweet, reeking sometimes of the finest dark, rich, brown sugar but with a smoky bite and surprisingly high acidity which make it almost refreshing.

CLASSIFICATION
The simplest Madeira, with no designation of age, must be at least three years old and is often misleadingly described as 'Finest'. The next category is Five Year Old. You need to go to the next level up, the 10- and 15-year old wines, to start to find real Madeira character. These ages are an indication as the wines are always blended for consistency. Vintage Madeira has to spend at least 20 years in cask before release but often this aging period lasts up to 80 years or so.

ORGANIZATION
The shippers tend to buy in wine or grapes from the smallholder growers, and then mature it before selling it. This is partly because aging any wine for so long is very expensive and requires tying up capital. Best producers: **Blandy's, Cossart Gordon, Henriques & Henriques** and **d'Oliveira**.

READING THE LABEL
Look for the name of a grape if you want a taste of what Madeira can really do. Cheaper wines – of five years old or less – will probably be from Tinta Negra Mole.

WHAT DO THEY TASTE LIKE?
Sweet or dry, Madeira has a biting, husky brown burnt flavour and a startling acidity which become more concentrated in aging.

ENJOYING THE WINE
Although cheap Madeira is used in cooking, good Madeira is best on its own. Sercial makes an excellent apéritif and can be served with soup, while the sweeter styles are less heady and more refreshing than Port for slow, after-dinner sipping with a bowl of nuts.

CONSUMER INFORMATION

WHAT DO I GET FOR MY MONEY?
Madeira is at last returning to being a fairly expensive but highly dependable quality wine. But before complaining about the price, remember that the costs of production are nearly double those of Port. Cheap wines of five years old or less will not give a true impression of what the wine can do, so pay more and buy a ten-year-old one.

AVAILABILITY
Not bad. The lesser wines are not too hard to find, and good outlets should have one or two wines of ten years old or more.

CONSUMER CHECKLIST
10-Year-Old Bual   *Quality 9* ★
(Blandy's)   *Price 8* ★
                           Value 9 ★

Good Years Vintage Madeira is very rare, but certain to be remarkable. But age is important in all good Madeiras, and good ones will be at least ten years old.
Taste Notes Madeira styles range from tangy and dry to intensely rich. The most recognizable characteristics in all the styles are a smokiness and an appetizing sharp acidity.

ENGLAND & WALES

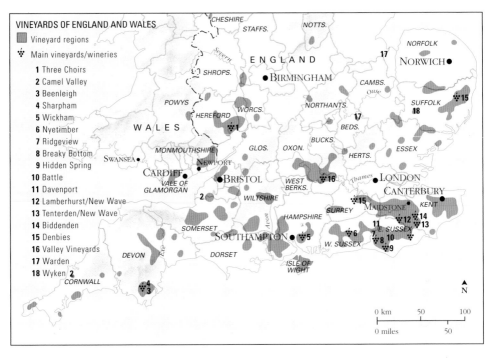

VINEYARDS OF ENGLAND AND WALES

▢ Vineyard regions

❦ Main vineyards/wineries

1 Three Choirs
2 Camel Valley
3 Beenleigh
4 Sharpham
5 Wickham
6 Nyetimber
7 Ridgeview
8 Breaky Bottom
9 Hidden Spring
10 Battle
11 Davenport
12 Lamberhurst/New Wave
13 Tenterden/New Wave
14 Biddenden
15 Denbies
16 Valley Vineyards
17 Warden
18 Wyken

We'd all love to think that the torrid vintage of 2003 was going to be the norm from now on. Cabernet and Shiraz ripening on the Sussex Downs? Bring it on! Well 2004 showed that the wretched old English weather is not going to go away that easily. But English *climate* – now that's another matter. You'd never know it some miserable August Bank Holidays, but the English climate really is warming up. Nowadays most if not all years are far warmer than the average over the last 50 years. And the grapes know it. Even 50 years ago the average Sussex and Kent temperature was only about 1°C below that of Champagne in France. That gap is now disappearing – and the result is a small but increasing number of sparkling wines in Kent and Sussex that are truly world class (**Nyetimber** and **Ridgeview** regularly beat any opposition you put them up against), as well as a rapidly increasing number of bright, tangy, scented whites and rosés all over the nation, and even a few light but delicious reds from grape varieties like Rondo and Regent specially bred to give good flavour and colour in cool conditions.

The industry is still minute; there are about 773 hectares (1910 acres) of vines, 330 vineyards, 115 wineries and an average annual output of about 2 million bottles. Concentrated in the warm South they even range as far north as Durham (off the map) and west into southern Wales. It is only the Gulf Stream that enables

wine to be made here at all, and wines need a sheltered south-facing site if they are to thrive.

GRAPE VARIETIES AND WINE STYLES

Until very recently the usual style for English wine (which is mostly white) was off-dry and vaguely Germanic. Most are, indeed, made from the vine crossings designed to cope with German-style cold, but which often produce better wine in England than in Germany. A newer style uses those same grapes to make dry wines, with body rather than sweetness to balance their high acidity. There are also a few good, botrytized wines and some outstanding Champagne-method fizz.

Producers have learnt which varieties are most successful – **Müller-Thurgau** was the most popular grape for many years but is in decline as producers turn to more quality varieties. The wine is often made slightly sweet. **Seyval Blanc** is now the most widely planted vine, and makes remarkably attractive wine: nettly and crisp when young, but able to age to a Chablis-like, nutty dry maturity. The grape is often blended or sweetened. **Bacchus** is proving to be a great success, with flavours resembling a good, tart Sauvignon Blanc. **Schönburger** produces somewhat Muscatty wines with low acidity but high sugar levels. Surprisingly, given the capricious and unreliable climate, there is also a little red wine from varieties such as **Dornfelder**.

Denbies Estate near Dorking is England's largest wine estate and picking can be done here by machine.

CLASSIFICATION
The UK's appellation system was introduced in 1994. The best wines are labelled either Quality or Regional Wine.

ORGANIZATION
This is changing as those growers determined to survive evolve strategies to combat English indifference to their own wines. Many growers still farm other crops as well, and spread their risks that way. Others band together in associations to market their wine, like English Wine Producers.

READING THE LABEL
Many wines are varietals, though blends are also popular. Labels should indicate whether a wine is dry or medium. The English Vineyards Association (EVA) seal is gold and black, and is a genuine quality pointer.

WHAT DO THEY TASTE LIKE?
The typical English flavour is of elderflower and grapefruit, nettles and hedgerows. Wines can be dry, medium, or sweet and botrytized.

THE GOOD YEARS
Most should be drunk young. 2004, 2003 and 2002 were all good years.

ENJOYING THE WINES
English white wines are some of the few wines to go well with Colchester oysters or Dover sole, but ideally, with their green, perfumed fruit they are best drunk on their own.

CONSUMER INFORMATION

WHAT DO I GET FOR MY MONEY?
English wines are not cheap and probably never will be: wine from the other side of the world can cost less. But a distinctive style of wine is gradually emerging.

AVAILABILITY
There are now a few larger operations making wine, but most producers are still small scale. Availability is often only local, sometimes only at the vineyard itself.

CONSUMER CHECKLIST
Seyval Blanc 2004   *Quality 7* ★
(Breaky Bottom)   *Price 6* ★
                          Value 8 ★

Good Years   Most English wines are best drunk young. Best years: 2004, 2003 and 2002.
Taste Notes   English wines should be delicate and aromatic with flavours of elderflower, nettles, hedgerows and grapefruit.

SWITZERLAND

WINE REGIONS OF SWITZERLAND

- Valais
- Vaud
- Geneva
- Neuchâtel
- Fribourg
- Bern
- Jura
- Eastern Switzerland
- Ticino

To record that Switzerland has Europe's highest vineyards at Visp, where grapes are grown on steep, terraced mountains at a chilling 1100m (3600ft) is not surprising. But to record that Switzerland until recently suffered from a grape glut, when such honours are usually only the bane of the sprawling vineyards of the Mediterranean south, where land is cheap to cultivate, is puzzling.

Switzerland is a mountainous land. The vines are regularly grown at altitudes that other winemakers would declare to be impossible. Her wines cost roughly four times as much as French wines to produce. And to all but the Swiss themselves the wines seem excessively dear to purchase. Little is exported; instead the Swiss lap up all they can produce, and import good reds from elsewhere into the bargain.

Yields have now been restricted, although at 75 hl/ha they are not low. But the vines have all the sunshine they could possibly want, and a warm, drying wind, the Foehn, helps to prevent rot in many places and keep the ripening grapes healthy. And believe it or not irrigation is often needed. We may think of Switzerland as being largely covered in snow, but in fact the vines can get very dry, and extra water is essential.

Vines are grown in all of Switzerland's 24 cantons, though most of the wine comes from the French-speaking parts. German-speaking Switerzland comes next, with 3000 hectares (7500 acres) compared to French-speaking Switzerland's 11,000 hectares (27,000 acres); Italian-speaking Switzerland has 800 hectares (2000 acres). The hot, wide valley of the Rhône, centred on the town of Sion which makes up the Valais area, is the main wine region, followed by the Vaud, a long arc of vineyards beginning at Martigny where the Rhône makes a very abrupt right turn northwards, and continuing in a wide and spectacularly scenic arc past Montreux and Lausanne round to Geneva. Geneva itself is the centre of a rather lesser area called the Mandement.

The German cantons don't have the mesoclimates to produce regular amounts of fully ripened grapes, but several have a fair reputation. Bern has the areas of Schafis and Twann. The Graubünden area near the Austrian border produces some quite big, chewy-tasting Blauburgunder (Pinot Noir); Zurich and Schaffhausen also make some light Blauburgunders. The Italian part of Switzerland has a totally different wine culture. The Sottoceneri is the main region, and the further south you go the more Mediterranean everything becomes – 'everything' meaning the architecture, the weather and, of course, the wine.

GRAPE VARIETIES AND WINE STYLES

The most exciting area is the **Valais**, where almost all of Switzerland's decent red is made.

The Swiss are the biggest buyers of Burgundy, as well as having a great love for Beaujolais, and this shows in the red grape varieties used in the Valais. Two-thirds of the red vines are Burgundy's Pinot Noir, with most of the rest Beaujolais' Gamay. They are often blended together – the better blends called **Dôle**, usually relatively light, but perfumed in a strawberryish way, and often with some bite. The reds which don't pass the tasting panel to gain the Dôle label are called Goron. There's a small amount of Syrah which is delicious.

However, two-thirds of the Valais vineyards are white, and the Chasselas, here called the Fendant, is the predominant grape; unless drunk very young it makes a rather flabby wine. Ironically for an Alpine country, many Valais vineyards are too hot for such a neutral grape. Much better are either the Sylvaner wines, here called Johannisberg, which are quite full and grapy, or the Muscat, Pinot Gris (called Malvoisie) and Riesling wines which can achieve a delicious delicacy, as perfumed as you could hope for. The Valais also has some remarkable rare old varieties, which are worth trying. Petite Arvine, Armigne and Humagne make big, honeyed whites. Best producers: **Charles Bonvin**, **M Clavien**, **J Germanier**, **Didier Joris**, **Mont d'Or**, **Orsat**, **Provins Valais** and **Zufferey**.

The **Vaud** makes the best Chasselas, here usually called Dorin, but often parading

Snow-capped peaks are never very far away from Switzerland's vineyards. These vineyards, near Sion in the Valais, nevertheless, get plenty of sun.

under the name of a village. The slopes of Chablais are perhaps the best Vaud vineyards, just before the Rhône runs into Lake Geneva, and the village of Aigle makes a sharp, slightly *spritzig* Dorin. **Dézelay**, from the lakeside hills between Montreux and Lausanne, is the best known Dorin appellation, and the wine is at its driest and stoniest here, again needing to be drunk young and slightly *spritzig*. Best producers: **Henri Badoux**, **Louis Bovard**, **Dubois**, **Massy**, **Obrist**, **Pinget** and **J & P Testuz**.

From Lausanne round to Geneva the vineyards become flatter, and so do the wines. There is light Chasselas (now called Perlan) from around **Geneva**, plus Müller-Thurgau and red Gamay, and more Chasselas from **Neuchâtel**, north of Lake Geneva. The Pinot Noir here is mostly light. Best producers: **d'Auvernier**, **Grillette**, **de Montmollin Fils** and **J-M Novelle**.

The 17 German-speaking cantons in eastern Switzerland produce far more red wine than white. **Schaffhausen**, indeed, rubs shoulders with south Baden, Germany's best red wine region. There's a lot of the Mariafeld grape as well as Blauburgunder. South of Zürich Blauburgunder is often called Clevner.

In the Herrschaft vineyards north of Chur, near the borders with Austria and Liechtenstein, the reds can be quite weighty and there are full sweet whites from the Completer grape. Pink wines like Weissherbst or Schillerwein (a blend of red and white grapes) are a speciality of the German cantons. The main white grape is Müller-Thurgau (here called Riesling-Sylvaner). Best producer: **Baumann**.

Switzerland's other red is the Merlot of the Italian-speaking cantons. Grapes ripen well in the Ticino vineyards around Lugano, and the best Merlot wines are designated VITI, a quality guarantee. Best producers: **Huber**, **Werner Stucky**, **Tamborini**, **Zanini** and **Zündel**.

CLASSIFICATION

Switzerland's appellation system seems to lack the easy logic of most other European systems. Wines may carry a place name, a combination of place and grape name, or they may have a generic title like Fendant. The places named can be a region within a canton, a canton or a region larger than a canton. In addition to all this each canton may have its own regulations.

In the Valais, a wine labelled Controlled Appellation of Origin (Appellation d'Origine Contrôlée) should have been made to stricter rules than one labelled Appellation of Origin (Appellation d'Origine). In Geneva, as well as these two categories, there are also Grand Cru and Premier Cru wines, the rules for which are still more restrictive.

The German-speaking cantons have a seal of quality – Winzer-Wy, or vintner's wine. In Ticino the best Merlots have the VITI seal.

ORGANIZATION

All over Switzerland, although many large companies make good wine, to get real individuality choose a domaine-bottled wine from an individual grower.

READING THE LABEL

Both the names of a single village and a single producer are good signs. Polish up your French, German and Italian: all three languages are used on Swiss wine labels.

WHAT DO THEY TASTE LIKE?

Most Swiss white is light, leafy and fairly neutral, though the Chasselas is good at reflecting the character of the soil which gives it some added interest. There are a few dessert wines, which can be surprisingly good and complex. The reds tend to be soft and juicy, with only a few having proper depth of fruit.

THE GOOD YEARS

Drink the youngest vintage available. Few of the wines improve with time.

ENJOYING THE WINE

With the strong Swiss Franc the first step toward enjoying Swiss wine is to get somebody else to pay for it. After that little barrier has been crossed you'll find that the wine goes pretty well with most everyday food. Chasselas is swamped by too much flavour in food; many of the reds can be chilled, and will go well with most light meat dishes.

CONSUMER INFORMATION

WHAT DO I GET FOR MY MONEY?
Well, not much, to be honest. One reason that Swiss wines are so little exported is that they are relatively expensive.

AVAILABILITY
Universal in Switzerland. Elsewhere, contact your local Swiss commercial office for details as they are not readily available.

CONSUMER CHECKLIST

Pinot Noir du Valais 2004	Quality 6 ★
(Caves Imesch)	Price 8 ★
	Value 2 ★

Good Years Few Swiss wines improve with age, and most just lose their freshness. So drink the youngest vintage available.

Taste Notes The white wines are dry, crisp and quite neutral. The reds are juicy, soft and seldom very dark in colour. Sweet wines are rare in Switzerland but they can be excellent, subtle and unusual.

AUSTRIA

It's all too easy to think of Austrian wines as being an offshoot of German wines. The language is the same, the grape varieties are often the same, many of the quality categories are the same – what's the difference?

The answer is, quite a lot. For one thing, Austria's geographical position gives her a climate quite different from that with which German vines have to battle. It's more continental, which means hotter in the summer and colder in the winter, and the grapes just don't have the same struggle to ripen. Anyone who needed further convincing should look at the way German research has been geared to developing new vine varieties that can tolerate cold autumns and winters. In Austria they don't worry about such things; instead they're increasingly concerned about making good international-style reds – wines that much of Germany would give its eye teeth to be able to produce.

Austria can already produce just about any style of white wine it chooses. Its sparkling wine appeals to local tastes more than to outsiders, but that's a minor problem. More important is the sheer variety. In fact this variety is part and parcel of the way that Austrian wine is produced, by smallholders who often run a Buschenschanke, or country inn. These places can be enchanting, and they are rightly popular with Austrians who will travel from the other side of the country in order to buy and drink wine in such congenial surroundings. You go in through a broad, high gateway, into a courtyard. There will be tables and benches there, arranged under the trees, as well as some rooms inside for chillier days. Your host and hostess will probably be wearing lederhosen and a dirndl, respectively. There may well be an accordionist. You will be offered only food that is home-made, and indeed home-grown – a few foodstuffs can be bought in, but by law the sausages, hams, pâtés and the like must be from home-reared and home-killed pigs.

Pig is the staple diet here. Every possible incarnation will be served, and it will all be delicious. The wine will also be home-made – often in a spanking new winery, fully equipped with stainless steel and temperature control, and quite possibly even some new oak barriques. Your host may choose to dress in traditional fashion, but the wine-making at the best inns is no more old-fashioned than the Mercedes cars which are stacked three-deep in front of the owner's house.

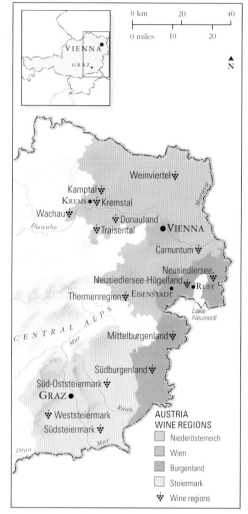

And you will be offered the full range of wines they produce: ten or a dozen different sorts, all identified by grape variety, and most made in the last couple of years. There may be a few older wines at the bottom of the list as a curiosity, but the Austrian taste is not for old wines. And while regional specialities do exist there are very few regions that stick to one grape in the manner of, say, Beaujolais.

GRAPE VARIETIES AND WINE STYLES
This is where Austria has changed dramatically in the last decade – not in grape varieties, but in the style of wines. Austria has always had the capability of making good dry whites. The climate is warm enough for the grapes to ripen properly, and the alcohol levels are quite high enough to support acidity with no sweetness. But because in one part of the country it is easy – almost too easy – to

produce botrytis-affected wines at relatively low prices, a market developed for these in Germany. To German consumers, used to the high prices inevitably charged for the rare sweet wines of their own country, the Austrian versions seemed a godsend. To the less scrupulous merchants of Austria (and to a lesser extent, of Germany) they seemed even more of heaven-sent, and they sold all they could get. Then, to have even more sweet wines at even lower prices, they started doctoring them with a chemical, diethylene glycol. This had the effect of making wines taste sweeter and fatter than they were, and while the chemical wasn't really harmful – nobody was reported as having become ill as a result of drinking the doctored wine – it was certainly illegal, and when the scandal broke in 1985 the merchants went to the wall, taking the reputation of Austrian wine with them.

The growers fought back by welcoming a strict new wine law, by slowly establishing themselves on the market to take the place of the merchants, and by embracing a new, bone-dry style of wine. Even in the places where nature clearly intended that sweet wine should be made, good dry wines started appearing. The right sort of expensive wine-making equipment was shipped into the cellars. Seldom has a wine industry reinvented iself so effectively as the Austrian one has in the last decade. Now, more than ten years on, what sometimes at first looked like a panic reaction can be seen to be a declaration of a

unique Austrian style. And the revolution is still continuing: now it's reds that are becoming better year by year.

There are four main wine regions. Vienna (**Wien**) is the smallest, and encompasses the green, hilly suburbs as well as the vineyards actually within the city boundaries. Then there is **Burgenland**, which makes the great sweet wines (yes, happily they never disappeared) and some good reds in the south. **Niederösterreich** (Lower Austria) makes wines that vary from top quality to distinctly everyday, and Styria (**Steiermark**) makes light, acidic wines that are a wow with German tourists hooked on the taste of Trocken wines back home.

Vienna first. The vineyards are west of the city (just follow the nearest tourist bus to the Buschenschanken, here called Heurigen). Grinzing, Heiligenstadt and Nussberg, all absurdly pretty suburbs, are the main centres of viticulture, and Grüner Veltliner is the main vine. This is a grape indigenous to Austria, though it is also found further east, in the territories of the old Austro-Hungarian empire. It makes attractive, light, slightly peppery white wine perfectly suited to being drunk, without too much attention, by the quarter- or half-litre. Wines made from Riesling and from Pinot Blanc (Weissburgunder) can be more serious, though are still drunk young.

But if Vienna is dedicated to quenching the thirst of her visitors, **Burgenland** produces very good wines indeed. In the north there is a remarkable lake, the Neusiedl, which is broad and shallow (indeed, it has occasionally dried up in the past). To the west the hills rise up, giving the region the name of **Neusiedlersee-Hügelland**; to the east the land is flat and dotted with countless small lakes. The Hungarian border cuts across the south of the lake – until 1921 the whole Burgenland was part of Hungary, and after World War Two it was part of the Russian zone of occupation. So it is only recently that proper investment in wine has been a possibility.

The secret of its success, at least here around the lake, is *Botrytis cinerea*. This is one of the very few places in the world where the botrytis fungus can be relied upon to show up every year. Great sweet wines can be made here without worry vintage after vintage, especially on the eastern side of the lake, where the humidity is greater and the climate even warmer. On the western side

The town of Rust on the shores of Lake Neusiedl in Burgenland is famous for its luscious sweet wines but also has a thriving basketware industry.

there is a narrow strip around the lake where botrytis is a regular visitor; further back from the lake good dry wines are made.

But fashion is now dictating that dry wines be made on the eastern side, as well. The most successful grapes here tend to be Traminer, Welschriesling and Weissburgunder, with Neuburger, Furmint, Ruländer, Bouvier, Scheurebe, Sämling and others joining these in Neusiedlersee-Hügelland. Strohwein – wine made from grapes dried on straw – and Eiswein are also made here. Best producers: **Feiler-Artinger**, **Heinrich**, **Kollwentz**, **Alois Kracher**, **Helmut Lang**, **Nittnaus**, **Willi Opitz**, **Schandl**, **Stiegelmar/Juris**, **Triebaumer**, **Umathum** and **Velich**.

The Hungarian border cuts across the south of the lake, curves south-westwards and then doubles back over **Mittelburgenland**. Here the grapes are 95 per cent red, and until recently the wine made from them was soft and sweetish, light in colour and distinctly jammy. Quite a lot of it still is like that.

But the Blaufränkisch grape can produce better things if it's encouraged to do so. If yields are kept down and the wine is fermented out dry; if a little Cabernet Sauvignon is blended in, on the principle that a blend can be more than the sum of its parts; if a few new or nearly-new oak barriques are brought into the cellar to give the wine a bit more structure, a bit more complexity. Then the

The vineyards around Rust benefit from their proximity to the broad, shallow Lake Neusiedl, which provides the humidity that allows the botrytis fungus to thrive.

reds from here can be distinctly interesting. They can have good depth of fruit and nice elegance. **Igler** and **Gesellmann** are two of the leading producers, both based in the village of Deutschkreutz.

The most remote part of Burgenland is the south, **Südburgenland**. Here there are none of the tourist buses that clog the streets of Neusiedlersee towns and villages like Rust. Fashions here change slowly, and when growers make good wine it has nothing to do with the latest fad from South Africa or Australia. They grow Zweigelt and Blaufränkisch for their reds wines and Welschriesling and Müller-Thurgau for their whites; Eisenberg is one of the best spots for red wines, and the Welschriesling is far superior in quality to the wines made from the grape in most places.

This in fact applies to the whole of Austria which seems to have the knack of getting fresh, appley wine out of a grape that in most countries is little better than flat and dull. It is this impression of general dullness and oxidation that has damned the grape – variously known as Welschriesling, Olaszriesling, Riesling Italico or Laski Rizling in central and eastern Europe – in the eyes and palates of most people. Yet the Austrians know better.

Welschriesling is grown widely throughout the country. It even makes some sweet wine, and that's pretty good, too.

But Südburgenland has another speciality, as well. It derives from the native American vines that were shipped over in an attempt to combat phylloxera: before grafting on to American rootstocks was accepted as being the best answer, many regions either tried planting these American vines to see what their wine would be like, or they tried crossing them with European varieties to produce hybrids. Many of these hybrids are doing well in Südburgenland; their wine, known locally as Uhudler, is light and juicy-fruity, with a curious mayflower and strawberry perfume.

But if Viennese wine has the distinction of being, well, Viennese, and Burgenland produces some of the world's greatest sweet whites, the region that can claim to produce more Austrian wine than any other is Lower

Austria or **Niederösterreich**. It spreads for miles each side of the Danube, and the smallest sub-regions are the best. Tiny **Wachau** produces world-class class dry whites, but the biggest one, **Weinviertel,** has no real identity abroad; the main production of its fertile, high-yielding vineyards is basic dry or dryish white from Grüner Veltliner and Welschriesling, though Weissburgunder can be better than this. Much of the base wine for the Austrian fizz producers is grown here.

Kamptal is the land around the river Kamp, a tributary of the Danube. **Donauland** is a much larger area stretching right up to the vinous boundaries of Vienna. Here and in nearby **Kremstal** is grown a lot of Austria's best Grüner Veltliner. It seems to have extra concentration and finesse here and can sometimes improve on its usual reputation as a simple, everyday white. Best producers: (Kamptal) **Bründlmayer**, **Fred Loimer** and **Schloss Gobelsburg;** (Donauland) **Bernhard Ott**; (Kremstal) **Malat, Nigl, Nikolaihof** and **Fritz Salomon.**

The Wachau is the star wine region of Lower Austria and produces Austria's top dry whites. Here, the terraced vineyards rise high above the Danube. Riesling is the best grape, and produces wines with the sort of knife-edge balance and refined structure otherwise found only in Germany. Yet these Rieslings could not be mistaken for German wines. They have neither the frail delicacy of the Mosel nor the fiery richness of the Rheingau, though they certainly have the ripeness and firmness of the latter. And they are bone dry. Best producers: **Hirtzberger, Högl, Knoll, Nikolaihof, Pichler, Prager** and **Schmelz.**

The final sub-region of Lower Austria is **Thermenregion**, named after its natural spas, though it used, until the new wine law that succeeded the scandal, to be called Gumpoldskirchen after its most famous wine village. Gumpoldskirchen wines are traditionally white and medium-sweet, made from

The Wachau hills rise high above the village of Weissenkirchen. Vines on these terraces are roughly three times as expensive to tend as those on flat land.

Zierfandler (or Spätrot) and Rotgipfler grapes. These grapes will happily ripen to Auslese level in this warm climate, but botrytis is not found here. Best producer: **Stadlmann**.

Styria or **Steiermark** is the most southerly of Austria's wine regions. But don't think that more southerly automatically equals warmer, because it doesn't. The climate is generally mild, but these rolling hills produce some of the leanest, most acidic wine in the country. But the wines also have some aroma, particularly when they are made from Sauvignon Blanc (sometimes called Muskat-Silvaner) or Gelber Muskateller (Muscat Blanc à Petits Grains). Pinot Blanc, Chardonnay, Rülander (Pinot Gris), Müller-Thurgau and Welschriesling are also grown.

Most of Styria's vineyards are in **Südsteiermark**; little **Süd-Oststeiermark** also has some and tiny **Weststeiermark** has a few, almost all of which are Blauer Wildbacher grapes, which make a light, acidic and assertive rosé called Schilcher. Best producers: **Polz** and **E & M Tement**.

CLASSIFICATION

Austria's way of classifying wine is broadly similar to that of Germany. Must weights are measured in degrees KMW, or Klosterneuburger Mostwaage; multiply the KMW figure by five to get the Oechsle equivalent.
Tafelwein The most basic category; **Landwein** Country wine from a specific region; **Qualitätswein** Quality wine from a single demarcated region; **Kabinett** In Germany this is a Prädikat category; not so in Austria; **Prädikatswein** There are six of these levels: **Spätlese**, made from fully ripe grapes; **Auslese**, from still riper grapes, and usually medium-sweet to sweet; **Eiswein**, made from grapes picked and pressed while frozen, and intensely sweet; **Ausbruch**, a uniquely Austrian category for sweet wine made from overripe, nobly rotten or shrivelled grapes, and **Trockenbeerenauslese**, sweet wine made from nobly rotten, shrivelled grapes.

Wachau, in addition, has its own classification: Steinfeder, Federspiel and Smaragd are all dry wines, but increasingly concentrated and ripe.

ORGANIZATION

The merchants were the producers most affected by the wine scandal of the 1980s – even if they weren't themselves involved, they were hit by the general fall in their reputation. Many growers started bottling their own wines and the result has been a tremendous rise in standards.

READING THE LABEL

Grape names may appear on the label either in their German form or in their more familiar international forms. It can be a shock to foreigners to see red wines described as Spätlese or Auslese. Dry reds may also be labelled Trocken as well.

WHAT DO THEY TASTE LIKE?

Austrian whites are mostly light and dry, with good acidity and backbone. The sweet whites can be immensely rich. The reds may be sweetish or dry, and with good fruit and sometimes even some oak aging.

THE GOOD YEARS

The light whites are best young, and only Wachau Rieslings, the sweet wines of Burgenland and a few other top examples will improve with age. Best years: 2004, 2003, 2002, 2001, 2000, 1999, 1998, 1997 and 1995.

ENJOYING THE WINES

The whites are drunk on their home ground with all manner of charcuterie and even Wiener= Schnitzel. They are very versatile and needn't be treated with reverence. The great sweet wines of the Neusiedlersee are big enough to cope with food, unlike most of their German equivalents, and will happily partner cheese and puddings.

CONSUMER INFORMATION

WHAT DO I GET FOR MY MONEY?

Fair value. Good Austrian wines – from low-yielding vines, made by a good grower – are not cheap, but they are of high quality. The sweet wines, in particular, are good value. The everyday wines are cheap, but not very thrilling.

AVAILABILITY

Still not good. Until the scandal of 1985 only one brand of wine was widely distributed. That is no longer seen, and interesting wines from individual growers can be hard to find.

CONSUMER CHECKLIST

Wachau Riesling Kabinett	*Quality* 7 ★
2004 (Hirtzberger)	*Price* 7 ★
	Value 7 ★

Good Years Most wines are best young. Best years: 2004, 2003, 2002, 2001, 2000.
Taste Notes Whites are dry and light or sweet and rich; reds can be sweetish but are increasingly dry and well-structured.

EASTERN EUROPE

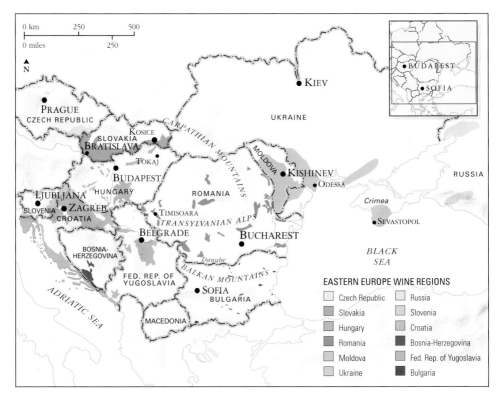

Scale: 0 km — 250 — 500 / 0 miles — 250

N

KIEV

BUDAPEST

SOFIA

PRAGUE
CZECH REPUBLIC

UKRAINE

KOSICE
SLOVAKIA
BRATISLAVA

TOKAJ

CARPATHIAN MOUNTAINS

MOLDOVA

KISHINEV
ODESSA

RUSSIA

BUDAPEST

HUNGARY

ROMANIA

Crimea

LJUBLJANA
SLOVENIA ZAGREB
CROATIA

TIMISOARA
TRANSYLVANIAN ALPS

SEVASTOPOL

BELGRADE

BUCHAREST

BLACK
SEA

BOSNIA-
HERZEGOVINA

Danube

FED. REP. OF
YUGOSLAVIA

BALKAN MOUNTAINS

ADRIATIC SEA

SOFIA
BULGARIA

MACEDONIA

EASTERN EUROPE WINE REGIONS

- Czech Republic
- Slovakia
- Hungary
- Romania
- Moldova
- Ukraine
- Russia
- Slovenia
- Croatia
- Bosnia-Herzegovina
- Fed. Rep. of Yugoslavia
- Bulgaria

We all know Bulgarian Cabernet Sauvignon. That was about the only wine that regularly penetrated beyond the Iron Curtain before 1989, with the possible exception of Hungary's Tokay, which never quite seemed worth the trouble. But then, gradually, the wines of Eastern Europe and the CIS states were revealed to us. And very strange the picture was, too.

The massive bureaucracy of Communism had planted collective vineyards over great swathes of the continent. Sometimes they were of good grapes, sometimes not. The priority had been to supply quantity, not quality. Gorbachev, alarmed at the consumption of alcohol, had ordered a huge vine pull programme; some regions had obeyed, some hadn't. The beginning of privatization introduced its own problems, and by no means guaranteed the quality of the wine made by the new owners. The collapse of the markets on which many of these countries had relied – those markets being other countries within the Warsaw Pact, none of whom had any money for buying wine now – created its own difficulties. In order to earn hard currency from abroad, these newly independent states had to export, and wine was an obvious possibility. But in order to make the sort of wine that would sell, they needed vineyard sprays and cellar equipment, many of which had to be bought with – you guessed it – hard currency. In some cases even obtaining corks, labels or clean bottles could be a nightmare.

In the event it is flying winemakers who have done most to bring these wines to us. Often Australian-trained, these winemakers specialize in providing expertise (and investment) for wineries that have the potential to make the sort of wines that Westerners want to drink. The initial task has often been to clean the winery – the importance of hygiene was not always properly understood and many of the problems with the wines in the past had stemmed from bad handling and dirty barrels. Picking the grapes at the optimum moment for ripeness (as opposed to the optimum moment for convenience) was also a new habit that had to be learnt.

But what has been most striking is the enormous potential that is present in all these countries. Some have been more forward-looking than others, but all have – or had – indigenous, highly characterful wine styles that have sometimes been almost lost to the world. What we are seeing now is a welcome revival – but which in most cases still has a long way to go.

CZECH REPUBLIC & SLOVAKIA

The 'velvet divorce' of the early 1990s left **Slovakia** with most of the vineyards of the former Czechoslovakia – two-thirds of them, to be precise. But then the Slovakian part of the country had always had the greater reputation for wine, while what is now the **Czech Republic** had long made excellent beer. Now both flying winemakers and Western investors are gradually taking an interest – though, ironically, rather more so in the Czech Republic than in Slovakia, where adjustment is not happening quite so quickly.

The grape varieties are much the same in both countries – and much the same as they are in Hungary and Austria. Both the Czech Republic and Slovakia are better suited to white wine than red, although there are some terrific reds – juicy, damsony St-Laurent and green, fresh Frankovka. But what really excel are whites like Irsay Oliver, with its nose of scented soap, and peppery, celery-flavoured Grüner Veltliner. There is Riesling, Müller-Thurgau, Pinot Blanc, Gewürztraminer and Léanyka as well – and at the eastern end of Slovakia, an extension of the Tokay vineyards of Hungary. This little enclave grows the same grapes as in Hungary: Furmint, Hárslevelü and Muscat Ottonel.

So what's been happening all these years? Why haven't we heard of these wines? Under

What a spot for a picnic, and increasingly I would be happy to drink the local Czech wine, provided I could catch it young and fresh.

the old Communist regime Czechoslovakia didn't export wine to the West and neither did it care that it had a chunk of Tokay, one of the world's most famous vineyard regions, in its back garden. Well, now it's changed its mind and throughout both countries there's a new mood in the air.

CIS STATES

Many of the CIS states grow grapes, but not always for wine. A few years ago, when we began to see bottles of a 1967 wine called Negru de Purkar, **Moldova** was a revelation. Gosh, it was good: like a wonderful old Pauillac, matured to mellowness and complexity. There was a bit of Cabernet Sauvignon in there, to be sure, but most of the blend was the Saperavi grape. Younger vintages – after we'd drunk all the old ones we could get – were nothing like as wonderful. But we'd seen what Moldova could do. Our appetites were whetted.

Now it is the so-called flying winemakers who are making good international-style wines. They are taking advantage of good red grapes like Saperavi and the large amounts of Cabernet planted here, and white grapes like Rkatsiteli, Riesling, Aligoté and Chardonnay, Sauvignon, Feteasca and Traminer. **Ukraine** and the **Crimea** come next in terms of quan-

tity. There are certainly vineyards in inland Ukraine, but the Crimea is the major region. And it has the **Massandra** winery – built to provide wine for the Tsar's summer palace at Livadia. This came to attention a few years ago when large stocks of historic dessert wines from its cellars were sold off. Again, the newer wines aren't as exciting, but they could be, they could be. There is sparkling wine, too, that goes under the name of **Krim**, but so far it's not brilliant.

Russia itself makes both red and white wines from familiar vines like Aligoté, Sémillon, Sauvignon Blanc, Pinot Gris and Cabernet, and less familiar ones like Black Tsimlyansky. But winters are harsh here and only the most favoured sites can grow vines.

Georgia has very individual historic winemaking traditions – including a liking for yellow, tannic whites – and **Azerbaijan** and **Armenia** make only small amounts.

HUNGARY

The name we used to see on every bottle of Hungarian wine exported from the country was Monimpex. If we read the small print we might have seen another name, too: Hungarovin. The first handled all wine exports, the second all the vineyards and wine-making. It was a system that worked perfectly well in its own terms – Hungary produced plenty of wine to sell to other Eastern Bloc countries – but that didn't exactly encourage quality. And yet quality seems to be something that Hungary is naturally good at. There are many wonderful indigenous grape varieties here – at least, there were. Some were't replanted after phylloxera and others suffered under the system of vast state farms that prized quantity above all else.

Look at The Great Plain, for example: there is something both magical and daunting about a place that states so simply its singularity and its vastness. The Great Plain is in the south of Hungary, just to the east of the Danube, which cuts the country in two lengthwise. Nearly half Hungary's vineyards are here, planted on easily cultivable land after phylloxera, partly because the louse could not live in the sandy soil. Quality is not overwhelmingly high.

Look at Bull's Blood, or Egri Bikavér. A terrific, gutsy red even as late as the 1960s, but thereafter increasingly debased. Look, too, at Tokay (or Tokaj in Hungarian). This wine, which should be wonderful, full of sweetness and richness, was under Communism blended to a saleable but dull norm. Safe but dull. The two things that Hungarian wine never used to be – and which images, increasingly, it is shedding.

GRAPE VARIETIES AND WINE STYLES

Just listen to this litany: Furmint, Ezerjó, Mezesfehér, Hárslevelü, Kadarka, Cirfandli (the Zierfandler of Austria), Léanyka (the Feteasca of Romania), Kékfrankos (the Blaufränkisch of Austria), or Zweigelt. They even sound exciting. And they should be: spicy, fiery, dry but rich. Some of the best come from the volcanic slopes north of the vast Lake Balaton in Transdanubia. The tempering affect of the lake softens the climate to produce big, rich wines. There are still Hungarian varieties planted here; south of the lake in **Dél-Balaton**, a more recent vineyard area, there are international grape varieties, including Chardonnay, Sémillon and Merlot.

The **Gyöngyös** estate in the North-East was one of the first in Hungary to benefit from Western input. **Eger** is the home of Bull's Blood, and the **Tokaj** region is rapidly transforming itself into the source of first-class sweet wine that it was always supposed to be.

Tokaji has been produced, in more or less its present form, for over two hundred years. In autumn mists rise off the Bodrog river and encourage the growth of *Botrytis cinerea*, or noble rot, on the grapes. The free-run juice, known as Eszencia, is fermented – it can take years to reach even a few degrees of alcohol, so intensely sweet is it. The grapes are then pounded to a sticky paste or *aszú* and macerated with dry base wine. After a day or two the mixture is pressed, and the wine left to mature. The final wine is categorized according to the amount of paste added: measurement is in 30-litre tubs called *puttonyos*. Three, four and five *puttonyos* are the usual qualities, in ascending order of sweetness. Szamorodni has had no aszú added, and may be dry ('száraz') or sweet ('édes').

CLASSIFICATION

There are 22 official wine regions according to Hungarian wine law. 'Minöségi Bor' means quality wine from a demarcated region.

Checking the clarity of the wine in the ancient cellars at the Tokaji Wine Trust. The future of the Tokay region itself has only just become clearer.

CONSUMER INFORMATION

WHAT DO I GET FOR MY MONEY?
The new-style table wines are excellent value. Tokaji is not cheap, but it can look inexpensive beside a bottle of Sauternes of equivalent quality.

AVAILABILITY
Most outlets will have some of the new table wines. Even Tokaji is not hard to find.

CONSUMER CHECKLIST
Furmint 2003   Quality 6 ★
(Disnókó)   Price 5 ★
                                  Value 6 ★

Good Years   The table wines should be drunk young. Only Tokaji can age, but at the moment, the producer is more important than the year.

Taste Notes   Tokaji ranges from dry to very sweet; the white table wines are dry and with plenty of fruit. Reds are vigorous.

The shores of Lake Balaton are popular with winemakers as well as with Hungarian holidaymakers. The wines from here tend to be rich and round.

ORGANIZATION
Tokaji has been the wine leading Hungary toward a brighter future. Western investment has had tremendous impact in the region and it is the only part of Eastern Europe to boast premium boutique wineries. Elsewhere in Hungary, flying winemakers have been making clean, fresh wines from grapes bought from growers and there is now a increasing band of young Hungarians keen to put their New World principles into practice, often helped by foreign investment. Best producers: **Arvay, Chapel Hill, Chateau Megyer, Chateau Pajzos, Disnókó, Atila Gere, GIA, Hétzóló, Hungarovin, Oremus, Istvan Szepsy, Szeremley** and **Royal Tokaji Wine Company**.

READING THE LABEL
This is easier than one might think, given that Hungarian is one of Europe's most difficult languages. Wines made with Western input tend to have Anglophone names, or at least a back label explaining it all. Most wines are varietals, and labelled as such.

WHAT DO THEY TASTE LIKE?
Tokaji from companies with Western investment is now a wonderful wine, all richness and complexity. Table wines from Furmint can have a marvellous smoky, dry fruit. Hungarian reds can be vigorous and full-bodied.

THE GOOD YEARS
So far, the wine produced each year has been better than in the one preceding it, with rising quality in the wineries and an increasing range of wines being exported far outweighing any vagaries of the weather. Table wines are best drunk young; Tokaji, however, ages very well in bottle.

ENJOYING THE WINES
The new-style wines are made to high standards and will match most foods. Tokay, since it is available in different degrees of sweetness, is a uniquely flexible dessert wine.

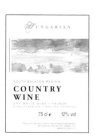

ROMANIA

It wasn't so very long ago that if you wanted to serve your friends Romanian Pinot Noir, you were best advised to decant it and hide the bottle. Nice wine, shame about the place. Romanian wine just wasn't something you could take seriously.

Well, that's all changing. Romanian wines are increasingly accepted as being both good and good value – but they're making an impact in a totally different way from, say, Hungarian wines. In Hungary you've got lots of foreign investment turning out wines tailor-made for export markets. In Romania there's less foreign input, and it was slower to arrive. Partly that was because the wineries were in more of a mess than in Hungary: foreign winemakers saw much less potential and more uphill struggle. Quality here is still more erratic. But when the wines are good they have a distinctive character that marks them out from any Australian-influenced product.

GRAPE VARIETIES AND WINE STYLES

There are plenty of international grape varieties, with Pinot Noir in great evidence. There is also lots of Cabernet Sauvignon and Merlot, Chardonnay and Sauvignon Blanc. Native varieties include the white Fetească and Grasă, and the Tămaîioasă, which makes individual sweet wines.

CLASSIFICATION

Wines are classified according to the ripeness of the grapes, rather on the German model. DOC wines come from a demarcated region. DOCG wines are the top quality wines.

ORGANIZATION

At the end of Communism in Romania vast collective farms were the rule. Privatization was set in motion, but has been slower here than elsewhere.

READING THE LABEL

Most wines sold abroad are varietals, and will state the grape name on the label. Tirnave is a cool-climate region in Transylvania, good for whites. Murfatlar is on the Black Sea coast and produces reds and sweet, late-harvest whites.

Plenty of Romanian families have made wine for generations but the legacy of Communism means that they have a lot of catching up to do.

WHAT DO THEY TASTE LIKE?

The reds are soft and jammy; the whites range from dry, crisp and often aromatic to intensely sweet and botrytis-affected.

ENJOYING THE WINES

The reds and dry whites go well with lighter foods, the sweet whites with puddings.

CONSUMER INFORMATION

WHAT DO I GET FOR MY MONEY?

Romanian wines are good value as well as having a distinctive style.

AVAILABILITY

Pretty good for Pinot Noir and some dry whites. The sweet wines are hard to find.

CONSUMER CHECKLIST

Dealul Mare Pinot Noir	*Quality 4* ★
2004	*Price 2* ★
	Value 7 ★

Good Years Drink the youngest Romanian wines available.
Taste Notes The reds are ripe and jammy without much tannin; and the whites are often aromatic, ranging from dry and crisp to sweet.

WESTERN BALKANS

Slovenia was the first of the republics of Yugoslavia to break away, in 1991, and the only one so far to establish any sort of independent reputation. Even so, it is still relatively unknown as a wine producer: that we are beginning to hear of Slovenia at all is because it joined the EU in 2004, and because some of its wines are good, although the potential for quality far outweighs most of what it is now being produced.

SLOVENIA

Most Slovenian wine is made in co-operatives, and while some of these are relatively careful about quality they don't have all the equipment they need to bring the wines up to a higher level. Private producers tend to be better equipped, particularly those in the west with vineyards over the border in Italy. Movement across the border was always easy even under Communism, and grapes grown in Italy could be sold for much-needed hard currency.

The centre of Slovenia is mostly flat and the vineyard areas are in the hills around the edge of the country adjacent to the borders with Austria, Italy, Croatia or Hungary. The region bordering Italy is called the **Littoral** or **Primorski**. It is an extension of the hills of Collio, and produces pretty similar wines: there is an acidic, tannic red from Refosco grapes, the best of which is called Kraski Teran, and other reds from Merlot, Barbera and both Cabernets. Whites are from Chardonnay, Pinot Blanc, Pinot Gris and, occasionally and deliciously, from Gelber Muskateller or Muscat à Petits Grains. There is also Tocai Friuliano and Picolit.

The **Sava Valley**, or **Posavski** region, stretches west from the Croatian border and makes whites from Sauvignon Blanc, Šipon (Furmint), Laski Rizling, Traminer, Pinot Blanc and others, and reds from Blaufränkisch, Cviček, Pinot Noir and Blauer Portugieser.

The **Drava Valley**, or **Podravski** region, is a continuation of the hills of Austria's Styria, and runs up to the Hungarian and Croatian borders. The whites are similar in style to those of Styria – light and fresh – and Laski Rizling from here can be excellent. The generally stale branded wines that have long been exported are no guide. There is also Traminer, Chardonnay and Pinot Blanc.

OTHER BALKAN WINES

All the states of the former Yugoslavia produced wine, although for obvious reasons we haven't seen much of it lately.

Croatia has two wine areas: Kontinentalna Hrvatska, the inland part along the river Drava, and Hrvatsko Primorje, bordering the Dalmatian coast. Inland the wine is mostly white; there are good reds from the coast, particularly those from the Plavac Mali grape.

Serbia used to produce a third of all Yugoslavian wine, and makes both red and white, of which the red is better – the native Prokupac is often blended with Pinot Noir and Gamay. Some of **Vojvodina**'s vineyards adjoin those of Croatia along the Danube Valley and produce similar styles. Others, near the town of Subotica and the Hungarian border, grow mostly Laski Rizling. In the south **Kosovo** makes mostly reds and in **Montenegro** the red Vranac grape, with its bitter cherry flavour, is the best bet. In **Bosnia-Herzegovina** there is both red and white, though, with its Muslim traditions, quantities have never been large. Warm **Macedonia** is better suited to producing table grapes than wine, though there is some decent red.

CONSUMER INFORMATION

WHAT DO I GET FOR MY MONEY?
Slovenian wines are not that cheap for their quality, though they can be good.

AVAILABILITY
Poor. Branded Laski Rizling is widely available, though it is not the best wine Slovenia has to offer.

CONSUMER CHECKLIST
Merlot, Provinces Illyriennes   *Quality 8* ★
(Slovenija Vino) 2004   *Price 6* ★
      Value 5 ★

Good Years   Drink the youngest vintage available.
Taste Notes   Most exported white wines are dry and slightly spicy. The reds should be lively and ripe.

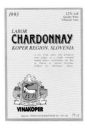

BULGARIA

How did it happen? How did Bulgaria burst on to the market back in the early 1980s, with those rich, soupy Cabernet Sauvignons thick with blackcurrant and vanilla flavours? And at those prices?

It was quite simple, really. Under Communism vast, rolling vineyards were planted in Bulgaria to service central wineries – as happened throughout Communist Eastern Europe. But then Pepsico, the American soft drink manufacturer, grew interested in selling their product east of the Iron Curtain and was less than enthusiastic about being paid in tractor parts. So it contacted the University of California at Davis, the main centre of viticultural study in the USA, and UCD became a prime advisor in the remaking of the Bulgarian wine industry. A product that would be saleable in the West was the aim – and it was achieved, in buckets. All that Cabernet Sauvignon. All that Merlot. But also all those dull, flat, often oxidized whites. How did the reds get so good, while the whites didn't?

The answer is that the improvement in Bulgarian wine was never uniform. The wineries whose reds we loved – **Suhindol**, **Sliven**, **Burgas**, **Preslav** and **Russe** among them – were the ones who were keen to change. Others weren't; many still aren't, even though privatization has begun and is continuing, and some wineries have been taken over by their managements. But the whites: well, they're still rarely good. They are better, sometimes. But I suppose the answer is that producing good, modern whites needs more technology, and even more investment, than producing good reds does. And that technology has been very patchily acquired.

GRAPE VARIETIES AND WINE STYLES
Cabernet Sauvignon is still the best-known Bulgarian wine, though now we've also seen good plummy Merlot, meaty Gamza, rich Mavrud and sturdy Melnik among the reds. But while those early Cabernets had several years age when they were released and trumpetted their crude, ripe flavours, somehow the well of sweetly, juicy grapes seems to have dried up. The old releases now generally lack heart and

Bulgarian wine-making today is full of contrasts – there are few substitutes for traditional pickers come the vintage, given the expense of harvesting machines.

guts and have a stale, dried-out feel to them. Efforts at a youthful 'fruit up-front' style are only intermittently successful since many wineries seem unwilling to make an effort for more than a few years in a row. But now Australian winemakers have begun to fetch up in Bulgaria and wineries like **Slavyantsi**, **Stork Nest** and **Vini Sliven** are learning the New World way and reinventing themselves.

The best of the whites were, until recently, usually from **Khan Krum** or **Varna** in the Eastern Region, though by no means everything from these wineries was particularly attractive. Popular white grapes include Chardonnay, Sauvignon Blanc, Riesling, Aligoté, Rkatsiteli, Dimiat and Misket.

The country is parcelled out into five wine regions. The **Northern Region** or Danube Plain makes reds and whites, of which the reds are the better; the Suhindol, Russe and Svishtov wineries are here. The **Eastern Region**, whose climate is moderated by the Black Sea, is white wine country; Khan Krum and Varna are both here. In the **Southern Region**, the Thracian Plain, the best-known wines are the reds of Plovdiv and Assenovgrad. The hot **South-Western Region** is also better for reds than whites, mainly from Melnik. And in the centre the mountainous **Sub-Balkan Region** is the home of the Sliven winery, Bulgaria's largest producer, making Cabernet, Merlot, Chardonnay and others in large quantities.

If the finished wines are to meet increasingly discriminating Western tastes, there must be investment in equipment, as here at Sliven winery.

CLASSIFICATION

Bulgaria has four quality categories and the system works reasonably well. Country Wines are, as the name suggests, roughly equivalent to France's Vins de Pays. They come from denominated regions and from grape varieties that can be named on the label. Varietal wine comes from a single grape variety only, from one of 43 geographical regions, and adheres to stricter rules.

Reserve or Special Reserve wines are superior varietal wines which have had longer aging (at least two years for whites and three for reds) and by no means always an advantage. One of Bulgaria's main problems is too much enthusiasm for long oak aging. The top category is Controliran wines. These come from a particular grape variety in a particular region; there are 27 Controliran wines.

ORGANIZATION

Under Communism the Bulgarian wine industry was structured around central wineries in each region – so Suhindol is both the name of a region and the winery from which all that region's wine came. Since 1989 there has been some privatization and a few estate wines are now making their way abroad.

READING THE LABEL

Labelling of Bulgarian wine is by grape variety. Different wineries produce different styles, but the quality is not always consistent and wineries can and do rise and fall in the quality stakes. So be open minded.

WHAT DO THEY TASTE LIKE?

The local Bulgarian market still loves the old-fashioned reds. That rich, soupy flavour of the early Cabernet Sauvignons is much thinner now, but many reds are still reasonably good and fruity. The whites are too variable for comfort.

THE GOOD YEARS

Drink the younger wines: the old red wines can be dried out.

ENJOYING THE WINES

Drink Bulgarian reds at any time, with just about anything: people have even been known to pass them off as red Bordeaux. I'm not sure the wines are good enough for this any more. Most whites are simply substitutes for when you can't find something better.

CONSUMER INFORMATION

WHAT DO I GET FOR MY MONEY?

Still good value. Okay, prices have risen since those early days and quality has become a bit more mixed, but there are still terrific bargains to be had, particularly among the young reds. The whites are less good value, simply because they're not, on the whole, particularly good.

AVAILABILITY

Pretty well universal. Very few wine shops don't stock any Bulgarian wine.

CONSUMER CHECKLIST

Country Red Cabernet/Merlot (Russe)

Quality 5 ★
Price 2 ★
Value 7 ★

Good Years Vintage variation isn't really a factor with Bulgarian wines. But drink fairly young wines if you want juicy fruit: wines more than three or four years old (which are often more expensive anyway) are frequently dried out and fruitless.

Taste Notes The Cabernets have good vanilla and blackcurrant fruit; the Merlots and Mavruds are plummy and rich, Melnik is good sturdy stuff and Gamza is attractively fruity when young, but ages well. Chardonnay at its best is fresh and often oaky, but that is a rare best. Few other whites are clean and fresh enough, though some young Country whites have a certain musky attraction.

EAST MEDITERRANEAN

The higher you climb the further you fall. There's every reason to believe that the cradle of our wine civilization was in the Middle East, and Greek wine was once the most famous in the world. But all that was a long, long time ago.

GRAPE VARIETIES AND WINE STYLES

Wine is still a staple drink in some of these countries – **Greece**, for example, where there is a slow but steady increase in standards as well as a welcome attempt at making fresher wines with native grapes rather than turning to the more international varieties.

Obviously, there's retsina (resinated white and rosé wine) which can be deliciously oily and piny, especially if it's young and fresh. But there are also unresinated wines from such grapes as the black Xynomavro, Agiorgitiko, Cabernet Sauvignon, Merlot and others, and the white Assyrtiko, Athiri, Robola, Mosofilero, Savatiano (which is the base of most retsina) and Muscat, as well as international grapes like Sauvignon Blanc. The sweet Muscats of Samos are tremendous; other appellations to look for include the red Naoussa and Nemea. Best producers: **Aidarinis**, **Argyros**, **Antonopoulos**, **Gentilini**, **Gerovassiliou**, **Hatzimichali**, **Kyr Yanni**, **Lazaridi**, **Mercouri**, **Papaioannou**, **Strofilia** and **Tselepos**.

In **Turkey** the vine is still vitally important, but for table grapes and concentrate, not for wine. Just three per cent of the grape harvest is turned into wine, and the results are – let's say – not attuned to foreign palates. The reds and rosés are robust though lacking in fruit (Buzbag is the most famous) and the whites are best avoided. Best producers: **Diren**, **Doluca**, **Kavaklidere** and **Turassan**.

Cyprus, half Greek and half Turkish, is a large producer of wine. Much of it used to be exported to the USSR, and much of the rest was cheap fortified wine sold as Cyprus 'sherry', a name which is now illegal. **Commandaria**, a sticky brown fortified, has centuries of fame but not a lot to recommend it now. **Keo**'s Othello and Aphrodite, and Semeli from **Etko**, are seen abroad. A three-year restructuring plan and EU membership in 2004 should help raise standards.

For years Lebanon was revered by all wine lovers for one reason: **Chateau Musar**. This red is blended from Cabernet Sauvignon and Cinsaut and ages for years to reach a supple, chocolaty complexity; the white is Obaideh and Merweh (which might be Chardonnay and Sauvignon Blanc respectively). The wines from the **Kefraya**, **Ksara** and **Massaya** wineries are also good and quality has much improved in recent years.

Israel's top winery, **Golan Heights**, is unfortunately located in a region which looks likely to be handed over to Syria. Admittedly, they could build a winery somewhere else, but Israel's best grapes have long come from here. The Yarden and Gamla labels are the best; grapes include Chardonnay, Sauvignon Blanc, Muscat, Merlot and Cabernet. These are kosher wines but of international quality, and have inspired **Carmel**, Israel's biggest producer, to invest in modernization. **Castel** and **Yarden** are also good.

CLASSIFICATION

Greece has 28 appellations of origin (AOs). Twenty of these are Appellations of Superior Quality (OPAP) for dry wines and the remainder are Controlled Appellations of Origin (OPE) for sweet wines. Réserve or Grande Réserve indicate wines that have had more aging. Vins de Pays (the French term is often used) obey more flexible rules.

Vines growing by the Sea of Galilee in Israel. Under kosher rules vineyards must be left fallow every seventh year.

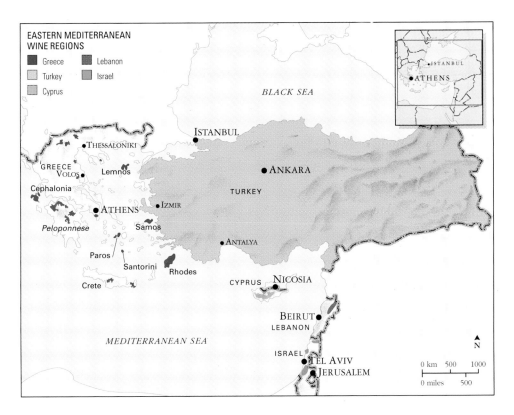

EASTERN MEDITERRANEAN
WINE REGIONS

- Greece
- Turkey
- Cyprus
- Lebanon
- Israel

BLACK SEA

ISTANBUL
THESSALONIKI
GREECE
VOLOS Lemnos
Cephalonia
ATHENS Izmir
Peloponnese Samos
Paros
Santorini Rhodes
Crete

ANKARA
TURKEY
ANTALYA
CYPRUS NICOSIA
BEIRUT
LEBANON
MEDITERRANEAN SEA
ISRAEL TEL AVIV
JERUSALEM

N

0 km 500 1000
0 miles 500

Cyprus has six delimited wine regions, some with sub-regions. Turkey has a quality wine scheme used for the top wines, from the main, state-owned producer. Israel has five wine regions, some with sub-regions.

READING THE LABEL
The most important piece of information, since standards are so erratic in this part of the world, is the name of the producer.

WHAT DO THEY TASTE LIKE?
There is a characteristic East Mediterranean flavour to the reds: they tend to be sturdy and tannic with some spice but also some decay. They may have some fruit. Whites stand up less well to the hot climate and old-fashioned wine-making. Except from the best producers these wines are flat and lacking in acidity.

THE GOOD YEARS
There is little vintage variation. Whites should be drunk young, but some reds, in particular Musar and the best Greek reds, age well.

ENJOYING THE WINES
Both red and white wines suit highly flavoured, garlicky food of the sort found all over the Eastern Mediterranean and you'll enjoy them more in situ. Drink retsina with Greek cheeses and classic meat dishes.

CONSUMER INFORMATION

WHAT DO I GET FOR MY MONEY?
The good wines are good value. Chateau Musar, in particular, is a bargain.

AVAILABILITY
Mixed. Chateau Musar is widely available abroad, as is retsina, but other Greek wines are now becoming easier to find.

CONSUMER CHECKLIST
Chateau Musar 1994   *Quality* 7 ★
Price 7 ★
Value 7 ★

Good Years There is little vintage variation from year to year. Many East Mediterranean reds will age (red Musar is supposed to be drunk at 15 years old) but the whites are best drunk young.
Taste Notes East Mediterranean reds are sturdy and spicy; the white wines at their best are fresh.

USA

Almost all of the United States' 50 states produce wine. Sometimes it's world-class, world-beating wine; sometimes it's of local interest only and seldom strays beyond the nearest town, far less the state boundary. Yet this was the country in which, from 1919 to 1933, the manufacture, sale or transportation of alcohol was illegal. How has this extraordinary volte-face come about? Where is it leading? And how far is the United States influenced by wine-making in other countries, and how much is it doing the influencing? These are the questions that fascinate me about wine in the USA at the moment. So I'm going to take a trip from coast to coast to try and find out.

One of the USA's great vinous achievements has been to take the classic wine styles of Europe and give them a new character. Domaine Mumm (left) in California makes sparkling wine that is often better than the Champagne of its parent company, Champagne Mumm in France; Frog's Leap Winery in the Napa Valley (above) grows good Merlot.

WINE REGIONS

As far as we can judge, there have always been vines in North America. Lief Ericsson, the Viking explorer, found wild vines in profusion when he landed on the north-east coast and named it Vinland; several hundred years later, the colonists of Virginia and Carolina set about making wine out of them.

They failed. Well, no, they didn't fail. The grapes fermented and turned into wine. But the wine didn't taste like anything those colonists could recognize as wine.

So as early as 1619 cuttings from European vines were used. They rooted and they grew; and then they died. It happened every time. Wine made from the native grapes didn't taste particularly nice; yet European vines turned up their toes. What those early colonists were seeing was a rehearsal of what was to happen in Europe, centuries later.

Wines from the native grapes didn't taste the same as European wines because the vines were of different species. European grape vines are *Vitis vinifera*; those native to north America are of various species, particularly *Vitis labrusca*. They lived where European vines could not because they were immune to a minute insect that during a phase of its life cycle lives on the vine roots and sucks the life out of them. The European vines, faced with this louse (later named *Phylloxera vastatrix*) had no natural immunity and succumbed.

When European vines were first planted on the West Coast, however, they lived. Those first plantings were of Mission grapes, tended by missionaries. But phylloxera in due course spread across the continent, and was spotted in California in 1873, just ten years after its first appearance in France.

However, North America, having exported the pest to the world, was also able to supply the cure. Rootstocks from those very vines whose wine had so disgusted the early colonists are now used, specially bred, all over the world, and European vines are grafted on to them.

Vitis labrusca grapes are still used for wine on the eastern seaboard and in some of the southern states, where the climate is problematical for vinifera vines. In New England it can be painfully cold in the winter for vinifera vines, although they are on the increase. In the south the problem is the opposite: too much heat and humidity in the summer, too little chill in the winter. So when I say that wine is made in almost all the states of the USA, I don't necessarily mean wine on the French model of Cabernet Sauvignon, Pinot Noir and Chardonnay. To find these vines – and indeed to find the wines with which the USA has made her international reputation – you will have to look in only a few places.

First and foremost, there's California. The Gold Rush of 1849 kick-started the vinous careers of the Napa and Sonoma Valleys, and the hotter San Joaquin Valley, further east. Then there's Oregon, where viticulture only really got started as late as the 1970s, was hyped too early and is now fighting to hold on to its reputation of being the USA's prime source of Pinot Noir. Washington State is just as young, indeed still young enough to warrant the label of 'emerging'. And then on the East Coast there's New York State, where the growers are beginning to find ways round their climate.

But I've jumped an awful lot of time. It wasn't all plain sailing between the conquest of phylloxera and the time when California wines started to take us all by storm. There was the little matter of Prohibition, when between 1919 and 1933 alcohol actually became an illegal drug in the USA.

The acreage of land under vine actually increased during Prohibition. It sounds daft, but there you are. Grape-growing wasn't forbidden, only the manufacture of wine – and even that wasn't actually forbidden if you did it in the privacy of your own home, using yeast and bought grape concentrate or even bought fresh grapes. Some commercial winemaking was allowed, too, for altar wine. Even so, from producing 55 million gallons of wine just before Prohibition, the USA produced only 3.5 million gallons in 1925. And this wasn't wine designed to tickle the palates of connoisseurs. Instead it was cheap and alcoholic and produced from inferior grapes. There was a lot of Alicante Bouschet and Thompson Seedless grown, neither of which is usually allowed near a serious winery. In order to survive (and most wineries didn't) wineries had to give up all thought of making decent wine. It was a period that did nothing to train the national palate.

After Repeal came the Depression and World War Two, so not until the 1970s did a new, revivified California wine industry start to take shape; and then it hit the headlines almost immediately. In 1976, at a blind wine tasting in Paris, Chateau Montelena Chardonnay 1973 beat top white Burgundies into a

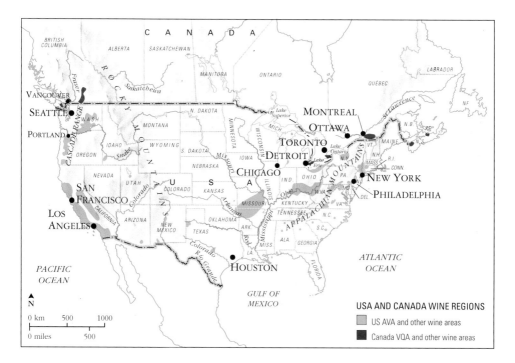

USA AND CANADA WINE REGIONS
- US AVA and other wine areas
- Canada VQA and other wine areas

cocked hat. Stag's Leap Cabernet Sauvignon 1973 did the same for the reds, beating leading red Bordeaux (to the apoplectic fury of the French). California wine was on its way. It hasn't looked back since.

CLASSIFICATION

An official classification of any sort is a new and still controversial idea in the American wine industry. In the early days no-one knew or cared where a bottle of wine came from – or how it was labelled. If it was white it might be called 'Chablis' or 'Sauternes', if it was red, then it must be 'claret' or 'burgundy'. If it was fizzy it was 'Champagne'.

Such borrowings are all very well for a local, infant industry, but when, in the 1970s, California wine grew serious and American wine began to hold its own at international level, a better system was needed. Accordingly, the first home-grown legislation came in 1983 with the introduction of the first American Viticultural Areas, or AVAs.

Based, like French Appellations Contrôlées, on topography, climate and soil types, AVAs do not attempt, unlike their European counterparts, to regulate grape varieties, wine-making methods or vineyard yields. They are thus purely an indication of origin. It is highly debatable whether most AVAs have their own identifiable character: from the consumer's point of view the name of the producer is probably a surer guide. There are now nearly 150 AVAs, of which more than half are in California.

MAJOR LABELLING REQUIREMENTS

Grape variety Varietal labelling is most common in the United States. If a variety is named on the label then 75 per cent of the blend must be of that variety. In Oregon the figure is 90 per cent, with an exception being made for Cabernet Sauvignon, where a minimum of 75 per cent is permitted to allow for Bordeaux-type blends which commonly use this variety.

Region of origin The winery and region of origin also appear on the label. If an AVA is named on the label, then 85 per cent of the grapes in the wine, regardless of variety, must come from that AVA. If a county is named, the minimum figure is the same. If the wine is a varietal 75 per cent of the named variety must come from the named AVA. (AVAs and counties do not generally coincide.) If the label simply names a state, then 100 per cent of the wine must come from that state. At the most basic level if the source is given simply as 'America', then the wine can be a blend of grapes from two or more states.

Health warning These have to be displayed not just on the label but also, prominently, in the winery (puritanical values die hard). The presence of sulphites must be stated on the label: sulphur dioxide, used as a preservative and anti-oxidant in wine-making, is a sulphite. Labels also must warn pregnant women or those in charge of heavy machinery against the consumption of the contents.

CALIFORNIA

It's not always hot in California. If it were it would not be possible to make fine wine there – not really fine wine of the type that we see from Napa, Sonoma, Carneros, Santa Barbara and elsewhere. What you need for this sort of wine is a long, cool ripening season of the sort found in the great European wine regions. What you don't need is baking heat, day after day after day.

But with modern high-technology wine-making methods, including cool fermentation, it is perfectly possible to produce good wine – attractive, everyday wine with fruit and freshness and no pretensions to anything more – from baking hot climates, too. That's the other thing California does so well: produce good, cheap everyday wine. Most of this comes from further inland, where south of Stockton the sun roasts the vast San Joaquin Valley. This used to be entirely fortified wine

country, and some impressive fortifieds are still made here. But if you want to see the scale of the California wine industry, this is the place to look. The huge Gallo corporation produces more wine here than is made in many decent-sized wine-producing *nations*! It's hardly memorable stuff, but it is generally sound. That's the flip side of California wine.

And the styles of wine: do they still imitate European prototypes? Well, they do and they don't. At the level of sophistication and quality of the best wines, imitation is no longer the word. The grapes are usually the classic grapes of Europe, and most good winemakers here take the great European wines as their lodestar, at least at first. But there are definite Californian styles, definite Californian ways of doing things. And European producers, particularly from Champagne, have been buying land and building their own wineries here.

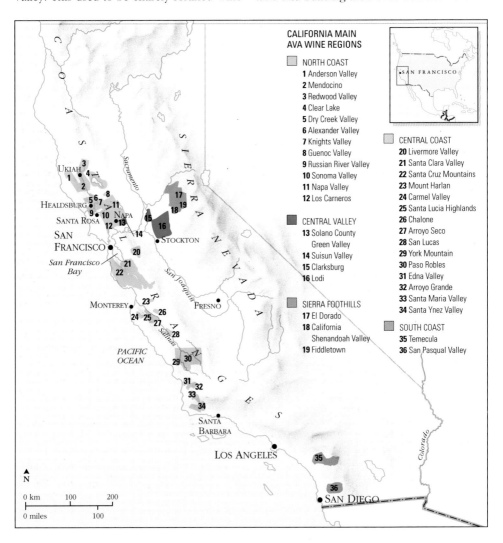

CALIFORNIA MAIN AVA WINE REGIONS

NORTH COAST
1 Anderson Valley
2 Mendocino
3 Redwood Valley
4 Clear Lake
5 Dry Creek Valley
6 Alexander Valley
7 Knights Valley
8 Guenoc Valley
9 Russian River Valley
10 Sonoma Valley
11 Napa Valley
12 Los Carneros

CENTRAL VALLEY
13 Solano County Green Valley
14 Suisun Valley
15 Clarksburg
16 Lodi

SIERRA FOOTHILLS
17 El Dorado
18 California Shenandoah Valley
19 Fiddletown

CENTRAL COAST
20 Livermore Valley
21 Santa Clara Valley
22 Santa Cruz Mountains
23 Mount Harlan
24 Carmel Valley
25 Santa Lucia Highlands
26 Chalone
27 Arroyo Seco
28 San Lucas
29 York Mountain
30 Paso Robles
31 Edna Valley
32 Arroyo Grande
33 Santa Maria Valley
34 Santa Ynez Valley

SOUTH COAST
35 Temecula
36 San Pasqual Valley

NORTHERN CALIFORNIA

One of California's characteristics – in fact probably the most important one as far as wine grape-growers are concerned, is the way the climate can change from hot to cool within just a few miles. The reason is geography: cool Pacific fogs sweep in through gaps in the coastal mountain ranges to cool the valleys – but only where they can reach. If the mountains are too dense, if there are no river valleys to allow them passage, then the fogs stay where they are and the vineyards heat up under the hot Californian sun. In Mendocino and Lake counties, on California's north coast, there are areas where the fog makes the days as cool as in northern Europe. Conversely, there are other parts where the fog cannot reach, and where the grapes planted must be those suited to hot climates.

MENDOCINO COUNTY

This is a microcosm of California's climatic extremes. At the cool end of the scale – well, the cold end of the scale, to be honest – there are sparkling wine companies busy making the **Anderson Valley** AVA one of the United States' best areas for fizz. When Roederer Estate, an offshoot of the Champagne house Roederer, decided to set up a US operation, it hunted high and low for somewhere as chilly as Champagne. It found it here, in Anderson Valley. It's a small, hilly area where it's not possible to plant many vines on the flat land, because there isn't much flat land, and most of the grapes grow in the chilliest parts, cooled by Pacific fogs.

The grapes grown for sparkling wines are usually Chardonnay and Pinot Noir – Pinot doesn't often get sufficiently ripe here to make serious red wine, but it's terrific for fizz. There's Gewürztraminer and Riesling, as well, both of which relish the cool climate.

But then, where the hills rear high above the fog line, something else happens: Zinfandel is planted here, some of the vineyards dating back to the original plantings by Italian immigrants at the end of the nineteenth century. These Zinfandels are big, strapping wines, full of spice and blackberry fruit and tannin, ripened by fog-free sunny summers. Mendocino Ridge is a newer AVA covering vineyards in western Mendocino located above 365m (1200ft).

In **McDowell Valley** AVA, a tiny area just east of the large **Mendocino** AVA, the sun also shines. It shines enough for the red Rhône varieties of Syrah and Grenache, and

Mendocino County produces a huge variety of styles of wine. These vineyards are in the hills near Hopland at the southern end of the county.

the Californian speciality of Zinfandel, to flourish. **Potter Valley** and **Redwood Valley** AVAs are likewise warm and grow good Zinfandel, Syah and Cabernet. Most wines are labelled Mendocino or Anderson Valley. Best producers: **Edmeades**, **Fetzer**, **Fife**, **Greenwood Ridge**, **Handley**, **Lazy Creek**, **Mariah**, **McDowell Valley**, **Navarro**, **Roederer**, **Scharffenberger** and **Steele**.

LAKE COUNTY

Across the Mayacamas Mountains from Mendocino Lake County was planted with vines in the nineteenth century, but Prohibition sealed their fate and wine was not made here again until the 1970s. Days here are warm and nights cool, and the long growing season favours Sauvignon Blanc and Cabernet Sauvignon; the latter is usually soft and ripe and made for early consumption. **Clear Lake** AVA is the main wine region, and the vineyards are mostly tucked in between the water and the hills to the west. There are few wineries here, though, as is common in California, a lot of the grapes are shipped to wineries elsewhere, often in Sonoma or Mendocino. Further south, **Guenoc Valley** AVA is tiny. **Fetzer** grows good Cabernet here; high-altitudes mean that cool nights can lengthen the growing season and keep the acid levels attractively high while the grapes ripen.

SONOMA

Now we're coming into the big time. Sonoma may not have quite the fame or pzazz of Napa, but at times it runs a close second and some of California's finest wines come from here.

Sonoma County is also important historically: Franciscan missionaries were the first to plant vines here, in 1825, and when the Mexican government secularized the area not long after, General Mariano Vallejo (after whom the town of Vallejo is named) took over the vineyards. In addition, near the old town of Sonoma is the site of Buena Vista Vineyards, where the Hungarian Agoston Haraszthy is generally reckoned to have introduced to California the great European grape varieties of Cabernet Sauvignon, Pinot Noir, Chardonnay, Riesling and dozens of others, which have since made California wine world famous.

Buena Vista means 'Beautiful View' in Spanish, and the Sonoma Valley, with the Mayacamas mountains running like a spine up the eastern flank, is a very beautiful area. A short way out of the town of Sonoma, Hanzell Winery, constructed to look like Burgundy's Clos de Vougeot, has a view of San Francisco which would make any property developer drool. Indeed, the beauty of the region and the proximity to San Francisco have already had an effect: property prices are sky-high, and it is difficult for many grape-growers to resist selling their land for urban development.

Sonoma style, though, is still different from Napa style. Napa is all fancy architecture and chi-chi restaurants; Sonoma is more relaxed, less smart. And whereas Napa is a sea of vines that lie carefully manicured all over the flat valley floor, Sonoma is more mixed. It looks more genuinely rural.

In general, too, the wines, both red and white, lack the intensity, the massive grandeur of the wines from the Napa. But that is no bad thing, because they make up for it with some of the most approachable, richly perfumed fruit in California.

GRAPE VARIETIES AND WINE STYLES

As always in California, the climate is the major deciding factor in the style of the wine. And the deciding factor in the climate is the topography: whether the cool Pacific fogs can find a way through the coastal hills to take the heat off the vineyards. Where they can, lighter, more elegant wines, often from cool-climate grape varieties, can be grown. Where they can't, the wine is robust, and altogether sturdier stuff.

The coolest parts of Sonoma are in the south. San Pablo Bay brings the fog right to the feet of the vines. I'll deal with **Carneros** separately (see page 268), but even just over its northern border good Pinot Noir and Chardonnay is grown in **Sonoma Valley** AVA. Go northwards up the valley and the climate warms as the influence of the Bay wanes, but many of the vines are grown on the steep valley sides, so sometimes altitude can provide coolness where the fog cannot. If the vines go even higher, above the fog line, then well-structured, long-lived Cabernet Sauvignon and Zinfandel can be grown. The Mayacamas mountains provide plenty of good sites of this sort, and so does the AVA of **Sonoma Mountain**.

Russian River Valley AVA is also cool, though here the coolness is provided by the

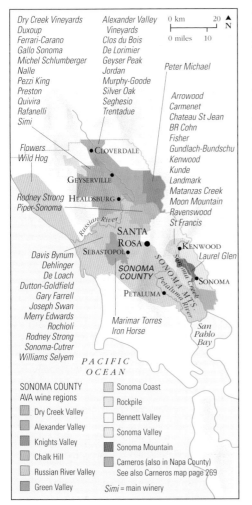

Dry Creek Vineyards
Duxoup
Ferrari-Carano
Gallo Sonoma
Michel Schlumberger
Nalle
Pezzi King
Preston
Quivira
Rafanelli
Simi

Alexander Valley Vineyards
Clos du Bois
De Lorimier
Geyser Peak
Jordan
Murphy-Goode
Silver Oak
Seghesio
Trentadue

Peter Michael

Arrowood
Carmenet
Chateau St Jean
BR Cohn
Fisher
Gundlach-Bundschu
Kenwood
Kunde
Landmark
Matanzas Creek
Moon Mountain
Ravenswood
St Francis

Flowers
Wild Hog

Rodney Strong
Piper-Sonoma

Davis Bynum
Dehlinger
De Loach
Dutton-Goldfield
Gary Farrell
Joseph Swan
Merry Edwards
Rochioli
Rodney Strong
Sonoma-Cutrer
Williams Selyem

Marimar Torres
Iron Horse

0 km 20
0 miles 10

CLOVERDALE
GEYSERVILLE
HEALDSBURG
Russian River
SANTA ROSA
SEBASTOPOL
KENWOOD
Laurel Glen
SONOMA COUNTY
SONOMA M'TS
SONOMA
PETALUMA
Sonoma Creek
Petaluma River
San Pablo Bay

PACIFIC OCEAN

SONOMA COUNTY
AVA wine regions

- Dry Creek Valley
- Alexander Valley
- Knights Valley
- Chalk Hill
- Russian River Valley
- Green Valley

- Sonoma Coast
- Rockpile
- Bennett Valley
- Sonoma Valley
- Sonoma Mountain
- Carneros (also in Napa County)
  See also Carneros map page 269

Simi = main winery

Pacific fogs, like this one blanketing vineyards in the Sonoma Valley, cause producers who want to make cool-climate wines to rub their hands with glee.

river valley itself, which heads more or less west towards the Pacific, and so cuts through the sheltering hills. There is lovely Pinot Noir here, plus Merlot, Chardonnay and Gewürztraminer. It used to be planted with Zinfandel, Petite Sirah and other hot-climate varieties; only with the change to more suitable grapes has it proved its worth – although it can, in places, produce tremendous Zinfandel.

The area gets its name because Russians established a fort and trading post nearby. Much of the land here is valley floor, and the area has traditionally been a major supplier to the jug wine market – **E & J Gallo**, the USA's biggest wine producer, still uses Russian River wine to improve its blends as well as to release a new Sonoma label. Yet, as always, the most interesting wines are being made on the hillside vineyards, or in the little side valleys. **Korbel**, which makes one of California's original sparkling wines, is established in the Redwood forests as the Russian River twines down to the Pacific Ocean; **Iron Horse**, producer of some of California's best sparkling wine, is in the foothills of the **Green Valley** AVA, while **Matanzas Creek** is making delicious reds and whites in the Bennett Valley, east of Santa Rosa.

Sonoma-Green Valley AVA is one of two sub-AVAs in the Russian River Valley AVA: it perches at the western end of Russian River Valley AVA, and is just that little bit cooler than the larger region. **Chalk Hill** AVA, the other, is small and cool, and grows mainly Chardonnay and Sauvignon Blanc.

Go north of Healdsburg, and you begin to realize that you are no longer in a cool region. There is only patchy fog here. Chardonnay and Sauvignon Blanc flourish in the **Alexander Valley** AVA, but so do Cabernet Sauvignon and Zinfandel, and Rhône varieties like Grenache and Syrah, so it grows just about anything the producers care to throw at it.

Much the same could be said of **Dry Creek Valley** AVA, although here it is pretty clear that Zinfandel ought to be given the pride of place it deserves. The Zinfandels from here are tremendous, brawny and ripe wines. Inevitably, though, given the demand, there is a lot of Cabernet Sauvignon planted, even though there are just as good Cabernets from elsewhere in California; top Zinfandel is far more of a rarity to be cherished.

One of the places where good Cabernet Sauvignon is to be found is in the small AVA of **Knights Valley**. **Beringer Vineyards** was

the first to spot the potential of this compact site; others have since followed.

Sonoma Coast AVA covers all sorts of odds and ends that have no particular reason to be joined together in a single AVA, except that a number of growers wanted them to be. The initial spur to create the AVA was political – big companies were trying to protect their right to use 'estate-bottled' on wines that were blended from large areas of Sonoma. However, the Sonoma Coastal region proved to have a number of brilliant sites for cool climate wines, and some of California's top Pinot Noirs and Chardonnays now sport the Sonoma Coast AVA. **Northern Sonoma** AVA, on the other hand, includes all of Sonoma except for Sonoma Valley itself. **E & J Gallo** use it on a lot of their labels. Best producers: **Arrowood, Alexander Valley Vineyards, Buena Vista, Carmenet, Chateau St Jean, Clos du Bois, B R Cohn, De Loach, Dehlinger, Dry Creek Vineyards, Dutton-Goldfield, Duxoup, Ferrari-Carano, Fisher, Gallo Sonoma, Gary Farrell, Geyser Peak, Gundlach-Bundschu, Iron Horse, Jordan, Kistler, Kunde, Laurel Glen, Matanzas Creek, Merry Edwards, Murphy-Goode, Nalle, Preston, Quivira, Rafanelli, Rochioli, St Francis, Seghesio, Silver Oak, Simi, Sonoma-Cutrer, Rodney Strong, Joseph Swan, Marimar Torres, Trentadue** and **Williams Selyem**.

Wild mustard blooming between the rows of still dormant vines is a common sight in early spring in northern California, here in Alexander Valley.

CLASSIFICATION

There is no official classification beyond the AVA system, but that's quite complicated enough here. The AVAs lie three or four deep in places: there is Northern Sonoma AVA, Sonoma-Green Valley AVA, Sonoma Mountain AVA, Sonoma Valley AVA and Sonoma Coast AVA, to name but a few.

ORGANIZATION

In California anything goes. You can grow grapes and sell them to a winemaker, or you can sell your own wine from your own grapes, either at the cellar door to passing trade or else worldwide. There are wineries of all styles and sizes here.

READING THE LABEL

These AVAs are all very well, but the amount of climatic variation within each one means that the name of the producer and the price of the bottle tell you far more about the probable quality of the wine. In California the appellation doesn't have the same influence on price that it does in Europe; instead the price indicates the producer's ambitions for the wine and where he or she sees its position in the market.

WHAT DO THEY TASTE LIKE?

Sonoma wines don't have quite such dramatic flavours as Napa's, but it is gradually becoming clearer which grapes do best where. Cabernet Sauvignon is often softer than the Napa equivalent, the best having a gorgeous juicy flavour, mixing blackcurrant fruit with lovely minty and eucalyptus perfume and some soft buttery oak. Zinfandel ranges from soft and gulpable to massive bramble and pepper styles. Coastal Pinot Noir is scented and seductive. Chardonnay is everywhere in Sonoma and can be delightfully savoury. Sauvignon Blanc can be zingy and grassy. There is excellent Champagne-method fizz of ever-greater finesse.

THE GOOD YEARS

There is more vintage variation in the cooler south of the county than in the warmer north, and Sonoma and Napa follow broadly the same pattern.

2004 One of the earliest harvests in decades in parts of Sonoma. Quality initially rated as excellent but could be patchy.

2003 High quality wines with good colour and flavour. Russian River Chardonnay especially good. Low yields.

2002 First rate Pinot Noir and Chardonnay, especially from Russian River.

2001 Good quality and big reds such as Cabernet and Zinfandel did best.

2000 A good, ripe crop. Pinot Noir and Chardonnay did better than Cabernet.

1999 Those who delayed picking made the best wine.

1998 An undersized crop of irregular quality.

1997 A very big harvest but not a great year.

1996 Small, variable crop.

1995 A good to very good vintage.

ENJOYING THE WINES

Most Sonoma wines have a freshness and a soft edge which makes them very suitable for drinking on their own. Even the reds are often made in a fruity, gulpable style. However, they have enough interest to partner strongly flavoured fish and meat dishes. The heftier, old-style Zinfandels positively demand the spicy, mouthfilling San Francisco cuisine.

CONSUMER INFORMATION

WHAT DO I GET FOR MY MONEY?

On the whole, the wines from Sonoma are fair value; the only problem is produced by exchange rates, which have an uncomfortable habit of making California wines seem rather expensive when they are exported to other countries.

Some wineries, notably Sonoma-Cutrer and Jordan, do charge high prices, but don't forget that California producers, if they decide to produce top-quality wines, don't stint on the investment or on the tiny, expensive details of grape-growing and wine-making that make the difference. There are plenty of lower-priced, more everyday wines from Parducci, River Oaks, Glen Ellen, Buena Vista and many others.

AVAILABILITY

This is good on the West Coast of the USA, but less consistent elsewhere. However, increasing interest in California wines generally on export markets means that most good outlets will stock some wine from Sonoma.

CONSUMER CHECKLIST

Dutton Ranch Chardonnay 2003 (Kistler)	*Quality 9* ★ *Price 10* ★ *Value 8* ★
Zinfandel 2001 (Ravenswood)	*Quality 8* ★ *Price 8* ★ *Value 8* ★

Good Years 2004, 2003, 2002, 2001, 2000, 1999, 1997, 1995.

Taste Notes Sonoma wines are often more subtle than their Napa equivalents, with softer, more approachable flavours. Some of California's best, spiciest Zinfandel comes from Dry Creek Valley AVA and some of the best Pinot Noir from Russian River AVA. There is good rich Cabernet Sauvignon and fresh, grassy Sauvignon Blanc from all over Sonoma. Chardonnay ranges from elegant and Burgundian in style to much fatter and oakier but it always manages to keep a soft, balanced core to the fruit.

NAPA

That's all it takes to conjure up a picture of world-class Cabernet Sauvignon or Chardonnay: just one word. Napa. And I don't mean the town of Napa, sitting at the south of the Napa Valley, just where it shades into Carneros. Nor do I mean Napa County, although it covers much of the same ground. I mean Napa Valley, a short, curving strip of some of the most valuable vineyard land in the world, stretching from the north of San Francisco Bay up to the snow-capped peak of Mount St Helena. In some places it's less than a mile wide, yet it is this patch of land that

forged the modern California wine industry, and which acted as the magnet that drew money, ambition and genius from other walks of life. It still sets standards against which not only the rest of California but also the rest of the world have to measure up.

The old Indian name for the Napa was 'Valley of Plenty', and on reaching the mouth of the valley, less than two hours' drive north from San Francisco, that plenty is vividly illustrated. The valley is about 5km (3 miles) wide here, and is a tightly meshed carpet of vines.

The Napa Valley was the obvious starting point for any fledgling winemaker, because its climate had long been considered ideal for viticulture – apart from some frost dangers, it had average rainfall, rich soil and a very long, reliable ripening period of hot but not sweltering days. These conditions make for pretty regular crops of perfect grapes, which allow the winemakers to exercise all their skills on moulding the grapes into their own personal styles of wine.

The styles that were to rocket the Napa to stardom began to appear in the 1970s. They were usually of a quite startling depth of flavour, both reds and whites having enormous personalities, tremendously impressive, though not always greatly refreshing. You couldn't fail to notice them – but at the same time they called to mind the old European adage that to make the best wine, the vine must suffer. The grapes must struggle to ripen. The vine must be forced to push its roots deep into unnutritious soil to find what nourishment it can. On the floor of the Napa Valley this struggle does not exist.

However, the Napa Valley is a freak flat spot in a very mountainous area. In the 1960s and 1970s, many winemakers did begin to find their wines a little too fat and ripe, and all the best recent vineyards have been established in the wooded mountains above the valley floor. It's cooler there and the soil isn't good – so vines do have to struggle. And of course, this being northern California, it's cool at the southern end of the valley, where the Pacific fog rolls in day after day, lowering the temperature. In the north, where the fog peters out, the climate is hot indeed. Between these extremes the Napa produces an astonishing array of wines.

GRAPE VARIETIES AND WINE STYLES

The Napa's reputation is based on Chardonnay and Cabernet Sauvignon, but these are by

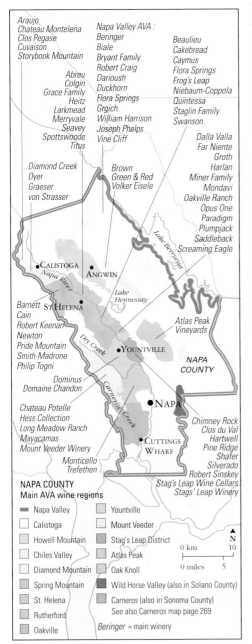

Araujo
Chateau Montelena
Clos Pegase
Cuvaison
Storybook Mountain

Abreu
Colgin
Grace Family
Heitz
Larkmead
Merryvale
Seavey
Spottswoode
Titus

Diamond Creek
Dyer
Graeser
von Strasser

Napa Valley AVA :
Beringer
Biale
Bryant Family
Robert Craig
Darioush
Duckhorn
Flora Springs
Grgich
William Harrison
Joseph Phelps
Vine Cliff

Brown
Green & Red
Volker Eisele

Beaulieu
Cakebread
Caymus
Flora Springs
Frog's Leap
Niebaum-Coppola
Quintessa
Staglin Family
Swanson

Dalla Valla
Far Niente
Groth
Harlan
Miner Family
Mondavi
Oakville Ranch
Opus One
Paradigm
Plumpjack
Saddleback
Screaming Eagle

CALISTOGA
Napa River
ANGWIN

Barnett ST HELENA
Cain
Robert Keenan
Newton
Pride Mountain
Smith-Madrone
Philip Togni

Lake Berryessa
Lake Hennessay

Dry Creek

YOUNTVILLE

Atlas Peak
Vineyards

NAPA
COUNTY

Dominus
Domaine Chandon

Chateau Potelle
Hess Collection
Long Meadow Ranch
Mayacamas
Mount Veeder Winery
Monticello
Trefethen

Carneros Creek

NAPA

CUTTINGS
WHARF

Chimney Rock
Clos du Val
Hartwell
Pine Ridge
Shafer
Silverado
Robert Sinskey
Stag's Leap Wine Cellars
Stags' Leap Winery

NAPA COUNTY
Main AVA wine regions

- Napa Valley
- Calistoga
- Howell Mountain
- Chiles Valley
- Diamond Mountain
- Spring Mountain
- St. Helena
- Rutherford
- Oakville

- Yountville
- Mount Veeder
- Stag's Leap District
- Atlas Peak
- Oak Knoll
- Wild Horse Valley (also in Solano County)
- Carneros (also in Sonoma County)

See also Carneros map page 269

Beringer = main winery

N
0 km   10
0 miles   5

no means the only grapes grown here. Pinot Noir can be excellent, particularly down in the south of the Valley where the cool climate gives red wines with vivid fruit and considerable finesse. Sauvignon Blanc can be either fat and oaky or, more rarely, sharp and gooseberryish. It is often called Fumé Blanc. There is some Riesling, here often called Johannisberg Riesling, but it is most successful when made as a sweet, nobly rotten wine; otherwise the warm areas can be too warm for it, and the cool areas tend to be given over to the more prestigious and profitable Chardonnay. The warmest areas of all make good Zinfandel and Petite Sirah that are full of chunky, chewy fruit.

But Cabernet, Merlot and Chardonnay are everywhere. Styles vary enormously, partly according to the winemaker and partly to the nature of the site. (Soils vary hugely in the Napa, but it is still climate that is the deciding factor in the style of the wine.) Many are made to be drunk young, and have abundant ripe fruit; others can be initially hard and tannic, but soften over four or five years to perfumed, cedary fruit. The prime areas for this latter style are **Rutherford**, **Oakville**, and the hilly AVAs like **Mount Veeder**.

Chardonnay is less fat and oily than it was a few years ago, and while many still have a fruit salad of flavours, with such delights as figs, melons, peaches or lychees all fighting for prominence, with some buttery oak to round it out, the best Napa Chardonnays are drier, steelier, with a slightly smoky, toasty taste from the partially charred oak barrels in which they are matured and often fermented.

So let's run through the main AVAs. **Napa Valley** itself is an AVA, but moving north from the southern end of the Valley there are the important AVAs of **Rutherford** and **Oakville**. You may have heard of the Rutherford Bench? Well, this is where it is. It's not terribly obvious to the eye – you could drive up the main road through the valley without being aware that anything had changed – but the Rutherford Bench is a slightly raised area of land on the western side of the valley. There have been Cabernet Sauvignon vines growing here for 100 years or more, and as you might expect, the exact delimitation of this prime Cabernet area has been contentious. It certainly continues into Oakville, which has its own AVA – indeed there has been a plan to define the boundaries of all the main towns of the Napa, rather like the communes of the Médoc. The new **St Helena** AVA doesn't claim the Bench but produces some pretty powerful Cabernets regardless. Rutherford, Oakville, St Helena,

This scene at Newton Vineyards might be the Napa of the future: vines climbing the slopes in search of structure and intensity, instead of just blanketing the valley floor.

Calistoga and Yountville are the first of these new AVAs.

In the hills along the eastern side of the valley are the AVAs of **Atlas Peak**, **Howell Mountain**, **Chiles Valley** and **Pope Valley**. All give long-lasting Cabernets (and other reds) of elegance yet power. There's Merlot and Cabernet Franc, too, because classic Bordeaux-style blends of the three grapes are increasingly popular in California as more winemakers see the advantages of filling out the leaner Cabernet varieties with the plummier Merlot.

On the edge of the eastern hills, and runing into the plain, is **Stags Leap District**. There is rich, beautifully balanced Cabernet and Merlot from here. In the Mayacamas Mountains, which form the western border of the valley, there are the AVAs of **Spring Mountain**, **Mount Veeder** and **Diamond Mountain**. The vineyards here can be planted at more than 600m (2000ft), and that's high. The wines, from low-yielding (often Cabernet Sauvignon) vines, are concentrated and slow to mature, and are some of California's best.

The higher you climb in the mountains – and the higher you plant – the more likely you are to escape the fogs. If you're growing Pinot Noir you may welcome the fog, in

which case you won't head for the mountains. But if you want to produce rich, ripe, dark Cabernets and Zinfandels then the sun is your friend. And though it's true that the huge fashionability of the Napa has led to just about every grape variety being planted, the return of phylloxera during the 1990s (phylloxera-affected vines take several years to die but 80 to 90 per cent of the valley's vines were affected) meant that a lot of replanting went on; and the growers didn't just replicate what they had before: they took the opportunity to plant better vines and made great efforts to match varieties to suitable terrain. Napa wine in the twenty-first century is the best it has ever been. Best producers: **Araujo**, **Beaulieu**, **Beringer**, **Caymus**, **Chateau Montelena**, **Chimney Rock**, **Clos du Val**, **Dalla Valle**, **Diamond Creek**, **Domaine Chandon**, **Dominus**, **Duckhorn**, **Dunn**, **Flora Springs**, **Harlan**, **Hartwell**, **Heitz**, **Hess Collection**, **Merryvale**, **Miner**, **Mondavi**, **Monticello**, **Mumm Napa**, **Newton**, **Niebaum-Coppola**,

Once the grapes have been picked (here at El Retiro vineyard on the Silverado Trail, Napa Valley) it's time to give the vines a good, long drink.

Opus One, **Phelps**, **Pine Ridge**, **Screaming Eagle**, **Shafer**, **Silver Oak**, **Silverado**, **Robert Sinskey**, **Spottswoode**, **Staglin** and **Stag's Leap Wine Cellars**.

CLASSIFICATION
In general the producer's name and his remarks on the label as to grape varieties, vineyards and wine-making style will tell you more than any particular AVA name.

ORGANIZATION
Small to medium-sized growers and wine-makers reign supreme here, even though some wineries are owned by large, multinational companies. Most wineries own some vineyard land, but there is a large group of farmers who concentrate purely on growing quality grapes on which to base their blends.

READING THE LABEL

Apart from the system of AVAs outlined above, labels (and not just those from Napa) may bear the name 'Meritage'. This is a fairly widely adopted term denoting a Bordeaux-style blend of Cabernet Sauvignon, Cabernet Franc and Merlot (for the reds) and Sauvignon Blanc and Semillon (for the whites), in whatever proportions the winemaker sees fit. Such wines may have names that relate to the vineyard where the grapes are grown, or they may be made up. Other wines are usually labelled with the name of the grape variety.

WHAT DO THEY TASTE LIKE?

They taste Big. If one generalization were possible it would have to concern the massive, ultra-ripe flavours produced from these bulging, sugar-filled grapes. For some years it seemed that the winemakers were straining to extract the maximum amount of flavours from their grapes, to ensure the maximum amount of alcohol, then were slamming the wines into highly perfumed, new oak casks to age. By the end you almost needed a knife and fork to tackle the result. Then for a while the wines became subtle and leaner – and in some cases too lean to be any fun.

Napa wines have been a pendulum of fashion in the last couple of decades, but now things have swung back towards the 'big is beautiful' style – but not too big, and they can be vaguely subtle with it, and have balance.

THE GOOD YEARS

The most marginal areas show the most vintage variations – this means in the cooler south of the county or those vineyards high in the hills above the valley floor.

2004 Prolonged heatwave hit the North Coast in the summer. Average year and quality patchy.
2003 Difficult weather conditions. Choose with care.
2002 A slightly cooler summer helped the whites.
2001 Big reds such as Cabernet did best.
2000 Good quality and quantity. Cabernets will take some aging but Chardonnay will be best in the short term.

1999 Moderate quantities of variable quality. Some good reds.
1998 Patient growers harvested fruit of optimum maturity.
1997 A monster crop with patchy quality.
1996 A good year for Chardonnay.
1995 Another small harvest.

ENJOYING THE WINES

The whites are excellent with the clear flavours of fresh-grilled fish and chicken, but can also cope with the spicy or creamy flavours of more exotic dishes. Despite some attempts to make a subtle 'Bordeaux' style, many Napa reds will overwhelm delicate cuisine. Rich red meat – roast, grilled or stewed – would be my choice, and game would go pretty well too, or even some of the less strong cheeses. The top fizzes make excellent apéritifs and often also have enough body to be drunk throughout the meal.

CONSUMER INFORMATION

WHAT DO I GET FOR MY MONEY?

Well, Napa wines are expensive. We're not talking bargain basement here. But there are cheaper wines too: Napa growers have as good a sense of the market as any growers in the world. If you buy a Mondavi wine, for example, you can pay an arm and a leg for the Cabernet Sauvignon Reserve, or much less for a straightforward Fumé Blanc. Remember, too, that in a milieu that equates high quality with a high price, there can be competition among leading producers to charge the most.

AVAILABILITY

Good. Napa wines are so famous that most outlets will have some, though the leading names are necessarily in shorter supply.

CONSUMER CHECKLIST

Barrel-Fermented Chardonnay	*Quality 9*★	
(Flora Springs) 2003	*Price 9* ★	
	Value 8 ★	
Merlot	*Quality 10* ★	
(Shafer)	*Price 10* ★	
	Value 9 ★	

Good Years 2004, 2003, 2002, 2001, 2000, 1999, 1998, 1996, 1995, 1994, 1991, 1990.
Taste Notes The keynote of Napa wines is ripeness, whether it is a blackcurranty, cedary Cabernet Sauvignon or a buttery Chardonnay, but balance is becoming important too. But expect to find lots of fruit in the wines as well, and often lots of new oak flavour.

CARNEROS

This must have been a terrific area for sheep. Why sheep? Well, it takes its name from sheep. And it used to be largely grazing land: the soil was too shallow for much else. And it's cool here: the sheep must have been glad of their wool. Carneros is on the same latitude as the toe of Italy, but the temperature is more like that of the very north of Burgundy. Carneros is the first stop for the ocean fog that moves in every day from San Pablo Bay, and it rolls over these low, barren hills to cool the climate to un-California-like levels.

GRAPE VARIETIES AND WINE STYLES

Carneros covers the extreme southern end of both Napa and Sonoma Valleys. It first began to attract attention in the mid-1980s, although vines had been planted here before that. And it was as a cool-climate region that it hit the headlines: this was the time when winemakers were beginning seriously to look for more finesse and less fat in their wines, and suddenly the answer was on their doorstep.

It's Pinot Noir and Chardonnay that excel here. There's good Merlot, as well and even Syrah, but these first two grapes acquire classic finesse and elegance. And while good Chardonnay is being made elsewhere in California, the regions that have proved themselves suitable for Pinot Noir are far fewer. So it is with Pinot Noir, the most temperamental of red grapes, that Carneros has really made its reputation.

So what does Carneros Pinot Noir taste like? If I say that, above all, it tastes of the grape, I'm not trying to avoid the issue. The wines have masses of strawberry and spice, cherry and chocolate fruit; they have lovely balance and structure. They're not doing a Burgundian me-too because they don't taste like Burgundy. They don't have that vegetal quality, that flavour of mature game that makes lovers of red Burgundy keep shelling out the money. Instead they have very seductive richness and freshness. And what they are proving, year after year, is that Burgundy is not the only region on earth that can produce Pinot Noir. And that the Burgundian style of Pinot is not the only valid one.

Best producers: **Acacia**, **Artesa**, **Buena Vista**, **Carneros Creek**, **Domaine Carneros**, **David Ramey**, **Kent Rasmussen**, **Saintsbury**, **Schug** and **Truchard**. In addition, many producers in other parts of Napa and Sonoma rely on Carneros fruit to improve their blends.

Vines just coming into leaf at Acacia Winery. The salt pans at the northern end of San Pablo Bay are just visible in the distance.

CLASSIFICATION

Carneros has its own AVA and there is no other official classification.

ORGANIZATION

Many producers with wineries in other areas are keen to buy Carneros grapes. But Carneros also has many wineries of its own.

READING THE LABEL

Wines from Carneros have the option of using the Sonoma Valley or Napa Valley AVAs if they prefer. But the growers have banded together to form the Carneros Quality Alliance to foster a sense of the region's identity, and many Carneros wines bear the Alliance's seal.

WHAT DO THEY TASTE LIKE?

The wines have great intensity of fruit, but with greater delicacy and more refined structure than is found in most of California. Pinot Noir has vivid strawberry and cherry fruit; Chardonnay is buttery but not over-fat.

THE GOOD YEARS

2004 Patchy quality so choose with care.

2003 Yields were down but quality excellent with well-balanced wines.

2002 Intense, ripe Pinot Noir.

2001 Long, cool growing season. Excellent quality wines.

2000 A bigger vintage than the previous two. Good quality.

1999 Variable Chardonnay but fine Pinot.

1998 An uneven vintage but good for Pinot.

1997 A huge crop of uneven quality.

1996 Small crop; good quality likely.

1995 Wines of good concentration.

ENJOYING THE WINE

These wines have the elegance and concentration to partner most dishes. Drink Chardonnay with fish and poultry, Pinot Noir with game and red meat.

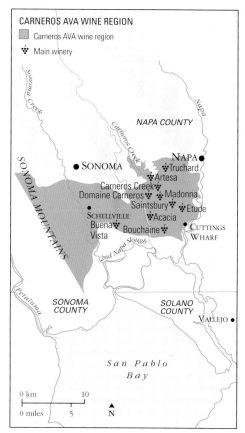

CONSUMER INFORMATION

WHAT DO I GET FOR MY MONEY?

Carneros wines aren't cheap. If you're thinking that the Pinot Noir might be a cheap alternative to the red Burgundy the bank manager won't let you buy, we-e-e-ll... they're still not exactly cheap. And that goes for Chardonnay, as well. But the quality usually justifies the price.

AVAILABILITY

The higher price means that they are really only found in the better wine shops.

CONSUMER CHECKLIST

Chardonnay	*Quality 9* ★
(Saintsbury) 2003	*Price 8* ★
	Value 9 ★
Pinot Noir 2002	*Quality 9* ★
(Kent Rasmussen)	*Price 8* ★
	Value 9 ★

Good Years 2004, 2003, 2002, 2001, 2000, 1999, 1996, 1995, 1994, 1993, 1992, 1991, 1990.

Taste Notes The Pinot Noir has bright, strawberry and cherry fruit with good structure and balance. Chardonnay is elegant and toasty, usually aged and often fermented in new oak, but never too fat.

CENTRAL COAST

L ook, I'm sorry if you're tired of fog. If it's any comfort, some people in California get tired of it too, unless they happen to grow vines or make wine. For them fog is crucial. Because in this huge AVA, which covers the coastal wine regions from south of the San Francisco Bay right down to Santa Barbara County, the fog can make the difference between those areas that are too hot for fine wine, those that are just right, and those that are too cold and are best-suited to lettuces.

It's all part of the great sorting-out process that is taking place in California: the deciding which vines grow best where. You can theorize and study the weather and take soil samples until you're blue in the face, but the only way to see if you're right or not is to plant vines, and wait a few years until they're producing the sort of crop you can make wine from. You may find that you were right, and that the wine is superb. Or you may find that the wine is just not what you want – it's too tannic, it's too green or it's too fat. In which case, you start again. And wait again. And try the wine again. Making good wine is a slow process. But this slow road of discovery is one of the most exciting things that's happening in California at the moment. It's leading to the gradual emergence of real excellence. And

This looks as parched as the popular image of Australia, except that the trees are the wrong sort. Instead, it's Firestone Vineyards in Santa Barbara County.

while these regions may not yet have the fame or the intensive plantings of the Napa, some of them are producing wines that are every bit as good, and sometimes better.

GRAPE VARIETIES AND WINE STYLES

I'll start immediately south of San Francisco Bay, in the area that is imaginatively called San Francisco Bay! In fact I'll start directly east of the Bay, in **Livermore Valley** AVA. It's warm here, since it's sheltered from the sea, and it's just the sort of spot you might choose to live – you and an awful lot of others. There's tremendous pressure on vineyard land here for housing, but the two main landholders, **Concannon** and **Wente Brothers**, are still there. In spite of the warmth, Sauvignon Blanc and Semillon do well.

Santa Clara Valley AVA used to be more important as a wine region than it is now – its modern alias is Silicon Valley. **Santa Cruz Mountains** AVA is also not exactly heavily populated with vines, but it does have a few, and these are low-yielding and packed with character. **David Bruce**, **Bonny Doon**, **Kathryn Kennedy**,

Mount Eden and Ridge make some stunning wines, particularly from Cabernet Sauvignon, Pinot Noir and, most recently, from Syrah, Marsanne and Roussanne.

That brings us to Monterey County whose northern reaches were heavily planted with vines in the late 1960s and early 1970s, but in more recent years the vines have quietly edged their way south, out of the cold air and fog that move in from Monterey Bay. Many of those early vines were red, especially Cabernet Sauvignon. Plant Cabernet in too cool a climate and the wine tasted of green peppers. Green peppers are all very well, but you don't necessarily want to drink them. Nowadays these cool areas are given over to white varieties and it is the smaller AVAs of Monterey and San Benito Counties – **Arroyo Seco**, **Carmel Valley**, **Santa Lucia Highlands**, **Mount Harlan** and **Chalone** – which are producing the most exciting wines.

Chalone Vineyard and **Calera** are both here, high up in the Gabilan Range, making superb, deep-hearted reds and well-structured whites. Their Pinot Noirs, in particular, are some of California's best.

San Luis Obispo County is a prime example of Californian extremes. In **Paso Robles** AVA, at the head of the Salinas Valley and separated from the Pacific by the high Santa Lucia mountains, it is hot enough for tremendously rich Zinfandel and Cabernet Sauvignon and there are new plantings of Rhône and Italian varieties. The small, cool **York Mountain** AVA also has some old plantings of Zinfandel.

By contrast, **Edna Valley** AVA, just down the road, is cool. Cool enough for wonderfully savoury Chardonnay, some of the best in the whole state, and good Pinot Noir and Gewürztraminer. **Edna Valley Vineyards** dominates production here. In **Arroyo Grande** AVA it is even cooler. So cool that the grapes are more likely to end up in sparkling wine than table wine. Even so good Chardonnay, Pinot Blanc and excellent Pinot Noir *do* come from here, and as usual in California, go inland a few miles away from the cooling fog and up goes the temperature. So Arroyo Grande can grow top heady Zinfandel, just a few miles away from elegant cool Chardonnay and Pinot. Best producers: (San Luis Obispo County) **Alban**, **Adelaida**, **Eberle**, **Edna Valley**, **Meridian**, **Peachy Canyon** and **Tablas Creek**.

Santa Barbara County was made famous overnight by the Hollywood film 'Sideways' and Santa Barbara Pinot Noir suddenly became a cult wine. Deservedly so, because the area has been producing top quality cool climate reds and whites for a generation. There are two main parts to Santa Barbara County. In the north, there's **Santa Maria Valley**, a wide flat river valley that is extremely foggy and cool at the seaward end but has outstanding cool climate sites, especially on the northern slopes of the valley, for Chardonnay, Pinot Noir and even Syrah. There aren't many wineries here – **Au Bon Climat** is one, making dark, broody Pinot Noir and rich, Burgundian-style Chardonnay. But plenty of producers have vineyards here, and they simply truck the fruit up to their wineries in the Napa Valley or elsewhere, where it does wonders for the finished wine.

Further south there are excellent vineyards at Los Alamos before you plunge into the

CALIFORNIA CENTRAL COAST

- San Francisco Bay
- San Benito County
- Monterey County
- San Luis Obispo County
- Santa Barbara County

MAIN AVA WINE REGIONS

1 Livermore Valley
2 Santa Clara Valley (sub-AVA San Ysidro)
3 Santa Cruz Mountains (sub-AVA Ben Lomond Mountain)
4 Mount Harlan
5 Carmel Valley
6 Santa Lucia Highlands
7 Arroyo Seco
8 Chalone
9 San Lucas
10 York Mountain
11 Paso Robles
12 Edna Valley
13 Arroyo Grande Valley
14 Santa Maria Valley
15 Santa Ynez Valley
16 Santa Rita Hills

heart of 'Sideways' wine country in the Santa Ynez Valley. The upper end of the Valley covered by the Santa Ynez Valley AVA is pretty warm and can ripen Cabernet, Merlot and the Rhône varieties. This is a landscape dotted with stud farms and ranches as well as vineyards and you can sense a certain 'Hollywood country playground' feel to the place. Even so, they make good wine. But as the river flows westward to the sea through an AVA called Santa Rita Hills, it gets colder by the mile, and this is where the really exciting wines are made. Pinot Noir and Chardonnay of such finesse but weight that this little region has been dubbed California's cool climate Nirvana. Well, it may be, but as our trip down California's west coast has shown, there are a lot more top cool climate regions than you might expect. Best producers: (Santa Barbara County) **Au Bon Climat, Beckmen, Brewer-Clifton, Byron, Fiddlehead, Foxen, Hitching Post, Lane Tanner, Andrew Murray, Ojai, Qupé, Sanford, Sea Smoke, Whitcraft** and **Zaca Mesa**.

South of Santa Barbara the vines peter out as homes and gardens take up more and more of the suitable land. But there is still one more area between Los Angeles and the Mexican border. The overall AVA is South Coast, but most of the action is in Temecula Valley.

CLASSIFICATION

Apart from the AVA system there is no other official classification.

ORGANIZATION

As well as boutique wineries making wine from their own grapes, many large companies based elsewhere in California have invested in the area.

READING THE LABEL

Because so many of these regions are packed with vineyards but short on wineries, a lot of the grapes are blended in with others from perhaps Napa and Sonoma – so you won't see these AVAs on many labels. But that doesn't matter because in California it makes sense to trust the producer rather than the region.

WHAT DO THEY TASTE LIKE?

TThe wines cover the full gamut of flavours, from rich, deep, raisiny Zinfandels, through supple, ripe Pinot Noirs, to elegant, Burgundian Chardonnays. Some of California's best wines are being made in some of these spots.

THE GOOD YEARS

The climate is more reliable than in North Coast California so vintages are less variable. There is a huge range of mesoclimates and grape varieties, even within individual AVAs, so it is difficult to generalise.

ENJOYING THE WINES

This enormous area makes wines for most foods. There's Chardonnay for the finest fish dishes and Pinot Noir for the best game. There is also Zinfandel for hearty casseroles, plenty of everyday reds and whites and fizz.

CONSUMER INFORMATION

WHAT DO I GET FOR MY MONEY?

As always in California, the value for money of these wines outside the USA varies according to the exchange rate. But the best Central Coast wines are certainly fair value, even if they are high-priced. Some are very expensive indeed but they are not necessarily any worse value than the cheaper wines.

AVAILABILITY

Quantities of wine from the smaller AVAs and the leading producers are fairly limited, and you'll need to go to a specialist.

CONSUMER CHECKLIST

Pinot Noir 2003   *Quality 9* ★
(Au Bon Climat)   *Price 9* ★
                        Value 9 ★

Good Years Vintages of the last decade have been of good quality.
Taste Notes Cool climates here give subtle flavours of great finesse. Vineyards in the warmer spots produce reds of tremendous richness and flavour.

CENTRAL VALLEY

This industrial complex is actually Franzia Winery in the Central Valley. This vast interior valley produces most of California's bulk wine as well as table grapes.

If you've ever sweltered under the Californian sun, and have become a touch confused by all this talk of fog and cool climates, then this is the place for you. This is where the sun beats down mercilessly, where the hills are too far away to offer shelter, and where the cool ocean is only a mirage. This is California's Central Valley, long and flat and up to 100km (60 miles) wide. If you go into any wine shop in the USA and buy a cheap varietal wine, the chances are it will have come from here.

But don't white grapes prefer cooler climates, I hear you ask? Yes, they do – but we're not talking about fine wines here. We're talking about sound, everyday stuff designed to be drunk within the year, or sooner – and if that's your aim as a producer, and you're prepared to sink telephone-number sums of money into vast wineries with every kind of technological gadgetry, then all you need are vast quantities of healthy grapes delivered promptly to your door. Forget about climate and soil and exposure to the sun and all that stuff. You're producing a commodity. This is where you do it cheaply and efficiently.

It's an achievement in itself. A few decades ago it would have been impossible: above all it is the advent of sophisticated cooling equipment that has made decent cheap whites possible here. Before that the wine that was made was mostly red, and mostly fortified – and mostly from beefy varieties like

Zinfandel. Zinfandel still does well here, and there are still some brilliant fortifieds being made, particularly from **Madera** AVA just north-west of Fresno, where it's hotter than hot and where **Andrew Quady** makes sensational Muscats. **Lodi** AVA is crucially a little cooler and has started to make quite a name for itself with rich, soft Zinfandel. **Clarksburg** AVA is up by the Sacramento River and is a bit cooler again – not very cool but good Chenin is grown along with soft reds. The overall AVA here is Central Valley, but there is a considerable difference between the cooler northern part near the Sacramento River, and the baking southern section as important for raisins and table grapes as for wine.

Finally, there are are the Gold Rush regions east of Sacramento, many of which were planted to quench the thirst of those first miners and you can still get a real sense of that if you drive up into the delightful mountains. And there are still patches of very old Zinfandel vines here which produce some of California's most characterful 'old time' reds. **El Dorado**, **Fiddletown** and **Shenandoah Valley** are all sub-AVAs of the **Sierra Foothills** AVA.

Best producers: **Quivira**, **R H Phillips**, **Ravenswood** and **Quady**.

PACIFIC NORTH-WEST

If the Californian wine industry had never existed would anyone have thought of planting wine grapes in the Pacific North-West? I suppose they might have done eventually. Wine freaks have a way of sniffing out likely spots in the most unlikely circumstances. But it was, in many ways, the California wine industry that gave birth to the wines of Washington, Oregon and Idaho, and it has tended to define their styles, too. Okay, the weather has done that, as well. But the Pacific North-West's main claim to fame over the last three decades or so has been that it makes wines that are different to California's; even, sometimes, that it makes the sorts of wine that California couldn't make if it wanted to. For Oregon it was the tantalizing possibility of making Pinot Noir and Chardonnay in the cool climate mould of French Burgundy that was the lure. For Washington it was the possibility of Riesling which first attracted a new wave of producers, but they soon realized that the growing conditions in the Yakima and Columbia Valleys had more similarities to

France's Bordeaux than any of the popular spots in California's Napa and Sonoma Valley, and so Cabernet and Merlot moved centre stage, to be joined more recently by Syrah. And with all of these grapes, Washington aims for a tauter, drier style than is generally possible in California.

Washington and Oregon, the two main wine states here, could hardly be more different. While Oregon's vineyards are cool and damp, most of Washington's are hot and dry in the summer and ice cold in the winter. You always thought that moving north meant cooler temperatures? Not if you travel east across the Cascades as well.

The Cascade Mountains run more or less north to south through both states. They're stunningly beautiful and if the eruption of Mount St Helens in 1980 affected the climate for a lot of us in the short term, the Cascades have a permanent influence on the climate of the two states they bisect. To the west rain moves in off the Pacific. It falls on Seattle, Portland and the wineries in Oregon's

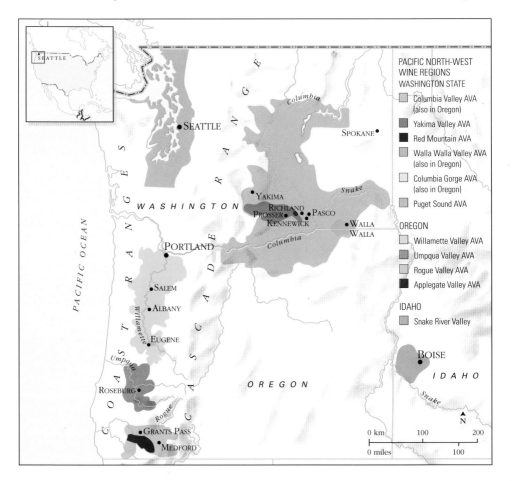

PACIFIC NORTH-WEST
WINE REGIONS
WASHINGTON STATE

- Columbia Valley AVA (also in Oregon)
- Yakima Valley AVA
- Red Mountain AVA
- Walla Walla Valley AVA (also in Oregon)
- Columbia Gorge AVA (also in Oregon)
- Puget Sound AVA

OREGON
- Willamette Valley AVA
- Umpqua Valley AVA
- Rogue Valley AVA
- Applegate Valley AVA

IDAHO
- Snake River Valley

Willamette Valley. But it doesn't cross the Cascades. To the east of the mountains there's a giant rain shadow – in fact it's a desert there. Only the Columbia River and its tributaries makes viticulture possible, and then only when the vines are irrigated.

But how can they be making subtle, European-style wines when it can be hot enough here to bake the life out of any crop that isn't irrigated? Well, the answer is that the wine vines are planted in the cooler places. Not cold, you understand, but cool enough for the first growers to see the region as a natural source of white wines rather than red. And the grapes ripen beautifully: the further north you get, the more hours of sunlight you get in the summer. That is far more important for quality wine than roasting the grapes on the vine over a short period. And what Washington State's vines lack in heat they gain in sun.

GRAPE VARIETIES AND WINE STYLES

The star grapes used to be just the cool-climate ones in all three states. For most of Oregon, this is still the case, though warm sites exist in the south and on the Washington border along the Columbia River. In Washington, the Bordeaux red grapes rule, along with increasing amounts of Syrah. Chardonnay and Semillon now make the best whites. In Idaho bitterly cold winters and hot summers create their own problems for the grower, and the most successful wines are Riesling and Chardonnay.

WASHINGTON STATE

This is the most important of the three states, as least as far as wine goes. There are a few vines west of the Cascades, now grouped into the **Puget Sound** AVA, but not many, because the climate is marginal at best.

Almost all the producers prefer to brave the arctic winters east of the mountains for the sake of the hot, dry summers and long hours of sunshine. But the vines have to be planted in spots that are a compromise between both extremes: the ripening grapes need sun yet not too much heat in the summer, and in the winter they need sites that are protected from the worst sub-zero frosts. However, the first necessity is water: the Columbia, Yakima and Snake rivers all have vines on their banks. Obtain water rights and you can grow vines.

The AVA that covers the whole eastern region is **Columbia Valley**. Within that are **Yakima Valley** AVA, which covers about one-third of the vineyards in the state, and **Walla Walla Valley** AVA. And the rest of the land here? It's planted with other crops where

Rolling hillsides of lush green vineyards, here belonging to Shafer Vineyard Cellars, are typical of the northern Willamette Valley west of Portland.

irrigation will allow, or is just left as desert. This is a sparsely inhabited, harsh landscape of bare sagebrush hills and monotonous plains. And even in the Yakima Valley there are still plenty of *Vitis labrusca* vines. Originally they were the only vines cultivated here, when the industry was established in the 1930s. Now they're grown for grape juice, grape jelly and grape concentrate. There are orchards of fruit trees, too, and vegetables, and in the Yakima Valley these are mostly grown on the flat ground near the river.

The vines are given the south- and south-west-facing slopes on the ridges bordering the river, where irrigation canals run across the hills. Vineyard yields are generally high, but flavour definition is nevertheless good, and the cool nights mean that the grapes preserve their natural refreshing acidity.

Until recently the whites have been the most successful, particularly the Rieslings, which can be sweet or dry but either way are increasingly unfashionable. Sauvignon Blanc can be good and grassy. Gewürztraminer should, one feels, be good, but hasn't so far been thrilling. Chardonnay is successfully fermented in new oak barrels, to give it some Burgundian polish. Semillon is good and getting better. Of the reds, Cabernet Sauvi-

There are no short cuts to good wine: before the harvest every barrel, here at Covey Run Vintners, must be washed out until it is spotlessly clean.

gnon produces some tremendous flavours, but can also bear some brutal tannins, which the producers are slowly learning to tame. Merlot also needed some taming but the rich flavours of blackcurrant and plum in both these varieties make the effort worthwhile. Syrah started out in Walla Walla but has now spread further afield and is producing dark, smoky, blackberryish wines. One delightful oddity is the Austrian Lemberger and there's also a little good Grenache. Best producers: **Andrew Will**, **Cadence**, **Cayuse**, **Chateau Ste Michelle**, **Chinook**, **Columbia Crest**, **Delille**, **Dunham**, **Hedges Cellars**, **Hogue Cellars**, **L'Ecole No 41**, **Leonetti**, **Matthews**, **Pepper Bridge**, **Quilceda Creek**, **Wineglass** and **Woodward Canyon**.

OREGON

This is where Pinot Noir outside Burgundy first rose to fame – in 1979 when a Pinot Noir from Eyrie Vineyards in the Willamette Valley came second to a venerable 1959 Chambolle-Musigny at a blind tasting in Paris. Had the USA at last discovered its own Burgundy Côte d'Or, people asked? Yes and no. In fact, the

Willamette Valley is on the latitude of Bordeaux rather than of Burgundy, but the ripening season is slow and the Pinot Noir's ripening pattern seems to match the Willamette Valley's warm and wet climate remarkably well. In spite of this, and in spite of that flying start and the hype that ensued, only a few producers have been able to deliver really convincing examples of the grape but as the obsession with Burgundy recedes, more good Pinot appears with a mellow restrained character all of its own.

Some producers are still determined to produce a Burgundian Pinot Noir, and the most obvious example is the leading Burgundian merchant Robert Drouhin who created Domaine Drouhin in the Willamette Valley's Dundee Hills. And there's no doubt some of his Chardonnays and Pinot Noirs have at times been almost more Burgundian than his Burgundy.

In the early days of the 1960s, planting vines here at all seemed pretty idiosyncratic. The University of California at Davis warned against it: wine could not be made from vinifera vines in Oregon, they said. How wrong they were. Admittedly, rot can be a problem. So can rain, when it falls during the harvest, but there's a long ripening season, and it is precisely the marginal nature of the climate for vines that makes it good for Pinot Noir – although this does not help growers seeking a consistent style.

With Pinot Noir so variable, some growers have been turning their attention to Pinot Gris. And they're making dry, nicely spicy but not overweight wines. Chardonnay and Riesling are the most widely planted grapes, but there is Sauvignon Blanc, Gewürztraminer and Müller-Thurgau as well, all of which can be good. There's some Cabernet Sauvignon, Merlot and even some Zinfandel in the warm spots, but none of these look set to displace Pinot Noir as the main red.

The main wine region is the **Willamette Valley** AVA, where the Coast Ranges keep off the worst of the Pacific weather and the Cascades keep off the continental extremes of climate of the interior. The Eola Hills near Salem also have some good sites. And if the

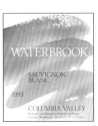

growers wanted Burgundian conditions, well, you'll find them praying for less rain at the wrong time and more rain at the right times, just like they do in Burgundy. The **Umpqua Valley** AVA is warmer, as is **Rogue Valley** AVA, down near California and there are some decidedly warm sites up by the Columbia River and Walla Walla. Best producers: **Adelsheim**, **Amity**, **Archery Summit**, **Argyle**, **Beaux Frères**, **Cameron**, **Cristom**, **Domaine Drouhin**, **Domaine Serene**, **Elk Cove**, **Rex Hill**, **Torii Mor**, **WillaKenzie** and **Ken Wright**.

IDAHO
Idaho's fame is for its potatoes, not its wine and good potato soil rarely produces exciting wine. But they were making good wine here in the nineteenth century, and there are now around 15 wineries farming 485 hectares (1200 acres) of vines, about 60 per cent red. It's not easy, though. You do get very hot days, but you also get ice cold nights up at 600m (1970ft) where the vineyards are, and you not only have a short growing season, but you are always at risk from frost. Even so, Idaho produces some tangy whites, especially Chardonnay, and excellent fizz. **Ste Chapelle** is the main winery.

CLASSIFICATION
The best sites are slowly being identified but there is nothing beyond the AVA system.

ORGANIZATION
Boutique wineries rule here, especially in Oregon where many producers moved north to avoid California's razamatazz.

READING THE LABEL
Oregon has very strict wine laws. Misleading terms like Chablis and Burgundy are forbidden. The label must state where the grapes were grown, and varietal wines must contain at least 90 per cent of the variety named. The exception is Cabernet Sauvignon, which may have up to 25 per cent of other varieties.

WHAT DO THEY TASTE LIKE?
Balance is a key word. High natural acidity is matched by good sugar, giving wines with body but also considerable fresh fruit and fragrance. Some of the reds are a little light, but the delicate fruit compensates.

THE GOOD YEARS
2004 Reduced yields. In Washington Merlot did especially well and in Oregon most wines have high alcohol levels and lots of flavour.

2003 Early maturing reds in Washington. In Oregon Pinot Noirs have plenty of tannin and high alcohol.

2002 Very long harvest produced high alcohol wines.

2001 High-alcohol, low-acid wines in Washington and good wines in Oregon.

2000 A medium to large crop of good quality in both Washington and Oregon.

1999 Record quantities of good, ripe fruit.

1998 Many top-quality, fruity wines.

ENJOYING THE WINES
The whites are marvellously refreshing and Riesling can be drunk at any time. There is some good sweet, late-harvest Riesling with excellent intensity and balance, which will partner most puddings. The reds and Chardonnay are usually delicate rather than massive, and shouldn't be matched with overpowering dishes.

CONSUMER INFORMATION

WHAT DO I GET FOR MY MONEY?
A varietal wine from Washington will normally be somewhat cheaper than from California but there are some star wines being produced from Cabernet, Merlot and especially Syrah – and they won't be cheap. Oregon Pinot Noir is no longer underpriced, and the wines can be variable, so keep to the top producers. Pinot Gris is less expensive and gives you a good idea of Oregon white styles.

AVAILABILITY
Outside the USA availability is mixed. For many of these wines you will need to go to the importers (who may also be retailers), though the better shops may well have wines from some of the bigger producers in Washington State. Idaho's tangy whites are a rarity.

CONSUMER CHECKLIST
Washington	Quality 10 ★
Cabernet Sauvignon 2001	Price 9 ★
(Andrew Will)	Value 10 ★

Good Years 2004, 2003, 2002, 2000, 1999, 1998.

Taste Notes Pacific North-West whites are mostly light and delicate, though as the vines mature so the intensity of flavour is becoming greater. Expect lean intensity from Idaho. The wines are often some of the best balanced on the West Coast. Delicate Pinot Noir (especially in Oregon) and gutsy Cabernet, Merlot and Syrah (from Washington State) are the best reds.

EAST COAST

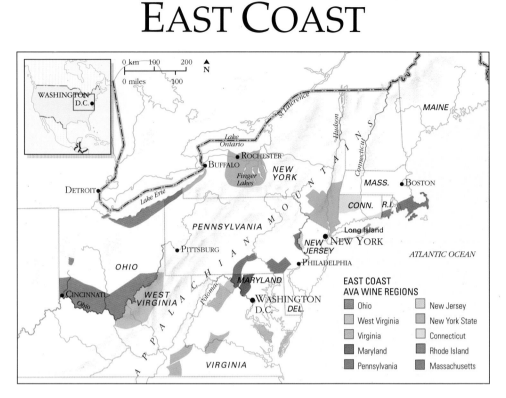

People always say that to make good wine, the vine has to struggle. Well, on the East Coast it's the growers that struggle. And my goodness, do they struggle. It's a constant battle here, and making wine has always been a a series of compromises. The first settlers made wine from the native grape varieties that grew in abundance, but the wines had a strange sweet, exotic perfume that didn't at all match up to the ideas of the colonists on what wine should taste like. But because of the presence of the phylloxera louse in the soil, classic European vines died, while the native varieties were immune. It wasn't until the nineteenth century that they discovered you could graft European vine varieties on to native American rootstocks and the vines would not only survive, they'd bear the European varieties' grapes. So that was the phylloxera problem solved.

But on the East Coast that still left the problem of the climate. Go too far north here and it quickly becomes too cold for European vinifera vines. Go too far inland and the winters are too long and too freezing. Go too far south and the heat and humidity will make your grapes rot. If you want to grow vinifera vines on the East Coast it is almost essential to have a large body of water close by, because lakes and seas – even rivers – can moderate extreme temperatures, easing the winter chill and providing humidity during hot, dry summers. The East Coast, luckily, has the Atlantic Ocean.

GRAPE VARIETIES AND WINE STYLES
Again, these are dictated by the difficulties of the climate. Native American *Vitis labrusca* vines are still grown, even widely grown, but the grapes make better jam or juice than they do dry table wine. Most of the vines grown nowadays are crosses of various sorts of American vine; the most familiar names are Concord, Niagara, Isabella, Catawba and Delaware; some make decent fizz, and Concord is often used for sweet kosher wines. But a new generation of hybrids, crosses of American labrusca vines with European vinifera vines, is proving better for wine.

Seyval Blanc is probably the best known and probably the most versatile. Make it in stainless steel and the wine will be crisp and aromatic; ferment it in barrel and it will be richer. Vidal and Vignoles make good sweet wine. Red hybrids, with such names as Baco Noir and Maréchal Foch can make attractive nouveau-style wines, but the red hybrids are gradually being squeezed out as growers find new techniques that will enable them to grow red vinifera vines in places that had previously seemed too cold.

Which brings me neatly to the best wines of the East Coast. There's Chardonnay here, of course: where is there not Chardonnay? There's also Cabernet Sauvignon and Cabernet Franc, Merlot, Pinot Noir, Riesling, Gewürztraminer, Pinot Blanc and Sauvignon

Blanc. The warmer sites of Long Island, New York State's trendiest vineyard area, are proving best for Chardonnay, Sauvignon Blanc, Merlot and Cabernet Sauvignon, and indeed Long Island, benefiting from the moderating influence of the Atlantic and with well-drained soils and a long growing season, may prove to be the best area on the whole East Coast. **North Fork** AVA, with its better climate and soils, is the leading region, though there are vines, too, in **The Hamptons** AVA on Long Island's South Fork.

But New York State has other wine regions as well, and they have been growing grapes and making wine for much longer. **Lake Erie** AVA grows mostly table grapes, **Hudson River Region** AVA boasts the oldest operating winery in the USA, **Brotherhood America's Oldest Winery Ltd**, and **Finger Lakes** AVA produces 90 per cent of the state's wine. Vinifera varieties are on the increase, though hybrids still rule. Ice Age glaciers carved the narrow, deep Finger Lakes, creating ideal conditions for the vine. The sub-regions of **Cayuga Lake** and **Seneca Lake** AVAs could prove the best bet for vinifera vines. Best producers: **Bedell, Chateau Lafayette Reneau, Fox Run, Dr Konstantin Frank, Galluccio, Heron Hill, Lamoreaux Landing, Millbrook, Palmer, Paumanok, Pelligrini, Pindar, Schneider, Wagner, Hermann J Wiemar** and **Wölffer.**

Elsewhere on the East Coast Pennsylvania, Virginia and Maryland are the main wine states. The growers tend to hedge their bets and grow both hybrids and vinifera vines, and Virginia, with Sauvignon Blanc, Riesling, Chardonnay and Viognier, but also Merlot and Cabernet, looks the best bet for quality. Best producers: (Virginia) **Barboursville, Horton, Linden, Valhalla, Veritas** and **White Hall**; (Maryland) **Basignani** and **Boordy**; (Pennsylvania) **Chaddsford.**

CLASSIFICATION

There is as yet no classification beyond the official AVA system.

ORGANIZATION

Most producers here are small or medium-sized, and many concentrate on local markets.

READING THE LABEL

Look out for the names of vinifera grapes on the label – though it's worth trying a labrusca wine just for the experience. They can be quite pleasant. They are also an exception to the rule that says that a wine must contain 75 per cent of the grape named on the label: the rule for labrusca grapes is 51 per cent.

WHAT DO THEY TASTE LIKE?

Labrusca wines are sweetly aromatic and juicy-fruity; vinifera wines are light to mediumweight and usually on the lean side.

THE GOOD YEARS

Erratic weather is the growers' biggest problem, and vintage variations can be huge. The best wines will often improve for three or four years, though most can be drunk young.

ENJOYING THE WINES

Labrusca wines don't really go with food, but they can be attractive on a hot day, chilled with ice. Vinifera wines will go with most foods, though avoid the heartiest dishes.

CONSUMER INFORMATION

WHAT DO I GET FOR MY MONEY?

The difficulties of production mean that these wines are not going to be cheap. And the proximity of large and rich markets, such as Washington DC and New York City, means that there's not much problem in selling the wines. So don't expect too many bargains.

AVAILABILITY

Very poor outside the USA and not all that good within it, apart from on the wines' home ground. You may find New York State wines in Manhattan, but you won't find them crowding out the shelves in Chicago or San Francisco.

CONSUMER CHECKLIST

Chardonnay 2003	Quality 7 ★
(Lamoreaux Landing)	Price 8 ★
	Value 6 ★

Good Years Most wines can be drunk young.
Taste Notes Labrusca wines have a sweet, exotic scent sometimes bafflingly described as 'foxy', though it bears no resemblance whatever to the scent of foxes. Vinifera wines from here are, at their best, subtle and mediumweight, with good balance and good structure.

CANADA

Canada is very cold indeed and not at all the sort of place you might think of as being suitable for viticulture. It has a climate of long, icy winters, and short blasts of torrid summer, yet there has been wine grown in Ontario since 1811. Of course, labrusca grapes were the secret of the early growers; and when hybrids became available they turned to them, as well. The former were strong-tasting, the latter rather dull, and they meant that although Canada produced some good port- and sherry-style wines, the table wines had a distinct grape jelly flavour.

Hybrids are still important to Canada's wine industry, because they can survive the long, cold winters more easily than vinifera vines; but they are less important than they were. For some years there has been a gradual increase in the amount of vinifera vines planted, and the recent Canada-US Free Trade Agreement gave this process a boost. It is much easier now for California wines to be sold on the Canadian market. Canadian drinkers decided that they didn't necessarily want to be restricted to local wines made from the likes of Seyval Blanc, Vidal, Baco Noir and Maréchal Foch. Not when they can have Chardonnay and Cabernet Sauvignon. With the end of tariff protection for Canadian wines on their own market, wines made from hybrids are of decreasing appeal. The result is that the amount of land planted with hybrids has declined sharply – by around two-thirds in British Columbia and by around a third in Ontario. But the best producers are thriving – because increasingly they can offer good wines made from noble vinifera grape varieties.

GRAPE VARIETIES AND WINE STYLES
Most of Canada's 8000 hectares (20,000 acres) of vineyards are in **Ontario**. **British Columbia** is next, with **Québec** and **Nova Scotia** each adding a little to the total. They're all cold in the winter: there's no escaping the cold in Canada, even though Lakes Ontario and Erie do help to ward off the worst of the chill, and soften the summer heat.

Most of the vineyards are on Ontario's **Niagara Peninsula** at the eastern end of Lake Erie on the lakeshore plain or on the benchland below the Niagara Escarpment, with the rest further west on **Lake Erie North Shore** and on nearby **Pelee Island**. The best dry whites here are from Chardonnay and they get better year by year; Rieslings are also good, and can be sweet or dry. There are

The temperature is well below zero and the grapes are frozen solid on the vine. The plan is to turn these Vidal grapes at Inniskillen Vineyards into Icewine.

even reds, from Merlot and Cabernet Franc, but both can be a bit lean and green.

The real stars of Canadian viticulture, here and elsewhere, though, are the Icewines. This is how the vintners take advantage of their early autumns: by leaving the ripe grapes to freeze on the vine. Just as happens in Germany with Eiswein, the grapes are picked and pressed while frozen, and the intensely sweet, sticky juice oozes from the press while the water is left behind in the form of ice. Both Riesling and Vidal grapes are used for Icewine, and the Vidal wines are often better.

British Columbia's **Okanagan Valley** was the first place in Canada to make Icewine. The nights are cold here but the days, in the short summer, are very, very hot, which gives the wines a combination of high sugar levels and high acidity. With most of the hybrids uprooted, the main grape varieties are Riesling, Gewürztraminer, Pinot Blanc, and Chardonnay but in the desert-like southern end of the lake they even grow Cabernet and Syrah. Hybrids are essential in Quebec and Nova Scotia if wine is to be made. Best producers: **Blue Mountain**, **Burrowing Owl**, **Cave Spring**, **Chateau des Charmes**, **Gehringer**, **Henry of Pelham**, **Inniskillin**, **Konzellmann**, **Mission Hill**, **Reif**, **Southbrook**, **Sumac Ridge** and **Thirty Bench**.

CLASSIFICATION
The best wines bear the seal of the Vintners' Quality Alliance, or VQA. To gain this seal each wine must pass a tasting panel, and must be made from local grapes. Minimum ripeness levels are also laid down. It's an appellation system, although it's not modelled precisely on any other, and the producers describe it as a 'contract between the vintners and the consumer'. So far it's working.

ORGANIZATION
In the upheaval following the Canada-US Trade Agreement only the best, most go-ahead producers are flourishing. Growers who have vinifera grapes for sale are immensely popular.

READING THE LABEL
Non-VQA wines from Ontario may contain up to 75 per cent grapes or must from outside Canada. And only wines from one of Ontario's three Designated Viticultural Areas (Pelee Island, Niagara Peninsula and Lake Erie North Shore) must by law be made entirely from vinifera grapes. Of course, many growers outside these regions also use only vinifera grapes in wines so labelled.

WHAT DO THEY TASTE LIKE?
In spite of Canada's hot summers, expect cool-climate flavours. Chardonnays tend to be elegant and fairly light. Sweet Rieslings and Icewines are intense and concentrated.

THE GOOD YEARS
Unlike Germany, Canada is able to make Icewine every year. Icewines are the best bets

CONSUMER INFORMATION

WHAT DO I GET FOR MY MONEY?
Canadian wines are unlikely ever to be cheap – the climate and the general conditions don't favour the production of inexpensive bulk wine. Instead the producers must concentrate on quality.

AVAILABILITY
Poor outside Canada. But the producers are trying to raise their profile abroad, so we should begin to see more, especially the Icewines.

CONSUMER CHECKLIST
Niagara Icewine 1998   *Quality 9* ★
(Inniskillin)   *Price 9* ★
     Value 9 ★

Good Years   Icewine: 2003, 2002, 2000, 1999, 1998.
Taste Notes   The dry wines are light and well-structured. Canada's sweet wines and Icewines are intense and concentrated.

for keeping, for up to ten years. Other Canadian wines are best drunk young.

ENJOYING THE WINES
Icewines, Canada's speciality, can be drunk young with all sorts of puddings. They can also deal successfully with traditional wine-killers like chocolate. The red wines are generally light and are best matched with quite delicate flavours. The whites make good partners for fish, poultry and all sorts of light to mediumweight dishes.

MEXICO

The Petite Sirah and Zinfandel from **L A Cetto**, and the Cabernet Sauvignon from **Domecq**, are only part of the story. These are the wines we've been seeing on Mexico's export markets, and they've attracted rave notices from people who had never even realized that Mexico made wine.

And, in fact, it doesn't make all that much. It may have nearly 50,000 hectares (123,548 acres) of land under vine, but many of those vineyards are produce table grapes and raisins. Most of the rest go to make brandy – and there has been a lot of inward investment from European companies like Martell, keen to take advantage of the local market. Wine production has in fact fallen in recent years.

Baja California, in the north, is the prime wine area with eastwest valleys and cooling breezes that mimic the California conditions in the USA. This is where virtually all of the good wine comes from, with Domecq and L A Cetto dominating production. In particular it is worth seeking Cetto's wines – they're not expensive and they're very good. Elsewhere in Mexico the only successful vineyards are usually very high to temper the savage heat. Zacatecas and Quevétano are have potential, and good wine is produced by Casa Madero west of Monterrey.

The grapes tend to be red, and those varieties suited to hot climates do best, in particular Merlot, Grenache, Zinfandel, Malbec, Nebbiolo and Carignan.

SOUTH AMERICA

Where is wine made in South America or, rather, where isn't it made? Most countries in this vast continent make wine of some description. Some of it is seriously good. Some of it is seriously bad – at least, to foreign palates. In fact, South America as a whole comes second only to Europe as a wine-producing continent – in spite of the fact that in a land mass ranging from tropical rainforest through desert to distinctly chilly, it has not been easy to find ideal spots for the vine.

European vinifera vines were brought here by the Spaniards. They needed wines to celebrate Mass, as well as something decent to drink, and importing wine from home was far too difficult. South American wine-making traditions still reflect Iberian influences, but nowadays French and New World influences are more important.

The main wine producers are Argentina and Chile, and I'll come to them later. But third on the list comes Brazil, surprisingly.

After all, the most noticeable thing about Brazil is how much of it is covered by rainforest. And a country tropical enough for rainforest isn't going to be suitable for vines.

Most of Brazil's vines are in the far south, often high on the hills, and though they're outside the rainforest belt there's still an awful lot of rain. The most commonly grown vine is the hybrid Isabella, and it is really only since the 1970s, when Moët & Chandon and Martini & Rossi invested here, that vinifera vines were planted in large quantities. Apart from the inevitable Chardonnay, there is Semillon, Trebbiano, Muscat, Welschriesling, Gewürztraminer, both Cabernets, Merlot, and Petite Sirah. The whites are the most successful, though yields are generally too high and the wines too dilute. Reds can be particularly light.

High humidity and high yields also rule in Uruguay. Commercial wine-making was unknown before the late nineteenth century. There's still plenty of Isabella, but there is also Tannat and Petit Manseng, both relics of Basque settlers. Muscat Hamburg is also popular. More recent plantings are of Chardonnay, Sauvignon, Pinot Blanc, Riesling, both Cabernets and Merlot. However recent efforts have gone in to trying to tame the Tannat's astonishing tough personality and trying to provide blending options from among the European classics. Obviously the Bordeaux red varieties are grown, but Tempranillo is showing good form, and the influence of Italian immigration shows with grapes like Nebbiolo and Sangiovese. Whites are largely based on Chardonnay, Sauvignon and Riesling and show attractive style. Uruguay is only a niche player, but one that is determined to punch above its weight.

Peru, on the other hand, is more suited to producing Pisco, a strong and aromatic brandy which is grown around the river and town of the same name. The other centre of viticulture is Ica, further to the south. Bolivia also concentrates on brandy, though there are table wines as well, often from Muscat. Paraguay, Ecuador and Colombia also make small quantities of wine.

0 km 1000 2000

0 miles 1000

WINE REGIONS OF SOUTH AMERICA

- Venezuela
- Peru
- Bolivia
- Brazil
- Uruguay
- Argentina
- Chile

CHILE

If you want the best quality wine in South America, you have to go to Chile. That was true a hundred years ago, and it's still true today. Argentina may produce more wine and Brazil may produce nearly as much, but quality-wise, they're just not in the same league. Chilean wine has been pretty heavily hyped for a few years – we were told they were the product of a land that was a paradise for vines. Now, at last, Chilean wines are showing real quality and they're getting better and better with every vintage.

The reason that vines are supposed to be so sublimely happy in Chile is that there is no phylloxera louse to chew their roots, there is ample irrigation water, if needed, in the form of melted snow from the Andes, and the climate can be remarkably temperate and even. The vineyards are mostly found in a narrow strip north and south of the capital, Santiago, and sheltered in the west by the coastal ranges of hills and in the east by the far higher Andes.

Not that Chile is all wine. The most northerly regions, Atacama and Coquimbo, are too hot for good wine and produce table grapes or Pisco, the brandy that is also made in Peru but right down the coast of Chile you'll find exceptional coastal conditions, and both Elqui and Limarí in **Coquimbo** have cool enough spots for excellent table wine. As you head south toward Santiago and then south of the city, it becomes more and more apparent that the old timers who established Chile's vineyards only got it half right. In **Aconcagua** and the **Central Valley** right down to Maule they established lots of vineyards that regularly produced large crops of decent grapes – every year. But with the exception of Maipo just south of Santiago, they never produced great wines. That's the trouble when you exist in a vine paradise and things are too damned easy – you plant the easy vineyards, you get an easy crop. But if there's one rule in wine it's that the vine needs to be challenged to produce thrilling fruit.

And in Chile, that means heading away from the flat fertile valley floor and up into the mountain sides or out into the foggy, chilly valleys that cut their way to the Pacific Ocean through the Coastal Ranges from the Andes. That's what's happening in the New Chile. From Coquimbo in the north, right down to Mulchén in the damp, cold south, challenging vineyard sites are being sought and planted, and year by year, more and more thrilling wines are being made.

GRAPE VARIETIES AND WINE STYLES
But thrilling grapes need imaginative wine-making. Helped by flying winemakers from Europe, California and Australia and led by a new dynamic young generation of Chilean winemakers and wealthy winery owners prepared to invest in top quality modern equipment, Chile has rocketed from old-fashioned to leader of the pack in scarcely a decade.

Two areas epitomize this change of spirit. First, **Colchagua**, a valley a few hours drive south of Santiago with baking temperatures, rich soil and a high water table. Everyone assumed it was only good for large volumes of bulk wine. Now the complacent, prosperous folk of Colchagua have become the leaders in dealing with one of the great weaknesses of Chilean wine – the lack of challenging, marginal mountain slope vineyards to tax the vine and produce small quantities of superlative wine. Around Colchagua, the hills are now draped in vines. Ten years ago they were bare.

Casablanca is a cool, foggy, infertile valley running to the sea west of Santiago. Too cold for vines they said. But all the traditional Chilean vineyards were too *hot* for decent whites. So despite frosts and fogs and lack of water a couple of pioneers began planting in 1982. There's now no room for any more vines. The Sauvignon, Chardonnay and Pinot Noir is world class and Casablanca is the role model for cool climate areas up and down the entire Chilean coast.

Though Chile makes increasingly good whites, it is the reds that have propelled her to the front. Cabernet, Merlot (usually blended with the intriguing powerfully flavoured Carmenère), Pinot Noir from the cooler sites and Shiraz/Syrah from the warmer ones. What marks them all out is the rush of irresistible ripe, crunchy fruit. In reds, cool and warm areas have equal amounts to offer. Cabernet from Maipo is most likely to have the thrilling combination of blackcurrant and eucalyptus, while that from Aconcagua and Colchagua is dense but less scented. Merlot/Carmenère can be superb right through the Central Valley while Pinot Noir likes the ocean valleys of Casablanca and Leyda or the cool south of Bio Bio. Shiraz, amazingly, likes cool and warm, producing brilliant results in the cool yet northerly climes of Elqui and Limarí and at San Antonio near Casablanca, but also in Colchagua and Marchihue.

Chile's white revolution required cool climate plantings, and Casablanca led the way

with fabulous Chardonnay and Sauvignon Blanc. Leyda and the southern region are continuing this exciting movement. Aromatic varieties are grown without success in warmer areas, but now delicate and enthralling Rieslings, Gewürztraminers and Viogniers are cropping up, from Casablanca, Leyda, San Antonio and Chillán and Bio Bio in the south. Best producers: **Canepa**, **Carmen**, **Casa Lapostolle**, **Concha y Toro**, **Cono Sur**, **Echeverria**, **Errázuriz**, **Mont Gras**, **Montes**, **La Rosa**, **San Pedro** (Churton label), **Santa Carolina**, **Santa Monica**, **Santa Rita**, **Tarapaca**, **Terra Noble**, **Torréon de Paredes**, **Torres**, **Valdivieso**, **Villard**, **Viña Casablanca** and **Viña Porta**.

CLASSIFICATION

The appellation system demarcates five main regions (Atacama, Coquimbo, Aconcagua, Central Valley and Southern Region) but they don't tell you much about wine styles, though you can presume that the Southern Region will be pretty cool.

ORGANIZATION

For many years the Chilean wine industry was dominated by a few large companies but increasingly grape growers are bottling their own wine. Chile has been a destination pop-

The Rothschilds of Château Lafite in Bordeaux have a half-share in these Cabernet Sauvignon vineyards belonging to the Los Vascos winery in Rapel.

ular with flying winemakers from Europe and the New World.

READING THE LABEL

The 1995 wine law has defined the regions. Most wine labels also state the grape variety.

WHAT DO THEY TASTE LIKE?

Varietal flavours are brilliant and individual. Expect plenty of fruit, with the vanilla taste of new oak on many of the reds and Chardonnays. The whites get better every vintage.

THE GOOD YEARS

So far choosing a good producer is more important than any vintage variation. Winemaking is improving so fast that younger wines are usually better than older ones.

ENJOYING THE WINES

The Cabernets and Merlots are versatile food wines, matching roast meats, casseroles and cheeses. The cool-climate whites have the crispness and subtlety to drink by themselvers or go with grilled fish, while the richer, oakier styles are good with creamy sauces or poultry.

ARGENTINA

It's strange to admit that you're still not quite sure what direction the fifth biggest wine producer in the world is headed in. The volume she produces is indeed awesome. The star wines – normally created with help from Chileans or Americans, Frenchmen or Portuguese – can be notably world class, but fabulously, fascinatingly different to their rivals. But the quality of the high-volume, good-quality, commercial wines which Argentina should be able to produce is still very erratic. A lot of the vines are still left-overs from the old days but they only figure in stuff made for local production. There is a serious amount of good-quality varieties like Malbec, Bonarda and Torrontes that can create outstanding – and unusual – wines, in large quantities – and for a very decent price. Several world-famous wine consultants say Argentina's vine-growing conditions are virtually unbeatable.

But the quality and consistency rarely delivers. A good commercial release is followed by a poor one. Well, Argentina's unstable political and economic situation has meant investment and long term vision has been extremely difficult. But you shouldn't lose heart. Argentina really does have massive potential, and in the twenty-first centry, more and more companies and regions are beginning to deliver.

All the scattered vineyard areas are on the eastern foothills of the Andes, where it is desert-dry, but where melted snow, running off the mountains, provides ample irrigation. The climate is reliable, with devastating hailstorms just before the vintage being the main problem. The main wine district is **Mendoza** where you are as likely to find classic Italian varieties as you are French. Cabernet Sauvignon from here is typically beefy and rich, and the high sub-

The snow-covered Andes provide an exciting backdrop to vineyards in the Tupungato Valley of the Mendoza region, as well as essential water for irrigation.

region of **Luján de Cuyo** has magnificent old Malbec vines, producing wine that can be ripe and plummy and perfumed in a way that most French growers of the grape would envy. Other wine regions include hot **San Juan**, dry **La Rioja**, and high-altitude **Salta**, where the quality is promising. Best producers: **Achaval-Ferrer**, **Luigi Bosca**, **Catena**, **Lurton**, **Nieto Senetiner**, **Norton**, **San Telmo**, **Terrazas de los Andes**, **Trapiche**, **Weinert** and **Zuccardi**.

CONSUMER INFORMATION

WHAT DO I GET FOR MY MONEY?

The good wines of Chile are still pretty good value, particularly since quality is so far improving year by year. The Merlots are particularly good value. In the case of Argentina quality is more erratic.

AVAILABILITY

Chilean wines are pretty well everywhere, though tracking down the best producers can be more problematic. Argentinian wines are increasingly available as more producers look to the export markets.

CONSUMER CHECKLIST

Chilean Merlot 2003	*Quality 7* ★
(Concha y Toro)	*Price 5* ★
	Value 9 ★

Good Years Always choose the most recent vintage available, though reds will age.
Taste Notes Chilean wines are notable for their juicy fruit. The better reds have oak aging to add depth and structure, and the whites are increasingly fresh and crisp. Argentine reds tend to be jammy and soft, and the whites tend to blandness.

AUSTRALIA

*A*ustralia's vineyards were established to aid the cause of temperance! Back in the early nineteenth century over-indulgence in rum was such a problem in the rowdy penal colony that successive governors hoped to wean convicts off ardent firewater and on to civilized – and civilizing – table wine. Some hope. Table wines of some quality did flourish fitfully in isolated parts of New South Wales, Victoria and South Australia, but the locals quickly demonstrated a preference for beer and sweet fortified wines. It really wasn't until the 1970s that a modern Australian wine industry became firmly established, and innovative and talented winemakers and grape growers learnt how to harness a harsh and arid environment.

The typical Australian vineyard (left) – a patch of irrigated green in a relentlessly parched land – is worlds away from Europe's lush landscape. This is Delatite Vineyards and Winery high up on the northern slopes of the Great Dividing Range at Mansfield in Victoria. The Muscat à Petits Grains grapes being harvested (above) grew in the equally arid Barossa Valley in South Australia.

WINE REGIONS

Anyone who has ever flown across Australia has already grasped the crucial point about the country's wine industry – the fact that Australia is very dry indeed. And it takes a long time to cross that vast red expanse of nothing in the middle. When the view from the window starts to become green, you know you're near the coast. When you start seeing suburbs, you know you're practically on the coast.

That's Australia: a fertile green fringe draped around a desert. And that's where the vineyards are, in that fertile fringe. Some of the oldest areas are certainly almost too warm, too humid, while some of the recent vineyard areas are certainly too fertile for high quality. And the current drift towards cooler, higher regions mirrors the changes that have overtaken the Australian wine industry since its earliest days.

The earliest vineyard areas were within a grape's throw of major cities. They produced big, alcoholic table wines or fortified wines that not only served the local markets but were given preferential duty rates when exported to the mother country – and as a result, in the 1930s, Britain drank more Australian wine than French. But the French wine was better: nobody thought of Australia as a producer of high-quality wine.

The first signs of change occurred in the 1950s. New technology showed the way: suddenly it was possible to ferment wine at low temperatures, in stainless steel vats. Suddenly wine from warm vineyards didn't have to taste like overboiled jam. Australians began to drink more table wine, and less fortified wine. But it took until the 1980s for the message to get through to the rest of us: that here was a country producing large amounts of wine that was reliably fruity, reliably well made and reliably inexpensive. As the winemakers have become ever more practised at making the most of their climate, so their wines have become still better and more varied. Now we can pay low prices and get appealing, simple everyday stuff, or we can pay considerably, but not ridiculously more, and get something to lay down for a special occasion a few years hence. Or anything in between.

To anybody versed in European viticulture, though, there are certain basic differences to be grasped. For one thing, you can plant a vineyard anywhere you like in Australia, and sell the wine for whatever you and your market think it is worth. That's not the case in Europe, where wine-making is hedged about with restrictions on what you can grow where, and what it ought to taste like. And in this driest of all continents, if there's no river nearby to provide irrigation water (and there often isn't), no worries: you dig a dam to catch winter rain (a reservoir, to non-Aussies), and suddenly you can fish, swim and irrigate your vines, all at the same time.

Irrigation is the reason that grapes can be grown in every one of Australia's states (even hot, humid Queensland is making a pretty good go of it in the south of the state). But the vineyards are concentrated in the south-east of the country, scattered in regions that grew up for reasons of history, or geography, or climate, or just whim. Because while Australian wine is predominantly made by big companies – around 80 per cent comes from the three largest companies – there are many, many companies of every size, right down to vineyards cultivated part time at weekends.

The first colonial settlements were in New South Wales; and the first vines were planted here, too. Now its most famous areas are the Hunter Valley, which has a far from ideal climate for viticulture – and yet manages to make some of Australia's best wines; Mudgee and Orange, higher up and further inland; and on the other side of the Great Dividing Range Riverina, where the Australian talent for producing vast quantities of good quality wine is manifest.

Victoria's vineyards are often where they are because they were planted in the wake of the Gold Rush. Nowadays the wines range from the distinctly warm-climate liqueur Muscats of Glenrowan and Rutherglen to the silky Pinot Noirs of the Yarra Valley.

South Australia produces more wine than any other state. In the Riverland it boasts another of those high-volume, decent-quality regions; in the Clare and Eden valleys, and the Adelaide Hills, it has cool climates to coax flavour from Riesling and Chardonnay, while the Barossa Valley and McLaren Vale revel in rich, ripe red styles and Limestone Coast and Coonawarra offer superb, fairly cool conditions in the far south.

Western Australia's wine regions are almost as far west as possible in this huge continent. The boiling hot Swan Valley is the most traditional region; the Margaret River and the Lower Great Southern are cooler and more exciting. Tasmania, with its obviously cool climate and Queensland, with its surprisingly temperate one, also make increasingly good wine.

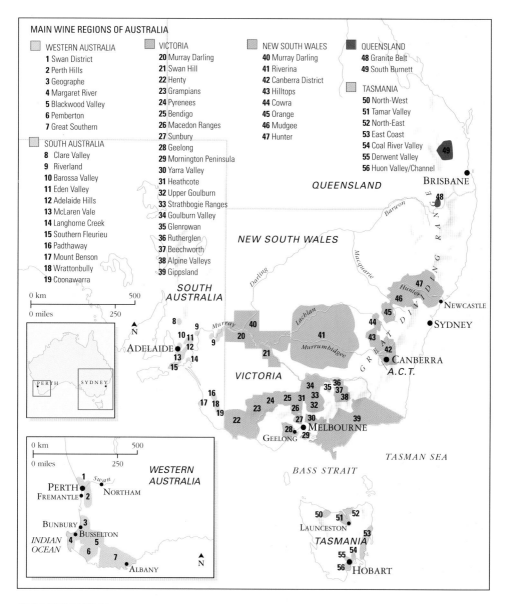

MAIN WINE REGIONS OF AUSTRALIA

WESTERN AUSTRALIA
1 Swan District
2 Perth Hills
3 Geographe
4 Margaret River
5 Blackwood Valley
6 Pemberton
7 Great Southern

SOUTH AUSTRALIA
8 Clare Valley
9 Riverland
10 Barossa Valley
11 Eden Valley
12 Adelaide Hills
13 McLaren Vale
14 Langhorne Creek
15 Southern Fleurieu
16 Padthaway
17 Mount Benson
18 Wrattonbully
19 Coonawarra

VICTORIA
20 Murray Darling
21 Swan Hill
22 Henty
23 Grampians
24 Pyrenees
25 Bendigo
26 Macedon Ranges
27 Sunbury
28 Geelong
29 Mornington Peninsula
30 Yarra Valley
31 Heathcote
32 Upper Goulburn
33 Strathbogie Ranges
34 Goulburn Valley
35 Glenrowan
36 Rutherglen
37 Beechworth
38 Alpine Valleys
39 Gippsland

NEW SOUTH WALES
40 Murray Darling
41 Riverina
42 Canberra District
43 Hilltops
44 Cowra
45 Orange
46 Mudgee
47 Hunter

QUEENSLAND
48 Granite Belt
49 South Burnett

TASMANIA
50 North-West
51 Tamar Valley
52 North-East
53 East Coast
54 Coal River Valley
55 Derwent Valley
56 Huon Valley/Channel

CLASSIFICATION

An agreement with the EU has led Australia to phase out the misuse of European generic wine names, like Chablis or Burgundy, and also to a system of Geographical Indications (not all the boundaries have yet been agreed).

The best-selling wine brands, like Jacobs Creek or Koonunga Hill, are generally blends of wines from all over the country; this practice, which is firmly enshrined in the Australian wine industry, will not change, and brands will not have to declare the precise origin of their grapes.

Label Integrity Programme This merely guarantees that all claims made on the label about vintage, variety and region are true.

Produce of Australia The most basic geographical indication. Many of these wines do not state a vintage or grape on the front label.

South-Eastern Australia This geographical designation is already widely seen. Since South-Eastern Australia incorporates South Australia, New South Wales and Victoria, it is quite hard for a wine not to qualify.

State of Origin The next most specific geographical designation.

Zones Zones are smaller than a state, and incorporate several regions.

Regions This is the next most specific designation. There are nearly 60 so far, with more in the pipeline.

Sub-regions Regions can be sub-divided into these smaller areas. There are over 12 so far, with many more to come. The Adelaide Hills region, for example, has two sub-regions, Lenswood and Piccadilly Valley. Politics sadly but inevitably will play a part in just where the boundaries are drawn.

NEW SOUTH WALES

New South Wales is the home of the **Hunter Valley**, a small, virtually subtropical area, which for years was presumed to produce the archetypal Australian wine: the reds big, strong, tarry, sweaty – real man's stuff – and the whites big, strong, oily, petrolly – man's stuff again.

You won't find much Hunter wine tasting like that nowadays, as the valley has become one of Sydney's tourist playgrounds and, if anything, too many of the wines actually need a bit of that old-timers 'grunt' in them. The Hunter is a conservative place, but they know when to be flexible and chase the tourist dollar and the finest wines are from winemakers who have the experience to deal with the Hunter's tricky growing conditions but know how to innovate.

The trouble with the Hunter is drought in the spring when the vines need moisture, downpours at the end of the summer, just when the grapes are ripening, and during the vintage period. The growing season is far too hot, and far too humid. Grapes get scorched, then go rotten. This could explain why the Hunter, which in the nineteenth century was Australia's first and finest vineyard, was almost extinct by the 1950s. Luckly, the enthusiasm for wine which has gripped Australia since the 1960s has revitalized the area.

Dams like this one at Montrose Wines in the Mudgee region are one of the reasons why Australia can produce such reliably good wine in such a dry climate.

The most historic part of the Hunter is the Lower Hunter, where the finest wines are produced. Here, the vineyards are small and frequently run in an eccentric manner. The Upper Hunter is flatter, more fertile, and the irrigated vineyards on rich, alluvial soil are mostly in the hands of large companies, intent on producing high yields of pleasant wines rather than low yields of brilliant ones. The exception to this is the Roxburgh vineyard belonging to Rosemount which can produce sensational Chardonnay and Semillon.

So that's the Hunter – still a producer of some top wines – but it's always a struggle. If we go west and south from the Hunter, we'll find New South Wales has a lot more to offer, and, frankly, better growing conditions too. **Mudgee** is due west, just over the top of the Great Dividing Range. It's fairly high here and the heavy clay soils mean the grapes are slow to ripen, but they don't get the Hunter's cyclonic vintage-time storms, so they generally get a pretty good crop of solid, sometimes tough-edged Cabernet and Shiraz, and broad, fleshy Chardonnay and Semillon. Due south of Mudgee is **Orange** – high, fertile tableland –

indeed the vineyards, up to 1000m (3280ft), are some of the highest in Australia. Orange was famous for cherries and apples and it wasn't until 1983 that Bloodwood planted a vineyard. But Orange quickly showed that it can produce fantastic Chardonnay and Riesling and pretty exciting Pinot Noir and Shiraz too. On the far side of the Dividing Range **Hilltops** and **Tumbarumba** are producing lean, fragrant, focused, cool-climate whites, and lower-altitude **Cowra** produces rich, lush Chardonnay which is in great demand for fattening blends. **Canberra** is another cool-climate area. The vineyards are all just outside the Australian Capital Territory because you can't own land freehold within it. Hot, dry days and cold nights sound encouraging, but spring frosts and wet autumns frequently spoil things. So far there has been some reasonable Riesling, Chardonnay, Shiraz and Cabernet Sauvignon.

But the forgotten giant of New South Wales is the **Riverina**, way out in scorched flatlands – a wasteland until they harnessed the waters of the Murrumbidgee River for irrigation, but now the state's biggest bulk producer and also the surprising source of some great sweet Semillon in the style of Sauternes. And if you're a fan of the Aussie phenomenon Yellowtail, well, this is where it comes from.

GRAPE VARIETIES AND WINE STYLES
There are over 60 different grape varieties grown in New South Wales, and the range of wines made is as wide as anywhere in Australia. Interestingly, for what is mostly a warm state, whites make the majority of the best wines, and the globally unheralded **Semillon** manages to produce two classic wines in styles that couldn't be more different. First, in the Lower Hunter it makes a wine that often starts out green and lean but over, 5, 10, 15 years a most astonishing transformation occurs as the wine takes on flavours of toast and custard, honey, petrol and lime. And the cyclone vintages which force growers to pick when the grapes aren't fully ripe, often produce the best wines of the lot.

Out in the Riverina, Semillon still makes a remarkably characterful dry white – an apple peel and lanolin wax – but also produces world class sweet wine. And I mean world class. De Bortoli's Noble One Semillon frequently beats France's top Sauternes in blind tastings. This is because the Semillon is the same grape as for Sauternes, and the 'noble rot' fungus, which attacks Sauternes' grapes and

massively concentrates their sugar, also attacks the Semillon in Riverina almost every year. The result is a viscous, waxy golden wine, packed with honey, barley sugar, peach and pineapple spice. Unexpected and fabulous.

Chardonnay can be exciting in the Hunter, and wines like Tyrrells Vat 47 and Rosemount Roxburgh have become world famous for their over-the-top, indulgent tropical flavours. Cowra, however, is a more reliable place to grow Chardonnay.

Most wine areas have something they do best, even if no-one quite knows why. Warm-climate Cowra should excel at Shiraz or Cabernet – but it doesn't. Its sandy soils and irrigation water from the River Lachlan produce a lush, creamy, almost syrupy Chardonnay style that is memorably Australian. Mudgee also produces fat but less irresistible Chardonnay, while Orange and Tumbarumba produce exciting, lean, savoury Chardonnay that may well become some of Australia's best in the future.

There are a lot of red grapes grown in the state but few of them produce wines of the quality of the best whites. **Shiraz** is certainly the most famous but its fame rests in the Hunter, and is based on wines of another era

In the Lower Hunter Valley there can be too much rain and usually it falls at the wrong time. Look at the lushness of the grass – and look at those clouds.

when there were few alternatives and wine faults were often lauded as 'regionality'. Now Australia is brimming with places able to produce top Shiraz and bursting open with talented winemakers who wouldn't allow the Hunter Valley 'sweaty saddle' flavours – aka excessive sulphides – within a mile of their winery. Yet when the vintage rains hold off, the Hunter can produce very good, rather restrained, savoury styles of Shiraz. Mudgee at its best adds a little blackcurrant spice to the taste, and Orange is showing real, cool-climate style with blackberry fruit and floral scent – and alcohol levels up to 14 per cent. Riverina Shiraz is a little fat and soft – she does a much better job of deep, dark fruit with the rare Durif. There's nowhere in New South Wales where **Cabernet** is an unqualified success – Hunter sometimes gets it right, as does Mudgee. Orange Cabernet verges on the leafy except in top years, but Riverina Cabernet is pleasant enough; jammy but tasty. **Pinot Noir** isn't much of a speciality but the Hunter has produced one or two star wines.

Best producers: **Allandale**, **Bloodwood**, **Brokenwood**, **De Bortoli**, **De Iullis**, **Hope**, **Lake's Folly**, **Lindemans**, **McWilliams**, **Meerea Park**, **Rosemount**, **Rothbury**, **Thomas**, **Tower**, **Keith Tulloch** and **Tyrrell's**.

CLASSIFICATION
Official boundaries for the official wine regions is about as complicated as it gets.

ORGANIZATION
A mixture of boutique operations and wineries sounding like boutiques but actually owned by the big corporations e.g. Rosemount Estate and Rothbury Estate. Riverina has several quite large family companies.

READING THE LABEL
Some like Tyrrell's use Vat numbers on special wines, others like McWilliams may use Bin numbers.

WHAT DO THEY TASTE LIKE?
In the Hunter there are still earthy, solid reds and thick, soupy whites, but mostly the modern Shirazes are midweight and appetizing and the whites are only slightly marked by their old phenolic waxiness. Semillon starts lean and ends up toasty and broad. The high altitude wines of Tumbarumba, Hilltops and Orange are elegant and scented, while Mudgee's are fairly dense in their fruit, and Cowra Chardonnay is rich and fat. Riverina reds are soft and jammy but the Semillon is exceptional.

THE GOOD YEARS
Most wines are for drinking young.
2004 High yields but good quality.
2003 Reduced yields but excellent quality.
2002 Rain at vintage spoiled some of the crop. Excellent in Riverina.
2001 Hunter reds suffered from vintage rain.

ENJOYING THE WINES
Riverina wines are simple, everyday wines. The great Chardonnays are fine enough to partner classic cuisine, while Hunter Semillons are often better with meat dishes than fish. Hunter reds go well with red meats.

CONSUMER INFORMATION

Lower Hunter wines are among Australia's most expensive, and are only good value from the top estates like Lake's Folly, Lindemans, Tyrrell's and Rothbury. Upper Hunter wines and Mudgee wines can be cheaper and good, while Riverina wines are cheap and good value.

AVAILABILITY
This is better than it used to be. The wines from the biggest companies in New South Wales, like McWilliams, Rosemount and Rothbury, are widely available.

CONSUMER CHECKLIST
Mount Pleasant	*Price 6* ★
Elizabeth Semillon 1998	*Quality 9* ★
(McWilliams)	*Value 10* ★

Good Years 2002, 2000, 1999, 1998, 1996, 1995, 1994, 1991.
Taste Notes New South Wales wines are full and fat with lots of taste. The whites are generally better than the reds.

VICTORIA

Victoria, more than any other Australian state, suffered from the devastation of the phylloxera louse and the shift in taste away from light table wine which occurred in Australia during the first half of the twentieth century. It suffered most because it was not only the biggest producer – its volume of wine in 1889, at over 7 million litres, was way ahead of South Australia's at 2.3 million and New South Wales's at 3.1 million – but the fame of its wines had spread worldwide, especially to Europe, and it already had to its credit a large number of awards both in domestic and international wine competitions. Geelong, Bendigo and the Yarra Valley were even then making delicate, balanced reds and whites which were building great renown for their areas in particular and Australia in general.

Frequently the spur to planting vines in the first place had been gold. Gold was found in Victoria in 1851; as soon as the secret was out would-be gold diggers started arriving from all over the world, desperate for their share of the wealth. And they wanted to slake their dry, dusty throats with – well, anything alcoholic. Avoca had been planted with vines since 1848, Bendigo planted its first vineyards in 1855, Great Western followed in 1858 and Ballarat joined the party in 1859. Anybody who had wine to sell was potentially in the money: flush with success or miserable with failure, miners would pay up to £5 a gallon for wine. In the normal, non-gold rush markets of southern Victoria, South Australia or New South Wales it would sell for only one-twentieth of that price.

But the Gold Rush came to an end, and a lot of these vineyards found themselves without buyers for their wine. Then, in 1875, along came the even greater blow of phylloxera, which hit Bendigo and Geelong so hard that the government ordered the uprooting of every single vine. In 1881, just eight years after the wines had been trouncing European competition at the 1873 Vienna Exhibition, the phylloxera louse and the Victorian government had, between them, destroyed the entire area. It was 85 years years before the next vine was planted in Geelong in 1966, 68 years before Bendigo saw another vine, and the Yarra Valley waited until 1968 for the re-establishment of its most famous vineyard, St Huberts. Since then, these three districts have shot to the fore of Australian wine-making once again, with the revived areas of Great Western (now renamed

The Grampians region was planted to slake the thirst of the Gold Rush miners; these vines at Montara Vineyards are of a more recent date.

as Grampians), Pyrenees and Central Goulburn Valley also reminding us of why they became famous in the first place.

If few of these names are very familiar, it is because of the almost complete demise of viticulture in Victoria during the first 60 years of the twentieth century. During that time South Australia and New South Wales continued to release small amounts of their great wines. North-East Victoria, and in particular the Rutherglen district – already famous for sweet Muscats and fortified wines – was able to survive phylloxera and the slump in demand for fine wine, but paradoxically is now struggling to find markets for its classic wines.

Several other tiny wine areas are beginning to flower again, like Goulburn, Gippsland, Ballarat and various spots in what are loosely termed Central Victoria High Country. And, of course, Victoria has its own grape basket irrigated area – this time along the banks of the Murray River, where some of the country's largest wineries process enormous quantities of fruit. In the last 20 years Victoria has begun to re-establish itself. Its wines are so fine, and so varied, that the next few years will see it fighting to regain its place as Australia's number one quality producer.

GRAPE VARIETIES AND WINE STYLES

Much of Victoria's strength lies in the fact that so many of her best vineyards have been planted – or re-planted – in the last couple of decades, and so the grape varieties chosen are mostly modern, effective performers. However, with this narrower range of classic grape varieties, the variations in style are still greater than in any other state. Endless trial, not much error, and all change every vintage is the order of the day, as Victoria's young winemakers probe further and further in the search for quality.

Let's start with the richest of all Victorian wines. These glories of the **North-East** region are the Liqueur Muscats and Liqueur Tokays of the **Glenrowan** and **Rutherglen** districts. Fortified and aged in old oak barrels for years, they combine the body and guts of great Madeira with a sweet beauty which is like the bottled essence of the ripest grapes on a late summer hothouse vine. The Muscadelle grape makes the sweet, raisiny Tokay, and both styles are world classics. They do table wines as well, and reds outshine whites with Shiraz and the beefy Durif sharing the honours. Best producers (fortifieds): **All Saints, Baileys, Brown Brothers, Bullers, Campbells, Chambers, Morris** and **Stanton & Killeen**.

The floor is earth and the roof is corrugated iron, but the Muscats and Tokays, in these old barrels at Morris Wines, are as fine as any in the world.

The great goldfield vineyards run in an arc from Ballarat, west of Melbourne, up through Ararat and Great Western and eastwards through Bendigo, Heathcote and Rutherglen to Beechworth. All vineyards were founded on the Gold Rush; **Ballarat** is largely known now as the base of Yellowglen fizz, but the **Grampians** region – taking in Ararat and Great Western – while famous for the fizz that Seppelt has produced at Great Western – is more famous for its reds and whites.

Vineyards are few and widespread in this part of the state, because a water supply is hard to locate, but wonderful scented Shiraz, savoury Chardonnay and delightful Riesling show the region's quality. **Bendigo** makes lovely eucalyptus-scented Shiraz but the deep, red soils of Heathcote which produce red wines of lush texture yet tremendous depth may yet prove to be some of Australia's best. Both Glenrowan and Rutherglen are best at rich fortifieds but **King Valley** has some excellent sites, often planted with Italian varieties like Nebbiolo and Sangiovese, and **Beechworth** perched on a high escarpment

over the Ovens Valley is proving to be an exceptional cool-climate area for reds and whites. Best producers (Goldfields): **Balgownie, Best's, Dalwhinnie, Delatite, Giaconda, Harcourt Valley, Heathcote, Jasper Hill, Mitchelton, Montara, Mount Langi Ghiran, Passing Clouds, Pizzini, Red Edge, Redbank** and **Seppelt.**

Victoria has several other cool-climate areas – **Geelong** and **Mornington Peninsula,** south of Melbourne, **Macedon** and **Sunbury,** north of Melbourne, **Gippsland,** a large zone to the south-east, but the most important and most famous is **Yarra Valley** virtually in the suburbs of Melbourne itself. It's cool here – cool enough for this region to be a prime source of silky, supple Pinot Noir, and also fine Champagne-method sparkling wine. But it's also warm enough to make intense, rich Shiraz and Cabernet. The secret is that the land is not just a straightforward up-and-down valley. Instead it offers sites at just about all useful altitudes (it can even get too high and too cold) and exposures. So it can turn its hand to just about all classic wine styles (except fortified – it never gets that hot) and make them in a deep, soft, approachable but always fascinating style. Best producers (cool climate regions): **Bannockburn, Bass Phillip, Bindi, By Farr, Delatite, Kooyong, Moorooduc, Rochford, Scotchmans Hill, Stonier** and **T'Gallant**; (Yarra) **Coldstream Hills, De Bortoli, Diamond Valley, Domaine Chandon/Green Point, Lillydale, Long Gully, Mount Mary, Tarrawarra, Yarra Burn, Yarra Ridge, Yarra Yering, Yeringberg** and **Yering Station.**

CLASSIFICATION
As elsewhere in Australia Victoria has sorted out its first official wine region boundaries.

ORGANIZATION
It is as hard here as anywhere in Australia for an independent producer to flourish. But new wineries are always starting up, even as others opt for mergers with larger companies.

READING THE LABEL
Straightforward labelling is the rule. Yarra Yering even names its main reds Dry Red Number 1 or Dry Red Number 2: the first is Cabernet-based, the second Shiraz-based.

WHAT DO THEY TASTE LIKE?
Victorian wines run the gamut from sweet, sticky and fortified (the Muscats and Tokays of the North-East) to supple, intense and cool-climate (the Pinot Noirs of the Yarra Valley).

THE GOOD YEARS
Victoria's wine regions have such different climates that what is good in the North-East may not be good at all in the Yarra Valley.
2004 Yields well above average and generally whites fared better than reds.
2003 The drought affected quantity but some great wines were produced, especially in Yarra and Mornington.
2002 Cool conditions affected the cool climate areas. Tiny yields. Pinot Noir and aromatic whites did best.
2001 Variable conditions with heat stress at vintage time. Reds fairly good.
2000 Nicely restrained, concentrated wines.

ENJOYING THE WINES
The Chardonnays are particularly good with seafood. The reds are best matched to simple meat dishes, but the biggest Shiraz can take on anything. Liqueur Muscat deserve your undivided attention (or some really good vanilla icecream), as does red sparkling Shiraz.

CONSUMER INFORMATION

Wines from the Yarra Valley tend to be expensive, though they are usually very good. Champagne-method sparkling wine looks good value next to Champagne. The great sweet dessert wines of the North-East are undervalued and irresistible.

AVAILABILITY
Variable, but better than it was. Far more top class wineries are now exporting.

CONSUMER CHECKLIST
Yarra Valley Chardonnay 2004 (Diamond Valley)

Quality 10 ★
Price 8 ★
Value 10 ★

Good Years 2004, 2003, 2002, 2001, 2000, 1999, 1998, 1997, 1996, 1995, 1994, 1991, 1990.
Taste Notes The flavours of Victoria wines range from elegant and silky to intensely sweet and sticky.

SOUTH AUSTRALIA

This is what makes Coonawarra great: a thin layer of rich, red topsoil over a deep, free-draining limestone ridge, an ideal environment for root nourishment.

South Australia is the biggest single wine-producing state in Australia. Victoria produces big volumes on the Murray River and New South Wales does the same in Riverina, but South Australia, tapping into the same vast river system, outdoes them both with the vast Riverland region, where the Murray River heads westwards across the state boundary on its way to the sea.

Yet if this makes South Australia sound like a mere bulk producer of anonymous hooch, we should think again. It took over the mantle of wine supplier to the nation in the late nineteenth century when much of the rest of Australia was devastated by phylloxera, and South Australia, protected from the louse by desert and sea, was untouched. Consequently, it had to satisfy all of Australia's thirst for wine. And that thirst was usually for heavy, sweet, cheap wine.

For a long while South Australia's reputation continued to be that of a supplier of big, flabby Barossa Valley Rieslings, scorching McLaren Vale reds and heady 'ports', rather than that of a quality producer of similar rank to the other states. But how out of date that now is. Yes, there's the Riverland, churning out the sort of cheap and cheerful wine that bulk regions in Europe would kill to make.

But listen to this tally of quality: Clare Valley; Barossa Valley; Eden Valley; Adelaide Hills; McLaren Vale; Langhorne Creek; Limestone Coast; Padthaway; Coonawarra. South Australia is in the forefront of the movement to high-altitude, cool-climate sites for viticulture. And there are dozens of brilliant sites, still undeveloped, and within easy reach of Adelaide into the bargain.

Sadly, many of these sites are destined always to remain undeveloped. Water is, as ever in Australia, the limiting factor in viticulture. And there's a general lack of subterranean water in South Australia, too – which means that sinking a well next to your planned vineyard won't necessarily yield the large quantities of water you'd hoped for and what you get may be brackish. Even in Coonawarra, whose water table is so high that if you stand in the wrong place for too long you're liable to get foot rot, the water is rationed to some extent. The water here comes from the Great Artesian Basin just below the surface – and the neighbouring states, perfectly reasonably, don't regard it as

South Australia's personal property. Victoria doesn't want its water supplies drying up because South Australia is busy watering its vines – and so there are agreed limits on how much water South Australia may take.

GRAPE VARIETIES AND WINE STYLES

Look at the address at the bottom of the labels of some of Australia's biggest wine companies. If you see the words 'Nuriootpa' or 'Tanunda' or 'Angaston', then they're in the **Barossa Valley**. This doesn't mean that the grapes were grown in the Barossa; in fact, they probably weren't. Barossa may be one of Australia's best vineyard areas but its commercial importance lies in the fact that the major companies process a large proportion of their grapes in mega-wineries there – even though they were probably grown in the bulk-producing Riverland, or Padthaway, or Clare, or even in places across the state borders. That's one side of the modern Barossa.

But the other side of the modern Barossa has its base in some of the oldest vines on the planet. When the Silesian settlers arrived from the 1840s onwards, they brought vines with them – Riesling, Shiraz, Grenache and others. The vine louse phylloxera destroyed most of the world's vineyards in the second half of the nineteenth century – indeed most of Australia's were devastated as well – but South Australia has never suffered the bug, so the vines from two centuries ago have survived in significant numbers. They give tiny crops of unbelievably intense fruit that until a generation ago was merely blended away, but is now recognized and revered for what it is – some of the most precious juice in the world of wine today. In particular old-vine Shiraz is greatly sought after and commands sky-high prices. Old Grenache is also highly regarded. There are less old Riesling vines since people have long realized the Barossa Valley floor is above all a red wine paradise. These Barossa Shirazes and Grenaches have remarkably rich, powerful black fruit, sometimes overripe, often merely super-ripe, always impressive.

However, it really does bake down in the Barossa Valley floor so for the best whites – and also for some stunning, more elegant reds, they headed for the hills, into the Mount Lofty Ranges just to the east of the Valley and in particular to High Eden and Eden Valley. Some of South Australia's most famous reds come from up here – Henschke's Hill of

Grace, for a start – but it is the thrilling flame-scented citrus Rieslings I mostly crave along with restrained but delicious Semillon and Chardonnay. Most of the great Barossa producers also make a refreshing and delicious white from up in these hills. Best producers: **Barossa Valley Estate**, **Grant Burge**, **Henschke**, **Peter Lehmann**, **Charles Melton**, **Orlando**, **Penfolds**, **Rockford**, **St Hallett**, **Torbreck**, **Veritas** and **Yalumba**.

But before we leave the Barossa altogether, I must tell you the story of Grange. Grange has acquired for itself, and with good reason, the unofficial title of Australia's Finest Red. It used to be called Grange Hermitage, in homage to the Rhône Valley, for this is one of the world's finest examples of the Shiraz or Syrah grape.

1n 1950 Max Schubert, chief winemaker at **Penfolds**, went to Europe. What struck him there, above all, was the quality and aging capacity of the great reds of Bordeaux. He came back to Australia determined to produce something just as good – and that, back in the days when nobody thought Australia capable of producing really good, serious wine, was nothing short of revolutionary.

But he couldn't produce a carbon copy of the red Bordeauxs – for one thing, while there

These rotary vinificators at Wynn's Coonawarra winery show how Australian companies have been at the forefront of new wine-making technology.

was plenty of Shiraz in South Australia, there wasn't much Cabernet Sauvignon. And while red Bordeaux is aged in French oak, he only had the more pungent American oak.

He made his wine, and he was thrilled with it. But few people agreed with him. It was just too different, too unfamiliar. The powers-that-be at Penfolds even ordered him to stop making it – so he carried on in secret. A few years later those same bosses were very glad he had carried on, because suddenly the wine began to be noticed. And praised.

Grange – and Schubert – never looked back. His wine became the prototype for a new generation of Australian reds. Nowadays, the grapes for Grange can come from anywhere, be it Coonawarra, McLaren Vale or Clare, as long as they're the very best.

To get to the **Clare Valley** from Barossa you head north. It gets hotter and hotter. The land becomes impossibly parched. Then suddenly, in a dip of land just north of the little town of Auburn, you feel a breeze in your face, and green vines stretch away in front of you. It's a real shock after the harsh slog of the ride from the Barossa. And you think – how can vines flourish here, well on the way to the parched heart of Australia?

Well, it's partly to do with height. Clare sits at over 400 metres (1312ft) above sea level and some vines are over 500 metres (1640ft). You do get cooling breezes and, crucially, the temperature really dives every night. And the result is tremendously focussed, intensive fruit flavours in red and white. But how can the famously cool climate, austere Riesling excel next door to Cabernet, Grenache, Shiraz and even the Portuguese Touriga Nacional? It's the great paradox of Clare. One vineyard will ripen the heat-loving Touriga in February. A few miles away, Riesling will struggle to be ripe by April. And those Cabernets and Shirazes do have a wonderful, dense, finely polished fruit quality, half cool climate elegance, half warm climate ripeness. The Clare in a nutshell. Best producers: **Adams**, **Barry**, **Grosset**, **Leasingham**, **Mitchell**, **Mount Horrocks**, **Petaluma** and **Wendouree**.

If the Clare is paradoxical, so are the **Adelaide Hills** – the beautiful, heavily wooded hills that dip and dive above Adelaide to the east. Famous for a damp, cool climate ideal for sparkling wines, Riesling, Sauvignon and taut, exciting Chardonnay, they can actully ripen the heat-obsessed Zinfandel up there, and Shiraz is scented and exciting. In a way this demonstrates one of the brilliant things about Australia – if you don't tie everyone's hands behind their back with restrictive appellation controls that tell you what you can and can't do, innovation can flourish. So wonderful new styles of wine develop that no one in the old, restricted world, had ever though possible. So-called typicity is fine, but imagination and inspiration are better. Best producers: **Ashton Hills**, **Chain of Ponds**, **Henschke**, **Knappstein Lenswood**, **Lenswood Vineyards**, **Nepenthe**, **Petaluma**, **Primo**, **Shaw & Smith** and **Geoff Weaver**.

The southern end of the Adelaide Hills slips imperceptibly into **McLaren Vale**, just south of Adelaide. This is a compact area famous for 'port' and ferreginous reds in the old days. It was presumed to be blindingly hot – but it isn't. Sunny, yes, but sea breezes cool the warm excesses of temperature down near the coast where rich, fruity Chardonnay excels. Further inland it gets hotter and the Shiraz and Cabernet vines bake to a memorable, black-fruited ripeness. This whole area south of Adelaide is called **Fleurieu** and there are vines scattered all over, particularly in **Langhorne Creek** down by Lake Alexandria, where very attractive soft reds and whites are grown in the flat fertile land. Best producers: **Chapel Hill**, **Clarendon Hills**, **D'Arenberg**, **Fox Creek**, **Hardy**, **Reynell** and **Wirra Wirra**.

Heading south there's one great last hurrah – the Limestone Coast – basically a semi-empty wilderness of sheep paddocks and cattle runs and sudden seriously impressive blocks of vines. There are a series of coastal ridges of limestone running right down to the bottom of Australia, and vines *love* limestone. The less well known areas are Wirrega, **Padthaway** – an excellent source of rich pineappley Chardonnay and sweetly ripe Shiraz – and **Wrattonbully** – a highly promising area for powerful, dark-hearted reds. There are some good vines right on the coast at **Mount Benson** and **Robe**, but the star is **Coonawarra**, the most famous limestone ridge with a red typical of weathered limestone and a record of producing sublime, musty, blackcurranty Cabernet and Merlot as well as peppery Shiraz, limey Riesling and pineappley, buttery Chardonnay. Best producers: **Brand's**, **Henry's Drive**, **Lindemans**, **Majella**, **Parker**, **Penfolds**, **Penley**, **Petaluma**, **Wynns** and **Zema**.

And last but not least, the **Riverland**. Tucked into the serpentine bends of the River Murray, and way inland where the sun really beats down, are vast mechanized vineyards, computer controlled, heavily irrigated with Murray water, and pumping out oceans of wine that ranges from the pleasantly forgetable to really good single varietal wines from grapes like Shiraz and Petit Verdot.

CLASSIFICATION

South Australia, as elsewhere in the country, now has official boundaries for its wine regions but new areas are still being developed where boundaries are understandably hazy at present.

ORGANIZATION

South Australia, especially the Barossa, is home to many of the country's largest wineries but there is also a very healthy number of independent producers.

READING THE LABEL

Most labelling is by grape variety, though some companies use bin numbers and fancy titles are increasingly common for the top wines.

WHAT DO THEY TASTE LIKE?

In general the cool areas of Coonawarra, Padthaway, Limestone Coast, Adelaide Hills and Eden Valley will give intense yet fragrant flavours, whereas those from the Southern Vales and parts of Clare Valley will be well defined but punchier. The Barossa can be rich and concentrated in both reds and whites.

THE GOOD YEARS

Coonawarra is the most susceptible to vintage variation, yet bad years are rare. Reds from here can age well, as can South Australia's whites, particularly Chardonnay, Semillon and Riesling from cooler regions. Barossa Shiraz can be very long-lived and Grange seems almost immortal. Drink Riverland wines young.

2004 Vintage was late and long and quality is mainly top-notch.

2003 Challenging conditions. Reds did better than whites. Shiraz was the star performer.

2002 Cool summer. Outstanding if atypical wines.

2001 Seriously hot even for South Australia. Reds did better on the whole than whites.

2000 A small crop but quality generally good.

ENJOYING THE WINES

Lamb, simply roasted, is the ideal partner for Coonawarra Cabernet Sauvignon. The richer Shirazes can cope with flavoursome game dishes and hearty casseroles: these are winter wines. The cool-climate Rieslings will go with fish dishes or, even better, with oriental, (particularly Thai) food. That touch of lime in the flavour makes these wines an ideal match.

CONSUMER INFORMATION

WHAT DO I GET FOR MY MONEY?

Riverland wines are very good value for money, but the labels won't necessarily identify them as the produce of the Murray River. South East Australia is a more likely designation. Companies like Yalumba, Orlando and Hardy offer great value. Clare, McLaren Vale and Limestone Coast all offer excellent flavours at a fair price. Barossa can be fairly priced or absurdly expensive.

AVAILABILITY

Distribution of the large companies' wines is very good, and the smaller companies have been increasing their exports in recent years. Clare Valley, Eden Valley, Barossa and Coonawarra wines should all be fairly easy to track down, though the top wines may only be available from the better specialists and then in small quantities.

CONSUMER CHECKLIST

The Footbolt Shiraz 2002	*Quality 8* ★
McLaren Vale	*Price 6* ★
(D'Arenberg)	*Value 10* ★

Good Years Coonawarra is the region most subject to vintage variation. Other regions are more reliable from year to year. Best years: 2004, 2003, 2002, 2001, 1999, 1998, 1997, 1996, 1994, 1991, 1990.

Taste Notes The flavours in South Australia range from the toast and lime of Riesling from the Eden and Clare valleys, the Adelaide Hills and the hilly sites in Barossa, through brilliant, vivid Cabernet Sauvignon from Coonawarra, to rich, intense, concentrated Shiraz from the Barossa Valley floor and further south in McLaren Vale. The Riverland region produces huge quantities of well-made, agreeable bag-in-box wine.

WESTERN AUSTRALIA

In South Australia the vine barely manages to sidle further west than Adelaide. It's about a four-hour flight westward before you hit the next vineyards, and they're on the far side of Western Australia. There's not much in between, either. Just a lot of desert and a lot of sea. That makes the Western Australian vineyards, and the state capital Perth, very isolated indeed – and explains why until recently the wines have made relatively little impact on the wider world. People weren't questioning their quality, they simply couldn't taste them. And until recently the only widely available WA wine was Houghton's 'White Burgundy' – HWB as it is now called – which was quite a big brand in the east of Australia.

Yet in this isolation, a remarkable wine culture has been born, has flourished and is now making a bigger and bigger impact on the wider world, especially as people look to Australia to provide more examples of relatively cool climate flavours. You wouldn't think so to look at the map – most of it seems to be arid desert but look to the little bulging knob of land at the very bottom corner of the state – that's Margaret River – and look across to Albany, the old whaling port to the east. Between these two are some of Australia's most thrilling vineyards – and they're all cool.

But that's not where wine started. As usual in Australia the first wines were planted near

the capital city – Perth – along the Swan River Valley. Now the **Swan Valley** *is* hot – the hottest of any of Australia's mainstream wine areas. Vines were established in the 1830s and fortified wines won a well-deserved reputation in the baking heat. The one company to make exciting table wines was Houghton, now Western Australia's leading company.

It wasn't until the 1960s when a bunch of doctors in **Margaret River** saw a report saying their little region jutting out into the Indian Ocean could be as good a cool climate region as the great Bordeaux in France that the modern wine era arrived. Those doctors established wineries – Vasse Felix, Moss Wood and Cullen were the first three – that have since proved that Margaret River *is* one of the world's most brilliant cool climate regions. And that has encouraged pioneering spirits to look for even cooler conditions further south where the mellow Indian Ocean's influence is replaced by the Antarctic chill of the Southern Ocean. An area called **Great Southern**, based on five different areas spreading eastward to Albany, has proved brilliant for cool climate whites like Riesling and delicate Chardonnay as well as florally scented Shiraz and tasty Pinot Noir. Frankland River and Mount Barker are the most important of the areas. And between Margaret River and Great Southern two other cool regions nestle – **Pemberton** and **Manjimup**, while north of Margaret River **Geographe**, **Peel** and **Perth Hills** get gradually warmer.

GRAPE VARIETIES AND WINE STYLES

Let's start with the Swan Valley. Most of its reds taste jammy or baked, though improvements in the wineries have led to improved flavours. But interestingly it's the whites I prefer – Chenin and Verdelho are surprisingly good and Semillon and Chardonnay aren't bad.

Perth Hills are higher and cooler than the nearby Swan and the wines have more style. Heading south from Perth we pass three vineyard areas, Peel, Geographe and Blackwood Valley, with Geographe the most important. The conditions are still quite warm here, but the reds and whites have attractive fruit. But as the coast curves away from Bunbury towards the town of Busselton we finally hit Margaret River, the jewel of the west.

There are two main areas to Margaret River. The first is around Wilyabrup towards Cape Clairault, and the second is a little further south around Margaret River itself. And even in those

few miles, the conditions have cooled. The original 1960s wineries around Wilyabrup made their reputation with Bordeaux blend reds which exhibit powerful blackcurrant fruit and restrained eucalyptus scent on a base of satisfyingly strong dryness. They're deep, long-lived and impressive. Shiraz, Pinot Noir and various white varieties also thrive. Down south of Margaret River township the most famous wines have been white, in particular Leeuwin Estates' Chardonnay, but wineries like Cape Mentelle and Voyager have produced excellent reds as well as whites. Grapes are now grown right down to Karridale in the south where the flavours are tangy and fresh, and inland from Wilyabrup at Jindong where reds in particular are fruity and soft.

For cool conditions, however, the vineyards of Pemberton, Manjimup and Great Southern excel. Some of Australia's best floral Rieslings are from Frankland River, some of its most scented Shirazes from Manjimup and Mount Barker and Chardonnays are focused and tasty right across the South. Best producers: **Alkoomi, Cape Mentelle, Cullen, Devil's Lair, Gilberts, Houghton, Howard Park, Leeuwin, Moss Wood, Pierro, Plantagenet, Sandalford, Suckfizzle** and **Voyager**.

CLASSIFICATION
There was an attempt at controlled Appellation in Western Australia, but now the effort is going into defining regional boundaries.

ORGANIZATION
Houghton is the dominant wine company. The rest of the industry is largely made up of small producers.

READING THE LABEL
Increasingly wines are being made from specific regions, though Great Southern has five subregions to blend from.

WHAT DO THEY TASTE LIKE?
Most reds and whites have exciting but restrained cool climate flavours. Chardonnays, Rieslings and Bordeaux blend reds are particularly good.

THE GOOD YEARS
Most of these wines are for drinking young, though the reds are well structured and will often age well for quite a few years.
2004 Bumper crop and excellent quality.
2003 A challenging mixed bag. The hot Swan Valley and Perth Hills did well.
2002 A cool, dry year which benefited the whites. Merlot also did well.

The stands of local red gum trees among Margaret River's vineyards are home to kangaroos and birds who eagerly devour the vines and ripening grapes.

2001 A top year for the classic styles.
2000 An excellent year.

ENJOYING THE WINES
Ripe, minty Cabernets are perfect with roast meat or game, and the Pinot Noirs also match game well. The whites, ranging from quite light to substantial, will go with grilled fish and chicken.

CONSUMER INFORMATION

WHAT DO I GET FOR MY MONEY?
Western Australian wines are not bargains, but there's plenty of individuality here. The massive wine companies further east can usually sell wines more cheaply.

AVAILABILITY
Apart from the large companies like Houghton (there aren't many others) quantities are relatively limited. But distribution is increasingly good.

CONSUMER CHECKLIST

Cabernet Sauvignon 2001	*Quality 9* ★
(Cape Mentelle)	*Price 7* ★
	Value 10 ★

Good Years 2004, 2003, 2002, 2001, 2000, 1997, 1996, 1995.
Taste Notes Flavours vary from light and fresh to very rich and intense.

TASMANIA

If there's one thing that nobody could deny, it is that Australia has established its own style of wine. Yes, there are a multiplicity of grapes, a multiplicity of flavours – but that clear, upfront fruit, those ripe, accessible tastes – those are what we all associate with Australian wine. There is very definitely an Australian national style.

And yet when it comes to seeking out new areas in which to plant vines, Australian growers are seldom without their atlases of Europe. They compare latitudes and temperatures, altitudes and rainfall patterns. Then they say, 'Well, this hillside is nearly as cool as Burgundy's Côte d'Or' or, 'This valley has almost the same climate as Bordeaux, except that it's drier' or, 'The soil here reminds us strongly of that in Champagne'. Because some of the most serious winemakers in Australia – those who want to produce wines in ever cooler climates to emulate the sort of complexity and elegance that they see in the finest European wines, or even outdo them – are always on the hunt for new sites. And in the 1970s it was just this sort of hunt that lead Andrew Pirie to Tasmania.

Tasmania is cool. In fact for years the Tasmanian government had reckoned that it was too cool for vines, and had thought apples the best crop. But Andrew Pirie had seen further than the bureaucrats, and had reckoned that parts of the north of the island – the Pipers and Tamar rivers, in fact – could be ideal for vines. He compared them to Burgundy.

Well, Burgundy is very cool. These days, if no vines were planted there, you'd have to be mad to start. Mad or very rich, and with money to throw away. For every wonderful vintage in Burgundy you probably get one dreadful one and a couple of okay ones. Those aren't the sort of averages that any winemaker with a bank loan could live with in the New World. Not when there are 20 other areas to hand turning out reliably ripe wines, year after year.

But Pirie persisted, and Pipers Brook Vineyard opened its doors in 1974. Others followed and there are now over 150 vineyards, most of them less than 5 hectares (12 acres). The vineyards are concentrated on the eastern half of the island: the west is too cool and wet. In Launceston in the north the Pipers River area is appreciably cooler than the Tamar, where the warm river estuary and the lower rainfall give reds a chance to ripen. The south of the island is surprisingly, rather warmer and a couple of patches on the East Coast are exceptional. There have been waves of planting – the first vineyards were established here in the 1820s, though more recently the 1950s saw some interest, followed by the Pirie-led influx in the 1970s. But the total output of the state (1150 hectares/2840 acres) is still less than that of some single wineries on the Australian mainland.

Tasmanian winemakers believe passionately in what they are doing. The difficulties of producing wine here might make them sigh wearily as the wind whipping through the springtime vines means yet another year of poor fruit set or the local birds descend uninvited on the ripening grapes. But the obvious potential of these wines must cheer them, even if they would like just a slightly larger share of the applause lavished on their mainland counterparts.

GRAPE VARIETIES AND WINE STYLES

So how do Tasmanian wines fit into the wider Australian picture? Well, for one thing they are more subtle. Any Europhiles who can't get on with the tropical fruit salad and vanilla oak flavours of a Barossa Valley Chardonnay should find solace here, with the citrussy, oatmealy, toast and butter flavours of, say, Pipers Brook **Chardonnay**. Tasmanian **Cabernet Sauvignon** is cedary and blackcurranty and the **Pinot Noir** supple and spicy. **Sauvignon Blanc** is grapefruity and grassy, and **Riesling** is balanced, perfumed and tends to be less toasty than that from the mainland. There's good intense Gewürztraminer, too.

The reason that many wineries here grow a good range of grapes is that the growers never know what the weather is going to do. unlike in parts of mainland Australia where things are pretty predictable. Tasmania takes unpredictability to extremes, so winemakers here spread their bets by growing a wide range of varieties.

But Tasmania has one supreme standby – Champagne-method sparkling wine from the classic Champagne grapes of Chardonnay and Pinot Noir – and some say it's the only thing the island will ever really be famous for. It's one way of making use of the cool climate – although the wind is still a problem, and keeps the yields uncomfortably low.

Tasmanian sparkling wines are certainly very good. But I love the still wines from here, too, with their concentrated, subtle flavours – even if I can't foresee a time when they'll cease to be overshadowed by their big brothers on the mainland. Best producers: **Clover Hill**, **Domaine A**, **Freycinet**, **Hardy** (Bay of Fires), **Stefano Lubiano**, **Moorilla**, **Pipers Brook**, **Tamar Ridge** and **Wellington**.

CLASSIFICATION
Tasmania has its own system of controlled appellations which is being incorporated into the new federal system.

ORGANIZATION
Tasmania is an island of smallholders, boosted by the investment of a few large companies, such as Yalumba whose Jansz fizz comes from Tasmania.

READING THE LABEL
Some sparkling wine companies on the mainland – Taltarni, for example – source some of their grapes from Tasmania, so you can find that cool-climate influence without seeing it mentioned on the label. Otherwise wines are labelled by grape variety.

WHAT DO THEY TASTE LIKE?
Tasmanian wines, typically, combine the subtlety of European-style cool climates with the classy wine-making and technological know-how of Australia. They are generally light but intense, with good balance.

THE GOOD YEARS
Vintages are more important here than in most Australian regions.
2004 Less than ideal weather. Lean wines with aromatic whites and Pinot Noir did best.
2003 Excellent wines including fizz.

The last autumn sunshine, here at Moorilla Estate, can make a difference between a fine Tasmanian vintage and a merely quite good one.

2002 High-quality wines thanks to a warm, dry autumn.
2001 Excellent Pinot Noir and Chardonnay.
2000 A big vintage of very good quality, especially Pinot Noir.

ENJOYING THE WINES
These are ideal food wines, versatile enough for most dishes, from grilled fish (Sauvignon Blanc) to game (Pinot Noir).

QUEENSLAND

Nobody could describe Queensland as cool. Nobody could describe it as obvious wine country – or even promising wine country. And yet make wine it does – because this is Australia, and anything is possible.

North-west of Brisbane, **Roma** is the hottest wine region in Queensland. The vines grow on fairly high ground but it's not high enough to produce cool temperatures. Even so, the winery here founded in 1863 does make some decent fortifieds.

For lighter wines you have to go south, toward the border with New South Wales, and then start climbing. The **Granite Belt** is where most of Queensland's vines grow, at altitudes of between 750 and 1000m (2500 and 3300ft). Now, that *is* high enough to make a difference. It's still not cool here, except by Queensland standards, but Cabernet Sauvignon, Shiraz, a little Pinot Noir, Chardonnay, Verdelho and Semillon are planted, for rather solid, sturdy wines. Shiraz often seems the most successful of the reds, and Semillon can be rich and good. New vineyards have also opened up at **South Burnett** north west of Brisbane and in small patches both south of Brisbane and west of Toowoomba. Best producers: **Boireann**, **Robert Channon**, **Preston Peak**, **Robinsons**, **Sirromet** and **Summit**.

NEW ZEALAND

The further south you go in New Zealand, the cooler it gets. At Rippon Vineyards, the broad expanse of Lake Wanaka helps to moderate the temperature.

New Zealand came from nowhere, and is now one of the most successful wine countries in the world. Her output isn't big – although it grows every year – but she plays brilliantly upon the drinkers' desire for wines that have the New World's powerful fruit yet which are not too blowsy and overblown. New Zealand is as 'New World' as you can get – its moribund wine industry was regarded as a joke by outsiders as recently as the 1980s – but it is also cool. Most 'New World' countries rely on heat and vintage consistency to build their reputations. New Zealand relies on the fact that its cool climate conditions create fabulously focused, tangy, intense – and refreshing – flavours. As for vintage consistency – there's no such thing. New Zealand's major vineyard regions frequently lose half their crop to spring frosts or vintage rains. What survives offers us some of the most exciting and individual wines the world has to offer.

The early settlers planted vines, but when they allowed themselves alcohol at all, they preferred beer to wine. In addition, the winemakers were constantly battling against ever more restrictive rules. It was only the votes of returning servicemen after World War One that saved the country from total prohibition.

Phylloxera took its toll, as did oidium (powdery mildew), and the industry made the grave mistake of replanting not European vines on grafted rootstock, but hybrids and labrusca vines, in particular Isabella. This last was known as Albany Surprise; it couldn't have been a very pleasant one. Even though the threat of prohibition had been avoided, wine was still not considered quite proper. You couldn't buy wine in restaurants until 1960; you couldn't get a drink at a theatre until 1969, and you couldn't buy wine in supermarkets until 1990.

It wasn't until the 1960s that New Zealand decided to take its wine industry in hand. Dr Helmut Becker, the great German viticulturalist, gave advice – and how sensible it seemed of New Zealand to seek advice from another cool-climate country. And how foolish it was of them to have taken it. For Dr Becker, whose life's work consisted of developing new vine crosses for the cold German climate, recommended not Riesling for New Zealand vineyards, but Müller-Thurgau. As a result, when Australia was streaking ahead producing its own versions of the great classic European wine styles, New Zealand was producing better versions of Liebfraumilch that were perfectly pleasant, but were never going to set the world on fire. It took another decade before the pioneers of fine wine in New Zealand started to probe the new frontiers.

When they did, they looked to cooler climates. Cooler climates in an already cool country? Ah, but not all of New Zealand is cool. The northern part of the North Island is subtropical; even the cooler parts of North Island equate roughly to Burgundian temperatures. It's an island made for Cabernet Sauvignon, Merlot, even Shiraz; for Chardonnay, Semillon and Sauvignon. And in the South Island, which was planted later, the climate suits Pinot Noir, Merlot, Chardonnay, Sauvignon, Gewürztraminer and, yes, Riesling. And though the Müller-Thurgau that dominated the vineyards was probably the best in the world – so what? It was Sauvignon Blanc that finally put New Zealand on the wine map.

New Zealand Sauvignon Blanc took the world by storm in the 1980s. Until then benchmark Sauvignon had come only from the Loire Valley; only these Loire vineyards had been able to produce Sauvignon with such pungency, such blackcurrant-leaf fruit, such gooseberry acidity. It took only a few vintages for New Zealand to knock the Loire off its perch – *it* now provides the benchmark: crunchy, brash fruit of startling vividness.

Vines started to be planted at a terrific rate. And in no time there was a glut of wine – particularly since many of the new vineyards were of high-yielding, inferior varieties. In the late 1980s New Zealand lost one-quarter of its vineyard area with a vine pull scheme. Now the New Zealand wine industry is leaner and fitter – and rapidly expanding – and proving itself to be perhaps the top cool climate country in the world.

CLASSIFICATION

A system of Certified Origin guaranteeing the origin of all New Zealand wines is being planned but will not go as far as regulating grape varieties and wine styles, as in many European appellation systems.

Certified Origin This means simply that 85 per cent of the grapes will come from the region, the vintage and the grape variety named on the label.

Geographical denominations These will be formally delimited under the new system. The most general designation will be New Zealand, with North Island or South Island being the next most general. There will then be named regions, for example Canterbury. Specific localities may also be named on the label. Individual vineyards will be the most specific origins of all.

ORGANIZATION

The industry is dominated by a handful of large companies who buy many of their grapes from growers, although they also own their own vineyards. Only the small wineries, of which there are many, do not depend at least partly on bought-in grapes and, as in Australia, it is common for wineries to be sited a long way from the vineyards.

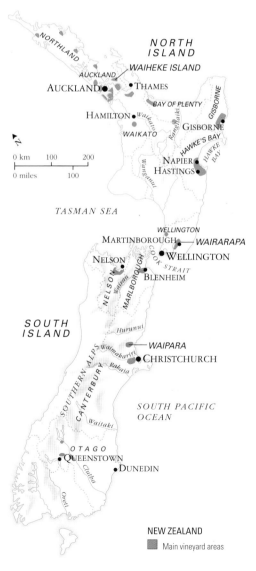

NEW ZEALAND

▮ Main vineyard areas

NORTH ISLAND

This is the warmest part of New Zealand. It's vital, when thinking about New Zealand wines, to remember that it is by no means a uniformly cool country – in fact, if you picked it up and took it to the same latitude in the northern hemisphere, one end would be resting on Paris, while the other stretched down as far as North Africa. And while the northernmost part of the North Island can be subtropical, it is cooler than its latitude would suggest because of the cooling effect of the Antarctic seas. (Northern Europe, conversely, is warmer than its latitude might indicate because of the Gulf Stream.)

So the North Island isn't all hot, but it does have plenty of places that are quite warm enough to ripen red grapes. And quite enough rain, in some places, to ruin the harvest, too. For much of the year the rain comes from the west – so, sensibly, most of the wine regions are on the east coast. But then in autumn the rain comes in from the north-east – so really there's no escape at all. Not surprisingly, New Zealand is a world leader in research into ways of pruning and training vines in warm, humid regions.

GRAPE VARIETIES AND WINE STYLES

Most of the North Island is very, very fertile. So fertile, so damp, that Müller-Thurgau will just go on yielding and yielding and yielding. That's fine if you just want to make soft, fruity, acceptable basic wine, but not if your ambitions lie in fine Cabernet Sauvignon or Chardonnay. And these grapes are nowadays the most popular red and white varieties respectively with North Island growers.

Hawkes Bay has been New Zealand's top red wine area for generations, huddled around Napier on the east coast, yet this isn't a perennially dry area, so vineyard selection is cruicial. In fact, despite being sunny, quite a few Hawkes Bay vintages are virtually destroyed by vintage rain. However, things have been greatly improved by the determined development of areas where drainage is good. The first to be developed were in the south side of the valley. At Te Mata where good wines were made generations ago, and

Waiheke Island off Auckland has seen a lot of new planting in recent years: it is new areas like this that are taking New Zealand to the next stage of quality.

John Buck created fine red wine in the 1970s and 1980s. Just north of Napier, at Esk Valley, warm well-drained sites produce top reds. But the most important developments have been in river valleys where there is gravel – warm and free-draining. The Tutaekuri river, and, above all, the Ngaruroro at the Gimblett Gravels are the most important areas, and both can produce top reds in most vintages. Best producers: **Alpha Domus**, **Craggy Range**, **Esk Valley**, **Matua Valley**, **Morton Estate**, **Ngatarawa**, **C J Pask**, **Te Mata**, **Vidal**, **Unison** and **Villa Maria**.

The North Island's other top quality region is **Wairarapa**, and, importantly, its sub-region of **Martinborough**. This warm, dry region usually avoids the autumn rains and has produced a succession of top Pinot Noirs. It also grows fine Sauvignon and Chardonnay, and good Cabernet and Shiraz, but patches of land able to produce fine Pinot Noir are rare, so that's what it's best known for. Best producers: **Ata Rangi**, **Dry River**, **Martinborough Vineyard** and **Palliser Estate**.

If you want Chardonnay go to **Gisborne** – at least, that's what the Gisborne growers say. They reckon it is the Chardonnay capital of New Zealand. Maybe they're right: the wines certainly have a soft, ripe, melons and peaches fruit that sets them apart from other New Zealand examples. Gewürztraminer also does well here too. Best producers: **Corbans**, **Millton** and **Montana**.

Auckland, as a grape-growing region, had been declining in importance, but now seems to be picking up again with the planting of more land, particularly on **Waiheke Island**. Cabernet Sauvignon blends do well here. But really Auckland is where wine companies are based, rather than where they grow their grapes. Grapes are trucked here from all over the North Island. Best producers: **Fenton**, **Goldwater**, **Heron's Flight**, **Kumeu River** and **Stonyridge**. And hot and humid **Northland**, jutting up towards the tropics? There are a few vines growing here, but not many.

READING THE LABEL

Wines are labelled varietally, and often with the name of a region and vineyard. It's all pretty logical.

WHAT DO THEY TASTE LIKE?

The Cabernet wines have intense berry fruit and the Pinot Noirs can be marvellously rich. Chardonnays from Gisborne are all peaches and cream, soft and ripe but well balanced.

THE GOOD YEARS

Vintages tend to vary quite a bit because of the cooler climate.

2004 A record vintage by a large margin in quantity. Some high-quality wines.

2003 Mixed quality due to wet conditions.

2002 Some outstanding wines, especially in Gisborne, Hawkes Bay and Wairarapa.

2001 Fairly wet season.

2000 Average to very good.

ENJOYING THE WINES

Very rich fruit makes these good wines to drink at any time. The reds increasingly have the concentration to match most meat dishes.

CONSUMER INFORMATION

WHAT DO I GET FOR MY MONEY?

The top wines aren't cheap, but they are good value. Leading Pinot Noirs like those from Martinborough or Ata Rangi, are delivering complexity and individuality and top Hawkes Bay reds, while not cheap, can stand up to similarly priced Bordeaux.

AVAILABILITY

Increasingly good. You won't necessarily find the top wines all over the place – some are available in quite small quantities – but the big companies like Villa Maria are widely available and can show what's happening in North Island.

CONSUMER CHECKLIST

Pinot Noir 2002 *Quality 9* ★
(Craggy Range) *Price 9* ★
Value 9 ★

Good Years 2002, 2000, 1999, 1998, 1996.
Taste Notes Generally ripe, rich flavours. The Chardonnays are creamy. The Pinot Noirs are concentrated and full of fruit while the Cabernets can be too leafy and stringy but at best are classic. The Merlots are generally rich and balanced.

SOUTH ISLAND

This is Sauvignon Blanc country, the source of some of New Zealand's most famous and world-beating wines. It's also cool country, and perhaps most surprisingly of all, it's very recently planted country. Recently planted with vines, that is. Until 1973 it was planted with, among others, cherry trees, garlic, and lots and lots of grass for lots and lots of sheep. But no vines. Vines had been planted on the South Island before, at various times, but none had outlived the first flush of enthusiasm. But during the years when hybrids and labrusca vines, and more latterly Müller-Thurgau were being planted on the North Island, the South Island was busy tending its sheep.

The year 1973 was when Montana arrived. New Zealand's biggest wine company was looking for more land – and the land had to be cheap and easy to work. Marlborough was the obvious spot. It's flat, it gets oodles of sun – and so they set about planting. They put in mostly Müller-Thurgau – but just for an experiment, having tasted one New Zealand Sauvignon Blanc, they included some of that, too.

It was an inspired guess. Marlborough Sauvignon Blanc is arguably the best in the world. Marlborough is certainly now the largest wine region in New Zealand. Others, like Nelson and Canterbury, are also building reputations for cool-climate grapes.

And the Müller-Thurgau? You hardly see it. Why would you? Riesling and Pinot Gris are much better if you want an aromatic style, but most of the world wants Sauvignon, Chardonnay or Pinot Noir – and that's what Marlborough does very well.

GRAPE VARIETIES AND WINE STYLES

Let's look at the Sauvignon Blanc first. **Marlborough** is the prime region, a broad, flat valley between two ranges of hills. It contradicts everything I've ever said about the importance of planting on hillsides to get extra sun and warmth, better drainage and so on. So let me try and talk my way out of it: Marlborough doesn't need better drainage or poorer soil because the soil is already as poor as you can get: almost pure gravel in places, as free-draining as you could want. And it already gets long hours of sunshine. In some places Cabernet and Merlot will ripen, except for Pinot Noir, which is increasingly good here as vines age and expertise improves. There are intense, buttery Chardonnays and beautifully structured Rieslings. Best producers: **Cloudy Bay**, **Forrest**, **Fromm**, **Hunter's**, **Isabel**, **Jackson**, **Nautilus**, **Saint Clair**, **Seresin**, **Vavasour**, **Villa Maria** and **Wither Hills**.

Nelson, to the north-west of Marlborough and marginally cooler, has a wide range of mesoclimates and grows most of the varieties grown in New Zealand. Best results are from Sauvignon Blanc, Chardonnay and Riesling. There are only a handful of wineries but they're good. Best producers: **Greenhough**, **Neudorf** and **Seifried (Redwood Valley)**.

With its arid, cool climate, **Canterbury,** too, has Chardonnay, and some top-class Pinot Noir. The sub-region of Waipara is developing an impressive reputation for Pinot Noir with terrific intensity and fruit. Best producers: **Mountford**, **Pegasus Bay**, **Daniel Schuster** and **Waipara West.**

Then there's **Central Otago**, way to the south; now here they really do have to plant on hillsides to catch the sun and reduce frost risk. Pinot Noir is thrilling; Riesling, Sauvignon and Chardonnay, not far behind. Best

The soil in parts of Marlborough is gravelly in the extreme – heat radiates onto the vines from the flat, round stones long after the sun has set.

Montana was the first company to plant vineyards in Marlborough – this vast swathe of vines, over 200 hectares (500 acres) in all, is its Brancott Estate.

producers: **Chard Farm**, **Felton Road**, **Gibbston Valley**, **Peregrine**, **Quartz Reef** and **Rippon Vineyards**.

READING THE LABEL
Wines are generally labelled very clearly, with grape, region, and perhaps vineyard name.

WHAT DO THEY TASTE LIKE?
Marlborough Sauvignon Blanc is the epitome of the style: gooseberryish, crunchy and pungent. Chardonnays and Pinot Noirs can be intense. Merlot can be surprisingly lush.

THE GOOD YEARS
These wines can be drunk young, though many can improve with a year or so of aging.
2004   Frost affected Central Otago.
2003   Frost in many regions reduced the harvest. Exceptional in Nelson and Central Otago.
2002   Slightly better than the North. Central Otago reds did especially well.
2001   South Island did better than the North.
2000   Yields in Marlborough were down but the wines are classically pungent.

ENJOYING THE WINES
Marlborough Sauvignon Blanc became the classic ultra-cool wine of the 2000s. Great by itself, it goes fascinatingly with much Chinese and Thai food. Chardonnay is rich enough for any fish and chicken and Pinot Noir is delicious with plain fish or lamb.

CONSUMER INFORMATION

WHAT DO I GET FOR MY MONEY?
The top Sauvignon Blancs are not cheap – although on second thoughts perhaps they are. You're getting the world's finest examples of the grape here. Quality in nearly all varieties is excellent; only Cabernet is usually too green.

AVAILABILITY
Cloudy Bay is so much in demand it hardly ever goes on the shelves. Other names are easier to find. Montana is available almost everywhere.

CONSUMER CHECKLIST
Sauvignon Blanc 2004   *Quality 8★*
(Wither Hills)   *Price 7 ★*
                                             Value 9 ★

Good Years   2003, 2001, 2000, 1999, 1997, 1996.
Taste Notes   Sauvignons are pungent and grassy, Chardonnays rich and buttery, and Rieslings, especially sweet and botrytis-affected, can be superb. Pinot Noirs at their best are intense and have delicious, sweet-centred fruit. Cabernets need the warmest years to be ripe and Merlot is a much better bet.

SOUTH AFRICA

There are times when I wouldn't have liked to have been a quality-conscious South African winemaker. One of those times was during the 1980s, when I couldn't buy the vines or the equipment I needed, I couldn't taste the wines my peers were making in other countries and, anyway, most of the world shunned my wine.

Another of those times was soon afterwards. Nelson Mandela had been released, apartheid was ending and the world was smiling in my direction once again. Everything, briefly, looked rosy. But then I would have looked around for people to buy my wine – and discovered just how far the world had changed in my absence. The wines I was making, that I had been proud of, that I thought others, too, might admire, were old-fashioned. They weren't what the world was drinking. I'd been left behind – and I was going to have to scramble like mad to catch up. That wouldn't have been an easy time to be a South African winemaker.

Would I like to be in that role now? Yes, I would. South African wine has transformed itself at astonishing speed, and it's poised on the brink of great success. Yes, I know I've said that before. It's been poised there before, and the great success has failed to happen.

But this time I think it will. I hope it will. Goodness knows, the winemakers deserve it. But to put things in context, let's go back to the seventeenth century when the first vines were planted in the new Cape settlement.

The man responsible was Jan van Riebeeck, who was aiming not to imitate the Grand Cru wines of Europe, but to find a cure for scurvy. (The Dutch East India Company ships sailing the spice routes had been at sea a long time when they docked at the Cape, and they had a long way yet to go. Scurvy would have been an ever-present danger.) The vine cuttings had come from western France, but they didn't guarantee good wine, and van Riebeeck's wines found little favour. That didn't occur until much later in the century, when Simon van der Stel planted the first vines at Constantia, near Cape Town. It was Constantia – sweet dessert wine – that was to prove the first great Cape wine, shipped all over Europe and sold for high prices.

Decline set in in the second half of the nineteenth century. In 1861 the British government removed preferential tariffs on Empire wines, leaving the market open to French imports. Then phylloxera arrived in the Cape; and when the cure (grafting European vines on to native American rootstocks) in due course followed, growers planted like mad. The resulting glut of wine found too few buyers. Growers were reduced to penury.

It was in order to bring some stability to this situation that the KWV was formed in 1918. The initials stand for Ko-operatiewe Wijnbowers Vereniging (van Zuid Afrika), or (South African) Co-operative Winegrowers Association. This body, in the ensuing years, regulated the market by acting as the official government control body as well as being the marketing arm of the industry and a producer in its own right. It established minimum prices and imposed production quotas, and it did indeed set the industry on a secure footing. But did it promote quality or encourage innovation? Well, no, it didn't. It ensured that grape growers received a minimum price, and turned out perfectly acceptable blends that for years were the face of South African wines abroad. But it was increasingly seen (by winegrowers who wanted to produce wines with more style, more individuality) as a dead

Wine kept in barrels will slowly evaporate and it must be kept topped up to prevent oxidation. This is at Hamilton Russell, a top-quality winery in Walker Bay.

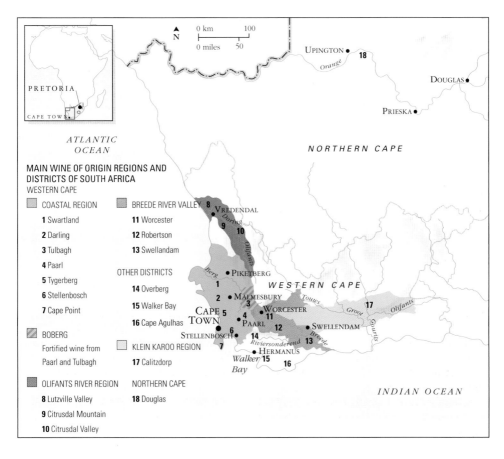

MAIN WINE OF ORIGIN REGIONS AND
DISTRICTS OF SOUTH AFRICA

WESTERN CAPE

COASTAL REGION

1 Swartland
2 Darling
3 Tulbagh
4 Paarl
5 Tygerberg
6 Stellenbosch
7 Cape Point

BOBERG

Fortified wine from
Paarl and Tulbagh

OLIFANTS RIVER REGION

8 Lutzville Valley
9 Citrusdal Mountain
10 Citrusdal Valley

BREEDE RIVER VALLEY

11 Worcester
12 Robertson
13 Swellandam

OTHER DISTRICTS

14 Overberg
15 Walker Bay
16 Cape Agulhas

KLEIN KAROO REGION

17 Calitzdorp

NORTHERN CAPE

18 Douglas

weight. It was reformed in the early 1990s and now, at last, quality-conscious producers have a freer hand. Confidence and optimism are high and new, quality-focused wineries are opening at the rate of one a week. However, co-operatives still process more than 80 per cent of the grapes.

South Africa comes ninth in the world in terms of production of wine but good wine-makers are still in a minority. For a start, just 75 per cent of the grape harvest is made into wine – brandy, grape concentrates, grape spirit or table grapes are alternatives. In addition, there are no limits on yields. For every producer aiming to make fine wines from 3 tons per acre or less, there are others farming irrigated vines in hot inland areas like the Orange River, taking up to seven times more per acre.

There are still vineyards planted with virus-affected vines producing poor quality wine from grapes that won't ripen properly, although they are less common than before, and there are still wineries making wine in the same old way, as though nothing in the world had changed. That's why I say that South Africa is on the brink of great success. It's not quite there yet.

Nevertheless, things have changed dramatically. For years vines were a huge problem

for the growers: there weren't many different clones available, they couldn't get virus-free vines, and strict quarantine regulations (as well as sanctions) made it difficult to try out new varieties. All those things are now better. Most growers admit they could still do with more clones to play with (all Chardonnay clones aren't alike, for example: some give higher yields, some lower, some more flavour, some less; and different clones adapt differently to different conditions).

GRAPE VARIETIES AND WINE STYLES

Cabernet, Shiraz and Merlot are the grapes showing the greatest increase but despite the fact that the country is making its reputation abroad at least as much on its Cabernets, Pinotages and occasional Pinot Noirs as on its Chardonnays, red varieties still take up only 36 per cent of South Africa's vineyards. Even so the percentage of reds has more than doubled since 1995.

Chenin Blanc is by far the most popular white grape. This is the country's basic white wine: fruity, clean, and made in every style from bone dry to ultra-sweet. It's known locally as Steen, and if it seldom hits the heights of quality it can nevertheless provide good, reliable, inexpensive drinking.

The Franschhoek valley was where the French Huguenot refugees settled after 1685. Today, Boschendal (above) is one of its best known estates.

Chardonnay is increasingly good, with balanced use of oak and good buttery fruit. But the two extremes of style are also available – light, dilute and overproduced, and massive and overoaked. Of the whites, Sauvignon Blanc has the most new plantings, though only the areas of **Constantia**, **Elgin**, **Durbanville** and the **Coastal Region** regularly produce those benchmark gooseberry flavours. Other versions are softer and more tropical-fruity, and have sometimes been aged in new oak.

There's more Colombard than there is Chardonnay or Sauvignon, and again we're talking simple, commercial whites. Attractive, but you wouldn't go out of your way. Even so, its green acidity, even when grown in hot, irrigated areas, is very useful.

Riesling can make some very good sweet wines indeed in South Africa. But if sweet wines are what you seek there's also excellent Muscat. Some is Muscat of Alexandria (known locally as Hanepoot), some is Muscadel, which can be red or white, is always richly sweet, and is a variant of the high-quality Muscat Blanc à Petits Grains.

Whites, overall, still have the quality edge on the reds. Sure, there are some stunning reds but there are still too many Cabernets with harsh, green austerity, too many Pinotages with a burnt rubber edge.

Cabernet Sauvignon is often blended with Cabernet Franc and Merlot in a classic Bordeaux-style partnership, and these usually are better than the pure Cabernets. Paarl and Stellenbosch are where you look for the best Cabernet; Paarl and Walker Bay are for good Pinot Noir. Each year there's a little more and three producers at least – **Hamilton Russell, Bouchard Finlayson** and **Glen Carlou** – seem to have the knack.

Pinotage is South Africa's speciality. It's a crossing of Pinot Noir and Cinsaut that is used for just about every red style from pink upwards. It works best in dark, rich, spicy numbers with plenty of damson perfume and perhaps a little barrel aging. Nearly all can be drunk young but the best will age.

Along with Cabernet, the most dramatic growth in new plantings has been in Shiraz, traditionally used for port-style wines but now increasingly being made into unfortified table wines. They're good, with raspberryish fruit, but so far aren't giving the best of Australia or France anything to worry about. Like Shiraz, Merlot has become suddenly seriously trendy in the Cape but with mixed results, and skilful producers are working out where – and how – to grow it in the cooler regions.

The greatest challenge now facing South African winemakers is to decide where, exactly, they should be planting all these varieties. The traditional way of growing vines is to grow as many varieties as you please on the same estate, and often on the flat, easy-to-work land. Planting higher up the hillsides in search of cooler climates is a new phenomenon, as is heading south east, away from the main winelands in the west of the country, in search of lower temperatures. But this is surely where the future lies.

Paarl, where the KWV is based, and **Stellenbosch** are the best-established quality areas. Paarl is basically a warm area and is the source of much of South Africa's good sherry-style and 'port'-style wines, but it does seem able to produce a diversity of styles, including sparklers. Wellington and Franschhoek are wards or smaller designated areas within Paarl. Stellenbosch is slightly cooler, and catches the sea breezes from False Bay, but in both regions, if you want to make whites with elegance and finesse then you must learn to manage the heat. Planting on sites that face away from the sun is one way; climbing up the hills is another. Chardonnay from these regions is ripe and rich, and there's some good Sauvignon Blanc too, more in the French Loire, than the New Zealand mould. Smaller units of origin (wards) are being demarcated to reflect more accurately the diverse soils and climates. Best producers: (Paarl) **Graham Beck**, **Boekenhoutskloof**, **Cabrière**, **Cape Chamonix**, **Diemersfontein**, **Fairview**, **Glen Carlou**, **Mont du Toit**, **La Motte**, **Plaisir de Merle** and **Veenwouden**; (Stellenbosch) **Beyerskloof**, **De Trafford**, **Neil Ellis**, **Kanonkop**, **Meerlust**, **Mulderbosch**, **Rust-en-Vrede**, **Rustenberg**, **Saxenburg**, **Stellenzicht**, **Thelema**, **Vergelegen** and **Warwick**.

The Coastal Region, to which the districts of Paarl and Stellenbosch both belong, stretches up the west coast to take in **Swartland**, as well as inland to the fortified wine country of **Tulbagh**. Swartland, a 'Black Land' of hills covered by dark scrub, is hot and dry, with low-yielding vineyards outnumbered by other crops. Pinotage is the best red; of the whites Chenin Blanc, Colombard and Sauvignon Blanc are worth noticing. Cooler-climate Sauvignon comes from **Groenekloof** and **Durbanville** (wards within Darling and Tygerberg respectively), to the north-east of Cape Town, but the biggest problem here is the expansion of bricks and mortar from the

city. To the south of Cape Town is cool-climate **Cape Point**, best known for whites, and **Constantia** – where it all began. That early dessert wine is now being made again, under the name of Vin de Constance, by **Klein Constantia**; **Groot Constantia**, now government-owned, and **Buitenverwachting** are the other two parts into which the original estate was split. Otherwise look for good grassy Sauvignons, nutty Chardonnays and good Bordeaux-style reds here. Best producers: **Buitenverwachtung**, **Klein Constantia** and **Steenberg**.

To the north-east and east, **Worcester**, **Robertson** and **Swellendam** comprise the Breede River Valley Region. Worcester is hot, fortified wine country, particularly good for red and white Muscats, but now also producing large quantities of light, fruity whites that sell for low prices. Robertson's table wines are capable of greater things, particularly Chardonnay and Sauvignon, but there are fortifieds too. Best producers: (Robertson) **Graham Beck**, **Bon Courage**, **De Wetshof** and **Springfield**.

Vineyards in the **Olifants River** region and in the **Northern Cape** along the Orange River also produce bulk table wines, and **Klein Karoo** makes fortified wines and some table wines when it isn't farming sheep or ostriches.

The most promising cool-climate areas include the coastal district of Walker Bay and

hilly Elgin (a ward within Overberg), with the small number of vineyards at Elim near Cape Alguhas claiming distinction as the most southerly wine area in the country. Sauvignon Blanc, Chardonnay and Pinot Noir are all good here, with elegant fruit, good varietal definition and complexity. Best producers: (Walker Bay) **Bouchard Finlayson**, **Hamilton Russell** and **Newton Johnson**.

CLASSIFICATION

Originally introduced in 1973, with various amendments along the way, the Wine of Origin system affects only the ten per cent or so of wines that are entered for it by their producers. Production areas, grape variety and vintage may all be certified. Production areas can range in size from a single vineyard (maximum size 5 hectares/12 acres) to a region, for example Coastal Region. If the production area is named on the label 100 per cent of the grapes must come from that area. If a grape variety is named on the label, then 75 per cent (85 per cent for export and from 2006 for all wines) must be of that variety.

ORGANIZATION

This has changed radically over the past decade, with the KWV, the producer that also had sweeping powers that included fixing quota limits and minimum prices, giving up much of its role in controlling the industry. It and other big companies still dominate in terms of volume, but life has become easier for the small independent producer.

READING THE LABEL

Labels are in Afrikaans and English, and several Afrikaans words are important. 'Oesjaar' means 'vintage'; 'oorsprong' means 'origin'; 'landgoedwyn' is the designation given to a single-estate wine. Most labels give the cultivar, or grape variety. Names like Premier Grand Cru, implying a French style, and Grünberger Stein, implying a German style, appear, but have no legal standing.

WHAT DO THEY TASTE LIKE?

The whites vary from the simple to the well-structured and complex, and from light to sturdy. The reds are increasingly fruity but are less reliable than the whites, unless you pick a leading producer. Many South African Cabernets are still too austere and lean; Pinotage can have an odd burnt rubber whiff about it. But the poor wine-making that can bring these problems is giving way to more modern practices and exciting results are flooding out of the country.

THE GOOD YEARS

The following notes refer to South Africa's cooler regions, where vintages can vary considerably. Most wines should be drunk young, although the best Pinot Noir and Chardonnay can improve with a year or two in bottle and Cabernet blends often need considerably more time and will develop for up to a decade.

2004 Excellent vintage. Reds have good colour, fruit and structure. Merlot and Shiraz especially promising.

2003 Outstanding year. Reds show good colour and flavour from berries smaller than normal. Some exceptional Cabernets.

2002 Varied conditions, so choose a good producer. Fine wines at the top level.

2001 Reds have excellent colour, fruit and concentration but some high alcohol levels.

2000 A hot year with powerful, concentrated reds.

ENJOYING THE WINES

The best Chardonnay and Sauvignon will match fish dishes well. Keep the oakier wines for creamier, richer foods. Many whites, particularly the simple everyday ones, are good on their own. Reds will go with all sorts of meat; keep Pinotage to drink with the heartiest dishes.

CONSUMER INFORMATION

WHAT DO I GET FOR MY MONEY?

Pretty good value at both extremes. At the lowest end there are some excellent everyday wines; at the top end quality matches the prices.

AVAILABILITY

A great deal better than it was a few years ago. Most retailers now see South African wines as 'must haves' in the way they do Australian wines, but distribution of the best wines can be patchy.

CONSUMER CHECKLIST

Pinotage 2003 *Quality 6* ★
(Beyerskloof) *Price 8* ★
Value 10 ★

Good Years 2004, 2003, 2001, 2000, 1998, 1997, 1995.

Taste Notes There is an ongoing revolution in South African red wine-making that is producing quite unexpected and decidedly delicious youthful flavours. Whites are still more reliable, and increasingly good and well-made, if sometimes a bit dilute.

NORTH AFRICA

If ever there was a region in need of a flying winemaker or two, it is North Africa. If ever there was a region unlikely to get them, it is North Africa.

There's no reason why North Africa shouldn't make good wine. Yes, it's hot and dry and on the edge of a desert. So are some wine regions in Australia. There are parts of Spain that get less rain than Algeria. Winds come off the Atlantic at up to 40 miles (65 km) per hour. But there are ways of protecting vines against high winds – you prune and train them differently so they don't get damaged. There are ways of overcoming all sorts of climatic problems. But there's no way of solving a lack of will.

North Africa used to make far more wine than it does now; in fact, in the 1950s North African wines accounted for between a half and a third of the whole international wine trade. That's impossible to imagine now. What happened was that the French left their North African colonies, and promptly reduced the amount of wine they bought from them. (Much of what France had bought before was in any case blended with its own native product.) Many of the best winemakers, too, left when Independence came, and the increasing influence of Islam has not exactly encouraged wine production.

The result was a glut of wine that could only be solved by uprooting vineyards. So effective has this been that **Algeria**'s vineyard area now stands at 65,000 hectares (160,600 acres) compared to 400,000 hectares (988,000 acres) in 1938. **Tunisia** now has just 26,000 hectares (64,200 acres) of vineyards, and **Morocco** 50,000 hectares (123,500 acres) and a lot of these are given over to table grapes.

One saving grace is that it is mostly the less good vineyards on the plains that have gone, while those that remain are up in the hills. Some of the grape varieties are perfectly good, like Syrah, Cabernet Sauvignon and Mourvèdre, and over 80 per cent of Algeria's vines are over 40 years old, so should be giving wines of great flavour and concentration. The trouble is that the largest single variety is the generally flavourless Carignan, with earthy varieties like Alicante Bouschet, Aramon and Cinsaut following behind. Add poor wine-making and an increasing Islamic influence, and the outlook is not rosy. All three countries have French-style systems of Appellation Contrôlée, but the best bets are the sturdy Muscats of Tunisia; Moroccan Syrahs and Cabernet from Meknès and Fès, in particular from **Cellier de Meknès** and **Castel Frères** who are investing massively in the country; and Algerian reds from Oran.

ASIA

If the vine is a Mediterranean plant, what's it doing in Asia? Well, the answer is that vines have been grown in the East for 2000 years or more – although the advent of European vinifera varieties is more recent. In **China** the preferred tipple is rice wine, with brandy for special occasions (Chinese abroad often favour Cognac), although wine has long been drunk there, too. The vines (many of which are better for table grapes) have such names as Dragon's Eye, Cow's Nipple or Cock's Heart; growing good old Chardonnay must seem dull in comparison.

But growing Chardonnay is what they're doing now. The north-eastern provinces of Shandong, Hebei and Tianjin have a moderate, maritime climate, and joint ventures with western companies Rémy Martin and Pernod-Ricard are aimed at producing wines that will sell to export markets. That means Chardonnay, Welschriesling, Sylvaner and others.

In **Japan** some wines are made to the western model, too: there are Bordeaux-style blends of Cabernet and Merlot, there is Chardonnay, and there are some sweet Sauternes-style dessert wines. But most Japanese wine is made from local varieties and hybrids, which can more easily withstand the rainy, humid weather. Only one of Japan's 47 provinces makes no wine, but only about ten per cent of the grape harvest is fermented.

In **India** only about 1 per cent of the 50,000 hectares (123,500 acres) of vineyards are used for wine. Chateau Indage, based in the Maharashtra hills above Mumbai, where the grapes need huge amounts of irrigation to survive, controls about 75 per cent of the market. Its best known wine is a Champagne-method fizz called Omar Khayyam. Other promising wineries are Sula, north-east of Mumbai, and Grover Vineyards in Bangalore, advised by Pomerol guru Michel Rolland.

INDEX of wines and main wine producers

Acknowledgments
All photographs supplied by Cephas Picture Library. Photographers: All photographs Mick Rock except: Jerry Alexander 265; Kevin Argue 280; Nigel Blythe 150, 157, 159, 161, 168, 169, 172, 189; Herve Champollion 138, Andy Christodolo 2, 6, 22, 161, 285, 290, 293, 296, 297, 304; David Copeman 232, 233; Xavier Desmier 103; Rick England 20, 284; Kevin Judd 308, 309; M.J. Keilty 245; John Millwood 252; Steven Morris 306; R&K Muschenetz 262; Alain Proust 311, 312; Ted Stefanski 23, 24, 25, 255.